W9-BZE-049

Justice at Nuremberg

Works by Robert Conot

Justice at Nuremberg

ROBERT E. CONOT

1817

HARPER & ROW, PUBLISHERS, New York
Cambridge, Philadelphia, San Francisco,
London, Mexico City, São Paulo, Sydney

Grateful acknowledgment is made for permission to reprint excerpts from *Nuremberg Diary* by G. M. Gilbert, copyright 1947 by Gustav Mahler Gilbert, copyright renewed 1975 by Gustav Mahler Gilbert.

Photographs courtesy of the National Archives, Washington, D.C.

JUSTICE AT NUREMBERG. Copyright © 1983 by Robert E. Conot. All rights reserved. Printed in the United States of America. No part of this book may be used or reproduced in any manner whatsoever without written permission except in the case of brief quotations embodied in critical articles and reviews. For information address Harper & Row, Publishers, Inc., 10 East 53rd Street, New York, N.Y. 10022. Published simultaneously in Canada by Fitzhenry & Whiteside Limited, Toronto.

FIRST EDITION

Designer: C. Linda Dingler

Picture layout: Jane Weinberger

Library of Congress Cataloging in Publication Data

Conot, Robert E.
    Justice at Nuremberg.
    Bibliography: p.
    Includes Index.
    1. War crime trials—Germany (West)—Nuremberg.
I. Title
JX5434.C66 1983   341.6'9'02684321   82-48395
ISBN 0-06-015117-X

83 84 85 86 87 10 9 8 7 6 5 4 3 2 1

341.41
.76
.1

603186

To
David Ginsburg
and all my friends and colleagues
on the National Advisory Commission on Civil Disorders

603138

Contents

A section of photographs follows page 242

Acknowledgments and Methodology

Justice at Nuremberg presented a particularly difficult problem in construction and organization because of the vast scope of the subject and the charges, the large number of defendants, and the enormous amount of material available. (I estimate that my research encompassed documents, papers, and books totaling some fifty million words.) Moreover, it was necessary to reconcile three complementary but sometime disparate elements: 1) The origins of and preparations for the trial, followed by the trial itself. 2) The characters and actions of the twenty-one defendants.* 3) The history of Nazi Germany applicable to the trial—particularly, the criminal acts perpetrated.

Compounding the problem was the duplication and lack of cohesion in the prosecution's presentation. In essence, the United States first presented the case *in toto* under Count 1, the Conspiracy to Wage Aggressive War. The other three prosecuting nations, Great Britain, France, and the Soviet Union, then offered their cases, which sometimes repeated and were often interwoven with the American case. The interpolation of charges against individual defendants occasionally triplicated the presentation of the evidence.

After considerable experimentation, a couple of false starts, and the receipt of valuable counsel from Buz Wyeth, executive editor at Harper & Row, I devised the following scheme for the book:

> *Part I: Crime and Punishment*—the origination of the trial concept and organization of the tribunal.
>
> *Part II: Interrogation and Indictment*—the imprisonment of the accused at Nuremberg and the preparation of the case.
>
> *Part III: Prosecution*—an account of Nazi criminality and the defendants' complicity, interwoven with the presentation of the evidence.
>
> *Part IV: Defense*—the testimony of the defendants and their witnesses.
>
> *Part V: Judgment*—the deliberations of the judges, their verdict, and the aftermath.

The book is composed for the most part from original sources and the trial record. The principal collections are Record Group 238—including the files of American prosecutor Robert Jackson—at the National Archives in Washington, D.C.; the papers of Murray C. Bernays, originator of the basic trial concept, at the University of Wyoming; the papers of Francis Biddle, the American judge, at the University of Syracuse; the papers of John J. Parker, the alternate American judge,

---

*Twenty-four were indicted. Of these, Robert Ley committed suicide before the start of the trial; Gustav Krupp was mentally incapacitated; and Martin Bormann was never found.

at the University of North Carolina; the papers of Father Edmund Walsh, founder of the School of Foreign Service at Georgetown University and a consultant to Jackson, at Georgetown University; the papers of Lawrence Egbert, deputy chief of the prosecution's Analysis Section and subsequently editor of the trial record, at Georgetown University,* and the papers of Commander James Donovan at Stanford University.

I am indebeted to the following people associated with the Nuremberg trial for the advice and information they provided in interviews:

Ralph G. Albrecht, who presented the individual case against the number-one defendant, Hermann Goering.

Roger Barrett, who had charge of the Defendants' Information Center.

Louise Bernays, the widow of Murray C. Bernays.

Smith W. Brookhart, a deputy to Colonel John Harlan Amen, the chief of the Interrogation Division. Brookhart had responsibility for questioning Himmler's second-in-command, Ernst Kaltenbrunner, and other SS and Gestapo personnel.

Elsie Douglas, longtime secretary to Supreme Court Justice and prosecutor Robert H. Jackson.

United States Circuit Court of Appeals Judge Murray I. Gurfein (now deceased), who prepared the economics case.

Sam Harris (now deceased), deputy to Gurfein.

Tom Harris, an aide to General Telford Taylor.

William Jackson, son of and aide to Robert H. Jackson.

United States Circuit Court of Appeals Judge Harold Leventhal (now deceased), who was a member of the prosecution committee preparing the charges on Crimes Against Peace.

Daniel Margolies, a member of the prosecution's Analysis Section.

James Rowe, one of the legal advisers to Judge Biddle.

Henry Sackett, a Midwestern prosecutor who had charge of the interrogation of Interior Minister Wilhelm Frick.

Richard Sonnenfeldt, principal interpreter in the Interrogation Division.

Drexel Sprecher, OSS labor expert, who helped prepare the cases against Fritzsche and Schirach.

Telford Taylor, dean of the Law School at Columbia University. General Taylor was in charge of the case against the German general staff and high command, and subsequently replaced Jackson as prosecutor-in-chief of the 185 accused in twelve follow-up trials.

I wish to thank the following persons for their assistance at the National Archives: Dr. Robert Wolfe, chief of the Modern Military Branch; Dr. John Mendelsohn, an expert on the Nuremberg records; Don Spencer, who served as an enlisted man at the Nuremberg trials, and is now engaged in the Immigration and Naturalization Service's effort to track down war criminals who entered the United States illegally; and Tim Mulligan, John Taylor, and George Wagner, archivists.

*The Egbert Papers had just been received at the time I conducted research for the book and had not yet been sorted, so that I am unable to provide box numbers or other locator identification for individual pieces.

Introduction

Supreme Court Justice Robert Jackson, the American prosecutor, observed: "Never before in legal history has an effort been made to bring within the scope of a single litigation the developments of a decade, covering a whole continent, and involving a score of nations, countless individuals, and innumerable events.... This trial has a scope that is utterly beyond anything that has ever been attempted that I know of in judicial history."

Norman Birkett, one of the two British judges, called it "the greatest trial in history. The historian of the future will look back to it with fascinated eyes. It will have a glamour, an intensity, an ever-present sense of tragedy that will enthrall the mind engaged upon its consideration."

The panorama was epic, the issues profound, the cast of characters unparalleled. For the first time, the leaders of a nation were charged with international crimes committed on a scale so vast as to strain belief. One of the defendants, Schirach, was three-fourths American. Another, Schacht, had been conceived in Manhattan. A third, Hess, had been born in Egypt and had parachuted into Scotland in the midst of the war. A fourth, Rosenberg, had never set foot in Germany until he was eighteen and never lived there until he was twenty-five. A fifth, Ribbentrop, had been a onetime emigrant to Canada. A sixth, Neurath, was a friend of Queen Mary of England. A seventh, Goering, was a drug-addicted larger-than-life figure, part Machiavelli, part Falstaff.

Yet, contrary to the expectations of the participants, the trial has never been fully explored. Although the record has furnished a documentary bonanza for histories of the Third Reich, there has been an absence of knowledge and comprehension of the trial itself.* As early as the summer of 1946, when the inquest was still in its final months, former American Undersecretary of State Sumner Welles expressed the fear that too little attention was being paid, even though it was imperative that the lesson become known.

No one who experienced the trial or has become familiar with the evidence and record can doubt that the case was proved conclusively; that, despite all the horrors that were brought to light, it was, if anything,

---

*The most widespread impression among the American public comes from *Judgment at Nuremberg*, a fictional TV drama (and later movie) based loosely on one of the subsequent proceedings following the trial of the major war criminals. Eugene Davidson, in *The Trial of the Germans*, published in 1967, provided comprehensive biographies of the defendants, but devoted only a single chapter to the trial per se. Other books about Nuremberg have consisted of personal accounts or have dealt with particular aspects of the proceedings.

understated.* None of the defendants attempted to refute the evidence. They sought instead to explain away their own participations and to shift the blame onto others. Schirach, the leader of the Hitler Youth, declared: "This murder decree of Hitler's seems to me the end of every race theory, every race philosophy, every kind of race propaganda, for after this catastrophe any further advocacy of race theory would be equivalent to approval in theory of further murder. An ideology in the name of which five million people were murdered is a theory which cannot continue to exist." Fritzsche, the leading radio commentator in Goebbels' Propaganda Ministry, said: "He who, after Auschwitz, still clings to racial politics has rendered himself guilty."

Not only were the documents the prosecution introduced the Nazis' own and the terror that had been unleashed spelled out in their own words, but the witnesses—both for the prosecution and for the defense—included some of the highest officials in Hitler's government. Far from denying what had taken place, each contributed additional information to the litany of murder. Dieter Wisliceny, one of Eichmann's half-dozen deputies, provided a detailed accounting of the 5,250,000 Jews (not including those in the Soviet Union) who had been exterminated. Otto Ohlendorf, the chief of Himmler's internal intelligence division and commander of an *Einsatzgruppe* in Russia, testified to the slaughter of the Jews in the East. Rudolf Höss, commander of Auschwitz, related that three million people, most of them Jews, had perished in his concentration camp—and he, most assuredly, was an authoritative witness. Erich von dem Bach-Zelewsky, the chief of the antipartisan forces, confessed to the indiscriminate extermination of the innocent. It was not as if the evidence were circumstantial or dependent upon secondary witnesses. It was direct and damning.

In his opening address to the tribunal Justice Jackson remarked: "What makes this inquest significant is that these prisoners represent sinister influences that will lurk in the world long after their bodies have returned to dust."

These influences, in fact, have regenerated like a poisonous weed. Anti-Semitism and the euphemistic catchwords that led to "the Final Solution of the Jewish Question" have reappeared hand in hand. A worldwide cult has arisen claiming that the Holocaust never happened. A hundred books, booklets, and pamphlets have been printed alleging that the slaughter was imaginary or exaggerated, and is but a Jewish invention.

*Because of the lack of cohesion in the prosecution's presentation and the huge range of the case, I have reorganized some of the material for the purposes of comprehension and concisiveness, without, of course, altering the testimony or documentary evidence in any way, except for abridgment.

All of this might be dismissed as the frustrated thrashing about of a radical, irrational fringe were it not for the haunting parallels to the pre-Hitler era, and the continuing employment of Nazi propaganda methodology. A leader of the French neo-Nazis, for example, asserts that those Jews who died had merely been victims of the wartime food shortage. The Nazis had, in fact, originally planned to starve the Jews to death, allocating 186 calories per capita daily for their sustenance, but had abandoned the scheme for more direct methods after the ensuing epidemics had decimated not only the Jews but threatened to spread to the relatively well-fed German population.

Similar in nature is the assertion that Zyklon B gas was employed only as a disinfectant at Auschwitz. This had been the case until the fall of 1941, when an enterprising SS officer had concluded that if Zyklon B killed lice it could kill people just as well. Thereafter, the gas had been used, first, to murder thousands of Soviet prisoners of war, and then hundreds of thousands of Jews—nearly all of them women, children, and old people unfit for "extermination through work." Hitler's dictum that "the magnitude of a lie always contains a certain factor of credibility, since the great masses of the people . . . more easily fall a victim to a big lie than to a little one" has once more come into vogue.

The most effective means to combat such distortions is to make the facts accessible, and, with them, expose the statements for what they are. At Nuremberg, General Telford Taylor, the prosecutor of more war criminals than any other man, said: "We cannot here make history over again. But we can see that it is written true." This book, I hope, fulfills that goal.

I

Crime and Punishment

1 Escape from Auschwitz

On April 7, 1944, two Slovakian Jews, twenty-six-year-old Alfred Weczler and twenty-year-old Rudolf Vrba, escaped from Auschwitz. They provided the first eyewitness account of the concentration and extermination camp to the western world, an account that set off the chain of events that led to the Nuremberg trial.

When Hitler dismantled Czechoslovakia in 1939, he had left the Slovaks nominally in charge of their own internal affairs, dependent on good behavior. The Slovaks had copied most of the German anti-Semitic laws, expropriated Jewish businesses, removed the Jews from government and the professions, and left them with little opportunity to earn a living. By the spring of 1942 most of the eighty thousand Jews were unemployed and compressed into a few blocks in two cities, Sered and Nováky.

In March, Adolf Eichmann, the head of the Gestapo's Jewish Section, offered to take seventeen thousand of the unemployed Jews off the Slovakian government's hands for, ostensibly, work in German arms factories. On April 13, Weczler, packed with threescore other men into a small freight car furnished with a single bucket of water, became part of a transport of 640 men destined for Auschwitz.

Auschwitz lay thirty miles west of Cracow, Poland's fifth largest city, and was on the direct railroad line to German Upper Silesia. Before the German attack in September 1939, Auschwitz had been a Polish army camp. In May 1940, Rudolf Franz Ferdinand Höss,* the adjutant at the Sachsenhausen concentration camp, was detailed with thirty men to establish a new compound at Auschwitz.

Until the early spring of 1941, Auschwitz, containing nine thousand inmates, was an installation approximately the same size as earlier German concentration camps, such as Dachau and Buchenwald. Then, as Hitler prepared the assault on Russia, Heinrich Himmler, the head of the SS and German police, came to Auschwitz and told Höss that the camp would have to be expanded to accommodate a population of 130,000—100,000 of them Soviet prisoners of war. The inhabitants of seven villages standing on the swampy, malarial ground between the Sury and the Vistula rivers west of Auschwitz were to be dispossessed and removed as farm laborers to Germany. Since this area was thickly covered with birch trees, the Germans called the new part of the concentration camp Birkenau ("in the birches").

---

*Not to be confused with Rudolf Hess, Nazi Party secretary until May 1941.

Weczler's transport arrived in Auschwitz after midnight on April 15 —arrivals were usually timed so that the twelve thousand residents of the adjoining town would not be witness to their coming. Stumbling stiff and bewildered out of the cars into the glare of spotlights, the men were lined up in a column of five. Carrying their heavy luggage—for they had been told to come well equipped—they were marched a mile to a building, where they were ordered to strip. Their heads and bodies were shaved roughly, they were given showers, and then were disinfected with Lysol. Each man had a number tattooed onto his left breast, a procedure so painful that many passed out. (Later, to simplify processing, the Germans changed the location of the tattoos to inmates' left arms.) It was ten o'clock in the morning before the operation was completed.

Outfitted with wooden clogs and Russian uniforms daubed with red paint, Weczler and his compatriots were taken to Birkenau. There he learned that only 150 of the twelve thousand Russian prisoners of war detailed in December 1941 to work on the camp's construction had survived the winter. Quartered in half-finished, unheated buildings, they had died of exposure, starvation, and disease. The Birkenau camp, a mile long and a half-mile wide, was encompassed, like Auschwitz, by two rings of electrified barbed wire. Along these, watchtowers were placed every 150 yards. Only a few buildings had so far been completed, though the ultimate goal was to expand the camp to an area covering some two hundred square miles.

The men were awakened at three o'clock every morning and marched off at four to clear land and work on the construction of factories for Siemens, Germany's largest electrical manufacturer; I. G. Farben, the nation's leading chemical company; and the Deutsche Ausrustungswerke (German Defense Works), an SS enterprise. Jews not capable of labor were executed.

Except for a half-hour break at noon, when the prisoners each received a bowl of filthy carrot, cabbage, or turnip soup, the work continued uninterrupted until 6 PM. For supper the men received one ounce—a little over one slice—of moldy bread made from ersatz flour and sawdust. They slept in almost windowless barracks with steeply pitched roofs resembling stables. Tiers of balconies, honeycombed with cells two and one-half feet high, each shared by three men, ran along the walls, giving the building the appearance of a giant beehive.

Lice and fleas tortured the men. Rats were so bold they gnawed at the toes and fingers of sleepers and stole carefully preserved crumbs of bread out of their pockets. A third of the prisoners died every week—the sick and injured were taken to the infirmary, where they were granted two to three days to recover or expire. If they did neither, they were spritzed—given a fatal injection of phenol directly into the heart. At the end of two weeks, only 150 of the 640 men Weczler had arrived with were still alive. By August 15, all but 159 of the 2,722 on the first four transports from Slovakia were dead.

It was possible to survive only by becoming part of the inmate administration that Höss needed to operate the concentration camp. In the middle of May, Weczler obtained assignment to the *Krankenbau* (infirmary), first as head nurse, then as manager. The infirmary constituted an assembly hall for death, through which two thousand passed weekly. Of these twelve hundred died without assistance; the remainder were killed.

In June and August of 1942 typhus epidemics devastated Auschwitz. In the women's compound, Dr. Josef Mengele, the SS physician, devised an ingenious solution. The 750 women in the first barracks were taken to the gas chamber, where humans and lice were exterminated together. The barracks was then sealed and disinfected. After it was habitable again, the inmates of the second barracks were deloused by less heroic means, and moved into the first barracks. The second barracks was then disinfected; and so on down the line.

Over 105,000 bodies had now been dumped into shallow trenches in the spongy fields of Birkenau. As they decomposed, the earth rose like a yeasty mixture of dough and bubbled up nauseating gases, which spread for miles. Rats multiplied and swarmed in packs. Fish died in the streams. The entire area's water supply was polluted. *Brigadeführer* Ernst Grawitz, chief medical inspector of the SS, ordered the bodies burned. A drunken, one-eyed, twenty-seven-year-old trumpeter, gardener, and pig farmer named Otto Moll was placed in charge of 150 inmates set to exhuming and incinerating the bodies on open pyres. Week after week, month after month, the towers of smoke rose into the sky. The stench of burning flesh permeated hundreds of square miles, as far as Cracow and the Vistula River. The ashes of the dead were used to fertilize the fields of nearby farms. Not a person in the area remained unaware of what was going on.

Rudolf Vrba, the second of the Slovakians, arrived at Auschwitz in midsummer 1942, after first having been sent to the Maidanek concentration camp. Together with three thousand other men, he was assigned to the construction of the artificial rubber plant for I.G. Farben. Before long his legs were so swollen that he barely managed to avoid being picked for the gas chamber at a "selection." When he heard of an opening in the *Aufraumungskommando*—the so-called cleaning squad—which promised easier labor, he volunteered.

The task of the *Aufraumungskommando* was to empty the freight cars after their arrival, and collect and sort the possessions of the people. A hundred Jewish prisoners were assigned to the squad. Luggage, rucksacks,

boxes, parcels of all kinds were stacked in mountainous heaps in warehouses. Vrba and his companions went through and separated their contents—toothbrushes, mirrors, cans of food, underwear, furs, chocolate,
drugs, cameras, photographs, watches, tobacco, fountain pens, eyeglasses,
money, jewels. The usable portion of the clothing went to the German
Winterhilfe (relief) organization, the remainder was sent to textile mills for
reprocessing. The punishment for pocketing any of the things was hanging for the inmates and prison sentences for the SS guards. But, in fact,
the SS joined with the *Aufraumungskommando* in plunder. In this way a
large amount of goods, including food, jewels, and money, entered the
camp—and even created a madcap inflation. Those inmates who had access
to the black barter—such as the *Aufraumungskommando*, the Kapos (trus-
ties), and the prison bureaucracy of block elders and camp clerks—represented a distinct class. It was only by providing the inmate elite with a
chance to survive, and thus binding them to the SS in an unholy alliance,
that Höss was able to govern his charnel house and squelch periodic waves
of rebellion.

Following the transportation of the seventeen thousand Slovakian
Jews to Auschwitz in the spring of 1942, thirty-three thousand relatives—
women, children, and old people—were left behind in Slovakia. The
Slovakian government had expected the men to send back money for
support. When none came, the government asked Dieter Wisliceny, Eichmann's deputy in Slovakia, what was to be done with the families. Eichmann offered to take them off the Slovakians' hands and resettle them.
President Tiso, a Catholic priest, agreed on condition that the several
thousand converted Jews among them would be able to follow the Catholic
religion—the Slovakians, though anti-Jewish, did not subscribe to the Nazi
racial anti-Semitism.

Assurances were given, and the thirty-three thousand were duly
shipped: directly to the gas chambers of Maidanek and Auschwitz. When,
by the end of July, no word had been received from the families, Tiso
summoned Wisliceny and, in the presence of the papal nuncio, asked what
had happened to them. Receiving no satisfactory reply, he demanded that
a Slovakian commission be permitted to travel to Poland to talk to them.

Wisliceny, taken aback, said he would have to go to Berlin to discuss
the request with Eichmann. Eichmann murmured: "It is too bad the
Slovakians won't be able to see their Jews anymore, because they no longer
are among the living." He advised Wisliceny to make up a story and apply
himself to having the thirty thousand Jews still remaining in Slovakia
shipped to Poland.

But, amid rumors of Jews dying by the tens of thousands, the Slovakians balked. No more Jews were transported.

By the winter of 1943 Höss had augmented his extermination installation with four crematoriums, each with its own gas chamber capable of killing two thousand people simultaneously. The number of workers to be salvaged from a transport was always determined beforehand according to the labor needs of the camp. If there had been an epidemic, or it was summer, when farmhands were required, as many as thirty percent of the arrivees might be reprieved momentarily. At other times, as few as ten percent were selected for work.

As soon as the ambulatory had left the boxcars, the *Aufraumungskommando* scrambled in. In addition to the corpses left behind amid the incredible jetsam and filth, there were frequently seriously ill and sometimes unconscious persons. Once a woman gave birth to a baby at the moment of arrival. Simon Gotland, one of the *Kommando*, wrapped it and put it next to the mother on the floor. A Romanian-born German SS guard named Stefan Baretzki stormed up and beat Gotland and the mother with his swagger stick. Yelling "Why are you playing around with this filth!" he kicked the infant out of the car like a football, then directed Gotland: "Bring the shit over here!" But the baby was already dead.

Everyone unable to stand on his feet was declared by the SS doctor to be officially "dead." The dead, the near-dead, and the infants were heaved indiscriminately onto trucks by the *Aufraumungskommando*. Driven to the burning pits that continued to handle the overflow of corpses even after the construction of the crematoriums, all were heaped together upon the pyre and incinerated. At Auschwitz there was no particular compunction about burning humans alive—newborn infants were sometimes thrust into the laundry furnace as a matter of convenience.

Escape from Auschwitz was made difficult not only by the physical barriers, but by the negative attitude of the general camp population, which suffered after every escape. If an escapee somehow made his way beyond the two electrified barbed-wire fences and watchtowers, blaring sirens alerted the whole countryside. Dogs were put into pursuit, and SS and military personnel began to comb the fields and woods. With his shorn head and prison uniform, an inmate could expect no help from the local populace, for assisting an escapee meant death.

Weczler and Vrba had, however, learned from the failures of others and been able to secrete civilian clothing, money, and food. On April 7, 1944, they slipped through the cordon at Birkenau, and within a week they were in Bratislava, Slovakia.

When, at first, they told their tale to members of the Jewish community remaining in that city, they were greeted with incredulity. The most common reaction to revelations of the Nazi plan to exterminate the Jews of Europe was that the informer was a lunatic. Not only did assertions of genocide (a word not yet coined) go against the grain of civilization and concept of self-survival, but the German emphasis on order and legality (an emphasis that the Nazis were superficially careful to preserve) served to put the stamp of fantasy on such reports. It was not until Weczler produced one of the stereotyped cards dated "Waldsee," describing the idyllic conditions of "resettlement" that the Czech Jews had been forced to send to relatives, that horrified acceptance of the truth replaced the disbelief. Rabbi Weissmandel transcribed Weczler's and Vrba's detailed account, containing names, figures, and diagrams, into a sixty-page report that he smuggled to Budapest. From there it was forwarded to Roswell D. McClelland, whom President Franklin D. Roosevelt had dispatched to Switzerland as a representative of the War Refugee Board. By early summer the document was in the hands of the President.

The Weczler-Vrba report reached the White House soon after the Germans initiated the mass extermination of Hungarian Jews. Until the spring of 1944, Hungary had escaped German occupation by following a policy of appeasement and alliance with Hitler. In mid-March, however, as the Russians closed in on the Hungarian border, Hitler summoned Admiral Nicholas Horthy, the head of the government, to Salzburg, Austria, and accused him of preparing to become "another Italy"—that is, to switch sides from Germany to the Allies. Horthy, after being kept incommunicado for three days, was forced to agree to the occupation of Hungary by German troops.

The deportation of the Hungarian Jews began April 28. Within two months, 470,000 people were taken to Auschwitz. Of these, 330,000 went directly into the gas chamber. The other 140,000, deemed capable of work and designated "Transport Jews," were shipped out to various concentration and labor camps, or assigned to details at Auschwitz.

But Hungary, still theoretically independent, was no sealed chamber like Germany; and news flowed out from Budapest as through a sieve. Copies of the Weczler-Vrba account went to the pope, the king of Sweden, and other leaders. Weczler and Vrba even provided a detailed breakdown of the arriving transports, the number and nationality of the people they contained, and the fate of the transportees. (By March 1944, 1,765,000 people had been put to death at the camp.) The world shuddered at the scandal of Auschwitz. The European neutral nations—mainly Sweden and Switzerland, but also Turkey and Spain—provided passports that saved thousands of Jews from extermination. The papal nuncio intervened on behalf of converted Jews. In the United States there was a crescendo of outrage. Jewish organizations, and leading American Jews like Secretary of the Treasury Henry Morgenthau, Jr., and Judge Samuel I. Rosenman, personal adviser to the President, pressured Roosevelt to take action. On June 12, Roosevelt declared:

"This nation is appalled by the systematic persecution of helpless minority groups by the Nazis. As the final defeat of the Hitlerite forces draws closer, the fury of their insane desire to wipe out the Jewish race in Europe continues undiminished.

"To the Hitlerites, subordinates, functionaries, and satellites, to the German people and all other peoples under the Nazi yoke, we have made clear our determination to punish all participation in these acts of savagery. In the name of humanity we have called upon them to spare the lives of these innocent people.

"Hungary's fate," Roosevelt threatened, "will not be like any other civilized nation's . . . unless the deportations are stopped." On July 2 his words were reinforced by a heavy air raid on Budapest and its railroad facilities.*

Horthy pulled himself together and ordered the deportation of Budapest Jews aborted. With the Russian summer offensive sweeping into Romania and eastern Poland, Horthy's hand was strengthened, and when Hitler, two weeks later, demanded the resumption of the transportations, Horthy stalled him by agreeing to gather the remaining Jews in assembly areas, but only within Hungary. He followed this up by insisting that Eichmann and his staff be withdrawn. On August 25 Himmler ordered them out.

2   The Sword of Justice

Nearly two years had passed since President Roosevelt, on October 7, 1942, had first declared: "It is our intention that just and sure punishment shall be meted out to the ringleaders responsible for the organized murder of thousands of innocent persons in the commission of atrocities which have violated every tenet of the Christian faith." Two months later, on December 17, British Foreign Secretary Anthony Eden had told the House of Commons: "The German authorities are now carrying into effect Hitler's oft repeated intention to exterminate the Jewish people of Europe. From all the occupied centers of Europe Jews are being transported in conditions

---

*In September, the British bombed the factories and railroad yards at Auschwitz. Prisoners who were wounded were given first-class medical treatment and even received flowers and chocolate from the SS. Then, with consistent incongruity, the Nazis exterminated the recovered inmates.

of appalling horror and brutality to eastern Europe. In Poland, which has been made the principal Nazi slaughterhouse, the ghettos established by the Nazi invaders are being systematically emptied of all Jews except a few highly skilled workers required for war industries. None of those taken away are ever heard of again. The ablebodied are slowly worked to death in labor camps. The infirm are left to die of exposure and starvation, or are deliberately massacred in mass executions."

The next year, Roosevelt, Churchill, and Stalin formally stated in the Moscow Declaration their determination to bring the guilty to justice. On October 26, 1943, the United Nations War Crimes Commission, composed of fifteen Allied nations (not including the Soviet Union) held its first meeting in London. Again, on March 24, 1944, Roosevelt warned: "None who participate in these acts of savagery shall go unpunished. All who share in the guilt shall share the punishment."

Yet nothing had been done to implement the multitude of declarations. Morgenthau was bitter at the State Department for its bureaucratic bumbling and failure to facilitate the escape of Jews; and President Roosevelt was concerned about the possible loss of the Jewish vote in an election year. In the weeks following the Normandy landing on June 6, Eisenhower became more and more incensed as scores of British, Canadian, and American prisoners of war were shot by the Waffen SS in what seemed like calculated policy. In Washington, G-1, the Office of the Chief of Staff of the Personnel Division, was charged with collecting evidence on crimes committed against American servicemen. In July, the task was delegated to Lieutenant Colonel Murray C. Bernays; and Bernays was to prove the guiding spirit leading the way to the Nuremberg trial.

Bernays, of Lithuanian Jewish stock, had emigrated with his family to the United States in 1900, when he was six. A brilliant student, he was admitted to Harvard, from which he graduated in 1915. He then attended Columbia and Fordham University law schools. In New York he met Hertha Bernays, a niece of Sigmund Freud. When they were married in 1917, he adopted her family name.

After serving in the army during World War I, he established a lucrative New York law practice. He was a friend of Judge Rosenman, who informed him of the Weczler-Vrba report and the lack of progress in preparing the prosecution of Nazi crimes. He read *The Voice of Destruction* by Hermann Rauschning, who, as the former president of the Danzig senate, had once supported Hitler and met with him a number of times, but had broken with him in 1934. Rauschning quoted Hitler as declaring: "Conscience is a Jewish invention. It is a blemish, like circumcision. . . . Providence has ordained that I should be the greatest liberator of humanity. I am freeing men from the dirty and degrading self-mortification of a chimera called conscience and morality." According to Hitler, Judaism and Christianity were locked in an apocalyptic struggle for world domination with the new Nazi-Nordic god and ethos. Rauschning's book struck a responsive chord in Bernays, who had a streak of mysticism in him, encouraged by his second wife, an Episcopalian. Viewing the history of western civilization as a synthesis of Judaism and Christianity, Bernays adopted the belief that the Nazis represented a barbarian reaction and were attempting to destroy the structure of the western world. But how to integrate such a philosophical perspective with the prosecution of war criminals was beyond him.

Bernays was still becalmed in his juridical Sargasso Sea when President Roosevelt met Prime Minister Winston Churchill in Quebec in early September. On July 11, Churchill had written to Foreign Secretary Anthony Eden: "There is no doubt that this is probably the greatest and most horrible crime ever committed in the whole history of the world, and it has been done by scientific machinery by nominally civilized men in the name of a great State. . . . It is quite clear that all concerned who may fall into our hands, including the people who only obeyed orders by carrying out the butcheries, should be put to death after their association with the murders has been proved."

Morgenthau, who advocated the division and deindustrialization of Germany, concurred with Churchill and the British Lord Chancellor,* John Simon, that the principal Nazi leaders should be charged with their crimes, then summarily shot. On the other hand, Colonel Mickey Marcus of the Army Civil Affairs Division, which was charged with formulating postwar policy for Germany, was disturbed by Morgenthau's emotional approach. At a meeting with Bernays, he agreed that retribution must not appear to be a Judaic act of revenge. Summary execution, no matter how justified, could never serve as a substitute for justice.

"Not to try these beasts would be to miss the educational and therapeutic opportunity of our generation," Bernays argued. "They must be tried not alone for their specific aims, but for the bestiality from which these crimes sprang."

Marcus reacted enthusiastically. He urged Bernays to formulate his ideas into a concrete plan, and provided him with an advance copy of Rafael Lemkin's book, *Axis Rule in Occupied Europe*. Lemkin, an international legal authority, had escaped from Poland after the Nazi attack and ultimately made his way to the United States, where he joined the OSS.

---

*The Lord Chancellor presides over the House of Lords, is the head of the judiciary, and has control over all judicial appointments. There is no comparable position in the United States government.

One of Lemkin's theses was that the SS, the Gestapo, and other Nazi groups were essentially criminal organizations of volunteer gangsters.

As Bernays pondered the problem day after day and lay sleepless in the dank, warm nights of pre–air-conditioned Washington, he was gripped by a creative fervor. International law, he came to believe, represented the soul and conscience and aspirations of mankind—it had to be shaped and reshaped according to the dictates of civilization. If one proceeded on the basis of trying individuals for specific offenses, one would never apprehend or convict more than a limited number of the criminals. It was this, Bernays thought, that the Nazis were banking on—that if crimes are widespread and hideous enough, justice will never catch up with more than a small proportion of the perpetrators.

But even if by some miracle every single guilty Nazi were found and convicted, the essential crime, the atrocity of Nazism, would still not have been touched. Attempting to reconcile demands, facts, and needs into a viable legal approach, Bernays expanded on Lemkin's view that organizations like the SS were criminal conspiracies. On the basis of that hypothesis, it could be understood that the killing of millions of Jews in Auschwitz and the shooting of scores of prisoners of war in Normandy were not unrelated events, but formed part of a gigantic pattern:

"The crimes and atrocities were not single or unconnected, but were the inevitable outcome of the basic criminal conspiracy of the Nazi party," he wrote. "This conspiracy, based on the Nazi doctrine of racism and totalitarianism, involved murder, terrorism, and the destruction of peaceful populations in violation of the laws of war.

"A conspiracy is criminal either because it aims at the accomplishment of lawful ends by unlawful means, or because it aims at the accomplishment of unlawful ends by lawful means. Therefore, such technicalities as the question whether the extermination of fellow Germans by Nazi Germans was unlawful, or whether this could be a 'war crime' if it was perpetrated before there was a state of war, would be unimportant, if you recognize as the *basic* crime the Nazi conspiracy which required for its success the killing of dissident liberal Germans and the extermination of German (and non-German) Jews before and after the war had begun.

"Therefore, the thing to do [is] to try the organizations along with the Nazi leaders on the conspiracy charge; and having convicted the organizations, the conviction should serve as prima facie proof of the guilt of any of their members."

Bernays proposed that an international tribunal should be established to condemn violence, terror, racism, totalitarianism, and wanton destruction; the tribunal should arouse the German people to a sense of their guilt and a realization of their responsibility. Otherwise, Germany would simply have lost another war; the German people would not come to understand the barbarism they had supported, nor have any conception of the criminal character of the Nazi regime. The fascist potential would remain undiminished, and the menace remain. Only the staging of a great trial—or, possibly, a number of trials—in which the conspiracy of the Nazi leadership would be proved and the utilization of the Nazi organizations in the furtherance of that conspiracy would be established, could all the objectives be attained, and all criminals, large and small, be caught in the same web.

At a meeting on October 24, Bernays's argument immediately appealed to Secretary of War Henry L. Stimson. He had been secretary of state under President Hoover from 1929 to 1933, and had adopted the view that the 1928 Kellogg-Briand Pact outlawed aggressive war and seizure of territories: "Individuals who violate this Pact by launching an aggressive war commit no less a criminal act than do individuals who violate the Hague and Geneva Conventions by murdering prisoners of war. They simply do it on a greater and more destructive scale."

A month later, on November 27, a joint memorandum, "The Trial and Punishment of European War Criminals," was submitted to the President by Stimson and Secretary of State Cordell Hull. It urged the immediate formation of an investigative body to gather evidence on the conspiracy so that it could be proved in a fair trial. "A condemnation after such a proceeding will meet the judgment of history," the memo asserted, "so that the Germans will not be able to claim, as they have been claiming with regard to the Versailles Treaty, that an admission of war guilt was exacted from them under duress."

In mid-January, Attorney General Francis Biddle put his stamp of approval on the Bernays plan (authorship of which was now more or less attributed to Stimson). A prosecutorial staff to collect evidence and prepare the case was to be immediately set up by the Big Four.* The American position would be put forward at the Yalta Conference between Roosevelt, Churchill, and Stalin in February.

At Yalta, however, the proposal was never placed on the agenda. Consequently, the first week in April, President Roosevelt sent a delegation headed by Judge Rosenman to London to negotiate. They were unable to prevail or even to make progress. Churchill and Lord Simon stuck to the proposition that "it is beyond question that Hitler and a number of arch criminals associated with him [including Mussolini, Himmler, Goering, Ribbentrop, and Goebbels] must, so far as they fall into Allied hands,

---

*The Big Four in this context were the United States, Britain, the Soviet Union, and France, though on other occasions the term embraced China but excluded France.

suffer the penalty of death for their conduct leading up to the war and for their wickedness in the conduct of the war. It being conceded that these leaders must suffer death, the question arises whether they should be tried by some form of tribunal claiming to exercise judicial functions, or whether the decision taken by the Allies should be reached and enforced without the machinery of a trial."

After weighing the pros and cons, the British concluded once more that the dangers of a trial outweighed the advantages and that "execution without trial is the preferable course."

The British reaction created a dilemma of major proportions for the Roosevelt administration. One of the Washingtonians with direct ties to the administration was Supreme Court Justice Robert Jackson. Jackson, who had been Roosevelt's solicitor general and attorney general before being appointed to the Supreme Court in 1941, was a fishing and poker-playing crony of the President's. He was, therefore, voicing not merely his own opinion when he prepared an address scheduled for delivery to the American Society of International Law on April 13:

"I am not so troubled as some seem to be over problems of jurisdiction of war criminals or of finding existing and recognized law by which standards of guilt may be determined. But . . . men of our tradition cannot regard as a trial any proceeding that does not honestly search for the facts. . . . The ultimate principle is that you must put no man on trial under the form of judicial proceedings if you are not willing to see him freed if not proved guilty. If you are determined to execute a man in any case, there is no occasion for a trial. The world yields no respect to courts that are merely organized to convict."

On April 12, the day before the address, President Roosevelt died. Judge Rosenman, still in England, returned to the United States and briefed Harry Truman. The Russians had opened the battle for Berlin. The American army had virtually cut Germany in two. The collapse of the Nazis appeared imminent. Rosenman impressed upon Truman that emphatic action was required to convince the British that the United States was determined to proceed with a trial, with or without the coopera-tion of its allies. On April 26, Truman sent Rosenman to offer Jackson the post of chief of counsel to prepare the case—an appointment that would place American prestige directly on the line.

Jackson, fifty-three years old, physically vigorous, by nature a partisan who relished a good fight, had been chafing throughout the war that he was unable to play a more relevant role in the great drama. When President Truman offered him the opportunity to organize and prosecute what promised to be a precedent-setting trial, and suggested, in fact, that he might be the advocate for all of the United Nations, Jackson responded like a high-strung racehorse led into the starting gate. On April 29 he told Truman: "I doubt the wisdom of delaying United States action pending agreement that I should prosecute on behalf of all the United Nations. I should be satisfied to represent the United States alone at the outset and such others as desire to entrust their cases to us. The best way to gain confidence in leadership is not to ask for it but to be the best prepared." Time was of the essence, he believed, not only because the world expected justice to be meted out swiftly, but also because he would have to return to the Supreme Court when it reconvened in October. "Hence, to some extent, I would sacrifice perfection for expedition."

Jackson, radiating self-confidence, independence, and power, proceeded without awaiting the formal announcement of his appointment. He converted the War Department group from its probing, exploratory nature into an operating nucleus. He endorsed, in addition to Bernays' earlier concepts, proposals to create an executive organization consisting of representatives from each of the Big Four to prepare the prosecution's case, and to establish a military tribunal of four judges and four alternates from the United States, Great Britain, the Soviet Union, and France.

On May 3, Rosenman and Secretary of State Stettinius, who had replaced Hull, met with Soviet Foreign Minister Vyacheslav Molotov and British Foreign Secretary Anthony Eden in San Francisco, where the foreign ministers of the Allies were meeting to establish the United Nations Organization. Only ten days before, the British government had again reiterated its opposition to a trial. On April 30, however, Hitler had committed suicide and been followed by Goebbels. Mussolini was captured and executed by Italian partisans. Two weeks later Himmler bit into a capsule of cyanide. With these men dead, the British opposition to a trial softened. The third week in May the foreign ministers agreed in principle to the American proposal.

Jackson, releasing the pent-up frustration of four years, dashed ahead and began assembling a staff around two longtime Washington friends, Assistant Attorney General Francis Shea and Sidney Alderman, general counsel for the Southern Railway. By May 17 the group had categorized types of evidence to look for, and Jackson was enlisting the services of a variety of government agencies, particularly the OSS, whose chief, Major General "Wild Bill" Donovan, had proffered his personal assistance.

When, a few days later, the United Nations War Crimes Commission decided to have a full-dress meeting of all participating nations on May 31 to discuss the indictment of Hermann Goering and other top Nazis, Jackson was disturbed that he might be preempted out of the prosecution. He decided to dash to Europe on a combined scouting and lobbying expedition—a journey that took on some of the aspects of a crusade as Jackson raised the sword of justice and made it clear he intended to wield it with or without the participation of the British, Russians, and French.

On May 28, Jackson met with Lord Chancellor Simon, Foreign Secretary Eden, and Attorney General Maxwell Fyfe in London, and overcame the British objections to the trial one by one. Although the trial must be fair and impartial, he argued, it need not be encumbered with the legalisms of Anglo-Saxon law. Nor need it give undue weight to precedents—international law had arisen out of the spread of civilization and the acceptance of certain standards; it changed with differing circumstances and requirements; it was not static, but in a continuous state of development. Since the United States already had a majority of top Nazis in its custody, it intended to proceed rapidly with an investigation and indictment—preferably in association with its allies, but alone if necessary. Jackson's whirlwind so unnerved the British that the next day Prime Minister Churchill appointed Attorney General Fyfe as Jackson's counterpart.

On June 1, Jackson returned to the United States, where his staff was rushing off in all directions to hunt for evidence. Colonel Telford Taylor, who had recently been assigned to Jackson after supervising the American processing of information from Bletchley, the British Ultra code-breaking center, advocated close cooperation with the British in the gathering of materials. They were, Taylor asserted, "far better staffed than we are with people who have achieved real expertise in knowledge of the Wehrmacht, the SS, the several police and intelligence services, and other German military, political, and economic organizations." The problem, Taylor pointed out, was not the obtaining of evidence—the record of German atrocities in France alone filled thirteen volumes—but of culling and organizing the material.

In the same fashion that Bernays had established the general approach to the trial of the Nazi leaders, Taylor outlined the procedure for the gathering of evidence and preparation of the case. Jackson, in a lengthy report to the President on June 7, incorporated many of the views of both men, and needed no convincing that the bulk of the evidence was to be found at the scene of the crimes. Jettisoning his earlier scheme of sending investigative teams to Europe while preparing the bulk of the case in Washington, Jackson decided to move his headquarters to London. Concurrently, he reached agreement with Fyfe that the chief prosecutors of the Big Four would meet in the British capital the third week in June to devise a protocol, establish rules for the trial, and select the defendants.

In London, Jackson, his two secretaries, his two aides (one of them his lanky young son, Bill, a navy ensign), and his two deputies, Alderman and Shea, moved into Claridge's, the city's most fashionable hotel. Bernays and other members of the staff were lodged in comfortable but less luxurious surroundings; it was the first manifestation of a divisiveness that was to assume a prominent role in the proceedings. The Americans hardly had time to adjust to their new environment—in fact, had not unpacked the boxes of documents that they brought with them—before the first meeting with the British took place on Thursday, June 21.

The British suggested that the trial might be held in Munich, the cradle of the Nazi movement; or, alternately, in Berlin or Leipzig. Jackson replied that he had no objection to Munich, which was in the American zone, but that the United States did not want the trial held in either of the other two cities, which were under Russian occupation. Fyfe proposed ten top Nazis as defendants: Hermann Goering, commander of the Luftwaffe, director of the Four Year Plan, founder of the Gestapo, and onetime heir apparent to Adolf Hitler; Rudolf Hess, party secretary and Hitler's right-hand man until 1941, when he had mysteriously parachuted from a Messerschmitt fighter over Scotland; Joachim von Ribbentrop, the foreign minister; Robert Ley, director of the German Labor Front; Alfred Rosenberg, party theoretician and minister for the Occupied Eastern Territories; Wilhelm Frick, interior minister; Field Marshal Wilhelm Keitel, chief of staff of the Wehrmacht; Julius Streicher, a gauleiter and notorious Jew baiter; Ernst Kaltenbrunner, head of the Reich Security Office, the second-ranking man in the SS after Himmler; and Hans Frank, governor of occupied Poland.

The British view was that "if we undertook to tell the whole story, as history may tell it in the future, it would take us years," but that, in fact, the trial could begin "about September 15 and last at most two weeks, with seven days for the four prosecuting nations to present their cases against ten defendants, and seven days for the defendants to present their cases." The British thought that the Americans were overly concerned with cataloging and indexing the evidence, since only bits and pieces were going to be plucked out and used.

Fyfe and Jackson agreed that preparations for the trial should move ahead without waiting for the arrival of the French and Russians. Four subcommittees were established, and Jackson assigned Alderman and Shea to the most important of these, concerned with preparation of the protocol. Alderman and Bernays were put on the committee charged with drafting the indictment.

Bernays, brooding, felt that he was being slighted and that the whole endeavor was likely to be twisted and crippled by men of lesser commitment than he. A chain smoker who liked to have a sherry or two for lunch and two or three drinks before dinner, he suffered from chronic bronchitis and a persistent cough. He was depressed by a city released from the tensions of war but without the benefits of peace—the people looked drab, there were long queues at every bus stop, and restaurants had elaborate menus but little food. He was pining for his wife, whom he called "Monkey Darling."

"I can't tell you how things are going," he wrote. "First it's a military secret. Second I don't know. The place is agog with resentments and intrigue. The atmosphere is hateful. An absolute gulf has been established between Claridge's and the slums. It's not only a social gulf, but also a yawning chasm within the organization. I try very hard but it's almost impossible to be creative within this atmosphere. At first people kept their feelings to themselves, then they began talking about it openly. Now it's becoming a subject for open comment."

The Russians arrived, together with the French, on June 25. Jackson had expected that reaching agreement would be a matter of no more than a few days. But he had no experience in international negotiations and was unrealistic about the difficulties of reconciling four divergent viewpoints, the holders of one of which had to refer each major question to Moscow for decision. The Anglo-American system of trial had little in common with the continental, followed by the French and Russians. Jackson was as ill-informed about continental practices as Major General I. T. Nikitchenko, the forty-five-year-old head of the Soviet delegation, was about American; and repeatedly one was unable to comprehend the other. Furthermore, it quickly became clear that the American and Soviet conceptions of the International Military Tribunal were startlingly at odds.

Nikitchenko maintained: "We are dealing here with the chief war criminals who have already been convicted by both the Moscow and Crimea [Yalta] declarations." The job of the court was merely to decide the degree of guilt of each individual, and to mete out punishment. The essence of the case would be determined before the start of the trial—in the continental system, the prosecutor assembled all evidence both against and in favor of the accused and presented it to an examining judge, who then decided whether the person should be brought to trial. If the judge ruled in the affirmative, he was, in effect, finding the person guilty, so that the burden of proof from then on rested on the defendant.

Unlike procedure in Anglo-American law, where the prosecutor and defense counsel are adversaries, with the judge acting as arbiter, in continental law prosecutor, defense counsel, and judge are all charged with the task of arriving at the truth. Thus, Nikitchenko did not really understand what Jackson meant when he emphasized that the judges must be independent and impartial, but replied that the Soviets did not accept the proposition that "the judge is a completely disinterested party with no knowledge of the case. The case for the prosecution is undoubtedly known to the judge before the trial starts and there is therefore no necessity to create a sort of fiction that the judge is a disinterested person. If such procedure is adopted that the judge is supposed to be impartial, it would only lead to unnecessary delays."

Nikitchenko's conception of the trial so shocked Jackson that he suggested, on June 29, that the best thing might be for each nation to go ahead and try the Nazis it held in custody according to its own customs.

The following day he recovered sufficiently to reiterate the American position that it was "necessary to authenticate by methods of the highest accuracy the whole history of the Nazi movement, its extermination of minorities, its aggression against neighbors, its treachery and its barbarism. . . . We envision it as a trial of the master planners."

But when, after the weekend, Nikitchenko introduced the draft of a proposed agreement, the gap seemed to widen further. The draft made no provision for the trial of organizations, such as the SS and the Gestapo—these, Nikitchenko asserted, had been outlawed by the Yalta Declaration and were now dissolved. A trial of them would be redundant.

Jackson responded that the concept of a conspiracy or common plan involving not only individuals but organizations was the heart of the American proposal, and if this were rejected, there was nothing left. The United States, he said, held 200,000 prisoners and it did not want to conduct 200,000 trials.

The next day produced new disagreement. SHAEF (Supreme Headquarters Allied Expeditionary Force) had conducted a survey of German cities as possible sites for the trial, Jackson revealed. The only undamaged facilities extensive enough to accommodate the trial were in Nuremberg, so Nuremberg should be selected as the location.

Nikitchenko was taken aback. The time had not yet come, he thought, to be talking about the headquarters of the tribunal, but he was certain that when it was selected it should be Berlin. Trials of individuals could be held wherever it seemed most appropriate. (Whether the International Military Tribunal would conduct one trial, a small number of trials, or many trials, had scarcely been touched upon.) Goering, for example, Nikitchenko suggested, might be tried in London.

When, following a three-day break, the Four Power meeting reconvened in London on July 7, Jackson said he was greatly encouraged by the documentary evidence being accumulated. "We are getting proof tracing the responsibility for these atrocities and war crimes back to the top authorities better than I expected we would get it. I did not think men would ever be so foolish as to put in writing some of the things the Germans did. The stupidity of it and the brutality of it would simply appall you."

Jackson, believing—quite rightly—that the United States possessed the trump cards, put all the pressure at his command on the other delegations. The United States held approximately 350 Nazis that it classified as major war criminals, and it was the only nation to have set up a full-scale investigating and evidence-gathering operation. Bulldozing ahead, he extracted a C-47 from the Army Air Corps, and told his confreres he was prepared to fly everyone to Nuremberg for a personal inspection.

All except Nikitchenko agreed to go. The pilot flew low over several German cities to give the passengers a view of the destruction. The reality shook Fyfe. City after city appeared as desolate as the ruins of Carthage; even though Fyfe had been through the blitz in London, he had had no idea of the devastation wrought by the British and American bombing. Approximately 600,000 Germans had died in the air raids, ten times the number of Britons killed, and more than twice the total of the 292,000 Americans killed on all battlefronts during the war.

In Nuremberg, the plane settled onto the runway as if it were landing on a dead planet—the city had not only suffered from some of the heaviest bombings, but was one of the few for which the Germans had made a determined fight against the Americans. For five days in April, tanks, artillery, and screaming fighter-bombers had ground down resistance street by street around the clock—at night the attackers had lighted the city by reflecting scores of searchlights from the clouds. On April 20, Hitler's last birthday, the city had been secured, and the next day the Americans had staged a thunderous parade to mock the Führer. By then, more than three-fourths of central Nuremberg was rubble.

The area commander and a large contingent of brass awaited Jackson's party on the tarmac. The VIPs were shepherded into a Packard sedan, and the remainder of the party climbed into GI vehicles. The convoy twisted through streets where rubble towered up like slag heaps, blackened girders contorted like frozen snakes, slabs of concrete fell in all directions like a giant's cookie pile, and a fine white dust sifted over everything. On jagged remnants of purposeless walls the saints of cracked and scarred frescoes lifted their arms in supplication. Shards of statuary and stained glass glinted jewellike in the sun. Here and there a German helmet perched atop a rock or a stake marked the grave of a Wehrmacht soldier buried where he had fallen. An estimated twenty thousand dead still entombed beneath the rubble wafted reminders of their presence up into the hot summer air. Half the population of 400,000 had fled, and much of the remainder were living in dugouts and cellars, from which they emerged blinking, like human moles.

"This cannot be rebuilt," Bernays thought, "this monumental wreckage of insolent wickedness brought crumbling down on the heads of the wrongdoers. It is too overwhelming. I am led to the feeling I have always had about Lazarus, that when he was resurrected and walked under the bright hot sun he still had upon him all the rest of his life the smell of the grave clothes. The city smells of broken pipes and shattered masonry and here and there of corpses not yet disinterred. They have come out of the teachings of death into its realization."

By the time the party reached the Palace of Justice, hardly a man would have argued that there was a more appropriate place to try the German leadership for the destruction, waste, cruelty, and suffering of the war. Although buildings had been leveled all around, the great complex spreading over several acres had suffered relatively little damage; some windows were smashed and boarded up, a few of the life-sized statues enniched in the walls had been blown off or decapitated, and a bomb had caved in a small portion of the roof. Inside, the area commander and Jackson led the way through dark corridors strewn with documents, books, empty cartridges, and the litter of war to the Court of Assizes, the largest of some twenty courtrooms on the second story. The GIs were using it for a recreation hall: a piano sat to one side, and a keg of beer graced the judge's bench. An engineer explained that the size of the court could be doubled by knocking out a wall and combining two rooms. To the rear of the Palace was a huge prison, its four buildings, radiating like the spokes of a half-wheel, capable of holding twelve hundred prisoners. A wall surrounded the entire complex.

The following afternoon the plane returned to London. Bernays was not optimistic. "It took a mighty coalition to defeat Germany," he mused. "It will take no less a coalition to keep her from renewing the battle and very likely winning it. It is not enough that the coalition shall be of nations. The coalition must be of the moral forces within nations. I do not feel easy about that."

The next day the negotiations recommenced. The tour had convinced the British and French of Nuremberg's appropriateness for the trial; and Nikitchenko revealed that, although he had not gone, he had recommended to Moscow that Nuremberg be accepted as the site for the first trial—providing, of course, that Berlin was chosen for the seat of the tribunal. Jackson grudgingly assented, making it clear he expected Berlin to be merely symbolic.

But if that issue was tentatively settled, it was the exception. The Russians and French would not go along with the concept of a criminal plan or conspiracy, and all three Allies deserted the Americans on the question of indicting the Germans for launching an aggressive war. Professor André Gros, who had been the French representative on the United

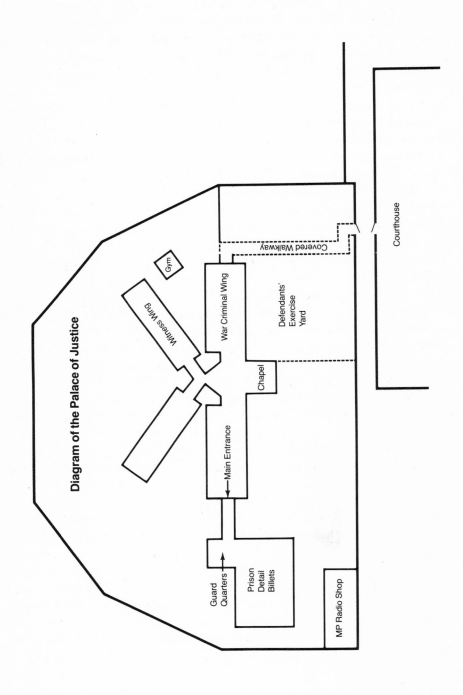

Diagram of the Palace of Justice

Nations War Crimes Commission, argued: "We do not consider as a criminal act the launching of a war of aggression." Fyfe was concerned that if the Germans were charged with attacking Norway, the British might be considered equally culpable, since their occupation forces had been only a destroyer's length behind. The Russians had been scarcely less rapacious than the Germans. They had occupied half of Poland after the Nazi attack, they had invaded Finland, they had annexed the Baltic countries and extracted Bessarabia from Romania. (All these areas, however, had been part of the Russian Empire, and had been detached from the prostrate Soviet nation after World War I.) Nikitchenko asked, realistically if cynically:

"Is it proposed then to condemn aggression or initiation of war in general or to condemn specifically aggression started by the Nazis? If the attempt is to have a general definition, that would *not* be agreeable."

Jackson argued forcefully and tenaciously: "We are trying to reach by our 'common plan or enterprise' device the planners. The zealots who put this thing across. . . . The reason that this program of extermination of Jews becomes an international concern is this: It was part of a plan for making an illegal war. Unless we have a war connection, I would think we have no basis for dealing with the atrocities . . . committed inside Germany, under German law, or even in violation of German law. . . . We must declare that they [the Nazi leaders] are answerable personally, and I am frank to say that international law is indefinite and weak in our support."

"Our difficulties are more or less this," Gros suggested. "The Americans want to win the trial on the grounds that the Nazi war was illegal, and the French people and other people of occupied countries just want to show that the Nazis were bandits."

In the midst of the debate, Fyfe arose and announced, "I must go and learn my fate at the polls." The British were in the throes of an election, and Fyfe had been dashing off nightly to his constituency in Liverpool, 150 miles to the north, where he was met by his wife with a car and cold cuts. After appearing at three rallies, Fyfe would take a Pullman back to London for the next morning's meeting.

The participants agreed that they would break for a day until the election results were in—everyone expected Churchill's Tory government to be returned to office. Churchill himself was at Potsdam, meeting with Stalin and Truman. Jackson parted with the admonition: "I am willing to recommend sending the question to Potsdam for a political decision if we cannot agree on a judicial disposition of it."

A few hours later Jackson decided that, rather than send the question to Potsdam, he would take it there personally, and flew off in semisecrecy to confer with Secretary of State James F. Byrnes. While he was there, the election results were announced—the Labour Party had pulled off a sweeping upset, (although Fyfe himself was reelected). The anti-imperialist Labourites were less concerned about the sticking point of aggressive war than the Tories. On August 1, Jackson, returning to London, met with the new Lord Chancellor, and received his backing for the American position. From Potsdam, Stalin, Truman, and the new British prime minister, Clement Attlee, signaled that an accord was to be reached speedily.

At the next and final negotiating session on August 2, Jackson continued to play the eternal pessimist. "This trial has a scope that is utterly beyond anything that has ever been attempted that I know of in judicial history, and we must attempt to do it in four languages," he declared. Unless the negotiators could agree on clear and streamlined procedures, it might yet be better to call the whole thing off: "I would much rather see us *agree* that the trial is impossible than to *demonstrate* the trial is impossible."

"As a matter of fact, we came here authorized to sign an agreement for the establishment of an International Military Tribunal," Nikitchenko retorted testily. "We have no power to sign an agreement saying we do not need an International Military Tribunal."

That settled the matter. Six days later the agreement and charter for the tribunal were signed, giving the Americans everything that Bernays and Jackson had originally asked for. Under the omnibus conspiracy charge, the Nazi leadership was indicted for (1) Crimes Against Peace, including the launching of an aggressive war; (2) War Crimes, that is, acts contrary to acceptable usages and against the provisions of the Hague and Geneva conventions; and (3) Crimes Against Humanity, covering any and all atrocities committed by the regime during its reign.*

Included in Bernays's task of preparing the indictment and selecting the defendants was the responsibility for gathering and systematizing the evidence in London. On August 8, the day after the signing of the charter, Bernays conducted an orientation for the Soviet, British, and French delegations on the state of the evidence.

In early July Bernays had complained: "We're deplorably behind schedule in the procurement of evidence; we have repeatedly won the case with glorious brave talk in conference, but the actual proof could be listed on a very few three-by-five filing cards." Since then, however, material had accumulated at avalanche proportions.

---

*Jackson's insistence on the umbrella-conspiracy concept subsequently resulted in a four-count indictment, of which the first was Conspiracy to Wage Aggressive War. The other three charges became Counts 2, 3, and 4.

The most spectacular of the finds were the records of Alfred Rosenberg, providing a detailed description of German operations in the East and of the looting of the various occupied territories. Discovered hidden beneath wet straw behind a wall in a Bavarian barn by an OSS lieutenant seeking photographic material, the forty-seven crates were flown to Paris, where Jackson had set up his continental document-collecting center. Though, by the end of July, the contents of the crates had been only cursorily examined, one of Bernays's investigators wrote him: "This is an almost unbelievable admission of *systematic* killings, looting, etc."

Bernays attempted to systematize the logging of the huge volume of documents, but thought: "To do the job we started out to do, in the time allowed, it looks very much as though we need a minor miracle." To the gathering in London he explained the method of summarization and analysis he had introduced; and Nikitchenko was impressed with his "scientific and efficient" approach.

Despite his frenetic efforts, however, Bernays felt himself more and more frozen out of the decision-making councils; and his assessment of the operation was acerbic:

"As usual in this bloody mission it's snafu, because there's no organization, no control," he wrote. "At bottom of the whole thing is the fact the mission has been from the beginning infested with self-seeking competition for publicity; for cushy assignments with the least possible to do and the most to be got out of it; and having started at the very top a situation like that spreads and becomes a general infection. . . . I'm not to blame if these glory thieves made away with my property. They're men, I'm only a dreamer."

Up to this juncture, Bernays had swallowed what he considered the slights and arrows of outrageous organization, and he was prepared to continue, even though Alderman and Shea had had their positions as Jackson's chief deputies solidified by being named associate counsel. On August 14, however, Bernays learned that on the previous day Jackson, subsequent to a Russian suggestion that responsibility for various aspects of the case be divided among the four Allies, had assigned Shea the task of preparing the American portion of the indictment on the Crimes Against Peace; Alderman was placed in charge of War Crimes and Crimes Against Humanity in the West; and Colonel Telford Taylor, who had completed his supervision of the compilation of the OSS studies, received responsibility for War Crimes and Crimes Against Humanity in the East. Jackson kept for himself jurisdiction over prosecution of the common plan, or conspiracy, to instigate the war. Bernays was devastated. From the beginning he had looked upon himself as the man who, by doing the work behind the scenes, would be the guiding force in the trial. It seemed to him now, probably erroneously as events were to demonstrate, that, at best, he could play only a subordinate role. Going to Jackson, he requested his release for reasons of health. Jackson did not try to dissuade him, and Bernays flew back immediately to the United States.

Jackson had never been comfortable with Bernays; and Bernays's idealistic concept of the trial already had planted the roots of many of the difficulties that were to be encountered during its staging. But, in Bernays's departure, the prosecution lost a capable organizer, a man driven by a mission, tireless in pursuit of his goal.

"Your knowledge of the subject, your enthusiasm, your energy, and your grasp cannot be replaced," another colonel on the prosecution staff wrote him.

3   The Accused

During his stay in London, Bernays had compiled a master list of the major German war criminals; by the time he departed, the number stood at 122. On the first ten of these, Goering, Hess, Ribbentrop, Ley, Rosenberg, Frick, Keitel, Streicher, Kaltenbrunner, and Frank, suggested originally by the British, the Americans immediately agreed. Only Hess, because of his disoriented mental condition, posed a question mark. The Americans proposed five others: Admiral Karl Doenitz, head of the submarine service until his elevation to command of the entire Nazi navy in January 1943; Arthur Seyss-Inquart, an Austrian who had played a pivotal role in Hitler's Anschluss in 1938 and subsequently had been head of the German administration in the occupied Netherlands; Albert Speer, chief of Nazi war production during the last three and one-half years of the war; Hjalmar Schacht, economics minister and head of the Reichsbank during the first five years of the Hitler regime; and Walther Funk, who had replaced Schacht as minister of economics and president of the Reichsbank. The latter three primarily interested the Americans, with their emphasis on the economic aspects of the Nazi aggression; but the British had no objection to them.

Almost everyone on the American and British delegations had his favorite candidate, and lists were compiled periodically. But by August 8, when the charter was signed, only Martin Bormann, who had succeeded Hess as party secretary, had been added. Since all the men were to be charged with a conspiracy, it was thought proper, and perhaps necessary, to list Hitler at the head of the group. The prosecutorial staff, nevertheless, hesitated to include him, for—although there was little doubt that he had killed himself—they feared that to do so might generate rumors of his survival.

No criteria had been established for inclusion in the list of defendants, and additions were arbitrary. The British suggested Baldur von Schirach, organizer and leader of the Hitler Youth, and subsequently gauleiter of Vienna. The Americans, adhering to the concept that each of the individual organizations should be represented by one or more of its leaders, had named Keitel for the armed forces, Doenitz the navy, and Goering the Luftwaffe, but were missing a man for the army. So General Alfred Jodl, the chief of the Wehrmacht operations staff, was included.

The OSS thought that to present a true panorama of Nazi crimes at least thirty defendants, including several industrialists, would have to be selected. The best known was Alfried Krupp, operating head of the world-famous armaments firm. His name was added, as was that of Fritz Sauckel, who had impressed workers from all over Europe into Hitler's labor program. By mid-August, however, no final determination had been made, and Jackson's list of potential defendants still contained seventy-three names.

After thinking the matter over, Jackson decided there was no point in trying a dead man, and dropped Hitler. However, Franz von Papen, who had preceded Hitler as chancellor and briefly been vice-chancellor in Hitler's cabinet, was tacked on.

When the tentative list was shown to the French and Russians in the third week of August, the French were chagrined that it contained no German held by them, and combed their roster for a candidate. They came up with Baron Constantin von Neurath, who had been living in retirement upon his estate in Württemberg, which was part of the French occupation zone. Neurath's tenure as Protector of Bohemia and Moravia and head of a "Secret Cabinet Council" placed him under suspicion. No one on the Allied staffs knew what this cabinet council had consisted of; but it sounded appropriately menacing.

On August 25, Jackson, Fyfe, Gros, and Nikitchenko agreed on a list of twenty-two defendants. Twenty-one were in custody. The twenty-second, Bormann, had, according to rumors, been captured by the Russians. Jackson repeatedly questioned Nikitchenko whether the Russians held Bormann; but Nikitchenko did not know, and apparently could not find out. A press release naming the accused was prepared, and about to be released on August 28, when Nikitchenko rushed in to announce that the Soviets did not hold Bormann, but that they had captured two Germans whom they wanted added to the list.

First was Admiral Erich Raeder, commander of the German navy until January 1943. Raeder had been a marginal candidate for the trial, so far as the British and Americans were concerned, but had gained importance by the discovery of a document indicating he had been a prime instigator of the invasion of Norway.

The other was Hans Fritzsche, a popular newscaster and second-rank official in Goebbels' Propaganda Ministry, who had not been on any of the many lists of top war criminals. Had he been suggested by a member of the American or British prosecutorial staffs, he would have been summarily rejected. But since the Americans were contributing thirteen defendants, the British seven, and the French one, it was a matter of national pride to the Russians that they be permitted at least two.

In the interim, the Americans had second thoughts about naming thirty-eight-year-old Alfried Krupp, who had been active in the company's affairs only since the start of the war, rather than his seventy-five-year-old father, Baron Gustav Krupp von Bohlen und Halbach. At the last moment, Gustav's name was substituted for Alfried's. It turned out to be an incredible error, but one typical of a case in which the charges were prepared and the defendants chosen before the facts had been more than cursorily investigated.

On August 30, the list of Nazi leaders selected for the first trial was released to the press. The investigation of the role each had played in the Nazi scheme was joined to the probe into the nature and development of the Nazi system already being pursued by Jackson's organization.

II

Interrogation and Indictment

4   The Prisoners of Ashcan

While the deliberations had been taking place in London, most of the defendants selected, together with other top-ranking Nazis, had been gathered together in the custody of Colonel Burton C. Andrus at Mondorf-les-Bains, a small town fifteen miles from Luxembourg. Andrus was a stocky, water-polo-playing regular army officer of medium height. His hard, humorless eyes glittered behind rimless glasses. He was a martinet who went strictly by the book, and if the book did not contain an appropriate paragraph, he added it in an appendix. Always accompanied by a riding crop, he would have been quite at home in the Prussian army. His career had had its inception in 1918 as prison officer of the Fort Oglethorpe, Georgia, stockade, which he had transformed from a condition of near riot into one of rigid discipline.

In Mondorf, the four-story Palace Hotel had been converted into a detention center, code named Ashcan. Four watch towers were erected, and strands of barbed wire looped around the building.

Hermann Goering, second only to Hitler in the Nazi regime, arrived at Mondorf the last week of May. Carrying 264 pounds on his five-foot-six-inch frame, he had surrendered in the Austrian Alps to the commander of the 36th Infantry Division on May 7. Looking, with his incredibly baggy pants tucked into his boots, like a parody of Jack Oakie lampooning Mussolini in *The Great Dictator,* he had been accompanied by four aides, his personal nurse, two chauffeurs, a five-member kitchen crew headed by a chef, his wife, his wife's maid, his young daughter, and his daughter's nurse. He was so corpulent that it took two men to lift him out of his car. He had left behind in an unfinished railroad tunnel in Berchtesgaden an entire train loaded with art purloined and extorted from every corner of Europe, and enough champagne, caviar, and pâté de foie gras to last a lifetime. He insisted that he would speak to no one but General Eisenhower, but instead was quartered in a castle in Kitzbühel, where General Carl Spaatz, commander of the American Strategic Bombing Force, threw a party for him. At this, he presented a photograph of himself to another American general with the inscription: "War is like a football game, whoever loses gives his opponent his hand, and everything is forgotten."

The next day he was flown to the American interrogation center at Augsburg, where he was met by General Patch, commander of the Seventh Army. Goering apologized that he was not clad in his full dress whites, which had been destroyed in the British pulverization of Berchtesgaden, but saluted with his bejeweled marshal's baton inlaid with twenty golden eagles.

Patch told him to hand it over.

"General, I can't give this to you," Goering huffed. "It is a symbol of my authority."

"You have no more authority. Hand it over!" Patch snapped.

To his utter dejection, Goering was lodged in a spartan three-room working quarter apartment. He held, nevertheless, a fascination for American officers and correspondents, who paid court to him. He was invited to eat at the officers' mess. When an officer sat down at the piano, Goering, who had a working knowledge of English, joined in the songs, then unpacked an accordion from his luggage and contributed to the revelry till two o'clock in the morning.

One by one the other Nazi leaders were taken into custody. Grand Admiral Karl Doenitz, named by Hitler as his successor, and Field Marshal Wilhelm Keitel and General Alfred Jodl, who had negotiated the surrender, were arrested in Flensburg, near the Danish border, where Doenitz had set up his government.

Foreign Minister Joachim von Ribbentrop was discovered hiding out in a Hamburg apartment on June 14. Rosenberg, the Nazi Party's ideologist, was arrested in a drunken stupor by the British, who had been seeking Heinrich Himmler. (Himmler, trying to escape from northern Germany to Bavaria, had been captured at a checkpoint on May 23, and had committed suicide by biting into a vial of cyanide.) Fritz Sauckel, the head of the forced labor program, was tracked down in a Thuringian cavern called the *Drachenhöhle* (dragon's lair) on a tip from a German-American gymnastics teacher who had been trapped in Germany by the war.

An American Jewish major, Henry Blitt, driving with three companions toward Berchtesgaden, stopped off at a farmhouse occupied by a short, bearded man. "What do you think of the Nazis?" Blitt asked.

"I am an artist and have never bothered about politics," the man replied.

"But you look like Julius Streicher," Blitt joked, referring to the man who had become notorious throughout the world as the Nazis' number-one Jew baiter.

"How did you recognize me?" Streicher blurted out.

Goering brought with him to Mondorf his valet, sixteen monogrammed suitcases, and a red hat box. The luggage contained his medals, 81,000 marks (worth perhaps twenty thousand dollars at the rather uncertain rate of exchange), and enough gold, silver, and precious stones to open a small jewelry store. Included were a diamond watch by Cartier, and three rings, one set with an enormous emerald, another with a ruby, and a third with diamonds, to match his varying moods. One suitcase was stuffed with twenty thousand paracodeine pills, which he took at a rate of forty a day. His finger and toe nails were lacquered bright red. His hands trembled. His face was flushed and moist; he breathed quickly and shallowly. He carried with him two glass vials of cyanide encased in brass cartridges. (These had been developed to enable German submariners disabled on the bottom of the ocean to commit suicide, and were the means by which Himmler had killed himself.) One was in a can of Nescafé given him by an American officer, the other sewn into his uniform.

Goering, along with the other leaders of the late Third Reich, was placed in the care of an elderly anti-Nazi prisoner of war, Dr. Ludwig Pflücker. A gradual withdrawal program, lasting two and one-half months, was instituted to get him off paracodeine. He complained continually about headaches, insomnia, and palpitations of the heart. Every few weeks he confided he had suffered a heart attack. One night a storm broke, lightning flashed about the hotel, and thunder rattled the windows. Goering, who had a childish fear of *Donnerwetter*, summoned Dr. Pflücker. The physician found him in a state of agitation. His face was pale, his pulse racing and uneven. Gasping, he complained of pains in his chest and vowed that he was near death. Though he recovered once Pflücker calmed him, Justice Jackson in London received reports that Goering might not survive until the trial. He ordered that the Reichsmarshal be given a complete physical examination. This showed that although Goering was suffering from some cardiovascular damage, it was not severe enough to be an imminent danger to his life.

Many of the other Nazi bigwigs were, like Goering, pronounced neurotics in deplorable physical condition; and some were borderline psychotics, with suicidal tendencies. Jackson had turned down requests from a number of prominent American psychiatrists who wanted to do a complete study of the accused, because he feared the Nazis leaders might claim insanity as the basis for their defense. But after receiving a report on the mental state of the prisoners, he issued orders to have a psychiatrist, Dr. Douglas M. Kelley, assigned full time to the staff.

As a group, the Nazi leaders had been plucked out of the most sybaritic of lives. The German military men, such as Keitel, Doenitz, and Jodl, were outraged that they were not being treated as prisoners of war and given the respect due their rank. They considered the Americans perfidious barbarians, and Andrus the prime specimen. Andrus tried to humble them by showing them a film of Buchenwald after its capture by American troops. But though they were nauseated by the mounds of corpses, they regarded the picture as propaganda and could not understand how it related to them. Ribbentrop walked out. Doenitz, missing the point entirely, inquired harshly: "If this is American justice, why don't they shoot me now?" Goering waved his hand cavalierly: "That's the type of atrocity picture we used to show our Russian prisoners."*

Early in August, Andrus had the notion that if a few of the bigger complainers were removed from Mondorf to what seemed like a friendlier and less strict environment, they might start talking among themselves and inadvertently reveal some of the secrets of the Third Reich. Enlisting the cooperation of a British signal corps unit, he converted a house three and a half miles away into a dummy German château. In the garden, a massive weeping willow tree was festooned with hidden microphones. On Wednesday, August 8, Andrus bundled Goering, Hungarian Admiral Nicholas Horthy, Franz von Papen (who had played a significant role in Hitler's rise, though he had never been a Nazi himself), and Field Marshal Albert Kesselring into a GI ambulance, whose windows had been blacked out so that they could not see where they were going, and for two hours bounced them in a circle over unpaved roads. After they were unloaded at their new location, Goering, delighted at believing he had escaped the tyranny of Andrus, assured the others that he recognized the place: they were in the vicinity of Heidelberg (actually more than one hundred miles off). Thursday they settled under the shade of the willow tree; and the British began cutting records of their conversation. Friday was rainy, and so consequently a washout. Saturday—three days after the charter for the Nuremberg trial was signed in London—Andrus received an order from Jackson to transfer all the prisoners to Nuremberg. Crestfallen, he was forced to abort his experiment.

Sunday the prisoners were loaded aboard two C-47s for the flight to Nuremberg. Only two guards accompanied them on each plane. When Andrus emphasized the importance and safety of the prisoners, the lieutenant in charge of the guards screwed up his mouth and nodded. "You mean no leaving the plane without a chute, sir?"

Nuremberg was typically gray and drizzly. The prisoners were rushed in enclosed ambulances to the Palace of Justice, where one wing of the prison had been prepared to receive them. Andrus, who had been worried to the point of incipient paranoia about the security of his prisoners in Mondorf and had unsuccessfully requested the camouflaging of the hotel against air attack, was not reassured by the sight of the Palace of Justice. The walls surrounding the prison still had several gaps that looked

*The reaction was much the same in many pro-German South American countries where the film was exhibited.

as if trucks had been driven through them. Two of the prison's wings continued to be occupied by German felons; and though a barrier was erected to separate these from the other two, holding the war criminals, the warders and guards of the regular jail were Nazis who had not yet been replaced; throughout Bavaria, occupied by General Patton's Third Army, Nazis were being retained in administrative positions. Patton remarked: "The Nazi thing—it's just like a Democrat-Republican election fight; to get things going we've got to compromise with the devil a little." And it wasn't until the protests became vociferous that Eisenhower eased Patton aside.

Andrus incarcerated his contingent in the four-story prison wing nearest the courthouse. Most were lodged individually in the six-foot by twelve-foot cells that lined both sides of the broad corridor on the ground floor, but others, not scheduled for prosecution in the first trial, were taken to upper tiers, whose walkways were encased in wire mesh after one general leaped to his death. At either end, steel staircases spiraled upward. The stone walls and floors, cool in summer but freezing in winter, imparted an eery, cavernlike stillness to the interior. Footsteps, or the turning of a key, were magnified, echoing and reechoing as through eternity. Each cell was supplied with a steel cot fastened to the wall, a clean though battered mattress, a chair scarcely strong enough to support Goering's weight, and a rickety, cardboard-topped table designed to collapse if anyone attempted to stand on it. In a niche recessed into one corner to the side of the door was the seatless toilet. Plexiglas was substituted for glass in the high, barred windows. The electrical fixtures had been removed and the outlets mortared over. At night the only light in the cell was provided by a bare bulb with a metal reflector directed into the cell through a rectangular flap in the thick, solid door. Through this flap, which was always open and formed a small shelf on the door's exterior, the guards observed the prisoners, and passed water and food.

The accused were completely isolated. They were not permitted to speak to each other or to the guards, and received no news of the outside world. When an officer entered their cell, they were required to stand up and bow. They were able to borrow books from a library installed in one cell; but in the evening the light projected from outside cast chiaroscuro shadows, and was difficult to read or write by. The lamp was not turned off after "lights out" at 9:30 PM, but was instead directed onto the floor, for the prisoners were under continuous observation by the guards. The half-hour's daily exercise in the yard consisted of walking around a square in well-separated single file without speaking or stopping. On Tuesdays and Fridays the men were taken to a cell outfitted with a wood-fired water heater and two showers, which produced a sprinkling of hot water.

On the second tier was a chapel, fashioned out of a double cell, and furnished with an organ and a makeshift altar. Adjacent to the chapel, Dr. Pflücker set up his dispensary, padding the walls with blankets to take the chill out of the stone. Other cells were converted into a dental clinic, a physiotherapy room equipped with a heat lamp, a laundry closet, and a baggage depository, where the prisoners' luggage was kept. (Goering's took up more space than all the others' combined.)

Food was prepared by German POWs in the kitchen on the top floor of the wing. The typical breakfast, served at 7 AM, consisted of coffee, poured into a handleless GI aluminum cup, oatmeal, and bread; dinner (the noon meal) was made up of soup, meat, vegetables, rice or potatoes, and coffee; for supper, bean stew, bread, and tea were served. On this fare of fifteen hundred to eighteen hundred calories daily, Goering, who used his bread to soak up the last bit of gravy from the mess kit, lost two pounds a week; and the others, most of whom had also been overweight, were relieved of their pot bellies.

5 The Documentation Division

Directly across the yard from the prison in the Palace of Justice, the Documentation Division worked feverishly to acquire and analyze the evidence to convict the Nazi leaders. When Bernays returned to the United States, Colonel Robert Storey, operating out of Paris, was elevated to the head of Jackson's evidence-gathering operation. Balding, chunky, his face adorned by rimless glasses, Storey was a fifty-year-old Texas lawyer who had been an air force intelligence officer before being recruited by Jackson.

With the conclusion of the war, the multitude of independently operating British and American intelligence-gathering agencies set up headquarters at various places in Germany. The most important of these was the MIRS (Military Intelligence Research Section) established by SHAEF. CIOS, the Combined Intelligence Objectives Subcommittee, was a creation of the Joint Chiefs of Staff, and dealt mostly with industrial intelligence. FIAT, a British agency similar in nature to CIOS, set up its interrogation center, code-named Dustbin, in Kransberg Castle near Frankfurt. OSS X-2 worked on German police and intelligence services.

When Doenitz and the other members of the government were transported from Flensburg to Mondorf, they left behind voluminous records of Hitler's regime and the war, including a complete set of admiralty documents and Jodl's official War Diary. The Luftwaffe files were dredged up from a salt mine near Salzburg.

Hans Frank, the ex-governor-general of Poland, facing capture by the Americans in Bavaria, had placed a record of Bach's *Saint Matthew Passion* on the phonograph, cut a deep gash in his left wrist, slashed his throat, and lain down to die. Consequently he had not destroyed the leatherbound, thirty-six-volume official journal of his administration in Poland. United States Army doctors snatched Frank from the brink of death; and the journal,* a record kept by Frank's staff of his speeches, decisions, meetings, and transactions, became a damning indictment.

A large cache, including one thousand pages of stenographic notes on Hitler's conferences, was uncovered at Berchtesgaden. Paul Schmidt, Hitler's interpreter at all of his meetings with foreign officials, turned over a complete set of his notes, bound in twelve volumes of several hundred pages each. Colonel Murray Gurfein, chief of the intelligence section of the United States Army's Psychological Warfare Division, had fifty-two investigators in the field, and himself discovered the Case Green (invasion of Czechoslovakia) plans in the rubble of Berchtesgaden, as well as the official German reports on the extermination of 500,000 Galician Jews.

A folder was discovered on the killings of mental defectives and in-mates of old aged homes, with the notation: "Hardly any mistakes have occurred so far. Thirty thousand attended to. Another hundred thousand to one hundred and twenty thousand waiting. Keep the circle of those in the know as small as possible. Today we will deal only with clear cases, one hundred percent executions. Later on this will be enlarged."

Since there was no coordination between the various agencies and none had any direct connection with Jackson's organization, Storey, with two or three assistants, scurried from one place to another scanning and collecting documents.

As the Document Room filled up, it began to look like the handiwork of a sorcerer's apprentice who, having waved his wand to start the flow of papers, did not know how to turn the stream off. Piles of documents, waiting to be filed in floor-to-ceiling racks, towered three feet high. Moving among them, stacking, sorting, and filing, were SS men from a nearby prisoner of war camp, where ten thousand of the Waffen SS were being held. They built shelves, cleared away the rubble, repaired the roof, and reconstructed the wall. Since there was only one guard for every fifty prisoners, men could easily have escaped. But they seemed as content working for the Americans as for the Hitler regime. The American major in charge of the camp boasted: "Those are my troops now. If I were to say 'Let's go fight'—they wouldn't even ask me who or where!"

---

*The journal has generally been referred to as Frank's "diary," giving the erroneous impression that it was a personal account.

By late September, nineteen hundred of some ten thousand documents assembled had been selected as having evidentiary value. But because of the shortage of linguists, only six hundred had been translated. A key member of the prosecution staff wrote Bernays: "The documentary evidence—original German documents—is just unbelievable. Their own reports illustrated with pictures are far better than any of the studies we have compiled on the persecution of Jews, crimes against humanity, etc. The Germans certainly believed in putting everything in writing."

6   Goering and Hess: The Flight from Reality

As the documents were translated and catalogued, they were made available to the second of Jackson's evidence-gathering groups, the Interrogation Division, which had responsibility for questioning some 120 high-ranking Nazis and potential witnesses, in addition to the defendants. The division chief was Colonel John Harlan Amen. The antithesis and rival of the scholarly Colonel Storey, Amen had been a member of the United States Attorney General's Anti-Trust Division, and from 1935 to 1938 had headed the Division's New York office, where he had conducted several large racketeering prosecutions. Subsequently New York Governor Herbert Lehman had charged him with investigating more than one hundred cases of corruption in state and local governments. Short and pixyish but tough, Amen's intimidating investigatory technique and prosecutorial approach were straight out of *Gangbusters*. A womanizer and coping alcoholic whose work was seemingly unaffected by his addiction, he had his first drink while whipping up his shaving lather and seldom went an hour without another during the day. One of his legs tremored involuntarily and was given to occasional small kicks. Bernays dubbed him "the glamorous knight of the bottle, the bed, and the ego."

Intensive interrogations began on August 27 with Goering, the key defendant, for whom Amen took personal responsibility. Goering was escorted the short distance across the yard to the east wing of the Palace of Justice. Ushered through a heavy iron gate that barred access to the interrogation section, he was led into a twelve-foot-by-fifteen-foot room. Amen, seated at a rectangular table, had his back to the windows so that his face was hidden in shadow, while Goering's directly opposite was illuminated—a standard police technique. Two guards took up positions at the far end of the room. A stenographer was seated two or three feet off from the table. Additionally, the room was bugged so that the entire conversation could be listened to and recorded from the chamber above.

At the end of the table to the right of Amen was the interpreter, Richard Sonnenfeldt, a slight, soft-spoken private first class, whose linguistic ability was to give him a distinguished place in the Interrogation Division.*

Facing Amen, Goering was a poised, glib, and imperious schemer, regaining confidence as he came once more to be the center of attention. When Amen asked Goering to take an oath, Goering wanted to know why he was being sworn and under what law: "I would like to know if this is a hearing, or if this is already a regular process, or what it is?"

Amen responded that *he* was going to ask the questions, and Goering was to respond to them.

"I have those objections because I don't know what my position is," Goering continued.

Amen did not tell Goering that he was to be the chief defendant in an international trial; indeed, none of the accused were officially informed until October 18.

Since Goering, however, was a man whose intelligence was matched by his shrewdness, he knew well enough what lay ahead. During a period of two months he was grilled thirty-five times. Every aspect of his life was examined, and every action he had taken during twelve years as the most powerful man in Germany after Hitler was subjected to scrutiny. Amen tried to intimidate him and treat him as he might a waterfront racketeer. But Goering was not to be cowed.

"I am trying to get you out of the habit of always wanting to see a document before you answer any of the questions that I give you," Amen chided when Goering kept asking to examine the papers from which Amen quoted excerpts.

"Well, the colonel has the documents to ask me from and I have nothing to rely on but my recollections. I did so many things, it is almost impossible. I can't think of all these details."

"Don't you know that you are responsible for all official communications going out of your office?"

"If you are going to apply this, you are going to hold me responsible for every little bit of nonsense that ever originated in my office. If you want to go on with this, you are going to have to hold me responsible for the porter, too."

"But you don't really think that these orders relating to the killing of

---

*Sonnenfeldt had fled Germany together with his family in 1938, and arrived in the United States after an incredible three-year odyssey that took him to Australia and India. Amen's deputy, Lieutenant Colonel Thomas Hinkel, had discovered him in an army reconnaissance unit near Linz, Austria, while investigating the killings of American and British officers at Mauthausen concentration camp. Sonnenfeldt's brother, Helmut, later became the aide of National Security Adviser and Secretary of State Henry Kissinger.

commandos and subsequent orders relating to the killing of fliers are a foolish matter or one of no importance?"

"No. I had nothing to do whatever with the killing of commandos and I have always been against the killing of aviators, and I have enough witnesses for that."

"Nevertheless, they were killed."

"Well, the population killed them, and the Führer had very strong objections to anybody intervening in that; and so we told him that if this went on that he would have to renounce the Geneva Convention; and he played with that thought. But later on he got away from it again because we talked him out of it."

So far as Germany's annexation of neighboring states had been concerned, Goering had no apology: "If one speaks of the acquisition of land, then it is as much land as possible at the lowest possible cost. Like you took part of Mexico when you needed it."

Prodded by Amen to relate the developments leading to the first Nazi aggression, the Anschluss of Austria, Goering responded frankly: "I don't want to deny that I was possibly the most active man in Berlin on that day. I might have been even more active than the Führer himself."

Pressed further during a subsequent session, Goering amplified: "Here is something that I want to say by way of explanation: I can only emphasize again that I spent a great deal of my youth in Austria, and therefore was very familiar with everything that went on in Austria. Moreover, my father, at the time of the Kaiser in Austria, had the following ideological concept of the Anschluss. This is only by way of explanation of how I came to have this opinion. So to speak, I spent half my youth in Germany, and half my youth in Austria."

The "father" to whom Goering referred in what was perhaps a slip of the tongue was not Heinrich Goering, listed on the birth certificate, but Ritter (Sir) Hermann von Epenstein, a dashing, foppish, Austro-German nobleman, who favored a reunification of the two nations along the lines of the Holy Roman Empire. Heinrich Goering, an upper-grade civil servant in the German Colonial Corps, had married his second wife, Fanny, in 1885 when he was forty-five and she was nineteen. A year later, when their first child was born, in Windhoek, the capital of German Southwest Africa, Fanny had been attended by Epenstein, a thirty-six-year-old physician who moved on the fringes of both the German and Austrian imperial courts. Though his father was Jewish, Epenstein had adopted Christianity upon marrying the daughter of a wealthy Gentile merchant.

In the early 1890s, the prematurely aging Heinrich, sinking into alcoholism and apathy, had been appointed consul general in Haiti, and Epenstein and Fanny had become lovers. When Hermann, named for Epenstein, was born in 1893, it was the childless Epenstein, not Heinrich, who arranged for Fanny's confinement and rushed to see the baby. A few weeks later, when Fanny sailed for Haiti, it was Epenstein who made provisions for the baby to stay with a family in Fürth, a suburb of Nuremberg. Fürth, only a streetcar ride removed from the Palace of Justice, was conveniently close to Epenstein's renovated castle, Veldenstein, thirty miles upstream on the Pegnitz River.

Hermann did not see his mother again until he was three years old; and, when the Goerings returned, Epenstein—whose wife meanwhile had died—installed the family at Veldenstein (which ultimately came into Hermann's possession). Here, in return for the favors of Fanny, whom the retired Heinrich now benignly neglected, Epenstein maintained the Goerings like gentry; and when Hermann's younger brother Albert was born, there was no question that Epenstein was his father.

Epenstein's principal place of residence was another, more elegant castle, Mauterndorf, deep amidst the peaks of the Austrian Alps. After Albert's birth, he adopted all of Fanny's offspring as his godchildren, and made Fanny his official hostess at Mauterndorf as well as at Veldenstein.

At the age of eleven, Goering was sent away to boarding school. When the pupils were required to write an essay on a notable German, Hermann picked Epenstein as his subject. Hardly had he turned the paper in than he was called to the office of the headmaster, who inquired scornfully what Hermann had in mind when he essayized a Jew as a notable German. For Hermann, the truth of Epenstein's ancestry was a terrible revelation, and the fact that he had to copy "I shall not write essays in praise of Jews" one hundred times was not the worst of his punishment; for his fellow pupils, apprised of his blunder, paraded him up and down with a placard, *"Mein Pate ist ein Jude,"** hung about his neck. Thoroughly humiliated, Hermann slipped away from the school and caught the train home.

Epenstein secured appointment at a military academy for him, and in 1912 Hermann was commissioned in the Imperial Army. Soon after World War I broke out, he fell ill with rheumatic fever. While convalescing, he went flying with a friend in the newly formed Observer Corps, and with Epenstein's aid secured a transfer to the air arm. By the end of the war he was, in addition to one of Germany's top surviving aces, with a total of twenty-two kills, commander of the famed Richthofen squadron.†

A few months after the armistice, Goering was hired by the Dutch

---

*"My godfather is a Jew."
†Baron von Richthofen, who shot down eighty Allied planes, had been killed on April 20, 1918.

aircraft designer Fokker as a barnstormer and airplane demonstrator in Scandinavia.

In Sweden one stormy night, he met Karin von Kantzow, the daughter of a nobleman. Five years Goering's senior, she was slender and stunning, but afflicted with tuberculosis and heart disease. Though she was married to an army officer and had an eight-year-old son, she and Goering became lovers.

Early in 1923, Goering went to Munich, where his mother was now living. There, he and Karin, who had obtained a divorce, were married. Seeking, like many other veterans, an outlet for his anger at Germany's reduced circumstances and political chaos, he attended a meeting at which Hitler was speaking. "That's the party for me!" Goering, swept away by Hitler's impassioned oratory, exclaimed, "Down with the Treaty of Versailles, goddamn it! That's my meat!"

Hitler, conversely, was impressed by the importance of his convert: "Splendid!" he exulted. "The war ace with the Pour le Merite.* Imagine it! Excellent propaganda!"

For six months Goering headed the SA *(Sturmabteilung)*, the Nazi Party's battle squad. On November 9, 1923, when Hitler unsuccessfully attempted to overthrow the Bavarian state government as a precursor to marching on Berlin, Goering was seriously wounded. Karin smuggled him into Austria. There, as microscopic pieces of dirt festered in his wound, he was given morphine to ease the pain. Not until May of 1924 was he well enough to travel; and then Karin, rounding up money here and there, took him to heal in the Italian sun. For a year, while Karin provided him with an education in art, they vagabonded around Venice, Florence, Siena, and Rome.

By the time Goering and Karin arrived back in Sweden in 1925, he was a confirmed dope addict. Floating through an opiate daze, the once intrepid pilot behaved like a whimpering child, dependent on the semi-invalid Karin to minister to his needs. Unfit to hold a job, he squandered the money provided by Karin's family and sold his and Karin's possessions to support his habit. Eventually committed to a hospital, he attacked a nurse in a homicidal rage. Placed in a straitjacket, he was, on September 1, 1925, transported to an insane asylum as a certified lunatic.

Following two lengthy stays in the asylum, he returned to Germany in the fall of 1927 when an amnesty for political offenders was declared. There his name still carried a certain ring, and through friends in Munich he obtained a position as the Berlin representative for the Bavarian Motor Works (BMW), whose proprietor was a Jewish Italian industrialist.

*The Pour le Merite was Germany's highest decoration.

A confirmed moocher, Goering had no compunctions about clamping his increasingly pudgy hand on anyone venturing into his orbit. But he was also a good companion; a facile conversationalist; a raconteur and connoisseur able to recount his aerial exploits in barracks-room argot or lecture on Italian art like Bernard Berenson; a linguist who could get along passably, if not grammatically, in English, Italian, and Swedish; a Bavarian *bon homme* stout enough to represent the stolid German burgher.

Karin arrived to provide him with a beautiful, tragic companion of noble mien, and Goering used her and Epenstein to worm his way into the vapid society of old court retainers. Life with little money was a ball of parties, outings, and lavish lunches. In the spring of 1928, when the Nazi Party was in difficulty and had only a few hundred thousand adherents, Hitler came to Berlin. Once more intent on exploiting Goering's record as a war hero, Hitler asked him to stand for election to the Reichstag.

Goering, it turned out, was one of the twelve Nazis among the 491 Reichstag deputies elected. His finances improved dramatically. He received, in addition to his parliamentary salary, a substantial stipend from Hitler for speaking at rallies around Germany. Lufthansa, the German airline, hired him as its Reichstag lobbyist—a peculiar but accepted custom. Word spread around German industry and commerce that the affable Goering not only could but was anxious to be bought; that he was not a wild-eyed Nazi, but a reasonable and corruptible man who understood that what was good for Krupp or I. G. Farben was good for Germany.

Moneyed people opened their checkbooks. Steel magnate Fritz Thyssen gave Goering 150,000 marks (nearly forty thousand dollars) to furnish an elegant new apartment.

In October 1929, the American stock market collapsed. A worldwide panic followed, and all the disasters Hitler had been predicting (but himself had not really expected) descended upon Germany. During the next three years industrial production was cut in half, and unemployment rose to more than six million. When elections for the Reichstag were held in September 1930, even Hitler was stunned by the results. The Nazi vote burgeoned from 810,000 to 6.4 million, eighteen percent of the total cast, second in number only to the Social Democrats. The Nazi representation in the Reichstag jumped from 12 to 107. Goering, as leader of the Nazi faction, overnight became one of the most powerful politicians in the land.

In Munich, which remained Hitler's headquarters, Rudolf Hess similarly found himself thrust into the limelight, first as Hitler's and then the party's secretary. A friend and admirer of Goering, Hess had been born in 1893 in Alexandria, Egypt, where his German grandfather had established an import-export business. Growing up in a villa surrounded by a luxuriant garden, Hess received a disciplinarian, Teutonic upbringing that clashed with his romantic temperament and the exotic Near East setting. Though he had no inclination for commerce and wished to pursue a liberal education at Oxford, his father insisted that he must prepare himself to take over the business. In 1908 he was enrolled in a boarding academy in Germany, and four years later he entered a school of commerce in Switzerland, where one branch of the family lived.

When World War I broke out, Hess embraced the opportunity to prove his manhood and patriotism, and simultaneously escape from studies in which he had no interest, by enlisting in the First Bavarian Infantry Regiment.

In 1916 he was wounded. Two years later he transferred to the Flying Corps, but the war ended before he saw aerial combat. His bushy eyebrows gave him a stern, almost fierce look, belying his personality. Because he was embarrassed by his jagged buck teeth, he seldom smiled. He enrolled in the University of Munich, but, disheartened and disoriented like so many other veterans, he yearned for a messiah. The night in April 1920 when he first heard Hitler speak, he rushed home laughing hysterically and crying over and over, "The man! The man!" One meeting transformed the despondent Hess into a radiant optimist convinced he had come upon the savior.

Within a few months Hess became Hitler's closest companion. The Führer treated him like a younger brother; an emotional bond developed between the two. When, in 1924, both were convicted and sent to Landsberg Prison, Hess assumed the role of Hitler's secretary. From Hitler's dictation he typed the manuscript of *Mein Kampf,* to which he contributed a number of passages. After Hitler's release, he acted more and more like Hitler's alter ego in dealing with the problems of party members, and so built up a personal following. When, after Hitler's assumption of power in 1933, the Führer moved to Berlin, Hess, subsequently appointed by Hitler as second in line to the succession after Goering, remained behind in Munich to handle party affairs.

Though Hess was verbally as anti-Semitic as any other Nazi, he did not have a stomach for brutality. Decent and honest, he came to be known as "the conscience of the party." At Nuremberg, Field Marshal Keitel described him as "a *Schöngeist;* that is, one interested in the fine arts." One of Jackson's investigators, who read all of Hess's private correspondence, wrote: "I am rather impressed with the type of friends he had and the manner in which he frowned upon favoritism, even in the case of his own family."

Unlike Hitler, Hess was a pacifist at heart. He believed, or tricked himself into believing, that Hitler was sincere in his oft-repeated declara-

tions that he was a man of peace. Gradually, Hess's position was eroded
by his distance from Hitler, and the growing gap between his beliefs and
the Führer's actions. Torn between his conscience and his loyalty, he was
overwhelmed by a sense of powerlessness. Consequently rationalizing that
life was governed by fate, he placed himself in the hands of soothsayers and
astrologers. He became prey to superstitions and obsessions. Psychoso-
matic gastrointestinal illnesses affected first one, then another of his or-
gans. Though, like Hitler, he was a vegetarian who neither smoked nor
drank and abstained from all stimulants except weak tea, he suffered from
colitis, imaginary gall and kidney stones, and angina. His face assumed a
jaundiced look. He had a pervasive fear of cancer. He had, without success,
a large number of his teeth pulled. When he went out to eat, he took with
him his own food containing "biologically dynamic ingredients." When
Hitler discovered that Hess was bringing his lunchpail to dinner at the
chancellery, he remarked with annoyance that he had a perfectly good diet
cook who could fix whatever Hess ordered, but that it was preposterous
for Hess to come lugging his own food. After that, Hess stayed away.

Since doctors were unable to help him, Hess turned to Tibetan nos-
trums and homeopathic remedies, magic healers and animal magnetists.
Above, beneath, and to the side of his bed he rigged up magnets to draw
away the evil influences.

One of Hess's closest friends was Albrecht Haushofer, the son of
Professor Karl Haushofer, a former Imperial Army general who had become an advocate of the new science of geopolitics. Hess had studied under
Karl Haushofer at the University of Munich, and had incorporated the
essence of some of Haushofer's theories into *Mein Kampf.* Hess and Albrecht—who was a talented poet and dramatist, as well as a geopolitician
—were kindred spirits.*

When Hess, following the fall of France, could not comprehend why
the British would reject Hitler's peace offer and prefer alliance with America to friendship with Germany, Albrecht, who had many British acquaintances, tried to explain to him in the mildest terms possible that
Hitler was anathema to British values and beliefs. Albrecht, nevertheless,
suggested to Hess that it might be possible to probe for peace through the
Duke of Hamilton, a high-ranking Royal Air Force officer who was a
friend of Albrecht's.

This suggestion planted in Hess the thought that he himself might
become an intermediary. Swearing Ernst von Bohle, the British-born state
secretary in the party's *Ausland* (foreign) bureau to secrecy, Hess, starting

---

*Since Albrecht was one-fourth Jewish by virtue of one grandparent on his mother's
side, Hess had him officially "Aryanized."

in October 1940, commissioned him to translate a variety of proposed peace messages to the British government. Though he had been forbidden by Hitler to fly, he covertly familiarized himself with a twin-engined Messerschmitt at the aircraft manufacturer's factory in Augsburg, just an hour's drive from Munich.

During the 1930s, Hess had helped Goering build up the Luftwaffe, and through the *Ausland* bureau he had come into contact with a group of conservative Royal Air Force officers who expressed the belief that Germany and Britain must stand together against Russia. When, by the spring of 1941, Hess had received no reply to the messages he had sent through private channels to the Duke of Hamilton, he rationalized that it was the 1939 Moscow Pact, linking Germany with the Soviet Union, that was the barrier between Germany and Britain.

On April 27, however, Hitler gave the order to launch the attack on Russia eight weeks hence. Now, Hess thought, peace with England could be achieved.

Having repeatedly told Felix Kersten, Himmler's masseur-psychologist, that he could not go on with his existence and wanted to stake his life on one great deed, Hess climbed into the twin-engined Messerschmitt fighter he had been test flying and had had fitted with extra fuel tanks. Once airborne, he headed the plane for the Duke of Hamilton's estate in Scotland, nine hundred miles away.

Soaring over the North Sea, Hess was euphoric, as if his tortured mind, which had been punishing his body, had at last been set free. Parachuting out of the sky near Glasgow that evening in his quixotic quest to meet the duke, he at first lay trancelike on the floor and stared fixedly at the ceiling of the room in which he was confined. The British, after ascertaining that he was not an impostor, were never able to make up their minds as to the degree of his sanity. The peace terms he proposed, calling for Britain to acknowledge Nazi hegemony over the Continent, had been rejected more than once and were clearly unacceptable, as Albrecht Haushofer had tried to impress upon him.

When it became evident that he was being rebuffed and that his overtures were not taken seriously, he attempted, on June 15, to kill himself by catapulting over the second-story bannister. But, plummeting to the stone floor below, he suffered only a fractured thigh.

Fearful that the Germans might try to rescue Hess, the British isolated him on a remote country estate, Mytchett Place, guarded by a sizable contingent of troops. He was attended continuously by three officers and a doctor, and examined periodically by psychiatrists. Though the British permitted him to do whatever he wished within the limits of his confinement, he developed the delusion that he was an object of persecution and was being poisoned. The initial psychiatrist who examined him recorded: "It is fair to say that the first glimpse of Hess produced an immediate reaction—'typical schizophrenic.' He was found sitting behind a table littered with papers, his skull-like face wearing a profoundly unhappy, grim expression, with his eyes staring into infinity."

In the dining room, where he ate with British officers, he sometimes demanded not only an exchange of plates, but a random shuffling around. He squirreled away pieces of bread, cheese, and other items for later chemical analysis. Utterly erratic, he suffered from a kind of revolving-door amnesia. Sometimes he howled like an animal in pain. Like Hitler, he had a paranoid obsession with the Jews—Hess believed that they exercised a hypnotic force over everyone in the world, including himself. After stabbing himself with a knife, he asserted that the instrument had been placed magically in his hands by the Jews to tempt him. Unable to reconcile his devotion to Hitler with the execution of his friend Albrecht Haushofer as a member of the July 20 conspirators, Hess, in July of 1945, took a turn for the worse.

The British, failing to resolve the question of whether they were dealing with a war criminal or a lunatic, did not fly Hess to Nuremberg until October 8. Hess brought with him a hoard of envelopes sealed officially with red and purple wax. They contained samples of the food that Hess suspected had been used to poison him over the years. On the outside of the envelopes Hess had made notations. One substance supposedly caused toothaches, another was a strong laxative, a third was a poison to damage the mucous membranes, a fourth caused bleeding in the mouth, and a fifth purportedly set the intestines to burn like fire. "Will cause headaches," he had written on a sample of cocoa, and "will cause shutting off of the intestines" on a sample of iron tablets.

Colonel Amen, convinced that Hess was shamming, had him brought into the interrogation room the morning after his arrival.

"Do you remember that you used to be in Germany?" Amen addressed Hess, who was clad in the same flying jacket and flying boots he had worn to England and refused to discard.

"Well, I think that is self-understood, because I have been told so repeatedly, but I don't remember. It has all disappeared. It is gone." Hess, exceedingly nervous, crossed and uncrossed his legs, blinked his eyes, and fumbled with his hands. He thought the fact that he was being "handcuffed like a cannibal" a personal disgrace.

"But don't you know what the proceeding is for?"

"I have no idea. I don't even know whether I was told what I am accused of. I know that it is a political trial."

"When did your memory go away?"

"The doctor told me yesterday that it has been this way since July."

"But you don't know yourself?"

"No."

That afternoon, Amen confronted Hess with his old acquaintances, one after the other. Goering was already seated when Hess was brought in, trailing bewilderedly behind the guard like a dog on a leash. Blinking, Hess stared without a sign of recognition at Goering.

"Don't you know me?" Goering asked.

"Who are you?" Hess was startled.

"You ought to know me. We have been together for years."

Hess shook his head. "I have lost my memory for some time, especially now before the trial. It is terrible, and the doctor tells me that it is going to come back."

"Listen, Hess, I was the supreme commander of the Luftwaffe, and you flew to England in one of my planes." Goering was irritated that he could not elicit the proper acknowledgment of his own importance from Hess. "Don't you remember I was the supreme commander of the Luftwaffe? First, I was a field marshal, and later a Reichsmarshal! Don't you remember?"

"No."

"Do you remember that the Führer at a meeting of the Reichstag announced that if something happened to him that I would be his successor and if something happened to me you were to be the successor? Don't you remember that?"

"No." Hess was distressed that he was unable to satisfy Goering. "This is terrible. If the doctors wouldn't assure me time and time again that my memory would return some day I would be driven to desperation." After a further exchange, he continued: "Do you think you could bring back my memory like this? The doctor told me it could only be done by shock."

"I can't shock you, but I can help you get your memory back." Goering began to view the encounter as a personal challenge.

"To concentrate means a terrible load on my mind and causes me headaches and for two hours afterwards I have to lie down on my cot and I don't know what is going on. My brain is in such a condition that I can't make any experiments with it right now."

"Now look here, Hess—"

"Yes—"

"It was not so simple for me to come here and talk to you because I too have to concentrate." Goering acted as if he were on his way to a state conference.

"Well, that is why I'm trying to answer you," Hess expostulated.

"Why the hell should both of us exert ourselves so much in here then?"

"All right, then, don't let's argue about it. A doctor of reputation told me to talk to you. He did not tell me to shock you, or to hit you over the head. I couldn't do that. I couldn't make a shock scene with you here. But if we discuss some points quietly something will come back to you. Do you remember the Führer?"

"Well, I know what he looks like. I had a picture in my room."

"Do you remember his manner of speech?"

"His picture didn't speak, so I don't remember his speech. You know it is not very good for my brain in its present condition to keep probing into these things. It is a natural reaction of self-defense—well, self-defense is not the right word, but if I work so hard on my brain it tries not to react in order to protect itself."

Professor Karl Haushofer and Ernst von Bohle were brought into the room, but were no more successful in jogging Hess's memory. Haushofer mentioned Hess's attachment to his World War I uniform, which he had worn all the time, and spoke of Frau Haushofer sitting before the fireplace and teaching him English. Taking a photograph of Hess with Frau Hess and their son out of his wallet, he handed it to Hess. Hess recognized them, but could recall no details.

"How old is he now?" He pointed to his son.

Later, after leaving the interrogation room, Haushofer shook his head. "Hess was my favorite pupil, and today I saw the ruin of it all. His heart and his idealism were greater than his intellect."

Amen resumed his grilling of Hess the following morning: "How is your memory today?"

"The same. It goes back a few days."

"How many?"

"You have to put it to the test. I can only find out the facts. I don't feel very well. I just had a cramp in my intestines."

Amen, never a patient man, assumed his racket-busting prosecutorial role: "When did you get the idea that it would be the smart thing to lose your memory?" he snapped.

"I don't quite understand that," Hess replied bewilderedly. "You mean to say that I thought that it might be a good idea to lose my memory and then deceive you like this?"

"That is just what I mean!"

"I can only say that that is not true."

"Well, it might be very helpful in connection with the coming proceedings, might it not?"

Hess shook his head. "On the contrary. I don't understand that. If I give the appearance that I lost my memory, then people will not like me and it will influence the trial in such a way that I will get a worse judgment."

"Do you remember Haushofer telling you that you read together a Swedish story by Selma Lagerlöf, which concerned students who lost their memory? That is where you got this idea of losing your memory, isn't it?"

"No! Certainly not!" Hess laughed out loud.

"What do you think is so funny about it?" Amen bristled.

"Possibly, the gentleman can put himself in my position. I won't be able to defend myself. I sit in my cell all the time and think about these things. It makes a terrible impression on me, and it hurts my mind very much. Then somebody says when did I get the idea to lose my memory because I read some story, and it leaves a very ridiculous impression on me."

"Well, Goering thinks that maybe he can help you get it back again in the near future."

"I don't know what I can give to him," Hess said, as if it were up to him to reward Goering. "Whether I can give him an order or a medal later. I don't know, but whatever I can give to him, I will willingly give to him."

Five days later, after another fruitless meeting between Hess and Goering, Amen inquired sternly: "Do you still think you would be better off at the trial if you refuse to remember anything?"

Hess shrugged. "It is all the same whether I say anything or not."

"Well, we will have to start giving you the shocks then, I guess," Amen threatened.

"Oh, yes, please." Hess nodded. "And also the papers you promised to give me."

7   Ribbentrop: The Wandering Aryan

If Hess seemingly represented a classic case of amnesia, Joachim von Ribbentrop, the number-three defendant, was as disoriented as a sleepwalker waking up in a strange city, and moved about in a trance. Born in 1893, he was the son of a demanding, whip-lashing Prussian artillery officer who expected his offspring to excel, a difficult feat for Joachim with his ordinary mind. During the early 1900s, after his mother's death and his father's remarriage to a woman of means, the family moved to Switzerland. There, Joachim began to study French, and, at the age of fifteen, was sent to a commercial school at Grenoble, in southern France. The next year he was befriended by an English family and invited to stay with them in Britain. He accepted, quickly adopted what he perceived as establishment manners and attitudes, and in 1910 crossed the ocean to Canada, where he was razzed for his airs. During the next four years he was a bank clerk in Montreal, a newspaper reporter in New York, and a worker on the Canadian transcontinental railroad. In danger of internment when World War I broke out, he sailed back to Germany.

Distinguishing himself during the war, he was awarded the Iron Cross, First Class. In 1919 he met Annelies Henkel, of the champagne-brewing family, at a tennis tournament, and the next year they were married. Through the marriage, he obtained the Henkel agency in Berlin, where he later established his own import-export liquor business. He traveled frequently to France and England. The snobbish circles in which he moved accentuated his social-climbing ambitions. At the age of thirty-two he had himself adopted by the widow of his father's brother—a general who had been knighted—and so acquired the coveted *von*.

Under normal circumstances, he would have lived out his life unremarkably as a pleasant, mildly successful bore. But the Depression had a shattering effect on his business, and the upsurge of the Communists threatened his capitalistic family and friends and his aristocratic pretensions. Like other men of commerce, he turned toward Hitler and the Nazis as a counterbalance to the Communists. Through a mutual acquaintance, he obtained an introduction to the Führer.

Overwhelmed by Hitler's personality and anxious to please, Ribbentrop became Hitler's unofficial eyes and ears when he traveled on business to England and France. Ribbentrop's accounts contained largely what Hitler wanted to hear (for Ribbentrop soon learned Goering's trick of covertly finding out Hitler's opinions before presenting his own). Soon Hitler asked Ribbentrop to establish a "Ribbentrop Bureau" at party headquarters across the street from the Foreign Ministry, and to prepare a daily summary of foreign news. Within a few months, Ribbentrop was established as Hitler's adviser on foreign affairs.

In June of 1935 Hitler appointed Ribbentrop an ambassador-at-large and dispatched him to negotiate with the British on a new naval treaty between Great Britain and Germany. Since both parties were, essentially, agreed beforehand on the terms, permitting Germany to rebuild its navy to a maximum of thirty-five percent of the British tonnage—thereby, in effect, bilaterally renouncing the military clause of the Treaty of Versailles —Ribbentrop had no difficulty in concluding the pact. Hitler hailed him as the conquering negotiator, and in 1936 appointed him ambassador to Britain—the most important Foreign Service post. Goering, who carried on a celebrated feud with Ribbentrop and referred to him as *Fatzke*—a uniquely derogatory term that might be translated as "fathead" or a "pompous ass"—protested that Ribbentrop had no qualifications for the post.

Hitler pointed out that Ribbentrop knew *this* lord and *that* viscount.

"Yes," Goering replied, "but the trouble is they know Ribbentrop too!"

In London, Ribbentrop committed one faux pas after another. Since he considered Hitler a titan and one of the great geniuses of all time, he patterned himself after his master. When he spoke, Hitler's voice emerged. He had not a single idea of his own; yet, sometimes pontificating for hours, he made others suffer through his insensate logorrhea. At a select Mayfair luncheon to introduce him to the Who's Who of the British Empire, he was asked one question, to which he responded by folding his arms across his chest, leaning back in his chair, and embarking on a forty-five-minute monologue justifying anti-Semitism—no one ever did the Jews a greater favor, Princess Stephanie Hohenlohe observed. Winston Churchill slyly shifted his chair so that Ribbentrop could not see him, and, to the scarcely suppressed hilarity of a number of the guests, mimicked every pompous word and pedagogic gesture—unaware that Frau von Ribbentrop, blushing scarlet, was watching him. By the end of the meal the air was icy, and Ribbentrop had irredeemably established himself as a German boor. His most memorable stupidity, however, was yet to come. At a reception held by King George VI, he suddenly, instead of shaking hands with the king, stiffened, clicked his heels, and shot out his arm in the Hitler salute—it was meant, Ribbentrop later explained, to demonstrate to the monarch the arrival of a new era.

Such behavior merely reinforced Hitler's confidence in Ribbentrop's astuteness. The dictator called his ambassador to Berlin so frequently to talk to him and employ him on special missions that *Punch* dubbed him "the Wandering Aryan."

In February 1938, after Hitler had committed himself to a course of aggression and wanted a foreign minister who would carry out his ideas without question or argument, he replaced Constantin von Neurath with Ribbentrop. Ribbentrop's career was climaxed eighteen months later when he concluded the German-Soviet Friendship Treaty in Moscow. Hitler thereupon characterized him as "one of the greatest men we have, and history will some day place him above Bismarck. He is greater than Bismarck."

Never was Hitler's opinion more at odds with the views of others. Prince Otto von Bismarck, a member of the great chancellor's family, characterized Ribbentrop as "such an imbecile he is a freak of nature." The

French ambassador remarked: "I could not talk to Ribbentrop; he listened only to himself." Goering referred to him as "Germany's number-one parrot," because of his endless repetition of meaningless claptrap.

Ribbentrop, in truth, was the perfect mouthpiece for Hitler's prevarications and chicanery. His career in futility was capsulized on his fiftieth birthday in 1943 when several members of his staff presented him with a jeweled casket, intended to hold the treaties he had negotiated. "We were thrown into great embarrassment," Ribbentrop's liaison at the Führer headquarters later told Hitler to the Führer's great amusement. "When we were about to fill the casket, there were only a few treaties we hadn't broken in the meantime."

An insomniac who could not go to sleep until three or four o'clock in the morning, Ribbentrop had customarily awakened between nine thirty and noon. Since at Nuremberg he was aroused at 6 AM, he was obtaining no more than two or three hours of sleep a night. He lost so much weight that beneath his gray, unkempt hair his skin fell away from his gaunt eyes loosely and without any texture. He had the haggard appearance of a man haunted by a thousand devils. His sight was failing and his state of mind suicidal. Despite exhortations and warnings, he could not be induced to make his bed or clean his cell. He scribbled endlessly, but had no sooner written something than he crumpled the paper and threw it on the floor. Pacing up and down, he kicked through the discarded papers as if they were an array of snowballs. Whenever the psychiatrist, Dr. Douglas Kelley, came to visit him, he implored: "Doctor, what shall I do? What shall I do?" Though he was twenty years younger than some of his co-defendants, his appearance placed him among the oldest of the accused.

The officer in charge of Ribbentrop's interrogation, Colonel Howard Brundage, had been deputy chief of the United States War Crimes Office. Gray-haired and mild mannered, he opposed the whole thrust of Bernays' and Jackson's "conspiracy" concept. To him, war crimes were such acts as the shooting of prisoners and the wanton killing of civilians. Employing a schoolmasterish approach, Brundage repeatedly lectured Ribbentrop and the other men he was questioning, some of them the most cynical and hardened in the entire Nazi regime: "We are trying to get up a record here for the benefit of the children of Germany so that when another time comes and a gang like this gets control of the government they will have something to look back on and be warned in advance. I find that most of these people who come in here are very evasive and they are trying to dodge their responsibility. Some of them claim to be still loyal to the Führer, but I don't find any of them who seem to acknowledge that they have got a duty to the German people."

Ribbentrop could get along quite well in English, he understood the questions before they were translated, and he frequently replied in English. His favorite expression was "you see," which he used over and over again in his rambling, interminable discourses. Seldom did he ever come to the point, for he usually forgot before he had proceeded far what he had intended to say. Replying to a question by Brundage about the persecution of the Jews, he explained that Hitler "was absorbed by the idea of the danger that in some way the Jewish question was behind the Communist question; and with communism coming from the East and being very strong, they would get together with the Jewish influences of the West, and by that way through the German Jewish influences disintegrate Germany and drive it into the arms of communism. This was a doctrine, more or less, which I may say I never quite grasped, and which I don't quite grasp to this very day." Ribbentrop, evidently feeling remiss at his lack of comprehension, stared disconsolately into space.

"Did you know there were hundreds of thousands of people killed in concentration camps?" Brundage inquired at another interrogation.

"No, I certainly did not," Ribbentrop said. "It may seem queer to you but I worked fourteen, sixteen, eighteen hours a day with my foreign political questions, so I knew perhaps less about the internal questions than the boy on the street or the porter in the hotel. But I was amazed during the latter months of the war when I heard for certain just by chance that there was a sister-in-law of mine that was put in a concentration camp. I suddenly got a glimpse of these police methods and things that were going on."

Brundage felt as if he were tilting against a chimera that he knew was there, but which darted this way and that out of reach every time he tried to get hold of it: "I can quite imagine a German saying, 'Yes, I knew about it but there was nothing I could do about it,' but to have one after another of the German leaders coming in saying, 'I knew nothing of that'—that, to me, is perfectly fantastic! You cannot have hundreds of thousands of people dying in concentration camps and not know."

"Is that true?" Ribbentrop asked wide-eyed.

"I think that is conservative. I think millions is nearer."

"I can't imagine that." Ribbentrop shook his head.

"There are lots of things you cannot imagine." Brundage was grim-faced. "You have an education coming to you!"

Hitler, Ribbentrop asserted, always maintained that only he himself was privileged to have an overview of the entire situation. He would not tell the military about foreign and domestic policy, the Gauleiters about military or foreign policy, or Ribbentrop about the military and domestic situations. "The personality of the Führer had such an influence on people, you see, and was so extraordinary, such an overawing personality, that you couldn't really discuss it with the Führer. I sometimes tried, but I very seldom got—and in later years since I became minister there was never a question of discussion. It was a question of the Führer saying, 'I will think that over,' and the next day he would call and tell me, 'I want you to do this, and that.' You see, that was the way it was done. It is perhaps difficult to explain."

"Hitler was his god," Ribbentrop's former doctor, Hans Conrad, summarized for Brundage.

At the end of one session, Ribbentrop, desperately wishing to please his interrogators, stood up slowly, slowly put on his coat, hesitated, then retraced his steps to the table and said: "If you will tell me where I have failed to tell all I know, I will be glad to say more." On October 2 he sent a letter to Jackson offering, in grandiose style, to take responsibility for the errors he had made in order to preclude the trial, which, he thought, would prevent a reconciliation between Germany and other nations, especially the United States.

The confrontation took place on October 5. "You have asked me to do something about preventing these trials because you say you think the German people would think that any verdict or decision as to war criminals would be directed at them." Jackson, his piercing eyes magnified by his glasses, regarded Ribbentrop, dressed in a frayed khaki shirt and baggy suit, like a Wall Street banker addressing a Bowery bum. "I am interested to know how the German people could think it was directed at them, as a whole, when you yourself say you disagreed with the policy but couldn't do anything about it?"

"I think this: I think that this war has been so terrible, and I want so much my people to come to a reconciliation—the German people with the other nations—especially also with the American nation."

"When did the war become terrible, Ribbentrop, when did this war impress you as terrible?"

"It became to me terrible—" Ribbentrop, as he often did, closed his eyes, then dropped his head into his hands as if wracking his mind, and finally looked up. "I can tell you the exact moment. From the moment of the African landing—I mean, of the English-American forces."

"That is just about when I thought it began to affect you that way," Jackson snapped, and a few days later wrote President Truman: "Without a trace of humor and after some deliberation, he said, 'I will tell you the exact moment. It was when I heard that the Americans and their allies had landed in Africa.' He inadvertently disclosed the underlying attitude of the Nazi crowd toward the war—it was a terrible war when it began to be a losing war."

Jackson relished the interrogation, for Ribbentrop confirmed his impression of the depravity, decadence, and weakness of the Nazi regime. "When the destruction was going on in other people's countries, this war never impressed you as being terrible, or having any terrible aspects," Jackson indicted him. "You knew Germany was running a course that was going to bring the whole world against her, and you let the German people in for this out of what you say is loyalty to the Führer. Now you say to me that the German people, if they know these facts, will think it is against them. It seems to me if the German people knew these facts, they are the people who would want to deal with you, and with the other men who led them into this, and I would like to know what you think about that."

"May I say this." Ribbentrop seemed verbally to be swaying from side to side. "I think I must say that quite frankly I was not satisfied with quite a number of things, as I said. Now, the Führer, of course, was of a different opinion, and he is dead, and it would be to me, disloyalty, and also I don't know—perhaps I have not the right and it would be presumptuous of me to judge such a big thing in history." Ribbentrop spoke in English throughout. Frequently he paused in midsentence as if suspending his answer over a precipice. Occasionally, fumbling for an English word, he reverted to German.

"We are to meet within the coming week to determine what we will do as to the indictment of yourself and others as war criminals," Jackson continued. "Do you really want me to go to my associates at this meeting and tell them that it is your position that as foreign minister of the Reich you didn't know what the foreign policy was?"

"I am sorry. I must say so. I am very sorry." Ribbentrop was at his most contrite. "The Führer never revealed his definite aims to anybody. I personally don't think the Führer had a real conception of it."

Jackson pursued his questioning throughout the morning. He quoted from Ribbentrop's multipage, tortuous letter: " 'If the necessity for finding responsibility can be satisfied by the voluntary assumption of such a responsibility by myself and perhaps other co-workers of the Führer, and in this manner the proposed trial of the Germans can be prevented, I stand ready to take such a step, as the former foreign minister of the Führer, who is taking over the political responsibility of the men and women of the regime who are imprisoned here.' Whom do you have in mind as to perhaps take responsibility with yourself?" Jackson wanted to know.

"I have already thought about it, but I have not come really to a definite conclusion about it. But I should think that a number should be found."

"What do you have in mind taking responsibility for? What is your proposal?"

"I can't take any responsibility for criminal matters, but I thought of a political responsibility."

"Do you take responsibility for the war of aggression?" Jackson demanded.

"I couldn't do that for the war of aggression." He seemed to shrink away.

"Are you willing to take any responsibilities for the killing of American airmen?"

"No. I couldn't."

"You don't take any responsibility for the policy of the deportation of slave labor?"

"Slave labor? No."

"And you don't take any responsibility, I suppose, for the killing, or the branding, or other mistreatment of Russian prisoners of war?"

"No. I couldn't."

"Do you take any responsibility for the killing of hostages?"

"No, I couldn't."

"The destruction of Lidice. You wouldn't take any responsibility for that?"

"No."

"And I suppose you take no responsibility for the concentration camps?"

"No. I can't."

"Nor for the extermination policy against Jews?"

"You mean for these criminal things? I can't."

"What about the SS? Do you take any responsibility for what they did?"

"I don't know what you are hinting at. What you mean by that I don't know."

"In other words, you take no responsibility for any war crimes or crimes of any kind?"

"Crimes, I can't take. But I mean, I assure you the Geneva Convention —we have sustained that Geneva Convention as much as we possibly could." He referred to Hitler's demand to renounce the Geneva Convention following the bombing of Dresden.

"I am rather afraid you are going to be surprised, if you knew so little about your own government. You are going to be surprised at some of the things that they did," Jackson continued. "If you took responsibility as you propose, what was your idea of the penalty that should be imposed?"

"I have not thought about that, I don't know." Ribbentrop seemed about to burst out crying like a child.

"What are you prepared to suggest as appropriate?"

"I would leave this entirely to the other side."

"I think that is all." Jackson dismissed him, leaving it for Amen to make the final summation later:

"I ask you, to see if maybe some day you will tell the truth about something. You have not yet, and I hope you will begin soon, because if you don't, it will be too late. You write letters, and say you want to assume responsibility, and then when Justice Jackson asks you what you want to assume responsibility for, it turns out it is nothing except the fact that you held a political position which, obviously, you could not dismiss anyhow."

8   Jackson: The Labors of Hercules

The entire preparatory work for the Nuremberg proceedings was attended by a kind of frenetic madness, as if the lunacy of the Nazi regime were a virus that had lingered in the atmosphere and infected those who had come to Germany. Never in the history of the world had there been a case of such scope and complexity, Jackson declared; yet, because of the pressure upon him to return to the Supreme Court, and the general anxiety to place the Nazi leaders in the dock as quickly as possible to assuage the outrage of mankind, Jackson aimed to commence the trial within two or three months. Within that time span he needed to gather the evidence and organize it for the presentation of the case; to repair the Palace of Justice and convert it into the seat of an international tribunal; to compose, in conjunction with the British, Russians, and French, the indictment; and to organize the machinery for the functioning of the court.

It was as if Jackson had taken upon himself the task of performing the labors of Hercules all at the same time. The man in his position needed to have a superhuman capacity for work, superb organizational talent, the diplomatic skills of a Metternich, and an incisive knowledge of German and European history.

Jackson, however, typified the Middle American. His father, descended from pioneer upstate New York settlers, had been a hotel and livery stable operator. Jackson attended Albany Law School for one year, but dropped out in 1913 to clerk in a Jamestown lawyer's office, where he learned law by "reading," a common practice of the times.

Trials were held not only in the courthouse, but in barns and taverns, where lawyers and judges gathered in the evening to swap law and lore. In this atmosphere Jackson picked up an ability for storytelling, a liking for risqué jokes, and a flair for expression. An Episcopalian and Freemason, he was one of the minority of Democrats in a solidly Republican region. His courtroom presence helped him establish a reputation as *the* lawyer in the county. By his early thirties he lived with his attractive wife and two children in one of the larger houses in the city of forty thousand, owned a farm and a cabin cruiser, and had an income of thirty thousand dollars a year. A staunch advocate of individual liberty, he defended suspected Communists during the Red scare of the early 1920s, even though his position was unpopular and his practice declined for a time.

Franklin D. Roosevelt came to know him when Roosevelt was governor of New York and Jackson was a member of the state's Commission on the Administration of Justice. In 1934 the President named Jackson general counsel for the Internal Revenue Service, and thereafter promoted him with regularity. In 1941, when Supreme Court Justice Harlan Stone was elevated to the chief justiceship, Roosevelt nominated Jackson to the court and gave him to understand—an understanding that Jackson was not loath to bruit about Washington—that it was but a stepping-stone to the highest judicial position in the land.

Despite his governmental experience, Jackson had an aversion to administration, and exercised little control over his staff, some of whom remained scattered. Francis Shea and Colonel Telford Taylor, the first working with the British on the Crimes Against Peace, the second with the Russians on War Crimes and Crimes Against Humanity in the East, were still in London. The economics group, operating entirely independently, continued delving through the records of the Fechenheim Center at Frankfurt. In the documentary shuffle between Paris, London, Washington, Frankfurt, and Nuremberg evidence appeared and disappeared, and no one knew where it had gone.

More convinced than ever that, were it not for the Americans, the entire prosecution of the trial would break down, Jackson told Storey on September 17: "Candidly, I think we must utilize Committee Four [the "Conspiracy"] as the basis for keeping control of the bulk of the case in American hands."

Since the French wanted no part of the Crimes Against Humanity committed in Germany prior to the war, the Americans assumed responsibility for these also. It was the Americans who had proposed the indictment of the organizations; who held the defendants and were questioning them. So, almost by default, they accepted primary responsibility for proving the individual guilt of the defendants and the liability of the organizations. "You can readily see this works out just as Jackson wants," Major Frank Wallis, an experienced trial lawyer who was an assistant to Storey, wrote to Bernays. "The United States tries the whole damn case, and the other nations make some speeches and offer some supplemental evidence."

Early in August, Jackson discovered that IBM had installed at the

League of Nations a system capable of translating four or five different languages simultaneously, thus providing a solution for what otherwise would have been an insuperable problem. Jackson arranged to transfer the system from Geneva to Nuremberg. For its operation, a brigade of linguists would be required—six interpreters, twelve translators, and nine stenographers for each of the four languages: a total of one hundred and eight.

Additionally, Jackson seemed intent on transferring a large portion of the American bar to Nuremberg. "My God, what are you doing with them all?" Washington plaintively inquired of Jackson's London office.

"We eat them," Shea replied.

The total complement built up by Jackson numbered 640 persons, including 150 lawyers and 200 women, who were lodged in billets that acquired the name Girls' Town. (The British staff, at its maximum, consisted of 168 people, and the French and Russian combined did not exceed half the British.)

So far, only the Americans had established themselves in force in Nuremberg. The activity to prepare the Palace of Justice for the great event was so frenetic that Storey's deputy, Lieutenant Colonel Andy Wheeler, observed: "The place is a regular Charing Cross all day with plumbers, chimneysweeps in silk hats, plasterers, furnacemen, maids, and gasmen, and even briefcase-carrying fellows who look like insurance collectors."

Stummelmen, Germans who worked for little or nothing as janitors and handymen so that they could salvage the cigarette butts *(Stummel)* discarded by the Americans and sell the tobacco on the black market, scoured the corridors. Suites of offices, consisting of small, dark, cheerless rooms, were prepared for each division on the second floor.

The building with its endless stone and marble corridors, mysterious nooks and crannies, and 650 rooms was being restructured into a self-contained entity embracing, in the basement, a cafeteria, a huge PX, a barbershop, mail room, money exchange, dispensary, travel service, and eventually, even a British pub! Signs were posted in four languages: "German first," Colonel Wheeler, explained, "because German is the language of the defendants; second, English, because there are two English powers; third, Russian, because they're the most sensitive; and fourth, French, because the French representative is a teacher whose spirit was crushed in a concentration camp."

The focus of the reconstruction was the courtroom, which was being doubled in size both vertically and horizontally to accommodate the trial. Portions of the paneled walls and ceiling disappeared. A magnificent clock and the ornate chandeliers were replaced by fluorescent fixtures. A press gallery for 250 reporters was constructed, and a spectator section hacked out of an attic.

On September 1 a huge beam, removed when the height of the courtroom was expanded from one to two stories, suddenly crashed through the floor into the basement. The edifice shook as if a bomb had exploded; Goering, who was at that moment in the interrogation room on the first floor, had the wits scared out of him. Though newspapermen at first sensationalized the event and reported that it would delay the trial for weeks and even months, the engineers were in fact relieved that the beam had solved, of its own accord, the problem of how to maneuver it out of the courtroom.

By mid-September the French had still done no work on their portion of the case, and had only appointed their prosecutor, François de Menthon, two or three days before. The Russians were equally remiss. Up to the end of August, Jackson and the Americans assumed Nikitchenko would be the Soviet prosecutor. But then Nikitchenko disappeared back to Moscow, and nothing more was heard from him. On September 17 the Russians suddenly showed up in London with an entirely different delegation, headed by a new prosecutor, Roman A. Rudenko, a cheerful thirty-eight-year-old Ukrainian of peasant stock, who bore the rank of lieutenant general of the Russian Judicial Service.

One key issue remained unresolved. The Americans and British had agreed early during the proceedings of the summer that the SS, SA, SD, Gestapo, Nazi leadership corps, and Reich cabinet should be indicted as organizations. Bernays, however, had pressed for the addition of the German general staff and high command, arguing that it was impossible to have an aggressive war without the participation of generals. Jackson backed him up, though there were obvious difficulties in the fact that no German general staff, as such, had existed since World War I, and it was hard to know whom the high command had consisted of when Hitler had sacked generals with every change of season. The Pentagon and the British general staff, supported by such men as Shea and Brundage in Jackson's organization, lobbied energetically against the indictment of the German generals, arguing that prosecuting them would denigrate American and British professional military men as well; and for a time it appeared that they would win their point. On October 1, however, Jackson made it known that he would not agree to any indictment not including the high command; and when the issue was bitterly disputed two days later, the Americans received the support of the French and the Russians, and carried the field.

On October 5 the printed document was flown to Berlin, where the prosecutors were to file it with the judges of the court.

9   *The Judges*

Jackson had tried hard to get President Truman to appoint Owen J. Roberts, his fellow Supreme Court justice, who had retired in June, as the American judge at Nuremberg. But this would have been judicially too incestuous an arrangement, bringing into question the impartiality of the tribunal. Truman, furthermore, had political questions to consider. Six weeks after taking office, the President had peremptorily requested the resignation of Roosevelt's attorney general, Francis Biddle, a wealthy, cosmopolitan New Deal liberal, with whom the plain-speaking Truman felt ill at ease and was out of sympathy. (Biddle had supported Supreme Court Justice William O. Douglas for the vice-presidency in 1944.) To mend his fences with liberal Democrats and salve Biddle's injured pride, the President asked Biddle to become the American judge at Nuremberg, and Biddle accepted.

At the same time, the President was under great pressure to appoint Judge John J. Parker of North Carolina to the seat vacated by Roberts. Parker had been nominated by President Hoover in 1930 for the opening that had ultimately gone to Roberts; but a massive campaign by the NAACP and labor had led to a 41–39 defeat of his nomination in the Senate. Parker's downfall had resulted from the fact that, as a United States Circuit Court judge, he had ruled "yellow dog" contracts, which compelled workers to agree not to join a union if they wanted to hold their jobs, legal; and from his 1920 comment that political participation by blacks would be "a source of evil and a danger to both races." Since then, Alabama's Hugo Black had been appointed to the Supreme Court and proved himself an outstanding civil libertarian despite having once been an honorary member of the KKK. Parker, in fact, was a man of great honesty and character, a southern Progressive Republican who supported worker and Negro rights, even though he was lukewarm toward unions and integration. Many prominent Americans, including columnist Drew Pearson, felt an injustice had been done to him, and thought the time had come to rectify it. For months an enormous lobbying campaign, supported by a large number of Democrats, was conducted to obtain the nomination for Parker. Truman, who believed the nomination would result in another divisive debate in the Senate, did not want to appoint him—the President had already settled on Senator Harold Burton, a liberal Ohio Republican who had been a member of the Truman Committee and could be confirmed without difficulty. Practical politics dictated that Parker should receive a consolation prize, so on September 12 Truman called him to the White House and offered him the post of alternate judge at Nuremberg.

Parker, more disappointed than mollified, divined correctly that the President was throwing him a sop. Truman, however, urged that he take the position as a matter of patriotism, and promised that if he went to Europe his chance of being nominated to the Supreme Court would not be adversely affected—which was true in a sense. Reluctantly, Parker accepted, though mourning: "I have never taken a journey for which I had less enthusiasm." (And five days later Truman announced Burton's nomination.)

United States Chief Justice Harlan Stone, who viewed the International Military Tribunal with great suspicion, refused to swear in Biddle and Parker, a refusal that did not add to the judges' morale or the tribunal's stature. Stone resented and thought demeaning Jackson's role as prosecutor. It was his opinion that Jackson was employing the war crimes trial as a means of garnering prominence to solidify his position as heir apparent to the chief justiceship. The tribunal, Stone huffed, was "Jackson's high-grade lynching party."

Biddle and Parker were a study in contrast. Parker, sixty years old, exuded the ambience of the small-town South. His speech at times seemed quaint. He was "right much depressed," he allowed; his stomach was queasy because there was "right much wind and a rolling sea." His knowledge of Germany was rudimentary, and his view of humanity idealistic. Before the start of the trial he tended to discount the stories of atrocities, because he simply did not believe people were capable of such actions; and for that very reason he was eventually perhaps more shocked and affected than any of the other judges.

Biddle, on the other hand, was cosmopolitan and sophisticated. On his father's side he was descended from wealthy seventeenth-century New Jersey landholders; on his mother's, his lineage went back to Pocahontas and the Randolphs of Virginia. An ancestor, Edmund Randolph, had been aide-de-camp to George Washington, and later the nation's first attorney general and second secretary of state. Francis Biddle had been born in Paris in 1886, while his parents were on a European sojourn, and he spoke fluent French. For a time he attended school in Switzerland, then went to the fashionable prep school, Groton, where he excelled as a boxer, and to Harvard, where he graduated near the top of his class despite a penchant for poker, bridge, social life, and debts. After graduation, he clerked for a year for Supreme Court Justice Oliver Wendell Holmes, about whom he later wrote a book. As a lawyer in Philadelphia, his clients ranged from the Pennsylvania Railroad to the Dionne quintuplets. In contrast to Parker, who had two decades of experience on the bench, Biddle had spent but one unhappy, undistinguished year as a judge on the United States Circuit Court of Appeals.

The British, for their part, first selected Norman Birkett to be their chief judge at Nuremberg. Birkett, born in Lancashire, was sixty-two years old, six feet three inches tall, and undoubtedly one of the ungainliest men ever to have been miscreated. It was not just that he was ugly, but that the various parts of his anatomy all seemed to have been taken from different persons, so that nothing matched. Beneath curly red hair his eyes drifted behind glasses perched on a hawklike nose accentuated by an odd, wedge-shaped head, broad in back and narrow in front. He was reluctant to smile, for his teeth were like a misaligned picket fence battered by the elements. He walked with one of his shoulders sloping, as if from a lifetime of edging sideways through narrow and low doors. In order to compensate for his physical appearance, he developed an articulateness and disarming manner that immediately charmed people and drew them to him. He loved music and literature, and wrote passable verse.

During the post–World War I days, Birkett developed into one of Britain's three or four great criminal lawyers, failing in only three murder defenses out of dozens. Perhaps his most difficult adversary, as well as good friend, was Fyfe; and in a system where king's counsel (prosecutor) was named by individual case, Fyfe might be prosecuting and Birkett defending in one case, then Birkett prosecuting and Fyfe defending in the next. As a result of his diffidence and circumspection, he was chosen to represent Wallis Simpson in the divorce that enabled her to marry Edward VIII. During the Depression he earned $150,000 a year, but was constantly torn by self-doubt. He had a duodenal ulcer, and wondered if he had made a mistake when he accepted a judgeship in 1941, for he dreaded passing sentence. His life's ambition was to be Lord Chancellor, governor-general of Canada, or ambassador to the United States. When he received notification of his selection for the International Military Tribunal on August 31, he immediately accepted and noted: "It is a great honor to be selected, and restores my confidence in myself."

Yet he had scarcely become elated when the Lord Chancellor called, most apologetically. The Foreign Office insisted that the appointment go to a law lord—a judge who was a member of the House of Lords, which performed the function of a high court of appeals. Birkett could only be offered the seat of alternate judge. Recording his "secret anguish to have been selected as member and then asked to be alternate merely because of the absurd snobbishness of the Foreign Office," he nevertheless swallowed some measure of pride and agreed to go.

In his place as chief judge came Lord Geoffrey Lawrence, a former Lord Chief Justice of England. Sixty-six years old, with a face as round and ruddy as his physique, he looked like a caricature of John Bull. He raised Guernsey cows on his country estate, was physically active if somewhat short of breath, and impressed everyone as a jolly good fellow. He had a tendency to confuse faces and occasionally his mind wandered. Sometimes he took catnaps on the bench. But he was impartial and could be resolute; and he had the good sense to let Birkett do most of the work, while he himself provided the diplomacy and image.

The French sent as their judges Donnedieu de Vabres and Robert Falco. Both were short, frail-appearing men, though de Vabres had considerable girth. The Americans and British nicknamed him "Nom de Dieu" (name of God) because he had a flair for dramatic, almost prophetlike oratory. He had an imposing white walrus mustache that he twirled with a flourish for emphasis at critical moments. He was formal, old-fashioned, and somewhat pedantic. Although he had spent most of his life as a professor and was a world-renowned authority on criminal and international law, he walked with a sailor's rolling gait. He spoke German and had lectured in Germany during the 1930s. He liked to show off the half-dozen words of English he knew, issuing them in hesitant malapropisms. When, once, accompanied by his wife, he met Biddle, he announced: *"Mon cher collègue,* permit me to introduce you to . . ."* He paused pregnantly. "My woman!" Madame de Vabres, who spoke English, flushed poppy red.

De Vabres's associate, Falco, had twenty-five years' experience as a member of the Court de Cassation, the highest in France. Though he spoke sparsely, he was a man of great humor, shrewdness, and patience, and understood English. His French was rhythmic and musical, as if a metronome were measuring the words.

The inscrutable Russians, who had recalled Nikitchenko to Moscow for consultation in his capacity as prosecutor, restored him, after long pondering, to the trial as the *judge!* He brought with him, as alternate, A. F. Volchkov, a man who, like Nikitchenko, was still in his forties, much younger than the other Allied judges. Volchkov's Slavic features were scarred and eroded. He had spent part of his career as a prosecutor and criminal judge, and part as a diplomat. Having once been assigned for three years to London, he could get along in English. His emotions were more pronounced than his intellect, and, after he had had a satisfactory amount to drink, his affability turned into positive affection, demonstrated with great bear hugs and exclamations of everlasting friendship.

The Berlin meeting had been scheduled, at the insistence of the Russians, to solidify the image of the former German capital as the permanent seat of the tribunal, even if the first trial was to be held in Nuremberg. But when Jackson, Fyfe, de Menthon, and Rudenko met in Berlin on October 6, the Russians had done no preparatory work, and Rudenko lamented that he and his staff did not even have a place to stay; so the British took them in like waifs.

On Tuesday, October 9, the judges met for the first time in the Allied Control Council building. One of the thorny issues that had been left in limbo in London was the question of who should preside over the trial. This was a matter not only of prestige and of rulings which the president would be called upon to make, but of pivotal power, for the charter provided that, in case of a 2–2 tie, the vote of the president would be decisive (except on the question of convicting, which required a 3–1 majority).

The British kept apologizing for their lack of preparation, and praising the extraordinarily efficient American organization. Nikitchenko was taken by Biddle's liberalism and quiet humor, which contrasted with the establishment airs of the French and British, and nominated Biddle for the presidency. "I really have been running this show," Biddle noted with satisfaction.

Jackson, however, as soon as he divined the drift of the proceedings, took Biddle aside and told him that under no circumstance must he accept. Jackson pointed out: "All of the arrangements are American, all of the defendants except three are prisoners taken by the Americans. [This was an exaggeration.] We have a staff three times that of all the other nations combined, and most of the evidence comes from our sources. In the division of the case, the major part of the trial work has been assigned to us because we are the people best prepared to carry it through. If we were also to provide the presiding officer, there would be danger that these trials would look like a purely American enterprise. If anything should go wrong, all of the animosities and blame would be centered upon the United States."

The British, Jackson had learned, were fully prepared to back Biddle for the presidency; but they must not be permitted to slide out from their responsibilities.

Reluctantly, Biddle suppressed his ego, withdrew from consideration, and seconded the French nomination of Lawrence for the presidency. "It would have been fun to preside, but this is the wisest choice," he mused, consoling himself with the thought: "Lawrence depends on me for everything, and I'll run the show."

Everything appeared ready for the swearing in of the tribunal and the filing of the indictment, scheduled for the tribunal's first public session on Monday, October 15. On the eleventh, however, Rudenko informed the tribunal that a problem existed with the indictment's statement: "Nine hundred and twenty-five Polish officers who were prisoners of war were killed in the Katyn Forest near Smolensk." Rudenko said that, according to later information he had received, the number was eleven thousand.

Though this seemed a simple enough correction to make, Rudenko, to the puzzlement and irritation of the judges, stalled for three days and demanded a postponement of the inaugural session.

The truth was that the Russians, when they had occupied the eastern half of Poland following the German attack on that country in September 1939, had taken 14,900 Poles prisoner. Eleven thousand of them were officers and reserve officers. For several months, the Soviets attempted to indoctrinate these men, and determine which of them might be "reeducated." During April and May of 1940, however, while the Germans launched their attacks in Scandinavia and the West, and concurrently decided to liquidate the cream of the Polish nobility, intelligentsia, and political leadership in the "AB Action," 14,500 of the Polish POWs in Russian hands disappeared.

Early in 1943, a German signal corps unit quartered on a former NKVD (Soviet secret police) installation in the Katyn Forest discovered a mass grave, from which 4,254 bodies of Polish officers were ultimately dug up. The Germans summoned an "international commission" of medical men from Axis and neutral nations, which concluded that the officers had been shot in the spring of 1940. Goebbels launched an intensive propaganda campaign, which soon resulted in a break in diplomatic relations between the Polish government-in-exile in London and the Soviet Union. A few months later, the Russians, on recapturing the area, formed their own commission, which exhumed 925 corpses and declared that the officers had been captured alive by the Germans but later shot by them.

The Russians assumed, somewhat naively, that they need only file the findings of their "Extraordinary State Commission" with the International Military Tribunal, and the commission's conclusions would be accepted and become part of history. When the figure of 925 appeared in the indictment, however, the Kremlin suddenly realized that, since more than 13,500 Polish POWs would be left unaccounted for, the issue would not be resolved. While the Soviet government agonized over the total number of victims to be ascribed to the Katyn massacre—925, or 4,254, or the 11,000 officers who were missing, or all 14,500 of the 14,900 men who had vanished—Rudenko was ordered to bring the process of filing the indictment to a halt.

The western judges, unaware of what lay behind Rudenko's request, were inclined to reject it, and the issue was still undecided late Sunday night. Nikitchenko asked which would be the greater evil: a postponement of a few days, or the harm that would come to Russia if the indictment were filed as it existed? Nikitchenko was so emotional that Biddle sensed disaster impending, and asked the Russian judges to leave so that he could discuss the situation with the others.

When the Russians absented themselves, Biddle said he believed they would walk out of the tribunal if the prosecutor were forced to submit the indictment in the morning. There seemed, consequently, no alternative but to grant a three-day postponement. After brief discussion, the others agreed.

On Thursday, October 18, the judges took their oaths, and the prosecutors delivered the indictment. The tribunal adjourned for Nuremberg. The defendants were served with the indictment. They would have thirty days to obtain lawyers and to prepare their cases. The greatest trial in history was scheduled to begin on November 20.

It was intended to set new standards for the world, but its foundation was pitted with inequities and self-serving restrictions. Seeds had been planted that many of those associated with the trial, including Jackson, feared would sprout into disaster. The Germans were charged with violating the Treaty of Versailles and rearming, but were not to be permitted to cite the fact that the French had refused to abide by the terms of the treaty or that the British had joined the Germans in bilateral negotiations circumventing it. No mention was to be allowed of the complicity of the four trial powers in German rearmament—the Russians had provided the Germans with training bases; the Americans had supplied the German air arm; the French, holding an interest in the Skoda works, had encouraged the Germans to buy weapons from the Czechs; and the British and German munitions industries had been interlocked.

Equality before the bar of justice was, in fact, impossible since the Allies had not only committed, but were in the process of committing, some of the very acts for which the Germans were to be tried. Churchill and Stalin had redrawn the borders of Poland and Germany as arbitrarily as Hitler and Stalin had reshaped European frontiers a half-dozen years before. When Bernays had wanted to charge the Germans with the dispossession and transportation of populations, Assistant Secretary of War John J. McCloy had warned him not to—some fifteen million Germans were, at that very moment, being driven out of their homes in the East. During the Berlin meeting, Jackson wrote to Truman, complaining that the Allies "have done or are doing some of the very things we are prosecuting Germans for. The French are so violating the Geneva Convention in the treatment of prisoners of war that our command is taking back prisoners sent to them [for reconstruction work]. We are prosecuting plunder and our Allies are practicing it. We say aggressive war is a crime and one of our allies asserts sovereignty over the Baltic States based on no title except conquest."

It was, of course, the realities of power politics that had led Jackson, in order to persuade the Allies to agree to the conspiracy and aggressive war charges, to suggest a trial framework that would prohibit the Germans from discussing the causes of the war, from pleading *tu quoque* ("I did it, but you did it too"), or from asserting that the law under which they were being tried was ex post facto. Professor Hans von Hentig, a German refugee teaching in the United States, protested to President Truman that every one of the defendants could be convicted under the laws of Germany or any other nation, but that the rules of the International Military Tribunal were similar to those of the French revolutionary tribunals during the Robespierre terror: "There is not a professor of constitutional or criminal law in this country or any other civilized state who would not ask you urgently to have those rules reconsidered. They are opposed to all legal standards."

Obliquely, even Jackson agreed: "This is not an ordinary trial," he told Biddle and Parker. "Some of the proprieties went by the way when General Nikitchenko, who had been the Soviet prosecutor, was made a member of the tribunal."

Thus, motivated by the necessity to mete out justice for the Nazi horrors and atrocities, but torn by apprehension that the trial would turn into a charade of expediency and retribution rather than a search for truth, the prosecutors and defendants, lawyers and judges came together at Nuremberg.

10   Ley: The Disaster of Anti-Semitism

Traveling from Berlin to Nuremberg with the American contingent on October 19 in response to a request from Colonel Andrus was Gustav Gilbert, a clinical psychologist. Two weeks earlier, Dr. Leonardo Conti, the former minister of public health, had hanged himself from the window bars in his cell. Colonel Andrus thereupon sought a German-speaking officer who could keep close watch upon and communicate with the defendants in their own language. (The psychiatrist, Dr. Douglas Kelley, did not speak German.)

The Vienna-born Gilbert, working in military intelligence in Berlin, eagerly grasped the opportunity. Given free and continuous access to the prisoners, he assumed the role of "resident observer." Since he doled out a few extra cigarettes and chocolate bars, the former leaders of the Reich looked forward to his daily appearances. In jail, he offered the principal opportunity for conversation; and, seeking to justify themselves, they poured out their souls to him.

Gilbert was faced with an immediate crisis in the person of Robert

Ley, the number-four defendant on the original British list. A fat, stubby little man, Ley, with his serrated nose and asymmetrical face, looked like a waterfront gangster. The son of a cattle dealer, he had been seriously wounded in World War I and had afterward gone to work as a chemist for I. G. Farben. The French occupation of the Rhineland in 1923 had radicalized him, and Hitler's trial in Munich had captured his attention. In 1925 he met Hitler for the first time and was appointed gauleiter of the Rhineland. At the beginning of 1933 Hitler named him head of the Party Organization; and, a few months later, following the Nazi assumption of power, gave him the task of liquidating the democratic labor movement and combining all 216 German unions into a Nazi conglomerate. Storm troopers controlled by Ley pounded into union offices, threw out the officials, and expropriated the unions' funds and property. The leaders and recalcitrant officials of the Social Democratic unions were shipped off to concentration camps. Other officials, willing to cooperate with the Nazis, were absorbed into the *Deutsche Arbeiter Front* (German Labor Front), the new organization created by Ley.

In the interest of "national solidarity," Hitler proclaimed an end to "class struggle." Strikes were prohibited. Wages and prices were frozen. In actuality, because of deductions by the Labor Front, take-home pay declined. Hidden inflation in the form of reduction of the quality of goods and disappearance of items from regular trade into the black market steadily eroded the purchasing power of the workers, who earned an average of $6.29 a week (compared to approximately $22 in the United States).

It was the fiction of the Labor Front that it united employers and employees in one vast "all for one, one for all" organization. The management of every factory of twenty or more workers was required to nominate a Labor Front leader approved by the party. It was the task of the factory Führer to keep the workers satisfied and the operation humming smoothly. Ostensibly, he protected the workers against abuses by management, and arbitrated grievances; but, in reality, he represented the interests of the party, and was a kind of factory ward boss.

Bureaucracy and social planning ran riot in Ley's imaginative mind. Almost a government in itself, the *Deutsche Arbeiter Front* contained no fewer than thirty-two separate bureaus and departments. Since the cost of entertainment and travel were beyond the means of most workers, Ley established the *Kraft Durch Freude* (Strength Through Joy) organization to regiment the leisure time of the masses. Strength Through Joy provided cut-rate prices through block booking and no-frills tours. By 1938 ten million Germans were taking Strength Through Joy vacations. A week at a German resort cost about 35 marks ($14) and a trip through Italy 155 marks ($62).

Ultimately, Ley encompassed thirty million workers in his paternalistic embrace, an apparatus of its kind dwarfing any in history outside of the Soviet Union and China. The dues paid by the workers represented the largest single source of capital in the Reich, and the assets of the Labor Front reached ten billion marks. Since Ley was responsible to no one but himself for the funds, he amassed enormous wealth. Industrialists showered gifts on him to stay in his good graces. He competed with Goering, Ribbentrop, and Goebbels in his ostentatious life-style. He collected 100 million marks in deposits from German workers for Volkswagen ("people's cars"). The original "beetle" was designed and ground broken for a factory that was to be the biggest auto plant in the world. The car was to sell for only 990 marks, but not a single depositor ever received a vehicle or his money back.

One of the champion alcoholics in a party noted for its heavy drinkers, Ley initiated a sobriety campaign in 1939, but never himself joined the crusade. He resembled Hitler in that it was almost impossible to hold a coherent conversation with him, for within two or three minutes he would monopolize whatever subject was being discussed. The Germans facetiously defined a "Ley" as "the maximum amount of time a man could speak without saying one sensible thing."

In 1938 he became impassioned with the statuesque blond daughter of a famous opera singer, and divorced his first wife. The Christian name of his new spouse was Inge, but he called her "Illegirl." He had three children by her in four years, but her pregnancies, aggravated by gallstones and heavy drinking, were difficult. She became addicted to morphine and was impossible to live with unless she was doped up. On December 29, 1942, after a trivial quarrel with Ley, she shot and killed herself. A few months later, Ley seduced a beautiful, seventeen-year-old Estonian girl, who was a dancer at the Strength Through Joy Sports Palace; and in July of 1944 she bore him a child.

Though privately Ley seldom spoke of Jews, publicly he rivaled Streicher as a Jew baiter. *"Juda muss sterben"* (Jewry must die) was a favorite phrase in the articles he wrote. He presaged the starvation of the Jews and Poles by postulating in a piece in the party newspaper, *Der Angriff,* on January 31, 1940: "A lower race needs less room, less clothing, less food, less culture than a higher race. The German cannot live in the same fashion as the Pole and the Jew." In 1943 he avowed: "We are not going to abandon the struggle until the last Jew in Europe has been exterminated and is actually dead."

When Goebbels in the spring of 1945 enunciated the concept that the German people would melt into the forest like Werwolves to carry on guerrilla warfare, Ley was placed in charge of organizing resistance in the

Alps, and promised Hitler that the party functionaries would "fight like lions, like heroes—just like the Russian partisans. They will ride silently through the woods on bicycles and mercilessly attack the enemy."

Upon the collapse of the Reich, Ley toyed with suicide, but fumbled an attempt to shoot himself and lacked the courage to take poison. On May 16, a detachment of the 101st Airborne Division, acting on a tip, discovered him in a mountain cabin south of Berchtesgaden. An incipient beard sprouting on his face, he insistently stammered out that he was not Ley, but Dr. Ernst Distelmeyer. He had been asleep when the troops burst in and was hustled off wearing blue pajamas, over which he threw a woolen cape. On his balding head was perched a green Tyrolean hat. "Distelmeyer," he kept repeating at his initial interrogation when asked his name, until suddenly party treasurer Franz Xavier Schwarz was brought into the room.

"Well, Dr. Ley, what are you doing here!" Schwarz burst out.

At Mondorf he was issued an ill-fitting jacket and pair of trousers. As soon as he arrived at Nuremberg, he addressed a letter to "Sir Henry Ford," suggesting that Ford take over production of the Volkswagen and make him the manager of the plant. All during the month of September he was left, except for one interrogation by Amen, to ruminate in his cell. His feverish brain, which had suffered some slight damage because of his drinking and a World War I injury, would not let him rest, and he filled scores of sheets of paper with his writing. He entiteld a seventy-four-page autobiography "The Fate of a Peasant." A lengthy political treatise received the caption "Life or Glory."

"I must go on America's side, and America must help us in her own interest against the Asian flood," he wrote. Germany had to become part of the American commonwealth, and National Socialism must be purged of anti-Semitism.

He spent a great part of his time in communion with his dead wife Inge, and hallucinated that she visited his cell: "You are bodily near to me. I am feeling you. You are embracing me with your love, your charm and your beauty. Illegirl, how beautiful you were! Beautiful in body, soul and spirit. You were a rare creation of our Lord. . . .

"She is silent, I lose myself in meditation, finally in a deep relaxing sleep and dream: Germany would have become so beautiful, Strength Through Joy, the most beautiful cities and villages had been planned, just wages, a great unique health program, social security for the aged, road construction and traffic lanes—how beautiful Germany could have been if, if, if, and always again if. God in heaven what have I done that I am treated under such conditions as a criminal. Lord God, give me an answer, I have a right to it."

Attempting to reconcile the Nazi disaster with his fanatic faith in the Führer, Ley told Major John J. Monigan, his interrogator: "I wish to say at this time that the Führer was one of the greatest men there ever was. But one thing broke us, that was our *Willensethos* [the belief that anything could be accomplished if it were willed powerfully enough] and our anti-Semitism, which were the things that finally undid us."

In his political testament addressed to the German people, Ley expatiated: "We deserted God and so God deserted us. In place of His divine grace we substituted our human will, and in anti-Semitism we violated one of the principal laws of His creation. Looking back upon all this today, I know and could recount dozens of examples how paralyzing and actually disastrously these two factors influenced us. *The anti-Semitic spectacles upon the nose of bold and defiant men were a disaster.* This must for once be courageously admitted. It is to no avail to evade the issue.

"Certainly, it is bitter and hard to admit mistakes. It is not enough to say we will no longer talk about anti-Semitism, we will tolerate the Jews, we are forced to do so. No, we must take the step completely, half steps are no good. We must eliminate suspicion and meet the Jew with an open heart. Judaism must make its peace with Germany, and Germany must make its peace with Judaism in the interest of world peace and world prosperity. Hatred and love dwell in close proximity."

A few days later, on October 19, Ley, together with the other defendants, was presented with the indictment, charging him with "Formulation of a common plan or conspiracy to commit Crimes Against Peace: Namely, planning, preparation, initiating or waging a war of aggression, or a war in violation of international treaties; War Crimes: Namely, violation of the law or customs of war [including] murder, ill treatment, deportation, the forced labor of civilian populations, the murder and maltreatment of prisoners of war or hostages, the plunder of private or public property, and the wanton destruction of towns or villages; Crimes Against Humanity: Namely, murder, extermination, enslavement, deportation, and other inhumane acts committed against any civilian population, before or during the war, or persecutions on political, racial or religious grounds . . . whether or not in violation of the domestic law of the country where perpetrated."

For the next half-dozen days, Ley, bewildered like his fellow prisoners by the omnibus "conspiracy" charge, wrote tirelessly in sanctimonious self-justification: "I understand that the victor thinks that he has to exterminate his hated opponent. I'm not defending myself against this—that he wants to shoot or kill me. I defend myself only against his endeavor to stamp me as a criminal. The war fitted into my plans like hail into a corn field. There is no question of a conspiracy or a common plan. The Führer, according to his habit, never spoke with anybody about things which didn't concern him. I always heard about the beginning of an operation out of newspapers or over the radio."

Disturbed and erratic, he paced up and down in his cell, gesticulating and muttering. To Gilbert and Dr. Kelley, he complained bitterly: "How can I prepare a defense? Am I supposed to defend myself against all these crimes which I knew nothing about?" Turning against the wall, he flung his arms out dramatically in the form of a cross, and cried: "Shoot me! Shoot me now as a German. You are the victors! But why should I be brought before a tribunal like a k-k-k-k-k . . ." he was unable to get the word "Kriminal" out of his mouth.

He became obsessed with the idea of martyrdom. His death would demonstrate that his motives were pure. If the Americans would not kill him, then perhaps he would kill himself. "Farewell. Farewell," he recorded. "I cannot stand this shame any longer. Physically, nothing is lacking. The food is good. It is warm in my cell. The Americans are correct and partially friendly. Spiritually, I have reading matter and write whatever I want. I receive paper and pencil. They do more for my health than necessary, and I may smoke and receive tobacco and coffee. . . .

"*I am reconciled with God.* I implore his mercy and his pity and I pray for it sincerely. Now comes sweet death, savior of all my suffering. To my Inge and to my Führer."

Since Conti's death, precautions against suicide had been increased— at night the chairs were removed from the cells, and in daytime it was forbidden to place them against the wall. But, at quarter to eight on the night of October 25, Ley tore the edge off a GI towel, soaked it in toilet water, and tied it around the toilet pipe that ran up the wall. Ripping some pieces from his underwear, he stuffed them into his mouth. He then looped the towel around his neck, twisted himself several times so that it tightened and cut off the circulation, and, in the process of losing consciousness, collapsed onto the toilet.

Through the opening in the door, only a prisoner's legs were visible when he sat in the recessed toilet alcove. Each guard was responsible for four cells. At 8:10 PM, when the corporal of the guard came by to collect the prisoners' eyeglasses, the sentinel had passed by Ley's door on four leisurely rounds, during which Ley had apparently not moved. To the demand by the corporal for Ley's glasses, there was no response. The corporal unlocked the door. Ley, his arms and head dangling limply, was suspended grotesquely by the towel. Though Dr. Pflücker administered a heart stimulant and attempted artificial respiration for twenty minutes, Ley could not be revived. After an autopsy was performed, his body, placed in a box lined with butcher paper, was taken that same night to the Nuremberg cemetery, where it was interred in an unmarked grave.

11   The Krupp Fiasco

On October 26, the day after Ley's suicide, Jackson met with the other prosecutors. There appeared little prospect that Martin Bormann would be discovered. Ley's death reduced the number of defendants to twenty-two; and serious question was arising whether the seventy-five-year-old Gustav Krupp von Bohlen und Halbach, the titular head of the Krupp steel and armaments empire, would be able to stand trial.

Krupp, whose mother had been American,* had had little use at first for the rabble-rousing upstart Hitler. He had, however, gradually been persuaded that Hitler was the only alternative to a bankrupt government and a Communist takeover. When Hitler had promised to quash the unions along with the Communists, Krupp had reluctantly joined the coalition backing the Führer.

For the next half-dozen years Krupp participated in the public adulation of Hitler and was rewarded with a flood of profits. Paying workers wages frozen at Depression levels, Krupp benefited both from the revival of the world's economy and the international arms race set off by Hitler. Like, however, his industrial compatriots, he supported rearmament only so long as it was good for business. He had a healthy respect for the British Empire and every desire to avert a war against the western powers.

By 1940, when he was seventy years of age, he was showing signs of cerebral arteriosclerosis and was slowly withdrawing from the management of the vast works. In 1941 he suffered the first of a number of strokes. Gradually he deteriorated. His mental powers declined. Unable to control his bowels and bladder, he wandered about in his soiled pants. Bertha took him to the family's eighty-room château, Blühnbach, deep in the Austrian Alps thirty-five miles south of Salzburg.

Unlike his father, Gustav's oldest son, Alfried, was fully a man of the Nazi era. Born in 1907, he became a member of the SS in 1931, when joining the purportedly knightly organization was in vogue among the

*Krupp's father, Gustav Halbach, was a member of a German-American family of coal mining entrepreneurs, with properties in the Ruhr and in Scranton, Pennsylvania. Gustav Halbach spent the early years of his life in Pennsylvania and married the daughter of a prominent Civil War hero, Colonel Henry Bohlen, who, when he was killed at the Second Battle of Bull Run, had sent the city of Philadelphia into mourning for a month. A few years later, Halbach, having joined the name Bohlen to his own, took his family back to his ancestral Germany, where the Grand Duke of Baden ennobled him as von Bohlen und Halbach. The junior Gustav, diminutive, intelligent, and ambitious, became a member of the German diplomatic corps, and was well known for his slavish devotion to the Kaiser. In 1906, when Gustav was thirty-six and balding, the Kaiser rewarded him by selecting him as consort for the tall, twenty-year-old Bertha Krupp, heiress to the Krupp fortune.

elite. In 1936 Alfried was appointed deputy director of the enterprise, and took his seat on the boards of no fewer than twenty-four other corporations and banks. As soon as the victorious Wehrmacht swept across Europe, Alfried joined with other German industrialists in the rush to acquire the spoils, consisting mostly of expropriated Jewish property. When one French entrepreneur, Robert Rothschild, was reluctant to sign over his plant and took refuge in the Italian-occupied area of France, the Krupp managers hired a bunch of thugs to kidnap him, and he wound up in the gas chamber at Auschwitz.

Under Alfried, Krupp became one of the principal firms involved in the gargantuan forced-labor program. The firm employed 100,000 foreign workers, prisoners of war, and concentration camp inmates. Not only did Alfried establish satellite concentration and labor camps in the vicinity of his plants—fifty-five in the area of Essen alone—but he proposed to construct a large automatic weapons factory at Auschwitz to utilize the labor of the prisoners there. Although Hitler and Himmler hesitated, Alfried personally pushed the project through. Part of Krupp's agreement with the SS was that the people who were injured, became worn out, or developed chronic illnesses could be exchanged for fresh workers. Since the smoking chimneys were part of the scene at every concentration camp, Alfried could have little illusion about the fate of those no longer capable of work.*

Though it was Alfried who had originally been selected for indictment, a member of Jackson's staff had realized a day or two before the announcement of the defendants that if all of the accused were to be charged with conspiracy to wage aggressive war, Alfried, who had not played a leading role in the company's affairs until after the start of the conflict, would have a ready defense. Gustav's name was thereupon substituted for Alfried's. That a seventy-five-year-old man was possibly not in condition to stand trial might have been suspected. But though during the next two months members of the prosecution staff were occasionally no more than an hour or two distant from Blühnbach, no one attempted to check on his physical state.

It was the British, learning of the true state of affairs from Alfried, who first brought up the question of Gustav Krupp's condition.

The judges decided to have a doctor accompany Jim Rowe, one of the three attorneys Biddle had brought along to assist him, when he went to serve Krupp with the indictment on October 19. Rowe found Krupp in the enormous hunting lodge that, with its thousands of stuffed animal heads,

---

*At the same time that Alfried was a participant in the Nazi spoliation of Europe, his second cousin, Charles "Chip" Bohlen, was working in the White House as President Roosevelt's liaison with the State Department and adviser on Soviet affairs.

tanned skins, and knickknacks made out of animal bones, looked like a museum dedicated to slaughter. The magnate lay incoherent, paralyzed, diapered like a baby, uttering no more than an occasional expletive. The doctor thought that any attempt to move him to Nuremberg would kill him.

A panel of six specialists dispatched by the judges to conduct a comprehensive examination confirmed the opinion. Charles Dubost, the assistant French prosecutor, noted: "The trial of a dying old man who is unable to attend is out of the question."

Jackson was in a quandary. He was about to lose the sole defendant representing the industrialists. The economics case, which was an integral part of the conspiracy concept, would be left hanging in limbo. On November 13, Jackson proposed to his co-prosecutors that Alfried should be substituted as a defendant for his father. The French and Russians were willing to go along. But to Sir Hartley Shawcross, the British prosecutor, Jackson's proposal seemed a cynical approach to justice. Shawcross, who had been appointed by the Labour government primarily as a matter of prestige and whose duty as Britain's attorney general kept him away from the trial except for four or five highlight appearances, told the judges, who were considering Jackson's motion: "This is a court of justice, not a game in which you can play a substitute if one member of the team falls sick."

Jackson was in an awkward position. He could scarcely reveal to the judges that, had it not been for the snarls in his organization, Alfried would have been the defendant all along. He even told the judges that he thought that Alfried, as a sporting gesture, might volunteer: "It would seem to me that in the first place he might be willing to step into his father's place without delay."

When the judges closeted themselves to consider Jackson's request, Birkett was unable to fathom Jackson's motive, and thought the idea advanced by the American prosecutor was shocking. Biddle, noting privately that Jackson had made a "cheap speech," told his fellow judges that the prosecution had had months to select the defendants, and adding another at the eleventh hour was unconscionable. Only Volchkov, in the absence of Nikitchenko, supported Jackson; and the judges voted three to one against the inclusion of Alfried.

12   Attorneys for the Defense

Biddle had suggested before leaving Berlin that the tribunal meet in Nuremberg on October 22 to enable the defendants to make motions and solicit counsel; but he was voted down. Instead, the tribunal established a secretariat to take care of clerical and administrative matters, and appointed a young British officer, Major A. M. S. Neave, to serve the defendants with the indictment and assist them in obtaining legal representation.* When Neave went to see the Nazi leaders on October 19, he took with him a list of some threescore attorneys for the accused to choose from if they wished.

A short time later, Goering was once more taken to the interrogation room in the Palace of Justice. Amen informed him that, since he was now officially a defendant, he was not required to participate in additional interrogations.

To the contrary, Goering responded. "I am absolutely ready to make further statements." Since, however, he was not familiar with any of the names on the list of lawyers, he wanted to consult with his fellow defendant Hans Frank about them.

"Sure!" Amen agreed.

"Good!" Goering, grateful, added that he would like to meet with Frank immediately.

"Right." Amen was accommodating. "We will try to arrange it this evening."

A number of the other prisoners made similar requests to talk to Frank, who had been the leading Nazi jurist. Born in 1900, he was the son of a lawyer who had been disbarred and sent to prison for embezzlement, reinstated, then disbarred again. Frank himself had studied law at the University of Munich. There, he told his interrogator, Lieutenant Colonel Thomas J. Hinkel, deputy chief of the Interrogation Division, he had, out of envy, joined the anti-Semitic Thule Society, and so come into contact with Hitler, Hess, and Rosenberg: "I was at that time a very poor man. I saw the Jews had all very rich positions and fortunes, and out of this youthful criticism I came to my judgment about the Jews."

Following his admission to practice, he had started his career as a teacher of law, but in 1927 had become the party's principal attorney, and subsequently had defended it in 2,400 of the 40,000 lawsuits launched against it in a half-dozen years. In 1929 he organized the Union of National Socialist Jurists, and the following year he became head of the NSDAP (Nazi) Legal Office. After the Nazi takeover he was named Bavarian minister of justice and president of the newly formed Academy of German Law.

*Neave, who had studied in Germany, had been captured by the Wehrmacht during the fighting in France in 1940, but two years later had escaped from Colditz prison, and was one of the relatively few men who succeeded in making his way back to England. He later was elected to Parliament and became a key adviser to Prime Minister Margaret Thatcher. He was killed in 1980 by a bomb planted in his car by the Irish Republican Army.

The Academy encompassed every member of the legal profession, and was designed to ultimately bring German law into conformity with National Socialist ideology.

Frank was so dazzled by the Führer that in 1935 he told a gathering of jurists: "Formerly we were in the habit of saying: 'This is right or wrong.' Today we must ask the question: 'What would the Führer say?' We are under the great obligation of recognizing as a holy work of our Folk Spirit the laws signed by Adolf Hitler. Hitler has received his authority from God."

On the one hand, Frank was intelligent, artistic, literate, a connoisseur of music, and a compendium of quotations. On the other hand, he was devious, venal, and vacillating, with a weathervane's constancy. After the conquest of Poland in 1939, Hitler named him governor-general of that part of the country not annexed to Germany or occupied by Russia. But when Hinkel questioned him about the events of that era, Frank's memory seemed to desert him. Though Auschwitz was only thirty miles from his headquarters in Cracow, he professed to have no idea of what had happened there:

"One passed it on the train. It was a huge camp. One could always see the barbed wire."

"Didn't you often also pass Maidanek?"

"I don't know about that. One passes a lot of things."

"In the course of your travels to Lublin, if you turned your head to your right or left you would have seen Maidanek, wouldn't you?" Hinkel challenged him.

"I was in the town. It was outside of town," Frank replied blandly.

"You never heard anything at all about Maidanek?" Hinkel, who had statements from Hans Lammers, state secretary in Hitler's chancellery, and other witnesses that Frank had known about the camp, inquired.

"No, never."

"And you were never curious as to what was going on there?"

"If I had known it at that time and if I had kept silent a single day, I would have been the biggest criminal that ever existed on God's earth! What took place at Maidanek I only heard later from the foreign press."

"You don't seem to know very much about what happened in the government-general in Poland, do you?"

"That is right," Frank was quick to agree.

"You were there only five and one-half years. You were not there very long, were you?"

"What has that got to do with it?" Frank shrugged uneasily. "This is no reason why I should know everything that happened."

Frank complained that he was being made responsible for all events and occurrences in his administration: "It seems that every leaf that falls from a tree and every fire that breaks out in the country is being attributed to me."

There was no limit to Frank's evasiveness and attempted rationalization. Periodically he became almost hysterical, waved his arms about, and in a rising voice expostulated: "I request that I not be charged with responsibility for a lot of crimes, or a lot of measures that had been taken, not by me, but by hundreds of others. How could I administer the country? I did not have any police. I did not have any railroads. How could I administer a country and feed them all?"

There was a kind of hypnotic quality to Frank's performance; and despite himself Hinkel found himself falling into the pattern. "What did you do? Don't tell me the things you didn't do!"

"I am telling you why I could not do more than this. The colonel should tell me what I should have done."

"I wasn't governor-general. You were."

"Colonel, it is easy for you to ask. You come from a country where laws are being adhered to. I had to carry out a position which caused me difficulties day and night."

"Your statements are that you did nothing."

"If that is not sufficient, the colonel should tell me what I should have done."

"I am not concerned with what you should have done or should not have done." Unknowingly, Hinkel was shouting. "I want to know what you *did.*"

"Please don't speak so loudly." Frank had managed to reverse roles. "I hear very well. We want to examine the things in quietness again."

"Yes." Hinkel sighed. "Let us just discuss them quietly."

Early in October, however, the thirty-six volumes of Frank's journal were brought to Nuremberg. At the interrogation of October 8, Hinkel stacked the red and green volumes up on the table; and when Frank caught sight of them, he said wryly: "Here you have the story of my life for five years. You are in the fortunate position of knowing everything about me in writing and printing."

Clearly, further prevarication would have its limits. In a desperate attempt to save himself, Frank, in addition to intensifying his previous attacks on Himmler, turned on Hitler and complained: "Things would have been different if Hitler had stuck to his word. But he never did." Passionately, Frank proclaimed: "I swear to God the mighty one, and I want to point out that I am a believing Christian, that I neither took part directly nor indirectly in the planning nor in the preparation nor in the buildup [of Hitler's extermination of the Jews]."

Frank, however, had a problem with swearing to God, since he had long ago rejected the Catholicism of his parents. To buttress his credibility in his calls upon the Almighty, he responded to the urging of the American Roman Catholic chaplain, Father Sixtus O'Connor, and on October 25 submitted to baptism.

A glove covering his left hand, partially paralyzed from his suicide attempt in May, he exulted in his new role of repentant sinner and turned the pages of the Bible with the little finger of his injured hand. "Many things have become clear to me in the loneliness of this cell," he told Gustav Gilbert. "Hitler represented the spirit of evil on earth and recognized no power greater than his own. God watched this band of heathens puffed up with their puny power and then simply brushed them aside in scorn and amusement. I tell you, the scornful laughter of God is more terrible than any vengeful lust of man! . . . Here are the would-be rulers of Germany—each in a cell like this, with four walls and a toilet, awaiting trial as ordinary criminals. Is that not proof of God's amusement with men's sacrilegious quest for power?"

When the judges reconvened in Nuremberg on October 29, the obtaining of counsel for the accused continued to be the most pressing matter. A week earlier, Biddle had recorded, "Time is running with no lawyers appointed yet. We are in a real jam." But, with the start of the trial barely three weeks off, twelve of the defendants still had been unable to retain counsel. No fewer than nine of the defendants asked for the same prominent Munich attorney, von Scanzoni, who had emigrated to Switzerland; but Scanzoni turned them all down.

Goering compiled a list of eight possible lawyers; some of them flatly refused to serve, and others could not be located. Goering then asked the British prosecutor, Maxwell Fyfe, to help him draw up a list of witnesses and prepare his case—a somewhat startling suggestion to anyone versed in Anglo-Saxon law, but less unusual in continental jurisprudence, where prosecution and defense are supposed to work hand in hand to uncover the truth. Fyfe suggested a Kiel lawyer of good reputation, Otto Stahmer, who had, however, little or no criminal experience.

Ernst Kaltenbrunner requested a lawyer from Vienna, but the man suffered a heart attack on the journey to Nuremberg and had to withdraw. Franz von Papen wanted his son, an army captain who was a prisoner of war, to represent him, and the judges agreed that he could be brought to Nuremberg. Hess refused to concern himself with such a mundane matter, told Neave he did not care who defended him or whether he was defended at all, and left it up to the tribunal to appoint his counsel.

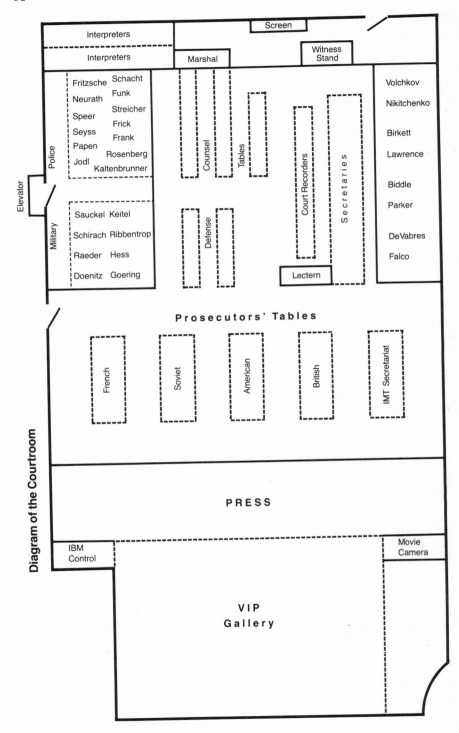

Diagram of the Courtroom

Admiral Karl Doenitz wanted a naval judge, Otto Kranzbühler, but continued: "If he cannot be reached I have requested that a British or American submarine admiral come here to defend me. You see, he can understand me. He did the same job."

The question of whether members of the Nazi Party were acceptable as defense counsel was discussed by the judges over the course of several sessions. Why not, Biddle asked? He thought it would be a grand idea to have Nazis defend the Nazi regime.

"It is a very difficult situation," Jackson remarked. "Frank, one of the defendants, was the head of the Nazi legal organization. Kaltenbrunner was a member of the bar. The only real assassins I have met were lawyers who were friends of Hitler."

Eighteen of the forty-eight German lawyers who eventually participated in the trial had Nazi backgrounds, but the membership of many had been perfunctory. Colonel Gill, the executive in charge of administration at the Palace of Justice, promised that the German attorneys would have complete freedom of movement. The army, in addition to feeding and finding lodging for them, would provide transportation. A Defendants' Information Center, in which the Americans would place copies of the documents they held, would be set up in the Palace of Justice for use by the attorneys.

While the clangor of hammers and saws still echoed through the building, the judges, sitting at a table covered with an army blanket in a chamber adjacent to the courtroom, thrashed out one issue after another. Schacht's attorney, Rudolf Dix, appeared in Nuremberg but returned temporarily to Berlin when the retainer of ten thousand marks he requested was not forthcoming. Biddle remarked: "It may be very difficult to find lawyers who will be willing to defend these men unless the tribunal pays."

A successful German lawyer earned between 30,000 and 40,000 marks ($7,500 to $10,000) a year. On October 30 the judges agreed to provide the lawyers with an advance of 4,000 marks, and pay them 2,500 marks a month —a decision that was almost academic, since the only viable currency in the Reich was now American cigarettes. Parker, nevertheless, thought the payments princely, and observed: "I am afraid we are going to be flooded with counsel."

The following morning the judges ruled that the defendants could not have conversations with each other prior to the start of the trial. That afternoon, however, they received a request from Rosenberg, who wanted Frank for his lawyer.

"If we admit that Frank can be Rosenberg's lawyer," de Vabres said, "the result is that he can have conversations with him."

"And we should also have to pay him four thousand marks," Birkett deadpanned, providing one of the lighter moments of the deliberations.

Some German lawyers refused to involve themselves in the trial because of their repugnance for the defendants. Others declined because of their antipathy toward the conquerors, their belief that the trial would simply be a political showpiece, or their fears that, in a future resurgent Germany, participation might be held against them. A greater number were reluctant to place themselves in the spotlight and subject themselves to investigation because of their past Nazi activities.

On the other side of the coin, a few attorneys sought positions as defense counsel in the hopes of making reputations, obtaining an income in a devastated land, or even garnering revenge. Robert Kempner, who had been legal adviser to the Prussian Ministry of the Interior until purged by Goering, and who was more familiar than any other member of the Allied staff with the German legal profession, assisted Neave in finding attorneys. One day he was visited by Dr. Josef Müller, chairman of the Bavarian Christian Socialist Union, who requested that he be assigned to defend one of the accused. No better man than he could be found, Müller averred. He would keep in touch with the prosecution throughout the trial and make certain that his client was convicted.

Kempner threw him out of the office and threatened him with arrest if he ever came back. Müller was astonished by Kempner's reaction—such deals had become routine under the Nazis.

While the judges were deliberating, the IBM multilanguage system was being tested daily in the courtroom. Though simultaneous translation was to become routine at the United Nations, Nuremberg was an experiment. Five channels were employed: channel one contained the verbatim transmission of the speaker; two, English; three, Russian; four, French; and five, German. Every participant in the trial had a headphone and could dial to whichever channel he wished. There were six microphones in the courtroom: one for each judge, one in the witness box, and one at the speaker's podium.

A monitor operating a control switch in the interpreting section could flash a yellow light by each microphone warning the speaker that he was going too fast, or a red light indicating that he was to stop and repeat what he had said. The trial would not be able to proceed at more than dictation speed—sixty words per minute—but, even so, that would be four times as fast as consecutive translation.

On November 13 and 14 the judges gathered in the courtroom for the first time to conduct a dress rehearsal. Biddle arranged for the seating of the judges. He placed Lawrence, as president, just to the right of center, with

Birkett to his right, followed by Nikitchenko and Volchkov. To the left of center came Biddle, then Parker, followed by de Vabres and the French alternate, Falco. Two interpreters sat to the rear, between the Russian-British and the American-French delegations. Everyone accepted this scheme as logical, since it placed the four English-speaking judges together. In the process, however, the wily Biddle managed to give himself equal prominence in the center with Lawrence; and since he was fluent in French, he made himself the fulcrum of the western delegations.

It was the American army with its sense of propriety and protocol that precipitated a near judicial crisis. For the judges in chief, Colonel Gill provided high-backed, thronelike seats, but the alternates received only modest armchairs. Parker's suspicions that he had been inveigled to come along simply for the ride flared up anew. Since arriving in Nuremberg, he had complained: "I am right homesick and blue. I wish the President had never asked me to undertake the job. It is unpleasant and I hate being away from home in this conquered country." The weather had turned dreary, there was "right much fog," and Jim Rowe, who had a bad cold, had used up all of his nose drops. Though he was an inveterate sightseer and enjoyed jaunting about, he had known so little about Germany that it was as if he had been dropped onto another planet, and he did not think that he would ever be able to acclimate himself. He felt, on his sightseeing trips, as if he were "driving through the Middle Ages."

As the tribunal broke for the noon recess on November 14, Parker was seething and unburdened himself to Biddle. He considered the two sets of chairs a deliberate slight, belittling the alternates. But the matter went beyond this. What were the alternates here for? What rights did they have? Waving a solemn forefinger, Parker declaimed: "The people of England will blame Sir Norman Birkett just as much as if he were an actual member." The alternates, Parker argued, should have the same rights as the principal judges to express opinions, ask questions from the bench, and even disagree with their countrymen.

The upshot was that the modest chairs were hastily removed, and all the judges henceforth received royal seats. The judges agreed among themselves that they were all to be equal, rewriting, in effect, if not in legal terms, the charter of the tribunal. Though officially only four votes were recorded on any issue, in practice eight voices were counted. So far as the Russians were concerned, it made no difference, since their position essentially was dictated from Moscow. But the judges from the western powers all influenced each other, and if Parker and Biddle, for example, disagreed, they resolved their disagreement before a vote was cast. With regard to the British, Birkett was by far the more influential member, and the chief judge in everything but name.

Biddle, in any case, sometimes assumed the initiative and acted as if he were the president of the court. On November 13 he informed his fellow judges that, because he had heard that the defense attorneys were complaining, he had scheduled an open meeting of the tribunal with the lawyers on the fifteenth. Birkett, who did not quite understand what Biddle was up to, thought it "a little unusual for the court to discuss with defending counsel how they should handle their case. A public sitting where the tribunal confers with the defending counsel might be very bad."

"I don't feel that at all," Biddle argued. "The great criticism of this trial is going to be that the defendants had very little time to prepare, were not properly represented, that their lawyers labored under impossible difficulties, that they were confused when they went on. This is an excellent opportunity not only to ask them if they have any questions, but to suggest some common method of procedure. I think the fact that this is unusual does not make it inappropriate. They may ask embarrassing questions, but they might ask those embarrassing questions any time during the trial."

It was, in truth, of great importance to give the attorneys the opportunity to familiarize themselves with the setting and the system with which they were to be confronted. Most of them were floundering about, unprepared to cope with the strange Anglo-Saxon legal system that was to be the basis for the procedure but had been amended to admit hearsay and other unsubstantiated evidence.

Schacht's counsel, Dix, was selected by the attorneys to be their spokesman. Sixty-one years old, he had been an administrator in the German colonies, served as chairman of the Association of German Lawyers prior to the Nazi takeover, and been the defense attorney in numerous political cases before People's Courts between 1933 and 1945.

Only eight of the defendants' chief attorneys had had substantial experience in criminal cases. The array of criminal lawyers one might have expected was missing partly because there was not as sharp a division between various fields in German as in Anglo-Saxon law, and partly because of the pressure to obtain lawyers of reputation whatever their background; but, primarily, because the defendants did not view themselves as criminals, but as men being subjected to an international political trial.*

Lawrence warned the lawyers that the judges would not involve

---

*Five of the attorneys, led by Dix's co-counsel, Herbert Kraus, were experts in international law. Kraus, initially asked to defend Kaltenbrunner or Streicher, had refused because he considered their cases to be "particularly repulsive." He had, after obtaining his law degree in Germany, studied at Columbia and Harvard, and at the Sorbonne. Later he had taught at the University of Chicago and at Princeton, and held the professorship of public and international law at Göttingen, from which he was ousted by the Nazis in 1937. His books included volumes on the Monroe Doctrine and the Treaty of Versailles.

themselves directly in the proceedings as in continental law: "When witnesses for the prosecution are called, it must be understood that it is a function of counsel for the defense to cross-examine the witnesses, and that it is not the intention of the tribunal to cross-examine the witnesses themselves." The general secretary would obtain for them whatever witnesses and documents they requested and the judges deemed relevant. Working space, complete with typewriters and other office materials, was to be made available to them in the Palace of Justice.

A graphic example of the adjustment that would have to take place was provided in an exchange between Lawrence and Alfred Thoma, the attorney for Rosenberg. Thoma, aware of the intensive interrogation that the defendants and potential witnesses had undergone, presumed that the questioning had been undertaken on behalf of an officially impartial prosecutor, and would be introduced in court.

"I should like to ask," he addressed Lawrence, "whether the defense will immediately get copies of the interrogation of witnesses?"

"Copies of the indictment?" Lawrence, who was slightly hard of hearing, responded rhetorically. "Those have been served upon each defendant."

"May I put my question more precisely?" Thoma repeated, and rephrased it.

Lawrence still did not understand: "If you mean a transcript of the evidence which was given before the tribunal, that will be taken down, and if it is given in any language other than German it will be translated into German and copies furnished to defendants' counsel. If it is in German, it will be furnished to them in German."

"Will we get copies of the interrogation of all witnesses?" Thoma tried again.

"Yes." Lawrence nodded. "That is what I meant by transcripts of evidence given before the tribunal."

"Thank you." Thoma retreated, without either man having comprehended the other.

13 Discord on the Prosecution

The spirit of the German attorneys would have been lifted had they known the prosecution's state of disarray. To a considerable extent, the hoard of documents that had been captured was not culled in time for the trial—repeatedly important documents turned up too late to be introduced by the prosecution. It was said that one hundred thousand documents had been screened, and of these ten thousand had been selected as having evidentiary value; but when Jackson ordered the search for further documentary evidence halted on November 3, the number was more in the neighborhood of five thousand, and of these only half had been translated. Jackson considered no more than five hundred of sufficient importance to be indexed for the Defendants' Information Center.

Jackson was under so much pressure to prepare the case, so frustrated by such difficulties as the Krupp imbroglio, and so disenchanted with the French and, especially, the Russians, over their lack of preparation and progress, that on October 26 he gave vent to his irritation, haranguing Fyfe about the fact that the French and Russians had still not come up with any translators and that the documents they proposed to introduce had not yet been rendered into German.* Dubost, the assistant French prosecutor, reacted by attempting to match the documents he had in French with the German originals in the Document Room. Storey, however, objected to Dubost's trespassing and ferreting about in his preserve. Major General Alexandrov, Dubost's Soviet counterpart, was similarly fascinated by the Document Room. On October 27, Jackson, taking the position that the French and Russians had no business snooping about the Anglo-Saxon documents, ordered Storey to ban all but American and British personnel from the room. In a message to the War Department, he complained: "My impression is the Russian delegation is devoting considerable effort to examining our materials for general intelligence purposes rather than for the case." He furthermore prepared a cable to the State Department, requesting notes be sent to Paris and Moscow protesting the Allies' failure to furnish translators.

When Dubost was turned aside from the Document Room, he sought out Fyfe and, in a towering rage sparked by four years of daredevil service in the Resistance, unburdened himself of what he thought of Jackson's action—Jackson was turning what was supposed to be an international trial into a purely American affair. Fyfe calmed Dubost down, promised him he would provide German originals for all but five of the French documents, and convinced the Russians to employ documents to be furnished by the British and Americans for the presentation of their case. He then persuaded Jackson that the employment of diplomacy in Nuremberg would serve better to solve the translator crisis than the stirring up of an international tempest.

*A few weeks later, when Jackson hosted a party for Colonel Gill upon his promotion to general, Gill gave Jackson a watch and quipped: "It is the best wristwatch we could buy back from the Russians." Jackson responded: "If it tells time accurately, it's the only information I ever got from the Russians."

"Usually, the unadvertising bloody British get no thanks," Fyfe recounted, "but both Rudenko and Dubost were almost tearfully grateful."

Jackson was more than ever convinced that the Americans, with some British help, were going to have to be the mainstay of the prosecution. Storey and his assistant, Lieutenant Colonel Wheeler, proposed breaking down responsibility for the American case into six sections, roughly following the lines of the indictment: (1) the conspiracy up to 1933; (2) economic planning for aggressive war; (3) utilization by the Nazis of control of the government for aggression; (4) war crimes, crimes against humanity, and crimes against the civilian population in Germany; (5) responsibility of the individual defendants; and (6) criminality of the groups and organizations. A seventh section, subsequently added to anticipate the defenses of the accused and prepare the cross-examinations, was placed under the direction of Kempner. Section chiefs were given full charge of preparing their particular portions of the case. Over them, a board of review was to act as a planning and coordinating agency. Storey, as author of the plan, was named both chief of the board of review and executive trial counsel —an overload of responsibility that was eventually to prove his undoing.

On November 5, Jackson, delighted to have the organizational task taken off his hands, selected some two dozen lawyers to introduce various aspects of the prosecution's case. At this juncture Jackson was of a mind to prosecute the entire case through so-called talking briefs, which were to contain all the documents plus, perhaps, a few sworn excerpts carefully culled from the interrogations of witnesses and defendants. Although he had told Nikitchenko in London that the calling of witnesses was necessary to satisfy American public opinion, he had shifted more and more to the view that the prosecution should rely principally on documents. Much of what potential witnesses had told interrogators was equivocal or contradictory, and frequently in the nature of self-exculpation. Jackson had little confidence in what Germans might say on the stand, and he foresaw an endless trial if some two dozen defense attorneys were given opportunity to cross-examine witnesses. His private, overriding concern was still to get the trial over with as speedily as possible so that he could return to the Supreme Court.

Jackson's decision generated virtual rebellion within the organization. Storey's Document Division and Amen's Interrogation Division were like two rival political parties. Each lawyer in the Documentation Division responsible for a particular portion of the case had his counterpart in the Interrogation Division. The interrogators had assumed that while the Documentation Division would prepare the indictment and organize the evidence, it was they who would prosecute the case—some had prepared lists containing as many as twenty witnesses they wished to place on the stand. Jackson's intent to reduce witnesses to a minimum or even scrap them entirely was a devastating blow to the morale of the staff. While half had little to do, the other half was working seventy to eighty hours a week attempting to meet a seemingly impossible deadline.

There were too many chiefs; consequently, disagreements flourished at the top. The head of the economics section left and was replaced. Francis Shea, who had played a key role in London, arrived in Nuremberg to discover his position usurped, and departed for the United States.

Colonel Brundage complained to Father Edmund Walsh,* the founder and regent of the School of Foreign Service at Georgetown University, that he had yet to find a Nazi leader willing to assume responsibility: "See, they all picture themselves as dutiful little boys who only did what they were told by someone else." Brundage was more than ever in disagreement with Jackson on the concept and latitude of the conspiracy charge. He feared that a massive trial would give the Nazis the opportunity to manipulate technicalities and loopholes. The defense counsel would employ delaying tactics, and the trial would turn into a mockery. He agreed with the German attorneys that a new theory of international justice was being introduced retroactively. Precedent was being established that would enable a victor in any future war to try a defeated government. Some day that precedent might backfire. It would have been far better to try the individuals by court martial and dispose of them summarily.

Brundage requested relief from his assignment and returned home at the end of October; but Walsh was able to persuade a number of other members of the staff, sympathetic to Brundage, from going with him. The Nazis, Walsh contended, have "violated the fundamental laws of society. It cannot be argued that now they can invoke the conventional canons of normal legal systems. There was a diabolical evil loosed in the world. Great power can be used without destroying justice. The challenge is to the purity of our conscience, and not to be dodged by the bare facts of being a victor possessed of might. The justice of God cannot be frustrated by lack of precedent."

The mild fall degenerated toward the end of October into a dark, dank prelude to winter. Storey, who was being overworked to the point of

---

*Father Walsh, who held a doctorate in law, had come to Nuremberg to prepare the case on geopolitics and assist in investigating the Nazi persecution of the churches. Having gone to Russia in 1922 to conduct famine relief and subsequently served as the Vatican's representative to the Soviet government, he had acquired a deep distaste for the Kremlin.

exhaustion, complained that there was never any heat in the frigid, depressing Palace of Justice on Sundays. Document books—consisting of manila folders in which all the materials pertaining to a single issue or defendant were collected—had to be compiled by the dozen. The mere task of typing, reproducing, collating, stapling, etc. required a gargantuan effort. The young SS men, wrapped in their greatcoats to ward off the cold, were guarded only perfunctorily as they performed clerical functions. Storey worried that discipline and security had become lax. Staff members talked freely in the cafeteria. Documents were left lying on desks and office doors sat open while German personnel roamed up and down the corridors.

Social life centered on the Grand Hotel. Its principal room was converted into an American-style nightclub and christened the Diamond Horseshoe. There, German jugglers, magicians, mimes, and dancers performed nightly for the entertainment of the packed GI audiences who overflowed into the VIP boxes.

At the Nuremberg Opera House, which remained unheated during the entire winter, German musicians provided excellent concerts and operas for audiences huddled in coats and blankets. Throughout Germany Eisenhower's antifraternization order had broken down so quickly and completely that it had become punningly known as "the antifertilization order"; and Biddle's driver told the judge that every GI had a German girl in his sleeping bag. Nothing would have capped Hitler's disillusionment with the German people more completely than the manner in which the German girls took to the American soldiers.

Nuremberg, however, had a special flavor since, thanks to Jackson's operation, it was the only German town with a sizable contingent of Allied women, many of them highly attractive. A Cotillion Club was formed to organize dances; and, with liquor plentiful and cheap, parties proliferated and romances flourished. Lieutenant Daniel Margolies and another staff member, Harriet Zetterberg, shared the only double bed in the Grand Hotel. This was officially permissible, since they were assumed to be single. Had the fact that they had been married in London become known, a crisis would have been engendered, since Jackson adamantly opposed any member of his organization enjoying the company of his wife.* (When General William Donovan showed up, he demanded a double bed, and it was whisked out from under the Margolieses.)

---

*Because of the lack of housing and food, Eisenhower had instituted the stricture against wives—he did not want high-ranking officers enjoying privileges unavailable to the lower ranks.

Parker's aide, Major Robert Stewart, fell in love with a stunning Russian interpreter named Tania, who was married to a Soviet brigadier but spoke slangy English, read *Life* and *Newsweek,* adored American movies, and dressed to perfection; when it appeared she might carry her predilection for American ways to the point of being lured to the United States, she was suddenly hustled back to Moscow.

The staff parties were punctuated by elaborate official celebrations staged whenever one of the numerous VIPs who visited Nuremberg appeared. On November 7, Andrei Y. Vyshinsky, who had been the prosecutor during the Russian purge trials and was the first Soviet ambassador to the United Nations, threw a party on the anniversary of the Russian Revolution—a fact that bewildered Storey, who could not understand why it was called the *October* Revolution when it was celebrated in November!* Jackson failed to attend, even though Major General Alexandrov went to fetch him personally. So that his absence would not be interpreted as a deliberate snub, Jackson felt called upon to host a party for Vyshinsky a few days later. After numerous toasts, when most of the celebrants were no longer seeing or hearing too clearly, Vyshinsky raised his glass and jovially exclaimed: "To the speedy conviction and execution of all the defendants!"

"Hear! Hear!" echoed about the room as glasses were drained. It was only afterward that Parker realized what he and the other judges had done —they had drunk to the execution of the defendants before the start of the trial! Later that night, Parker, visiting Biddle in his room, was as conscience-stricken as if he had hanged a man in error. Biddle tried to console him by assuring him that no one had noticed, and that, in any case, such a bibulous faux pas was nothing to worry about. But Parker kept shaking his head. "Supposing Drew Pearson gets hold of it? Can't you see the headline: 'American Judges Drink to the Death Sentences of the Men Whom They Are Trying!'"

14   *The Eve of Trial*

The United States expected that, when the trial began, diehard Nazis would launch demonstrations and make attempts to disrupt the proceedings. These efforts, a political intelligence officer prophesied, would coalesce about the families of the defendants. The United States Army, there-

---

*The apparent discrepancy was caused by the fact that Russia did not switch from the outdated Julian to the modern Gregorian calendar until 1918.

fore, planned to intern the immediate family members, and for this purpose commandeered twin villas on a bucolic dead-end street in the suburb of Erlenstegen.

As housekeeper of what was called the Detention House, the army installed Ingeborg Kalnoky, a stunning Hungarian countess of German birth.* Before any of the accuseds' dependents were brought to Erlenstegen, however, the military government changed its mind about rounding up the families en masse.† The Detention House was employed, instead, as a place of light arrest for men who had been associated with the regime but now worked for the prosecution or were considered potentially friendly witnesses. Soon, even opponents and victims of the Nazis were lodged there, and the name was changed to the Guest House.

The initial "guest" had been Professor Karl Haushofer, when he was brought to Nuremberg early in October. The second, who became a permanent resident, was Heinrich Hoffmann. Hoffmann, whose daughter Henriette was married to the youngest of the defendants, Baldur von Schirach, had joined the Nazi Party at the same time as Hitler. The proprietor of a small, struggling photography shop, Hoffmann had been Hitler's personal photographer and had gleaned a fortune through this privileged position. Adept at storytelling, card tricks, and impersonations, he had also served as Hitler's court jester and frequent chauffeur. When Hitler, who during his forties had a penchant for teenaged girls, had manifested an interest in Henriette, Hoffmann had gently steered him to another seventeen-year-old, Eva Braun, who was employed in his shop.

The Americans, after arresting Hoffmann and confiscating his collection of a half million negatives for use in the trial, decided that they needed Hoffmann to identify and catalog the pictures. Hoffmann, consequently, was installed as curator. Dressed in a Bavarian jacket and formal striped pants about four sizes too big, he was, after a few days, given the run of the Palace of Justice and of Nuremberg.

Skilled at sketching humorous drawings, he swapped them to GIs and members of the prosecution staff for cigarettes, whiskey, and chocolate, which soon overflowed his trunk. He dyed his white hair with laundry bluing so as to make a younger impression on the girl he was pursuing at the neighborhood tavern. The soldiers called him "Uncle Heini." He had no qualms about working for the prosecution against his son-in-law—it

---

*Countess Kalnoky, several months pregnant, had fled with her three children from Budapest upon the advance of the Russians. The United States Army, coming across her in Czechoslovakia, had informally adopted her. A Chinese-American doctor had brought her to Nuremberg and arranged for her hospitalization when she gave birth.

†Himmler's wife, Margo, and sixteen-year-old daughter Gudrun were, nevertheless, imprisoned for a time in the witness wing at the Palace of Justice; and Goering's and Schirach's wives and children were also held for several months.

was, after all, an apolitical job, proving his contention that he had never bothered his head about such matters. When word of his presence spread among the defendants, Goering groused: "The swine made a million marks on my pictures, and now he's sorting photographs to hang me!"

Relatives of two other defendants were also permitted to work in the Palace of Justice. Papen's son, Franz, Jr., was retained as his assistant defense attorney; and Luise Jodl, the wife of General Alfred Jodl, became the secretary to Jodl's lawyer, Franz Exner.* Like the attorneys, she received a yellow pass for the Palace of Justice, a red pass for the cafeteria, a third pass authorizing her to obtain quarters, and a fourth enabling her to buy household fuel. The Americans, in addition to paying the defense attorneys, provided them with all necessities, ranging from soap and food to typewriters and transportation.

One room in the Palace of Justice, furnished with four plain tables and a dozen chairs, was set aside for consultations between the lawyers and defendants. A partition, consisting initially of a screen and later of glass, ran down the center of the tables. Head-high boards, intersecting the partition, created fourteen cubicles. But, amid the hubbub of voices in the crowded room, it was difficult for the accused and their counsel to concentrate.

A few feet behind each prisoner stood a guard—following Ley's suicide, security had been tightened even further. Jackson had succeeded, despite the continuing reduction of American forces in Europe, in having another company of military police allocated to the Palace of Justice, and the Nazi leaders were kept under observation every minute, twenty-four hours a day. Guards, rotated every three hours, were assigned one per cell. At night the Nazi leaders were required to sleep with their hands outside their blankets, and were not permitted to turn their faces toward the wall. Whenever one rolled over in his sleep, the guard took the long pole designed for opening the high windows, pushed it through the porthole in the door, and poked and awakened the sleeper.

Shakedowns of cells were conducted frequently. Despite the fact that the defendants were searched whenever they returned to the prison, they managed to squirrel away an assortment of odds and ends. Jodl was relieved of a nail, a six-inch piece of wire, some tooth powder, and a bunch of old rags; Schacht, of three feet of cord and ten paper clips; Doenitz, of five shoelaces, part of a bobby pin, and a screw; Keitel, of a fragment of sheet metal, a tube of aspirin tablets, and two nails. Within a few months

*Luise, who was twenty years younger than her husband, had been a secretary in the High Command and had married the general, who was a widower, only a few months before the end of the war. Her maternal grandfather had been British, and she spoke fluent English.

men who had been the leaders of one of the most powerful nations in the world had been conditioned by prison life to behave like old cons.

Not only Hess and Ribbentrop, but a number of other defendants gave indication of being mentally disturbed. Many of them suffered from physical ailments resulting from licentious living, overindulgence in food and drink, and questionable medical treatment.

The prisoner evincing the greatest ravages from a combination of mental and physical afflictions was Ernst Kaltenbrunner, who in early 1943 had replaced the assassinated Heydrich as chief of the RSHA (Reich Security Office). A forty-two-year-old lawyer born in Linz, he came from a respected Austrian family—both his father and grandfather had been attorneys, and his mother had been the adopted daughter of the Belgian ambassador to Romania. Kaltenbrunner was a hulking man, nearly six and one-half feet tall, with an elongated, horselike face, one side of which had been deeply scarred in an automobile accident (Kaltenbrunner preferred to attribute the disfigurement to his membership in a dueling fraternity). A chain smoker, alcoholic, and habitué of cafes, he had been unable to go five minutes without a cigarette or an hour without a drink. (Felix Kersten, Himmler's psychologist-masseur, observed that Kaltenbrunner had to get drunk in order to be capable of reasoning.) Though devoted to his three legitimate children, he carried on a series of affairs and was continually in debt—his latest mistress, the Countess Gisela von Westaup-Wolf, had given birth to twins only a few weeks before Kaltenbrunner's arrest.

Unlike most of the other defendants, Kaltenbrunner had never been at Mondorf, but had undergone intensive grilling from May to September at an interrogation center near London. Separated from alcohol and repeatedly threatened with hanging, he had taken on a haggard, almost imbecilic appearance. His unkempt hair cascaded down in streaks, and his mouth habitually hung half open. Dressed in a lumber jacket and boots, he wandered about with his hands dug deep into the pockets of his baggy breeches. Exhibiting the emotional maturity of a child, he frequently broke out in fits of bawling.

On the morning of Saturday, November 17, three days before the scheduled start of the trial, Kaltenbrunner awakened sick to his stomach. Complaining of an excruciating headache and obviously seriously ill, he was rushed to the hospital. A tap showed blood in his spinal canal—he exhibited all the symptoms of spinal meningitis.

Momentarily, Andrus and his staff were panicked. It seemed possible that everyone in the environs of the jail and the Palace of Justice might have been exposed to the highly contagious disease, and the trial would have to be postponed indefinitely. The next day, however, it was determined that Kaltenbrunner had suffered a subarachnoid hemorrhage—the rupture of a small blood vessel in the membrane covering the brain. Though not incapacitating in the manner of a stroke, such a hemorrhage was potentially fatal; and Kaltenbrunner was to spend many weeks during the trial in a hospital bed instead of in the courtroom.

III

Prosecution

15   The Conspiracy

On Monday night, most of the prisoners, tortured by the knowledge that
if they happened to turn the wrong way they would be poked awake, slept
badly, as usual. While the prison clock metallically struck the hours, the
guards, bored and restless, shifted about, whispered among themselves,
and leaned on the porthole flaps. Occasionally these gave way, causing the
light and the guards' elbows to collapse with a clatter. Boots tramped and
chains rattled as the guards were changed.

At 6 AM, two hours before dawn, the Nazi leaders were awakened.
Crawling from beneath their half-dozen blankets, they pulled on the felt
boots that protected their feet against the icy stone floor. (Though a steam
pipe ran along the wall of the cells, the heat it radiated evanesced in the
damp cold.) At seven o'clock the defendants were served a breakfast of
oatmeal and coffee, and their chairs and spectacles were returned to them.
They were shaved by a German POW, then issued their "court" clothing
—uniforms with the insignias removed for the military men, suits and ties
for the civilians. (For those dressed nondescriptly when captured, blue
serge outfits had been tailored.) A few minutes before nine o'clock they
were lined up for Andrus's inspection. Striding up and down like the
headmaster of a reform school, Andrus flicked his swagger stick and gave
them a small lecture: He hoped that they would cooperate and engage in
no action that might disrupt the trial—if they behaved they would make
the best impression, and he would not have to take punitive measures
against them.

Then, in groups of three and four, they were marched out of the
prison and through the covered walkway that had been built early in the
fall after an SS dagger had mysteriously plummeted out of the sky and
imbedded itself near Goering's feet. Guards equipped with field telephones passed each group from one checkpoint to the next. Admitted into
the Palace of Justice, the defendants were halted before an iron door. This
opened to reveal a large elevator with a cage for the prisoners in back and
space for the guards in front.

On the second floor, the men were led from the elevator through a
door that opened directly into the prisoners' dock in the courtroom. Two
long wooden seats, resembling park benches, and divided by an aisle,
received them. In these cramped, uncomfortable accommodations the defendants were placed in the order they were listed in the indictment.
Goering, Hess, and Ribbentrop led off the front row, followed by Field

Marshal Wilhelm Keitel, Kaltenbrunner (who, of course, was absent), Alfred Rosenberg, Hans Frank, Wilhelm Frick, Julius Streicher, Walther Funk, and Hjalmar Schacht.

The tall Keitel, sixty-three years old with bristling gray hair, projected the mien and moustache of a major domo. Though his back pained him so much that he had once sat up three nights in succession, he never complained, praised the American doctors, and composed himself rigidly, seldom moving a muscle in court.

Alfred Rosenberg, fifty-two years old, was aloof and pedantic, with a face so unremarkable it would have posed a major challenge to a caricaturist. The so-called philosopher of the party and its high priest of anti-Semitism, he had been born in Estonia, and had never resided in Germany until he was twenty-five.

Next to Rosenberg was Frank. Following him came the sixty-eight-year-old Wilhelm Frick, who, with his gray crewcut and relatively youthful appearance, seemed as if he might just have retired as a GI sergeant major. A lawyer and onetime civil servant in the Bavarian police, he had been Hitler's minister of the interior.

Julius Streicher, the ninth defendant, was sixty years old, and a muscular five feet two inches tall. Bald-headed, with a fringe of white hair, he had been, as gauleiter of Nuremberg, notorious throughout the world for his scatological Jew baiting. One of a handful of men who had been on familiar *du* (thou) terms with the Führer, he had sometimes been referred to by intimates as "the other Hitler."

According to the order of the indictment, the defendant positioned next to Streicher should have been the supercilious, stiff-necked banker, Schacht. But Schacht, who had been the president of the Reichsbank and the regime's economics minister prior to the war, maneuvered to place Walther Funk between himself and the repulsive Streicher, thus simultaneously obtaining a more comfortable corner seat.

The short, rotund Funk, whose protuberance was second only to Goering's, might well have served as the model for a comic strip character. Though he had considerable intelligence and musical talent, and had followed Schacht as president of the Reichsbank and economics minister, he was bald, effeminate, and whining. Having once had gonorrhea, he suffered from a scarred urethra, chronic bladder trouble, and a hypertrophied prostate gland. He had spent two months prior to the trial in the hospital.

The second row started off with the two admirals, Karl Doenitz and Erich Raeder, followed by Baldur von Schirach, Fritz Sauckel, General Alfred Jodl, Franz von Papen, Arthur Seyss-Inquart, Albert Speer, Constantin von Neurath, and Hans Fritzsche.

The seventy-year-old Raeder, a naval officer whose code and traditions were more of the nineteenth century than of the twentieth, had little use for the younger Doenitz, who was a Nazi through and through. In January 1943, Raeder had retired and been replaced by Doenitz after a bitter quarrel with Hitler. The Soviets had arrested him in Berlin and interned him comfortably in a dacha near Moscow. Together with the other Soviet captive, Fritzsche, Raeder had not been brought to Nuremberg until October 30. Suffering from heart disease and a hernia, which he kept aggravating because he insisted on exercising like a seventeen-year-old cadet, Raeder sat trussed up stoically, maintaining his innocence and deeply humiliated by his position as a defendant.

The next two accused, Schirach and Sauckel, had both joined the Nazi Party in Weimar, but there the similarity ended. Schirach, who had come under Hitler's influence as a teenager, had been the former leader of the Hitler Youth, and was only thirty-eight. Handsome and intellectual, he was descended from an artistic, aristocratic family, and had had ambitions to be a writer. Under different circumstances, he might have become a professor of literature.

Sauckel, on the other hand, was as unattractive as Schirach was good-looking. His bald head, pasty skin and Hitler mustache reminded onlookers of the features of a pig. The least talented and most obtuse of all the accused, he had, as Plenipotentiary for the Allocation of Labor, conducted the forced labor program.

The fifty-five-year-old Jodl, chief of the Wehrmacht Operations Staff, had planned all of Hitler's major campaigns. His slanted eyes, pointed features and reddish nose gave him the appearance of a turkey. Though he had a barbed tongue, he was otherwise dour, disciplined, withdrawn, and without a trace of humor; so, naturally, the Americans nicknamed him "the Happy Hooligan."

Papen, aged sixty-five, had been the last chancellor of the Weimar Republic, and had subsequently served for a year and a half as vice-chancellor under Hitler. A member of a wealthy, landed family, he was distinguished by his grizzled hair, bushy eyebrows, and sartorial pretensions: a white handkerchief not only adorned the breast pocket of his coat in court, but was transferred by him to his fatigue jacket in jail.

The tall, introverted Seyss-Inquart, who had led Austria into the Anschluss with Germany, limped badly as the result of a World War I wound that had left one leg shorter than the other. A highly intelligent sophist and opportunist, his studious, slightly fish-eyed appearance was accentuated by his thick-lensed glasses.

Speer, next to him, had the quiet good looks that made women's hearts in the courtroom go out to him; before he had attained prominence, Leni Riefenstahl, the leading film producer of the Reich, had clipped his picture out of a newspaper with the idea of using him in one of her movies.

The baronial Neurath, at seventy-two the oldest prisoner in the dock, had served for five years as Hitler's foreign minister. He considered himself the victim of a hysteria similar to that which had led to the trial of aristocrats during the French Revolutionary terror. Suffering from heart disease and cerebral arteriosclerosis, he periodically nodded off with his head on Fritzsche's shoulder.

Fritzsche, who was in the dock only because he had called himself to the Russians' attention by offering, after the suicide of Hitler, to go on the air as Germany's leading radio commentator and announce the surrender of Berlin, resembled Seyss-Inquart in his intellectualism and cynical opportunism. It mattered not to him whom he served so long as he held a position of prominence—he was quite prepared to adapt his politics and his morality to facilitate his advancement. Since it was unlikely that he would receive a severe sentence, he retained a certain detachment and viewed the proceedings almost from the perspective of a journalist.

As a group, the defendants were sophisticated, well-educated, and intelligent—during the week preceding the start of the trial Gustav Gilbert had administered IQ tests to all of them; and Schacht, Seyss-Inquart, Goering, Doenitz, Papen, and Raeder had scored in the near-genius range.* Most had traveled abroad and several were multilingual (Schacht, Schirach, Papen, Neurath, and Ribbentrop were fluent in English, and a number of others, including Goering and Hess, could read and understand the language). Frank, Kaltenbrunner, Seyss-Inquart, and Frick were lawyers, Schacht and Funk financiers. (Additionally, Rosenberg, Speer, Schirach, Fritzsche, and Neurath possessed university degrees.) Papen, Schirach, and Neurath were members of titled families. Neurath's lineage was among the most distinguished in Germany: one of his childhood companions had been Mary of Teck, who had married King George V of England.

Only Sauckel was of blue-collar origin. Even Streicher, whose father had been a teacher, came from a middle-class, albeit poor, family. The backgrounds of the others ranged from middle and upper-middle class to patrician. They were the antithesis of a rabble. Nor, with a few exceptions, were they wild-eyed agitators and flaming anti-Semites—a fact that they cited repeatedly in attempted self-justification. They were, in truth, representative of the type of men that might be found in any government; and for that reason an explanation of the manner in which they had led Germany to perdition was as important for the purpose of preventing a re-

*The defendants tested out as follows: Schacht 143; Seyss-Inquart 141; Goering 138; Doenitz 138; Papen 134; Raeder 134; Frank 130; Fritzsche 130; Schirach 130; Ribbentrop 129; Keitel 129; Speer 128; Jodl 127; Rosenberg 127; Neurath 125; Funk 124; Hess (estimated) 120; Sauckel 118; Kaltenbrunner 113; Streicher 106.

petition as for the clarification of history and the execution of justice.

Ten guards, outfitted in white helmets, white belts, and white billy clubs made out of mop handles, were positioned behind and to the side of the dock. Only Colonel Andrus, who wore a shoulder holster secreted beneath his uniform, and the officer in charge of the detail were permitted to have firearms in the court.

Scores of heavily armed military police were, however, stationed outside the Palace of Justice, and others patrolled the corridors. Admittance to the court was restricted to defense attorneys, members of the staff, the press, and eighty VIPs with passes to the gallery.

At nine thirty, the doors to the court were opened. Constructed like an amphitheater, the room was slightly raised on all four sides, with steps leading down to a depression in the center. The walls were paneled in dark wood, the doors outlined by magnificent, ornate carvings topped with figurines. (Above the paneling, however, in what had once been, before the removal of the ceiling, the next story, the walls were a prosaic off-white.) The IBM system's spaghettilike tangle of cables snaked over the silver-gray carpet. Two dozen defense attorneys garbed in robes of black, purple, and red, according to the schools from which they had graduated, took their seats at desks in front of the dock. To the side of the dock, semi-enclosed in glass booths, sat the interpreters. The witness box stood next to the interpreting section. In the wall directly behind was a disappearing motion picture screen. Halfway across the room, directly opposite the witness box, was the speaker's lectern, from which the prosecutors and defense attorneys conducted examinations and addressed the court. A score of court reporters and stenographers sat facing the attorneys' desks. Behind them rose the judges' bench, punctuated by the flags of the four trial nations. Light green velour curtains were draped from ceiling to floor to cover the windows. Five counsel tables, one for each of the participating nations and a fifth for the tribunal's secretary, occupied the west side of the room in front of the press section.

Two hundred and fifty journalists and newspapermen, jostling in, stared at the defendants, compared notes, and, speaking in a multitude of languages, created an electric hubbub. Eighty-five were from the United States, fifty from Britain, forty from France, five from the Soviet Union, ten from Scandinavia, ten from South and Central America, five from Belgium, three from Switzerland, and the remainder from Germany.*

---

*Adjacent to the court, an elaborate, presidential-nominating-convention-style press room, novel to the Europeans, had been established for the reporters. The rattle of typewriters, the ringing of telephones, and announcements from loudspeakers orchestrated a continuous cacophony; from behind a barrier, a secretary kept piling up copies of documents at such a rate they were impossible to digest.

Although there was no official regulation prohibiting the mingling of the German with the non-German reporters, there was, in practice, segregation. A large separate workroom was furnished the German press, who were provided (because of the difficulty of obtaining anything in the ravaged land) with typewriters and other materials. Barred from the cafeteria, they ate instead at a nearby cafe, whose food supply was supplemented by American rations.

At ten o'clock the judges filed into the room. The marshal called the court to order. The hush of a cathedral descended over the five hundred occupants. But the trial could scarcely have gotten off to a less auspicious start.* The whole of the initial day was taken up by the reading of the indictment and its three appendices. The high-powered lights installed for the benefit of the motion picture cameras, which filmed every minute of the proceedings, produced incubatorlike conditions that caused Lawrence and Parker to mop their brows and the defendants to fall into a state of somnolence. The accused found the courtroom more conducive to sleeping than their cells, and several of them had to be prodded awake by the guards. A large number of the newsmen grew restive. Although court regulations forbade anyone to leave his seat during the proceedings, droves of newsmen, pleading "castle disease," disappeared. At the end of the first day the regulation was revised, and reporters, visitors, and members of the prosecution staff came and went as they pleased.

In the dock, Funk fidgeted like a little boy seemingly on the verge of wetting his pants. Hess, wracked by intestinal cramps, grimaced, contorted, and groaned loudly until a doctor gave him a shot to relax him and quiet him down. Ribbentrop kept blinking back tears, and finally was taken out into the corridor to give vent to his sobs. On the bench, Biddle amused himself by twirling the dials and listening periodically in French and German instead of English. He tried to familiarize himself with the defendants—few of whom, except Goering, Hess, and Ribbentrop, he could identify—and wondered why Kaltenbrunner was missing.

At noon the regimentation that had enchained the defendants for four months finally broke down. No one had considered the manner in which they were to be fed; so the GI trays were brought into the courtroom, and the defendants were permitted to sit and eat at the desks of their attorneys. (The next day and thereafter they were served in two rooms on the top floor of the building.)

Andrus did not attempt to keep them from speaking to each other, and

---

*Only the afternoon before, the Russians, who seemed unable to organize themselves, had demanded that it be postponed. Rudenko, they claimed, was ill with malaria in Berlin. When, however, the tribunal turned down their request, the Soviet prosecutor showed up quite healthy in Nuremberg the next morning.

there was an excited outpouring of conversation. Many of them had never met before. Others, like Speer and Doenitz, Keitel and Jodl, and Goering and Funk were old acquaintances. Enmities and feuds among them were legion. Everyone avoided speaking to Streicher, who hated Goering and Hess. Schacht was the archenemy of Goering, and withdrew as far as possible into his corner, as if any contact with his co-defendants might contaminate him. Ribbentrop was despised by Rosenberg, Papen, Neurath, and Goering. Speer was scarcely on speaking terms with Goering and Sauckel. Raeder considered Doenitz an upstart and Goering and Keitel military nincompoops largely to blame for the loss of the war.

Everyone protested his innocence and placed responsibility for his predicament on Himmler, Bormann, and one or two others. Ribbentrop tried to explain the reason for the trial to Hess, who stared bemusedly and gave some indication of alertness only when Ribbentrop mentioned the atomic bomb, which Hess had apparently never heard of. Schirach, in a wry mood, commented on the food to Gustav Gilbert: "I suppose we'll get steak the day you hang us!"

The following morning, after the defendants had all pleaded innocent to the charges, Jackson presented his opening statement: "The wrongs which we seek to condemn and punish have been so calculated, so malignant, and so devastating, that civilization cannot tolerate their being ignored, because it cannot survive their being repeated. That four great nations, flushed with victory and stung with injury, stay the hand of vengeance and voluntarily submit their captive enemies to the judgment of the law is one of the most significant tributes that Power has ever paid to Reason."

The quality of Jackson's Rooseveltian mellifluence was conveyed even to the men who could not comprehend the language. Dressed in a three-piece, pin-striped suit, with a watch chain gracing his vest, Jackson spoke with an air of informality not entirely appreciated by the British and European lawyers unaccustomed to seeing men throw their coats back and slip their hands in and out of their pockets.

"It is hard now to perceive in these men as captives the power by which as Nazi leaders they once dominated much of the world and terrified most of it," Jackson continued. "Merely as individuals, their fate is of little consequence to the world.

"What makes this inquest significant is that these prisoners represent sinister influences that will lurk in the world long after their bodies have returned to dust. We will show them to be living symbols of racial hatreds, of terrorism and violence, and of the arrogance and cruelty of power. . . . We will give you undeniable proofs of incredible events. The catalog of crimes will omit nothing that could be conceived by a pathological pride, cruelty, and lust for power. These men created in Germany, under the 'Führerprinzip,' a National Socialist despotism equaled only by the dynasties of the ancient East. . . . Against their opponents, including Jews, Catholics, and free labor, the Nazis directed such a campaign of arrogance, brutality, and annihilation as the world has not witnessed since the pre-Christian ages. They excited the German ambition to be a 'master race,' which of course implied serfdom for others. They led their people on a mad gamble for domination. . . .

"Never before in legal history has an effort been made to bring within the scope of a single litigation the developments of a decade, covering a whole continent, and involving a score of nations, countless individuals, and innumerable events. . . . Unfortunately, the nature of these crimes is such that both prosecution and judgment must be by victor nations over vanquished foes [but] we must never forget that the record on which we judge these defendants today is the record on which history will judge us tomorrow. To pass these defendants a poisoned chalice is to put it to our own lips as well. We must summon such detachment and intellectual integrity to our task that this trial will commend itself to posterity as fulfilling humanity's aspirations to do justice. . . .

"If these men are the first war leaders of a defeated nation to be prosecuted in the name of the law, they are also the first to be given a chance to plead for their lives in the name of the law."

The leaders of the government, Jackson contended, could not escape responsibility by arguing that they had been acting on behalf of the state. "The idea that a state, any more than a corporation, commits crimes, is a fiction. Crimes always are committed only by persons. . . . It is quite intolerable to let such a legalism become the basis of personal immunity.

"The charter recognizes that one who has committed criminal acts may not take refuge in superior orders nor in the doctrine that his crimes were acts of state. These twin principles working together have heretofore resulted in immunity for practically everyone concerned in the really great crimes against peace and mankind. Those in lower ranks were protected against liability by the orders of their superiors. The superiors were protected because their orders were called acts of state. Modern civilization puts unlimited weapons of destruction in the hands of men. It cannot tolerate so vast an area of legal irresponsibility." The German military code itself, Jackson pointed out, stated that neither a subordinate nor a commander could escape punishment if he carried out an order he knew to be illegal or criminal.

"These defendants were men of a station and rank which does not soil its own hands with blood. They were men who knew how to use lesser folk as tools. We want to reach the planners and designers, the inciters and leaders without whose evil architecture the world would not have been for so long scourged with the violence and lawlessness, and wracked with the agonies and convulsions of this terrible war."

On the afternoon of the next day Major Frank Wallis, a Detroit lawyer in civilian life, took the microphone to introduce the first part of the prosecution's case, "The Nature and Development of the Common Plan or Conspiracy." Wallis told the court that he would cover "the aims of the Nazi Party, their doctrinal techniques, their rise to power, and their consolidation of control over Germany between 1933 and 1939 in preparation for aggressive war."

Only one of the defendants, Alfred Rosenberg, had participated in the founding of the Nazi Party. The prosecution charged: "The political career of the Defendant Rosenberg embraces the entire history of National Socialism and permeates nearly every phase of the conspiracy. . . . As the apostle of neo-paganism, the exponent of the drive for *Lebensraum,* and the glorifier of the myth of Nordic superiority, and as one of the oldest and most energetic Nazi proponents of anti-Semitism . . . he provided the impetus and inspiration for the National Socialist movement. . . . Rosenberg was a member of the National Socialist movement even before Hitler himself."

Almost six feet tall, thin, tight-lipped and unemotional, Rosenberg had been born into a family of ethnic German artisans in Reval, Estonia, then part of the Russian Empire, on January 13, 1893. Studying architectural engineering in Riga and Moscow, he had prolonged his schooling until he was twenty-five, and thus escaped service in the Russian army during World War I. Bilingual in Russian and German, he had, when civil war broke out in 1917, become a man searching for an identity. Though he was anti-Communist, the White (conservative) forces suspected him because of his German, Jewish-sounding name. When, toward the end of 1918, the German troops that had occupied Latvia and Estonia began to withdraw, Rosenberg went with them. At the beginning of the new year he arrived in Bavaria.

Rosenberg brought with him a copy of *The Protocols of the Wise Men of Zion,* an anti-Jewish tract that was the most outrageous forgery in literary, religious, and political history. Throughout Europe, but especially in the semi-feudal eastern lands, the Jews had been, due to their tradition of literacy, a mainstay of the intelligensia and the middle class. Democratic politically and progressive socially, they had provided the founders and leaders of the Social Democratic Party in Germany and similar liberal parties in other nations. They were, therefore, anathema to the reactionaries, who joined with the large landholders and peasantry (both affected adversely by the Industrial Revolution) in league against the Jews.

Nowhere had the cleavage been sharper than in czarist Russia, which had absorbed the most concentrated Jewish population in the world with its annexations of the Ukraine, Lithuania, and eastern Poland in the seventeenth and eighteenth centuries. To separate the masses of urban workers from the Jewish leadership in a land devoid of democratic traditions, the Okhrana (secret police) instituted a policy of calumny and terror against the Jews. Organizing looting and rioting, the Okhrana introduced a new word, "pogrom," into western languages. Then, focusing on the 1897 founding of the Zionist movement in Basel, Switzerland, and inspired by the Dreyfus Affair,* the Okhrana concocted the *Protocols*, which purported that the Jews planned to dominate and divide the world among themselves.

For source material, the Okhrana relied on three books:

The first, *Dialogue in Hell Between Machiavelli and Montesquieu*, had been published by a Frenchman, Maurice Joly, in 1854. Joly's volume, a satire upon Emperor Napoleon III, presented a primer on the subversion of democracy, the art of demagoguery, and the employment of money and secret agents to dominate the world.

The second, *Biarritz*, was a novel authored in 1868 by a German writer, Hermann Gödsche. In this, twelve rabbis representing the tribes of Israel meet in a Prague cemetery, and there, chanting like the witches in *Macbeth*, celebrate the triumph of the Jewish bankers, who have bought control of the entire world.

The third, *The Book of the Kahal*, was the work of Jacob Brafman, a Russian Jew orphaned and subjected to a Dickensian childhood. Embittered at Jews and Judaism, he had converted to Orthodox Christianity and become a teacher in a theological seminary. His book was a fairly accurate translation of the minutes of the Minsk Kehillah, or Jewish council. Struggling to survive in a hostile land untouched by the ideas of the Enlightenment, the Jews of the Kehillah had been both clannish and bigoted. Brafman characterized the Kehillah as "a state within a state," and propagandized that the Jews were engaged in an international conspiracy.

Transforming these three works into the *Protocols*, the Okhrana alleged that the Zionists declared: "We shall everywhere arouse ferment, struggle, and enmity—we shall unleash a world war—we shall bring the people to such a pass that they will voluntarily offer us world domination."

---

*In order to protect a corrupt but aristocratic colleague who had sold secret documents to the Germans, the head of the intelligence section of the French army forged evidence against a Jewish captain, Alfred Dreyfus, who was convicted and imprisoned for several years on Devil's Island.

The Freemasons, as espousers of liberalism, antiauthoritarianism, and international fellowship, were linked by the Okhrana to the conspiracy.

The *Protocols* were so obviously fictitious that the czar himself was moved to say: "We must not fight for a pure cause with unclean weapons."

But, in the wake of the World War, followed by the Russian revolution and the upheavals in Central Europe, the *Protocols* were receiving new respect, as well as worldwide notoriety—events seemed to be catching up with the Okhrana's fiction.

Germany verged on anarchy. With the abdication of the Kaiser and the transition to parliamentary government, the liberal, Jewish-influenced Social Democrats, who were the largest single party in the fragmented Reichstag, inherited the government of a nation economically devastated by war, unable to feed its population, burdened with a huge arms debt, and on the brink of runaway inflation. The militarists and reactionaries who were responsible exploited every opportunity to divert the blame onto the Social Democrats. Civil war broke out in various places between Communists and discharged veterans recruited by right-wingers into *Freikorps* (volunteer legions). In Bavaria, a Communist republic, soon bloodily crushed by the *Freikorps*, was proclaimed the first week in April by Eugene Leviné, a St. Petersburg–born Jewish German army veteran.

Rosenberg's translation of the *Protocols* into German thus found a ready audience and became known throughout Bavaria. Dietrich Eckart, a fifty-year-old lawyer, alcoholic, and drug addict who was the editor of a small reactionary weekly, the *Münchner Beobachter,* hired him as a writer.

In January of 1919, Rosenberg joined the German Workers' Party, founded by Anton Drexler, a bespectacled toolmaker, as a counterweight to the Social Democrats and the Communists. "It was not the French who defeated us, but the Jews," Rosenberg lectured to the party members.

In September, a meeting of the German Workers' Party was visited by Adolf Hitler, an intelligence operative for the army's political division, which kept a multitude of political groups under surveillance; and soon thereafter the Austrian-born German army veteran joined the party.

So it was that Hitler—whose venom had previously been generalized and included women, Jews, moneygrubbers, fossilized civil servants, the Church, and the aristocracy—had his anger at the world given direction by the writings of Drexler, Eckart, and Rosenberg. The *Protocols* he accepted as gospel: "With positively clarifying certainty they reveal the nature and activity of the Jewish people and expose their inner contents as well as their ultimate final aims," he proclaimed. "Russia and Germany had to be overthrown in order that the ancient prophecy might be fulfilled! So the whole world was lashed into a fury! And so it was that Judah won the World War!"

To formulate the Nazi dogma, Rosenberg and Eckart amalgamated the Byzantine plottings of the *Protocols* with the German racial anti-Semitism expounded by Wilhelm Marr and Stewart Houston Chamberlain. Marr, an atheistic anarchist, had declared in 1879 that the Germans must preserve their "Aryan" purity by halting the rapid assimilation of the Semitic Jews into the population, and had thus coined the word "anti-Semitism." Twenty years later, Chamberlain, an upper-class Englishman who had settled in Bavaria and married the daughter of composer Richard Wagner, suggested that the Prussians represented the genetic acme of the Aryans, and that the task of the future was to preserve Prussian stock from adulteration and concentrate it by inbreeding. Hitler, with his extraordinary oratorical instinct and dramatic talent, translated the abstruse philosophies into the argot of the masses. Before meeting Hitler, Eckart had postulated the kind of man that was needed: "A fellow who can stand the rattle of a machine gun. The rabble has to be scared shitless. Best of all would be a worker who's got his mouth in the right place."

Until Hitler's arrival, the German Workers' Party had had no more than a handful of adherents.* But the chemistry and excitement provided by Hitler attracted an increasing number of people.

"At a meeting of the German Labor Party held on 24 February 1920," Major Wallis recounted to the court, "Hitler announced to the world the 'twenty-five theses' that subsequently became known as the 'unalterable program' of the National Socialist German Workers' Party"—a name that was adopted on March 4.

The first three of the twenty-five points demanded the unification of all Germans, the abrogation of the terms of the Versailles Peace Treaty, and *Lebensraum* commensurate with the German population. Point four declared: "Only a member of the race can be a citizen. A member of the race can only be one who is of German blood. Consequently, no Jew can be a member of the race."

What rankled the Germans most throughout the decade of the 1920s was a sense of betrayal. They believed they had been tricked into suing for an armistice based on President Wilson's Fourteen Points and Peace with Justice, but had then been coerced into signing a treaty that did violence to most of the clauses except those disadvantageous to Germany. Although President Wilson had promised self-determination on the basis of ethnic identity, the Sudetenland, with its largely German population, had been incorporated into Czechoslovakia. The almost unanimous desire of the

---

*Hitler was not the party's seventh member, as he claimed, but its fifty-fifth.

Austrians to unite with Germany was vetoed by the French. The new borders of Poland, separating East Prussia from the main body of Germany, were an invitation to eternal friction. The reparations of thirty billion dollars imposed by the French, British, and Italians hung like a Damocles sword over the economy; and though only a tiny fraction of the sum was ever paid, the psychological effect on the German people was devastating. The French exploitation of the Saar, the loss of Germany's foreign markets, and the trade barriers that were erected all wreaked havoc with the German economy, heavily dependent on foreign markets. Germany barely avoided all-out civil war during the 1923 crisis, when Hitler's putsch was but one of a number of violent actions. Six years later, when the collapse of Wall Street precipitated a universal depression, the Nazis got their second chance.

To the Nuremberg tribunal Jackson acknowledged: "The democratic elements, which were trying to govern Germany, got inadequate support from the democratic forces of the rest of the world, including my country. It is not to be denied that Germany, when worldwide depression was added to her other problems, was faced with urgent and intricate pressures which necessitated bold measures."

That bold, and even radical, measures were required had become evident to the industrialists and financiers who composed the leadership of the right-wing German Nationalist Party and were interested in exploiting the Nazis as a counterforce to the Communists. On January 1, 1931, Goering invited a representative of the Nationalists, Hjalmar Horace Greeley Schacht, to a New Year's party to meet Hitler. It was the first step in the developments that led the prosecution to charge: "At least up until the end of 1937 Schacht was the dominant figure in the rearming of Germany and in the economic planning and preparation for war."

Schacht, who derived his two middle names from the famous editor of the New York *Tribune,* had been conceived in Manhattan. His father, a newspaper editor, had emigrated to the United States, joining five brothers there, in 1870, and subsequently had become an American citizen. In 1872 he had married a German girl in the Madison Avenue Episcopal Church, and their first child had been born in America. Hjalmar had missed becoming an American only because his mother was homesick and her husband had heeded her plea to return to Germany.

After obtaining his university degree in Germany, Schacht had studied economics and commerce in France and England. His first job was with one of Germany's leading banks, the Dresdner, and by the age of forty-one he was its manager. In 1923 he was appointed head of the Reichsbank, Germany's central bank, and his contribution to bringing inflation to an end and stabilizing the currency engendered the ditty: *"Wer hat die Mark stabil gemacht, das war allein der Doktor Schacht"* ("Who stabilized the mark? Dr. Schacht all by himself").

In the spring of 1930, however, Schacht resigned his position in protest at the deflationary philosophy of the government and the restrictive trade policies of the western nations. A superegotist who destroyed opponents with biting sarcasms, Schacht had become convinced by his experiences in international negotiations that Germany could never obtain equality at the bargaining table until it rebuilt its armed forces.

Schacht thus shared Hitler's views on rearmament, on the desirability of curbing the influence of Jews and their liberal allies, and, most of all, on the need to impose a totalitarian government on the nation. Neither the Nationalists nor the National Socialists were in position to come to power independently. But each was possessed of elements vital to the other. The Nationalists had respectability, influence, and money. The Nazis had a growing popular following and a paramilitary force. Schacht believed the Nationalists could exploit Hitler as a *Hetzer*—an agitator to stir up the masses in support of the reactionaries. Hitler, conversely, viewed the Nationalists, as he did everyone else, as a stepping-stone to the achievement of personal power. So, although the rank and file of the Nazis hated the barons and industrialists scarcely less than the Jews, Hitler, starting with the New Year's day meeting, embarked on a drive to woo the right-wing establishment.

His campaign reached its climax in a two-and-a-half-hour speech before the ultraprestigious Dusseldorf Industrialists Club on January 17, 1932. Appearing in a dark pin-striped suit, Hitler asserted that he came not to overthrow the existing order, but to defend it. He represented Germany's and the western world's last stand against Asiatic Bolshevism. Denying that the National Socialist German Workers' Party was socialist or worker oriented, he declared that, far from wishing to socialize industry, he intended to convert the government to capitalistic autocracy. Democracy, he pointed out, could not be permitted to exist in the army, and was incompatible with private property; no proprietor could run his enterprise if every worker were permitted to have a say in the management. Capitalism and the army were, therefore, bound to become alienated from a democratic state. Under his leadership, however, the three would once more be brought into harmonious relationship: "If the present course continues, Germany must one day land in Bolshevik chaos, but if this development is broken, then our people must be enrolled in a school of iron discipline."

Hitler's audience was delighted. The Nationalists, however, were not alone in the belief that they could exploit Hitler. General Kurt von Schleicher, the head of the Reichswehr's political department and real power in the army, had thoughts along similar lines. Like the reactionaries and the Communists, Schleicher perceived parliamentary democracy as defunct, and had for some time been contemplating the transformation of the government into a de facto military dictatorship controlled by himself. Since the army was not strong enough to enforce totalitarian rule by itself, Schleicher intended to use his friend, Prince August Wilhelm (the Kaiser's youngest son), whom Hitler had made a general in the SA, to wean the Nazi storm troopers to the side of the army and convert them into an auxiliary.

Opening a dialogue with Hitler, Schleicher undermined the government of Chancellor Heinrich Brüning, a member of the Catholic Center Party. To President Paul von Hindenburg, Schleicher proposed the appointment of fifty-two-year-old Franz von Papen in Brüning's place.

"The key to von Papen's activities," the prosecution asserted, "is that, although perhaps not a typical Nazi, he was a political opportunist and ready to fall in with the Nazis when it suited him. . . . So variable and so seemingly contradictory were von Papen's activities and utterances regarding the Nazis that it is not possible to present the picture of Papen's part in this infamous enterprise unless one first reviews the steps by which he entered upon it."

Descended from landowning gentry, Papen had at one time been a professional army officer, and was a cousin of the famed Jewish-Gentile, German-American Warburg bankers. His wife came from a wealthy family of French-Belgian extraction, more fluent in French than German. As a youth he had attended military school and later became a page at the Imperial Court. In 1907 he had been selected for the general staff, and in 1913 appointed military attaché in Washington. (The American government demanded his recall after he was suspected of involvement in German sabotage activity in the United States during the first part of the World War.) Later he served on the staff of the German-Turkish forces in the Middle East. Like Brüning, he belonged to the Catholic Center Party, which expelled him when it became known that he was a willing tool in Schleicher's intrigues. Though scarcely anyone took him seriously, Papen could be trusted to do the army's bidding, and had the confidence of Hindenburg. When one of Schleicher's acquaintances expressed incredulity that a man of such little intelligence and perspicacity should be appointed chancellor, Schleicher smiled. "I don't need a head. I need a hat."

While the nation prepared for the next Reichstag election, scheduled for July 31, the antagonism between storm troopers and Communists erupted into new heights of violence. On July 17 seven thousand Nazis marched into the Hamburg working-class suburb of Altona, and full-scale guerrilla war broke out. The fighting left seventeen dead and scores seriously injured. Papen, prompted by Schleicher, thereupon used the Altona battle as an excuse to stage a coup d'état against the government of Prussia.

Prussia, with 38 million of Germany's 65 million population and most of its heavy industry, was the giant of the republic. It was under the leadership of Prussia and its great minister-president Otto von Bismarck that the various German states and principalities had been united in 1871. (Even more than in the United States, however, the individual states had been left sovereign in their domestic affairs). Prussia dominated Germany. Its importance was such that, prior to the overthrow of the monarchy, the prime ministry of Prussia and the chancellorship of Germany had always been lodged in the same person. Berlin was the capital of both the *Land* (state) and the nation.

The Prussian government, controlled by the Social Democrats, was the most democratic in the republic. Because of the threat of a right-wing coalition of Nationalists, Nazis, Junkers, and Reischswehr, the Prussian Social Democrats were wooing the Communists for an alliance of the center-left. Since this threatened Schleicher's plans, he directed Papen to invoke the chancellor's emergency powers under Article 48 of the constitution. Deposing the Prussian prime minister and minister of the interior, Papen substituted himself as Reich commissioner of Prussia. Schleicher sent a detachment of the Reichswehr to oust the officials and occupy the state government buildings.

The result of the July 31 election was a triumph for Hitler. The Nazis took 230 of the 608 seats in the Reichstag, a margin of nearly one hundred over the Social Democrats, the next ranking party. It was the most decisive mandate in the thirteen-year history of the republic.

Hitler was jubilant. He believed that Hindenburg must now offer him the chancellorship and the opportunity to form a government. The president, however, had no such intention. Although he had suffered a stroke and was weary and feeble, he was firmly committed to the republic, utterly mistrusted Hitler, and believed the Nazi tide was an economic phenomenon that would recede when business improved.

Papen was Hindenburg's choice to continue as chancellor. But, as soon as the Reichstag assembled, Goering—elected president as the leader of the largest single faction—maneuvered with the Communists to bring Papen down. The deputies voted 512 to 42 against him, the most humiliating defeat ever for a chancellor.

Another round of elections was set for November 5. To Hitler it seemed a do-or-die struggle, for, if he was unable to obtain a clear-cut victory this time, the door to power might be closed for good. It was taking all his efforts to keep the hungry, bloody SA men in the streets from launching an attack to overthrow the government by force, an attempt that Hitler believed would fail.

The election, in fact, demonstrated that the Nazi tide was ebbing. The party received two million fewer votes, and lost thirty-four Reichstag seats. A month later, in the Thuringian state election, the Nazis mustered only sixty percent of their previous support.

The government, however, was paralyzed. Schacht, envisioning himself as the economic savior of a resurgent Germany, continued to promote a Nationalist-Nazi alliance. On November 12 he wrote Hitler a letter that Jackson and the prosecution presented as a key exhibit of the banker's involvement:

"I am confident that the present system is doomed to disintegration. The present development of things can only lead to your becoming chancellor." With that goal in mind, Schacht collected the signatures of two score leading industrialists and financiers on a petition to Hindenburg requesting the president to suppress the Communist Party and appoint Hitler as chancellor of a coalition cabinet.

Schleicher concurrently concluded that Papen had outlived his usefulness, and that, instead of having a politician front for the army, he himself would assume the chancellorship.

Schleicher's jettisoning of Papen, however, provided a new opening for Schacht and Goering. Papen still had the backing of Hindenburg; and the landowner class to which they belonged were fearful that Schleicher might initiate land reforms and expose the scandals of the *Osthilfe*—agricultural loans that had been intended to help the peasants, but instead had been appropriated by the proprietors of large estates. On January 4, 1933, Schacht induced Baron Kurt von Schröder, the leading German banker, to invite Hitler and Papen to his Cologne mansion.

Papen proposed that he and Hitler become, in effect, co-chancellors, sharing power equally. Hitler, somewhat chastened, replied that he was willing to share power, so long as *he* was named chancellor. To Schröder, Hitler promised that he would act legally and responsibly, declaring that he intended only to remove all Jews, Social Democrats, and Communists from leading positions in public life—a proposal that the baron and his anti-Semitic, reactionary friends might have made themselves. The meeting concluded with Hitler and Papen agreeing in principle, and Schröder committing himself to pulling the party out of its financial hole.

There remained the necessity for Schacht and Schröder to convince their friend, sixty-five-year-old Alfred Hugenberg, the leader of the Nationalist Party, to join the coalition so as to provide Hitler and Papen with a parliamentary majority. The proprietor of a motion picture and publishing empire and onetime board chairman of Krupp, Hugenberg had little use for either Hitler or Papen. He demanded so many ministries for his party—including two, economics and agriculture, for himself—that Hitler flew into a rage, and it was all Goering could do to convince him not to abandon the negotiations.

On Sunday, January 29, the marathon talks between Papen and Hitler continued. During the fall President Hindenburg had refused to appoint Hitler as the chancellor of a presidential cabinet because he feared "a presidential cabinet led by you would inevitably lead to a party dictatorship."* But Germany had not had a functioning government in more than a half year; and the alternatives now seemed to be between a right-wing coalition led by Hitler and a Schleicher dictatorship with the likelihood of civil war.

The agreement finally reached seemingly made Hitler little more than a figurehead chancellor. Hindenburg, intending to control foreign policy and the armed forces himself, insisted that Neurath be retained as foreign minister, and that General Werner von Blomberg, a Prussian officer, be named war minister. Papen, as vice-chancellor, would hold the prime ministry of Prussia. Two other members of Papen's short-lived "cabinet of barons" were retained. Hugenberg obtained the Economics and Agriculture ministries for himself, and placed two of his followers in the cabinet as well.

Hitler secured only three positions for his adherents. Goering was named minister without portfolio, and Goebbels was promised a soon-to-be-established Ministry of Propaganda—two posts that inspired Papen and Hugenberg to more chuckles than apprehension. Wilhelm Frick, the senior parliamentarian in the Nazi hierarchy, was appointed minister of the interior. Since, however, in Germany, as in America, each state was responsible for its own law enforcement, the minister of the interior did not, as in most other European countries, control the police; and Frick's position, consequently, seemed reasonably innocuous.

All in all, Hugenberg and Papen were content. Hugenberg was confident that Hitler had been boxed in, and that "nothing much would be able to happen." Papen congratulated himself that, since he alone had the confidence of Hindenburg, he would wield the real power. "We've hired him for our act," he declared.

Beneath the surface, however, there were ominous undercurrents.

*A presidential cabinet was one not requiring the approval of the Reichstag.

Hitler, through the SA, had 400,000 men at his disposal. Goering, as minister without portfolio, was taking over the Prussian Ministry of the Interior, control of which had been stripped from the state by Papen the previous July. Though Goering would, theoretically, be subordinate to Vice-Chancellor and Prime Minister of Prussia Papen, the fact was that Goering, by obtaining direction of the police in the dominant German state, became one of the most powerful individuals in the nation. On the night of January 30, Hitler stood at a window of the chancellery and watched for hours as thousands of torch-bearing SA men marched by to memorialize the triumph. It was an awesome, ominous, hypnotic spectacle as the stream of fire, accompanied by rolling drums and thudding feet, flowed through the streets and was reflected from the windows on the dark winter night.

"That is the end of the prologue as it were, to the dramatic and sinister story that will be developed by the prosecution in the course of this trial," Major Wallis informed the court, before continuing with his account of the chronology of events. "On January 30, 1933, Hitler held his first cabinet meeting and we have the original minutes of that meeting which will be offered in evidence. . . . They seized control upon securing the passage of the 'Law for the Protection of the People and the State' on 24 March 1933. The steps leading to this actual seizure of power are worthy of recital."

Initially, it was not Hitler and the Nazis, but Hugenberg and the Nationalists who had taken the lead in proposing the most repressive measures. Hugenberg declared it was imperative to suppress the Communist Party. Unless that was done, it would be impossible to achieve the two-thirds Reichstag majority required for the passage of an enabling act empowering the cabinet to rule by decree. Hitler, responding skeptically, "It appears flatly impossible to suppress the six million people who stand behind the Communist Party of Germany," instead advocated once again dissolving the Reichstag and holding new elections. Over the opposition of the Nationalists—who feared that the Nazis would gain seats at the Nationalists' expense—Hitler prevailed.

With the assistance of Schacht, Hitler solicited a three-million-mark election fund from business leaders, who applauded his statement that he was determined to crush the Communists and establish an authoritarian state.

Goering, concurrently, prepared to smooth the way by terrorizing the opposition. Expanding the Prussian political police, which had heretofore been a minor department charged with keeping track of subversives, he transformed it within a few months into the *Geheime Staats Polizei* (Secret

State Police), whose postal designation, "Gestapo," was to become a synonym for terror. To confront the Communists in the streets, he deputized forty thousand storm troopers as auxiliary police.

Despite these maneuvers, it was clear to Hitler and Goering that they could never achieve their goal of unfettered power so long as Germany remained a democracy and they were the minority partners in a coalition. Some great, cataclysmic event was required to stampede the nation in the direction the Nazis wished to herd it.

"On February 27, 1933, less than a month after Hitler became chancellor, the Reichstag building was set on fire," Jackson had narrated in his opening address. "The Nazis immediately accused the Communist Party of instigating and committing the crime, and turned every effort to portray this single act of arson as the beginning of a Communist revolution. Then, taking advantage of the hysteria, the Nazis met this phantom revolution with a real one."

On February 18, Marinus van der Lubbe, a twenty-four-year-old Dutchman dressed in a soft peaked cap, worker's jacket, tattered pants several inches too short, and cracked shoes, arrived almost penniless in Berlin. His father, a drunkard, had deserted the family, and his mother had died when he was twelve. While he was in his teens working as a bricklayer, most of his sight had been destroyed when lime was splashed into his eyes. Once a member of the Young Communist League, then again an adherent of a small anarchist group, he had wandered around Europe for several years, a miserable, half-lunatic outcast angry at the world.

For nine days van der Lubbe slept in flophouses, begged food, harangued the unemployed in front of a district welfare office, shivered in the cold, and, like any other anarchist, reported his presence to the police, as was required. Since he was completely down and out, the police let him sleep in a cell. Goering's political police almost surely became aware of his presence in the city.

A few minutes after 9 PM on February 27, a pedestrian hurrying against the damp, subfreezing breeze was startled to see a figure waving a flaming brand at a second-story window of a restaurant located on the right side of the dark, locked Reichstag building. Twenty minutes later, the entire central Reichstag chamber was a mass of flames. At 9:27 PM, the fire cracked the huge glass dome two hundred feet above the chamber. At that very moment, van der Lubbe, disheveled, sweating, and bare to the waist, ran directly into the path of a police officer in a hall at the rear of the building.

Van der Lubbe was immediately hustled off to a nearby police station, where he laughed and gibbered senselessly. No papers were found upon him. A few minutes later, Goering, enveloped in a voluminous trenchcoat and accompanied by an entourage of bodyguards and aides, strode into the Reichstag. Since the basic stone structure was essentially fireproof, and the smoke and heat were being funneled upward, it was quite safe to move about. Giving directions to firemen and talking to police officers, Goering suddenly shouted to a newsman: "This is a Communist outrage! One of the Communist culprits has been arrested!"

Hitler and Goebbels arrived shortly. The group went to the balcony projecting into the chamber from one of the upper floors, and, as the flames subsided, looked directly into what appeared the glowing crater of a volcano. Hitler, staring as if hypnotized, suddenly jerked about and screamed: "Now we will show them! Anyone who stands in our way will be mowed down! Every Communist official must be shot. All Communist deputies must be hanged this very night!"

"The whole thing was the signal for a Communist uprising!" Goering echoed. The official Nazi version issued by Goering to the press was that at four o'clock in the morning, the Communists, having observed flames shooting from the Reichstag, were to take to the streets all over Germany to torch public buildings, assassinate officials, batter in the doors of the populace, and slaughter women and children.

This was somewhat surprising since no Communists, except those routed out of their beds by the police and the SA, were to be seen abroad. Goering, however, had providentially had a list prepared ahead of time, and within twenty-four hours nearly five thousand opponents of the Nazis were in custody.

The fire and the strident propaganda unleashed by Goebbels created an atmosphere of mass hysteria. The Nationalists in the cabinet led the way on the following day in preparing an emergency measure, "Decree for the Protection of the People and the State." This suspended Article 48 of the German constitution, the equivalent of the American Bill of Rights. The inviolability of personal freedom, the right of habeas corpus, the sanctity of one's home, the right to secrecy of postal and telephone communications, the right of free speech, the prohibition of censorship, the right of assembly and free association, and the powers of the *Länder* (states) were all temporarily abrogated. The suspension of the article in an emergency was intended to protect the government against violent overthrow, and such a suspension had accomplished its task in 1923. What the drafters of Article 48 had not foreseen was that the insurrectionists might already be *in* the government; and that they would be so clever as to stage their coup at a time when the Reichstag, which might have voted the chancellor and cabinet out of office, had been dissolved.

Thus, the police were authorized to search and arrest without warrants, and empowered to take people into "protective custody" for an indefinite period without filing charges or bringing them before a judge. It was the initiation of the Gestapo–concentration camp state, yet such was the panicky fear of the Communists that the befuddled Hindenburg, who only a few weeks before had been apprehensive that Hitler would transform the government into a dictatorship, signed the decree without a murmur.*

Despite the Reichstag fire, a massive propaganda campaign, the staging of Wagnerian spectacles, and the terrorizing of the opposition by the SA, the Nazis did not stampede the voters in the election of March 5. A million workers were intimidated into casting their ballots for the Nazis instead of the Communists, but the Nationalists, the Catholic Center Party, and the Social Democrats all held their own.

Still well shy of a majority in the Reichstag, Hitler would have to continue to depend on the votes of the fifty-two Nationalist deputies, unless he could push through the enabling act that would permit the cabinet—and, in reality, he himself—to govern by decree without the consent of the Reichstag. The act furthermore empowered the cabinet to "deviate from the Reich constitution," and thus, in effect, supersede it. Trying to sugarcoat his poison with conciliation and reasonableness, Hitler vowed he had no intent to endanger the existence of the presidency or the Reichstag. The Länder would retain their form and their rights. His only aim was to speed up the legislative process so that he could get the country on its feet again. Papen, Hugenberg, and their Nationalist companions, still thinking of Hitler as the figurehead for their collegiate dictatorship, gave him their full support.

To trick Hindenburg, now capable of reading and grasping only the most elementary things, into signing the decree, it was given the euphemistic designation "Law to Remove the Distress of the People and the State." This practice, together with the device of hiding the most significant clauses deep in the body of the text, was to be continued in all of the Reich's legislation.

On March 24, the Reichstag met in the Kroll Opera House to consider the enabling act. For its passage, the constitution required two-thirds of

---

*Van der Lubbe was executed in January 1934 after a sensational trial, throughout which he remained manacled and never emerged from a semi-catatonic state. Four Communist co-defendants, against whom charges had been trumped up, were acquitted. The sole point on which everyone—prosecutors, defense attorneys, expert witnesses, observers, Communists, and Nazis—agreed was that van der Lubbe could not have been a lone arsonist, if, indeed, he himself had set any part of the conflagration.

the members of the Reichstag to be present; and, of these, two-thirds had to cast their ballots in favor. Consequently, the 120 Social Democratic and 81 Communist deputies, plus a smattering of others, could have frustrated Hitler's plans by simply boycotting the 647-member body.

Major Wallis read to the court Frick's statement to the cabinet explaining how this danger would be obviated: "The Communists will be prevented by urgent labor elsewhere from participation in the session. In concentration camps they will be reeducated for productive work. We will know how to render harmless permanently subhumans who don't want to be reeducated."

Goering's Gestapo and the SA detained or barred entry into the Reichstag of more than a score of key Social Democratic deputies, who were then ruled by Goering as president of the Reichstag to be "present." Members of the Catholic Center Party were intimidated and inveigled into acquiescence. The deputies voted 441 to 94 to pass the enabling act. Goering, whom Hitler characterized as "brutal and ice cold in crises," had already told the nation:

"Fellow Germans, my measures will not be crippled by any legalistic hesitation. Here I don't have to give justice, here I have only to destroy and exterminate, nothing more." He would use the power of the SA and the police equally. "Each bullet which leaves the barrel of a police pistol now is my bullet. If one calls this murder, then I have murdered. I ordered all this, I back it up. I assume the responsibility, and I am not afraid to do so."

16   "A Ring of Evil Men": The Röhm Purge

Hitler was now prepared to convert the nation into a dictatorship. Frick was given the task of drawing up and promulgating the measures.

"Frick's great contribution to the Nazi conspiracy was in the field of governmental administration. He was the administrative brain who devised the machinery of state for Nazism," Robert Kempner told the court.

Priority was placed on bringing the entire German press under Nazi control. (Since broadcasting was under the direction of the government, no special action was required by Hitler to make himself the master of radio.) On March 13 the Reich Ministry for Public Enlightenment and Propaganda was created specifically for Goebbels. Decree by decree the press was turned into a Nazi choir. Under the pretext of weeding out libel and licentiousness, the "Decree for Protection Against Treacherous Attacks on the Government" clamped a lid on all criticism: "Whoever purposely makes or circulates a statement of a factual nature which is untrue or grossly exaggerated or which is apt to seriously harm the welfare of the Reich or the reputation of the national or state governments or the party supporting these governments" was liable to two years in prison.

Henceforward any statement could be declared "untrue" by the Nazis and its author clapped into jail. The following year the decree was reissued under the designation "Combating Griping and Defeatism" to specifically place the Nazi Party, government, and officials beyond censure. Newspapers were turned into unwitting parodiers of the regime. The death of a Social Democratic Reichstag deputy in a concentration camp was announced as follows:

"Although treated with the same tolerance as all other people in protective custody, he acted in an unfriendly and provocative manner toward the supervisory personnel."

On April 7, "The Law for the Reestablishment of the Professional Civil Service" was enacted. Communists, liberals, Jews, and part-Jews were dismissed from all positions.

Journalists were incorporated as a body into the civil service. Since Jews could not be civil servants, it followed that they could not work on newspapers.

With ruthlessness, chicanery, and intimidation Hitler and Goering emasculated not only their opponents but their allies. On April 20, a month after the passage of the enabling act, Goering replaced Papen as prime minister of Prussia, thus eliminating Papen's theoretical check on Hitler's power. Through a series of edicts in June and July, all political parties except the Nazi were dissolved. The inept Hugenberg was forced to resign. Those Nationalist ministers who remained became completely subservient to Hitler.

On July 14 the Führer Principle was established by law. It was explained that, in the future, the cabinet was to be "de facto and also de jure nothing more or less than the Führer."

"The Law to Secure the Unity of the Party and the State" followed on December 1. The party, the law declared, "is the bearer of the concept of the German state and is inseparable from the state." Henceforth, any attack on the party was equated with an attack on the state. The spoils system was institutionalized; party bosses became the dispensers of government jobs in their jurisdictions.

To consolidate his totalitarian control, Hitler, in direct contravention of his pledge not to alter the status of the *Länder*, stripped them, like the Reichstag, of legislative power. Except in Prussia, Hitler superimposed

Reichstatthalter (Reich governors) over the government of each *Land,* and transformed the states into quasi-colonies.

One measure after another was directed against the Jews. On April 25 "The Law Against the Overcrowding of German Schools" limited the number of Jews permitted in institutions of higher education to the same percentage as their presence in the general population. Since Jews accounted for less than one percent of the population, but ten percent of university students, nine out of ten were ejected. After disposing of the Jews, the party gave vent to its general anti-intellectualism and male chauvinism by forcing the reduction of university enrollment from 118,000 to 51,000. Of those remaining, only 6,300 were women—down seventy-five percent!

On November 1, a Reich Chamber of Culture was established under the aegis of Goebbels to supervise the arts. Only Aryans were admitted to the chamber, and only a member of the chamber could work as a writer, actor, musician, or painter. In parallel fashion, the creation of the Academy of German Law eliminated Jews from meaningful participation in the legal profession. A "Homestead Law" prohibited Jews from farming or owning land.

"The German people were in the hands of the police, the police were in the hands of the Nazi Party, and the party was in the hands of a ring of evil men, of whom the defendants here before you are surviving and representative leaders," Jackson charged to the court.

It had taken Hitler and Goering less than a year to convert Germany from one of the principal democracies in the world to an iron-fisted dictatorship. They demonstrated with what ease a demagogue, once he obtains control of the government, can employ the apparatus to destroy the constitution. Through Goering, Hitler ruled Prussia, and through the *Reichstatthalter* (governors) the other *Länder.* Never before in German history had the central government, much less one man, exercised such control over the nation.

But while Hitler had smashed his enemies, the Nazis themselves were badly divided. The roughnecks and street fighters of the SA had always been a breed apart from the bureaucrats and politicians of the Party Organization, abbreviated "PO," and derisively referred to by the SA storm troopers as "P-Zero." Both, of course, hailed Hitler as *"der Führer,"* but neither had any use for Goering or his cronies: the reactionaries, financiers, and monopolists whom they had vowed to bring down, together with the Communists and the Jews, in their revolution.

Hitler, however, with his unlimited contempt for the "masses," had no intention of hanging the fate of his government on the whim of the rabble. Though he had exploited the "revolutionaries," his was a revolution of reaction. He wished to reverse the course of social development, not to advance it; and he warned his followers that Goering and his supporters were now part of the coalition:

"The revolution is not a permanent state of affairs. We must therefore not dismiss a businessman if he is a good businessman, even if he is not yet a National Socialist. History will not judge us according to whether we have removed and imprisoned the largest number of economists, but according to whether we have succeeded in providing work."

As prime minister of Prussia, Goering controlled the machinery of internal affairs in the preponderance of Germany. To buttress himself in his struggle against the SA, Goering rapidly built up a private army of police. He placed the burgeoning Gestapo under the control of a cynical young right-wing Lothario, Rudolf Diels (who liked to display his toughness by chewing beer steins to pieces after draining them), and made it personally responsible to him. He recruited three thousand men for a new Investigations Department, which kept him informed of the results of the telephone and telegraph taps they installed.

In the streets, dominated by the SA, terror reigned. Between the spring and autumn of 1933, the storm troopers, encouraged by Hitler's grant of amnesty to Nazis convicted of "political" killings during the Weimar regime, murdered between five hundred and seven hundred persons. More than thirty thousand others were dragged off to illegal detention centers in storm trooper barracks, old army camps, abandoned breweries, and so-called *Heldenkeller* (heroes' cellars). Some fifty of these existed in Berlin alone. There, Communists, Social Democrats, liberals, Catholic activists, Jews, "reactionaries," and personal enemies were starved, beaten, whipped, and tortured.

When outraged members of the *Herrenvolk* (elite) stormed into Goering's office to protest that some of their followers had disappeared into the *Heldenkeller,* Goering ordered Diels to take action. After raiding one detention center, Diels reported: "The victims whom we found were half dead from starvation. 'Interrogation' consisted simply of beatings, a dozen or so guards being employed in fifteen-minute shifts to belabor their victims with iron bars, rubber truncheons, and whips. When we entered, these living skeletons were lying on rows of filthy straw with festering wounds." During the fall and winter of 1933–34, Goering closed down all but two of the SA concentration camps, and placed these under his control.

The conflict between the Gestapo and conservatives on the one hand and the SA on the other was attended by the personal antagonism between

Goering and Ernst Röhm, the chief of the SA. Röhm, who, as head of the Reichswehr political department in Munich, had been Hitler's superior in 1919, had been wounded several times in World War I, and had the looks of an unsuccessful pugilist. An unabashed homosexual, his soul was that of a soldier of fortune. His ambition was to convert the SA, which had doubled in a few months and now outnumbered the hundred-thousand-man Reichswehr eight to one, into an army reserve, and make himself the nation's military leader. The prospect of being inundated by a howling horde of street fighters led by a homosexual horrified the aristocratic, tradition-encrusted officer corps, which allied itself with Goering against the SA.

The development that sealed Röhm's fate was Goering's weaning of Heinrich Himmler* and Reinhard Heydrich away from loyalty to Röhm. Himmler had taken over the SS, which Hitler had established as a personal bodyguard, in 1929, when it had 280 members. A born bureaucrat who had a mystic vision of transforming the SS into a latter-day version of the Teutonic Knights, Himmler expanded the organization into fifty thousand members in four years. He emphasized elitism. For the leadership he recruited heavily among nobility and intellectuals. For the rank and file he established severe tests of "Aryan" heritage and looks, robustness, and dedication (but not intelligence or character). Since he was responsible for Hitler's safety, he took over the Bavarian political police when Hitler came to power. Within a few months he insinuated himself into control of the small political police departments in the other *Länder* outside of Prussia also, and, naturally, staffed them with his SS men.

To keep himself apprised of the activities of his enemies—without and within the party—Himmler established in 1931 the *Sicherheitsdienst*—Security Service—abbreviated SD. As head of the SD he named the twenty-seven-year-old Heydrich, a tall, angular blond, who was a multifaceted athlete and had just been cashiered from the navy by Admiral Erich Raeder because he had impregnated the daughter of an influential businessman but had declined to marry her.

In the fall of 1933 the Gestapo had dealt as summarily with the improvised concentration camps of the SS as those of the SA; and when Heydrich had appeared in Berlin to set up an office, Goering had run him back to Bavaria.

---

*Himmler was the grandson of the onetime chief of the Munich gendarmes, the son of a headmaster who had once been a tutor at the Bavarian court, and the godson of Prince Heinrich of Bavaria. A study in contradiction, he was a myopic, slope-shouldered, spindle-chested weakling who wanted to be an eagle-eyed warrior; a darkhaired, stub-chinned Asiatic-featured Bavarian who dreamed of reincarnation as a Nordic blond; an apostate from Catholicism haunted by his conscience; a vapid prude with a voyeur's prurience.

Six months later, however, the patterns of power were shifting. President Hindenburg's health was worsening rapidly. Upon his death the monarchists proposed to abolish the presidency and name Prince August Wilhelm as regent. Hitler, however, had every intention of merging the chancellorship and the presidency in his own person, thus becoming head of state as well as head of government. As such an action would be a violation of the constitution, as well as of his pledge not to alter the status of the presidency, he was in critical need of the support of the Reichswehr. Wooing the generals, he promised them in April 1934 the rearming of Germany, the independence of the army, and a two-thirds reduction in the size of the SA. Röhm, whom Hitler only a short time before had praised "for the imperishable services which you have rendered to the Nationalist Socialist movement and to the German people," was to be sacrificed in return for the adherence of the generals. In a dramatic meeting a month later, the generals agreed to abandon the last redoubt of constitutional government to Hitler.

Goering concurrently negotiated a compact with Himmler. Though Himmler and Heydrich were close to Röhm (Himmler had been a member of Röhm's unit during the 1923 Putsch), the elitist SS was the antithesis in concept of the demotic SA. Dismissing Diels, Goering named Himmler deputy chief and operating head of the Gestapo under himself. Goering thus gained the SS as an ally. Himmler's position, conversely, was enhanced and solidified. Since Himmler, however, had neither interest in nor aptitude for police work, it was Heydrich, who rivaled Goering in intelligence, ruthlessness, and a passion for power, who aimed to become the security chief of the Reich. On June 9, the SD was officially proclaimed the party's (and hence the Reich's) intelligence organization; and Heydrich took a giant stride toward his goal.*

Hitler had achieved power through the political legerdemain of combining the reactionary right with a portion of the revolutionary left to crush the center. During the first few months in office he had managed to generate a patriotic fervor resembling the spirit of a religious revival. Yet to hold together such a disparate coalition united by nothing more than nationalism and anti-Semitism was quite a different matter. The disillusionment of the reactionaries was as notable as that of the SA. Though the industrialists could congratulate themselves that the Communists and the unions had been crushed and that the economy was reviving, the threat represented by the workers was being replaced by the meddling of the Nazi Party. There were intimations that a fair-sized portion of the profits

*Subsequently, Heinrich Müller, the head of the anti-Communist desk in the Munich police department, was named chief of the Gestapo.

were going to be siphoned off by hidden taxation, such as "voluntary" contributions to various Nazi funds, and payoffs to the *Bonzen* (big shots). Goering, whom they had not minded keeping in style so long as he resembled a grubby grafter, had been transformed into a smiling, sword-wielding god of extortion, appeased only with repeated sacrifices. Hitler, whom they thought they were hiring as a ringmaster for their circus, had become, instead, the undisputed master of the nation. Uneasily, they longed to put a halter on the Führer. It was thus Papen, as the spokesman for the right, not Röhm and the SA, who forced the issue.

The vice-chancellor's vaunted ties with Hindenburg were fading into insignificance as Hindenburg's condition worsened. While Hitler, keeping abreast of Hindenburg's decline, hovered like a vulture, Papen's friends urged him to speak out. Edgar Jung, a talented Munich lawyer and writer, composed a speech with the help of Papen's staff. Jung was no shining democrat, but a typical believer in the divine right of the *Herrenvolk*. So long as the heads being crushed were those of the Communists, he had been in full agreement with Hitler. "Violence is an element of life," he had written. "A nation that has become incapable of employing violence must be suspected of biological decline." But the continuing ferment, the crudeness of the SA, and the clear threat that the *Herrenvolk* were to be treated no differently than other Germans sparked Jung's cry of danger. Since it was impossible to attack Hitler directly, Goebbels and Röhm were selected as scapegoats.

Papen delivered his speech at the University of Marburg on June 17. "The government is well informed concerning the elements of selfishness, lack of character, mendacity, beastliness, and arrogance that are spreading under the guise of the German revolution," he said. "Not by whipping people up, especially whipping up the youth, and not by threats against helpless parts of the nation can confidence and eager commitment be intensified. Every word of criticism must not instantly be dubbed ill will, and despairing patriots must not be labeled enemies of the state. . . . No nation can live in a state of permanent revolution from below. . . . It is only weaklings who suffer no criticism. . . . Great men are not created by propaganda."

His speech was received with repeated applause, and created a stir throughout the country. When Heydrich and Goering informed Hitler that Schleicher was making overtures to Papen and Röhm to stymie Hitler by having the SA join in support of Prince August Wilhelm, Hitler concluded to wipe them all out with one blow—he would deal with the right under the guise of crushing the left, and crush the left under the pretext of acting as the guardian of Germany's morality.

"On the thirtieth of June, and 1 and 2 July 1934 the conspirators proceeded to destroy opponents within their own party by wholesale murder," the prosecution informed the court.

Empowering Goering to take all necessary actions in Prussia, Hitler boarded a plane for Munich at two o'clock in the morning of Saturday, June 30. Some time before he had proclaimed: "We are ruthless. I have no bourgeois scruples. They think I am uncultured, a barbarian. Yes, we are barbarians. That is an honorable epithet. This old world is done for." Landing at four o'clock, he rounded up a handful of men, and descended on Röhm, who was vacationing at the Bad Wiessee resort, at dawn. After arresting the SA leader and his immediate followers, Hitler flashed the code word "Hummingbird" to Goering to commence the purge in Berlin.

Throughout Germany, two days of slaughter, the climax of a year and a half of chaotic lawlessness produced by Hitler's vaunted "law and order" regime, followed. Hitler himself put the toll at seventy-seven. Two decades later at the Munich trial of some of the survivors and perpetrators, the number was raised to one thousand. In addition to Röhm and the SA leaders, all principal opponents, past, present, and potentially future, were liquidated. Anyone possessing embarrassing information about Hitler or Goering was killed. Some were bumped off gangster-style in their homes or taken for rides. Others were arrested, and executed in the prisons. Röhm and his men were shot in Munich. Karl Ernst, the Berlin SA leader, at whose wedding Goering had been the best man, was snatched in Bremen as he was about to board ship for his honeymoon, and executed. General von Schleicher and his wife were shot down by Gestapo agents in their home. Jung, following his arrest, was dispatched in the cell of his jail. Father Bernhard Stempfle, an anti-Semitic priest who had helped edit *Mein Kampf,* but had in his possession a compromising letter written to him by Hitler's niece and suspected paramour, Geli Raubal, was found in a forest with his neck broken and three shots in his chest. Gustav von Kahr, the Bavarian strongman who had first supported, then opposed Hitler during the Munich putsch, was hacked to death in a swamp near Dachau. Undersecretary of Transportation Erich Klausner, a leading Catholic spokesman, was assassinated at his desk.

The same fate befell Papen's press aide, Major von Bose, who had come into possession of documents damaging to Himmler. Papen and the other members of his staff were arrested. Papen was confined in his apartment, and for three days his life hung in the balance. It was, however, one thing to dispatch a homosexual ruffian like Röhm, and another to bump off the vice-chancellor of the nation. Besides, though Papen was an intriguer, he had a gelatinous spine, and had never been dangerous. When Papen was finally able to get through to Goering on the telephone, Goering expressed solicitous astonishment that Papen should have thought himself confined. It was all a misunderstanding.

The next day, July 3, Papen attended the cabinet meeting at which Hitler was presenting his version of the events of June 30. In the morning-after assessment, it had dawned on Hitler and Goering that hundreds of people had been killed contrary to German law. In a specious attempt to legalize the murders ex post facto and exculpate himself, Hitler presented to the cabinet a decree entitled: "Law Relating to National Emergency Defense Measures." This declared: "The measures taken on June 30 and July 1 and 2, 1934, to counteract the attempt at treason and high treason shall be considered as national emergency defense." Subserviently and hypocritically, the cabinet passed the measure. Henceforth the law in Germany would be whatever Hitler said it to be. He could do nothing wrong, for he could legalize—before or after—whatever action he might take.

For five hours, starting at 8 PM on July 13, he addressed the Reichstag in the Kroll Opera House and all of Germany over the radio. His hands clutching the lectern, a wild look in his eyes, he presented at one and the same time a rambling, disjointed, often illogical exposition and a fascinating tour de force. It was as if Ivan the Terrible had been reincarnated, and, availing himself of the marvels of the Industrial Revolution, was recounting how he, the head of government, had gone about personally hacking off heads in the interest of justice. "I was responsible for the fate of the German people and thereby I became the supreme judge of the German people. I gave the order to shoot the ringleaders in this treason, and I further gave the order to cauterize down to the raw flesh the ulcers of this poisoning of the wells of our domestic life.

"If anyone raises his hand to strike the state, then certain death is his lot."

The Nazi deputies, listening spellbound, gave Hitler their tumultuous support. Papen, who momentarily had seemed resolved to demand that the perpetrators of the murders be brought to justice and had informed Hitler that he intended to resign, returned, quaking, to character and wrote Hitler that his willingness "to accept responsibility even for these acts which, at a time of great mental excitement and antagonism, took place without your knowledge" exhibited outstanding magnanimity. "Allow me to say how manly and humanly great of you I think that is. The crushing of the revolt and your courageous and fine intervention have met with nothing but recognition throughout the entire world."

The denouement was ironic. Less than two weeks after Hitler's speech, the Nazis in Austria, incited by Hitler's example, assassinated the Catholic Chancellor-Dictator Engelbert Dollfuss. When the rebellion collapsed, Hitler washed his hands of the Austrian comrades, pretended shock at the affair, and recalled the German minister in Vienna, who had let himself be implicated. Desperately needing a German whom the Austrian government could regard with confidence, Hitler called Papen in the middle of the night on July 26, and asked him to take the diplomatic post in Vienna. Papen, as one good Catholic conservative speaking to others, would have the best chance of smoothing the troubled relations.

And Papen, with his need to be wanted and his longing to cast a shadow in the sun, accepted.

On August 1, the members of the cabinet affixed their signatures to Hitler's measure combining the presidency with the chancellorship the moment Hindenburg breathed his last—which he did the next day.

Eighteen months before, Hitler might have been brought down by the Reichstag, the cabinet, or the president. Now he had eliminated them or turned them into his pawns. To bind his minions to him even tighter, he exacted an oath of loyalty to his own person from all officials and members of the armed forces.

Theoretically, following the consolidation of power in the national government, Frick now had as Reich minister of interior all the *Länder* interior ministries and their police departments under his authority. With the presumed elimination of Germany's internal enemies, Frick believed that the time had come to reinstitute order in the penal system. He decreed that all motions for protective custody must be fully documented, that each person apprehended must be granted a hearing, and that the status of all those held had to be reviewed at intervals of no more than three months.

In reality, tables of organization meant nothing in the Third Reich. Himmler, as chief of the SS, was responsible only to Hitler, and as operating head of the Gestapo he was beholden to Goering, not to Frick. In 1935 Frick complained: "The decree on protective custody by the Reich Minister of Interior has been made invalid long ago by the actions of the political police. It is almost impossible to receive an adequate report of protective custody."

Citing the "unquestionable lawlessness" in which the SS and Gestapo were engaging, Frick proposed to Hitler that "it be settled once and for all who is to bear responsibilities in all matters pertaining to the political police. *Either:* this responsibility rests with the Reich Minister of the Interior. Then he has to be vested with altogether different powers. *Or:* this responsibility with all its consequences is borne by the Reichsführer SS, who is already actually claiming the management of the political police in the Reich."

Hitler responded in February 1936 by combining all the *Länder* political police under Himmler. Four months later, prior to the Olympic games, he went one step further and appointed Himmler chief of a united German police. Nominally the police were left in the Ministry of the Interior, but, in actuality, Frick had no control over Himmler.

Since there was no national police law, Himmler was free to undertake whatever tasks he saw fit, following only Hitler's dictum that he should act according to "the good sense of the people."

Heydrich assumed control of all security and investigative police functions. He combined the Gestapo and the Kripo (Criminal Police) under a new designation, the *Sicherheitspolizei* (Security Police), with himself at the head. Then, when war broke out in September 1939, he created an umbrella organization, the *Reichsicherheitshauptamt* (RSHA), embracing both the Security Police and the SD, of which he also remained the chief. Since he was responsible to both Himmler and Goering, but neither took an active interest in his operations, he could play them off against each other when necessary, and in practice act virtually independently.

By Goering's directive, only the Gestapo could decree protective custody (that is, commitment to a concentration camp). The Gestapo exercised political and judicial control over the camp inmates. The SS Operations Department furnished the guards. The SS Economic and Administrative Department (WVHA) was responsible for financing. The commander of each camp received orders from and had to deal with all three authorities, as well as with a concentration camp inspectorate established subsequently. The fragmentation and interweaving of party and governmental agencies (e.g., the SD remained a party apparatus, paid out of party funds, while the Gestapo and Kripo were governmental organizations) increased in complexity as time progressed.

For the judges and other participants in the Nuremberg trial, the comprehension of the Nazis' governmental structures proved a major challenge; and Lawrence, to a certain extent, remained puzzled by the snarls, overlapping, and confusion until the end.

17   The Hossbach Meeting: A Split in the Alliance

Following the Röhm purge, Hitler was, in accordance with his agreement with the Reichswehr, ready to press ahead with rearmament. Since Hitler's knowledge of finances was nonexistent and his comprehension of economics badly askew, he needed an ingenious and skilled administrator to fine tune the economy and coordinate industrial production with the needs of the armed forces. On August 1, 1934, he named Schacht, who had

The Structure and Chief Wielders of Power in the Third Reich

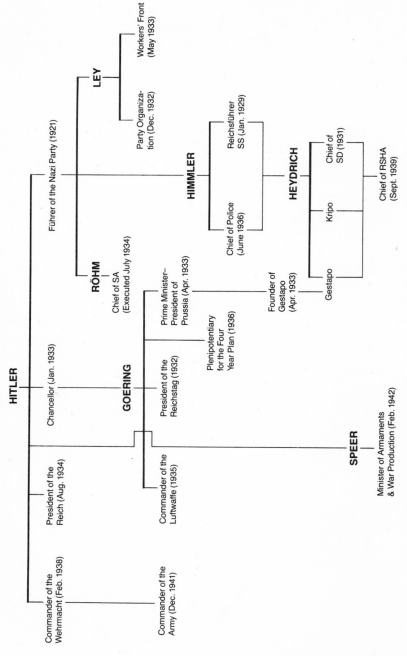

HITLER
- Commander of the Wehrmacht (Feb. 1938)
  - Commander of the Army (Dec. 1941)
- President of the Reich (Aug. 1934)
- Chancellor (Jan. 1933)
- Führer of the Nazi Party (1921)

RÖHM
- Chief of SA (Executed July 1934)

LEY
- Party Organization (Dec. 1932)
- Workers' Front (May 1933)

GOERING
- President of the Reichstag (1932)
- Commander of the Luftwaffe (1935)
- Prime Minister–President of Prussia (Apr. 1933)
- Plenipotentiary for the Four Year Plan (1936)
- Founder of Gestapo (Apr. 1933)

HIMMLER
- Reichsführer SS (Jan. 1929)
- Chief of Police (June 1936)

HEYDRICH
- Chief of SD (1931)
- Kripo
- Gestapo
- Chief of RSHA (Sept. 1939)

SPEER
- Minister of Armaments & War Production (Feb. 1942)

become president of the Reichsbank in March 1933, to the additional post of economics minister.

By March 1935 Hitler felt on solid enough footing to decree the reestablishment of universal military conscription, and Goering, as minister of air, announced the creation of the Luftwaffe. "The defendant Schacht was designated Plenipotentiary for the War Economy* on May 21, 1935, with complete control over the German civilian economy for war production," the prosecution related.

The establishment of a half-million-man army and the initiation of such public works as Autobahn construction solved the unemployment problem. Soon, however, as the economy revived, critical shortages of many raw materials developed. Germany needed to import oil, rubber, tin, nickel, cobalt, high-grade iron ore, and many other basic elements. Most important of all, it could produce only eighty percent of the food its population consumed. The generation of foreign exchange through trade was, therefore, essential. But one of the Nazis' first acts—blocking all foreign accounts and permitting the repayment of foreign loans and debts only in marks—alienated Germany from its traditional markets. No one was willing to do business unless paid in gold, and Germany's gold reserves were negligible. The situation was aggravated by the adverse reaction abroad to the Nazis' persecution of the Jews and harassment of the Catholic Church. The initial measures against the Jews, barring them from government jobs, from all positions of influence, and from the arts, had benefited principally the Nazi *Bonzen* and professionals. So far as the masses could see, the middle-class Jews still prospered. The former Nazi street brawlers took out their frustrations in spontaneous beatings and atrocities, which were punished cursorily if at all, but played up in the world press. Schacht, who was the recipient of the repercussions in his foreign dealings, excoriated the violence as "barbarous and infamous." On August 18, 1935, in a speech at the Königsberg Fair, he brought the matter to a head.

"There are those of our contemporaries about whom it is best to pray: 'Lord, save me from my friends,' " he declared. "Those are the people who heroically smear windowpanes in the middle of the night, who brand every German who trades in a Jewish store a traitor, who condemn every form of Freemason as a bum, and who, in the just fight against priests and ministers who talk politics from the pulpit, cannot themselves distinguish between religion and misuse of the pulpit. The goal at which these people aim is generally correct and good. But the solution of these problems must

*The plenipotentiaries appointed by Hitler were superministers empowered to exercise authority over all departments and ministries in a specified field.

be brought about under state leadership and cannot be left to unregulated individual actions. Since our economy is closely allied with that of foreign countries, not one of us can be indifferent to what consequences these disturbances can have at home and abroad. It is absolutely necessary that confidence in Germany as a constitutional state remain unshaken. No one in Germany is deprived of his rights.

"According to Point Four of the National Socialist Party program, the Jew can neither become a citizen or a fellow German. But that means he must not be subjected to arbitrary action, but regulated by law. *This legislation is being prepared and must be awaited.*"

Little, actually, had been done to prepare the legislation alluded to by Schacht. But, spurred by Schacht's speech, Hitler ordered Frick, as well as Hess and the Party Organization, to get busy, and the laws were introduced at the Nuremberg rally the next month by Goering. The Nuremberg Laws deprived the Jews of German citizenship and all political rights. They were forbidden to marry or have extramarital relations with "Aryans," or employ Aryan girls in their homes.

For the moment, the legislation had minimal practical effect on the German Jews. It did nothing to satisfy the party stalwarts, but merely egged them on, since Jews were now officially outcast and could be accused of the new sexual crime, *Rassenschande* (disgracing the German race). The psychological effect abroad was exactly the opposite of what Schacht had intended, for the clear implication was that Jews were a subspecies unfit for association with their betters.

Consequently, the economic boycott against Germany continued. The party's *Bonzen* (big shots) and *Ausland* (foreign) organization kept on spending money to import luxury goods and support Nazi activities in other countries. When Schacht, who had never been a party member, was unable to prevail against the Nazi nabobs, he complained to Hitler that continuance of the pattern would lead to bankruptcy and the inability to obtain strategic materials. Hitler thereupon, in early 1936, appointed Goering as comptroller of foreign exchange, on the presumption that Goering had the clout to make the rules stick.

Furthermore, the Führer a few days later named Goering as commissioner of the first Four Year Plan, designed to achieve autarchy. Gasoline, rubber, and other products were to be produced synthetically so as to make Germany independent of foreign sources. (One result was to introduce the word *Ersatz* into languages throughout the world.)

Predictably, Goering, rather than acting as a planner and coordinator, set about to establish himself as economic czar. Beneath him a new bureaucracy sprang up. The Hermann Goering Works, embracing coal and iron mines, steel mills, and various other enterprises, developed into Goering's personal industrial empire. Providing him with a new source of graft, it transformed him into one of Germany's richest men.

In his drive to increase production, Goering ignored costs, and the Germany economy began to stagger under his inefficiencies. The iron he wrested from the low-grade ores of the Salzgitter mine in Brunswick cost twice as much as imported iron. The manpower he siphoned off from the now fully employed work force could have been used far better to produce goods for export. Instead of contributing to the solution of the trade problem, he intensified it. "We have no butter, comrades," he flamboyantly told a mass rally in Hamburg. "But I ask you—would you rather have butter or guns? Shall we bring in lard or iron ore? I tell you, preparedness makes us powerful. Butter only makes us fat!" Slapping his paunch, he drew a roar of laughter and support.

Goering's "guns or butter" comment achieved worldwide renown, but did not impress Schacht. Schacht considered Goering a cross between an economic ignoramus and mad hatter. "I have never taken orders from Goering and I never would," he declared during an interrogation. "Goering didn't like me, and I hated him."

In April 1937, Schacht told Goering that, unless various schemes under the Four Year Plan were cut back and the pace of rearmament curtailed, the economy would be out of control by the end of the year. When, by August, he had had no satisfactory response, he refused to associate himself further with what he perceived as a portending economic crisis, and submitted his resignation to Hitler. On August 11, Schacht met with Hitler and argued that it was impossible to forge cannon out of air and paper money.

Though Hitler refused to be dissuaded from his intent to continue with the rapid buildup of the armed forces, he took up Schacht's argument and twisted it to his own purpose. On November 5, shortly after Schacht's decision to resign became irrevocable, Hitler called Goering, Minister of War Werner von Blomberg, Foreign Minister Constantin von Neurath, and the army and navy chiefs, General Werner von Fritsch and Admiral Erich Raeder to the Reich Chancellery to explain to them his views on Germany's economic condition and foreign relations. The notes of the meeting were kept by Hitler's adjutant, Colonel Friedrich Hossbach. They composed, Sidney Alderman told the court, "one of the most striking and revealing of all the captured documents."

Except for Goering, all the men present at what came to be known as the Hossbach Meeting were from the Nationalist camp, and Hitler's primary intent was to wean them away from Schacht's gradualist conception of rearmament. But, carried away and ranging, as was his wont, from the Creation to the Apocalypse, he conducted a four-and-a-half-hour monologue during which he presented his blueprint for aggression.

The attainment of total autarchy was impossible, Hitler said, and even partial autarchy was beyond achievement in agriculture. The amount of foreign currency spent on food imports was considerable even in years of good harvests and increased catastrophically in bad. After two decades of little population growth, the German people were now increasing by more than half a million per year, so the problem could only get worse. To rely on exports for the earnings required to import raw materials and food was foolish because of the continuous fluctuations in the world economy, and because to do so was to leave Germany at the mercy of the British, who could cut the sea lanes at any time. Consequently, Germany's aim had to be to secure its food supply in Europe. "It is *not* a case of conquering people, but of conquering agriculturally useful space," Hitler asserted. "Every spatial expansion can only be effected by breaking resistance and taking risks. Even setbacks are unavoidable; neither formerly nor today has space been found without an owner; the attacker always comes up against the proprietor.

"The question for Germany is where the greatest possible conquest can be made at the lowest cost."

War would have to come at the latest between 1943 and 1945, for after that Germany's strength vis-à-vis other nations would decline. But since any year could bring a food crisis, since the maintenance of a large standing army would be a burden, since the leaders of the Nazi movement would be aging, and since it would be in the near future that the Wehrmacht and especially the Luftwaffe would have their greatest comparative advantage, one should think in terms of striking sooner rather than later.

If Austria and Czechoslovakia were incorporated into the German Reich, and one million people (Jews and Slavs) were forced to emigrate from Austria and two million from Czechoslovakia, then these two areas might produce sufficient surplus food for five to six million Germans. In any case, preparations for the attack would have to be completed in detail, so that it could be carried out *"blitzartig schnell"* (lightninglike) and other powers would be faced with a fait accompli before they could react.

Hitler's exposition shocked his audience. For years, even while steadfastly building up the armed forces, Hitler had been proclaiming his peaceful intentions; and both at home and abroad, the wishful tendency had been to believe him. The Wehrmacht's staff, as Hitler chagrinedly remarked, was not the mastiff straining at the leash he had once imagined it to be, but a reluctant mule needing to be pushed and prodded every step of the road toward war.

Blomberg joined Fritsch in observing animatedly that if France and England were to get wind of Germany's intentions, Germany would be in dire peril, and that Czechoslovakia, its "Little Maginot" line protected by an army equal in size to Germany's , would be no easy conquest. The elderly Neurath so disagreed with Hitler's assessment that the Führer became quite belligerent, and the foreign minister went out and had a mild heart attack.

Neither Hitler nor his listeners left the meeting in a happy frame of mind. Hitler could hardly miss that, far from instilling a martial spirit in the generals, the scenario he had projected had generated skepticism and anxiety. The generals, for their part, were shaken by what they considered Hitler's irresponsible and dangerous resolution to pursue an aggressive course alienating all of Europe's major powers. The covert, disorganized opposition to Hitler in the army and among the Nationalists drew together. Convinced that war would be a disaster for Germany, they planned in their haphazard, disjointed way to forestall the Führer when the time came by deposing him one minute before midnight.

18   Goering's Coup: The Blomberg-Fritsch Crisis

By 1937 Goering had firmly cemented his position as subdictator of the Third Reich under Hitler. He was, in effect, Hitler's prime minister, and executor and administrator of his will. Had Hitler not existed, he would, in his own right, have been one of the most powerful despots in the world. As Plenipotentiary for the Four Year Plan, he had taken over control of the economy. As prime minister of Prussia, he ruled more than half of Germany as a personal fief. As president of the Reichstag, he was the leader of the Nazi deputies and therefore a power in the party. As director of the Hermann Goering Works, he funneled government contracts to himself. He was Reich Minister for Air, and commander of the Luftwaffe. He owned a leading newspaper in the industrial Ruhr, the *Essener Zeitung.* He held numerous secondary titles like the Reich Director of Television* and Master of the Hunt.

Still, he was symbiotically dependent upon Hitler. "Only with the Führer, and with the Führer standing behind him is one really powerful," he confessed. "In Hitler the rare union has taken place between the most acute logical thinker and truly profound philosopher and the iron man of action. I follow no leadership but that of Adolf Hitler and of God."

After Karin died in 1930, he had gone back on drugs. The paracodeine

---

*Germany was the world's leader in development of TV, and experimentally telecast the 1936 Olympics.

pills he took to lift his spirits were not as addictive as morphine, but year by year he required more of them to stay in a frame of mind optimistic enough so that he could function. The pills stimulated his already hefty appetite to the point that he became voracious. He had a eunuch's baby-pink skin without the vestige of a beard, and rouged his cheeks like a woman. The nails on his stubby fingers were manicured daily and lacquered pale pink. In bed he wore frilled and embroidered nightshirts. He glowed like a little boy at the faintest word of approbation from Hitler, but rushed off to gorge himself at the hint of a scowl.

As Master of the Hunt he appropriated the hundred-thousand-acre Schorfheid hunting preserve two hours north of Berlin for himself. There, by the side of a forest lake, he built the replica of an enormous thatched-roof feudal manor that was never completed but continued to be expanded like a miniature counterpart of Hitler's megalomanic conquests. Its principal room, the size of a castle hall, was paneled in oak and bedecked with armor, weaponry, hunting trophies, Gobelin tapestries, and old masters. For this estate, christened Karinhall, as well as his other residences, Goering plundered private collections and requisitioned paintings from public museums, so that by 1938—when he was scarcely started—Karinhall contained fourteen Cranachs, seven Rembrandts, five Raphaels, several primitive altars, and innumerable wood carvings, rare prints, Byzantine art works, and gold and silver ornaments. Stained-glass windows filtered the dappled sunlight penetrating the woods, completing the slightly ominous Gothic effect. A separate wing was added to provide a palatial state dining room. An Olympic-sized swimming pool took shape in the basement. For entertainment there was a movie theater, for exercise a tennis court and an archery range, and for physical rehabilitation a gym and a Turkish bath. For the complement of guards, servants, gardeners, foresters, and game wardens a village of outbuildings arose. Wild animals, including lions, were imported from America and Africa. One of Goering's diversions was to play with the lion cubs as if they were kittens.

He welcomed notable guests from all over the world—including the Duke and Duchess of Windsor shortly after the former Edward VIII's abdication from the British throne—standing legs akimbo in the courtyard, a six-foot Scandinavian hunting spear in his hand. His ensembles combined features from the Middle Ages, a Wagnerian opera, and the lurid costumes displayed in the dives of Berlin's West End. Since he perspired fearfully, he preferred loose-fitting garments, and would sometimes lounge about in a toga, his legs encased in a cardinal's red silk stockings.

Shortly before Karin's death, he had met a divorced actress, Emma Sonnemann, who was as sturdily built as Karin had been wraithlike. A goodhearted though self-indulgent simpleton Goering's own age, she was the daughter of a Hamburg merchant, and no great beauty. She became his mistress. When he decided to marry her in 1935, the wedding, staged in Berlin's Lutheran Cathedral with the Berlin Opera providing a choir and orchestra, put many a royal ceremony to shame.

The obvious reluctance of the nation's military leaders to support Hitler at the Hossbach Meeting appeared to Goering an opportunity to aggrandize further power to himself—he would add the title of minister of war. Blomberg, the current occupant of the post, was a strapping, handsome man whose wife had died five years before. He had taken as mistress Erna Gruhn, a woman half his age with an embarrassing past. Passionately in love with her, he wished to marry her. Goering, expressing the greatest sympathy, helped facilitate the nuptials by arranging for Fraülein Gruhn's former lover to be offered a lucrative position in South America. Goering pointed out that he himself had made an honest woman of Emma, and encouraged Blomberg to follow his example.

On January 12, 1938, Blomberg, with Hitler and Goering attending, married Erna, and went off on a honeymoon. Almost at once the telephones at general staff offices began ringing, and coy, seductive female voices, proffering their services, indicated interest in emulating the success of Fraülein Gruhn. The trap had been sprung.

Through the Gestapo and his Investigation Department, Goering, of course, had access to the Reich's police files. Erna Gruhn's mother had operated a Berlin brothel, camouflaged as a massage parlor, and there Erna had been introduced into the ways of Aphrodite. Later she had served as a model for pornographic photographs, some of which were still extant. Police in no fewer than seven major German cities had files on her. Field Marshal Blomberg was hopelessly compromised.

On January 24, Goering, shedding crocodile tears, called Blomberg in and told him that his fellow officers were demanding his resignation—he had disgraced the honor of the officer corps. The following day Goering advised Hitler of the state of affairs, and on January 26, Hitler, who cared nothing for bourgeois morality but a great deal about the sensitivity of the Junkers, personally accepted Blomberg's resignation.

The Wehrmacht's leadership unanimously favored General von Fritsch as Blomberg's successor. Fritsch's reactionary views were shared by the generals, he was highly popular, noted for his political independence, and known as a Wehrmacht man through and through.

Goering, however, also had a file on General von Fritsch. This had first been compiled by the Gestapo in 1935, upon the arrest of a blackmailer and petty criminal named Hans Schmidt, who made a habit of loitering around homosexual pickup spots. Schmidt asserted that in November 1934 he had observed an officer engaging in a sex act with a youth. After threatening the officer with exposure, he had accompanied him to his home in suburban Lichterfelde and obtained fifteen hundred marks as the price for keeping quiet. The officer's name was von Fritsch.

On the same day that Goering apprised Hitler of the Blomberg scandal, he advised the Führer that it was obviously impossible to replace Blomberg with a bachelor officer who stole around railroad stations to pick up boys.

At a confrontation with Hitler at the chancellery, Fritsch appeared white-faced and agitated, unable to fathom what the scandal was about. Then a side door opened and the blackmailer, Schmidt, was marched in.

"Is that the man?" Hitler asked, pointing at Fritsch.

"That is the man!" Schmidt averred.

Fritsch shouted that Schmidt's declaration was "a stinking lie," but Hitler was only too ready to believe the worst. Goering rushed off to a small dining room in the chancellery. "He did it! He did it!" he shrieked at the top of his lungs as he threw himself on a couch. "He did it! He did it!"

But Hitler had no more intention of naming Goering minister of war than he had of picking Fritsch. Though he was fairly certain he had the measure of Goering, he would not risk giving a subordinate, who already had control of the economy, Prussia, and the Gestapo, command of the armed forces as well.

So Hitler threw Goering a sop, naming him field marshal, thus appointing him with Blomberg's retirement Germany's highest-ranking officer. Simultaneously, however, the Führer abolished the Ministry of War and announced: "From now on I take over directly the command of the entire Wehrmacht. The Armed Forces office with its function as Supreme Command of the Armed Forces, hitherto within the Reich War Ministry, will come directly under my command and serve as my military staff."

"All that remained," the prosecution asserted, "was to provide . . . military chiefs whose conscience was sufficiently elastic to allow them to play the part of faithful executives."

In place of the War Ministry, Hitler created the *Oberkommando der Wehrmacht* (OKW), the High Command of the Armed Forces, and appointed General Wilhelm Keitel to the post of chief of staff, responsible directly to himself. Keitel, whose son was engaged to Blomberg's daughter, had been chief of staff to the dismissed field marshal, but was of such plodding mediocrity that Blomberg protested he was nothing but a housekeeper, unfit for any major command.

"Yes," Hitler agreed. That was why Keitel was the ideal man for the post.

On February 5, the *Völkischer Beobachter* bannered: "Strongest Concentration of All Power in the Führer's Hands!"

There was no one who would dispute that claim. Hitler was the leader of Germany's only party. He was, as chancellor, the head of the government; as president, the head of the state; and he had, all along, been his own de facto foreign minister. Now he held the reins of the Wehrmacht. Never in German history—not even in the heyday of Frederick the Great—had power been so concentrated.

Deciding to make a clean sweep and get rid of all the Nationalist deadwood he had allowed to float along for the past five years, Hitler dismissed sixteen top generals and transferred another forty-four.

On January 31, Colonel Alfred Jodl, Keitel's aide, recorded: "Führer wants to divert spotlight from Wehrmacht. Keep Europe gasping and by replacements in various posts not awaken the impression of an element of weakness but of a concentration of forces. Schuschnigg (the Austrian chancellor) is not to take heart but to tremble."

On February 4, Neurath was replaced as foreign minister by Ribbentrop, and the cabinet, meeting for the last time in the history of the Third Reich, perfunctorily approved Hitler's abolition of the Ministry of War. The German envoys in London, Tokyo, Rome, and Vienna were replaced. Ulrich von Hassell, the ambassador to Italy, noted with German fatalism: "This man—Hitler—is Germany's destiny for good and for evil. If he now goes over the abyss—which Fritsch believes he will—he will drag us all down with him. There is nothing we can do."

19 Goering as Machiavelli: The Anschluss

The first, and unexpected, effect of the Blomberg-Fritsch, crisis was that Austria tumbled into Hitler's domain, and the Führer was transformed from a domestic tyrant into an international menace. Papen, a friend of Fritsch's, was one of the diplomats recalled by Hitler on February 4. Appearing at Berchtesgaden like a bewildered schoolboy wondering what he had done wrong, Papen bewailed the fact that he was being dismissed just at a time when he was about to persuade the Austrian chancellor, Kurt von Schuschnigg, to meet with Hitler.

Hitler, like a bird dog sniffing a quarry, exclaimed: "But that is splendid!" Papen was to go back to Vienna and send Schuschnigg to him.

The Austrian political scene was as fragmented as Germany's had been in 1933, and in a country of seven million the effect was somewhat as if every cafe and beer garden had its own party. The dominant influence in the country was the Catholic Church, and in 1932 the Christian Socialist (Catholic) chancellor, Engelbert Dollfuss, had established a de facto dictatorship. In February 1934 the Social Democrats and Communists had staged an unsuccessful uprising, which was followed by the Nazis' attempted putsch, during which Dollfuss was assassinated.

For a time, Schuschnigg, who succeeded Dollfuss, had benefited from the Austrian Nazis' own internecine quarrels and Hitler's preoccupation with internal German affairs. At the time of the Olympics in the summer of 1936, when Hitler was anxious to project a pacific image, he had agreed to a modus vivendi with Schuschnigg. A German-Austrian commission was established to arbitrate differences between the two countries. The pact provided for a measure of political freedom for the "legal" branch of the Austrian Nazi Party, which promised not to engage in subversive activities. The "illegals," who continued their underground attempt to overthrow the government, were disowned by Hitler. Seyss-Inquart was selected as liaison between the legal Nazis and the government. Though sympathetic to the Nazis, the cautious Seyss-Inquart had never formally joined the party and, despite political differences, was personally on good terms with Schuschnigg.

"He was a traitor to the government to which he owed allegiance and in which he held high office," the prosecution's indictment of Seyss-Inquart declared. "With full knowledge of the ultimate purpose of the conspirators, he bent every effort to integrate Austria into the Reich and to make its resources and manpower, as well as its strategic position, available for the Nazi war machine."

On the morning of February 12, 1938, Schuschnigg, persuaded by Papen, motored across the border to Berchtesgaden. Hitler had only a vague conception of what would be discussed or what he would demand —to a large extent that depended on Schuschnigg's character and his reaction to Hitler. Never asking Schuschnigg to sit down, Hitler plunged into a series of tantrums: "Herr Schuschnigg, I say to you, Austria did in the whole of its history nothing other than to oppose German aims. That was the task of the Habsburgs, that was the task of the Catholic Church; and it is the task of your government. We have only difficulties with Austria. Austria is our enemy."

Creating an atmosphere of intimidation, Hitler refused to negotiate at all but had Ribbentrop and a representative of the Austrian Nazis work out the terms to be presented to Schuschnigg. Taking a leaf from the

Allies' diplomacy at Versailles, Hitler presented these to Schuschnigg on an "accept-them-or-else" basis. What the "else" would be was left to Schuschnigg's imagination, though Germany, which still had only one far-from-battle-ready armored division, was in no shape militarily to precipitate an international crisis.

Losing his nerve, Schuschnigg agreed to the terms: Seyss-Inquart was to be appointed minister of interior with control over the police, thus placing him in the same position as Goering in Prussia in 1933. Another Nazi was to be named minister of economics. The most outspoken anti-Nazis in the cabinet were to be dismissed. All Nazis held in jail for political crimes, including those involved in Dollfuss's assassination, were to be released.

On February 20, Hitler, speaking about the agreement to the Reichstag, mixed lukewarm conciliatory remarks with further threats. Four days later, Schuschnigg, who now regretted not having been more resolute, declared he had made the last Austrian concession.

His speech set off a violent reaction by the radical Nazis. The situation deteriorated so rapidly that, at the end of the first week in March, Schuschnigg felt called upon to take a desperate gamble. He decided that on Sunday, March 13, he would hold a national plebiscite, asking the people: "Do you want a free and independent Austria?" Various devices were to be employed to stack the vote against the Nazis. If the outcome was as expected, the Nazis would be dealt a major propaganda defeat, and an Anschluss with Germany would be postponed.

To the Austrian Nazi leaders, this was the equivalent of a call to arms. On the evening of March 9 they appealed to Hitler and Goering, who at the time was eating dinner in Berlin with his Austrian brother-in-law, Franz Hüber. Goering took the initiative. A courier was put on a plane to Vienna with instructions that Schuschnigg was to be forced to resign. Seyss-Inquart was to be installed in his place and was then to send a telegram to Berlin: "Because of unrest, murder, and bloodshed on the streets of Vienna, I, Seyss-Inquart, chancellor of Austria, request assistance from German troops."

"We have at hand another document which permits us virtually to live again through the events of March 11, 1938, and to live through them in most lively and interesting fashion," Alderman told the court as he conducted his narrative and initiated the reading of the transcript of Goering's telephone conversations.

All through the day Goering, giving directions to Seyss-Inquart and other members of the Nazi cabal, was on the phone to Vienna. Vacillating,

Schuschnigg proposed one half measure and compromise after another, each of which was rejected and merely made the situation worse. Finally, at eight o'clock that evening he resigned; but Austrian President Miklas refused to accept the resignation.

"OK. I shall give the order to march in," Goering told Seyss-Inquart, "and then you make sure you get the power."

A few minutes later Goering informed the German military attaché in Vienna: "It will be best if Miklas resigns."

"Yes, but he won't," the attaché replied. "It was very dramatic. He declared that he will under no circumstances yield to force."

"What does this mean? So he just wants to be kicked out?"

"Yes, he does not want to move."

"Well, with fourteen children one cannot move as one likes," Goering, referring to Miklas's prolific family, wisecracked. "Well, tell Seyss that he'll take over."

Six thousand storm troopers, many of them slouching around like legionnaires at a convention, took control of the radio station, invested public buildings, and hoisted swastika flags everywhere. Fifty SS men knocked on the door of the chancellery and were politely admitted by a guard. In one room an official of the Foreign Office continued to send out desperate pleas for help to countries all over the world, while down the hall Seyss-Inquart and his cohort met. One of them, Friedrich Rainer, brought a typewriter and asked whether anyone understood anything about forming a government. No one was sure. The scenario seemed straight out of a comic operetta, had it not been such a pivotal event in world history. In the end, the Austrian government simply dissolved; and Hitler, like a ferocious-looking hermit crab, crawled into the empty shell and appropriated it. Rainer recalled, "Once a door opened and a strapping guard arrived with beer and seltzer bottles and ham sandwiches for us. That was the first sign that we had assumed power."

When Hitler made a triumphal entry into Austria later that day, he was greeted by a kind of hysterical relief. On Sunday morning, Goering, left behind to mind the government in Berlin, spoke on the telephone to Ribbentrop, whom Hitler had dispatched to London to deal with the British during the crisis.

"There is overwhelming joy in Austria," Goering declared. "This story that we had given an ultimatum, that is just foolish gossip. The Austrian National Socialist ministers asked us to back them up, so they would not be completely beaten up again and be subjected to terror and civil war. Then we told them we would not allow Schuschnigg to provoke a civil war. One could not know that they would capitulate like that and therefore Seyss-Inquart who had already taken over the government asked us to march in immediately. These are the actual facts. The absolute complete enthusiasm for National Socialism is surprising even to us. . . . The whole affair is rolling as it is supposed to roll and it has crystallized into a march of joy. . . . We have a clear conscience, and that is the decisive factor."

Alderman, not cognizant of Goering's ubiquitous telephone-tapping organization, explained: "Evidently the defendant wanted to keep a record of important telephone conversations," a statement that elicited from Goering a half-stifled grin. Punctuating Alderman's recitation with gestures, grimaces, laughter, and silent applause, he appeared ready to leap to center stage to assume his own role in the drama. Reliving the triumph of the event, he was foremost in the amusement occasioned by the spurious telegram he had composed for Seyss-Inquart, calling for the assistance of German troops to put down nonexistent rioting in the streets. When Alderman said to the court, "Well, of course, he [Seyss-Inquart] did not need to send a telegram because Goering wrote the telegram: he already had it," Goering could not have been prouder had his name been mentioned in the same breath with Machiavelli's.

Goering, in fact, exploited every opportunity throughout the trial to attract attention to himself, and performed a continuing pantomime. When he agreed, he nodded his head; when he disagreed, he shook it violently from side to side; at mention of the Luftwaffe, he straightened his shoulders and sat up; when Thomas Dodd said Hitler had chosen Hess as his successor, he glowered, motioned vigorously in dissent, and kept pointing to himself; when Dodd subsequently corrected the declaration, he beamed with pleasure. He ogled every girl that went by, and particularly had his eye on a redheaded secretary with the French prosecution. He seemed, in fact, to feel almost personally responsible for the conduct of the trial. A few days into the proceedings he recognized Murray Gurfein, one of his interrogators, and vigorously motioned for him to come over to the dock. Holding up a sheaf of papers, he explained: "You've got to do something about this!"

"About what?" Gurfein responded, startled.

"The transcript! The translations are terrible! Something's got to be done! They can't go down in history this way."

Hess, seated next to Goering, daily brought a different book with him to read, opened it but never turned a page, and stared absentmindedly into space. The guards kept taking the book away from him, but, after a few days, Biddle told them not to bother; it seemed pointless. Keitel and Jodl studiously took notes. Papen listened to the speakers in English and French. Frank, Schirach, and Doenitz regularly wore dark glasses to ward off the glare of the lights; and the Hollywood touch heightened the resemblance of the accused to an array of Mafia chieftains.

It was the trial's eighth court day as the prosecution recounted the history of the Anschluss. Session by session, Jackson's failure to organize the presentation better took its toll on the judges. In the attempt to relate all the diverse events of the era to the "conspiracy," and associate all twenty-two defendants (including Bormann) with them, the prosecution repeatedly wandered far afield. A bewildering array of documents was introduced, and long quotations cited from them. Dodd, who had responsibility for the case on the economic preparations for war, apologized: "I am aware, if your honors please, that the material I am pursuing here is a little tedious." Jackson's "talking briefs," delivered at the translation speed of sixty words per minute, took the drama out of the trial even when the evidence was inherently interesting and intriguing. The newsmen, provided with advance copies of the presentation, felt no need to sit through the recitations and absented themselves a good part of the time.

One of the problems that had been sloughed off by Jackson and Storey was that of providing German copies of all the documentary evidence and written material that they were introducing. No translation at all had been made of the briefs upon which the American lawyers were basing their cases, and the defense attorneys had not even been given the texts in English. On the third day of the trial, Lawrence suggested that the defense counsel should have "at least one copy between each two of them here in court."

Storey promised that copies would be placed in the Defendants' Information Center, and that the prosecution would assign "German-speaking officers in the Document Room who will translate for any of them who may not be able to read German—pardon me, to read English," a slip of the tongue that produced merriment. A list of the documents, but not the documents themselves, had been placed in the Defendants' Information Center on November 1; and Storey pointed out that each attorney had been at liberty to request a copy of whatever document he desired. He had to agree with Lawrence, however, that "the defendants' counsel wouldn't know which out of that list of documents were going to be relied upon."

Additionally, only a fraction of the 2,500 documents that formed the core of the prosecution's case had been included in the original list. On the afternoon of Friday, November 23, Walter Siemers, Admiral Raeder's counsel, protested: "This morning a list was made available to us in Room 54. I have it in my hand. This morning nine documents were named. Of these nine documents, only one, contrary to what the prosecution said, was found in the old list; the other eight documents were neither in the old list nor in the new list. The other eight documents are, as I ascertained at lunchtime today, not in the Document Room. Neither are they available in photostatic copies."

Storey kept pleading a poverty of facilities and an overworked staff: "I wonder if the tribunal and defense counsel realize the physical problems that are imposed?" His organization was working twenty-four hours a day, but, "again, sir, I call attention to the physical problems that are almost insurmountable: to make twenty-three photostatic copies which are required of every document . . ."

Alderman chipped in: "I understand that both our photostatic facilities and our mimeograph facilities are right up to the hilt with work. It is a very difficult mechanical problem."

Upon the convening of the court on Monday, November 26, Lawrence ruled: "In the future, only such parts of documents as are read in court by the prosecution shall in the first instance be part of the record." A photostatic copy of the original of all such documents was to be deposited in the Defendants' Information Center. Ten copies of the trial briefs and five copies of the document books were to be furnished to the defendants' counsel, each of whom was also to receive a copy of the transcript in German.

The issue resurfaced that afternoon when Goering's counsel, Otto Stahmer, objected that one of the documents referring to Hitler's Obersalzberg meeting on August 22, 1939, ordering the attack on Poland, had been given to the press, although it was not introduced into evidence.

Alderman admitted, "I feel somewhat guilty. It is quite true that, by a mechanical slip, the press got the first documents . . ."

"The tribunal would like to know how many of these documents are given to the press," Lawrence asked.

"I think about two hundred and fifty copies of each one, about two hundred or two hundred and fifty mimeographed copies," Storey replied.

It took a moment for this information to sink in. Biddle looked at Lawrence, then held a hurried conversation with him. Storey's pleadings were exposed as specious—the prosecution seemed to have been more interested in trying the case in the press than in furnishing the defense with copies of its evidence. Biddle was indignant, and Nikitchenko was as upset as the German defense attorneys: the Russians, too, wanted copies of the documents before they were given to the press.

"The tribunal thinks that the defendants' counsel should have copies of these documents before any of them are handed to the press," Lawrence told Storey. "I mean to say that in preference to the gentlemen of the press, the defendants' counsel should have the documents."

Storey appeared unable to comprehend what Lawrence was saying, and kept protesting that copies were now being placed in the Defendants' Information Center.

"You don't seem to understand," Lawrence finally repeated for the third time, "what I am putting to you, which is this: That if you can afford to give two hundred and fifty copies of the documents in English to the press, you can afford to give more than five copies to the defendants' counsel—one each. Well, we do not need to discuss it further. In the future that will be done." Henceforth, one hundred copies of the briefs and fifty of the document books were to be reproduced so that each judge and every defense counsel could be provided with a copy prior to the presentation.

This chastening of the prosecution by the judges was heartening to the defense. But a far more important ruling was to follow, as Jackson's plan to pick and choose excerpts from interrogatories and depositions started to unravel.

First, Raeder's attorney, Walter Siemers, objected to the prosecution's introduction of an extract from the admiral's interrogation: "I am surprised that the prosecution wishes to furnish proof by way of records of interrogations, taken at a time when the defense was not present. I should be obliged to the court if I could be told whether, in principle, I, as the defense counsel, may resort to producing evidence in this form; that is to say, documents in which I myself interrogated witnesses the same as the prosecution without putting witnesses on the stand."

That, of course, was putting the question squarely as to whether there was going to be one set of rules for the prosecution and another for the defense. Lawrence, for the moment, sidestepped the issue, though the answer could not be in doubt. He declared that, if any portion of an interrogatory were to be used by the prosecution, all of it would have to be made available to the defense beforehand, a ruling that in itself tended to have an inhibitory effect upon Jackson's employment of the defendants' statements.

It was evident even to Jackson that it was necessary to spice up the trial. He decided, therefore, to introduce, following the exposition of the Anschluss, an hour-long film on concentration camps. When, on November 29, the court prepared to adjourn for its ten-minute afternoon break, Alderman informed the judges: "Logically we should proceed at this point with the story about Czechoslovakia [but] it is planned by our staff to show a motion picture."

During the intermission, the defendants were in a light mood. Chuckling, they recalled the bouquets with which the Wehrmacht had been greeted in "The War of Flowers," and Hitler's triumphant entry into Vienna. Then, the seats in the press and visitor galleries filled up, court reconvened, the lights went out, and a row of dim bulbs recessed into the balustrade of the dock went on so that the guards could continue to observe the defendants. The screen filled with images of skeletal men and women, crematoria and gas chambers, the scarred and disfigured bodies of women who had survived medical experiments, mound upon mound of cadavers whose sticklike arms and legs gave the appearance of jumbled piles of driftwood, displays of human lampshades, Germans holding their noses as they were compelled into sightseeing tours through the camps and impressed into burying details, and tractors pushing the dead into mass graves like contaminated jetsam. The juxtapositioning of the motion picture with the levity that had preceded it heightened the effect and horror. The accused were graphically confronted with the product of the regime whose leaders they had been. Funk, biting his knuckles, cried like a baby; Sauckel shuddered; Schirach gasped; tears welled in Ribbentrop's eyes; Hess appeared bewildered. None watched the movie in its entirety. Schacht turned his back and later exploded: "How dare they make me sit there with those criminals and watch a film on concentration camp atrocities!"

In his cell that evening Fritzsche exclaimed: "No power in heaven or earth will erase this shame from my country—not in generations—not in centuries!" Frank, similarly emotional, burst out: "To think we lived like kings and believed in that beast! Don't let anybody tell you they had no idea! Everybody sensed that there was something horribly wrong with this system, even if we didn't know all the details. They didn't want to know! It was too comfortable to live on the system, to support our families in royal style, and to believe that it was all right. May God have mercy on our souls!"

Sauckel and Ribbentrop were still trembling and shaking hours afterward. Hess kept muttering over and over, "I don't understand, I don't understand."

Goering, deflated, shook his head: "It was such a good afternoon, too —and then they showed that awful film, and it just spoiled everything!"

20 Conflict: Donovan versus Jackson

The following day, Jackson, attempting to stem the grumbling of his staff and still press criticism of his conduct of the case, introduced a former Austrian army intelligence officer as the prosecution's first witness. Ironically, Major General Erwin Lahousen had already been the catalyst for a major split in the Office of the Chief of Counsel.

Forty-eight years old, Lahousen, a major at the time of the Anschluss, had petitioned to be absorbed into the Abwehr (Wehrmacht intelligence) following Hitler's annexation of Austria. Within a few months he had become executive officer to the Abwehr chief, Admiral Wilhelm Canaris. As such, his name had become familiar to General William Donovan, head of the OSS, all the more so because a number of high-ranking Abwehr officers had been at the nexus of the opposition to Hitler.

Donovan, having made the OSS manpower available to Jackson and facilitated the gathering of evidence, had expected to play a role in the trial second only to the justice's. But he had been in the Far East from the middle of July until October, and had not returned to Europe until the issuing of the indictment in Berlin. When he arrived in Nuremberg, he became a focal point for the former members of the OSS, most of whom idolized him but rarely saw Jackson. He made no secret of his opinion that the case required more administrative control, intellectual direction, and cohesiveness, and that "because it was a lawsuit plus something else it needed an affirmative human aspect with German as well as foreign witnesses."

He stepped into the middle of the high-command controversy by calling the procedure used to indict the German general staff "unbecoming to our country." He believed it dishonest and hypocritical to ignore the fact that, whatever their motives, a large number of the Wehrmacht leaders had opposed Hitler's bellicose plans and had been, from 1938 to 1944, among the men plotting to depose him. He urged a revision of the indictment "so that such members as were participants be charged individually and not by position and by function. I have never agreed with those of our regular army who think that there should be no criminal charge against the general staff. Perhaps it would have been better to shoot the guilty ones. Since we elected to proceed by indictment I think we should do it properly. It is repugnant to me that there should be any pretext as we find in the trial today for the defendants to assert that the prosecution is unfair."

Aside from Jackson's lack of appreciation for this criticism, he resented the fact that Donovan had absented himself during the preparatory work, then popped up again a month before the trial was scheduled to get under way. Although the two men were on "Bob" and "Bill" terms, they had been longtime political opponents in New York State. Donovan had once run for governor on the Republican ticket, was a supporter of Thomas Dewey, and, as a cosmopolitan, big business, Wall Street lawyer, represented all that was anathema to the Democratic, small-town, upstate Jackson.

In meetings with Storey and the board of review, Donovan repeatedly expressed the opinion that the trial could not be prosecuted merely on documentary evidence. On November 7, Jackson assigned Storey the task of discovering what role Donovan had in mind for himself. Donovan was affronted that Jackson did not personally ask that question of him, and interpreted it as "indicating that you considered that you saw no place for me. I am sorry you did not take a different means of telling me. I told Storey that you had the right—as you had the responsibility—to prepare and try the case as you wanted, and to make your decision without asking my opinion." Accordingly, Donovan advised Jackson, he would finish up his business at Nuremberg and leave.

Jackson replied immediately that there had been a misunderstanding. "I anticipated you would prefer to work with live witnesses or cross-examination of defendants and defense witnesses. But it is not likely that the defense part of the case will be reached until after the first of the year." He did not plan to make a determination on the use of witnesses until after the completion of the documentary case. Since he understood that Donovan intended to return to his law practice by January, there seemed to be an obvious conflict. "If you are of the opinion that the trial as it is now shaping up does not present a place of interest to you, I shall understand and accept your decision. But I do not want you to reach that conclusion on any misunderstanding of the motives either of myself or of Colonel Storey."

On this note, Donovan's position in the trial was left suspended for two weeks. Donovan was well acquainted with Colonel Murray Gurfein who, in preparing the economics case, had been questioning Schacht and Goering, and with Commander Ralph G. Albrecht, another New York lawyer, who had responsibility for the individual case against the Reichsmarshal. He accompanied both Gurfein and Albrecht, as well as Amen, to interrogations. The OSS chief had the knack, born of a man skilled at intelligence gathering, of projecting a sympathetic air. Schacht, who had ultimately joined the July 20 conspiracy, was anxious to divorce himself from his co-defendants. He wished to testify against Hitler, so long as he was able to act the part of a German Nationalist, and not appear to be a handmaiden of the prosecution. On November 14 he sent a message to Donovan:

"I am among the few people who have watched and gone through the frightful events of the last twelve years in Germany from nearby and with open eyes. Thanks to my official position I think I know more of the background of Hitler's policy than many others.

"I welcome the installation of the International Military Tribunal. I submit myself voluntarily to this court, in the justice of which I have full confidence. I do it the more willingly as the trial will prove that I am in no way guilty of any crime or any immorality.

"I would therefore be very grateful if an officer of your high standing, of your experience and wisdom and of your well-known international reputation, would be willing to look into a brief summary of the underlying reasons and conditions of the dreadful Nazi regime, as I have experienced them."

Donovan immediately talked the matter over with Gurfein, and they agreed that Schacht would make a useful and dramatic witness. Donovan addressed Jackson:

"Schacht made possible the rearmament project. It was his support in financial matters that strengthened Hitler's position. Aided by influences and what he should have known about Hitler's character, we may have enough to hold him for aggressive war. There is strong argument in this.

"[But] Schacht claims that Roosevelt sent him a message that he would be needed after the war. He worked with the resistance movement and finally found himself in a Gestapo prison and then in a concentration camp.

"It is also true that Don Heath of the American Embassy in Berlin in 1940 was keeping in touch with Schacht on behalf of the State Department. Heath says that our advance notice of the attack on Russia was given to Heath through Schacht.

"In view of all this I return to the suggestion that consideration be given to the possibility of giving him the opportunity to fight his way out by actual testimony dealing with the facts. He could strengthen our case considerably and without promises he could be given the chance in the direct case to state his position."

Jackson did not reply. Goering, however, got wind that Donovan was open to offers, and might be willing to make him the star of the drama. Goering and Donovan were skilled, well-matched antagonists, each intending to manipulate and make use of the other.* The former Reichsmarshal indicated that he was willing to testify against the dead Himmler and Heydrich, as well as some of his co-defendants, such as Ribbentrop, Kaltenbrunner, Streicher, Schacht, and Speer, with whom he had never gotten along.

While Jackson attempted to deal with Donovan by ignoring him, Amen voiced his irritation at Donovan's horning in on his preserve. He considered Lahousen, who was ever ready to jump to the winning side and

---

*Goering had taken an almost avuncular interest in Sonnenfeldt, whose family he had hounded out of Germany a few years before. At one point, Sonnenfeldt translated a statement by Goering as, "I don't admit that." Donovan, taking issue with the translation, corrected: "I think he said 'I don't agree to that.' " Goering, bristling that the accuracy of his favorite should be impugned, declared in guttural English: "I *said* I don't *admit* that."

had offered to tell all he knew about Admiral Canaris, the Wehrmacht, the atrocities, Keitel, and the German High Command as potentially his star witness.

Early in November, Lahousen was moved from the witness wing of the jail to the Guest House. There he joined the Hitler-hating Wehrmacht historian Wilhelm Scheidt, who had turned over his records to the American army and had now fallen in love with the Countess Kalnoky. Scheidt's rival was Rudolf Diels, the macho, charming, debonair and lying first head of the Gestapo, who viewed himself as irresistible to women. Diels grated on the onetime (1930 to 1933) president of the Reichsbank, Dr. Hans Luther, who was forced to take his meals listening to Hoffmann's tales of Hitler's fascinating personality and Diels's accounts of the charms of Goering.

Lahousen, accompanied by a guard, kept mostly to himself and was a terrible sight. Tall, cadaverous, hollow-eyed from insomnia, he suffered from a heart condition, and chewed his nails so persistently they seemed to have receded into his fingertips. His only clothes consisted of a dirty, battered army jacket, threadbare trousers, a frayed silk scarf, and a dark blue beret perched atop his bald head—it was an attire made all the more incongruous by his habit of bowing mechanically whenever he met or passed anyone, even if it was on the way to the bathroom. To improve Lahousen's appearance, the Americans requisitioned one of the suits belonging to Herr Krulle, the absent owner of the house, and had it retailored for Lahousen. (Frau Krulle, like the proprietors of other requisitioned homes, lived in the basement.)

But since Lahousen appeared shattered internally as well as externally, and was given to fits of weeping, more concrete measures seemed necessary to build him up for his ordeal as a witness. When it became known that he longed for his girl friend, a young woman half his age, the Americans rushed her to Nuremberg. The guard who had been sleeping in his room was ejected, and the more complaisant companion installed in his place.

Late in the afternoon of Thursday, November 22, Lahousen received a message that General Donovan wanted him to come to his house for dinner that evening. Amen had previously informed Lahousen that he was to work with Sonnenfeldt on the preparation of his trial testimony that night. But since a general outranked a colonel, and a meeting with Donovan promised both potential advantages and an elegant dinner, Lahousen decided to go.

Amen, furious, brought Lahousen in for a grilling the next morning, and threatened to put him back in jail. Lahousen, wringing his hands, asserted that he could not refuse the command of a general: "I am here in the position of an object—nothing more. I can't protest like I used to do in my better days."

Amen, in a stew, went to Jackson and voiced the opinion that Donovan was trying to usurp the role of chief examiner and cross-examiner in court, and was threatening to throw a monkeywrench into the whole proceedings. Jackson immediately issued a memorandum that, in effect, placed Donovan under the authority of Amen. Only persons authorized by the Office of the Chief of Counsel were to be permitted to be billeted in the Guest House. There was to be no entertainment of anyone held in custody. "Witnesses shall be interrogated, communicated with or interviewed on behalf of this office only by persons authorized in writing to do so. No agreement shall be made with any defense counsel on behalf of this office for the use by the United States of any defendant as a witness except upon written authorization. It will be the general policy that no defendant will be used as a witness for the prosecution who does not in advance make a written and signed statement incriminating other defendants against whom other evidence in our possession is deemed weak or insufficient to establish guilt. No promise of leniency, or promise to recommend it, and no intimation that leniency will or may follow shall be given to any defendant or his counsel."

Donovan replied in a conciliatory tone that he had kept both the review board and Jackson apprised of his talks with Schacht and Goering: "I have informed the planning committee it was my purpose to ask a decision from you as to the use of the defendant Goering only after I submitted to you through the committee a full written question and answer statement containing the necessary safeguards usually surrounding a confession." Donovan requested that Goering be made available Sunday afternoon and thereafter for questioning. "This is damn hard work and, if he is to be ready, the present momentum must not be lost."

Jackson did not immediately reply, but agitated over the matter all day Sunday. Monday he responded:

"You and I appear to have developed certain fundamental differences in viewpoint about this case. Time alone will tell which of us is right, but there can be no doubt that the case cannot follow both our lines.

"During your long absence from the case, my own confidence grew with study of the document analyses that our case could safely rest wholly on documents and that witnesses need be used, if at all, only incidentally. I was and am willing to consider use of any witness but only if he has made a complete written statement of what his testimony is.

"Meanwhile, other differences of viewpoint have developed. I understand you have expressed complete disagreement with the indictment of the General Staff and High Command. Obviously if the work you're doing with the witnesses or with such a defendant as Goering reflects this attitude, it is at odds with the policy of the case as settled by the indictment and may result in serious embarrassment. . . .

"Now the question as between you and John Amen as to which shall examine and cross-examine defendants and witnesses is not simply a personal one, or one of military rank. He has been for months at work with these defendants and witnesses. So far as I know, John has worked fully in accord with my view of the policy of the case. Frankly, Bill, your views and mine appear to be so far apart that I do not consider it possible to assign you to examination or cross-examination of witnesses.

"Time may prove you right and me wrong. I do not claim any great wisdom in so novel and complex a matter. I only have responsibility."

Jackson was, in effect, terminating Donovan's association with the case. Donovan replied the following day, reiterating that he had kept the review board fully informed, that he had no disagreement with the lodging of charges against the general staff, only with the method that was employed, and that there never had been a question of negotiating or bargaining with the defendants. Jackson was, of course, to have had final approval of the use of Goering as a witness.

"I agree that the case is foolproof and of itself needs no such statement. But a confession from the last sane leader of the gang might well be of value in a larger sense. This was not intended as a 'stunt,' or as a dramatic episode, but as a very practical means of bringing home to the German people the guilt of these men.

"To accept or exclude this kind of testimony after reading it is an exercise of judgment. To exclude it before doing so—is something less.

"There is not—and never has been, so far as I am concerned—any question between Amen and me on examination of defendants or witnesses. That is just absurd. If one exists in your mind, you have been tilting at windmills. Amen can do the job. Your mind may work that way—mine does not." He would leave within a few days. Gurfein, who had wanted to use Schacht as the focal point for the economics case, decided to go with him.*

Having bested Donovan, Jackson was immediately embroiled in a dispute with the court over Lahousen's projected appearance.

Nikitchenko, suspicious of American intentions, objected to the calling of any witness before all four prosecuting nations had concluded their documentary cases. Finally, after an hour's deliberation, the judges agreed

---

*Both Jackson and Donovan were closemouthed, and went to their deaths without revealing the nature of their disagreement.

to permit Lahousen to testify, but ruled that he must be restricted to Count One: The Conspiracy. Since, however, Lahousen's testimony had nothing at all to do with the conspiracy, per se, Jackson responded that it would be impossible to abide by the ruling: "I think, perhaps, the best way to do is to swear the witness, and that the other prosecutors, if they feel their field is being trespassed upon, or the judges, if they feel that we are exceeding, raise the objection specifically; because I don't know how we can separate, particularly on a moment's notice, Count One from the other counts."

The defense counsel protested that they had been under the impression that they were going to be notified a day in advance whenever a witness was going to be called.

"I know of no agreement to inform defendants' counsel of any witness, nor of his testimony; nor would I want to make such," Jackson retorted. "There are security reasons involved in disclosing to defense counsel the names of witnesses, which I don't need to enlarge upon, I am quite sure.

"These witnesses are not always prisoners. And the protection of their security is a very important consideration where we are trying this case, in the very hotbed of the Nazi organization with which some of defense counsel were identified."

It was the kind of off-the-cuff remark that Jackson's best friends wished he would refrain from. No more than a third of the attorneys had had even a vague connection with the Nazi Party, and a number had been as staunchly anti-Nazi as it was possible to be in the Third Reich. Lawrence himself was taken aback:

"I think, Mr. Justice Jackson, that that is sufficient. If you tell the tribunal that there was no such agreement, the tribunal will, of course, accept that."

Biddle, taking notes, wrote: "Jackson's talk about security reasons is bunk." The truth was that if Heinrich Hoffmann could lodge with the witnesses, have the run of the Palace of Justice, and visit the Gasthaus zum Stern, the tavern that had become the favorite gathering place of the defense attorneys, reference to "security" was laughable. The reporters, for one, were snickering. The prosecution had informed all 250 of them the previous day about Lahousen's upcoming appearance. Jackson simply did not wish to give the defense an opportunity to prepare for cross-examination.

Lahousen looked startlingly like an ambulatory figure from a wax museum as he traversed the courtroom with a stiff, stiltlike walk, halted before the judges' bench to bow, and moved on to the witness stand. Amen's specific intent was to forestall any public criticism by Donovan of

the indictment of the general staff and the High Command; and he therefore directed his examination of Lahousen toward the Wehrmacht leadership's complicity in war crimes and atrocities. Without laying any foundation or providing any background for the court, Amen conducted
Lahousen through a recitation of a bewildering variety of largely unrelated events: a plot to kill French Generals Maxime Weygand and Henri
Giraud to preclude their rallying of French forces in North Africa; the
starvation and systematic murder of Soviet prisoners of war; Hitler's order
to kill British commandos after they surrendered; and a plan to foment an
uprising by Polish Ukrainians against Poles and Jews.

The overall effect was one of confusion and stupefaction. The design
against the French generals hardly seemed criminal in the context of war;
and the incitement of discord was within the accepted practices of psychological warfare. The remainder of Lahousen's testimony was anticipatory
of the development of the case in the weeks to come. While the evidence
he gave would have been relevant in a month, it lost most of its force in
its anachronistic presentation.

Subjected to cross-examination, Lahousen became evasive, and his
posture as an anti-Nazi man of principle cracked. Fritz Sauter (representing Ribbentrop, Funk, and Schirach) was the principal defense attorney
to impeach Lahousen's honesty.

"Witness," Sauter declared, "your memory deceives you, because immediately after Hitler's attack on Austria you called on the general staff
in Berlin and there you tried to get a commission in the German Wehrmacht, and you now deny this. You also filled in and signed a questionnaire
in which you declared your complete allegiance to the Greater German
Reich, and to Adolf Hitler; and shortly afterward you took the oath of
allegiance to Adolf Hitler."

"I can easily explain why my rise in office was so rapid," Lahousen
tried to exculpate himself. As an Austrian military intelligence officer his
efforts, he said, had been specifically "directed against the neighboring
country of Czechoslovakia. Czechoslovakia was the country that was next
on the list after Austria. Therefore, it was natural that my later chief,
Canaris, was very interested in having me promoted in his department."

"Then it is true you did go to Berlin and apply to be transferred into
the German Wehrmacht, which you at first denied?" Sauter continued.

"No, that is not true, I did not apply. Others made the request. I can
even say that I did not go there: I flew there!" Lahousen protested, as
Biddle's eyebrows arched.

Sauter, who for a short time had been a member of the Nazi Party but
had been expelled for defending Jews and Communists, for his part revealed an astonishing sophistry and psychological obtuseness that was

characteristic of a large number of the defense counsel throughout the trial. "You have told us about murderous designs on which you or your department or other offices were employed or which you were charged to carry out. Did you report these to any police stations as the law required?" Sauter asked in all seriousness, as if he were a hybrid of Candide and Rip Van Winkle. "May I point out that, according to German law, failure to report intended crimes is punishable with imprisonment or in serious cases with death." Such puerile casuistry made it, in a sense, more comprehensible how Hitler had been able to exercise his mastery over the German people.

When the defendants were taken to the elevator at the conclusion of court Friday afternoon. Hess and his attorney remained in the room. After a forty-five-minute break, during which the judges partook of tea and delicacies in their conference room, court was reconvened to consider the question of Hess's sanity.

In the week prior to the trial, Hess had been examined by no fewer than ten psychiatrists—two American, one French, one Canadian, three British, and three Russian. They all agreed that he was a paranoid psychopath suffering from hysterical amnesia, generated as a defense mechanism. He would be able to comprehend the proceedings, though his ability to present his case would be limited.

"The experts themselves are," Hess's attorney, Gunther von Rohrscheidt, contended, "obviously not quite sure whether the defendant Hess, beyond his inability to plead, is insane or at least not of sound mind." He suggested that Hess be subjected to a more extensive psychiatric investigation.

Jackson opposed the motion: "He has refused every simple treatment that has been suggested. . . . The medication which was suggested to bring him out of this hysterical situation was the use of intravenous drugs of the barbital series. . . . He is in the volunteer class with his amnesia. When he was in England, as the reports show, he is reported to have made the statement that his earlier amnesia was simulated. He came out of this state during a period in England, and went back into it. It is now highly selective. That is to say, you can't be sure what Hess will remember and what he will not remember.

"So we feel that so long as Hess refuses the ordinary, simple expedients, even if his amnesia is genuine, that he is not in a position to continue to assert that he must not be brought to trial."

Rohrscheidt pointed out that Hess had had a lifelong aversion to standard medical treatment, and had even founded the Rudolf Hess Hospital in Dresden, which treated patients with nothing but homeopathic remedies.

Hess, listening to the debate over his sanity, was anxious to voice his own opinion. As a weak, dependent character, he had loved good, kind "older brother" Adolf. But as a basically decent and honest person (despite his paranoid obsession with anti-Semitism), he had been baffled by the cruel, malicious, brutal, war-loving Hitler.

The attempt to escape from his dilemma through amnesia was, however, now generating a new conflict. Earlier in the day Gilbert had told him that he would probably be ruled incompetent to defend himself. Consequently, he would not be coming to court anymore, but would be separated from his co-defendants. Hess was visibly upset. For more than four years he had been isolated in an alien country among people out of sympathy with his National Socialist beliefs. Less than two months before, he had been returned to the milieu of his compatriots, and their companionship gave him psychological security. The thought of being removed and isolated from them once more was unbearable.

Lawrence and Nikitchenko opposed permitting Hess to speak. But Biddle, supported by de Vabres, once more imposed his wishes upon the tribunal's president. Hess, informed he could have his say, jumped up from his seat and began reading from a slip of paper:

"In order to forestall the possibility of my being pronounced incapable of pleading, in spite of my willingness to take part in the proceedings and to hear the verdict alongside my comrades, I would like to make the following declaration before the tribunal although, originally, I intended to make it during a later stage of the trial:

"Henceforth my memory will again respond to the outside world. The reasons for simulating loss of memory were of a tactical nature. Only my ability to concentrate is, in fact, somewhat reduced. But my capacity to follow the trial, to defend myself, to put questions to witnesses, or to answer questions myself is not affected thereby.

"I emphasize that I bear full responsibility for everything that I did, signed, or co-signed. My fundamental attitude that the tribunal is not competent is not affected by the statement I have just made. I also simulated loss of memory in consultation with my officially appointed defense counsel. He has, therefore, represented it in good faith."

Momentarily, everyone was stunned by Hess's declaration. The judges, who had been faced with a difficult decision, were relieved. After Hess's assertion that he had been shamming, it was virtually impossible for the tribunal to rule that he was incapable of defending himself, though no impartial observer could question his mental instability. (Parker pointed out that the law did not recognize amnesia as a defense.)

For the next few days, Hess, pleased with the sensation he had generated, appeared better. Then he relapsed, and his mind slipped back into its apathetic meanderings and paranoia. He thought that the extra K-rations, which Dr. Pflücker weekly divided among the defendants, were intended to poison him, and one day passed a note around the dock inquiring if any of his co-defendants were willing to offer themselves as guinea pigs. Fritzsche volunteered; and, as Hess looked on with alarm, tipped the packet of sugar that Hess handed him into his mouth. The next day, Hess wanted to know what had happened; and Fritzsche, willing to conduct further "tests," informed Hess that he had suffered some discomfort, but it was too early to tell. Goering jealously offered to join Fritzsche as a test subject; and together the two of them strove to relieve Hess of his sweets and supplemental rations.

21   The Rape of Czechoslovakia

On Monday, December 2, Alderman resumed his recitation of the Nazi conspiracy to wage aggressive war with, as he termed it, "the rape of Czechoslovakia."

The lesson perceived by Hitler from his sudden, bloodless Austrian triumph had been that the same tactics of bluff, terrorization, propaganda, and precipitate action that had worked so well in the domestic sphere could be employed with equal success on the international scene.

Czechoslovakia, which had been carved out of the Austro-Hungarian Empire like a drumstick after World War I, was an agglomeration of seven ethnic groups, totaling thirteen million people. Their cohesion stemmed from the natural borders within which they were contained, but they otherwise had little to hold them together. The inclusion of three and a quarter million Sudeten Germans had been an anomaly from the start. Their natural ties were with Germany; but removal of the Sudetenland from the territory of Czechoslovakia—a process upon which Hitler now embarked—would make the survival of the rest of the nation problematical at best.

Hitler's initial plans for "Case Green," the assault against Czechoslovakia, were, he instructed Keitel and Jodl, predicated on the arising of some "especially favorable opportunity" within the context of European developments. Since, however, a large number of the German generals were of the opinion that, with the current condition of the Wehrmacht, an attack on Czechoslovakia resulting in a general European war would be suicidal, they were leaking information to western intelligence. This, in turn, led to the misconception in Czechoslovakia and the West that the assault Hitler was contemplating at some future time was imminent. In late May, a crisis along the border resulted.

Hitler, thereupon, lost patience. On May 23, he altered the preamble of Case Green to read: "It is my unalterable decision to smash Czechoslovakia by military action in the near future." A week later, on May 30, he signed the directive initiating preparations for the attack, to begin no later than October 1.

Hitler was now determined to go to war, come what might. His minimum demands, he pointed out, were such that the Czechs could not accede to them without committing national suicide. "I can see now that Clausewitz was right," he remarked at maneuvers in August. "War is the father of all things. Every generation has to go to war once. At first we shall take the thirty-five-year-olds; and then we shall carry the big thing [war against the West and Russia] with the younger generation."

On September 1, the Nationalist finance minister, Count Lutz Schwerin von Krosigk (one of the last remaining members of the original Hitler cabinet) appealed to Hitler to change course. Germany's national debt had tripled during the past six years; and, with the increased tempo of armaments production and the expansion of the Wehrmacht, a financial crisis was impending. The treasury was empty. Fear of war and inflation had caused both consumers and industry to initiate a buying spree and to refuse to subscribe to government bonds. German public opinion was overwhelmingly against going to war over Czechoslovakia and risking a general European conflagration.

"Whether or not the war stays localized in the event of a showdown with Czechoslovakia depends mainly on England," Krosigk, who had graduated from Oxford, believed. Britain's "repeatedly expressed attitude to take action is *no* bluff. The fact that England is not ready for war militarily does not prevent England from entering it. Because she possesses two great trump cards. One is the soon expected active participation of the United States of America in the war—American industry, now only occupied to the extent of twenty-five percent, would at once be converted into a war industry of unimaginable productive capacity. The second trump card is Germany's financial and economic weakness, although she has a head start militarily. In my opinion, it is Utopian to think we can secure the necessary raw materials with imports from the Southeast and the exploitation of our own resources. Economically, we are in a position which corresponds with Germany's situation in 1917. The western powers would not run against the West Wall but would let Germany's economic weakness take effect until we, after early military successes, become weaker and weaker and finally lose our military advantage due to delivery of armaments and airplanes by the United States."

In the Third Reich, the messenger bearing unwelcome news was barred from the presence of the the Führer thereafter; and Krosigk, although he continued as minister of finance to the end of the regime, never again had a personal audience with Hitler. Beyond that, his warning had the opposite of the intended effect. For if the German economy was about to go into crisis, war would preempt that cataclysm. And if England was going to stand by her principles in any case, it was certainly better to challenge her while she was unprepared than after she had had time to modernize her forces.

Goering, eyeing the industrialized Sudetenland as a boost for his empire, railed before the massed party ranks at the Nuremberg rally on September 10: "A trifling segment of Europe is making life unbearable for mankind. This miserable [Czech] pigmy race is oppressing a cultured people; and behind them can be seen Moscow and the eternal mask of the Jewish fiends."

The French, whose high command shared the view of the German generals that war would bring disaster, begged sixty-nine-year-old British Prime Minister Neville Chamberlain to try to head off a conflict. Chamberlain, as petrified as the French by German air superiority, envisioned clouds of Luftwaffe planes dropping poison gas on London. On the night of September 13 he sent a message to Hitler: "I propose to come over at once to see you with a view of trying to find a peaceful solution."

Twice during the next two weeks Chamberlain met with Hitler, who had not the slightest interest in defusing the crisis; whenever one of his demands was met, he simply raised another. On the night of September 26, he stood shrieking and gesticulating before a jammed audience at the Sportspalast, and hurled his gauntlet at the world: "I approached all apparently impossible problems with the firm determination to solve them in a peaceful manner even at the cost of more or less heavy German concessions," he prevaricated. "I am a front line soldier myself and I know the hardships of a war. I wanted to spare the German people. . . . Now we are confronted with the last problem which must be solved. It is the last territorial claim which I have to make in Europe. . . . And that, I will guarantee. We don't want any Czechs at all. But I must also declare before the German people that in the Sudeten German problem my patience is now at an end." If by 2 PM on the twenty-eighth his demands were still unmet, Germany would mobilize (officially), and war would follow.

By and large, this was too much for all but the most bellicose members of Hitler's entourage, such as Ribbentrop and Speer. "My Führer, do you wish to start a war under any circumstance? Of course not," Neurath, acting as foreign policy adviser, argued rhetorically, and was supported by Goering, intent on achieving Germany's goals by scheming and manipulating, not fighting.

Hitler, faced with the reality that his generals, a large part of his inner circle, and the preponderance of the German people all lacked the spirit for war, reluctantly permitted Neurath to arrange the Munich Conference with Mussolini and Prime Ministers Chamberlain of England and Daladier of France. Goering and Neurath devised a wily scheme to have the German plan, incorporating all the Nazi wishes, introduced as a "compromise" by Mussolini. Daladier acted more like a dazed spectator than a participant in one of the most important gatherings in the history of Europe. Chamberlain was isolated. Since no agenda had been prepared, there was a general atmosphere of confusion. From 1:30 PM on September 29 until the signing of the pact at 2:30 AM on the thirtieth, people wandered in and out, small groups huddled here and there, and sometimes three, four, or five persons spoke simultaneously.

"Actually, the whole thing was a cut-and-dried affair," Goering remarked to Gilbert in the jail after the presentation of the evidence on the Munich Pact. "I was simply amazed at how easily the thing was managed by Hitler. After all, they knew that Skoda, and others, had munition plants in the Sudetenland, and Czechoslovakia would be at our mercy. We got everything that we wanted. Just like that!" He snapped his fingers.

22 Kristallnacht: *The Plot Against the Jews*

Hitler had not the least intention of keeping the Munich agreement. To Schacht he grumbled: "That damn Chamberlain has spoiled my parade into Prague!" To Keitel he issued a directive: "Liquidation of the rest of Czechoslovakia."

"The preparations for this eventuality are to continue on the assumption that no resistance worth mentioning is to be expected. To the outside world too it must clearly appear that it is merely an act of pacification, and not a warlike undertaking."

"In a conference on October 14, 1938," the prosecution continued its chronology, "the Defendant Goering stated that the Führer had instructed him to carry out a gigantic program, by comparison with which the performances thus far were insignificant."

It was true, Goering told the economics and production ministers, that as a consequence of the armaments buildup and the decline in international trade associated with the Austrian and Czech crises the treasury was empty. Foreign credits were greatly overdrawn. German industrial capacity was booked with orders for years ahead. But all this, he declared, would be "overcome with utmost energy and ruthlessness." Exports were to be increased. The construction of railroads, highways, and canals was to be accelerated. Armaments production was to be multiplied "to an extraordinary extent, the air force having first priority. Within the briefest time the air force is to increase fivefold, the navy shall be armed more rapidly, and the army should procure large amounts of offensive weapons at a faster rate, particularly heavy artillery pieces and heavy tanks."

If necessary, Goering continued, he would "make barbaric use of the plenipotentiary powers given me by the Führer." Plants producing for domestic consumption were to be converted to the manufacture of armaments and export goods. "A retraining of hundreds of thousands of people will have to take place. Much more work will have to be performed by women than until now. Work periods of eight hours do not exist anymore. Wherever necessary, overtime is to be performed, double and triple shifts are a matter of course. When the workers will protest, as in Austria, [I] will proceed with forced labor, and create camps for forced labor. It is a fact that one generation has driven the cart into the mud as a result of the mutiny of the workers, and because it was guilty of not having shot these workers on the spot. Therefore, we have to put the thing in order again."

In addition to the Sudetenland, the remainder of Czechoslovakia was to be turned into a dominion and exploited for the benefit of Germany. The Jews, Goering went on, would have to get out of the economy. Jewish labor units should be established. The Jews would then emigrate of their own accord.

Where would they go? That was *their* problem.

Those with assets abroad had no difficulty procuring visas, but not a single nation in the world, including the United States, was willing to expand its quota or accept those that might become public charges.

Hungary and Poland refused to permit the return of Jews who had previously migrated to Germany. Several score Hungarian Jews wound up cast away on an island and on barges on the Danube. The plight of the Polish Jews was no less difficult. Some sixty thousand had gone to Germany between 1918 and 1933 because of the anti-Semitic policies of the Polish regime. Most had managed to improve their condition despite the hostility of the Nazis, the Nationalists, and many German Jews, who regarded the orthodoxy of the Polish Jews as a throwback to the Middle Ages. When the Nazis announced their intention to deport these Jews back to Poland, the Poles deprived them of citizenship and closed the border to them. Thousands became stranded without shelter and little food in the border area between the two nations.

Among the emigrants was Zindel Grynszpan, who had been born in western Poland when it was part of the Imperial Reich and had moved to Hanover, where he established a small store, in 1911. On the night of October 27 Grynszpan and his family were rousted out of their home. Grynszpan's store and the family's possessions were confiscated. Penniless, famished, soaked to the skin and freezing, they were herded over the Polish border.

Zindel Grynszpan's seventeen-year-old son, Herschel, was living with an uncle in Paris. When he received a letter from his father containing an account of the expulsion, he decided to strike back in order to demonstrate that "Jews are not animals." Resolving to assassinate the German ambassador, he went to the embassy on November 7. When he was unable to get near his target, he settled on a more accessible diplomat, Third Secretary Ernst vom Rath. Rath, who, as it happened, was an anti-Nazi, was critically wounded.

Grynszpan's action was doubly unfortunate in that it came two days before the annual party ceremony commemorating the November 1923 putsch in Munich. Hitler was just leaving the evening festivities in Munich on November 8 when Goebbels brought him word that Rath had died. Grynszpan's provocation could be turned to good account, just as van der Lubbe's firing of the Reichstag had been, Goebbels argued. For years the party had been fighting a futile battle against Germans' shopping in Jewish stores, where prices were lower and quality better. Goebbels's perpetual propaganda that the failure of the standard of living to improve was due to the plotting of the international Jewish financiers was wearing thin. Here was the opportunity to give the average Nazi a chance to vent his spleen in a "spontaneous" outburst of indignation, to terrorize the Jews into a mass exodus, to take the wealthy ones hostage for ransom, and to dramatize to Jews in other countries what would happen to their coreligionists in Germany if they did not cease to speak out and halt their economic boycott.

Hitler, in a state of high excitement, agreed. To him, the assassination was not the act of a desperate Jewish youth, but a conspiracy by the "International Jews." The victim was not a minor foreign office official, but, symbolically, he himself. Goebbels, returning to the party leaders who remained gathered, reported that anti-Jewish demonstrations during which shops were demolished and synagogues set on fire had broken out in two districts. The Führer, at his, Goebbels's, suggestion, "has decided that such demonstrations are not to be prepared or organized by the party, but so far as they originate spontaneously, they are not to be discouraged either."

The Gauleiters (district chiefs), Kreisleiter (county chiefs), and SA and SS leaders were accustomed to reading between the lines of such declarations. If they had any doubts, they were resolved by a teletype message sent out a few minutes before midnight by Heinrich Müller, the head of the Gestapo, to all central police stations. "1. Actions against the Jews and in particular against their synagogues will occur in a short time in all of Germany. However, it is to be made certain that plundering and similar lawbreaking will be held to a minimum. 2. Insofar as important archive material is present in the synagogues, it is to be secured by immediate measures. 3. The seizure of some twenty to thirty thousand Jews in the Reich is to be prepared. Wealthy Jews above all are to be chosen. More detailed directives will appear in the course of this night."

This message was followed an hour and a half later by one from Heydrich. Heydrich directed that the police leaders were immediately to confer with the party leaders "about the handling of the demonstrations. Only such measures may be taken which do not jeopardize German life or property (for instance, burning of synagogues only if there is no danger of fires for the neighborhood). Business establishments and homes of Jews may be destroyed but not looted. The police have been instructed to supervise the execution of these directives and to arrest looters. Subjects of foreign countries may not be molested even if they are Jews. . . . For the performance of the measures of the Security Police, officers of the Criminal Police as well as members of the SD, the special troops, and the SS may be used. . . . After the arrests have been carried out, the appropriate concentration camp is to be contacted immediately with a view to a quick transfer of the Jews to the camps. Special care is to be taken that Jews arrested on the basis of this directive will not be mistreated."

Since these teletypes were open to considerable leeway in interpretation, officials in various jurisdictions reacted differently, and these differences were exacerbated as the directives were passed on from one level to the next. The casuistry, hypocritical criminality, and moral perversity of the orders were typical of the Nazi regime. The *Kristallnacht,* * as it came to be known, joined the Saint Bartholomew's Day Massacre as an example of an aberrant government's insensate incitement of riot against a portion of its own subjects.

The attacks were intended to take place under the cover of darkness; and in some places the riots got under way at two or three o'clock in the morning. But since, in most areas, a few hours of organization were required, people on their way to work in the bleak hours of the dawn were greeted by the astonishing sight of men and youths shattering the doors

---

*The term *"Kristallnacht,"* coined by Funk, was a measure of poetic license, and referred to the fact that the shards of glass from the thousands of broken windows glittered like crystal in the streets.

and windows of synagogues, applying gasoline, then setting the structures afire—while all the time firemen and their engines stood by to keep the flames from spreading, and police officers were on hand to preserve order.

The assault against Jewish stores was launched concurrently with the firing of the synagogues—and here confusion reigned. In some cases merely the windows were smashed; in others the windows were smashed, the shelves ripped off the walls, and the contents chopped to pieces; in still others, the goods were heaved into the streets; in a lesser number, the entire establishment was put to the torch. To Germans starved of consumer goods and squeezed by inflation, it seemed madness to destroy what was in short supply; so widespread looting—or, in many cases, simply scavenging—set in.

This was the visible element of the *Kristallnacht,* and it was met by the average German, steeped in law, order, and the sanctity of property, with numbness and incomprehension; the same Nazis who had rioted against the Communists, Social Democrats, and Weimar Republic now seemed to be rioting against themselves. (No one, of course, was fooled by the pretense of spontaneity or noninvolvement of the Nazi Party when the burning of the synagogues was orchestrated in every detail, and the men leading the rampages were the neighborhood block leaders and SA *Scharführer* [sergeants]. If there was one element lacking in the German character, it was spontaneity.)

Yet it was the invisible and theoretically unsanctioned activity that was by far the more horrifying. Armed Nazis broke into Jewish homes throughout the land, smashed furniture, threw belongings into the street, looted money and valuables, and raped women and girls as young as thirteen before the eyes of their families. Any sign of resistance—even a word or a gesture—was suppressed with ruthless brutality. Women as well as men and boys were beaten, knifed, and shot. Pets were hurled out of upper-story windows alongside their owners. Jews were plunged into ice-cold rivers. When they tried to claw their way out, German boys were encouraged to throw bricks at them, onlookers were ordered to spit at them, and party members kicked them in the face. A number of the victims drowned. Those few Germans who dared come to the defense of the Jews were beaten and threatened with incarceration. A few prominent Germans who protested were arrested. Goebbels announced that there was "a spontaneous wave of righteous indignation throughout Germany as a result of the cowardly Jewish murder of Third Secretary vom Rath." Jews were imprisoned for assault when they tried to defend themselves, and for arson when their shops were burned down. More than one hundred Jews were killed; and thirty thousand men between the ages of sixteen and sixty, nearly twenty percent of the total, were picked up and packed off to concentration camps. Goebbels, lying with inimitable crudeness and aplomb, told foreign reporters: "Not a Jew has had a hair disturbed." All stories to the contrary were "stinking lies."

It was typically Hitlerian that the Nazis acted without fully considering the consequences; thus it was not until the day after that the government was made startledly aware that many of the stores, although they carried Jewish names, had previously been purchased by Gentiles. Even more distressing, most of the Jewish stores were located on Christian-owned property and insured by German firms, who were now faced with staggering claims. The amount of plate glass broken equaled half a year's production of the entire Belgian glass industry, the only source for Germany (which did not manufacture plate glass itself). On November 12, Goering convoked what was, essentially, a cabinet meeting. He himself was furious; and Hitler, whose spleen had come home to roost, was fed up.

"The stenographic report on this meeting is an extraordinary document," Commander Albrecht remarked to the judges, "and it does not make pretty reading."

"Gentlemen! Today's meeting is of a decisive nature," Goering announced. "I have received a letter written on the Führer's orders requesting that the Jewish question be now, once and for all, coordinated and solved one way or another.

"Since the problem is mainly an economic one, it is from the economic angle it shall have to be tackled. Because, gentlemen, I have had enough of these demonstrations! They don't harm the Jew but me, who is the final authority for coordinating the German economy.

"If today a Jewish shop is destroyed, if goods are thrown into the street, the insurance companies will pay for the damages; and, furthermore, consumer goods belonging to the people are destroyed. If in the future, demonstrations which are necessary occur, then, I pray, that they be directed so as not to hurt us.

"Because it's insane to clean out and burn a Jewish warehouse, then have a German insurance company make good the loss. And the goods which I need desperately, whole bales of clothing and whatnot, are being burned. And I miss them everywhere. I may as well burn the raw materials before they arrive.

"I should not want to leave any doubt, gentlemen, as to the aim of today's meeting. We have not come together merely to talk again, but to make decisions, and I implore the competent agencies to take all measures for the elimination of the Jew from the German economy, and to submit them to me."

The conference marked the pivotal point in the history of the German Jews. It was more important in sealing their fate than the Nuremberg Laws or the developments that were to follow after the onset of the war. Having been stripped of their citizenship, they were now to become pariahs, open to exploitation and terrorization by every petty bureaucrat and tyrant, and totally subject to the caprice of a government wallowing in corruption and hypocrisy.

"The Jew being ejected from the economy transfers his property to the state," Goering continued. "The Aryanizing of all the larger establishments, naturally, is to be my lot. The trustee of the state will estimate the value of the property and decide what amount the Jew shall receive. Naturally, this amount is to be set as low as possible. The representative of the state shall then turn the establishment over to the Aryan proprietor.

"There the difficulties start. It is easy to understand that strong attempts will be made to get all these stores to party members. I have witnessed terrible things in the past; little chauffeurs of gauleiters have profited so much by these transactions that they are now worth about half a million. You, gentlemen, know it. Is that correct?"

A chorus of assents responded, though a few smiles were suppressed. Goering, who had arrived broke in Berlin ten years before, was now one of the world's plutocrats. The chief robber was decrying petty larceny.

Goering went on: "Of course, things like that are impossible. I shall not hesitate to act ruthlessly in any case where such a trick is played. . . . We must agree on a clear action that shall be profitable to the Reich. . . . Anyway, the Jew must be evicted pretty fast from the German economy."

After Goering promulgated the robbery of the Jews, Goebbels took over to institute their segregation. "In almost all German cities, the synagogues are burned," he announced.

"How many synagogues were actually burned?" Goering asked.

"All together there are one hundred and one synagogues destroyed by fire," Heydrich responded. "Seventy-six synagogues demolished. And seventy-five hundred stores ruined in the Reich."

"I am of the opinion that this is our chance to dissolve the synagogues," Goebbels spoke animatedly. "We shall build parking lots in their places or new buildings. [Furthermore] I deem it necessary to issue a decree forbidding Jews to enter German theaters, movie houses, and circuses. Our theaters are overcrowded. We have hardly any room. I am of the opinion it is not possible to have Jews sitting next to Germans. It is still possible today for a Jew to share a compartment in a sleeping car with a German. Therefore, we need a decree from the Reich Ministry for Communications stating that separate compartments for Jews shall be available. They shall not mix with Germans, and if there is no more room they shall have to stand in the corridor."

"We'll kick him out and he'll have to sit all alone in the toilet all the way," Goering interjected humorously.

Goebbels, who had the sense of humor of a vulture, clattered on: "There ought to be a law. Furthermore, there ought to be a decree barring Jews from German beaches and resorts. It'll also have to be considered if it might not become necessary to forbid the Jews to enter the German forests. In the Grünewald [the famous Berlin woods] whole herds of them are running around."

Goering nodded. "We shall give the Jews a certain part of the forest, and the Alpers shall take care of it that various animals that look damned much like Jews—the elk has such a crooked nose—get there also and become acclimated."

"Further"—Goebbels barely paused at Goering's interruption—"Jews should not be allowed to sit around in German parks. I am thinking of the whispering campaign on the part of Jewish women in the public gardens. They go and sit with German mothers and their children and begin to gossip and incite. Furthermore, Jewish children are still allowed in German schools. That's impossible. It is out of the question that any boy should sit beside a Jewish boy in a German *Gymnasium* [classical high school] and receive lessons in German history. Jews ought to be completely eliminated from German schools." So long as Jews had contact with the Germans, they were able to communicate the truth about what was being done to them, and that, to Goebbels and Hitler, was "provocation and incitement."

Goering then had the national insurance commissioner, Hilgard, summoned. Hilgard explained that the victims of fire and theft had been both Jews and Christians. "As for the glass insurance, which plays a very important part in this, the situation is completely different. The majority of the victims, mostly the owners of the buildings, are Aryans."

"In these cases the Jew will have to pay," Goebbels piped up without a tremor at the ludicrous injustice of his statement.

"It doesn't make sense!" Goering snapped. "We have no raw materials. It is all glass imported from foreign countries and has to be paid for in foreign currency! One could go nuts!"

As Hilgard continued his exposition, Goering ejaculated: "This cannot continue! We won't be able to last with all this! Impossible!"

"The jewelry store of Margraf [suffered] damage that was reported to us as amounting to 1.7 million dollars because the store was completely stripped," Hilgard related.

Goering turned to Heydrich and to Kurt Dalüge, the commander of the *Ordnungspolizei* (uniformed police). "You'll have to get me this jewelry through raids staged on a tremendous scale."

Dalüge answered with alacrity: "The order has already been given. According to reports, one hundred and fifty were arrested by yesterday afternoon."

Hilgard requested that, in order to maintain the international integrity of the German insurance industry, insurance companies not be prevented from paying claims.

Heydrich had the answer: "The insurance may be granted, but as soon as it is paid, it'll be confiscated. That way we'll have saved face."

"One moment!" Goering resumed command. "You'll have to pay in any case because it is the Germans who suffered the damage. But there'll be a lawful order forbidding you to make any direct payments to Jews. You shall also have to make payment for the damage the Jews have suffered, but not to the Jews, but to the minister of finance."

"Ah ha!" Hilgard exclaimed.

"We estimate that the damage to property, to furniture, and to consumer goods amounts to several hundred million," Heydrich reported.

"Most of the goods in the stores were not the property of the owners but were kept on the books of other firms, which had delivered them, which definitely are not all Jewish but Aryan," Dalüge went on.

"I wish you had killed two hundred Jews," Goering groaned, "and not destroyed such valuables."

"There *were* thirty-five killed." Heydrich apologized that the number was not greater. (The final figure, actually, turned out to be over a hundred, and innumerable others died as a result of maltreatment in the concentration camps.)

"Now for the damage the Jew has had." Goering turned to the next item. "He is the one who has to suffer the damage. As far as the jewels may be returned again by the police, they belong to the state." Goering, who loved to trickle his growing horde of gems through his fingers, was already envisioning his share.

"I wonder to what an extent insurance companies in foreign countries might be involved in this?" Hilgard mused.

"Well, they'll have to pay. And we'll confiscate that." Goering had the answer. "The Jew shall have to report the damage. He'll get the refund from the insurance company, but the refund will be confiscated." Since the insurance companies would have to pay the full damages, Goering complimented Hilgard on making a profit.

Hilgard was mystified. "The fact that we won't have to pay for all the damages is called profit?"

"If you are compelled under the law to pay five million, and all of a sudden there appears an angel in my somewhat corpulent form and tells you: you may keep one million—why cannot that be called making a profit? I should actually split with you, or whatever you call it." With Goering, that was not an idle suggestion. "I can see it, looking at you— your whole body is grinning! You made a big profit!"

"It ought to be considered whether or not the United States might take measures against German property," the representative from the Foreign Office suggested when the question was raised whether foreign Jews should be compensated.

"That country of scoundrels does not do business with us according to any legal rules," Goering exploded. "You can do it with a regular country but not with one that cares for rights as little as the United States." He said he had told the American Ambassador there would be no more zeppelin flights to the United States because "it goes without saying that one cannot fly to such gangster states."

Heydrich turned to practical aspects: "In spite of the elimination of the Jew from the economy, the main problem, namely to kick the Jew out of Germany, remains. We have set up a Center for the Emigration of Jews in Vienna [headed by Adolf Eichmann], and that way we have eliminated fifty thousand Jews from Austria while from the Reich only nineteen thousand Jews were eliminated during the same period of time."

Goering acted as if he did not believe a word of it: "This story has gone through the whole world press. During the first night the Jews were expelled into Czechoslovakia. The next morning the Czechs grabbed them and pushed them into Hungary. From Hungary they were returned to Germany, and from there into Czechoslovakia. They traveled around and around that way. They finally landed on an old barge in the Danube."

Heydrich protested that only one hundred Jews had been involved in this particular caper, with a total of perhaps five thousand pushed secretly over the borders into other countries at night. "We extracted a certain amount of money from the rich Jews who wanted to emigrate," he ex-plained, understating as much as Goering exaggerated. "The problem was not to make the rich Jews leave, but to get rid of the Jewish mob."

Heydrich suggested that a similar plan should be implemented for the rest of Germany. There were, nevertheless, going to be major problems: "The highest number of Jews we can possibly get out during one year is eight thousand to ten thousand. Therefore, a great number of Jews will remain. Because of the Aryanizing and other restrictions, the Jews will become unemployed. The remaining Jews gradually become proletarians. Therefore, I shall have to take steps to isolate the Jew so he won't enter into the German normal routine of life. For example, whoever is Jewish according to the Nuremberg Laws shall have to wear a certain insignia.

That way we could also put an end to the molestation of foreign Jews, who don't look any different from ours."

"One more question, gentlemen," Goering proffered as the lengthy conference drew to a close. "What would you think if I announced today that the Jews should have to contribute one billion marks as a punishment?"

Everyone agreed that such a confiscation, representing one-fifth of Jewish wealth in Germany, would be a splendid idea.

"I shall close the wording this way," Goering announced. "That German Jewry shall, as punishment for their abominable crimes—and so forth —have to make a contribution of one billion marks. That'll work. The swine won't commit another murder. Incidentally, I'd like to say again that I would not like to be a Jew in Germany."

Finance Minister Schwerin von Krosigk nodded. "Therefore, I'd like to emphasize what Herr Heydrich said in the beginning. That we'll have to try everything possible, by way of additional exports, to shove the Jews into foreign countries."

"If in the near future, the German Reich should come into conflict with foreign powers," Goering declared, "it goes without saying that we in Germany should first of all let it come to a showdown with the Jews. Besides that, the Führer shall now make an attempt with those foreign powers which have brought the Jewish question up to solve the Madagascar project. He explained it all to me on November 9. There is no other way. He'll tell the other countries 'What are you talking about the Jew for? Take him!' "

Thus the tragedy was set in motion. The implications were clear, though no one at the conference (including Goering, Interior Minister Wilhelm Frick, and Economics Minister Walther Funk) yet had an inkling that the final destination would be Auschwitz. Still, that a government composed of men (Nationalists and apolitical bureaucrats as well as Nazis) capable of such psychopathic actions as victimizing the victims of a terror officially unleashed should bring a nation to such an end can hardly be surprising.

One after another the measures proposed against the Jews were enacted during the next few weeks. Their cars, trucks, and motorcycles were confiscated, and their drivers' licenses stripped from them. They were banned from certain districts, from the best parks, from theaters, opera and symphony halls, and from all but a few second-rate movie houses. Children were segregated in the older, least desirable schools, and expelled entirely from institutions of higher education. Christians were placed under enormous pressure not to speak to Jews, so that Jewish families were, in effect, ostracized. All Jews were ordered to report to police stations, where they were fingerprinted like criminals. One decree forced them to register their gold, silver, and jewelry; and the next ordered them to turn their valuables into Goering's state pawn shops, where they received ten percent of their value. They had to deposit all their securities with the government. They were forbidden to own factories, retail shops, income-producing real estate, or to hold management or supervisory positions. They had to register with a Reich Association of the Jews, formed to facilitate their emigration.

Despite Goering's injunction that he was to be the supervisor and principal beneficiary of the "Aryanization of property," every Nazi from *Blockleiter* to *Reichsleiter* (and some influential non-Nazis as well) jumped at the opportunity to acquire property at ten percent of its value. Goering, to be sure, got the choicest plunder, including the coal and iron works and Viennese palace of Baron Louis Rothschild. Count Wolf von Helldorf, the venal SA leader and Police President of Berlin (who was to become involved in the conspiracy against Hitler, and die as a result), extracted as much as a quarter to a half million marks from individual Jews in return for passports and exit visas. The aristocratic and upstanding Baron von Neurath acquired a quarter-million-mark villa in Berlin. "The Aryanization of Jewish capital was largely a political plum," one prominent gauleiter admitted.

Yet, whatever satisfaction and riches the Nazis obtained from the *Kristallnacht* and its followup, the more important consequence was the final alienation of Germany from the western democracies. No matter how much geniality Goering might display, the depravity of the regime could no longer be masked. The American consul in Leipzig reported: "This flagitious attack upon a helpless minority very probably has had no counterpart in the course of the civilized world." The American consul in Stuttgart wrote: "The Jews of southwest Germany have suffered vicissitudes during the last three days which would seem unreal to one living in an enlightened country during the twentieth century if one had not actually been a witness of their dreadful experiences."

When French Foreign Minister Georges Bonnet brought up the riots in a meeting with his German counterpart, Joachim von Ribbentrop, Ribbentrop's only response was to explode in invective. "The Jews in Germany without exception were pickpockets and thieves," he ranted. The property they possessed had been acquired illegally. The German government had therefore decided to assimilate them with the criminal elements of the population. The property that they had acquired illegally would be taken from them. They would be forced to live in districts frequented by the criminal classes. They would be forced to report to the police like other criminals. The German government could not help it if some of these criminals escaped to other countries which seemed so anxious to have them.

Ribbentrop was merely mouthing Himmler's views, which had appeared in the SS publication, *Das Schwarze Korps*, a few days before: "The program means the elimination of the Jews and their economy. They must be chased out of our dwelling houses and our residential districts and quartered among themselves. A mark of recognition must be given them. In this isolation, the parasitic people unwilling or unable to work will become impoverished. All of them will sink into criminality. But let nobody suppose that we shall look calmly on the results. We do not intend to permit hundreds of thousands of Jews to become breeding places for Bolshevism. At this stage of development we should therefore face the hard necessity of exterminating the Jewish underworld in the same fashion we exterminate criminality with fire and sword."

23   Schacht: An Economy in Ruins

For Hjalmar Schacht and other apologists for Hitler, the *Kristallnacht* marked a bitter end to rationalization. For years Schacht had proclaimed that the disabilities imposed upon the Jews were for their own benefit. After the passage of the Nuremberg Laws, Schacht told President Roosevelt's personal emissary: "I called Mr. Warburg [a leading Jewish banker] in to see me the other day and explained to him the protection Germany now guarantees to Jews; they can engage in their businesses from now on and will have proper governmental protection. I told Mr. Warburg to have his people stop making a noise and accept this protection."

Such statements now having been given the lie, Schacht, who unlike so many others retained at least a measure of integrity, told Reichsbank personnel at a Christmas party: "The deliberate burning of Jewish synagogues, the destruction and looting of Jewish businesses, and the ill-treatment of Jewish citizens was such a wanton and outrageous undertaking as to make every decent German blush with shame." On another occasion, he remarked to a woman dinner companion: "My dear lady, we have fallen into the hands of criminals. How could I have known that?"

As long as Schacht had been economics minister, his policy of keeping communications open had paid off to the extent of even convincing Jewish bankers to continue participation in the floating of Reich bonds. But now the break was complete. So Schacht, whose Reichsbank was desperately short of funds, became engaged in an attempt to trade Jewish émigrés for money.

In December 1938, he met George Rublee, the representative of the Jewish American Joint Distribution Committee, in London. Schacht proposed, and Rublee tentatively agreed, that 150,000 Jewish men in the work force should each be provided with an immigration loan of ten thousand marks raised by American and British Jews—a total of 1.5 billion marks. A considerable part of this loan would be spent in Germany, and so provide the government with foreign exchange. Germany would sequester the property of the departing Jews and repay the loan over a period of twenty-five to thirty years from the proceeds.

It was late January before Schacht, who by then had resigned as president of the Reichsbank, was able to speak to Hitler about the plan and overcome Ribbentrop's resistance to bringing Rublee to Berlin. But then Schacht dropped out of the picture, and it was not until, after many difficulties, Rublee was able to gain access to Goering that negotiations recommenced. Goering said flatly that the remaining Jews in Germany were to be considered "exports" to raise foreign exchange. Part of the deal, furthermore, would be that American Jews end their campaign of boycott against German goods. Hitler suggested that the émigrés could be settled in Madagascar—the Madagascar scheme had originally been proposed by Theodore Herzl and the Jewish proponents of immigration from Poland and Russia at the turn of the century. Alternatively, Goering wanted to know why the British talked so much and did not set aside some of their wide open spaces in Canada or Australia for a Jewish enclave.

Rublee received the cooperation of Goering, but had difficulty winning British and American Jews over to any plan that would prop up the Hitler regime at a time when Hitler was intensifying his campaign of vituperation and persecution.

On January 7, 1939, Schacht told Hitler he was sitting atop an inflationary volcano that was about to explode the economy. During the first five years of the Nazi regime the amount of currency in circulation had increased from 3.6 to 5.3 billion marks. Although consumer goods production fell far short of keeping pace, rigid price controls, sometimes enforced by the SA, and covert manipulation that sacrificed quality for quantity kept the rise in prices under control. But the money required to finance the Anschluss, the Sudeten acquisition, and the preparation for war resulted in a *near doubling of money in circulation*, from 5.3 billion to 10.2 billion marks, in ten months.

"*Beginning in March,* and through the period of the Austrian and Sudetenland invasion and the actions connected therewith, the *wage and price structure totally fell apart,*" Schacht stated. "The overemployment of the economy was accompanied by scarcity of materials and labor and by lowering of quality. At the same time the relative production of consumer goods for daily needs lagged. The excess of orders and the pressure for quick production have caused the failure of all planning by the authorities [and] force the manufacturers to corner material and labor which has caused *an excessive price and wage racket* because of the shortage of materials and labor. Especially in the field of *daily requirements* for the home and clothing, the lack of supply and above all the decline of quality is most evident. Children's clothes, workers' clothes, and so forth, which formerly lasted for years now last for only months, but cost the same or even more than the previous good merchandise. *The unlimited growth of the government* expenditures nullifies every attempt for an orderly budget and brings the *government's finances to the verge of bankruptcy* despite a tremendous increase in taxes. Due to *Treasury deficits* running into billions, the Minister of Finance during the last months was continually placed in the position to declare insolvency or to cover the deficit in the Reich finances through inflationary means of using the printing press. Gold or foreign exchange reserves of the Reichsbank are extinct. *The unfavorable balance of imports over exports is increasing rapidly. The reserves, created through the annexation of Austria and the requisitioning of foreign securities and domestic gold coins are exhausted.*"

To Hitler the answer seemed simple: issue new currency backed by the real estate, securities, and valuables obtained from the Jews through the billion-mark fine—the real purpose of the confiscation. Schacht, however, replied: "Covering the expended money with real estate, securities, and so forth cannot retain the currency value. An increase in the production of goods is not possible by the increase of scraps of paper money— one can only increase prices and wages, but not production."

Schacht and the directors of the Reichsbank were of the opinion that "it is now time to put a stop to it." The budget must be brought into balance. The treasury, which had run out of funds to pay current obligations and government employees, must stop printing money ad infinitum. The Reichsbank's independence to control the money supply must be restored.

"This is rebellion!" Hitler sputtered, and on January 20, summoned Schacht to unburden himself of his grievances. Remarking, "You don't fit in to the National Socialist scheme of things," he dismissed Schacht and two other Reichsbank directors. Ticking off charges one by one, he transfixed the impassive banker: "You have criticized and condemned the events of November 9!"

"Had I known that you approved of these events, I should have said nothing," Schacht replied imperturbably.

For once, Hitler was speechless. "I am too upset to continue this conversation," he burst out, and indicated Schacht should take his leave.

Hitler had reached the end of Germany's economic tether. By drawing men from agriculture into industry and the armed forces, he was aggravating the shortfall in food production. One bad harvest had already necessitated a doubling of grain imports, and another (which was to come in 1940) portended disaster. Having led Germany from depression into bankruptcy, he was left with his final option: to retreat or go to war. And he would never retreat.

"I will once more be a prophet," he shouted to the Reichstag on January 30, the sixth anniversary of his accession to power. "If the international Jewish financiers in and outside of Europe succeed in plunging the nations once more into a world war, then the result will not be the bolshevization of the world, and thereby the victory of Jewry, but the annihilation of the Jewish race in Europe!"

Harking back to *The Protocols of the Wise Men of Zion*, Hitler thus announced beforehand that the Jews were responsible for the war that he himself was determined to precipitate. To complete the absorption of Czechoslovakia and obtain the remainder of her badly needed resources and foreign exchange, Hitler kept increasing the pressure on the new Czech president, an aged and infirm former supreme court justice, Emil Hacha. On February 18, 1939, Goering wrote Ribbentrop: "In view of the increasingly difficult currency position, I must insist most strongly that the thirty to forty million Reichsmark in gold which are involved come into our possession very shortly."

Proclaiming that "Czechoslovakia without Slovakia is still more at our mercy [and] air bases in Slovakia are of great importance for the German air force for use against the East," Goering prodded the Slovak leaders to agitate for independence. Otherwise, he warned, Slovakia might be annexed by Hungary—an eventuality that the Slovaks, who had been under the thumb of the Magyars for centuries, feared greatly.

Precisely a year after the Anschluss, Hitler's and Goering's machinations succeeded in convincing the Slovaks to declare their independence, thus rending Czechoslovakia asunder. When the despairing Hacha appealed to Hitler, the Führer invited him to Berlin, and informed him that, since Czechoslovakia had disintegrated of its own accord, he intended to establish a "protectorate" over Bohemia and Moravia.

To the world, Hitler announced, "The territories of the erstwhile Czechoslovakian Republic are hereby incorporated into the territory of the Greater German Reich as the 'Protectorate of Bohemia and Moravia' [because] the German Reich cannot tolerate everlasting disturbances in these areas [and] the German Reich has proven that it alone is chosen by virtue of its greatness and the qualities of the German people to solve this problem."

Both the French and British governments delivered stiff protests, declaring they would not recognize the legality of the occupation. It was evident to all the world that the next territory on Hitler's agenda of conquest was Danzig and the Polish Corridor. Chamberlain, faced with an alarmed but vacillating Polish government, and a more militant but still reluctant French, abandoned his pacific posture and launched a diplomatic offensive. In a speech on March 18 he asked: "Is this the end of an old adventure, or the beginning of a new? Is this the last attack upon a small state or is it to be followed by others? Is this, in effect, a step in the direction of an attempt to dominate the world by force? ... No greater mistake could be made than to suppose that because it believes war to be a senseless and cruel thing, this nation has so lost its fiber that it will not take part to the utmost of its power in resisting such a challenge if it ever were made."

Thirteen days later the prime minister offered a unilateral British guarantee to the Poles: "In the event of any action which clearly threatens Polish independence and which the Polish government accordingly considers it vital to resist with their national forces, His Majesty's Government would feel themselves bound at once to lend the Polish government all support in their power. They have given the Polish government an assurance to this effect."

Hitler believed not a word, although the German ambassador in London warned that a fundamental change in British attitude had occurred. On April 3, Hitler ordered the drafting of plans for an attack on Poland, code-named *Fall Weiss* (Case White), on September 1.

24   *"War Is Still a Law of Nature":* *The Moscow Pact*

Up to this point the trial had been a purely American show; and if Jackson had had his preference, it would have remained so for several weeks more. After the United States had completed its presentation of the all-embracing Conspiracy count, there would have been nothing left for the other three nations except to fill in the details and tidy up.

The British, however, were not of a mind to play along docilely. Having responsibility for Count 2, the Crimes Against Peace, which overlapped and was interwoven with Count 1, they insisted on opening their case at a logical point of the prosecution's progression. Since, until Hitler's violation of the Munich Pact, they had acceded, however reluctantly, to Hitler's expansionism, they were hardly in a position to prosecute the Nazi leaders for Germany's actions before 1939. But once the chronology

arrived at Hitler's preparations for the assault on Poland, they could enter
the fray with clear conscience. Both Sir Hartley Shawcross, the nominal
British prosecutor in chief, and Fyfe, who headed the British prosecution
in practice, were sensitive about the American "poaching" on their case.
Under pressure, Jackson agreed to the British interpolation of Count 2
into the midst of the American presentation on Count 1.

Flying in from London, Sir Hartley made the opening statement for
the British prosecution on Tuesday, December 4. He argued eloquently
that all contentions that law was being applied ex post facto were specious:
"The rights of humanitarian intervention on behalf of the rights of man,
trampled upon by a state in a manner shocking the sense of mankind, has
long been considered to form part of the recognized law of nations. Here
too the charter merely develops a preexisting principle. If murder, rapine,
and robbery are indictable under the ordinary municipal laws of our
countries, shall those who differ from the common criminal only by the
extent and systematic nature of their offenses escape accusation? . . . Can
it really be said on behalf of these defendants that the offense of these wars,
which plunged millions of people to their death, which brought about the
torture and extermination of countless thousands of innocent civilians,
which devastated cities . . . which has brought the world to the brink of
ruin from which it will take generations to recover—will it be seriously
said by these defendants that such a war is only an offense, but not a crime
justiciable by any tribunal? . . . If this be an innovation, it is an innovation
long overdue—a desirable and beneficent innovation fully consistent with
justice. . . . If this be an innovation, it is an innovation we are prepared
to defend and to justify, but it is not an innovation which creates a new
crime. . . .

"It may be said that many of the documents which have been referred
to were in Hitler's name, and that the orders were Hitler's orders, and that
these men were mere instruments of Hitler's will. But they were the
instruments without which Hitler's will could not be carried out; and they
were more than that. These men were no mere willing tools, although they
would be guilty enough if that had been their role. They are the men
whose support had built Hitler up into the position of power he occupied;
these are the men whose initiative and planning often conceived and
certainly made possible the acts of aggression done in Hitler's name. . . .

"The government of a totalitarian country may be carried on without
representatives of the people, but it cannot be carried on without any
assistance at all. It is no use having a leader unless there are also people
willing and ready to serve their personal greed and ambition by helping
and following him. The dictator who is set up in control of the destinies

of his country does not depend on himself alone either in acquiring power or in maintaining it. He depends upon the support and the backing which lesser men, themselves lusting to share in dictatorial power, anxious to bask in the adulation of their leader, are prepared to give. . . .

"It is no excuse for the common thief to say, 'I stole because I was told to steal,' for the murderer to plead, 'I killed because I was asked to kill.' And these men are in no different position, for all that it was nations they sought to rob and whole peoples which they tried to kill. . . . There comes a point where a man must refuse to answer to his leader if he is also to answer to his conscience. Even the common soldier, serving in the ranks of his army, is not called upon to obey illegal orders. . . .

"The total sum of the crime these men have committed—so awful in its comprehension—has many aspects. Their lust and sadism, their deliberate slaughter and degradation of so many millions of their fellow creatures that the imagination reels are but one side of this matter. . . . Perhaps their guilt as murderers and robbers is of less importance and of less effect to future generations of mankind than their crime of fraud—the fraud by which they placed themselves in a position to do their murder and their robbery. That is the other aspect of their guilt. The story of their 'diplomacy,' founded upon cunning, hypocrisy, and bad faith, is a story less gruesome no doubt, but no less evil and deliberate. And should it be taken as a precedent of behavior in the conduct of international relations, its consequences to mankind will no less certainly lead to the end of civilized society. . . .

"Let us once again restore sanity and, with it, also the sanctity of our obligations towards each other."

Responsibility for presenting the British case on Poland was vested in one of the assistant prosecutors, Lieutenant Colonel J. M. G. Griffith-Jones.

Until Hitler had disposed of Czechoslovakia, his relations with Poland had been relatively cordial. In 1934 he had concluded a friendship treaty with Poland's pro-German dictator, Marshal Jozef Pilsudski; and at the time of the Munich crisis he had wooed Poland as a possible ally in a war against the Soviet Union and the West. "We realize that here are two peoples which must live together and neither of which can do away with the other," he had said on September 26, 1938.

A week after the occupation of Bohemia and Moravia, however, Ribbentrop called in Polish Ambassador Jozef Lipski and peremptorily told him that Hitler demanded an immediate settlement of German-Polish differences over the Corridor and the preponderantly German city of Danzig, which had been turned into a "Free State" after World War I.

On April 6, Poland and Britain announced they were prepared to conclude a treaty of mutual assistance. Three weeks later, on April 28, Hitler unilaterally denounced the German pact with Poland. "Poland, like Czechoslovakia a year ago," the Führer orated, "believes under the pressure of a lying international campaign that it must call up troops although Germany, on her part, has not called up a single man and had not thought of proceeding in any way against Poland."

"There was Hitler," Griffith-Jones commented acidly, "probably with a copy of the orders for *Fall Weiss* in his pocket as he spoke, saying that the intention to attack by Germany was an invention of the international press."

On May 22, Mussolini, provided with false assurances by Ribbentrop that the Führer had no intention of launching a war until 1942 at the earliest, concluded a military alliance—grandiloquently titled the "Pact of Steel"—with Hitler. Now confident that the Italian dictator was prepared to tie down the French in case the West should come to Poland's assistance, Hitler the following day summoned his military chiefs to the chancellery in Berlin.

"Here again the careful and meticulous record keeping of the Adjutant Schmundt [who had replaced Hossbach] has provided us with a document that lets the cat out of the bag," Alderman related to the court.

Ever since the Hossbach Meeting, Hitler had been working to win his commanders to the view that "armies for the preservation of peace do not exist," and that "war is still a law of nature. It serves the survival of the race and state, and the assurance of its historical future. This high moral purpose gives war its total character and its ethical justification."
Once more reviewing Germany's position in the world back to the dawn of history, Hitler was like an actor playing several roles. His statement was a crazy quilt of contradictions, non sequiturs, and disorganized ramblings tied together by a few premises:
"A mass of eighty million people has solved the ideological problems," he declared. "So, too, must the economic problems be solved. The solution of the problems demands courage [and] is impossible without the invasion of foreign states or attacks upon foreign property.
"Living space, in proportion to the magnitude of the state, is the basis of all power. Danzig is not the subject of the dispute at all. It is a question of expanding our living space in the East and of securing our food supplies. Food supplies can be expected only from thinly populated areas. Over and

above the natural fertility, thoroughgoing German exploitation will enormously increase the surplus. There is no other possibility for Europe. . . .

"If it is not certain that a German-Polish conflict will not lead to war in the West, then the fight must be primarily against England and France. Fundamentally, therefore, conflict with Poland—beginning with an attack on Poland—will only be successful if the western powers keep out of it. If this is impossible, then it will be better to attack in the West and to settle with Poland at the same time. It is not impossible that Russia will show herself to be disinterested in the destruction of Poland.

"England cannot deal with Germany and subjugate us with a few powerful blows. It is imperative for England that the war should be brought as near to the Ruhr basin as possible. The possession of the Ruhr basin will determine the duration of our resistance.

"The Dutch and Belgian air bases must be occupied by armed force. Declarations of neutrality must be ignored. If England and France intend the war between Germany and Poland to lead to a conflict, they will support Holland and Belgium in their neutrality and make them build fortifications, in order finally to force them into cooperation.

"Therefore, if England intends to intervene in the Polish war, we must occupy Holland with lightning speed. We must aim at securing a new defense line on Dutch soil up to the Zuider Zee [Amsterdam and northern Holland].

"The moment England's food supply routes are cut she is forced to capitulate. The import of food and fuel depends on the fleet's protection. If the German air force attacks England, she will not be forced to capitulate quickly. But if the fleet is destroyed, immediate capitulation will result.

"The army will have to hold positions essential for the navy and the air force. The occupation of Holland and Belgium and the defeat of France will establish fundamental conditions for the successful war against England."

Despite the twistings and turnings of the long delivery, the end results of Hitler's thoughts and aims were clear: Poland, still largely an agricultural country of horse carts and dirt roads, with ill-equipped armed forces and an ethnically fragmented population of 20 million Poles, 9 million Ukrainians, 3.5 million Jews, 1.5 million Germans, and a smattering of other ethnic groups, could be expected to fall in a quick campaign. Danzig was just a pretext. The real aim was to create Lebensraum for German expansion and to augment the nation's food supply. If war with the western powers resulted, England would be the key enemy, and the Ruhr industrial basin would be, in the era of air power, Germany's Achilles heel. (It was to the great astonishment of both Hitler and his generals that the

French and British strategists seemed unable to grasp this at the beginning of the war.) Consequently, Holland must be seized to protect the Ruhr, and Belgium conquered to provide the Luftwaffe with bases for attack on the British fleet, which was the sine qua non for England's survival.

During the same week, Prime Minister Chamberlain, under great pressure from Churchill and the House of Commons, agreed to dispatch a delegation to Moscow to discuss a possible alliance with the Soviets. The Conservative prime minister, however, conducted the negotiations with all the enthusiasm of a girl contemplating a shotgun marriage. Chamberlain's reluctance was not lost on Stalin, who in any case could see little profit from allying himself with the West.

As the lack of enthusiasm became more and more evident, Hitler, always ready to exploit an opportunity, jumped in to offer Stalin an alternative. During the first three weeks of August, he courted the Russians more and more precipitously, and indicated a willingness to grant all of Stalin's demands. On August 19 Stalin informed the Politburo that a trade treaty was about to be signed with Germany, and would be followed after a suitable interval by the conclusion of a nonaggression pact, a draft of which had been prepared and was being forwarded to Hitler by Molotov. A supplementary protocol, which was the key to the pact, would define each power's "sphere of interest."

The trade treaty was signed on August 20; but Hitler, whose timetable now called for the troops to attack six days later, pressed for immediate further talks: "The substance of the supplementary protocol desired by the Soviet Union," Hitler wired Stalin, "can, I am convinced, be clarified in the shortest possible time if a responsible German statesman can come to Moscow himself to negotiate. The tension between Germany and Poland has become intolerable. A crisis may arise any day. I therefore again propose that you receive my foreign minister on Tuesday, August 22, but at the latest on Wednesday, August 23."

Since Hitler had, at this point in time, no taste for embroiling Germany in the "big thing" with the British Empire, he hedged his approach to the Soviet Union by encouraging Goering to make a personal appeal to Chamberlain.

Many of the more important British and German firms, which were interlocked and cartelized, had a mutuality of interest, and found a go-between in a Swedish businessman, Birger Dahlerus, who was the employer of Goering's stepson, Thomas von Kantzow (Karin's son by her first marriage). Early in August, Dahlerus arranged for a group of British businessmen to come to Germany and be enlightened personally by Goering about his antipathy toward war. Exploiting the channels opened by Dahlerus, Goering, on August 21, informed the British ambassador, Sir Nevile Henderson, that he had obtained Hitler's permission to fly to

London in a corollary to Chamberlain's mission to Berchtesgaden the year before. Chamberlain agreed to see him in secret on August 23.

The meeting never took place. For late on the night of August 21, Stalin wired Hitler that he would receive Ribbentrop on August 23 for the signing of a Soviet-German nonaggression treaty.

Since the parties were agreed in principle upon the terms, only the details of the secret protocol had to be negotiated. Lithuania was determined to be in the German sphere, Latvia, Estonia, and Finland in the Russian. Poland was divided along the Narew, Vistula, and San rivers, giving the Russians all the territory east of Warsaw. "The question whether the interests of both parties make the maintenance of an independent Polish State appear desirable and how the frontiers of this state should be drawn can be definitely determined only in the course of further political developments. In any case, both governments will resolve this problem by means of a friendly understanding," the protocol concluded.

While Ribbentrop was in Moscow, Hitler convened his military commanders for the last peacetime meeting on the Obersalzberg. "Now Poland is in the position in which I wanted her," the Führer told his audience in another of his rambling monologues. "We will hold our position in the West until we have conquered Poland. Russia has no interest in maintaining Poland. We need not be afraid of a blockade. The East will supply us with grain, cattle, coal, lead, and zinc. I am only afraid that at the last minute some *Schweinhund* [dirty dog] will make a proposal for mediation.

"For us it is easy to make a decision," Hitler continued. "We have nothing to lose; we can only gain. Our economic situation is such that we cannot hold out more than a few years. Goering can confirm this. We have no other choice, we must act."

At the conclusion of the speech, Goering, as was his custom and privilege as the highest-ranking officer, jumped up to pledge the loyalty and support of the Wehrmacht to the Führer.

Privately, however, he was beset with a host of doubts. A year before he had told the forty-three gauleiters at a meeting at Karinhall that the conduct of German foreign policy would have to be directed toward avoiding a conflict under any circumstance—the shock of the last war was still being felt, the German people were not ready for another, and even the outcome of a war against France alone was doubtful. The morning after the Obersalzberg meeting he telephoned Dahlerus to come to Berlin at once—the situation had become critical. Meanwhile, trying to play one side against the other, Goering told Ambassador Lipski that it was the British who were stirring up the pot; left to themselves, the Poles and Germans could reach agreement without difficulty. On the other hand, he asked Dahlerus to inform the British that the Moscow Pact had improved Germany's strategic position to such an extent that he counted on the good sense of England to restrain the Polish troublemakers and influence them to accept a peaceful solution.

Chamberlain, however, disappointing both Goering and Hitler, warned: "Whatever may prove to be the nature of the German-Soviet agreement, it cannot alter Great Britain's obligation to Poland."

The declaration threw Hitler into a seething rage. Mussolini, caught unaware by the Moscow Pact, refused to commit Italy to war on Germany's side. Although Russia had been neutralized, Hitler did not relish the prospect of combating Poland, Britain, and France by himself. "I will have to see whether we can eliminate British intervention," he told Goering. Eight hours before the attack on Poland was due to commence, he postponed it until the original date, September 1.

He then set out to create such a whirlwind of confusion that the British and French would be unable to disentangle the situation and would hesitate while the Wehrmacht, *blitzartig schnell*, grabbed those portions of Poland Hitler wanted. Presented with another fait accompli, the western powers, Hitler hypothesized, would once more recognize the futility of declaring war.

When the British ambassador, Sir Nevile Henderson, arrived at the chancellery on the evening of August 29, Hitler rehashed all the German grievances against Poland, those "barbaric actions of maltreatment which cry to heaven." In a dispatch for Chamberlain he avowed that he had "never had any intention of touching Poland's vital interests or questioning the existence of an independent Polish state"—a communication Griffith-Jones characterized as "the letter of some common swindler rather than of the government of a great nation."

Next, Hitler assumed his long-suffering but magnanimous posture; because of his friendship for Britain, he would make one last attempt to bring the Poles to reason and "accordingly agree to accept the British government's offer of their good offices in securing their dispatch to Berlin of a Polish emissary with full powers. They count on the arrival of this emissary on Wednesday, August 30, 1939."

It was all a charade. Hitler's scenario called for the Poles to be confronted with a list of impossible demands upon their arrival. The British and French would be handed a set of different proposals, so as to drive a wedge between them and the Poles. On the thirty-first the negotiations would break down, and at dawn the following day the attack would be launched.

After the Poles refused to fall into the same trap that had swallowed the Austrians and the Czechs, Hitler issued the final order for the attack at noon on the thirty-first, and the following morning the German troops jumped off.

25 Keitel and Jodl: "A Child's Game in a Sandbox"

The campaign against Poland had been planned, like all the other German operations, from the march into Austria to the invasion of the Soviet Union, by General Alfred Jodl, chief of the Wehrmacht Operations Staff. Born in Würzburg, sixty miles northwest of Nuremberg, in 1890, Jodl came from a family of Bavarian military officers on his father's side and Austrian farmers on his mother's. As a boy he read omnivorously and loved sports, especially mountain climbing. After attending cadet school on a scholarship, he joined an artillery regiment commanded by an uncle. Introverted but at times unusually outspoken, he had the soul of a writer, but, over the years, gradually developed the demeanor of a cynic. Though Catholic by antecedence, he was, like Hitler and many of the Nazis, antireligious. Following World War I, he had thought of studying medicine, but instead had remained in the Reichswehr. Psychologically as obtuse as intellectually he was capable, he had little insight into either his own mind or the minds of others. Revering Hindenburg, to whom he was once assigned as an aide, he had viewed Hitler with Hindenburg's skepticism until the Nazis' assumption of power, but was subsequently dazzled by the Führer's skein of triumphs. After the signing of the Munich Pact, he criticized the army general staff for their opposition to Hitler: "The genius of the Führer and his determination not to shun even a World War have again won the victory without the use of force. The hope remains that the incredulous, the weak and the doubtful people have been converted and will remain that way." Later Jodl heard the Führer, referring to the character of the respective commanders, complain over and over: "I have a reactionary army, a Christian and Imperial navy, and [only] a National Socialist air force."

Jodl was a protégé of Keitel, who had been born in 1882 on a large farm in Brunswick. In 1900 he had been enrolled in the Kaiser's field artillery, and thirteen years later he had married into a well-to-do brewing and landowning family of former French Huguenots. He escaped most of the misery of World War I as a general staff officer. During the years of peace, his stolid industriousness and bureaucratic administrative ability earned him, eventually, the position of chief of the army's organization department. Though honest and well meaning, he was devoid of imagination, dependent, and given to rambling. He served Hitler so slavishly that other generals referred to him as a *"Nikesel"* (a toy donkey that nods its head when wound up) and *"Lakeitel"* (a pun on "lackey"). Goering remarked that he had "a sergeant's mind in a marshal's body."

Theoretically, when Hitler had dismissed Blomberg and abolished the Ministry of War in February 1938, taking over the functions himself, he had unified all three services of the Wehrmacht and placed Keitel, as chief of staff, at their head. Actually, the Luftwaffe remained entirely independent under Goering, as did the navy under Admiral Raeder. Since the army had its own commander in chief, and under him a chief of staff, Keitel was little more than Hitler's aide-de-camp, and his function was that of a military bureaucrat. Authority gravitated to whoever was capable of seizing it. In one interrogation at Nuremberg several of Germany's top-ranking generals argued for an hour, without resolution, what the structure of command had been.

To the prosecution, nevertheless, Keitel and Jodl represented the military's participation in Hitler's crimes. During an interrogation at Ashcan, Keitel had said: "Personally I was a faithful follower of Adolf Hitler and my political conviction was National Socialist. Even today I am a convinced adherent of Adolf Hitler." Jodl, questioned before the commencement of the trial about Hitler's statements at the time of the attack on Poland, raged: "I don't believe your evidence and your documents. . . . Had that man been the criminal which your question implies, I would not have obeyed him for a single day. A man who has such a warm heart for women and children could not have made such utterances."

"I submit that the case against these two men is overwhelming," G. D. "Khaki" Roberts, the hulking, rugby-playing chief assistant to Fyfe charged to the court. "No doubt all these wicked schemes germinated in the wicked brain of Hitler, but he could not have carried them out alone. He wanted men nearly as wicked and nearly as unscrupulous as himself."

The basic strategy followed by the German army in World War II had been worked out by General Hans von Seeckt, the Reichswehr commander during the 1920s. Compelled to improvise due to the limitation on manpower, he had restructured the army as a mobile striking force. Amplifying on Seeckt's tactics, Hitler directed that tanks were not to be employed in set battles or for infantry support, but as armored cavalry: "It is the task of motorized forces to bridge areas free of the enemy. When an attack opens up a large free space, the commitment of motorized forces is justified. It is catastrophic for tanks to have to stop and wait for infantry. Tanks are used up, and are not available for the subsequent territorial-seizing operation."

In September 1939, however, the panzer forces at Hitler's disposal were still severely limited. During the past eighteen months the number of armored divisions had been increased from one to five, but two of these were only half fleshed out. The Germans had no heavy tanks to match those of the French and British. The light tanks were armed only with machine guns, and the medium tanks with thirty-seven-millimeter cannon —popguns by artillery standards.

It was the Luftwaffe that in combination with the panzers gave Germany its devastating one-two punch. Goering's 2,700 combat planes, representing the world's largest and most modern air force, cut up Poland's World War I–style army and enabled the panzers to stab as far as 350 miles into the country in two and one half weeks.

The complete reversal of the static trench combat of World War I astonished military men. Even Hitler was surprised. Jettisoning all thoughts of a limited goal, he decided to reincorporate into the Reich all the territory annexed by Prussia during the eighteenth-century partitions of Poland but lost by Germany after World War I. Aboard his headquarters train on September 12, Hitler declared that the Poles would have to surrender unconditionally. "It is imperative," he ranted, as Keitel, Ribbentrop, and Admiral Canaris stood by stupefied, "to break all elements of the Polish will to resist. It is especially necessary to eliminate the clergy, the aristocracy, the intelligentsia, and the Jews." All were to be expelled from the four westernmost provinces of Poland, which were to be annexed to Germany. The most prominent and vigorous of the men were to be exterminated, so as to extirpate all nationalism and ethnic identity, and leave the masses without leadership. When Canaris privately pointed out to Keitel that the world would hold the Wehrmacht responsible for such outrages and killings, Keitel shrugged. Hitler, Keitel told Canaris, had stated that if the Wehrmacht did not want any part of these occurrences, it would have to accept the SS and Gestapo as rivals. For each military district, besides the military commander, a civil commander would also be appointed. The latter would then be in charge of the "extermination of folkdom."

On September 17, the Russians applied the coup de grace by joining the attack on Poland. On September 27, the day that Warsaw fell, Ribbentrop met once more with Molotov and Stalin in Moscow. Stalin, taking a pragmatic approach, proposed an amendment to the Moscow Pact of the month previous. Germany would keep the territory it had already captured, thus pushing the boundary seventy-five miles east. In return, Lithuania would be transferred to the Soviet sphere of interest.

Hitler readily agreed to the modification. Since Stalin was not interested in the establishment of a rump Polish protectorate, Hitler designated a 39,000-square-mile area—centered on Warsaw in the north, Lodz and

Cracow in the west, and Lublin in the east—as a German-administered "government-general." This, together with the annexed territory, embraced slightly less than half of the land and two-thirds of the population. Stalin, thereupon, forced the three Baltic nations to agree to the stationing of Soviet troops on their soil, and so prepared the way for the reabsorption of these countries the following year. Hitler, well satisfied with his "limited" test of the Wehrmacht, was prepared to conclude the war, then go ahead with the buildup for the "big thing."

The German press launched a peace campaign. Stalin cynically joined Hitler's scheme. The Soviet Union and Germany, the two dictators declared, "had definitely settled the problems arising from the disintegration of the Polish state and created a firm foundation for a lasting peace in eastern Europe. [Consequently] it would serve the true interest of all peoples to put an end to the state of war between Germany, and England and France."

Neither the German nor the French people, nor the French and German armies were in any mood to wage war against one another. All was so quiet on the western front that the British army did not suffer its first battle death until mid-December, and the Germans, with their propensity for coining words, dubbed it the *Sitzkrieg*. The Wehrmacht staff, Jodl related to Lieutenant Colonel Thomas Hinkel, deputy chief of the Interrogation Division, held "the opinion that if we did not do anything at all, the war might just fall asleep."

But as soon as Hitler was certain the French had no intention of moving out of their fortifications, and even before Chamberlain rejected peace without honor or the restitution of Poland and Czechoslovakia, Hitler directed Jodl to prepare plans for an offensive in the west. Troops were to be concentrated along the Dutch and Belgian frontiers, he decreed, "in order to incite the British and French armies to march into Holland and Belgium." Such a move by the democracies would save Germany from becoming the aggressor, for, as the Wehrmacht War Diary noted, "The intention of attacking through Belgium and Holland is certain from the start. From the very beginning it is the Führer's idea not to repeat the Schlieffen Plan, but to attack in approximately a west-northwest direction through Belgium and Luxembourg and to gain the Channel coast."

The Schlieffen Plan, employed by the Imperial Army at the start of World War I, had been a sweeping end run through Belgium, intended to surround and trap the French army along the German border. Hitler, however, believed that combat between the massed German and French armies would merely bring about a repeat of World War I's bloody stalemate. His goal, therefore, was more modest: "To gain as large an area as possible in Holland, Belgium, and northern France as a base for conducting a promising air and sea war against England." He would fight the British with their own methods. If they aimed to blockade Germany into economic submission, he would cut their lifelines with submarine and air attacks. Though he publicly guaranteed to Denmark, the Low Countries, and Luxembourg the inviolability of their frontiers, he privately told his generals: "Breach of the neutrality of Holland and Belgium is meaningless. No one will question it when we have won."

The generals were, to say the least, skeptical. The combination of their reservations and of unfavorable flying weather postponed the date of the attack repeatedly. Originally scheduled for November 12, 1939, it did not take place until May 10, 1940. By that time German industry and transportation were so rundown that the assault *had* to succeed if Hitler was to continue the war. Steel reserves had dwindled to the vanishing point. The stocks of gasoline and other essential raw materials were so low that the offense would exhaust them. If the Wehrmacht could not capture stockpiles in the west, it would grind to a halt of its own accord.

In the meantime, the plan of the attack underwent one modification after another. It was not until mid-February that Hitler proposed concentrating the bulk of the panzers on the southern wing for the purpose of intercepting the main British and French forces as they moved forward to the assistance of the Belgians and Dutch. Since this routed the panzers through the Ardennes Forest, considered unsuitable terrain for tanks, Jodl, reflecting the skepticism of the generals, was concerned about being "surprised by the god of war."

It was, however, the element of unexpectedness that proved the decisive factor, and resulted in developments foreseen by neither the German nor the Allied generals. Forewarned of the attack by the German resistance, the Allies advanced into the Low Countries to meet the German threat from the north so rapidly that when the panzers broke out of the Ardennes they slashed in behind the bulk of the British army and French armored forces. The confused reaction and irresolution of the Allied generals resulted in the trapping of the entire British army and French mobile forces in Belgium.

Though Hitler's hesitancy to commit the panzers to a set battle, combined with the slowness of the advance by conventional German forces through Belgium, enabled the British to rescue the preponderance of their forces from Dunkirk, to Hitler and Keitel this scarcely seemed a mitigation of the Allied disaster. The British lost everything but their men, and the Wehrmacht was able to replenish its stockpiles. "I never before in my life saw such quantities of motors, raw materials, gasoline, etc. as I saw at Dunkirk," Keitel recalled to his interrogator, Thomas Dodd.

France was cracked open. The German tanks traversed unhindered across the country, as they had Poland, while the cream of the French army continued to sit immobile and untested in the Maginot Line. On June 16 the French sued for an armistice. Hitler, having launched a campaign with a limited objective, had achieved the total victory that had eluded the Kaiser's generals.

In two years Hitler had absorbed Austria and Czechoslovakia, occupied Denmark and Norway in a quick thrust to protect Germany's iron ore supplies prior to launching the assault in the west, conquered Holland and Belgium, and crushed the two major powers on Germany's eastern and western borders. He had outdone Napoleon, at far less cost. "Our campaigns in Poland and France cost us practically nothing in material or casualties," Jodl told Colonel Hinkel. "It was simply ridiculous."

Hitler, moreover, had done it in opposition to the skepticism and cautious advice of many in his entourage. Little wonder that more and more he considered himself omniscient and infallible, and was unresponsive to any counsel.

In a great victory speech to the Reichstag on July 19, the Führer, spraying sarcasm, appealed to the British people over the head of Churchill, who had replaced Chamberlain. "I can see no reason why this war must go on," he declared.

He nevertheless expected, he wrote Mussolini, that it would continue: "I have made Britain so many offers of agreement, even of cooperation, and I have been treated so shabbily that I am now convinced that any new appeal to reason would meet with a similar rejection."

Three days before the Reichstag speech, Hitler issued the order for the preparation of Operation Sea Lion, "to eliminate the English homeland as a basis for the carrying on of the war against Germany, and if it should become necessary, to occupy it completely. The *landing* must be carried out in the form of a surprise crossing on a broad front approximately from Ramsgate to the area west of the Isle of Wight, in which air force units will take the role of artillery, and units of the navy the role of engineers." The Royal Air Force was to be defeated beforehand. Both ends of the English Channel were to be sealed off by mine barriers, and the Channel cleared of the British fleet. Since the German navy, after its losses in the Norwegian campaign, had only four dozen submarines, a handful of destroyers, and one capital ship operational, it was evident that help would have to be secured from other sources. Ships might be seized, Hitler suggested, from France and Belgium, and the Italian navy employed to combat the British. (Mussolini had declared war on France and Britain a week before the French sued for an armistice.)

Hitler had by this time become convinced that by demanding the impractical he could achieve the impossible; but the unreality of the invasion strategy boggles even the nonmilitary mind. The proposed invasion area covered a coastline of 120 miles. River barges, which would be swamped in even a light to moderate sea, were to be used for landing craft. The sealing off of the English Channel at both ends was an absurd concept, and its clearing of British warships was a pipe dream—in actuality, the British had the almost uncontested run of the Channel. The utilization of the Italian fleet to challenge the British was, perhaps, the biggest illusion of all—in one action, the British eliminated half the Italian navy while it was at anchor in Taranto.

As for the Luftwaffe, Goering's fliers had looked like world beaters against the puny and outmoded air forces of the continental nations. Their exploits were magnified both by German propaganda and the terror stories of Allied news reporters. But the Luftwaffe had no heavy, four-engined bombers (since several small planes could be built at the cost of one large), and its tactical bombers were inadequately armed against fighter attack.

These shortcomings became manifest as soon as Goering launched the Battle of Britain in mid-August in order to knock the RAF out of the sky. The slow, gull-winged Stuka dive-bombers fell like clay pigeons before the British Spitfires and Hurricanes; after a few days, they were withdrawn from combat. Though the Luftwaffe had an approximate superiority in numbers of two and one half to one, its losses were in the same proportion. The two air forces, therefore, seemed engaged in a battle of mutual attrition.

Since Hitler could not understand why Britain was continuing a war that to all appearances had been won by Germany, he rationalized, without any basis in fact, that Britain must have a secret understanding with the only military power left to contest Germany on the continent: the Soviet Union.

During the winter of 1939–40, the Russians had fought a limited campaign in Finland, annexed a strategic strip, and forced the nation to grant it bases. While Germany and the world were preoccupied with the conquest of France, the Russians annexed Estonia, Latvia, and Lithuania, massed troops on the Romanian border, and demanded the cession of Bessarabia and Bukovina. Momentarily, the Germans were near panic at the thought that their precious Romanian oil supply might go up in smoke; and even when the crisis ended peacefully, with the Romanians buckling in to the Russian demands, the end result was that the Soviets advanced to within 125 miles of the Ploesti fields. Toward the end of June, Hitler, while traveling through the Black Forest following a tour of France, remarked offhandedly to Keitel and Jodl: "Now we have shown what we are capable of. Believe me, Keitel, a campaign against Russia would be like a child's game in a sandbox in comparison."

During the last week of July, Hitler ordered Jodl to initiate provisional plans for an attack on the Soviet Union. When Jodl passed this news on to his staff, they reacted with consternation—it was as if the victory celebrants had been doused with ice water. "We couldn't help feeling a bit chickenhearted," Jodl recalled to Hinkel. "Up to that moment we considered the war as won, and now came an entirely new variation."

On August 9, Hitler gave the order for *Aufbau Ost*, the buildup of communications and transportation facilities in Poland. A few weeks later, he ordered the transfer of twelve divisions to Poland, where, beyond the Carpathians, they would be able to menace the Russian flank if the Soviets decided to advance farther in Romania; and it was only with difficulty that Jodl persuaded him a campaign against the Soviet Union could not possibly be initiated that fall. On September 20, Hitler directed German troops to be sent to the Balkan nation as "advisers," though, he emphasized, "the real tasks—which must not become apparent either to the Romanians or to our own troops—will be to protect the oil districts against seizure by third powers [and] to prepare for deployment from Romanian bases of German and Romanian forces in case a war with Soviet Russia is forced upon us."

The true reason underlying Hitler's declaration was the fact that he could not at one and the same time continue to conduct war against Britain, build up the Wehrmacht, and meet his trade commitments to the Soviet Union. Even as he spoke, a crisis was impending: Russia was delivering twice as many goods to Germany as Germany was to Russia under the August 1939 pact; and the Soviets were threatening to curtail their shipments if Germany did not start fulfilling its commitments. Talks between the two nations took place in Moscow from August 24 to September 12, and then were broken off. On September 28, a German economics expert composed a memorandum:

"The execution of the armament program ordered by the Führer permits neither an adjustment of the existing deficit of 73 million Reichsmarks nor the fulfillment of the remaining German quota within the time specified. There is furthermore the directive of the Reichsmarshal to avoid deliveries to Russia which directly or indirectly would strengthen the Russian war potential. If these decisions remain in force, then we shall have to expect an interruption of the Russian deliveries to Germany within a short period.

"This means that the large imports of raw materials, especially of grain, mineral oil, cotton, rare metals and nonferrous metals, and phosphates will at least temporarily cease and at best will be resumed later on a much lower scale and with great sacrifices in German deliveries." Additionally, the 1940 European harvest was bad, and portended Hitler's long-feared crisis in the German food supplies. "To date Russia has delivered us almost one million tons of grain. Russia is the only country which has a good grain crop and which therefore would be in a position to make further grain deliveries. The Reich Food Ministry points to the fact that the national grain reserve will be used up, so that we will start the next grain year without such a reserve.

"The Reich Economic Minister, the Reich Food Minister, and the OKW [Wehrmacht] have requested to ask the Führer once more for a decision regarding the continuation of the economic relations with the Soviet Union. Since it is principally a question of deliveries of machines, rolling mill products, and coal, such an arrangement can only be made at the expense of the armament orders."

Adding to Russian unhappiness were Hitler's troop deployments in Finland and Romania, and the concluding of a Tripartite Military Pact between Germany, Italy, and Japan on September 27. Further complicating the situation was the fact that Germany's only means of obtaining strategic materials such as rubber, tungsten, copper, platinum, tin, and asbestos from the Far East and South America was by transshipment across the Soviet Union. To Hitler there seemed only two alternatives: Either Stalin must make economic concessions and unite with the Axis in bringing Britain to her knees, or else the Reich would once more take by force what it could not gain through negotiations.

On November 12 Soviet Foreign Minister Molotov arrived in Berlin for a discussion that was as important to the course of history as Ribbentrop's journey to Moscow the summer before. From the very first the talks went badly. Hitler spoke vaguely about dividing up the world. Molotov, cold-bloodedly pragmatic, asked about Finland and the Balkans, and refused to be diverted by Hitler's magniloquent promise of India for the Soviets. Soviet terms for joining Germany, Italy, and Japan in an alliance, Stalin informed Hitler a few days later, were the withdrawal of German troops from Finland, the acknowledgment of Soviet hegemony over the Bosporus and Dardanelles, the placement of Persia (Iran) in the Soviet sphere of interest, and Japan's renunciation of claims to Soviet territory.

These were demands clearly unacceptable to Germany, as Hitler had anticipated they would be. On the very day of Molotov's arrival in Berlin, the Führer had ordered Jodl to solicit plans from all three branches of the Wehrmacht for a campaign against the Soviet Union. To the Führer, it seemed the only way of extricating the Third Reich from its chronic economic and industrial crises. Directly after the fall of France, he had told

Fritz Todt, the minister of armaments and production: "The course of the war shows that we went too far in our autarchical endeavors. It is impossible to try and manufacture everything we lack by synthetic procedures. For instance, it is impossible to develop our motor fuel economy to a point where we can entirely depend on it. All these autarchical endeavors demand a tremendous amount of manpower, and it is simply impossible to provide it. One has to choose another way. What one does not have, but needs, one must conquer. The commitment of men which is necessary one single time will not be as great as that needed for the running of the synthetic factories." It was better to lose two million men on the battlefield than to keep them unprofitably engaged in the manufacture of *Ersatz*.

Meeting with his generals on December 5, Hitler touched upon the theme with which he was obsessed: "No further doubt is possible. England is hoping for this final sword thrust against us on the continent, else she would have stopped the war after Dunkirk. Private or secret agreements have certainly been made. The Russian deployment is unmistakable. One day we shall suddenly become the victim of cold-blooded political extortion, or we shall be attacked."

Hitler's long-range plans included the annexation of Finland in order to obtain its nickel mines, and the transformation of Sweden into a satellite. With Russia taken out of the picture, Britain would at last realize its position was hopeless, and sue for peace.

"As to the case on aggression against the Soviet Union, they had a code name, 'Case Barbarossa,' " Alderman explained.

"How do you spell that?" Lawrence inquired.

"B - a - r - b - a - r - o - s - s - a—after Barbarossa of Kaiser Friedrich," Alderman elaborated.

On December 18, Hitler issued the first directive for the Russian operation:

"The German Armed Forces must be prepared to crush Soviet Russia in a quick campaign even before the end of the war against England. The mass of the Russian army in western Europe is to be destroyed in daring operations by driving forward deep wedges with tanks, and the retreat of intact battle-ready troops into the wide spaces of Russia is to be prevented. The first goal of operations is the protection from Asiatic Russia of a general line Volga-Archangelsk."

Hitler expected that this massive endeavor, one of the greatest military operations in history, necessitating a drive forward of some nine hundred miles and the setting up of a defense line more than fifteen hundred miles in length, would be concluded by late summer or early fall of 1941. When Otto Bräutigam, a high-level Foreign Ministry expert on the Soviet Union, suggested the conquest might take as long as three months, he was warned by an associate against publishing his assessment: If he did, he would be branded a defeatist!

"It was for us not a pleasant but an extremely painful surprise," Jodl confessed to Colonel Hinkel, "because we had rather counted to have Russia as an allied power."

26   *"The Train of the Dead"*

To cap the prosecution's presentation on Counts 1 and 2, the Americans on December 11 showed a four-hour movie, *The Nazi Plan*. Excerpted from German propaganda films and newsreels, especially Leni Riefenstahl's epic *Triumph of the Will,* the film had been prepared by Hollywood novelist-screenwriter Budd Schulberg, director George C. Stevens, and Hungarian producer Alexander Pathy under the direction of thirty-year-old Commander James G. Donovan, the general counsel of the OSS. A man with a giant-sized ego, Donovan had boasted prior to the trial's start: "I am riding high in Jackson's favor because I planned things so that some of the most important parts of the trial are controlled by me—as the time draws near he must turn to me more often."* Venting his opinion of *The Nazi Plan,* he explained: "It's terrific!" and thought it might win an Academy Award.

The movie began with Rosenberg, plump in his party uniform, providing the pompous narration for *Triumph of the Will.* Dominated by torch-light parades and massed ranks of Hitler Youth, workers, and soldiers, the first two hours of the film composed a frequently stirring, dramatic spectacle. Goose-stepping to martial music and the roll of drums, the Wehrmacht was supported by hundreds of thousands of Germans chorusing *"Sieg Heil!"* and *"Ein Reich, ein Volk, ein Führer."* At the Nuremberg rallies, Speer's powerful, yet simultaneously ethereal setting, with walls of searchlights transforming the field into a "cathedral of ice," created an aura of Walpurgis Night for Hitler's frenzied orations.

*Donovan, nevertheless, in keeping with his OSS background, was a partisan of General William Donovan (to whom he was not related) and did not like Jackson. At the time the dispute broke out between the chief of the US prosecution and the intelligence agency head, Commander Donovan wrote: "I have both respect and affection for the general, but little of either for Jackson." After being discharged, Commander Donovan joined General Donovan's law firm in New York and, drawing on his OSS experience, played a prominent role in Cold War politics. He defended Colonel Rudolph Abel, the Soviet master spy, and negotiated his exchange for downed U-2 pilot Gary Powers. Following the disastrous Bay of Pigs landing, Donovan arranged with Castro for release of the prisoners.

In another scene, Goebbels appeared like a goblin out of the darkness to preside over the bonfires of books: "My German men and women! The era of the overemphasized Jewish intellectualism is now finished. The German to come will be not only a man of learning but rather a man of character. Forget the fear of death in order to gain reverence for death, that is the task of this young German generation and therefore you do well to entrust to the flames the demon of the past at this hour of midnight."

Promulgating the Nuremberg Laws at the 1935 Party Congress, Goering apotheosized Hitler: "To our Führer, the savior and creator, *Sieg Heil!*" Schirach dedicated the Hitler Youth to Hitler. Seyss-Inquart welcomed the Führer amid jubilation in Vienna. Goering rubbed his hands in glee and laughed so hard that he quivered following the signing of the Munich Pact. Goering presided and Speer listened intently as Hitler prophesied on January 30, 1939, that, if war broke out, the result would be "the annihilation of the Jewish race in Europe!" His statement was greeted by a storm of applause.

During the three days following the showing of *The Nazi Plan*, the United States prosecution launched into an overture to War Crimes and Crimes Against Humanity. As a coherent presentation of evidence this was a failure. But as a kaleidoscopic flashing of shifting impressions, it was overwhelming and horrifying.

Certain phrases and images leaped out at the judges from the German documents: "We are a master race, which must remember that the lowliest German worker is racially and biologically a thousand times more valuable than the population here" . . . "What the nations can offer in the way of good blood of our type we will take, if necessary, by kidnapping their children" . . . "The Army Group Center has the intention to apprehend forty thousand to fifty thousand youths of the ages of ten to fourteen—this action is aimed at not only preventing a direct reinforcement of the enemy's military strength but also of a reduction of its biological potentialities" . . . "The policemen meanwhile ignited the houses. The people fall on their knees and kiss their hands, but the policemen beat them with rubber truncheons and threaten to burn down the whole village. They are now catching humans as the dog catchers used to catch dogs" . . . "I have even proceeded to employ and train a whole staff of French and Italian agents of both sexes who for good pay, just as was done in olden times for 'shanghaiing,' go hunting for men and dupe them, using liquor as well as persuasion in order to dispatch them to Germany" . . . "I mean the clearing out of the Jews, the extermination of the Jewish race. Most of you must know what it means when one hundred corpses are lying side by side, or five hundred or one thousand. To have stuck it out and at the same time to have remained decent fellows, that is what has made us hard. This is a page of glory in our history—!" . . . "On Christmas 1944, a number of prisoners were hanged at one time. The prisoners were forced to view this hanging. By the side of the gallows was a decorated Christmas tree" . . . "To lock men, women, and children into barns and to set fire to them does not appear to be a suitable method for combating partisans, even if it is desired to exterminate the population."

A ninety-second amateur movie taken by an SS man of a ghetto clearing depicted naked girls dragged by the hair and chased through streets littered with bodies. Placed on exhibit was a piece of tattooed human skin, tanned at Buchenwald concentration camp, together with the affidavit of a former guard, Andreas Pfaffenberger: "After the tattooed prisoners had been examined, the ones with the best and most artistic specimens were kept in the dispensary and killed by injection. . . . The finished products were then turned over to SS *Standartenführer* [Colonel] Koch's wife, who had them fashioned into lampshades and other household articles."

Thomas Dodd cited the regulations applying to forced laborers: "For every case of sexual intercourse with German men or women application for Special Treatment is to be made for male labor from the original Soviet territory, transfer to a concentration camp for female labor . . . Special Treatment is hanging." A graphic example was displayed on the table: a young Pole's shrunken, preserved head used as a paperweight at Buchenwald.

Keitel muttered, *"Furchtbar! Furchtbar!"* ("Frightful! Frightful!"). Goering, later pacing up and down in his cell, pretended bewilderment: "I still cannot see how he [Hitler] was capable of ordering those mass murders. I keep thinking—it is such a mystery—the whole thing!" Hess had a simple, resigned explanation: "I suppose every genius has a demon in him. You can't blame him—it is just in him."

Schirach shrugged. "It's all over. I wouldn't blame the court if they just said, 'Chop off all their heads!' Even if there are a couple of innocent ones among the twenty, it wouldn't make a bit of difference among the millions who were murdered."

The defense attorneys, generally appalled by the evidence, felt in desperate need of breathing space to digest the information, analyze the prosecution's case, and determine the nature of their defense. Awash in a sea of documents, they met nightly until 9 or 10 PM with the defendants. A number of the lawyers were unable to establish rapport with their clients, who continued their evasive rationalization. The charge of conspiracy, holding all the accused responsible for the actions of one, and one for the actions of the others, complicated the task of the defense as much as it simplified—at least in theory—that of the prosecution. The attorneys pleaded for the court to adjourn over Christmas and New Year's so that they could organize their cases.

Jackson, his staff growing more restive by the day, opposed the request. Former members of the OSS were unhappy about the mysterious departure of General Donovan. Many of the attorneys had lucrative law practices awaiting them at home. With the briefs prepared and no more than a dozen lawyers required for court appearances, they were itching to return to the United States. Wanting to complete the prosecution's case as rapidly as possible, Jackson suggested that the court break only a single day for Christmas. The French and British, however, with the opportunity to go home for the holidays, looked favorably upon the attorneys' request. Lawrence consequently announced: "In a trial of this complexity and magnitude the tribunal considers that it is not only in the interest of the defendants and their counsel but of everyone concerned in the trial that there should be a recess." Court would adjourn for two weeks from December 20 until January 2.

"I should like, in justice to my staff," Jackson protested, "to note the American objection to the adjournment for the benefit of the defendants."

It seemed a singularly ungracious observation to those not familiar with his problems. But he had, in fact, to issue "An Appeal to the Loyalty and Sportsmanship of the American Staff" to forestall a wholesale departure. He decided to rearrange and contract the American case so as to allow the maximum number of people to go home. "Don't moon over the documents that won't be introduced—they will be available to historians," he tried to placate his rebellious workers.

Alderman's deputy, Lieutenant Colonel John B. Street, nevertheless gave voice to the widespread dissatisfaction at the prosecution's general sloppiness: "Time and again some member of the American staff would appear in court to present part of the case without having made any study of the subject matter and without any knowledge of what was contained in the documents he intended to introduce."

Storey's assistant, Major Andy Wheeler, summarizing the trial's early weeks, was more specific: "Colonel Storey has been greatly overloaded with duties and responsibilities, and, having to be in court all day, has little time to consider questions as they arrive. . . . [He] has been running around like the proverbial decapitated chicken at a time when we ought to be pretty well advised as to how the case should go in. Last week it got so bad that everyone was grumbling over having to prepare their case on totally insufficient notice, first in extenso, then only to hit the high spots, then to sandwich parts in between the various sections of the aggressive war case, then after the U.S. and British had finished the aggressive war case, then with, then without witnesses, etc. Sidney Alderman has read his documents at length and complains of neck and shoulder and larynx pains as he drones on. Nevertheless, his part of the case has gone over very well, with enough time for the press to cover it.

"The sudden, more or less desperate interpolation of the movie on concentration camps . . . although utterly illogical at the time, did achieve a phenomenal impression on the defendants and the press, and worked out undeservedly well. The offering of General Lahousen, of Canaris's Abwehr, by Colonel Amen, however, seems to have proved practically nothing that could not have been proved better by documents or left unproved."

Wheeler was equally concerned about what was to come: "Storey is planning to present some of the case on the criminal organizations, and we are hoping that he will not be interrupted by the court or by objections from the defense, because he cannot possibly have had time to become thoroughly familiar with the details, or even with the main points."

When, on December 17, Storey launched into the culpability of the organizations, Wheeler's worst fears came to pass. Presenting material by rote that had been prepared by his staff, Storey became mired in a morass of confusion. Since he did not comprehend the relationship between the antagonistic SS and the party leadership corps, or between the intellectual SD and the demotic SA, he could scarcely educate the judges, who tried bewilderedly to disentangle the maze. Lines ran this way and that on organizational charts without reference to the time bodies had been formed or existed.

Lawrence had not yet succeeded in disentangling the Reich's leading personalities, and asked Alderman: "Will you tell us at some time who these people are? Who is the Reichsmarshal?"

Alderman: "The Reichsmarshal is the defendant Goering."

Lawrence: "And who was the Reichsführer of the SS at that time?"

"Himmler."

"Himmler?" Lawrence seemed astonished.

Three days into Storey's presentation, Lawrence was still unable to differentiate between the SD and the Gestapo. Repeatedly Lawrence or Biddle asked Storey for what purpose he was reading documents and what meaning he placed on them: "Colonel Storey, may I ask you what has that to do with the criminality of the Reich cabinet?" . . . "Colonel Storey, may I ask you what these three documents are supposed to prove?" . . . "Is that relied upon as evidence of criminality, that he took the trouble to find out what other ministers thought?"

Time and again Lawrence interrupted Storey to remark that a document had already been read once, twice, or three times, or that it was merely cumulative and added nothing. Storey would contritely nod. "Yes sir, and I will forgo that at the moment." . . . "Yes, all right, sir. It may be strictly cumulative. I will omit the next reference, which will probably also be cumulative."

Lawrence urged Storey to try to organize himself so that the documents "which you wish to read are read at one time, rather than to read one sentence, then come back to another sentence, and then possibly come back to a document for a third sentence."

When the court adjourned for Christmas, the participants dissolved into their various worlds. Many of the American attorneys went home permanently. "Piddle and Barker," as the British punningly referred to the American judges (for no particular reason), took off in different directions. Parker departed on a grueling trip home to North Carolina. Biddle accompanied Birkett to England for the holidays, and the two judges spent a considerable portion of the time reading poetry to each other. Jackson, together with his son Bill and comely, plumpish, adoring secretary, Elsie Douglas, who were his constant companions, went junketing to Rome, Athens, Bethlehem, and Cairo. Others went sightseeing to Berchtesgaden or skiing at Garmisch-Partenkirchen at a cost of a dollar a day. The defendants and their attorneys embarked on a feverish attempt to discover documents that might contradict the damning directives introduced by the prosecution, but were unsuccessful.

Kaltenbrunner, who had come to court for the first time on December 10, was ignored by the other defendants, who shrank away from him as if he were the ghost of Himmler. Even his defense attorney, Kurt Kauffmann, a staunchly Catholic former party member, studiously clasped his hands behind his back when Kaltenbrunner offered his own. The rejection so shattered Kaltenbrunner that as the Christmas recess began he suffered another hemorrhage and went back into the hospital for two more months.

Hess and Seyss-Inquart had requested and been furnished typewriters by Colonel Gill, and spent a large part of their time clattering away on them. Hess seldom spoke, but intimated that he was now in communication with mysterious forces that would abort the trial; certainly, none of the defendants would be executed. Jodl occupied his time mapping out military campaigns that would have won the war. Schacht wrote an indictment of Adolf Hitler. Streicher, like Rosenberg a primitive artist, drew and drew, and daily swept the sketches out of his cell in a heap. Speer decorated his cell walls with red and blue crayons; and, when the duty officer objected, pointed out that Colonel Andrus's comprehensive regulations contained no prohibition against murals on the walls, thus winning his point.

Fritzsche, Frank, and Schacht engaged in competitive poetry writing, which Schacht won hands down. Schacht, calling Goering a "born criminal," exuded an air of confidence, delighted in the exposure of the atrocities, and considered his presence among the defendants an accident and miscarriage of justice that would be rectified by the verdict. Ribbentrop wrote with the energy of despair and asked: "Why can't the victors accept this as a historical tragedy that was inevitable, and try to work toward a peaceful solution? It is no use heaping hatred upon hatred. All the persecutions and atrocities are revolting to all of us, I assure you. It just isn't German. Can you conceive of me killing anybody? Tell me frankly, do any of us look like murderers?"

Frank, more realistic, suggested that Hitler had been a genius at cultivating the evil in men: "Just imagine—I was a minister at thirty; rode around in a limousine!" Highly suggestive, he yearned now to identify himself with the other side: "Such fine men, those judges and the prosecuting attorneys, such noble figures, the Englishmen, the Americans—especially that tall fine Englishman [Birkett]. And they sit on the opposite side, and I sit here among such repulsive characters as Streicher, Goering, Ribbentrop." One day in the dock he had been gripped by an apocalyptic vision in which Hitler had appeared and, beckoning, said: "You have sworn faithfulness to me unto death—come!" In a kind of ecstasy he had written a poem entitled "Hitler on August 22, 1939":

"We sit opposite the court—and silently the train of the dead goes endlessly by—it is unbroken—pale and wan—without sound, in the dim yellow-gray light of eternity, this stream of misery flows on— All, all surge on without pause, enshrouded in dim mist, whipped by the flames of mankind's agony— Hither— Thither— On and on, and no end is in sight . . . And one voice cries: 'This war must come, for only as long as I live can it come about!' Ah, what hast thou suffered to come to pass, almighty God!"

Frick, on the other hand, had perceived a real vision—one day his young wife had succeeded in obtaining a pass and smuggled herself into the VIP gallery. To catch his attention, she had waved her umbrella; and Frick, who had not an iota of artfulness or subtlety in him, had stared and stared at her until all eyes in the court had turned toward the gallery, and Frau Frick had been discovered and hustled off.

(The innocent victim of her appearance was Luise Jodl, whose permit to work in the Palace of Justice as secretary to her husband's lawyer was revoked.)

Goering, the charming hypocrite, informed the Lutheran pastor, Charles Gerecke, that in order to help save his fellow Protestants' souls he would set a good example. He always led the way into the second-floor chapel. Army blankets had been hung over the bare walls of the double cell, a cloth-covered table on which a candle and a crucifix were set served as an altar, and a small organ had been installed to one side. Rosenberg, Streicher, Jodl, and Hess, remaining true to their beliefs, never attended. Separate services were held for the four Catholics, Frank, Schirach, Seyss-Inquart, and Papen. On Christmas Eve Catholics and Lutherans together stood before the tiny Christmas tree with its flickering candles, and sang the traditional hymn "Silent Night, Holy Night," and other carols.

It was a poignant moment. Frank was quite certain that it was his last Christmas, and his thoughts were shared by a number of the other defendants. Goering continued his bravado: "If I've got to die, I'd rather die as a martyr than a traitor. Don't forget that the great conquerors of history are not seen as murderers—Genghis Khan, Peter the Great, Frederick the Great. The time will come when the world will think differently about all this!"

At the Guest House, Christians and Jews, Nazis and anti-Nazis, Hitler's friends and would-be assassins mingled in a scene that would have seemed fantastic a year before. Sonnenfeldt dropped by with cigarettes, whiskey, and a large box of toys for the Kalnoky children. He helped the boys array the lead soldiers in formation, and, after several drinks, conducted a sham battle. "Let 'em have it, boys! Get the bastards!" he called out as soldiers were strewn in all directions.

27   The Ravages of Euthanasia

Until the start of the war, events in Germany had been well reported in the world's press; and the presence of foreign reporters had had some inhibiting effect on the scope and degree of Hitler's terror. But as one after another of the nations on Germany's borders were swallowed up and the Third Reich was increasingly isolated, Hitler had accelerated his program to "Aryanize" Germany and get rid of everyone who did not fit into the scheme of the New Order.

With the expulsion of the Jews progressing satisfactorily, the Führer had initiated the so-called euthanasia program to destroy the carriers of inferior genes and eliminate "useless eaters" from the economy. Since Frick had jurisdiction over public health, it was at his feet the prosecution laid responsibility.

"One category of Frick's contribution . . . deserves special notice," Robert Kempner asserted to the court. "This is the systematic killing of persons regarded as useless to the German war machine, such as the insane, the crippled, the aged, and foreign laborers who were no longer able to work."

The euthanasia action had had its wellspring in a passage of *Mein Kampf*: "The right of personal freedom recedes before the duty to preserve the race. There must be no half measures. It is a half measure to let incurably sick people steadily contaminate the remaining healthy ones. This is in keeping with the humanitarianism which, to avoid hurting one individual, lets a hundred others perish. If necessary, the incurably sick will be pitilessly segregated—a barbaric measure for the unfortunate who is struck by it, but a blessing for his fellow men and posterity."

Implementation of this philosophy had begun on July 14, 1933, the same day that the Führer Principle had been promulgated, when the cabinet enacted "The Law for the Prevention of Offspring with Hereditary Diseases," providing that "Anyone who is suffering from a hereditary disease can be sterilized by a surgical operation."

Though the law established a "eugenics court" to which a sterilization order could be appealed, the procedure was a fiction. As in so many of the other Nazi measures the appearance of legality served merely to cloak the dehumanized application of Hitler's aberrant concepts.

In the summer of 1937, a year after Hitler remilitarized the Rhineland, he had ordered the secret roundup and sterilization of all the "Rhineland bastards"—children fathered by the French and Belgian occupation troops. Neither their parents nor guardians were informed, and no public acknowledgment of the action was ever permitted. As was the case throughout the Nazi regime in all the various professions, Hitler had no difficulty finding doctors, nurses, and hospitals to execute his designs.

During the same period that Hitler decreed the Rhineland sterilizations, a German medical economist pointed out, in an article entitled "The Fight Against Degeneration," that the care of a deaf-mute or cripple cost 6 marks a day, that of a reform school inmate 4.85 marks, and that of a mentally ill or deficient person 4.50 marks. The average earnings of a laborer, on the other hand, were only 2.50 marks, and those of a civil servant 4 marks daily. (The exchange rate at the time was about forty cents —2.50 marks to the dollar.) The economist lamented: "The state spends far more for the existence of these actually worthless compatriots than for the salary of a healthy man, who must bring up a healthy family," and hinted that it was too bad that a more radical program than sterilization could not be employed.

The economist's dissertation took on added meaning upon the outbreak of the war, when the Nazis' earlier elimination of Jewish physicians generated a medical crisis. (Approximately ten percent of doctors in Germany and half in Austria had been Jewish.) Because of Hitler's neglect of the civilian economy, jampacked, rundown institutions for the aged, the insane, and physically and mentally handicapped were turning into veritable snakepits. "In connection with the limited space, this question of euthanasia came up," Dr. Hermann Pfannmüller, chief psychiatrist at the Egglfing-Haar Asylum near Munich, related to Major John J. Monigan, a handsome Newark, New Jersey, lawyer who had responsibility for investigating euthanasia and medical experiments. For three thousand patients there had been only fifteen doctors, and some of these had been diverted to care for war casualties.

Writing a report on what was required to maintain the patients, Pfannmüller's superior, the director of Egglfing-Haar, expressed the opinion: "These days when our worthy men must make the hard sacrifice of blood and life teach us impressively that it is not possible on economic grounds to continue operating the installations of living corpses. The conception is unbearable for me that, while the best young blood lose their lives at the front, the tainted asocial and unquestionably antisocial in the institutions have a guaranteed existence."

Such an opinion fitted in completely with that of Hitler and his personal physician, Dr. Karl Brandt, the Reich Commissioner for Health and Sanitation. Early during the campaign in Poland, Brandt suggested to the Führer the necessity of weeding incurables out of the institutions.

When the Reich Public Health Director, Dr. Leonardo Conti, and Hans Lammers, the state secretary and chief of the Reich (government) Chancellery, proved too bureaucratic and legalistic to work out practical implementation of such a program, the Führer put it in the hands of Brandt and the director of his personal chancellery, Philip Bouhler.

"*Reichsleiter* Bouhler and Dr. Brandt," Hitler wrote, "are charged with the responsibility of expanding the authority of certain officially appointed doctors, so that after a critical diagnosis incurable persons may be granted a mercy death."

Hitler vested operational authority for the exterminations in Himmler, who was immediately to close down the institutions in the annexed portion of Poland and liquidate the inmates.

In Germany itself, the first category of unfortunates to be victimized were the so-called *Ausschusskinder,* translatable either as "committee children" or "garbage children," who had previously been institutionalized or sterilized. On October 12, the SS expropriated the Grafeneck crippled children's institution, operated by the Samaritan Brothers in a bucolic section of Württemberg, halfway between Stuttgart and Ulm. Under the supervision of Christian Wirth, criminal police commissioner of Württemberg, the children of Grafeneck were killed with overdoses of drugs secreted in their food. If they would not eat, they were dispatched with suppositories or injections. Setting up a front organization, the Public Corporation for Nursing Homes, Bouhler and Brandt sent questionnaires, to be filled out for every patient, to all child-care institutions in Germany. On the basis of the completed questionnaires, children who were considered "incurable" or had hereditary diseases were picked for *"Besonderes Heilverfahren"* (special healing procedure) and transported to Grafeneck and a half-dozen similar installations subsequently set up throughout Germany. In most cases the directors of the children's institutions were unable to find out where their charges were going. Occasionally, if an official balked, he was told that the children were to be submitted to a new heroic treatment. The weak would die, but the stronger would be cured.

Then, early in 1940, with the liquidation of the children well under way, the exterminations were expanded to adults. Every institution caring for the mentally or physically afflicted was required to fill out patient questionnaires. On the basis of these, commissions of doctors and medical students made the selections for transportation—soon, in fact, the selections became pro forma, and the asylums were cleared en masse.

"The reason was to make room for sick soldiers, but otherwise also the reason was to relieve these people from their suffering," Pfannmüller pleaded to Major Monigan. "I didn't murder them," he continued, though admitting: "I already heard that they died from gas."

Another doctor, named Hallervorden, spoke more bluntly and truthfully: "Most institutions did not have enough physicians, and what physicians there were were either too busy or did not care, and they delegated the selection to the nurses and attendants. Whoever looked sick or was otherwise a problem patient from the nurses' or attendants' point of view was put on a list and was transported to the killing center. They got to simply taking out those whom they did not like, and the doctors had so many patients that they did not even know them, and put their names on the list."

Around Grafeneck signs were posted: "Danger—Epidemic," and all access was barred. The exterminations rose to an average of more than thirty a day. Since it was awkward, time-consuming, and too expensive to kill so many with drugs, Criminal Police Commissioner Wirth devised a method for mass extinction. The people, upon arrival, were undressed, given a one-minute physical examination, then herded into a shed whose walls had been mortared and sealed. Since many of these patients, removed from their accustomed surroundings, were in a state of great agitation, Wirth tried to calm them by leading them to believe that they would be given showers. The shed, in fact, was equipped with dummy shower heads. Once all were inside the doors were locked, and coal gas or carbon monoxide was pumped in.

To dispose of the bodies, a crematorium was erected. Dr. Hallervorden, however, thought it a shame that so much "scientific" material should go up in smoke. In a deposition for the trial he related: "I went up to them and told them, 'Look here now, boys, if you are going to kill all these people, at least take the brains out so that the material could be utilized.' They asked me, 'How many can you examine?' And so I told them an unlimited number—the more the better!"

Since Grafeneck was situated on a ridge adjacent to a Wehrmacht training area and the town of Munsingen was but three miles away, it had not taken long for people to make the connection between the transports on which thousands arrived and no one ever departed and the nauseous smoke that continually wafted over the countryside from the high chimney. By July 1940, Grafeneck created such a tempest in Württemberg that Bishop Wurm, the head of the Lutheran Church in the province, addressed a letter to Frick:

"For some months past, insane, feeble-minded, and epileptic patients have been transferred on the orders of the Reich Defense Council. Their relatives are informed a few weeks later that the patient concerned has died of an illness, and that, owing to the danger of infection, the body has had to be cremated. Several hundred patients from institutions in Württemberg alone must have met their death in this way, among them war-wounded of the Great War.

"The *manner* of action, particularly of deceptions that occur, is already sharply criticized. Everybody is convinced that the causes of deaths which are officially published are selected at random. When, to crown everything, regret is expressed in the obituary notice that all endeavors to preserve the patient's life were in vain, this is felt to be a mockery. The air of mystery gives rise to the thought that something is happening that is contrary to justice and ethics and cannot therefore be defended by the government. It also appears very little care was taken in the selection of the patients destined for annihilation. The selections were not limited to insane persons, but included also persons capable of work, especially epileptics.

"What conclusions will the younger generation draw when it realizes that human life is no longer sacred to the state? Cannot every outrage be excused on the grounds that the elimination of another was of advantage to the person concerned? There can be no stopping once one starts down this decline. God does not permit people to mock Him. Either the National Socialist state must recognize the limits which God has laid down, or it will favor a moral decline and carry the state down with it."

No response to the letter was forthcoming. Frequently, if a critic did not take on the system publicly and the issue was likely to be embarrassing, the Nazis preferred to let the matter disappear in the caverns of the bureaucracy. There, with exquisite, polite casuistry, officials communicated with each other in such terms as: "I have the honor to inform you that the female patients referred from your institution on November 8, 1940, to the institutions of Grafeneck, Bernburg, Sonnenstein, and Hartheim all died in November of last year."

In truth, the euthanasia exterminations were just getting in full gear. On September 5, 1940, Bishop Wurm wrote Frick again, deploring that, since his last letter, "this practice has reached tremendous proportions. Recently, the inmates of old-age homes have also been included. The basis for this practice seems to be the opinion that in an efficient nation there is no room for weak and frail people. If the leadership of the state is convinced that it is an inevitable war measure, why does it not issue a decree with legal force, which would at least have the good point that official quarters would not have to seek refuge in lies? Is it necessary that the German nation should be the first civilized nation to return to the habits of primitive races?"

Soon all pretense of eliminating only "incurables" ceased. Small institutions were shut down, and larger ones left operating as fronts with a minute fraction of their former patients. A young, hardworking farmer by the name of Koch was ordered to report for sterilization because he was an epileptic. He wrote his mother he was feeling fine and asked her to send him some tobacco. The next his mother heard was that he had died of an incurable disease. His neighbors had no doubt that he had met a violent death and expressed great indignation.

Unintentionally, macabre humor crept into the coverup. One family received notifications several weeks apart that a beloved had passed on— at different places and of different diseases. Another was informed that their relative had died of acute appendicitis—but his appendix had been removed ten years before; a third that the institutionalized member had succumbed to a degenerative disease of the spinal cord—but the family had visited him only eight days before, and he had been in excellent health.

As 1941 progressed, attention shifted to the small town of Hadamar in a famous cheese-making region near the Dutch border. There, with the Nazi knack for conspicuousness, an extermination installation was set up in a former monastery situated on a hill overlooking the community. Children, with their instinct for cruel truth, taunted each other: "You're crazy! You'll be sent to bake in Hadamar." The bishop of Limburg addressed Justice Minister Gürtner: "The population cannot grasp that systematic actions are carried out which, in accordance with Paragraph 211 of the German criminal code, are punishable by death."

But it was not until late July of 1941 when Count von Galen, the bishop of Münster, spoke up, that anyone dared to bring the matter of the killings into the open. Von Galen's family had been renowned in Germany for hundreds of years, and his name was so famous it provided him with a certain immunity. "Citizens of Münster," the bishop addressed his parishioners, "wounded soldiers are being killed recklessly since they are of no more productive use to the state. Mother, your boy will be killed too if he comes back home from the front crippled." The recent British air attacks on Münster, the bishop warned, should be interpreted as God's vengeance on the German nation.

Walter Tiessler, Goebbels's deputy for propaganda and public enlightenment, responded by suggesting "that we adopt the only measure that can be taken as good propaganda as well as legal punishment— namely: to hang the bishop of Münster. A general public notice of the execution of the death penalty as well as a detailed justification of the measure should be made."

By this time, the preponderance of "useless eaters" and "lives unworthy of living" had been exterminated. Brandt and Bouhler were ordered to deemphasize but not discontinue the euthanasia program. "Directors of asylums," one official reported, "were instructed that 'useless eaters' who could not work very much should be killed by slow starvation. This method was considered very good, because the victims would appear to have died a 'natural death.'"

The pedantic Dr. Brandt told Major Monigan that he had disagreed with Hitler's emphasis on secrecy: "I presume that people anticipated the objections that would be brought by opponents of such a program. From this rather peculiar attitude, a number of differences and practical complications resulted. I am of the opinion that these matters should have been discussed in public. It was a miscalculation if one thought that it would be possible to keep secret an affair that was as widespread all over the Reich as this one."

The euthanasia program, serving as the prototype for the extermination of millions that was to follow, demonstrated how, through fragmentation of authority and tasks, it was possible to fashion a murder machine. Hitler had enunciated an offhand, extralegal decree, and had not wanted to be bothered about it again. Brandt had ordered the "scientific" implementation of the program and, like Hitler, wished to hear no complaints. The directors and personnel of institutions rationalized that matters were out of their hands and that they were just filling out questionnaires for the "experts" in Berlin, though in reality each form was the equivalent of a death warrant. The specious "experts" perused the questionnaires only to cull out prominent persons that might have been accidentally included, then passed them on to Himmler's myrmidons, who transported the afflicted to the annihilation installations. The personnel at the end of the line excused themselves on the basis that they were under compulsion, had no power of decision, and were merely performing a function. Thousands of people were involved, but each considered himself nothing but a cog in the machine and reasoned that it was the machine, not he, that was responsible.

"I have a clear conscience in this issue, a better conscience than in most issues in my life," Brandt asserted to Major Monigan. He thought that 60,000 people had been killed in all, though the estimate of a Czech commission that 200,000 mental cases and 75,000 aged had been done away with is surely more accurate. "It would be more practical," Brandt suggested, "and I am trying to project myself into the future, to call things of this nature by their true name. Then reason and conviction will support them."

28   Frank: The Ant and the Aphid

Concurrent with the start-up of the euthanasia exterminations, Hitler authorized Himmler to establish a Race and Resettlement Office under the aegis of the SS. It was the Race and Resettlement Office that was to be responsible for the "racial" purification of the Reich and the establishment of a Nordic empire. On October 17, 1939, Keitel summoned the victorious Wehrmacht generals for a lecture from the Führer, who ranted: "The increased severity of the racial struggle permits of no legal restrictions. Jews, Poles, and similar trash are to be cleared from the old and new Reich territories." Eight million Poles and 800,000 Jews were to be transported from the annexed portion of Poland into the government-general, and replaced by ethnic Germans repatriated from the Baltic lands, the Balkans, Russia, and the Italian Tyrol—even though, in large part, these Germans had emigrated generations before.

To "render harmless" the Polish intelligentsia, political and religious leaders, Jews, and anyone else who might, theoretically, rally an opposition, Heydrich established SS *Einsatzgruppen* (action groups). The *Einsatzgruppen* rampaged over the land, terrorizing and killing. Selections for execution were haphazard. Sometimes the commandos erred and included ethnic Germans whom they mistook for Jews. Shootings were carried out publicly to heighten the climate of fear. A Wehrmacht intelligence officer reported: "*Arrests were almost always accompanied by looting.* Evacuations were carried out and blocks of houses were cleared at random, the inhabitants loaded into lorries at night, then taken to concentration camps. Actions against the Jews were carried out with the most serious excesses. A number of Jews were driven into a synagogue, where they had to crawl, singing, between the benches. Forced to take down their trousers, they were continuously whipped by the SS men on their bare behinds. A Jew who out of fright dirtied himself was forced to smear the excrement onto the faces of the other Jews.

"After about fifty Jews, who had been used during the day to repair a bridge, finished their work in the evening, two SS men drove them into a synagogue and shot them all *without any reason.* "

Himmler directed that a million Jews and Poles were to be herded into the government-general before spring. Ten thousand persons daily were driven from their homes into unheated boxcars and cattlecars for the journey into the government-general, where they were dumped without food, shelter, or means to support themselves.

Forty-five thousand Jews were shipped before the end of the year to a marshy area at the headwaters of the Pripet and Bug rivers east of Lublin, where Himmler intended to establish a reservation until the Jews could be transported to Madagascar, or wherever else they might eventually go. Since there was little food, and they were supposed to construct their own shelter with primitive tools, thousands succumbed.

A few months later, after the conquest of France, Himmler explained to the SS division *Leibstandarte Adolf Hitler* the necessity for the similar clearance of Frenchmen and Jews from Alsace-Lorraine, which was to be annexed to the Greater German Reich. "Exactly the same thing happened in Poland," Himmler rhapsodized, "in weather forty degrees below zero where we had to haul away thousands, tens of thousands, hundreds of thousands. Where we had to have the toughness—you should hear this but also forget it again immediately—to shoot thousands of leading Poles. In many cases it is much easier to go into combat than to suppress an obstructive population of low cultural level or to carry out executions, or to haul away people, or to evict crying and hysterical women."

Since Himmler was dead, the prosecution concentrated on Frank's culpability in the atrocities. "The defendant Frank was chosen executor of this program," the prosecution charged, emphasizing that much of the evidence had unwittingly been provided by Frank. "These facts, if the tribunal please, are from the diary of the man himself."

Initially, upon being appointed governor of the government-general, with its eight million Poles and two million Jews, Frank had wholeheartedly endorsed the concept of rapine. It was, he announced, "The will of the Führer that this area shall be the first colonial territory of the German nation. This territory in its entirety is the booty of the German Reich."

The Poles, Frank declared, were to be reduced to the status of drones:

"A seasonal laborer—the eternal nomad." The Catholic Church was to be transformed into a Nazi tool: "The priest will be paid by us, and will, in return, preach what we wish him to preach. If any priest acts differently, we shall make short work of him. The task of the priest is to keep the Poles quiet, stupid, and dull-witted." Thousands of Polish priests, of whom 850 died in Dachau, were arrested.

Throughout Poland, art and valuables in private as well as in public collections were confiscated and carted off to Germany or directed to the residences of Frank and other high occupation officials. Industrial enterprises were dismantled and transferred to Germany. Goering even intended to tear up one track of all double-track railroads for the benefit of the hard-pressed German transportation system. Much of the harvest had been lost as a consequence of the German attack. The economy was in chaos and the condition of the people desperate. In the cities little food was available except at soup kitchens, which were set up to keep people from starving.

Though Frank was quite willing to exploit his "colony" to the hilt for Germany, he realized, within a few weeks, that if matters continued as they were he would be left governor of a wasteland. During one of his numerous interrogations by Colonel Hinkel, Frank asserted: "The government-general kept on protesting and opposing all this looting. I cannot use a different word although we speak of Germans. If I had not fought against it with all my power, the most gruesome catastrophe would have taken place."

Pleading to slow down Himmler's slapdash resettlement and ameliorate the government-general's economic woes, Frank proposed to Hitler and Goering that "one should remove cheap labor temporarily by the hundreds of thousands, employ them for a few years in the old Reich, and thereby hamper their native biological propagation."

Hitler wanted the Poles kept quiet until he had dealt with the West, and Goering needed raw materials, agricultural products, and a million workers for the labor-short Reich. On February 12, 1940, Goering called a conference attended by himself, Frank, Himmler, and other Reich leaders. Frank argued that until the population was stabilized and the economy revitalized, Poland would be of little use to the German war effort. Goering, perceiving the validity of Frank's contention, dressed down Himmler: "The strengthening of the war potential of the Reich must be the chief aim of all measures to be taken in the East. Therefore it is necessary that conditions be stabilized as soon as possible."

Frank's attitude toward the Poles and Jews was, indeed, as cynical as Himmler's was tyrannical. "My relationship with the Poles is like the relationship between the ant and the plant louse [aphid]," he explained.

"When I treat the Poles in a helpful way, so to speak tickle them in a friendly manner, I do it in the expectation that their performance will redound to my benefit. If in spite of all this the performance does not improve, I would not hesitate to take the most draconian action."

When, by May 10, only 210,000 of the promised million laborers had reluctantly allowed themselves to be "tickled" into compulsory labor in Germany, Frank reflected bitterly that "the Poles, out of malevolence and guided by the intention of harming Germany by not putting themselves at its disposal, refuse to enlist." He thereupon issued a decree for forced labor service, and told Friedrich Krüger, the *Höhere SS und Polizeiführer** in the government-general to round up the workers—both men and women—in any way he could.

Krüger's response was typical of the simplistic barbarity the Nazis employed in their occupation policy—he directed himself to the points of public assembly, such as movie houses and churches, where he could gather up the most people with the least effort. The SS and police scooped up the moviegoers and worshipers, and loaded them onto freight trains to Germany. Since these measures resulted in predictable outcries from the Poles, together with an intensification of passive resistance and attempts to avoid shipment to Germany, an *Ausserordentlich Beruhigung* (extraordinary pacification) operation was scheduled for June 15. This AB Action, as it came to be known, was an extension to the government-general of the extermination of the Polish intelligentsia and leadership ordered by Hitler in the annexed territory the previous fall.

"There is no need to send these elements to Reich concentration camps, and by so doing involve ourselves in dispute and unnecessary correspondence with their relatives," Frank told his officials. "We will liquidate our difficulties in the country itself, and we will do it in the simplest way possible. I frankly admit that it will cost the lives of some thousands of Poles."

Thirty-five hundred prominent Poles were shot, whereupon Frank congratulated the SS officer in charge of the killings: "What you, *Brigade-führer* Streckenbach, and your people have done in the government-general must not be forgotten; and you need not be ashamed of it."

Once it became evident that the British would not make peace and that Madagascar would not become available for the resettlement scheme —impractical as it might have been—the Nazi policy toward the Jews turned murderous. After Hitler ordered *Aufbau Ost* in August 1940, the

---

*The Higher SS and Police Leaders, appointed by Himmler in each region or district, represented the Reichsführer SS's fusion of the police and the SS. As the direct deputies of Himmler, they were supposed to coordinate the activities of the two organizations, a goal seldom achieved.

sweeping of Jews from the countryside and their confinement into metropolitan ghettos and resettlement camps accelerated. When, in mid-November 1940, Warsaw became the Wehrmacht headquarters for Operation Barbarossa, an eight-foot-high wall was erected around the one and one-third square miles of the ghetto, encompassing more than 400,000 people. Simultaneously, because of the poor German harvest, Hitler directed that Poland be stripped of all agricultural supplies. Delivery of food was halted altogether to the ghetto. The concept of "useless eaters" was extended from the mentally and physically afflicted to the Jews. The penned-up Jews were to be starved to death.

The effect of malnutrition and overcrowding—an average of thirteen persons per room—manifested itself speedily. Typhus became epidemic in the ghettos of Warsaw and other large cities, where the death rate rose to twelve percent. Five thousand Jews died monthly in Warsaw, yet the population did not diminish, since the Germans kept shipping in Jews rounded up in the provinces. On the first anniversary of assuming power in Poland, Frank told an assembly of officials and Wehrmacht officers in Cracow that their friends and relatives in Germany might worry. "My God, there he sits in Poland where there are so many lice and Jews, perhaps he is hungry and cold. It would not be a bad idea then to send our dear ones back home a picture and tell them, 'Well, now, there are not so many lice and Jews anymore, and conditions here in the government-general have changed and improved somewhat already.' Of course, I could not eliminate all lice and Jews in one year's time"—Frank paused—"but in the course of time, and above all, if you help me, this end will be attained."

29   Barbarossa: The Commissar and Partisan Orders

In planning the attack on the Soviet Union, Hitler decreed that even the minimal restraints practiced in Poland were to be abandoned. Under the tutelage of Rosenberg, he had written in *Mein Kampf:* "Fate itself seems desirous of giving us a sign. By handing Russia to bolshevism, it robbed the Russian nation of that intelligentsia which previously brought about and guaranteed its existence as a state. Today it can be regarded as almost totally exterminated and extinguished. It has been replaced by the Jew. And the end of Jewish rule in Russia will also be the end of Russia as a state."

Therefore, Hitler now ordered that the Jews, bolshevism, and Soviet Russia were to be exterminated together so that Germany could colonize and exploit the lands of the East. On March 31, 1941, Keitel, at Hitler's behest, issued the first of a number of directives to the Wehrmacht on the "Treatment of Political and Military Russian Officials." This, which came to be known as the "Commissar Order," stipulated: "The Armed Services must rid themselves of all those elements among the prisoners of war considered as the driving forces of bolshevism. The special conditions of the eastern campaign demand *special measures* which they can carry out on their own responsibility, free from bureaucratic and administrative influences.

"Political representatives and commissars are to be *eliminated*. . . . Identification as a political functionary is sufficient proof."

Presenting the account of Barbarossa to the tribunal, Sidney Alderman turned the focus to Rosenberg: "Equally elaborate planning and preparation were engaged in by the conspirators to ensure the effectuation of the political aims of their aggression. For the accomplishment of their purpose the Nazi conspirators selected as their agent the Defendant Rosenberg."

On April 2, Rosenberg, who had been drifting in the backwaters of power, was summoned by Hitler and named Reich Commissar (upgraded three months later to Reich Minister) of the Eastern Territories. At last the Baltic German, who had longed to be foreign minister but had had to content himself with the leadership of the party's *Aussenpolitischer Amt* (Foreign Political Bureau), felt vindicated. As political head of the occupied lands he would be able to give vent to his hatred of the Soviet Union and indulge his misanthropic philosophy.*

"Military conflict with the USSR will result in an extraordinarily rapid occupation of an important and large section of the USSR," Rosen-

---

*Hitler once said, "Rosenberg is rabid against the Russians only because they would not allow him to be a Russian." In 1930 the party's ideologist had published a seven-hundred-page book, *The Myth of the Twentieth Century,* that became, along with *Mein Kampf,* one of the two great unread bestsellers of the Third Reich. "We now realize," Rosenberg wrote, "that the central supreme values of the Roman and Protestant churches, being a negative Christianity, do not respond to our soul. Liberalism preached: Freedom, generosity, freedom of trade, Parliamentarianism, emancipation of women, equality of mankind, equality of sexes, etc., that is to say, it sinned against a law of nature, that creative actions can only come from the working of polarized potentials, that a potential of energy is necessary to produce work of any kind, to create culture. The German idea today demands in the midst of the disintegration of the old effeminate world: Authority, type-creating energy, self-elimination, discipline, protection of racial character, recognition of the eternal polarity of the sexes.

"The idea of honor—national honor—does not permit Christian love, nor the humanity of the Freemasons, nor Roman philosophy."

berg postulated. "It is very probable that military action on our part will very soon be followed by the military collapse of the USSR. . . . After the military collapse of the Soviets in Europe, very small forces would be needed to dispose of the Moscow tyranny in Central Asia." Germany would annex the most strategic areas of the Soviet Union and break up what was left into a half-dozen or more subject states.

Both Hitler and Goering were obsessed with the necessity of keeping the German people well fed and content, no matter what privation the populations of conquered lands might undergo. Despite all of Hitler's victories, the preponderance of Germans longed for peace; and if their stomachs started growling, the rebellious spirit that had undermined support for the troops in World War I might revive. Goering decreed: "In the occupied territories only those people who work for us are to be supplied with an adequate amount of food. . . . All food supplies for the troops in the Eastern Territories have to be furnished by the occupied territories themselves. On no account will I permit an increased supply from the Reich, which would lead to a decrease of rations for the German civilian population. The morale at home would suffer. The home front has to take enough already."

Rosenberg informed his officials: "The job of feeding the German people stands, this year, without a doubt at the top of the list of Germany's claims on the East." Dividing European Russia into a "black soil" agricultural zone of the south and an industrialized "forest zone" of the center and north, Rosenberg continued: "We see absolutely no reason for any obligation on our part to feed also the Russian people with the products of that [agricultural] surplus territory. We know that this is a harsh necessity, bare of any feelings.

"The consequences will be cessation of supplies to the entire forest zone, including the essential industrial centers of Moscow and St. Petersburg [Leningrad].

"All industry in the deficit area, particularly the manufacturing industries in the Moscow and Petersburg region as well as the Ural industrial region, will be abandoned.

"Germany is not interested in the maintenance of the productive power of these territories, except for supplying the troops stationed there. . . . The population of these areas, in particular the urban population, will have to face the most serious distress from famine. . . .

"Many tens of millions of people in this area will become redundant and will either die or have to emigrate to Siberia. Any attempt to save the population there from death by starvation by importing surpluses from the black soil zone would be at the expense of supplies to Europe. It would reduce Germany's staying power in the war, and would undermine Germany's and Europe's power to resist the blockade. This must be clearly and absolutely understood. . . .

"One must always bear in mind that the Great Russian people, whether under czarism or bolshevism, is always an irreconcilable enemy not only of Germany, but also of Europe."

With utter callousness and tyrannical calculation Hitler and his cohorts were preparing to turn the clock back to the Dark Ages when the Mongol hordes had swept out of Asia to raid and devastate Europe. This time, however, the barbarians would issue out of the West to savage the East.

To Field Marshal Gerd von Rundstedt, Hitler predicted: "You have only to kick in the door, and the whole rotten structure will come crashing down." In the weeks immediately following the onslaught of June 22, 1941, the prediction seemed astute. By mid-July the German army was two-thirds of the way to Moscow. Hitler met with Goering, Rosenberg, Keitel, Lammers, and Bormann to proclaim the victory and gloat over the spoils. "It is essential that we do not publicize our aims before the world; there is no need for that," the Führer cautioned. "The main thing is that we ourselves know what we want. We ought to act here in exactly the same way as we did in the cases of Norway, Denmark, Holland, and Belgium [which Hitler intended to absorb into the Greater German Reich]. In these cases too we did not publish our aims. Therefore we shall emphasize again that we were forced to occupy, administer, and secure a certain area. Nobody shall be able to recognize that it initiates a final settlement. This need not prevent our taking all necessary measures—shooting, resettling, and so forth—and we shall take them!

"But," Hitler continued, "we do not want to make people into enemies prematurely. Therefore, we shall act as though we wanted to exercise a mandate only. At the same time we must clearly know that we shall never leave these countries. On principle, we now have to face the task of cutting up the giant cake according to our needs, in order to be able: First, to dominate it; second, to administer it; and third, to exploit it."

In accordance with Rosenberg's proposals, Hitler announced that the Baltic countries, the Crimea, the Caucasus oil region, the Volga basin, and the nickel-rich Kola Peninsula were to be annexed outright. The Ukraine would become a protectorate governed by Nazi overlords. Even allies were not to be trusted: "One ought not to be dependent on the good will of other people. We have to plan our relations with Romania in accordance with this principle. This we have to consider, and we have to draw our frontiers accordingly."*

*Mussolini once remarked that, after the Führer finished dividing up the world, "there was nothing left but the moon."

In accordance with his perceptions of pacification, Hitler had, prior to the attack, amplified his prescription for terror: "In view of the vast size of the occupied areas in the East, the forces available for establishing security in these areas will be sufficient only if all resistance is punished not by legal prosecution of the guilty, but by the spreading of such terror by the occupying forces as is alone appropriate to eradicate every inclination among the population to resist." So that the troops might have a free hand to rampage, Hitler ordered "the prosecution of offenses against civilians through courtmartial only if it is considered necessary for the maintenance of discipline or the security of the troops; for instance, to cases of serious offenses which are based on sexual acts without restraints, which derive from criminal tendency, or which are a sign that the troops threaten mutiny."

To Hitler's great irritation, however, he now discovered that many of the Wehrmacht commanders were sabotaging both this and the Commissar Order by failing to pass them on through the chain of command. Dismissing the protestations of the army generals that the Commissar Order constituted a violation of international law and would lead to retaliation by the Soviets, Hitler snapped that Russia was not a signatory to the Geneva Convention and would kill the Germans taken prisoner anyway; so German treatment of Soviet captives was immaterial. Jodl, unburdening himself to Colonel Hinkel, related: "For five and a half years he did not stop denouncing the lack of brutality of the German army."

The task of segregating and liquidating commissars and Jews from the ranks of the POWs was, consequently, turned over to Heydrich, who, drawing on the experiences of the ad hoc "action groups" that had operated in Poland, had previously established four *Einsatzgruppen*, totaling three thousand men, to operate in the conquered territory. Specifically included in the extermination order by Hitler were "leading personalities of the state authorities; the leading personalities of the business world; members of the Soviet-Russian intelligentsia; all Jews; all persons who are found to be agitators or fanatic Communists."

To reassure the executioners that, in performing their dirty work, they were an elitist group pursuing the highest goals of the Third Reich, Hitler directed that "the members of the *Einsatzkommando* must be constantly impressed with the special importance of the missions entrusted to them."

The Commissar Order undermined the task of the counterintelligence officers of the Abwehr who were responsible for extracting information from Soviet prisoners of war and enlisting intelligence agents. In mid-September, when there were already 1.5 million men in the camps, and more pouring in every day, Admiral Canaris, the head of the Abwehr, made an attempt to have the order rescinded. Since he knew that any appeal on humanitarian grounds would simply harden Hitler's resolve, he based his argument on German self-interest:

"The Russian decree for prisoners of war complies with the principles of International Law and to a very large extent the Geneva Convention. Since the eighteenth century there has gradually been established that war captivity is neither revenge nor punishment, but solely protective custody. This principle was developed in accordance with the view held by all armies that it is contrary to military tradition to kill or injure helpless people, and in the interest of all belligerents in order to prevent mistreatment of their own soldiers in case of capture."

By giving the *Einsatzkommando* free rein to weed out and execute prisoners "along principles which are *unknown to the Wehrmacht authorities*," Canaris argued, "the will to resist of the enemy troops will be extremely strengthened by the enemy intelligence service. . . . Instead of taking advantage of the tensions among the populations of the occupied territories for the benefit of the German administration, the mobilization of all internal opposition forces of Russia for unified hostility will be facilitated." Finally, Canaris pointed out, the result would be Soviet retaliation: "It will be impossible to protest against the bad treatment of German soldiers in Soviet Russian captivity."

To the last argument, Keitel, whose youngest son had already been killed on the Russian front, retorted: "I consider it useless! The objections arise from the military concept of chivalrous warfare! This is the destruction of an ideology! Therefore, I approve and back the measures."

The barbarity and horrors of the Commissar Order were exacerbated by the chaos of its implementation. At Nuremberg, General Lahousen told Colonel Amen during a pretrial interrogation: "It was left entirely to the judgment of the man in charge of the detail whom he wished to call a Communist. So in practice anybody whom he did not like he could call a Communist and thus have him executed." Testifying before the tribunal, Lahousen continued: "Particularly, of course, if someone were a Jew or of a Jewish type or could otherwise be classified as racially inferior he was picked for execution. Other leaders of the *Einsatzkommando* selected people according to their intelligence. Some had views all of their own and usually most peculiar, so that I felt compelled to ask [Gestapo Chief] Müller: 'Tell me, according to what principles does this selection take place? Do you determine it by the height of a person or the size of his shoes?' "

The two basic criteria, in fact, were whether a man had been circumcised or had the "Mongolian" features that Himmler and Goebbels proclaimed as the mark of "subhumans." Though several ethnic groups, especially Muhammadans, were prepared to break away from the Soviet Union, they, like the Jews, were circumcised, and the *Einsatzkommando* consequently cut as wide a swathe through Islam as through Judaism. Veli Gajun Chan, the president of the National (Liberation) Movement of Turkestan, who had his headquarters in Berlin, was, at the start of Barbarossa, arrested, together with his family. For two weeks he was examined by the Gestapo for Semitic origins, and then released. Since the Russians had deported all of the Turkestani intelligentsia and nobility, together with their families, and many had settled in Poland, several hundred thousand of them came under German control. The *Einsatzkommando* herded them, together with Turkestani prisoners of war from the Russian army, into sixteen camps, where they all—including women and children —were paraded before SS officers. Those who had long, hooked noses or slanted eyes or were circumcised were ordered to turn left, taken to a nearby ditch, and shot. Gajun, who was allowed to visit the camps after being classified "reliable," was horror struck. When he returned to Berlin, Gajun (who spoke fluent German but no Russian) went to see Count von der Schulenburg, the former German ambassador in Moscow, and told him: "People are wretched, starved, underfed, living in holes in the ground, and now and again the Gestapo shot some, actually shot some in front of my eyes!" Schulenburg reported to Ribbentrop, who, after checking with Hitler, relayed the message that nothing could be done. Gajun, thereupon, informed the International Red Cross in Switzerland and the Turkish ambassador in Berlin, and stirred up such a brouhaha that a commission was formed by Rosenberg to look into the conditions in the camps, where typhus had become epidemic.

In practice, however, little changed. "It is a matter of common knowledge," Gajun recounted to Colonel Hinkel, "that the execution of circumcised men still went on during the invasion of the Crimea. Every German who was there can tell you. I met a colonel who told me how astonished he was when he saw agents of the Gestapo execute Turks." All together, Gajun estimated, between 300,000 and 400,000 Turkestanis had been shot or had died in the camps.

Although Hitler ordered that Jews and commissars were to be screened out before they reached POW camps, the procedure proved impractical, and many were not "selected" before they arrived in the Reich. Those weeded out were then sent to concentration camps for execution. At Auschwitz, to which Russian prisoners were dispatched to clear land and build factories, the officers and "commissars" were initially executed one at a time with a shot in the back of the neck at the so-called Black Wall, adjacent to the *Bunker* (camp prison). This was a laborious procedure that wore on the nerves of the SS executioners. In October 1941, however, an SS officer named Arthur Johann Breitwieser noticed that one of his companions, charged with delousing the camp laundry, was instantly knocked out when exposed to a whiff of Zyklon B, the gas that was used as a disinfectant.

To Breitwieser, this seemed to offer the possibility of more efficient and less time-consuming executions. After ordering the half-submerged lower level of the *Bunker* sealed, Breitwieser had several cans of the blue pellets, which vaporize when exposed to air, dropped in among the one thousand Russians awaiting execution.

Two days later the camp inmates detailed to remove the bodies were met by a fearsome sight. Men with contorted faces had locked themselves together in their death agonies, torn out each other's hair, and bitten off their fingers. Their flesh and their clothes had fused into gelatinous blobs that sometimes disintegrated when the members of the detail tried to pick them up.

Infamous as the Commissar Order was, it was responsible for only a relatively small proportion of the deaths among the Russian POWs. Since Goering and Rosenberg postulated that the Germans had no obligation to feed Russians, and the Wehrmacht had difficulty supplying its own troops, most prisoners were left to starve to death, either deliberately or through indifference. A high-ranking Wehrmacht officer reported to Keitel: "The fate of the Soviet prisoners of war [is] a tragedy of the greatest extent.

"The native population within the Soviet Union is absolutely willing to put food at the disposal of the prisoners of war. Several understanding camp commanders have successfully chosen this course. However, in the majority of cases, the camp commanders have forbidden the civilian population to put food at the disposal of the prisoners, and they have rather let them starve to death.

"Even on the march to the camps, the civilian population was not allowed to give the prisoners of war food. In many cases, when prisoners of war could no longer keep up on the marches because of hunger and exhaustion, they were shot before the eyes of the horrified civilian population, and the corpses were left."

Since the occupiers were, in fact, intent on stripping the land of everything edible, the captives were herded onto open ground fenced with barbed wire, and there, without shelter or tools, left to graze like cattle on grass, roots, and bark. Men died in layers huddling together for warmth. The living ate the dead, and cannibalism became epidemic.

Goering, his corpulence covered with a great sable coat that the Italian foreign minister, Count Ciano, described as "something between what automobile drivers wore in 1906 and what a high-grade prostitute wears to the opera," chucklingly told the Italian foreign minister that the Soviet prisoners, "after having eaten everything possible, including the soles of

The Structure of the SS and Police

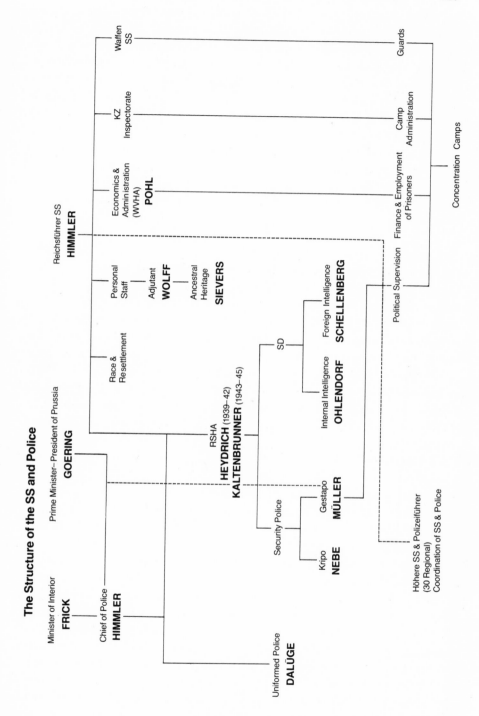

their boots, have begun to eat each other and, what is more serious, have eaten a German sentry."

One SS leader suggested to Himmler that two million prisoners be shot immediately so as to thin out the ranks and give the remainder a better chance for survival. A high-ranking German political officer noted: "It is especially peculiar that the food supplies are deficient only for prisoners of war from the Soviet Union, while complaints about the treatment of other prisoners of war, Polish, Serbian, French and English, have not become vociferous. It is obvious that nothing is so suitable for strengthening the power of resistance of the Red Army as the knowledge that in German captivity a slow, miserable death is to be met."

By and large the Russian soldiers did, indeed, cease to surrender. The fighting took on the savagery of the hegira that Hitler had proclaimed. Units overwhelmed by the Wehrmacht's tidal wave but never subdued resurfaced everywhere behind the German lines and were augmented by stragglers and escaped prisoners until they totaled at least a quarter million men, often joined by women and children. The partisans assumed control of a third or more of some areas, imposed their own quotas on the harvest of local farmers, and interdicted the tenuous German supply lines by raiding convoys and blowing up trains to gather booty.

At first, Hitler professed to see but one more opportunity for his brand of nihilism in the flare-up of guerrilla warfare. "The Russians have now ordered partisan warfare behind our front," he told his intimates on July 16. "This partisan war, again, has some advantage for us. It enables us to eradicate everyone who opposes us."

On September 16, Keitel, at Hitler's behest, followed up by issuing the "Partisan Order":

"Since the beginning of the campaign against Russia Communist insurrections have broken out in all the areas occupied by Germany. It can be seen that this is a mass movement centrally directed by Moscow. In view of the considerable political and economic tensions in the occupied areas, it must moreover be anticipated that nationalists and other circles will take full opportunity to cause difficulties for the German occupation forces by joining the Communist uprising. In this way, an increasing danger to the German conduct of the war is developing.

"The measures taken so far to meet the general Communist insurrection movement have proved inadequate. The Führer has now given orders that we must take action everywhere with the most drastic means in order to crush the movement.

"Every case of rebellion against the German occupation forces, regardless of circumstances, must be concluded to be of Communistic origin.

In order to suppress these machinations from the beginning, the strongest means have to be employed. . . . As atonement for the life of one German soldier, the death penalty for fifty to one hundred Communists is generally considered as proper."

The difficulties with the Partisan Order, beyond its terrible implications of massive and indiscriminate retaliation, was that, like the Commissar Order, it was impractical. Communists were almost as difficult to identify as commissars; and, even if most of them should be uncovered, their numbers would be exhausted rather quickly at the rate of fifty or one hundred for each German. Substitutes would have to be found. Since the decree stated that "a clever campaign of propaganda" should emphasize that these "strict measures free the native population from these Communistic criminals and are thus to their own advantage," the substitutes would have to be people with whom the inhabitants did not identify.

On September 19, three days after the issuance of the Partisan Order, Kiev, with a population of 850,000, fell. Unbeknown to the Germans, the Red Army had planted more than ten thousand mines in the city. Every major building and strategic location was implanted with the wireless-controlled explosives linked to the electrical system.

Five days later, on September 24, the Soviet engineers, having given the Germans time to settle in, began pressing the buttons. The two major hotels, the central post office, the radio station, the telegraph office—all came crashing down upon the heads of the invaders. Many of the burning buildings exploded like giant firecrackers, showering all those in the vicinity with flaming shards. By the time the fire was controlled on September 29, approximately one thousand Germans (as well as countless inhabitants) had been killed, and three-fourths of a square mile of the downtown area lay devastated. The Germans were so shaken that, for fear of further explosions, they did not restore power in the city for weeks thereafter.

There was, of course, no question that the occurrence had *not* been the result of partisan activity. The Soviets had merely turned Kiev into the biggest and most sophisticated booby trap in history, and the Germans had fallen into it like klutzes. But Field Marshal Walther von Reichenau, the ardent Nazi general commanding the area, was in need of scapegoats. Applying the Partisan Order, he could shoot at least fifty thousand Communists. Of course, there was no way of identifying fifty thousand Communists, or even a fraction of that number. The only segregatable group approaching such a multitude and included on Hitler's list of "enemies" were the Jews.

On September 29, the same day the fire was controlled, placards went up ordering the 170,000 Jews of Kiev to report immediately for "resettlement." Those that failed to do so, the notices warned, would be subject to severe penalties. Approximately one-fifth of the Jews responded. They were marched to the Jewish cemetery, abutting the Babi Yar ravine, within earshot of the center of the city. For two days and nights rifle and machinegun fire crackled uninterruptedly. Before it ceased, nearly 34,000 men, women, and children lay sprawled in the ravine—the greatest single slaughter of the war.

According to the report of a German captain, "The population took the execution calmly, many with satisfaction. The newly vacated homes of the Jews were turned over for relief of the housing shortage."

Obviously, the extermination at Babi Yar was no secret. Stories and rumors spread through much of the Ukraine, and created such a sense of bewilderment in the German army that ten days later Reichenau issued an explanatory order designed to excise the troops' unease:

"The soldier must have full understanding for the necessity of a severe but just revenge on subhuman Jewry. The army has to aim at another purpose, that is the annihilation of revolts in hinterlands, which, as experience proves, have always been caused by Jews. The most essential aim of the war against the Jewish-Bolshevistic system is a complete destruction of their means of power and the elimination of Asiatic influence from European culture. In this connection the troops are facing tasks which exceed the one-sided routine of soldiery. The soldier in the Eastern Territories is not merely a fighter according to the rules of war, but also a bearer of ruthless national ideology and the avenger of bestialities which have been inflicted upon Germany and racially related nations. This is the only way to fulfill our historic task to liberate the German people once and forever from the Asiatic-Jewish danger."

30   Einsatzgruppen

Hitler thought Reichenau's order so exemplary that he directed its distribution to troops throughout the East, where the terror of the *Einsatzgruppen* was now in full sway and leading to friction with the Wehrmacht.

Since the Jews ranged from fifty percent of the skilled and professional workers in central Poland to ninety percent in Russia and the Ukraine, the Wehrmacht depended heavily upon them in the support areas. "The attitude of the Jewish population was anxious—obliging from the beginning," a Wehrmacht armaments officer reported to Berlin in one of the documents introduced at the trial. "They tried to avoid everything that might displease the German administration. That they hated the German administration and army inwardly goes without saying and cannot be surprising. But it cannot be said that the Jews as such represented a danger to the German armed forces. The output produced by the Jews, who, of course, were prompted by nothing but the feeling of fear, was satisfactory to the troops and the German administration."

Himmler complained so much about the "close relations between the Wehrmacht and the Jews" that Keitel issued an order: "Any cooperation of the Wehrmacht with the Jewish population who are openly or secretly anti-German, as well as the use of a single Jew in any preferred auxiliary position, will have to cease." Employment of Jews was to be limited to back-breaking jobs in the building of roads, repair of railroads, and the like. "Care is to be taken that Jewish labor is used only in those productions which will later suffer no noticeable interruption in case of a rapid withdrawal of these labor forces. It is to be avoided in every case that Jewish workers become indispensable in essential production."

This was an impossible stipulation, since the Jews were essential from the very beginning. The officials of Rosenberg's civilian administration joined the Wehrmacht in attempting to tone down the SS executions, which tore up the whole fabric of the occupation.

Since the number of men in the *Einsatzgruppen* was inadequate for the task, the SS recruited from among the native populations, who more often than not had fewer scruples than the Germans, and frequently constituted the preponderance of the extermination squads. In the Baltic port of Libau, the rampaging SS and their Latvian auxiliaries swept thousands of Jews off the streets and machine-gunned them at the naval base, where the day previous they had been the principal workers. As blood coursed down the gutters of the streets and desperate people scurried to find hiding places, the economy was paralyzed. Hinrich Lohse, a prominent Gauleiter whom Rosenberg had named commissioner for the Baltic and White Russia, threatened to throw the *Einsatzkommando* leader out of the territory if the shootings did not cease. Himmler brought the dispute to Hitler's attention. An immediate explanation was demanded from Rosenberg, who petulantly wrote Lohse:

"The RSHA has complained that the Reich Commissioner for the East has forbidden execution of Jews in Libau. I request a report on this matter by return mail."

"I have forbidden the wild executions of Jews in Libau because they were not justifiable in the manner in which they were carried out," Lohse wrote back. "I should like to be informed whether your inquiry of 31 October is to be regarded as a directive to liquidate all Jews in the East? Shall this take place without regard to age and sex and economic interests of the Wehrmacht; for instance, specialists in the armaments industry?"

"Yes," Rosenberg responded. "Economic considerations should fundamentally remain unconsidered in the settlement of the problem."

Although Lohse's objections resulted in some key workers being exempted, the SS had no mercy on Jewish doctors and dentists, and so eliminated more than half the medical personnel in Lithuania. At this point, the Germans, discovering that they were facing epidemics of catastrophic proportions, were forced to import doctors from the physician-short Reich. (The medical musical chairs later continued with the conscription of Ukrainian doctors and nurses to work in German hospitals.)

In neighboring White Russia, the *Einsatzkommando* with their indigenous footsoldiers swept over the land like ravenous locusts feeding on Jews. At Borisov, a town fifty miles east of Minsk, an army intelligence officer learned on Friday, October 17, 1941, that the extermination was to take place on Sunday and Monday. The chief of the Russian security police, Ehof, an ethnic German appointed by the SD, had served the czarist government in a similar capacity, and then adapted himself to the Communist regime. In fact, the intelligence officer reported, "these security men are said to consist largely of old Communists, but nobody dares to report them because they are feared. To my astounded question whether it would be possible to dispatch eight thousand persons into Eternity in the course of a single night in a fairly orderly manner, he [Ehof] replied that this was not the first time he had done this and he was no longer an amateur." About fifteen hundred Jews were to be spared temporarily, since they were specialists such as cobblers, tailors, blacksmiths, locksmiths—in other words, artisans who were urgently needed.

"Although the shootings of Jews were to be kept secret, they were already known in the ghetto on Saturday," the officer continued. "I gave my own boots for repair to a Jewish cobbler. There I learned that a delegation was on its way to the mayor to obtain a temporary reprieve from these executions so that they might present a petition to the general. The mayor promised them to speak to the general and he himself could only say that the conduct of the Jews had been exemplary in every respect —the performing of the work imposed on the Jews, the raising of 300,000 rubles, the turning in of all gold and silver, etc."

On Saturday night, in preparation for the event, a great party entitled "Celebration of the German Police" was held. All of the town's prominent personalities participated in the enormous consumption of liquor. A great ditch, one hundred yards long and nine feet deep, had already been dug by Russian prisoners of war. "At three o'clock in the morning the shootings began. First the men were brought out. They were driven to the place of execution in Russian trucks, escorted by men of the Russian security police. The women and children of all ages whimpered and screamed for help as soon as they saw a German soldier. In this manner one vehicle followed another during the whole day in the direction of the place of execution, located in the woods near the former staff headquarters of Army Group Center. Besides, since there were not sufficient vehicles, groups of women and children were constantly being herded down the aforementioned road, and other groups, even mothers with babies in their arms, were standing waiting to be picked up. In the distance the noise of rifles could be heard all day. The women and children cried and screamed, cars raced through the streets bringing new victims—all before the eyes of the civilian population and German military personnel who happened to come along.

"The scenes which took place in the streets were ghastly. The non-Jews may have believed on the preceding evening that the Jews deserved their fate, but the following morning their sentiment was: 'Who ordered such a thing? Now it is the Jews' turn, when will it be ours? What did these poor Jews do? All they did was work!' The executions continued all day Monday. Late in the evening the shooting could be heard not only from the woods, but also spread to the ghetto and the streets of the city, since many Jews broke out of the ghetto and tried somehow to save themselves."

In the bitter cold, those Jews who managed to flee into the countryside had little prospect other than to succumb to exposure and starvation. The police, most of whom were never sober during the exterminations, looted the emptied residences. Fires broke out and cast a reddish glow visible even from the execution site, where people were made to jump naked into the pit, and were then shot from above. Those who followed were forced to arrange the bodies in neat rows, place a thin layer of dirt over them, then tamp down both the dirt and the bodies with their feet before being shot in turn. The heaps of clothing and other articles carried back to the city on the trucks presented a graphic spectacle to the civilians and German troops, some of whom participated in the action as volunteers.

Exactly a week later a battalion of *Einsatzkommando*, composed half of Germans and half of Lithuanians, appeared in Sluzk, sixty miles south of Minsk. Rosenberg's local commissioner, named Carl, reported: "I protested violently, pointing out that a liquidation of Jews must not be allowed to take place in an arbitrary manner. These Jewish tradesmen were simply not expendable because they were indispensable for maintaining the economy. White Russian tradesmen are, so to say, nonexistent, therefore all vital plants would have to be shut down at once if all Jews were to be liquidated."

Carl thought he had the battalion commander's acquiescence to spare essential workers and their families who had proper papers and identification. However, he continued, when the shootings began, "all Jews without exception were taken out of the factories and shops. The town itself offered a picture of horror during the action, which bordered on sadism. With indescribable brutality by the German police officers and particularly the Lithuanians, Jews were taken out of their dwellings and herded together. Everywhere in the town shots were to be heard, and in different streets the corpses of Jews accumulated. The White Russians themselves were worked over with rubber truncheons and rifle butts. There was no question of an action against the Jews anymore. It rather looked like a revolution."

At the grave site, the *Einsatzkommando* had orders to shoot low, so as not to miss the children. Consequently, many Jews collapsed into the trench with excruciating abdominal wounds. The executioners did not bother to finish them off.

Rosenberg's commissioner for White Russia, Gauleiter Wilhelm Kube, protested that "peace and order cannot be maintained in White Russia with methods of that sort. To bury seriously wounded people alive who worked their way out of their graves again is such a base and filthy act that this incident should be reported to the Führer and the Reichsmarshal."

Kube, however, had no reluctance about proceeding with the killings in an *orderly* fashion. During the dead of winter when the ground froze, so that it was impossible to bury the bodies, the killings were interrupted. In the spring they resumed. On July 31, 1942, Kube reported that, in cooperation with "the exceedingly capable leader of the SD, *Obersturmbannführer* Dr. Strauch, we have liquidated in the last ten weeks about 55,000 Jews in White Russia. In the city of Minsk approximately 10,000 Jews were liquidated on July 28 and 29, 6,500 of them Russian Jews, predominantly aged persons, women and children, the remainder Jews unfit for commitment to labor who had been deported to Minsk in November of last year from Vienna, Brünn, Bremen, and Berlin on order of the Führer.

"After completion of the action against the Jews in Minsk," Kube continued, "SS *Obersturmbannführer* Dr. Strauch reported to me tonight with just indignation that suddenly a transport of one thousand Jews had arrived from Warsaw for the Luftwaffe Administrative Command. I beg the Reich Commissioner to prevent transports of such a kind. The Polish Jew is, exactly like the Russian Jew, an enemy of Germanism. He presents a politically dangerous element, far exceeding his value as a skilled worker. I fully agree with the commander of the SD that we shall liquidate every shipment of Jews which is not ordered or announced by our superior offices."

This, of course, was the ultimate insanity: The SD exterminated the indigenous skilled workers the Wehrmacht desperately needed; the Wehrmacht imported more; and as soon as they arrived, the SD murdered the newcomers as well.

The prosecution had been in the midst of the account of *Einsatzgruppe* operations in central Russia when the trial had recessed for Christmas; and Colonel Storey resumed on January 2 by presenting the affidavit of Hermann Gräbe, a German construction manager who had worked in the Ukraine for more than two years.

On July 13, 1942, Gräbe had witnessed a violent roundup of Jews in the town of Rovno on the Polish-Russian border: "All through the night these beaten, hounded, and wounded people moved along the lighted streets. Women carried their dead children in their arms, children pulled and dragged their dead parents by their arms and legs down the road toward the train. Again and again the cries, 'Open the door! Open the door!' echoed through the ghetto.

"I saw dozens of corpses of all ages and both sexes in the streets I had to walk along. The doors of the houses stood open, windows were smashed. Pieces of clothing, shoes, stockings, jackets, caps, hats, coats, etc. were lying in the street. At the corner of a house lay a baby, less than a year old, with his skull crushed. Blood and brains were spattered over the house wall and covered the area immediately around the child."

A few months later, in October 1942, Gräbe had come across a mass execution: "Moennikes and I went directly to the pit. Nobody bothered us. Now I heard rifle shots in quick succession, from behind one of the earth mounds. The people who had got off the truck—men, women, and children of all ages—had to undress upon the order of an SS man, who carried a riding or dog whip. They had to put down their clothes in fixed places, sorted according to shoes, top clothing, and underclothing. I saw a heap of shoes of about eight hundred to one thousand pairs, great piles of underlinen and clothing. Without screaming or weeping these people undressed, stood around in family groups, kissed each other, said farewell, and waited for a sign from another SS man, who stood near the pit. An old woman with snow-white hair was holding a one-year-old child in her arms and singing to it, and tickling it. The child was cooing with delight. The couple were looking on with tears in their eyes. The father was holding the hand of a boy about ten years old speaking to him softly; the boy was fighting his tears. The father pointed toward the sky, stroked his head, and seemed to explain something to him. At that moment the SS man at the pit shouted something to his comrade. The latter counted off about twenty persons and instructed them to go behind the earth mound. I walked around the mound, and found myself confronted by a tremendous grave. People were closely wedged together and lying on top of each other so that only their heads were visible. Nearly all had blood running over their shoulders from their heads. I looked for the man who did the shooting. He was an SS man, who sat at the edge of the narrow end of the pit, his feet dangling into the pit. He had a tommy gun on his knees and was smoking a cigarette. The people, completely naked, went down some steps which were cut in the clay wall of the pit and clambered over the heads of the people lying there, to the place to which the SS man directed them. They lay down in front of the dead or injured people; some caressed those who were still alive and spoke to them in a low voice. Then I heard a series of shots. I looked into the pit and saw that the bodies were twitching or the heads lying already motionless on top of the bodies that lay before them."

This was the type of account that, no matter how often it was repeated, never failed to stir the tribunal. Still, it would have had an even greater impact had Gräbe, who was easily available, been called to testify for himself. And Jackson, under pressure from his staff, finally agreed to permit the use of a few key German witnesses in person.

No one, however, quite anticipated the sensation generated by Otto Ohlendorf when he appeared the next day. Thirty-eight years old, short and blond, he would have been overlooked in any gathering. Yet he was, in some ways, the Savonarola of the Nazi era. A militant anti-Semite, he had joined the party, of which he had the most idealistic conception, at the age of eighteen. After graduating with a degree in economics, he had gone to work at the Institute for World Economics in Kiel. He had an eighteenth-century belief in laissez-faire, and his vision of the party was of an organization that would simultaneously smite the Communists and big business, and nurture the development of small businesses and independent enterprise. With his intellectualism and insistence on speaking the truth, he would, had he been Catholic, have found a natural home among the Jesuits. Disillusioned by Hitler's alliance with Schacht, Krupp, and the other Rhineland bankers and industrialists, outraged by what he considered Ley's bolshevization of the German workers, and shocked by the corruption that flowered in the Party Organization, he had generated consternation among local party leaders by his outspokenness. At one point he had been arrested and interrogated by the Gestapo.

Friends had obtained a job for him in Berlin, where within a year his intellect and analytical ability had come to the attention of Heydrich. In 1936 he had joined the SD for the purpose of establishing a network of economic intelligence. Heydrich found him invaluable; but when the party functionaries awoke to the fact that the SD, purportedly the party's intelligence organization, was turning its eye inward, they raised such a howl that Himmler severely curtailed Ohlendorf's operation.

Upon the outbreak of the war, nevertheless, Ohlendorf's talents were too valuable to be left lying fallow; and he was made chief of Amt III, the Internal Intelligence Service.

When Barbarossa was launched, Heydrich pressed his principal subordinates to take charge of the *Einsatzkommando*, so as to tie them to him irrevocably through bonds of blood. Ohlendorf was placed in command of *Einsatzgruppe* D, which had responsibility for the southern Ukraine and the Crimea. He had spent a year in Russia, then returned to Berlin in June of 1942 to resume his post. His "Reports from the Reich," which presented the only unvarnished, factual account of conditions in the nation, had circulated among the top echelon of the government and the party.

The pretrial interrogation of Ohlendorf had been conducted by Lieutenant Colonel Smith W. Brookhart, Jr., the rock-jawed son of a famous midwestern senator, Wildman Smith Brookhart. Ohlendorf, after first offering to establish a German intelligence organization for the Allies, formed an attachment to Brookhart, and wanted the American to help him write a book. He could not understand why any of the high-ranking Nazis incarcerated at Nuremberg should take offense at his recounting of the truth. "Every individual will have to stand for what he has done and be held responsible for what he has done, and also make a complete statement of what he has done," he assured Brookhart. Nothing upset him or dejected him more than the accusation by Major Leon Goldensohn, who had replaced Dr. Kelley as the prison psychiatrist, that he must be a sadist, a pervert, or a lunatic. Goldensohn could not understand how else a man of such integrity and incorruptibility could have commanded an *Einsatzgruppe*.

The fact of the matter was that Ohlendorf, as Himmler had indicated when he called him Nazism's "Knight of the Holy Grail," was gripped by the fanaticism of a crusader. He would slay the heretics not because he liked to kill them, but because he believed their slaughter necessary in pursuit of his faith.

It almost beggared belief that such a gem of veracity should have been discovered among the prevaricators; and a thorough interrogation of Ohlendorf on the witness stand might have done much to bring the true state of affairs in the Reich into focus and appreciably increase the comprehension of the judges. Logic dictated that the adept Brookhart, who had worked with him for months, should be the one to question him; but Colonel Amen, of course, was not about to let such a prize get away from him; and Amen was interested only in Ohlendorf's leadership of the *Einsatzgruppe* and had little knowledge of the mass of additional material Brookhart had developed.

After taking his oath, Ohlendorf, since he had not specifically been told or granted permission to sit down, remained standing during much

of his testimony. As he spoke, precisely, clerically, the normal hum of
activity in the courtroom died away and everyone's eyes became riveted
on his jockey-sized figure.

"What was the ultimate objective of Group D?" Amen asked.

"The instructions were that in the Russian operational areas of the
Einsatzgruppen the Jews, as well as the Soviet political commissars, were to
be liquidated."

"And when you say 'liquidated' do you mean 'killed'?"

"Yes." Ohlendorf nodded imperceptibly. "I mean killed."

"Did you, personally, have any conversations with Himmler respect-
ing any communication from Himmler to the chiefs of army groups and
armies concerning this mission?"

"Yes. Himmler told me that before the beginning of the Russian
campaign Hitler had spoken of this mission to a conference of the army
groups and the army chiefs—no, not the army chiefs but the commanding
generals—and had instructed the commanding generals to provide the
necessary support."

"Did you have any other conversation with Himmler concerning this
order?"

"Yes, in the late summer of 1941 Himmler was in Nikolaev," Ohlendorf continued. Nikolaev was a city on the shores of the Black Sea halfway
between Odessa and the Crimea. In this pleasant setting Ohlendorf had,
in fact, been procrastinating, and had hoped to avoid a mass execution by
registering all Jews and selecting only the "Bolshevists" from among them.
When Himmler found out what Ohlendorf had (or had not) done, he was
furious, and demanded that the exterminations be initiated immediately.

"He assembled the leaders and the men of the *Einsatzkommando*,"
Ohlendorf declared, "repeated to them the liquidation order, and pointed
out that the leaders and men who were taking part in the liquidation bore
no personal responsibility for the execution of this order. The responsibility was his, alone, and the Führer's."

"Do you know how many persons were liquidated by *Einsatz* Group
D under your direction?"

"In the year between June 1941 and June 1942 the *Einsatzkommando*
reported ninety thousand people liquidated."

"Did that include men, women, and children?"

"Yes," Ohlendorf acknowledged.

"On what pretext, if any, were they rounded up?"

"On the pretext that they were to be resettled." Ohlendorf paused.

"Will you continue?"

"After the registration, the Jews were collected at one place; and from
there they were later transported to the place of execution, which was, as

a rule, an antitank ditch or a natural excavation. The executions were carried out in a military manner by firing squads under command."

"What was done with the personal property and the clothing of the persons executed?"

"All valuables were sent to Berlin, to the RSHA or to the Reich Ministry of Finance. At first the clothing was given to the population, but in the winter of 1941–1942 it was collected and disposed of by the NSV [the Nazi relief organization]."

"How about watches, for example, taken from the victims?"

"At the request of the army, watches were made available to the forces at the front."

Though occasionally Ohlendorf's voice seemed on the verge of breaking, he might have been detailing the latest economics statistics. He was the antithesis of the image of Nazi brutality; and Biddle began to wonder if the Allies were confronted with a nation of Jekylls and Hydes, as Frank seemed to indicate when he mused: "Barbarism must be a strong German racial characteristic—how else could Himmler have gotten men to carry out his murderous orders?" Ohlendorf's bureaucratic, dispassionate manner only heightened the shock with which his recitation was received.

Contrapuntally, during the next few weeks, the judges were to be treated to flesh and blood accounts from eyewitnesses and people who had been on the lethal end of the weapons.

A man named Kamenev stated in his affidavit: "We reached the trench. We were lined up facing it, and the Germans began their preparations to shoot us in the nape of the neck. The shots rang out and my son instantly jumped into the trench. I threw myself in after him. Dead bodies began to fall upon me in the trench. About three PM an eleven-year-old boy stood up from among the pile of corpses and began to call, 'Little fathers, those of you who are still alive, get up. The Germans are gone.' I was afraid to do so, since I thought that the boy was shouting by order of the policemen. The boy called out a second time, and then my son answered him. He stood up and asked, 'Dad, are you still alive?' I could not say anything and merely nodded. My son and the other boy dragged me out from under the bodies. We saw some others who were still alive and who were shouting, 'Help us!' Some were wounded. All the time, while I had been lying in the trench, under the bodies of the dead, I could hear the shrieks and wails of the women and children. The Germans had started shooting old men, women, and children after shooting us."

A youth, Anatol Bombarenko, related: "I got up and the two of us began to drag out the living from beneath the corpses. I was covered with blood. A light mist hung over the trench—steam arising from the rapidly congealing mass of dead bodies, from the pools of blood, and from the last breath of the dying."

Himmler, the one time he witnessed an execution, would have fainted had he not been propped up by his adjutant, Karl Wolff. Consequently, Ohlendorf testified, in the spring of 1942 he had received "a special order from Himmler to the effect that women and children were not to be exposed to the mental strain of the executions; and thus the men of the *Kommando,* mostly married men, should not be compelled to aim at women and children." In order to accomplish this goal, a young SS university graduate, *Untersturmführer* Becker, had devised a truck with a sealed body into which carbon monoxide was pumped from the engine.

The vans, which came to be called "soul destroyers" by the populace, had had their own drawbacks, however. Ohlendorf and his subordinates preferred the strain of shooting people to that of unloading the corpses from the vans. In Ohlendorf's opinion, "The unloading of the corpses [was] an unnecessary mental strain [because of] the terrible impression created by the position of the corpses themselves and by the state of the vans—certain functions of the body had taken place leaving the corpses lying in filth."*

The *Einsatzgruppen,* Ohlendorf related, had obtained their personnel from all the various organizations in Himmler's domain, and Ohlendorf himself had augmented his unit of five hundred Germans with five hundred Tatars. Attempting to explain to the court the structure of the *Reich Sicherheitshauptamt* (Reich Security Main Office), he narrated: "The RSHA as such never actually had official validity. Party and state offices with different authority were amalgamated. Under this designation RSHA, no directives or laws or orders could be issued on a legal basis, because the state police, in its ministerial capacity, was still subordinate to the ministry of the interior, whereas the SD, despite this setup, was an organ of the party. The RSHA was therefore nothing more than a camouflage designation which did not correctly represent the actual state of affairs but gave the chief of the Sipo and the SD [Heydrich] the opportunity of using one or the other letterhead at any time."

After Ohlendorf continued further in this vein, Lawrence, overstating his degree of comprehension, commented: "I'm not sure that I follow altogether what you have been saying."

---

*Becker protested that the unfortunate consequences were not his fault: "The application of gas usually is not undertaken correctly. In order to come to an end as fast as possible, the driver presses the accelerator to the fullest extent. By doing that the persons to be executed suffer death from suffocation and not death from dozing off as was planned. My directions now have proved that by correct adjustment of the levers death comes faster and the prisoners fall asleep peacefully. Distorted faces and excretions such as could be seen before are no longer noticed."

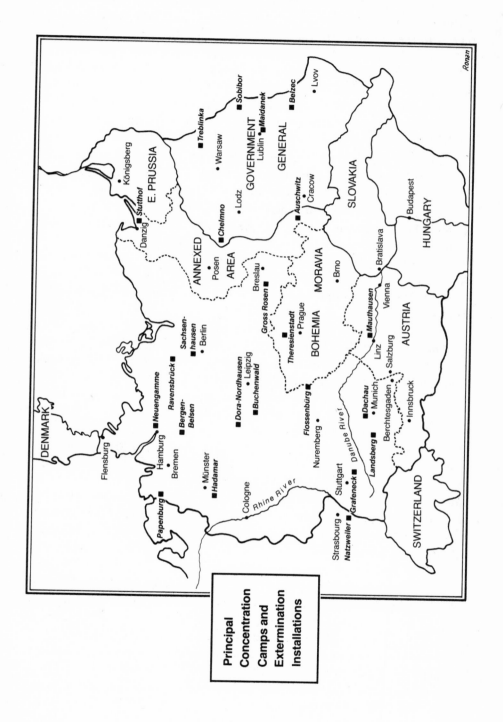

Principal
Concentration
Camps and
Extermination
Installations

Ludwig Babel, the attorney for the SS, attempted to elicit some explanation for the Ohlendorf phenomenon: "Did you have no scruples in regard to the execution of these orders?"

"Yes, of course," Ohlendorf replied.

"And how is it they were carried out regardless of these scruples?"

"Because to me it is inconceivable that a subordinate leader should not carry out orders given by the leaders of the state," Ohlendorf answered, astonished.

"Was the legality of the orders explained to these people under false pretenses?" Babel desperately sought to discover some exculpatory factor.

"I do not understand your question," Ohlendorf retorted icily. "Since the order was issued by the superior authorities, the question of legality could not arise in the minds of these individuals, for they had sworn obedience to the people who had issued the orders."

"Could any individual expect to succeed in evading the execution of these orders?"

"No, the result would have been a court martial with a corresponding sentence."

This was not entirely true, since one of the aspects of the Nazi system was that it operated on two tiers. While introducing its own pragmatic immorality, it never dismantled the old legal structure. Anyone who evaded a clearly immoral or illegal order with enough determined diplomacy or deviousness had not been called to account.

31   Speer and Sauckel: Slave Labor

Theoretically, by the late fall of 1941, Hitler had achieved his objectives of destroying the bulk of the Soviet army, conquering the Ukraine with its wealth of agriculture and natural resources, and converting the Baltic into a German lake on which ore ships from Scandinavia could sail without fear of attack.

The German thesis had been that, at this point, the Soviet Union would collapse. But nothing of the sort occurred. Repeatedly the Russians suffered terrible defeats, yet dragged themselves off the battlefield to fight again. In the Ukraine, where Hitler had expected to come into possession of seventy-five percent of the Soviet arms industry and enough food to make up the deficit in the Reich, the Russians had carted off a large part of the harvest, dismantled factories and shipped the machines to the Urals, and put out of commission a good part of what they left behind. All of the economic suppositions on which Hitler had predicated the attack were collapsing.

In mid-December, Field Marshal von Brauchitsch, commander in chief of the army, suffered a heart attack and was dismissed. Hitler, already minister of war and head of the Wehrmacht, thereupon appointed himself commanding general of the army as well. For the subsequent three and a half years of his life he devoted most of his time to the eastern battlefront.

By the end of the winter the German army had suffered a million casualties, and the loss of equipment was comparatively even greater. Soviet industry, transported to the Urals, soon started to outproduce the German. Propelled into the forefront of this disaster was Albert Speer, who within months became one of the most powerful men in the Reich, and by his ruthless exploitation of manpower and reorganization of German industry strove his utmost to stave off a collapse.

Speer had been born in 1905 into one of the top twenty families in Mannheim. His father and grandfather were architects and industrialists, and in 1927 Albert received his own architectural degree. Marrying the attractive and engaging sweetheart of his teens, Speer became an instructor at the Technical Institute in Berlin.

In January 1931, some of his students persuaded him to attend a Hitler rally. Speer, bored, his architectural career stymied by the Depression, was so inspired by Hitler's vision of a resurgent Reich that, without having more than cursory knowledge of Nazi aims, he joined the party.

Ownership of an automobile made him important to the party from a practical standpoint; and his ancestry was of value to the Nazis, attempting to recast their image in a mold of respectability. Speer became a close companion of his *Kreisleiter*, Karl Hanke, who himself was an intimate of Goebbels, the Berlin Gauleiter as well as Nazi propaganda chief.

As the party's fortunes increased, Speer was commissioned, first, to refurbish its Berlin headquarters, and then, early in 1933, the Propaganda Ministry. As a result of his acquaintance with Hanke and Goebbels, Speer was charged with preparing the setting for the first Nuremberg rally. This led to his introduction to Hitler and his selection as assistant architect for the renovation of the chancellor's residence in Berlin. Speer's entire career was, in truth, linked inseparably to the Nazi Party.

"For the commission to do a great building, I would have sold my soul like Faust. Now I had found my Mephistopheles," Speer later commented in his memoirs. By the end of 1933, he had been absorbed into Hitler's immediate circle. To Hitler, Speer was the personification of his own architectural ambitions—could Hitler have been reborn as someone else, he would have chosen to be Speer. The two men shared the same artistic soul; they had like visions of megamonumental buildings designed to erase the inferiority complex of Germans in general and Hitler in particular. "Why always the biggest?" Hitler asked, then answered: "I do this to restore to each German his self-respect. In one hundred years I want to be saying to the individual, 'We are not inferior. On the contrary, we are the complete equals of every other nation.' "

To accomplish his aim, Hitler, with Speer as his architect, dreamed of developing Berlin into a city of monuments dwarfing any other ever built before, including the pyramids. In 1936 he ordered plans prepared for a stadium seating 450,000 people, a hall with a capacity of 150,000, topped by an 825-foot-diameter dome surpassing St. Peter's, a 400-foot-high Arch of Triumph into which the French Arc de Triomphe would fit forty-nine times, a statue of a German woman forty-six feet higher than the Statue of Liberty, and a palace covering 22 million square feet for himself. To accommodate the parades of the victorious armies, avenues were to be laid out hundreds of feet wide. But these were simply the centerpieces of a gigantic complex whose construction would have sapped the resources of Europe for a generation, cost tens of billions of dollars, and had little or no practical value. Yet Speer was intoxicated by Hitler's fantasies; and Hitler, fascinated by plans and drawings, made a habit of peering over Speer's shoulders and rambling on for hours. One day, a friend asked Speer: "Do you know what you are? You are Hitler's unrequited love."

During the first two years of the war, Speer continued to employ no fewer than 65,000 workers. To transport building materials—including a vast quantity of granite and marble from Scandinavia, the Low Countries, and Italy—Speer established a shipyard and put together his own fleet of one thousand ships. Near Trondheim on the Norwegian coast, Hitler decided to construct one of the world's great naval bases, and assigned Speer the task of laying out a city to accommodate a quarter million German colonists. Similar fortress towns were to be placed by Speer along the French coast and in the heart of Russia. On November 29, 1941, while disaster was overtaking the troops assaulting Moscow, Hitler instructed Speer not to dally: "The building must begin even while this war is still going on. I am not going to let the war keep me from accomplishing my plans."

When, however, Speer broached the question of transporting construction materials and workers to and from Russia to officials of the railroads, on which wounded soldiers were freezing to death in unheated boxcars because of the clogged lines, they were horrified. Speer thereupon suggested to Hitler that thirty thousand of his workers be assigned to the repair and laying of track. Fritz Todt, chief of public works and minister of armaments and munitions, proposed that Speer take responsibility for the rebuilding of the railroads in the Ukraine. In January 1942, Speer began dispatching daily contingents of German engineers and workers to an area devastated by the SD's shooting of the local Jewish transportation technicians.

In February 1942, Todt was killed in an airplane crash; and Hitler appointed Speer, who had missed the flight only because he overslept, to succeed him. Word quickly spread through the hierarchy that "the Führer looks upon Speer as his principal spokesman, his trusted adviser in all economic spheres." By the latter part of March 1942, a somewhat apprehensive official of the Wehrmacht's Armaments Office reported: "Speer is the only one who today can say anything. He can interfere in any department. He already disregards all other departments. We must join the Speer Organization and pull together, otherwise Speer will go his own way."

Because Hitler had insisted consumer production not be reduced beneath the prewar level and pet public work projects had not been curtailed, arms manufacture at the beginning of 1942 was only a quarter of what it had been in 1918. German aircraft production was a fraction of British and American combined. The swollen government bureaucracy, spawned of infinite Nazi suspicions, was a perpetual source of production bottlenecks. (An armaments firm, for example, urgently needing a single quart of alcohol, had to make application to four different agencies, and after a merry-go-round of ten weeks had still been unable to fulfill its requirements.) To avoid disaster during the coming summer, Speer was confronted with no less a task than the reequipment of a substantial part of the armed forces within four months.

Speer proceeded ruthlessly to bend industry to war production. Exploiting Hitler's indecisiveness, he ended Autobahn and nonessential building construction. To get the supplies up to the front, he refurbished the railroads and built Rollbahnen (military highways) through Galicia and southern Russia. For this purpose, Jewish men were conscripted and placed in labor camps. Their families, left without sustenance, were relegated to slow starvation, and then, within a few months, to the quick expedience of extermination.

Since the army and navy chronically complained that, under Goering's dual role of Plenipotentiary for the Four Year Plan and commander of the Luftwaffe, they were being shorted in the allocation of materials and production of weapons, Speer suggested that a Central Planning Board be established as a coordinating agency beneath the aegis of the Four Year Plan. He himself would represent the army and the navy, and Erhard Milch, the operating chief of the Luftwaffe under Goering, the air force. Paul Körner, Goering's World War I comrade and later benefactor, was appointed delegate for the Four Year Plan. (Funk, as economics minister, was added in 1943 when Speer gained control of civilian production as well.) Theoretically, the Central Planning Board was under the authority of Goering; but since Goering, as Speer expected, did not interest himself in its functioning, it was left to Speer, with some input from Milch, to make the decisions.

As early as October 1941, Keitel noted: "The lack of workers is becoming increasingly dangerous for the future German war and armament industry. The expected relief through discharges from the armed forces is uncertain. However, its ultimate extent will by no means correspond to expectations and requirements in view of the great demand." When, following the disaster before Moscow during the winter of 1941, Hitler decided to pull 370,000 more skilled workers out of factories to replenish the army, a gigantic mobilization of labor was required to fill the gaps. Speer knew that the gauleiters would resist every attempt to transfer industry or workers from one area to another, and that they, together with the entrenched bureaucracy in the Labor Ministry and the German Labor Front, were likely to undermine a transfer of manpower from the hundreds of thousands of nonessential jobs created during the 1930s to war production. Speer, therefore, proposed to Hitler the appointment of a Plenipotentiary for Labor Action, capable of imposing his will on the various bureaucracies. He suggested his mentor and friend Karl Hanke, who had become gauleiter of Lower Silesia, for the post.

Bormann, however, perceived that if Speer, who was accumulating power at a rate unprecedented since the early days of the Third Reich, gained control of labor as well as of production, he would pose a unique threat to the civilian dominance of the party and the gauleiters. Bormann, therefore, proposed the appointment of Fritz Sauckel, who, during the 1920s, had been a co-worker of his in Thuringia, and would be under the primary influence of Bormann, not of Speer.

Born in 1894 to a mailman and a seamstress, Sauckel had gone to sea at the age of fifteen, and spent the next five years traversing the oceans on German and Scandinavian sailing ships. At the outbreak of World War I he had been on a voyage to Australia. After the ship was captured by the French, Sauckel had languished for five years in an internment camp. Upon returning to Germany, he had become an apprentice locksmith and toolmaker in his native town of Schweinfurth, famous for its ballbearing works. For a time, Communists had captured control of the state, and Sauckel had seriously considered emigrating to the United States with his wife, whose sister had, with her husband, already established herself in New Jersey.

The east wing of the Palace of Justice, where the trial was held. The courtroom is behind the large curtained windows in the center.

The tribunal *(left to right)* consisted of A. F. Volchkov, the Soviet alternate; I. T. Nikitchenko, the Soviet judge; Norman Birkett, the British alternate; Lord Geoffrey Lawrence, the British judge; Francis Biddle, the American judge; John J. Parker, the American alternate; Donnedieu de Vabres, the French judge; and Robert Falco, the French alternate. Seated in front of the tribunal are members of the secretariat and stenographers.

Colonel Murray C. Bernays originated the trial concept.

Brigadier General Telford Taylor, a key figure in the first trial and chief prosecutor in the follow-up trials, confers with the American prosecutor, Supreme Court Justice Robert Jackson.

Guards, watching the defendants around the clock to prevent suicides, stand outside the cells.

Spectacles are returned to prisoners through the cell portholes in the morning.

Colonel Burton C. Andrus, the prison commandant, left, walks with another officer through the covered walkway leading from the jail to the Palace of Justice.

In the dock, Goering seems bored while Ribbentrop, second from right, chatters away, and Hess, in the middle, looks on bemusedly. Field Marshal Keitel is to the right of Ribbentrop. In the second row, left to right, are Admirals Doenitz and Raeder, and Schirach and Sauckel.

Francis Biddle *(above)* pins ribbon on Brigadier General Mitchell, head of the tribunal secretariat, while most of the other judges look on, and Norman Birkett focuses on the camera. The British and American prosecutors, Maxwell Fyfe and Robert Jackson *(below)* are dwarfed by an assistant British prosecutor, K. C. Roberts.

Goering confers with Hitler and
Field Marshal Blomberg, against
whom he intrigued.

Hans Bernd Gisevius, the most important witness
against Goering *(left)*, and Goering *(above)* are
shown in the witness stand.

Hess and Streicher stand to the right of Hitler at the 1935 Nuremberg rally, at which the anti-Jewish laws were announced.

At Nuremberg, Hess was interrogated by Colonels John Harlan Amen and Smith W. Brookhart, Jr., who sits to the right of Amen.

Financier Hjalmar Schacht, who helped prompt the Nuremberg Laws, eats lunch in the Palace of Justice.

Speer engages Hitler in planning on the Obersalzberg.

Hitler moves around the pieces in a model of a workers' complex as Sauckel, center, and Speer look on *(above)*. Speer talks to his attorneys in the Nuremberg consultation room *(below)*.

Ribbentrop and Hess *(front row)* and Schacht and Funk *(second row, right)* were seated with Hitler when he prophesied the extermination of European Jews on January 31, 1939.

At the signing of the Moscow Pact, Ribbentrop and Stalin were all smiles.

Among the prisoners at Nuremberg were Luise Guyon Witchel, an SS woman of intrigue, left, shown with Himmler's wife Margo, center, and daughter Gudrun.

Hans Frank, governor of Poland, in whose territory most of the extermination took place, is shown greeting Santa Claus at a Christmas Party in Cracow.

Hans Frank carrying a blanket from the courtroom.

Frank's attorney, Alfred Seidl, created a furor over the Moscow Pact.

Otto Ohlendorf, *Einsatzgruppe* commander who testified to supervising the execution of 90,000 Jews, is dwarfed by his American guards

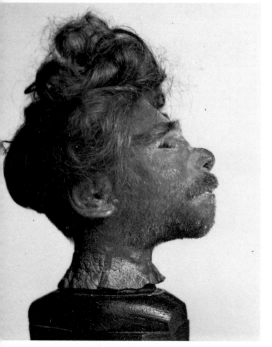

The shrunken head of a hanged Polish worker, used as a paperweight at Buchenwald concentration camp, was introduced as an exhibit at the trial.

Luise Jodl, who made a gallant attempt to save her husband, talks with Jodl's attorney, Franz Exner *(above)*. Doenitz's counsel, Otto Kranzbühler *(below, left)*, sparkplugged the defense. Following their acquittal, Papen, left, signs autographs; Schacht, center, still looks dour; and Fritzsche, right, grins from ear to ear *(below, right)*.

The defendants are shown in the dock while Jodl, standing, makes his final plea. Front row, left to right, are Goering, Hess, Ribbentrop, Keitel, Kaltenbrunner, Rosenberg, Frank, Frick, Streicher, Funk, and Schacht. Second row, left to right, are Raeder, Schirach, Sauckel, Jodl, Papen, Seyss-Inquart, Speer, Neurath, and Fritzsche. *(Doenitz, second row, far left, is not in the picture.)*

Instead, he had, in 1921, become an adherent of Hitler, and held the low party number of 1395. After making hundreds of speeches for the Nazis, he was appointed gauleiter of the region in 1927. When the independence of the *Länder* was eliminated, Hitler named Sauckel *Reichstatthalter* (Reich governor), in addition to gauleiter. This appointment made Sauckel, in effect, a subdictator. Like the other gauleiters, he attempted to resist Himmler's takeover of the police, which represented both muscle and an important part of the spoils system for the gauleiters. "Himmler was purely a police tyrant," Sauckel complained to Major Monigan. "All gauleiters, and, for that matter, all party members, hated him. We, all the National Socialists, didn't want any police state. We wanted a people's state." Had it been pointed out to Sauckel that he was upset because the tyranny of the party had found a rival in the tyranny of the SS, he would have been astonished.

On March 21, 1942, Speer took Sauckel to the Führer headquarters for his official appointment. Burdened with a mammoth inferiority complex, Sauckel had an overeager cub scout's anxiety to please. In the circle of Gauleiters he felt so much of an outsider when they discussed their World War I experiences that once, in order to prove his own fighting spirit, he stowed away aboard a submarine, and Admiral Doenitz had to recall the vessel. "Now," Hitler told him, "you have a chance to fulfill your obligations as a soldier, as we are all soldiers now."

For the prosecution, Thomas Dodd introduced the evidence on the slave labor program, contained in a document book lettered "R."

"The Nazi foreign labor policy," Dodd asserted, "was a policy of mass deportation and mass enslavement . . . of underfeeding and overworking foreign laborers, of subjecting them to every form of degradation, brutality, and inhumanity . . . a policy which constituted a flagrant violation of the laws of war and the laws of humanity.

"We shall show that the Defendants Sauckel and Speer are principally responsible for the formulation of the policy and for its execution."

A million foreign laborers—mostly Polish and French—were already working in Germany as a result of the program initiated by Frank and Goering in the government-general a year earlier. The Poles, upon arrival in Germany, were degraded to the status of slaves. Working mostly on farms, they were quartered in barracks, stables, and sheds. They were forbidden to be on the streets after dark. They were to labor six days a week from dawn to dusk. They could be whipped or cudgeled for the slightest infraction, or simply at the whim of their masters. Any employer who did not keep them at arm's length, or treated them as fellow human beings, could himself be punished severely. Where work camps were established, Himmler threw barbed wire around them and guarded them with the SS in order to prevent contamination of the German "race."

At the commencement of Barbarossa, Hitler, who looked upon communism as a germ that could spread from person to person and infect everyone, had decreed that not a single Russian POW was to be brought into the Reich itself. Now, however, he was forced into acknowledging that the prisoners represented an immense pool of manpower, and directed: "Even the working power of the Russian prisoners of war should be utilized to a large extent by large-scale assignments for the requirements of war industry." Since the Russians, Hitler asserted, were accustomed to living in caves, their accommodations could be minimal. Political "infection" was to be prevented by quarantining the prisoners from the German people.

In truth, of the 3.9 million Russians taken prisoner of war, 2.8 million were already dead, and of the remainder only a few hundred thousand were in good enough shape to make them useful as workers. "We now experience the grotesque picture of having to recruit millions of laborers from the occupied Eastern Territories after prisoners of war have died of hunger like flies," Otto Bräutigam, head of Rosenberg's political department, wrote scathingly.

Sauckel announced that he would import 1.6 million men from the occupied territories, three-fourths of them from the Soviet Union. In conversations of several hours with Hitler and Goering, he broached the possibility of following the British example and utilizing women fully in war production. Even before the outbreak of the war there had been fourteen million women in the German labor force of forty million; and Goering had at that time declared: "Compulsory work for women in wartime is of decisive importance."

Hitler, however, would not hear of a mass assignment of women to factories. He considered that, since tens of thousands of men were being killed, women's most important task was to be breeders, not workers. "German women and girls must, under any circumstance, be protected from moral and mental harm," Hitler declared. They were not to engage in "jobs unsuitable for women, namely endangering their health, the birthrate of our nation, and family and national life."

Nor was there to be any curtailment of the program which assigned unmarried German girls as house servants to Nazi families, "an instrument of political breeding through which the German girls are made politically more reliable." Since, nevertheless, a shortage of servants for party nabobs developed, Hitler a few months later "ordered the immediate importation of 400,000 to 500,000 female domestic workers from the Ukraine between the ages of fifteen and thirty-five."

A miniature white-slave trade was, in fact, being conducted by officials and Wehrmacht officers returning from the East. The Germans enticed, or forcibly carried back, to the Third Reich attractive girls for themselves and their families, or, as Sauckel recounted to Major Monigan, "to give away as presents to friends." Hitler thought this quite all right, stipulating only that the girls must be of "Nordic" appearance. "The illegal bringing of housekeepers into the Reich by members of the Wehrmacht is not to be prevented," Hitler decreed.

To Rosenberg, Sauckel burbled: "It has always been natural for us Germans to refrain from cruelty and mean chicaneries toward the beaten enemy, even if he had proved himself the most bestial and implacable adversary. . . . The principles of German cleanliness, order, and hygiene must therefore also be carefully applied to Russian camps." If the Russians needed any convincing of the benefits awaiting them in the Reich, "they would have to be handled so roughly by the German administration in the East that they should come to feel that they would prefer to go to Germany for work."

Hitler demanded that 300,000 of these men, women, and adolescents, fifteen years and up, be brought to Germany each month. Sauckel sent seven hundred officials east, where they in turn enlisted one thousand natives of the Soviet Union as assistants. Even though elaborate promises of good pay and working conditions, as well as of future preferential treatment in the Greater German Reich, were made, the voluntary response was but a small fraction of the gigantic levy.

Before a month was out, Sauckel's recruiters replaced persuasion with methods that Bräutigam noted "probably have their origin in the blackest periods of the slave trade." Quotas were established for each district and community, and native officials made responsible for fulfilling them. If a village failed to produce the prescribed number of people, it was raided by mixed squads of Germans and indigenous militia. As in Poland, except on a much greater scale, people were snatched indiscriminately from churches, weddings, marketplaces, and festivals, and even from pilgrimages to monasteries.

Rosenberg, complaining to Sauckel, quoted a letter: "You cannot imagine the bestiality. The order came to supply twenty-five workers, but no one reported. Then the German militia came and began to ignite the houses of those who had fled. The fire became very violent, since it had not rained for two months. In addition, the grain stacks were in the farmyards. You can imagine what took place. The people who had hurried to the scene were forbidden to extinguish the flames, beaten, and arrested. The people fell on their knees to kiss the hands of the policemen, but the policemen beat them with rubber truncheons and threatened to burn down the whole village. During the fire the militia went through the adjoining villages and seized the laborers. That is how they raged throughout the night. They have already hunted for one week, and have not yet enough. The imprisoned workers are locked in the schoolhouse. They cannot even go out to perform their natural functions, but have to do it like pigs in the same room. Among them are lame, blind, and aged people. They are now catching humans like dog catchers used to catch dogs."

Upon arrival in Germany, the people were regarded as so many bodies. During the initial period of recruiting, when an attempt was made to obtain volunteers, those signing up had been promised that they would be employed at their specialties. But these promises were never fulfilled. One of Rosenberg's officials reported scarcastically that "Gauleiter Sauckel does not seem to be informed about the real conditions, in which doctors, engineers, teachers, qualified skilled laborers, and such are employed as unskilled workers, mechanics as farmers, and farmers as industrial workers."

An anti-Communist engineer, who had left his family and had come to Germany of his own will, wrote: "I have unloaded coal, have dug up the ground, and have stacked lumber. This is supposed to be 'employment of specialists' in their own line of work. The question constantly arises, why did I go to Germany? Maybe I am to be transformed into an outcast prisoner. What misdeeds did I commit against Germany? Our food ration consists at four o'clock in the morning of three-fourths of a liter [a little less than three pints] of tea and in the evening at six o'clock of three-fourths of a liter of soup and 250 grams [about nine ounces] of bread. On account of the undernourishment and heavy work, I am weak and exhausted. There is no possibility of surviving like this."

To Major Monigan, Sauckel expressed astonishment at the charges of mistreatment: "The foreign workers got more food than the ordinary German citizen. Not even myself and my family got as much food." Seeking to justify himself, he said: "I hope that it does not seem that I am speaking in my own defense. According to my inner conscience, the German women and foreign workers could not have had any better man to look after their health than myself."

In truth, Sauckel's demand that workers should be provided adequate nourishment was never given serious credence. Instructions went out: "The Russian is easily satisfied. He should not be spoiled or accustomed to German food. Therefore, he should be fed lightly and without serious reduction of our own food balance." In theory, this meant that the Russian was to be provided with eleven hundred calories a day—even if he performed the heaviest labor—but in practice such a quantity was seldom attained. A German factory foreman related: "The Russians' food consisted of a dirty, watery soup containing a few foul potatoes and a bit of cabbage. When the food containers were opened, the whole works stank. Our people often held their noses. The Russians were so hungry that they were never satisfied. They would let themselves be beaten half to death for a piece of bread and never murmur."

The workers were expected to make do with whatever clothing they brought along; for, together with the food and labor shortage, the textile scarcity was such that the *Winterhilfe* charity organization depended for its clothing distribution to Germans largely on items stripped from Jews prior to their extermination. Since the roundup of workers took place primarily in the spring and summer, their dress was unsuited for the German winters. Hence they used the single blanket they were issued not only as a bed cover but as an overcoat—when it rained or snowed, they had no choice but to roll up in it sopping wet at night. (To sleep without any cover was still worse.) They received no underclothing, for, according to the Nazi view, "Underwear is scarcely known or customary to the Russians." Many were reduced to wearing nothing more than a sack with holes cut in it. Although they had to march as many as ten miles a day to and from work, the only shoes they were issued were wooden. These wore out so quickly, were so uncomfortable, and caused such sores, that a large part of the workers preferred to go barefoot or to wrap their feet in rags even when the ground was frozen. Frostbite resulted almost routinely, and there were numerous cases of death from gangrene. (Rosenberg suggested the manufacture of concrete shoes, to go along with Goering's proposal for concrete locomotives.)

Women made up 900,000 of the 1.7 million workers transported from Russia. Hitler, with his tender regard for the health of German girls, had no interest at all in the welfare of the foreigners, and they were treated precisely the same and performed the same labor—shoveling coal, hardening steel, hammering boilers, and handling heavy machinery—as the men. Men and women alike were housed in filthy, decrepit accommodations almost beyond imagination. Twelve hundred were crammed into an abandoned school, where the lavatory contained ten children's toilets. Supplied only sporadically with water, these overflowed within days, and eventually the entire lavatory turned into a vermin-infested cesspool. Thousands slept without cots or mattresses in dripping tunnels, coal mines, cellars, barns, and old baking ovens.

A doctor at one facility recalled in a deposition: "The floor was cement, and the paillasses on which the people slept were full of lice and bugs. Every day at least ten people were brought to me whose bodies were covered with bruises on account of the continual beatings with rubber tubes, steel switches, or sticks. Dead people often lay for two or three days on the paillasses until their bodies stank so badly that fellow prisoners took them outside and buried them somewhere. The dishes out of which they ate were also used as toilets because they were too tired or too weak from hunger to get up and go outside. At 3 AM they were awakened. The same dishes were then used for washing, and later for eating."

A physician at Krupp had reported: "One could not enter the barracks without being attacked by ten, twenty, and up to fifty fleas. I visited this camp with a Mr. Grene on two occasions and both times we left the camp badly bitten. We had great difficulty in getting rid of the fleas and insects which had attacked us. As a result, I got large boils on my arms and the rest of my body." After the doctor repeatedly complained he had not even the most basic medicines to administer to the sick, he was given one hundred aspirin tablets for three thousand workers. In a typical factory camp for Russians, the survival expectancy was eighteen months—shorter than in one of the milder concentration camps, such as Dachau.

Contrary to Hitler's edict, these miserable human beings rapidly replaced and were completely integrated with German workers. Scarcely anyone in the Reich's cities remained unaware of their plight.

At the end of July 1942, Sauckel reported that he had added 1,640,000 foreigners to the German labor force, 1.3 million of whom were Russians, and that there were now 5.1 million non-Germans (of whom 1.6 million were POWs, three-fourths of them French) working in the Reich.

Early in the fall, as the losses from Stalingrad mounted, Hitler decided that he would have to draft another half million industrial workers into the army, and would need an additional two million foreigners. Sauckel, unable to understand how more than one and a half million workers could have been swallowed up so quickly, became involved in a bitter dispute with Speer and other Reich ministers, and protested to Hitler. But Hitler brushed him off.

"The orders which I received from the Führer and from the Central Planning Board I had to enforce rigidly," Sauckel recounted to Major Monigan, and pleaded he was being blamed for things over which he had had no control. "I could do nothing about it since Speer had in all his decrees and dealings been in cooperation with Hitler."

Goering, during an interrogation by Colonel Amen, corroborated Sauckel: "I know that there were differences before the Führer, and they were very vivid between Sauckel and Speer. Speer only requested workers. It didn't matter to him how he obtained them. The Führer would make demands. Speer would say he could not meet them without so and so many more workers, and would get the Führer to give a direct order in that direction."

Whenever he was criticized, Sauckel, in the fashion of hierarchies and bureaucracies, turned and lashed out at others. After Agriculture Minister Backe requested Sauckel "to refrain from the execution of the measure [importing two million more men] until a better food situation for the workers from the East can be assured," Sauckel lectured him stridently: "Party member Backe has only to solve the organizational problem. The reference to the difficult transportation conditions does not impress me in the least. I would find ways and means to utilize the harvest and the cattle from the Ukraine, even if I had to draft the whole Jewry of Europe and use them as a human road. If the food rations for both the Germans and the foreign workers are not increased shortly, then a scandal of the greatest proportion will take place. The decreased resistance of the bodies—especially with the shortage of doctors—will give rise to great epidemics."

Sauckel ordered Backe to get cracking, using Jews who no longer existed to transport cattle that had been slaughtered and eaten the previous year at Rosenberg's behest, and garner a bountiful harvest that was as illusory as most of the other German conceptions about the Soviet Union. Hitler grumbled that he could not understand why the heroic Germans, battling for the future of Europe, were going hungry while the Ukrainians, Hungarians, Dutch, and French (the latter of whom were shipping two-thirds of their grain to Germany) were feasting on milk and wheat. Ill and chronically out of temper in his Ukrainian headquarters during the summer and fall of 1942, Hitler was irritated by Bormann's account of the multitude of purportedly healthy children running about the countryside, and directed the implementation of measures to reduce this "biological material." As for the nourishment of the eastern workers in Germany, Hitler remarked that this could be augmented by shifting some of the food supply from "lazy Dutchmen or Italians."

By January 1943, following the surrender of the German Sixth Army at Stalingrad and the wholesale collapse of the Romanian forces, the manpower situation reached a stage of chronic crisis. In March, Sauckel initiated a new drive to dragoon ten thousand Russians a day. Wherever Sauckel's "recruiters" appeared, people fled into the countryside, where they augmented the resistance. By the winter of 1942–43 the partisan movement had become so strong, and the "Sauckel actions" served so effectively to add to the guerrilla ranks, that the Wehrmacht petitioned Hitler to call Sauckel off. The Wehrmacht was supported by Rosenberg and his subordinates, who warned: "The compulsory conscription of labor in the occupied Eastern Territories must be restrained immediately. If we do not accomplish this change of course at once, then one can say with certainty that the power of resistance of the Red Army and the whole Russian people will mount still more, and valuable German blood must flow more and more." The voices of opposition were so insistent that, surprisingly, Hitler paid heed to them and temporarily ordered suspension of the roundups.

Sauckel, called by Goebbels "one of the dullest of the dull," was stunned. In only a year he had become the model bureaucrat, who later bragged to Major Monigan: "I was glad I did not work unbureaucratically as Speer did. I worked on correct principles!" With Hitler Sauckel pleaded: "My Führer! To fulfill my task I ask you to abolish these orders. I think it impossible that the former Soviet people should be given more consideration than our own German people. I myself report to you that the workers belonging to all foreign nations are treated humanely, correctly, and cleanly, are fed and housed well, and are even clothed. I go so far as to state that never before in the world were foreign workers treated as correctly. Our National Socialist Reich presents a shining example compared with the methods of the capitalist and Bolshevik worlds."

Hitler, pleased to hear this, reversed himself once more. Authorizing Sauckel to renew his "recruiting," he nevertheless directed that "injustices, insults, trickery, mistreatment, etc. must be discontinued. Embezzlements, usurious prices, etc. by supervisory bureaus or administrative offices will be punished as if the act were committed against Germans. They are not only punishable from the point of view of nonpolitical crimes, but also can be punished for treasonable crimes."

For 1944, Hitler demanded another four million workers. Sauckel promised that he would "attempt with fanatic determination to obtain these workers, but, with the best of intentions, I am unable to make a definite promise." He enlisted SS formations in the hunt by providing them with extra rations, cigarettes, and liquor, but by July had been able to conscript only 560,000 people, three-fourths of them from the East. He considered this "a scandal, and the complete bankruptcy of authority in Italy and France." He was outraged that "wide circles in the Wehrmacht saw in the labor recruiting program something disreputable. It has actually occurred that German soldiers endeavored to protect the population from being taken by the German labor service."

By early autumn, the German armies had been ousted from all of France and much of Poland, so that Sauckel, thrashing about in frustration, had only a few remnants of the Greater German Reich in which to "recruit." Nine months later, when the war ended, there were 4.8 million foreign laborers and 1.9 million prisoners of war (excluding American and British) working in German industry.*

As for Speer, he was completely uninterested in the human condition of the workers, but looked upon them like an army of ants, too minute to be seen as individuals. So long as they marched this way and that with their

*Of these, 2.5 million were Russians, 1.5 million French, 900,000 Poles, 600,000 Italians, and a half million Belgians and Dutch.

burdens, dug holes in the ground, and operated machines, he was concerned only that they appeared in the numbers demanded by him.

Rightly contending that modern wars were won with superiority in technology and fire power, not manpower, Speer resisted Keitel's efforts to draw every last German capable of fighting out of the factories. While Sauckel, spurred on by Keitel, sent investigators out to uncover nonessential workers "hoarded" by Speer, Speer argued that it made no sense to draft highly skilled workers when only two million out of nine million men in the Wehrmacht ever saw combat.

In truth, Speer was as zealous to prove himself a master of production as Sauckel was to show himself a supplier of manpower. Not only was he as wasteful of labor as Goering had been in his drive to make Germany self-sufficient, but he countenanced corruption, black marketing, and profiteering as incentives for industrialists. The quarrel between Speer and Sauckel went deeper than the disputes over workers—it personified once more the struggle in the Nazi Party between big business on the one hand and the gauleiters on the other; and Sauckel more than once suggested many problems would be solved if a few industrialists had their heads chopped off.

Speer's position with Hitler, however, was invulnerable. In order to impress the Führer, he inflated his considerable accomplishments and submitted exaggerated figures on armaments. When the generals protested that the weapons were not being received in the numbers Speer said they were being produced, Hitler, believing Speer, became all the more distrustful of the army. During one interrogation Speer recalled that Hitler had raved "that the officers were without honor, without intelligence, that they were liars, that he was dealing with nothing but a bunch of crooks!"

Surrounded by a retinue of incompetents, the Führer looked upon Speer as a kind of magician. If Speer protested at the magnitude of a task, Hitler waved him off: "You've made so many things possible, Speer, you'll manage that too." Before long, Hitler informed Speer that he would make him second in the succession after Goering. Speer, admitting in his memoirs that he was "intoxicated by the desire to wield pure power, to assign people to this and to that, to say the final word on important questions, and to deal with expenditures in the billions," reveled in his ascendancy. Like an industrious weevil he hollowed out Goering's Four Year Plan. Adding control, one after another, of civilian production, airplane manufacture, mining, and transportation to his "Speer Ministry," he left the once-powerful Reichsmarshal with nothing but a shell.

In April 1944, the British *Observer* called Speer the most important personage in Germany, "the man who actually directs the giant power machine. The Hitlers and the Himmlers we may get rid of, but the

Speers, whatever happens to this particular man, will long be with us."

Speer never questioned Hitler's policies until the Führer's manic ways finally impinged upon his own sphere. With the beginning of the retreat in the East, Hitler decreed a scorched-earth policy: "The aim to be achieved is that when areas in the Ukraine are evacuated, not a human being, not a single head of cattle, and not a railway line remain behind. That not a house remain standing, not a mine is not destroyed for years to come, not a well is not poisoned." When the first Allied troops reached German territory in September 1944, Hitler extended this apocalyptic policy to the Reich. The enemy was "to find every footbridge destroyed, every road blocked—nothing but death, annihilation, and hatred will meet him."

Not surprisingly, industrialists, directors of utilities, and other wealthy Germans opposed the wanton destruction of their property. Speer was torn between his personal attachment to Hitler and the desires of the men who were his constituency; and when it became clear to him the war was lost, his instinct for self-preservation caused him to start detaching himself from the Führer. By March of 1945 Speer the technocrat was thinking about measures of postwar reconstruction, while Speer the architect was still engaged with Hitler the artist in never-never fantasies of megamonumental buildings, as if they were children dreaming over their erector sets. When Speer objected that the flooding of mines, blowing up of bridges, and destruction of all power and transportation facilities would result in "eliminating all further possibility for the German people to survive," Hitler retorted:

"It is not necessary to worry about what the German people will need for elemental survival. On the contrary, it is best for us even to destroy these things. For the nation has proved to be the weaker, and the future belongs solely to the stronger eastern nation. In any case, only those who are inferior will remain after this struggle, for the good have already been killed."

These words finally catalyzed Speer into action. Supported by the industrialists, mayors, and to some extent the Wehrmacht and gauleiters, Speer moved to partially undercut the implementation of Hitler's order. Indeed, in the chaos that was Germany, Hitler had lost much of the power to enforce his decisions, and Speer's vacillating intervention served mainly to exacerbate the confusion—between March 18 and April 7, twelve contradictory edicts were issued on the scorched-earth policy.

It was not until April 24, when Berlin was almost completely surrounded by the Red Army, that Speer tore himself away from Hitler and the ruins of the chancellery which he had designed. Like most of the regime's leading figures, he was entering a twilight world where escapism confounded reality. Upon reaching Admiral Doenitz's headquarters at Flensburg, he had a flying boat outfitted for an expedition to Greenland, where he intended to hibernate while writing his memoirs.

Persuaded to abandon this impractical plan, Speer remained at Flensburg, and told Doenitz he intended to work for the Allies in the reconstruction of the country. After being taken into custody the third week of May, he spent only two weeks at Mondorf. He was then driven to SHAEF headquarters at Versailles, and passed the next four months in confinement resembling comfortable house arrest. Along with Schacht, Alfried Krupp, and other German businessmen and industrialists, he was questioned regarding all phases of German industry, war production, and the effects of the air attack. Gradually, the nature of the meetings was transformed from interrogations to colloquies, in which all of the participants were more or less on equal footing. A lieutenant even took Speer on an outing to Paris.

When, in July, Eisenhower's headquarters was moved to Frankfurt, the prisoners were lodged in Kransberg Castle (Dustbin), a magnificent edifice that Speer had renovated for Goering's use during the campaign against France. The detainees received the same rations as Allied personnel; and Speer recuperated from the enormous tensions and overwork he had labored under during the last years of the war. During scores of sessions with British and American engineers, economists, and technicians, Speer gained insight into western democratic thinking, and adapted himself to it as easily as he had to Hitler's megalomania.

Accepted more and more as part of the Allied technical management team, Speer was in the midst of conducting a two-week symposium, "Organization of German War Production," when it was announced in London that he was to be tried as a major war criminal.

On September 5, Speer was told that, in return for his continuing cooperation, none of the information he provided would be made available to the Nuremberg prosecution. Not until early October was he transferred to the stringent captivity of Nuremberg, where, displaying the adaptability of a chameleon, he stripped to the waist on sunny days, and, placing a blanket on the floor, followed the small patch of sunlight about his cell in a desperate attempt to sunbathe. Though he sketched well, he had very little ability to visualize. "My fantasies run into musical channels," he told Gustav Gilbert. "I can entertain myself here in the cell for hours by running over classical music. But I can't visualize very well." Lacking empathy for others as well as understanding of himself, his mind tended to be an emotional desert. On October 17, he wrote to his wife: "I must regard my life as concluded. I have no right to consider all of you or myself. Strange as it may sound, I am in good spirits when I have relinquished all hope, and become uncertain and nervous as soon as I think I have a chance. . . . Perhaps, by my bearing, I can once more help the German people. Perhaps I shall accomplish it. There are not many here who will."

In truth, Speer's agile mind was working to extract every possible advantage from his perilous position. On November 17 he wrote Jackson at length that at Dustbin he had not only volunteered all the information at his command, "but quietly eliminated the scruples of co-workers to give information. British Colonel Lawrence can testify to that." There was, of course, the implicit suggestion that he could perform the same role at Nuremberg.

(While still at Flensburg, he had provided the Strategic Bombing Survey with a detailed analysis of the successes and errors made by the Allies in their aerial warfare, so that the United States could improve upon its performance in the bombing of Japan.)

The American chief of economic warfare and his deputy, as well as Lieutenant General Anderson, would vouch for him, Speer noted: "You can rely on the fact that I carried out this task from conviction. I have always emphasized that I did not undertake this task in order to gain personal advantages for the future. I would feel miserable, however, if I would be forced by third persons to furnish this information again—I would prefer any personal sacrifice to such a possibility."

In other words, it would be wise not to press him too hard on some matters, so that the Russians wouldn't find out. All in all, Speer wanted Jackson to know of the valuable service he had already rendered to the Allied cause, and his readiness to continue his cooperation.

Although Jackson did not respond, Speer made clear to Gustav Gilbert that he was prepared to recant and identify himself with the Americans. Using every opportunity to persuade Fritzsche and Schirach to join him, Speer strove to break up the united front that Goering endeavored to have the defendants present.

When, following Ohlendorf's testimony for the prosecution, the time came for the defense attorneys to cross-examine, Speer launched his campaign for survival.

"Is it known to you that the defendant Speer," Egon Kubuschok* asked Ohlendorf, "contrary to Hitler's order, took measures to prevent the destruction of industrial and other installations?"

"Yes," Ohlendorf replied.

*Since Speer's lawyer, Hans Flächsner, was absent, Speer had Kubuschok, the counsel for Papen and the Reich Cabinet, temporarily represent him.

"Do you know that the defendant Speer prepared an attempt on Hitler's life in the middle of February of this year?"

"No."

"Do you know that Speer undertook to turn Himmler over to the Allies so that he could be called to account and possibly clear others who were innocent?"

"No."

Ohlendorf could have said much more if Amen, on reexamination, had asked him: but Amen did not, and Ohlendorf was too disciplined to volunteer.

The truth was that Speer's scheme to do away with Hitler, engendered when the Führer was clearly no longer in full possession of his faculties, had been—as Speer acknowledged a quarter century later—the product of a "romantic and fantastic state of mind." To accomplish his goal, Speer had turned to his good friend and personal physician Dr. Karl Brandt, who, in addition to being Reich Commissioner for Sanitation and Health, was the chief of chemical warfare. Speer asked Brandt to supply him with a quantity of Tabun, a deadly nerve gas, which he planned to release in the Berlin bunker's ventilation system, killing not only Hitler, but scores of people with him. Tabun, however, could be activated only by an explosion, and so was useless for Speer's scheme.*

The fact was that Speer, in his momentary thought to do away with Hitler, had merely fallen in with a growing number of Hitler's entourage. Ohlendorf had earlier told Brookhart: "I may assume that it was known that both Himmler and several SS leaders [including Ohlendorf himself] were playing with the thought half a year or even a year or two before to try a coup d'état to establish a new government in Germany."

The judges, nevertheless, were left with the impression that here was one defendant who had, at least toward the end, seen the light. Goering had difficulty controlling himself until the afternoon recess, when he flew halfway across the dock as if to throttle Speer. He was still raging in his cell that evening when he conversed with Gilbert: "This was a bad day. Damn that stupid fool Speer! Did you see how he disgraced himself in court today? *Gott im Himmel! Donnerwetter nochamal!* How could he stoop so low as to do such a rotten thing to save his lousy neck! I nearly died with shame! To think that Germans will be so rotten to prolong this filthy life —to put it bluntly—to piss in front and crap behind a little longer! *Herr Gott, Donnerwetter!* Do you think I give that much of a damn about this

---

*In his memoirs Speer related that he had been thwarted because the chimneys of the ventilating system had, in the meantime, been raised too high for accessibility. "The whole idea of assassination vanished from my consideration as quickly as it had come," Speer wrote in his book.

lousy life? For myself, I don't give a damn if I get executed, or drown, or crash in a plane, or drink myself to death! But there is still a matter of honor in this damn life! Assassination attempt on Hitler!—ugh!—*Gott im Himmel!* I could have sunk through the floor!"

To Ohlendorf, Speer's suggestion that he had endeavored to hand Himmler over to the Allies seemed even more ironic and outlandish than his plan to kill Hitler, since no one in the hierarchy had cooperated more closely with Himmler than Speer, and it was to Himmler that Speer had turned for support in his disputes with Sauckel and the gauleiters. Speaking before a meeting of gauleiters and *Reichsleiter* at Posen on October 6, 1943, Speer had warned that he would no longer tolerate their obstructionism: "I can assure you I am prepared to apply the authority of the Reich government at any cost. I have spoken with Reichsführer SS Himmler, and from now on I shall deal firmly with the districts that do not carry out these measures."

The gauleiters, interpreting this as a threat to have them hauled off by the SS, were left seething by Speer's words, but were thrown into even greater agitation by Himmler, who followed Speer to the podium. The Reichsführer SS regarded himself as misunderstood and unappreciated: The other Nazi leaders, instead of being grateful that he was carrying out the regime's dirty work, were sniping at him and sanctimoniously pretending they were unaware of what was going on. The time had come, Himmler decided, to force them into acknowledgment of their complicity in the policy of murder decreed by Hitler.

"The sentence 'The Jews must be exterminated,' with its few words, gentlemen, can be uttered easily," Himmler addressed the Reich's leaders icily. "But what that sentence demands of the man who must execute it is the hardest and toughest thing in existence. I ask you really only to hear and never to talk about what I tell you in this circle. When the question arose, 'What should be done with the women and children?' I decided here also to adopt a clear solution. I did not deem myself justified in exterminating the men, that is to say, to kill them or let them be killed, while allowing their children to grow up to avenge themselves on our sons and grandchildren. The hard decision had to be taken—*this people must disappear from the face of the earth.*"

Himmler's speech sent the gauleiters and *Reichsleiter* out reeling, and there was no one attending the Posen meeting who could be left with any illusions.*

*Speer later lamely excused himself on the basis that he had departed before Himmler's speech; but this was a contradictory statement since, the next day, he self-righteously asked Hitler to chide those in attendance for the orgy of drunkenness they engaged in after his and Himmler's addresses.

32 "The Final Solution of the Jewish Question"

To the judges and the world it was Dieter Wisliceny who, following Ohlendorf to the witness stand, explained the meaning of the phrase "the Final Solution of the Jewish Question."

Wisliceny's interrogation, like Ohlendorf's, had been the responsibility of Colonel Brookhart; and since Amen did not regard Wisliceny's appearance as a witness as highly as Ohlendorf's, he permitted Brookhart to conduct the examination in court.

"Do you know Adolf Eichmann?" Brookhart inquired of the thirty-four-year-old Wisliceny who, as Eichmann's deputy for Slovakia, had supervised the shipment of Alfred Weczler, Rudolf Vrba, and the other Slovakian Jews to Auschwitz.

"Yes, I have known Eichmann since 1934."

"Under what circumstances?"

"We joined the SD about the same time, in 1934. Until 1937 we were together in the same department."

"How well did you know Eichmann personally?"

"We knew each other very well. We used the intimate '*du*,' and I also knew his family very well."*

In response to Brookhart's questions about Eichmann's position, Wisliceny replied: "Eichmann had special powers from Gruppenführer Müller, the Chief of Amt IV [Gestapo], and from the Chief of the Security Police. He was responsible for the so-called solution of the Jewish question in Germany and in all countries occupied by Germany."

Wisliceny related that when—at the time of the shipment of the Slovakian Jews—he had requested verification, "Eichmann told me he could show me this order in writing if it would soothe my conscience. He took a small volume of documents from his safe, turned over the pages, and showed me a letter from Himmler to the Chief of the Security Police and the SD [Heydrich]. The gist of the letter was roughly as follows:

"The Führer had ordered the final solution of the Jewish question; the Chief of the Security Police and the SD and the Inspector of Concentration Camps [Richard Glücks] were entrusted with carrying out this so-called

---

*Six weeks before, during an interrogation, Wisliceny had been more specific: "Eichmann personally was an extreme coward. He did not start anything, he did not do anything, he did not attempt anything without being completely covered down to the slightest detail by both Müller and Kaltenbrunner. He feared every responsibility."

final solution. All Jewish men and women who were able to work were to be temporarily exempted from the so-called final solution and used for work in the concentration camps. This letter was signed by Himmler himself. I could not possibly be mistaken since Himmler's signature was well known to me."

"Was any question asked by you as to the meaning of the words 'final solution' as used in the order?" Brookhart continued.

"He said that the planned biological annihilation of the Jewish race in the Eastern Territories was disguised by the concept and wording 'final solution.' In later discussions on this subject the same words 'final solution' appeared over and over again."

"Did you make any comments to Eichmann about his authority?"

"Yes. It was perfectly clear to me that this order spelled death to millions of people. I said to Eichmann, 'God grant that our enemies never have the opportunity of doing the same to the German people.' In reply to which Eichmann told me not to be sentimental; it was an order of the Führer and would have to be carried out."

Eichmann, Wisliceny said, "was in every respect a confirmed bureaucrat," a characterization given graphic meaning by a communication dispatched in 1942 by Eichmann's representative in France, *Hauptsturmführer* Theodor Danneker. In June of 1942, Eichmann had pressured the Vichy government, through Ribbentrop's ministry, to hand over fifty thousand Jews from the unoccupied territory for shipment to the east. Premier Laval, however, had refused to expel French citizens and agreed only to hand over "stateless" Jews—those unfortunates who had managed to flee from the Nazis in Germany, Austria, Czechoslovakia, and Poland. On the evening of July 14, 1942, Eichmann had telephoned Danneker from Berlin and testily demanded to know why the transport scheduled for the next day had been canceled.

"The train due to leave on 15 July 1942 had to be canceled," Danneker replied, "because, according to information received by the SD Kommando at Bordeaux, there were only one hundred and fifty stateless Jews in Bordeaux. There was not time to find enough other Jews to fill the train."

Eichmann, Danneker had related in his message, was furious: "SS *Obersturmbannführer* Eichmann replied that it was a question of prestige. [He] had to conduct lengthy negotiations about these trains with the Reichsminister of transportation, which turned out successfully; and now Paris canceled the train. Such a thing had never happened to him before. The matter was highly shameful. He did not wish to report it to SS *Gruppenführer* Müller right now, for the blame would fall on his own shoulders. He was reflecting whether he would not do without France as an evacuation country altogether."

Unfortunately, Eichmann had not adhered to his threat to leave the Jews of France alone because of the insult he had suffered. But the episode revealed the inhuman banality of the perpetrators of the Final Solution—Eichmann had not thought in terms of human beings, of despair and agony, terror and torture, but of *Judenmateriel:* So and so many Jewish carcasses that he had contracted to deliver.

"Were there distinct periods of activity affecting the Jews?" Brookhart asked Wisliceny.

"Yes."

"Will you describe to the tribunal the approximate periods and the different types of activity?"

"Yes. Until 1940 the general policy was to settle the Jewish question in Germany and in areas occupied by Germany by means of a planned emigration. The second phase, after that date, was the concentration of all Jews in Poland and in other territories occupied by Germany in the East, in ghettos. This period lasted approximately until the beginning of 1942. The third period was the so-called final solution of the Jewish question, that is, the planned extermination and destruction of the Jewish race; this period lasted until October 1944, when Himmler gave the order to stop their destruction."

As early as September 15, 1935, Hitler had, in speaking about the Nuremberg Laws, employed the term "final solution." If the laws did not "create a ground on which the German people may find a tolerable relation toward the Jewish people," the Führer had said, then the problem "must be handed over by law to the National Socialist Party for a final solution."

In January 1939, at the time George Rublee and the American Joint Distribution Committee had attempted to work out a plan for the immigration of Jews, Goering had vested responsibility for the expulsion of Jews in Heydrich; and Heydrich had delegated the task to Eichmann, who was already at work in Vienna, where half of the remaining Jews in the Reich were concentrated.

On July 31, 1941, after the Commissar Order, equating Jews with Bolshevists, set the murder machinery in operation in the captive Soviet territory, Goering instructed Heydrich to accelerate the removal of Jews from the territory of the Greater German Reich: "I hereby charge you with making all necessary preparations with regard to organizational and financial matters for bringing about a complete solution of the Jewish question in the German sphere of influence in Europe."

Heydrich established a second, convenient headquarters in Prague, almost equidistant between Berlin, Vienna, and Frank's capital of Cracow. Taking over from Neurath the additional title of Protector of Bohemia and Moravia, he assumed concurrent responsibility for "Germanizing" the protectorate by eliminating not only Jews but all others whom the Nazis considered racially unsuited for assimilation.

By mid-November 1941, the disappearance of a large portion of the remaining Jews in Germany and Austria, the rumors of mass executions in the East, and the unpopularity of the war caused Goebbels to issue a shrill statement, broadcast and published throughout Germany under the heading: "The Jews Are Guilty."

"The historical guilt of world Jewry on the outbreak and expansion of this war is so amply proved that it is not necessary to lose another word over it. The Jews wanted this war and they have it now. But they must also keep in mind the prophecy of the Führer of January 30, 1939—the outcome will not be the victory of Jewry, but the extermination of the Jewish race in Europe. We now see the fulfillment of this prophecy. Pity, to say nothing of sympathy, is entirely inappropriate. We must win this war against the Jews. Should we lose it, then the harmless-appearing Jewish good fellows would exact on our people, women and children, a revenge for which history gives no precedent."

A month later, Frank informed his cabinet in Cracow: "As far as the Jews are concerned, I want to tell you quite frankly they must be done away with in one way or another. I know that many of the measures carried out against the Jews in the Reich at present are being criticized—there is talk about cruelty, harshness, and so forth. Before I continue, I ask you to agree with me: We will have pity on the German people only, and nobody else in the whole world. The others, too, had no pity on us. As an old National Socialist I must say: This war would be only a partial success if the whole lot of Jewry would survive, while we would have shed our best blood in order to save Europe. My attitude toward the Jews is therefore based on the expectation that they must disappear. They must be done away with. But what should be done with the Jews? Do you think they will be settled in villages in the Ostland? We were told in Berlin: Why all this bother? We can do nothing with them in the Ostland. So liquidate them yourselves."

The Jews, Frank complained, represented "extraordinarily malignant gluttons"—186 calories per capita daily were allocated for their sustenance. Yet the epidemic of typhus that afflicted the Jews in their starving condition was spreading to the Poles, and threatening the pure-blooded Germans. A German doctor reported to Frank: "The majority of Poles eat only about six hundred calories, whereas the normal requirement for a human being is twenty-two hundred calories. The Polish population is enfeebled to such an extent that it would fall easy prey to spotted fever [typhus]. This health situation represents a serious situation for the Reich, and for the soldiers who are coming into the government-general. A spreading of the pestilence into the Reich is absolutely possible."

Consequently, Frank informed his staff: "We must annihilate the Jews. We have now approximately 2.5 million of them in the government-general, perhaps with the Jewish mixture and everything that goes with them 3.5 million. We cannot shoot or poison those 3.5 million Jews, but we shall, nevertheless, take measures which will lead to their annihilation."

A great discussion, Frank said, would take place in Berlin in January under the leadership of Heydrich to consider means to implement the *Ausrottung* (extirpation) of the Jews.

On January 20, 1942, the head of the RSHA, accompanied by Eichmann and Müller, hosted the Conference on the Final Solution of the Jewish Question at the former Wannsee headquarters of Interpol in Berlin. To the undersecretaries from the various ministries in attendance, Heydrich announced that Himmler had ordered further emigration of Jews halted. They could not, as dedicated opponents of National Socialism, be permitted to augment the ranks of Germany's enemies. Instead, they were to be transferred to the East. Everyone was familiar with the disadvantages connected with this operation, Heydrich noted, but it must, nevertheless, be continued until Europe had been cleared of Jews—a total of some eleven million, ranging from two hundred in Albania to five million in Russia. Those Jews capable of work would, segregated by sex, be placed in great labor camps, where the larger part would be decimated by natural reduction. The survivors would have to be subjected to "special treatment," since they otherwise might form the nucleus of a Jewish resurgence. In order to eliminate protests that otherwise might arise, some 85,000 elderly and prominent German Jews, plus wounded and highly decorated veterans of World War I, would be permitted to live out their lives in the ghetto established by Heydrich in the Czech fortress town of Theresienstadt two months before. (Since this number, however, far exceeded Theresienstadt's capacity, a high mortality was expected.)

Everyone, then, gathered for drinks around the cozy fireplace. None wished to intrude into the details of the Final Solution—Wisliceny related that Eichmann had told him: "You should have seen the faces of the old idiots!"

To initiate the Jews' *"Vernichtung Durch Arbeit"*—Extermination Through Work—Himmler decided to convert the Polish region between Lublin and Zamosc, previously intended as a Jewish reservation, into the first of his proposed SS soldier-peasant settlements along the lines of Roman military colonies.

"Just imagine!" he exulted. "The greatest piece of colonization the world will ever have seen linked with a most noble and essential task, the protection of the western world against an irruption from Asia!"

Heydrich more practically addressed himself to the question of how to get rid of the "useless eaters" after the laborers had been culled out. The drawbacks and difficulties of shooting women and children had become evident in Russia, and led to the invention of the gas vans. Although the vans were employed at one location, Chelmno, in western Poland, a more efficient means was required to exterminate millions of people.

Providentially, the euthanasia killings had served to demonstrate how mass murder could be accomplished. At Heydrich's behest, Eichmann consulted Philip Bouhler and Viktor Brack,* then summoned Württemberg Criminal Police Commissioner Christian Wirth to Berlin and directed him to set up a manifold expanded version of his Grafeneck extermination works in eastern Poland.

Under his supervision, four concentration camps with carbon monoxide chambers arose: Treblinka, eighty miles northeast of Warsaw; Maidanek and Sobibor, in the vicinity of Lublin; and Belzec, near Lvov in Galicia. Auschwitz, already in existence for two years, was to receive the Jews from Cracow, plus central and western Europe. Since each commander was the satan of his own hell, Höss declined to use carbon monoxide, but relied on Zyklon B, to which the Russian POWs had first been subjected. (Wirth, peeved, thereupon jibed at Höss as "my untalented disciple.")

On March 27, 1943, Goebbels noted:

"Beginning with Lublin, the Jews in the general-government are now being evacuated eastward. The procedure is pretty barbaric, and not to be described more definitely. Not much will remain of the Jews. On the whole it can be said that about sixty percent will have to be liquidated, whereas only about forty percent can be used for forced labor. . . . A judgment is being visited upon the Jews that, while barbaric, is fully deserved by them. . . . One must not be sentimental in these matters. If we did not fight the Jews, they would destroy us. It's a life-and-death struggle between the Aryan race and the Jewish bacillus."

Nothing but the extraordinary ingenuity and skills of the Jews had kept the death rate in the Polish ghettos to ten percent during the winter

---

*Dr. Karl Brandt attempted to convince Major Monigan that "there should be a distinction between using the words 'extermination' and 'euthanasia.' Our euthanasia program had nothing to do with Himmler, and Himmler's program had nothing to do with us. I have never exchanged a word with anybody who had anything to do with exterminations in concentration camps." After making this statement, however, Brandt hedged: "Maybe Hitler mentioned it to me, but professionally he did not."

of 1941–42. By liquidating their valuables, the Jews were able to buy food on the black market. German businessmen, who had acquired Jewish factories and other enterprises at forced sales, continued to operate them with Jewish managers and workers, and thereby reaped enormous profits. The Wehrmacht derived substantial supplies of uniforms, accessories, and even ammunition from within the ghettos. The sub-rosa trade between Germans and Poles on the one hand and the Jews on the other was forty times the official exchange. The black market pipeline stretched all the way to Berlin. Most, if not all, of Frank's burgeoning bureaucracy of forty thousand Germans, as well as members of his family, benefited from the corruption. Frank's wife and sister, together with other relatives, made repeated trips into the ghettos to exchange a few eggs and apples or a pound of butter for jewelry, watches, and antiques. During the "fur action" of December 1941, when all fur coats were confiscated from Jews for use by the freezing soldiers in Russia, Frau Frank accumulated fur coats and jackets by the dozens for herself. Staggering quantities of food were extracted by Frank from the starving country and shipped to his estate in Bavaria. One consignment included 200,000 eggs, a year's production of dried food, 150 pounds of beef, 130 pounds of ham, pork, and sausage, 170 pounds of butter, 120 pounds of sugar, 50 pounds of coffee, and 70 chickens and geese. One of Frank's officials reported: "The big dinners at the castle with meat, magnificent salads, fruit and dessert were always a feast. . . . A life such as one reads about in the *Arabian Nights.* An oasis where no one notices the war."

The corruption prevalent among Nazi Party officials, nevertheless, played only a small part in the enormous shortages of goods arising in German-occupied territory. From the very start, Hitler's rationale for launching the war had been to augment the Reich's stock of raw materials and, especially, its food supply. But, in consequence of Nazi brutality, mismanagement, killings, forced labor, devastation, and massive diversion of manpower to combat, the result instead was to reduce agricultural production drastically in all of Europe. In December 1941, a Wehrmacht economics officer in the Ukraine asked rhetorically: "If we shoot the Jews, let the prisoners of war perish, condemn parts of the urban population to death by starvation, and also lose a part of the farming population by hunger during the next year, the question remains unanswered: Who in all the world then is supposed to produce economic values here?"

The answer was self-evident. The 1942 harvest was reduced by one-half to two-thirds. The number of cattle dropped by fifty percent and the number of sheep by seventy-five percent. Since Hitler and Goering were determined to continue to feed—or at least try to feed—the German population at prewar levels, the only possibility was to cut back further and further on the rations of people of lower standing in the Nazi caste system. Sauckel's forced laborers and the citizens of occupied countries would be provided only with enough sustenance to permit them a gradual death from malnutrition, prisoners in concentration camps would starve more quickly, and "useless eaters" like inmates of asylums and Jewish women and children would get nothing at all.

On August 24, 1942, Frank, convening forty-five members of his administration, told them:

"The Reichsmarshal has the reports concerning the almost catastrophic developments of the food situation in Germany. Unless a considerable improvement can be achieved in a short time, serious consequences for the health of the people, especially the German working people, would result. In hundreds of thousands of illnesses one can already see the tragic consequences not only of this food shortage, but also of the deterioration of foodstuffs, which endangers health—especially the quality of bread distributed to the German people within the last few weeks.

"A serious situation has, therefore, arisen. We must take care that during the coming winter sufficient food will be distributed to the German people that they will be able to withstand the great nervous strain of the coming months. Before the German people are to experience starvation, the occupied territories and their people shall be exposed to starvation. We here in the general-government must have the iron determination to help the great German people, our fatherland."

Poland was to contribute half a million tons of grain, six times the amount of the previous year, to the feeding of the German people. Rations for the Poles were to be cut to four hundred calories per capita daily for all but essential war workers. Since, Frank pointed out, "the previous quantities of food were already not enough, in view of the worsening living conditions an extraordinary hardship will set in for railroad workers and others." Beginning in March 1943, all Poles, except essential workers, would receive no bread at all.

Then, casually, Frank revealed: "The feeding of the Jewish population, estimated at 1.5 million,* will drop off to an estimated three hundred thousand Jews, who still work for German interests as craftsmen or otherwise. The other Jews, a total of 1.2 million, will no longer be provided with foodstuffs.

"It must be done coldbloodedly and without pity—exclusively at the expense of the foreign population. The *Germans* in this area shall not feel it. Whatever difficulties you observe, you must always remember that it is much better that a Pole collapses than that a German succumb. That we

---

*Frank's figure of 1.5 million, compared with his earlier estimate of 2.5 to 3.5 million, is indicative of the rapidity with which the Jews were being decimated.

sentence 1.2 million Jews to die of hunger should be noted only marginally. It is a matter of course that should the Jews not starve to death the result would be, we hope, that the anti-Jewish measures will be speeded up."

The anti-Jewish measures to which Frank referred had been in full swing since June, following Heydrich's assassination in Prague by four British-trained Czech agents. Hitler, in his rage, initially ordered forty thousand to fifty thousand Czechs shot as a reprisal, and desisted only when Heydrich's deputy, Karl Frank, warned that such a slaughter would lead to a mass uprising and destroy Czechoslovakia's value to the German war machine.

Hitler, thereupon, once more took out his wrath on the Jews. Fifteen hundred German Jews were executed, 3,000 Czech Jews were exterminated at Mauthausen concentration camp, and 2,359 members of Czech Jewish families were gassed at Auschwitz. Concurrently, the village of Lidice, suspected of having harbored the assassins, was laid waste. One hundred and seventy-two men and boys over sixteen were shot; the women were taken to Ravensbrück concentration camp; and the children were placed with Reich families for "Germanization." (Only a handful were found and returned to their families after the war.) Though Lidice was in actuality the lesser of Hitler's reprisals, and but one of hundreds of villages deracinated during the war, its visibility enabled Allied propaganda to turn it into a symbol for Nazi atrocities.

On the other hand, the emptying of the Polish ghettos produced only a tepid response from Allied propaganda. To memorialize Heydrich, Himmler initiated "Operation Reinhard," the ruthless intensification of the Final Solution. Only those Jews employed at hard labor for the benefit of Germany, and, primarily, the SS, were to be temporarily exempted.

As in other Nazi actions against the Jews, Operation Reinhard had, beneath its strident racial rationale, an economic foundation. As a consequence of the Führer's disappointment with his generals, he was encouraging Himmler to build up the Waffen SS, which had started with one division in 1939, into a full-fledged army. By 1942 Himmler commanded eight divisions, and within the next three years that number quintupled. Himmler, furthermore, had the advantage that, unlike the Wehrmacht, he was able to recruit in the occupied countries; and since the German manpower pool was nearly dry, ultimately more than half of the SS's forty divisions were composed of citizens of foreign countries.*

*Virtually every continental nation contributed one or more divisions to the SS. There were Scandinavian, Balkan, Muslim, Galician, Latvian, Estonian, Albanian, Hungarian, Croatian, Flemish, Walloon, Italian, White Russian, French, two Dutch and three Cossack divisions, plus smaller Bulgarian, Romanian, Indian, Caucasian, and Turkestani units. Four hundred thousand German nationals, 310,000 ethnic Germans from foreign countries, and 200,000 non-Germans served in the SS.

Since the SS was, at least in theory, still a party organization not financed out of the national treasury, and Himmler had interminable disputes with Party Treasurer Schwarz over the amount of money he requested, the Reichsführer SS was constrained to develop the funds to pay and equip his 600,000-man legion himself. The most direct means was to kill the Jews and rob them of their property—Jews were encouraged to bring their valuables with them when they were "resettled," and the SS sometimes spent weeks hunting through the emptied dwellings in the ghettos. Wealthy Jews, whose riches were not so accessible, had their fortunes extracted from them in return for their release and safe conduct out of Nazi territory. Himmler thus built up an SS industrial empire ranging from the bottling of soft drinks to the production of V-rockets.

To operate his enterprises, Himmler employed concentration camp inmates. The excess were farmed out to German industry, which paid the wages to Himmler instead of to the workers. The concentration camps, consequently, were transformed into holding areas for vast pools of labor to be exploited for profit. Because of the camps' expansion coupled with the high death rate, Himmler's demand for new slaves became voracious. Thirty thousand Jews and foreign workers were swallowed up monthly on manufactured charges or for the most petty offenses. The SS acquired the appellation of "a state within a state"—the designation previously applied by Jacob Brafman to the Jewish Kehillahs.

On July 22, 1942, the "resettlement" of the half-million persons in the Warsaw ghetto, the largest single concentration of Jews in Europe, commenced. At the rate of six thousand to seven thousand a day they were shipped to Treblinka and the Lublin reservation. As usual, the first to go were the sick, the aged, the poor, the homeless and friendless, and the orphaned children. The starving were lured by promises of bread. Transitory thoughts of resistance were undermined by the suicidal nature of such action, by the total lack of arms, and by the desperate hope that the plague might stop short of oneself and one's family. The discord between the SS on the one hand and the Wehrmacht and German businessmen on the other helped foster such hopes. The Nazis' ostensible commitment to legality, specious and bordering on the lunatic as it was, reinforced the illusions born of despair. For example, all Jews holding passports from foreign countries not occupied by Germany, including Britain and the United States, were removed from the ghetto for safekeeping, so as to avoid retaliation against German nationals. Throughout the entire campaign of terror and murder the diplomatic niceties were scrupulously maintained; and no Jew of a neutral or noncontinental enemy power was deliberately harmed.

A million and a quarter Jews were cleared from the ghettos of Warsaw and other Polish cities during the late summer of 1942. By the second week of September, according to the Nazi count, only 35,000 of 400,000 Warsaw Jews remained, all exempted from transportation by virtue of the fact that they were employed in manufacture for the Wehrmacht, or in the Jewish administration, police, and hospital. (In actuality, an additional 45,000 "illegals" remained in the ghetto.) On September 13, General Curt von Gienanth, the Wehrmacht's commander in Poland, ordered further deportations halted because "immediate removal of the Jews would lead to a considerable reduction of Germany's war effort; supplies to the front and to the troops in the government-general would be held up." Until the situation could be remedied, Gienanth requested an order from Keitel "that Jews working in industry be exempted from evacuation."

In response to Gienanth, Himmler blustered: "I have ordered that ruthless steps be taken against all those who think that they can use the interests of war industry to cloak their real intentions to protect the Jews and their own business affairs."

Keitel, exhibiting that combination of amoral servility and stultifying stupidity for which he was noted, relieved Gienanth and messaged his successor: "OKW is in entire agreement with the principles laid down by the Reichsführer SS that all Jews employed by the armed forces in auxiliary military services and in war industries are to be replaced immediately by Aryan workers."

This, however, was a practical impossibility, since Polish peasants being shipped to Germany as farm laborers could not simultaneously replace Jews in Poland or instantly be transformed into educated and skilled craftsmen. In practice, therefore, as so often happened when inane directives were issued without regard for reality, nothing changed. The essential workers were provided safe conduct certificates by the Wehrmacht, and the transportation of the fraction of the Jews still in the ghetto remained, for the moment, in abeyance.

By mid-fall, when escapees from the trains to Treblinka trickled back, the fate of the deportees became known. "It seems a nightmare and yet it is a reality," the Jewish Anti-Fascist Organization reported in its exposé, entitled "The Liquidation of the Jews in Warsaw," on November 15. As rumors about the exterminations in Poland and Russia spread to Germany itself, Bormann and Goebbels felt constrained to publish some kind of explanation, together with guidelines for party officials:

"In the course of the work on the final solution of the Jewish problem, rumors about 'very strict measures' against the Jews, especially in the Eastern Territories, have lately been taking place within the population of the various areas of the Reich. Investigations showed that such rumors were passed on by soldiers on leave from various units committed in the East, who had the opportunity to eyewitness these measures.

"It is conceivable that not all 'Blood Germans' are capable of demonstrating sufficient understanding for the necessity of such measures. Since even our next generation will not be so close to this problem and will no longer see it clearly enough, the whole problem must be solved by the present generation.

"A complete removal or withdrawal of the millions of Jews residing in the European economic space is therefore an urgent need in the fight for the security of the German people. It lies in the very nature of these problems, which in part are very difficult, that they can be solved only with ruthless severity."

When Anthony Eden and Lord Rothschild early in December informed Parliament of the Nazi extermination measures, Goebbels jeered the revelation as "a tearjerker bemoaning the fate of the Polish Jews!"

On virtually the same day that Eden spoke in London, Himmler directed the further augmentation of his slave force:

"In accordance with the increased recruitment of manpower into the concentration camps, which was ordered by 30 January 1943, the following may be applied to the Jewish sector.

"Total amount: 45,000 Jews.

"Breakdown: the 45,000 Jews consist of 30,000 Jews from the Bialystok district, 10,000 Jews from the Theresienstadt ghetto, 3,000 Jews from the occupied areas in the Netherlands, and 2,000 Jews from Berlin, which equals 45,000. As heretofore, only the Jews who have no special connections or relations, and who have no important decorations, have been earmarked for deportation. In the total of 45,000 are included *physically handicapped* and others (old Jews and children). In making a distribution for this purpose, at least *10,000 to 15,000 laborers* will be available when the Jews arriving in Auschwitz are assigned."

Franz Kafka himself would have had difficulty devising a directive of more incredible bureaucratic cold-bloodedness. Ten thousand to fifteen thousand workers were to be channeled to the SS enterprises. In order to obtain them, forty-five thousand men, women, and children would have to be sifted. Of these, two-thirds or more were to be directed to the gas chamber.

Accidentally, some of the tens of thousands of Jews who were partners in mixed marriages were included in the roundup. Himmler, bombarded with petitions, petulantly complained in a speech to SS generals: "And then there come eighty million worthy Germans, and each one has his decent Jew. Of course, the others are vermin, but this one is an A-1 Jew. . . . Among ourselves it should be mentioned quite frankly—but we will never speak of it publicly—just as we did not hesitate on June 30, 1934, to do the duty we were ordered to stand comrades up against the wall and shoot them, so we have never spoken about . . . cleaning out the Jews, the extermination of the Jewish race. Most of *you* must know what it means when a hundred corpses are lying side by side, or five hundred, or a thousand. To have stuck it out and at the same time remained decent fellows, that is what has made us so hard. This is a page of glory in our history which has never been written and will never be written."

In early January 1943, Himmler visited Warsaw and discovered that tens of thousands of "unessential" Jews were still present in the ghetto. Himmler ordered an immediate operation to once again weed out the "useless eaters."

The Jews, however, refused to cooperate in their "resettlement" as they had in the past. When, on January 18, the SS squads, composed largely of Balts and Ukrainians, attempted to sweep through the ghetto, the inhabitants responded with sniper fire and hit-and-run tactics. Since the Jews had but some 140 small arms, most of them pistols and revolvers worthless except for close combat, the toll on the defenders was terrible —one thousand were killed and fifty-five hundred captured.

On the other hand, Himmler's entire pursuit of the Final Solution was predicated on the premise that there would be no organized or mass resistance. The few hundred police he had available were insufficient to conduct a clearing operation against opposition.

During the ensuing four months, while Himmler scraped together a brigade to reduce the ghetto, the inhabitants worked frantically to prepare for the assault. Passages were burrowed through the walls separating adjoining buildings, thus eliminating the need for people to emerge into the open. Bunkers were dug and false walls erected in cellars to hide and shelter families. Some additional arms—a few hundred at the most—were obtained at exorbitant cost from the Poles. But the stock of ammunition did not exceed ten rounds per weapon, scarcely enough for a single action. It was Masada, 1943, but without a vestige of hope.

On April 19 a force of nearly 2,100 men, consisting of 825 Waffen SS, 230 SS security police, 530 Polish police and firemen, 335 Lithuanian auxiliaries, and 100 German soldiers, renewed the operation broken off on January 22. This motley, ragtag force—the Waffen SS were members of reserve battalions and had had only three to four weeks training—was commanded by the Warsaw *SS und Polizeiführer*, Jürgen Stroop, a surveyor by profession.

Stroop's seventy-five-page, day-by-day account of the operation, prepared for Himmler and first displayed by Jackson for the judges during his opening address, was entitled *The Warsaw Ghetto Is No More*. The assistant prosecutor dealing with the persecution of the Jews referred to it as "the finest example of ornate German craftsmanship, leather bound, profusely illustrated, typed on heavy bond paper . . . the almost unbelievable recital of the proud accomplishment by Major General of Police Stroop."

The first morning that the SS force entered the ghetto, it was met with a shower of explosives and Molotov cocktails. The accompanying tank was twice set on fire, but the flames were quickly extinguished. (A tank can be disabled by a Molotov cocktail only if it is hurled directly into the engine vent or down a hatch.) After initial surprise at the fierceness of the resistance, the SS force regrouped, and, by raking upper-story windows with cannon and machine-gun fire, drove the defenders back.

Some twenty thousand Jews, encouraged by their employers to believe they could wait out the latest storm as they had earlier ones, huddled in the Wehrmacht workshops, some of which were inside the old but outside the new ghetto boundaries. Stroop ordered the German managers to clear the workers out and have them marched to the railroad station for transportation to the Lublin Reservation. When he received no response, the work places were stormed. The Jews taken from them accounted for the preponderance of the twenty thousand killed or captured during the operation's first four days.

Though resistance in the ghetto itself diminished after the first day, Stroop found it almost impossible to comb out the inhabitants. The majority holed up in the bunkers during the day and scurried back to their rooms at night. Others escaped through the sewers, or by various ruses—such as hiding among the dead being carted to the cemetery—into the Polish part of the city. (Many of them were subsequently betrayed by Poles who, in a practice dating back to the Inquisition, were rewarded with one-third of the property of the captured Jews.)

Stroop's casualties were light—at the end of the first seven days of action he had suffered five dead and fifty wounded. (In contrast, each side often lost one hundred men in a single day's combat for a solitary block in Stalingrad.) But, given the difficulty of ferreting out the residents from their underground hiding places, Stroop decided on April 23 to raze the ghetto.

Building after building, one block a day, was blown up or set afire. Some Jews leaped or dashed from the structures in order to escape the flames. Many others—among them innumerable children—risked being buried or burned to death in the cellars. One thousand to two thousand a day were flushed out by the troops using explosives and smoke grenades. As a group, the Jewish Women's Battle Association (Chaluzim) offered the most tenacious resistance, sometimes concealing grenades in their bloomers and unleashing them in suicidal actions that earned the grudging respect of the Germans. "The Jewesses, arms in hand, fought the men of the Waffen SS and police to the end," Stroop observed in his report.

By the fourth week of the operation the daily count of dead and captured was steadily declining, but the resistance, consisting almost entirely of youths under twenty-five, was stiffening. A significant number of people continued to escape. On one occasion three dozen young men emerged from a sewer, jumped into a truck, and got away without difficulty. When the headquarters of the resistance was captured, 50 of the 150 defenders were able to flee into the forest.

On May 13, Stroop ordered an air strike against the last strongpoint. Three days later, after twenty-eight days of killing and burning, he called off the operation. He had exterminated 7,000 Jews and ferreted out 49,000. (Seven thousand of the latter were sent to Treblinka for gassing. The remainder were shipped to Lublin, where most of them either died or were later executed.) He had captured nine rifles and fifty-nine pistols. His own casualties had been sixteen dead (two of them killed accidentally in the Luftwaffe attack) and ninety wounded.* Fifteen thousand Jews remained in hiding in Warsaw, perhaps a few thousand more had succeeded in reaching the countryside, and three hundred holding foreign passports had been carefully assembled by the SS for preservation.

The Warsaw resistance resulted in a decision by Himmler to eradicate every remaining ghetto in the East. "Nothing but catastrophic conditions were found," an SS report recounted. "The Jews tried every means in order to dodge evacuation. Not only did they try to flee, but they concealed themselves in every imaginable corner, in pipes, chimneys, even in sewers. They built barricades in passages of catacombs, in cellars enlarged to dugouts, in underground holes, in cunningly contrived hiding places in attics and sheds, within furniture, etc. The access was concealed in such a manner that it could not be found by persons not acquainted with the locality. Here nothing succeeded but the assistance of some Jews to whom anything whatever was promised."

The terror and degradation of those days make *The Diary of Anne Frank* read like a charming fable in comparison. Condemned to dark holes filled with filth, people coexisted with swarming rats and were covered with lice

---

*A writer's comment in the *Jewish Encyclopedia* that "it is conjectured that the German casualties were in fact much higher" is surely without foundation. Stroop's figures were intended for Himmler, and Stroop would have risked his head had he falsified them. Stroop would, in any case, have preferred to report higher casualties in order to prove how "heroic" his operation against the "Jews, bandits, and subhumans" had been. Several romanticized versions of the ghetto resistance, depicting Jews fighting with automatic weapons and blowing up tanks with hand grenades, have appeared in novels and on the screen; but the truth was more nightmarish than any fiction.

and fleas. Tens of thousands suffered from typhus, a disease that, despite inoculations, spread to the ferreting security police.

At the Lublin reservation, execution squads appeared from Maidanek and from Auschwitz, headed by the same *Scharführer* Otto Moll who supervised the gas chamber at the latter concentration camp. The Jews were herded together and machinegunned by the tens of thousands. The bodies were burned in huge pyres, the smoke from which darkened the sky day after day and filled the streets of the city with ash as if from a volcanic explosion. The German managers of the enterprises were stunned and complained that the massacre "resulted in losing much of the available labor supply. The factories were left with a tremendous stock of raw materials. There were no more people to work the machines."

The *Vernichtung* of eighty percent of the 3.5 million Polish Jews (and a somewhat smaller proportion of Ukrainian) destroyed the Polish and Ukrainian economies, and left the lands for whose riches Hitler had launched Barbarossa in such confusion that they were more of a burden than an asset to the Germans. The problem, to the annoyance of Hitler and Himmler, even surfaced sporadically at the Führer conferences. In June 1943, during the period of Himmler's last great "action," Rosenberg urged the enlistment of Ukrainians and the build-up of Ukrainian nationalism in the fight against the Soviet Union. But Rosenberg's commissioner in the Ukraine, Gauleiter Ernst Koch, complained:

"Here I lost five hundred thousand Jews. I had to take them away because the Jews are the elements of revolt. But in my area, actually, the Jews were the only tradesmen. Now they [Rosenberg] want to set up high schools and grammar schools, thereby building a national Ukrainian state that should in the future fight against Russia. I am not even in a position to have a worker, who must work here, have his boots repaired. I can't do that because the Jews are all gone. What is more important, that I train the Ukrainians how to mend boots, or that I send them to high schools so that they can build the Ukrainian state?"

During the late spring of 1943, following the finding of the bodies of the Polish officers at Katyn, Himmler was beset by terrors over what would happen when it was discovered by the advancing Russians that the *Einsatzkommando* had exceeded the Katyn massacre a hundredfold. He therefore, in one of history's most extraordinary examples of a psychopathic mentality, ordered that the hundreds of thousands of bodies lying in mass graves all over the East should be exhumed and burned. One of the *Einsatzkommando*, Paul Blobel (the man who had directed the Babi Yar massacre), was placed in charge of this revolting, nauseating task, for which Jews, naturally, were selected.

A deposition by Gerhard Adametz, one of the men assigned to guard the Jewish *Sonderkommando* (special squad), enlightened the tribunal on the conduct of a typical body-burning operation.

"The place smelled of corpses," Adametz related. "We felt faint, stopped our noses, and tried not to breathe. *Oberleutnant* Hänisch addressed us: 'You have to come to the place where you are to serve and support your comrades. You already smell an odor coming from the church behind us. We must all get used to this, and you must all do your duty.' The work of the internees consisted of exhuming corpses which were buried here in two common graves, transporting them, piling them up into two enormous piles, and burning them. It is difficult to estimate; however, I believe that on this spot were buried from forty thousand to forty-five thousand corpses. On the day of our arrival, about 10 September, 1943, there were three or four small piles of corpses on the field. Every such pile consisted of about seven hundred corpses. With the aid of iron hooks, the corpses were dragged to certain spots and then piled on a wooden platform. Then the whole pile of corpses was surrounded with logs, petroleum was poured on, and ignited. We, the policemen of Detachment 1005-B, were then led back to the cemetery and to the church. However, not one of us could eat because of the terrible smell and because of all we had seen." Since Himmler was determined, as in concentration camp gassings, to salvage everything of value, twelve- and thirteen-year-old boys were detailed to pull gold teeth from the cadavers.

Concluding his questioning of Wisliceny, whom he called "a walking adding machine on the Final Solution," Brookhart asked: "In your meetings with the other specialists on the Jewish problem and Eichmann, did you gain any knowledge or information as to the total number of Jews killed under this program?"

"Yes," Wisliceny replied. "He [Eichmann] expressed this in a particularly cynical manner. He said he would leap laughing into the grave because the feeling that he had five million people on his conscience would be for him a source of extraordinary satisfaction."*

Wisliceny, eager to extricate himself from his predicament by switching sides, volunteered to track down Eichmann for the Americans. He suggested Eichmann might be hiding in a cave in the Tennen Mountains of Austria or even have gone to Palestine, since "he looked like a Jew."†

The fact of the matter was that Eichmann had been captured by the

---

*On November 15, Wisliceny had told Brookhart that, of the total of 5.25 million, two-thirds had come from Poland, 458,000 from Hungary, 420,000 from Romania, 250,000 from Czechoslovakia, 220,000 from France, 180,000 from Germany, and the remainder from a variety of other countries.

†Wisliceny's efforts were in vain. He was extradited to Czechoslovakia, where he was tried and executed.

Americans in May, and, betrayed by his SS blood mark, had had to acknowledge his affiliation. First giving his name as Barth, then Eckmann, he claimed to have been a member of the Waffen SS, and had since been in a prison camp for SS officers at Oberdachstetten, scarcely more than thirty miles from Nuremberg.

On January 5, when an account of Wisliceny's testimony reached the POW camp, Eichmann began to feel uneasy. The sense of loyalty among his former comrades seemed to be waning. With the help of the SS camp leader, he obtained identity papers under the name of Otto Heninger and, with relative ease, disappeared from a work detail. Taking a train north into the British zone of occupation, he found a job as a lumberjack on the Luneberg Heath, fifty miles south of Hamburg. There he remained three years before leaving Germany; and it was more than ten years before Israeli intelligence finally discovered him in Argentina.

33   Partisan Warfare

The presentation on the SS was followed by Colonel Telford Taylor's on the German general staff and high command. When Jackson had had his disputation with General Donovan, Taylor had argued forcefully that the high command should not be deleted from the indictment. "Because of the difficulty of defining the high command, it may or may not have been wise to include them, but that's water over the dam," Taylor declared. The Russians had supported the United States with great vigor on the issue, and would feel betrayed if the Americans now changed their mind. The object was to stamp out the German military tradition by discrediting it, and dropping the top generals from the indictment "might lend force to the view that the entire proceedings has always been a sham."

Taylor, however, had serious differences with Jackson over the manner in which the case against the high command should be presented. Taylor believed his part of the prosecution to be "relatively more dependent on oral testimony than certain other portions." He had obtained statements from a dozen officers, and these, he contended, would reinforce the documentary evidence: "I believe it is fundamental that we cannot sacrifice the evidence contained in the statements under oath. It being known that we have obtained these statements, we will in the future be in a very vulnerable position if we do not make use of them, not because the statements are valueless, but because they are so significant and valuable."

Jackson's opposition to oral testimony, nevertheless, continued to be so strong that Taylor agreed to place only a single witness on the stand. This was Erich von dem Bach-Zelewski, the SS general in charge of antipartisan warfare—a phase of combat on the conduct of which, Taylor believed, the high command was most vulnerable.

One of the most disreputable and contradictory of all the SS leaders, Bach-Zelewski had been born in Pomerania, much of which had gone to Poland after World War I. In 1914, at the age of fifteen, he had enlisted in the German army, and been twice wounded and twice decorated before he reached draft age. Though two of his sisters were married to Polish Jews, he had joined the Nazi Party in September 1930. Enlisting in the SS when it contained only a few hundred members, he had become a favorite of Himmler's. He had killed several Communists during the street fighting of 1932 and 1933, and capitalized on the Röhm purge to have one of his own rivals in the SS murdered. By the time the war began, he was one of the twelve highest-ranking SS officers.

Following the onslaught on the Soviet Union, Bach-Zelewski became *Höhere SS und Polizeiführer* in central Russia. In 1942 he suffered a nervous breakdown and was hospitalized. Tortured by guilt, he writhed and screamed, and was oppressed by horrible visions. "Don't you know what's happening in Russia?" he asked his doctor. "The entire Jewish people is being exterminated there."

Dr. Ernst Grawitz, the chief SS medical officer, reported to Himmler: "He is suffering particularly from hallucinations connected with the shooting of Jews, which he himself carried out, and with other grievous experiences in the East."

Within a few months Bach-Zelewski recovered sufficiently to be named chief of all antipartisan units. Throughout 1943 he flew from one headquarters to another organizing antipartisan task forces out of units of the Wehrmacht, the SS, the SD, and the police. Occasionally, when he considered an action especially important, he led it himself.

While, individually, many of the partisan groups were more a nuisance than a danger to the Germans, collectively, by their very numbers and the vast territory over which they spread, they posed a major threat. Attacks on trains averaged eight hundred to a thousand a month. In the northern Ukraine the series of "partisan republics" stretching from the battlefront all the way to the Romanian and Hungarian borders left only tenuous communications between the German Central and Southern Army Groups. In much of the Ukraine, including the district around Zhitomir, where Himmler had his headquarters, the Germans controlled only one-fifth of the forested and two-fifths of the cultivated areas. Of the greatly reduced harvest, not more than one-third to one-half went to the Germans.

By its very nature, the warfare was savage. The partisans had no facilities to keep prisoners or to treat wounded, so captured soldiers were shot as a matter of course. Hitler, conversely, reiterated that whoever was involved in antipartisan warfare had carte blanche:

"The enemy employs in partisan warfare Communist-trained fanatics who do not hesitate to commit any atrocity. It is more than ever a question of life or death. If the fight against the partisans in the East is not waged with the most brutal means we will shortly reach the point when the available forces are not sufficient to control this pest. It is therefore not only justified but it is the duty of the troops to use all means without restriction even against women and children as long as it insures success.

"No German employed against the partisans will be held accountable for the fighting against them or their followers either by disciplinary action or by court-martial."

Every village from the vicinity of which resistance emanated was given the Lidice treatment—the men and boys lined up on one side, the women and children on the other, and the women informed that, unless they pointed out the perpetrators, the men would be shot and the village burned. More often than not, however, the guerrillas had no connection with the village, and seldom did anyone know the identity of the guilty, so that the inhabitants were helpless to avoid the slaughter.

In mixed Polish-Ukrainian communities, where the Poles were usually numerically, educationally, and economically dominant, they frequently managed to maneuver the Germans into picking Ukrainians, though it was the Ukrainians who had been favorably inclined toward the Germans. The leader of the Ukrainian minority lamented: "In the village of Nodosow eight pro-German Ukrainians who had been persecuted by the Poles because of their patriotic views were shot on 30 October 1942. Thus the purpose of exterminating anti-German elements quite to the contrary annihilates or weakens positively pro-German elements and creates bad feeling and bitterness. In the district of Lublin about four hundred such Ukrainians perished."

Frank routinely received reports like the following: "On 29 January 1943 in the village of Sumyn forty-five Ukrainians, including eighteen children between the ages of three and fifteen, were shot, and on 2 February 1943 in the villages of Pankos and Scharowola nineteen Ukrainians were shot, including eight children aged one to thirteen years."

During the first two and one-half years of the occupation, the security police in the government-general shot seventeen thousand Poles, a figure that led Frank to comment: "We must not be squeamish when we learn that a total of seventeen thousand people have been shot; these persons who were shot were nothing more than war victims." In 1943, executions in Poland and Russia accelerated, even though Kaltenbrunner directed that, "as a rule, no more children will be shot [and] special treatment is to be limited to a minimum." So that this order would not be misunderstood, he explained that "if we limit our harsh measures for the time being, that is only done [because] the most important thing is the recruiting of workers. Wherever prisoners can be released, they should be put at the disposal of the labor commissioner. When it becomes necessary to burn down a village, the whole population will be put at the disposal of the commissioner by force."

But with hundreds of hostages shot each week and most of the adult males either in forced labor camps, employed in key positions, or gone underground, the Germans—all directives to the contrary—relied increasingly on old people, women, and children to absorb the fire of the execution squads.

Innumerable communities were eradicated without a trace by the Nazis. The SD had principal responsibility for anti-insurgency warfare. But since the SD consisted only of a cadre and, Goering pointed out, "generally speaking, soldiers are of no use in carrying out such measures," Bach-Zelewsky relied heavily on indigenous mercenaries to contest the partisans. Exploiting traditional antagonisms, the SD recruited Tatars to fight Ukrainians, Ukrainians and Lithuanians to combat White Russians and Poles, Cossacks to battle Communists, and some members of all groups to exterminate the Jews. In all of central Russia there were only two regiments of German security police. The remainder of the units consisted of Lithuanians, Latvians, Estonians, White Russians, and Ukrainians. In major operations against guerrilla-infested regions, the practice was to kill everybody, carry off everything movable, destroy what could not be taken away, and leave nothing but a wasteland behind—regardless of the fact that the great majority of those caught up in the sweeps were simply residents of the area and had played no active guerrilla role. Thus, in a typical action in the Pripet Marshes between February 8 and 26, 1943, the SD reported: "Losses of the enemy: 2,219 dead; 7,378 persons who received special treatment; 65 prisoners; 3,300 Jews. Our own losses: 2 Germans and 27 non-Germans dead; 12 Germans and 26 non-Germans wounded." Eight machine guns, 172 rifles, 14 pistols, 150 hand grenades, and 8 land mines were captured. Ten villages, containing 1,900 houses, were burned; and 559 horses, 9,578 head of cattle, 844 pigs, 5,700 sheep, 223 tons of grain, and 3 church bells were carried off.

Shortly afterward, Kube, Rosenberg's commissioner in White Russia, made the obvious comment when apprised of another operation: "If only 492 rifles are found on 4,500 enemy dead, that is, to my mind, proof that among those dead were numerous ordinary peasants." Kube's superior,

Lohse, added: "What is Katyn compared to this? Think of what would happen if the enemy found out about these things and made use of them! I suppose such propaganda would be ineffective because listeners and readers would simply refuse to believe such things."

Under Hitler's directives, the only German reaction to resistance was to intensify terror. In Warsaw, the security police commenced in October 1943 to hold impromptu public executions. A block would suddenly be cordoned off and hostages trucked in. On a street that a few minutes before had been a thoroughfare, the condemned were lined up against the walls of the houses and, as residents watched from the windows, shot down. The names of the dead, together with a list of those to be executed the next time if further acts of resistance occurred, were posted on the walls. The bodies were then transported for burning into the ruins of the former ghetto, and the street was reopened to traffic.

In midsummer of 1944, as Soviet troops approached Warsaw, the pent-up hatred of the Poles exploded. Although Kaltenbrunner had received numerous reports that the Warsaw underground was about to rise, the Germans were unprepared when, on the first of August, 35,000 nationalist partisans—including a thousand Jews who had fought in the ghetto the year before—took over the city.

All regular Wehrmacht and Waffen SS units, trying desperately to stem the Red Army's advance in the East and the Allied sweep through France in the West, were already committed. Himmler, who lacked the most basic knowledge for directing troops but had a passionate hatred for Warsaw, took personal command. Decreeing that no prisoners were to be taken, he threw a pair of notorious SS brigades into the fighting. One, led by a sex deviant and necrophiliac, Oskar Dirlewanger, was composed of habitual criminals recruited from concentration camps; the second, headed by a convicted White Russian criminal, Bronislav Kaminski, consisted of Russian and Cossack volunteers. (Its officers, however, came from the Wehrmacht.) Drunk more often than sober, they conducted mass executions without regard to age and sex, plundered and raped at will, burned civilians alive, sexually abused and murdered children, dangled rows of women by the heels from balconies, and impaled babies on bayonets like spits of meat.

Confusion reigned as Germans and Poles controlled blocks in a checkerboard pattern. It was often difficult to tell friend from foe. Himmler, after a few days of bumbling about, turned command of the chaotic operation over to Bach-Zelewski. Bach-Zelewski halted the indiscriminate slaughter of civilians and promised prisoner-of-war status to the partisans in order to encourage their surrender.

The fierce fighting, nevertheless, continued, and waned only gradually through August and September. The Russians, alienated from the Poles by the controversy over the Katyn massacre, made no attempt to cross the Vistula. While the partisans and the SS slaughtered each other, soldiers of the Red Army and the Wehrmacht, observing an informal truce, splashed about on opposite banks of the Vistula.

Enlisting the aid of the Polish archbishop and the Red Cross, Bach-Zelewski suggested that the Poles and Germans would be better off fighting the Russians together instead of each other. Having been named in a BBC broadcast as one of the SS leaders who would have "to answer for the crimes against the people of Warsaw," he was anxious to improve his image. As a token of good faith, he rousted Kaminsky's brigade out of the distillery that was its headquarters, and had Kaminsky himself shot for disobeying orders to stop looting.* Early in October, the Poles surrendered.

Warfare between guerrillas and German troops in western Europe was scarcely less savage. On February 3, 1944, the commander in chief of the forces in the West directed: "It is of little importance that innocent people should suffer. It will be the fault of the terrorists. All commanders of troops who show weakness in suppressing the terrorists will be severely punished. On the other hand, those who go beyond the orders received and are too severe will incur no penalty."

When, the following month, 35 German soldiers were killed in an attack in Rome, 382 people of all genders and ages were mowed down in the Ardeatine Caves. While retreating north through Italy, the SS killed and burned as wantonly as in the East.

In France, thirty thousand people were shot and forty thousand died in Nazi prisons during the war. The violence reached its height following the Allied landing in Normandy. The Wehrmacht, and especially the SS, came under relentless attack from the Maquis, supplied and loosely coordinated by the Allies. Sniped at, blown up by mines, their stragglers picked off and their wounded killed, their columns bombed by British and American planes directed by the guerrillas, the SS cut a swathe of terror in revenge.

The division *Das Reich*, ordered from Bordeaux to the Normandy front, required seventeen days to make what was normally a three-day journey and suffered hundreds of casualties en route. When a popular battalion commander was killed in the village of Oradour-sur-Vayres, near Limoges, the troopers descended in error on Oradour-sur-Glane. Unable to extract any information, they machine-gunned the 190 men of the com-

*Dirlewanger escaped after the war to Egypt, where he lived out his life in comfortable retirement.

munity in the square, and burned 245 women and 207 children alive in the church.

The account of an eyewitness was introduced into evidence: "Outside the church the soil was freshly dug; children's garments were piled up, half burned. Where the barns had stood, completely calcinated human skeletons, heaped one on the other, partially covered with various materials, made a horrible charnelhouse."

Juxtaposed was the report of a German judicial inquiry, issued January 14, 1945: "The reprisals appear to be absolutely justified for military reasons."

In an effort to apportion responsibility, Colonels Taylor and Hinkel confronted the genial-appearing Bach-Zelewski, who looked more like a Boy Scout leader than an SS commander, with General Heinz Guderian, who had ended the war as the army's chief of staff, and Major General Walter Warlimont, who had had, as Jodl's deputy, charge of coordinating antipartisan warfare between the Wehrmacht and the SS.* Guderian and Warlimont both professed ignorance. Guderian, at one point (during a later interrogation) revealed the indifference, amorality, and self-limitations of the German military mind by excitedly blurting out: "The whole thing was a matter of complete indifference to me, and I can tell you that I know nothing of this persecution of the Jews and their being put in ghettos. As to all the problems of the people, to preserve or to exterminate the people, we never wasted any thought on that!"

Bach-Zelewski, after listening for some time, suggested to Guderian and Warlimont that they should be ashamed of their know-nothing pretensions, and pointed out that, after all, *someone* had been providing him with troops and material. Warlimont thereupon admitted that everyone had known what was going on, but nobody had had the inclination or the power to do anything about it.

During his early interrogations Bach-Zelewski was agitated, given to contradictory statements, and evidently undecided about the stance he should take. By December 5, however, he had made up his mind to cast himself in the most favorable light possible by pinning responsibility on the Wehrmacht and Army High Commands. Declaring himself willing and anxious to testify, he prepared a statement that Taylor introduced when the antipartisan chief appeared in court on January 7:

"Leaders at the top who are conscious of their responsibilities can-

*Warlimont was married to the daughter of a German nobleman and Paula Anhaeuser-Busch of the St. Louis brewing family. During the 1930s he had, as an exchange officer, attended the United States Staff College and become friends with a number of high-ranking American officers, including General Donovan and General Hermann Wedemeyer.

not abandon the execution of reprisals to the caprice of individual commanders. If lack of direction leads to a chaos of reprisals and no clear orders are given, then the only possible conclusion is that this chaos is intended by the leaders at the top. There is no question but that reprisals both by the Wehrmacht and by the SS and police units overshot the mark by a long way. This fact was repeatedly established at conferences with generals. The fight against partisans was gradually used as an excuse to carry out other measures such as the extermination of Jews and Gypsies, the systematic reduction of the Slavic population by some thirty million souls in order to assure the supremacy of the German people, and the terrorization of civilians by shooting and looting. The commanders in chief with whom I collaborated, Field Marshals von Weichs, von Küchler, Bock, Kluge, Colonel General Reinhard, and General Kitzinger were as well aware as I of the purposes and methods of antipartisan warfare."

Goering, Keitel, and Jodl were stunned by Bach-Zelewski's appearance and the critical affidavits Taylor had obtained from a number of their fellow officers. Keitel was aghast at Field Marshal Blomberg's characterization of him: "He became a willing tool in Hitler's hands for every one of his decisions. He did not measure up to what might have been expected of him." Since Keitel's son was married to Blomberg's daughter, it seemed almost like the public airing of a family dispute.

During a brief intermission to permit the attorneys to confer with their clients following the direct examination of Bach-Zelewski, Goering stomped up and down the dock: "Why, that dirty, bloody, treacherous swine! That filthy skunk! God damn, *Donnerwetter*, the dirty son of a bitch! He was the bloodiest murderer in the whole goddamned setup! The dirty, filthy *Schweinhund*, selling his soul to save his stinking neck!"

Jodl's face turned almost purple as he directed his attorney, Franz Exner: "Ask him if he knows that Hitler held him up to us as a model partisan fighter! Just ask the dirty pig that!"

Exner succeeded in eliciting during his cross-examination that only SS, not Wehrmacht, officers had been present when Himmler had declared that among the goals of the Russian campaign was the elimination of thirty million Slavs, and that it was the SS, not the Wehrmacht or the Army High Commands, through which key orders had been channeled.

The cross-examination by a half-dozen other defense attorneys was, at best, mediocre, and frequently silly. Stahmer, on behalf of Goering, asked: "Don't you know that Hitler and Himmler singled you out for praise and decorated you because of your hard and pitiless conduct of partisan warfare?"

"No," Bach-Zelewski answered only half the question, and that speciously, since Hitler had said: "This Bach-Zelewski is one of the cleverest of men," and awarded him the Knight's Cross, the highest Nazi medal. Goering, who itched to cross-examine witnesses, fumed as Stahmer dropped the inquiry, and Bach-Zelewski escaped unscathed.

Rosenberg's attorney, Alfred Thoma, intent on disassociating the philosophy that Rosenberg expounded from the atrocities, asked Bach-Zelewski how he could reconcile his conscience with his leadership of the *Einsatzgruppen?* Bach-Zelewski, of course, replied that he had never been the chief of an *Einsatzgruppe*. To Thoma's question whether Himmler's speech projecting the extinction of thirty million Slavs was consistent with National Socialist philosophy, Bach-Zelewski replied: "I am of the opinion today that it was the logical result of our philosophy."

Then how could it be, Thoma inquired, that Ohlendorf, though admitting his *Einsatzgruppe* had killed ninety thousand people, had testified that this action had not been in accord with National Socialist ideology?

"I am of a different opinion," Bach-Zelewski answered. "If one year after year predicts that the Slavic race is a subrace, and that the Jews are not human at all, then such an explosion has to come."

Up to this time, the translating system had performed its stately minuet remarkably well. The prosecution's lawyers had adjusted themselves to speaking in measured tones; and, when witness and interrogator conversed in different languages, they were forced to halt until the translation came through.

Since, however, the attorneys and Bach-Zelewski both spoke German, they tended to forget themselves. As the questions and answers volleyed back and forth at normal conversational speed, the translators were unable to keep up. The judges frequently found themselves listening to a translation of Bach-Zelewski while an attorney was speaking, and vice versa. Lawrence repeatedly told the Germans that they must wait for the translation of a question before they could give an answer, or of an answer before they could ask the next question; but the problem kept resurfacing throughout the trial.

Biddle wanted to know how many troops the Germans had committed to antipartisan warfare. Bach-Zelewski replied: "Perhaps three divisions." This was a statement that was true insofar as it went, but was completely misleading as to the extent of the combat. The fact of the matter was that at the height of the fighting there had been 253,000 men employed in battling the guerrillas, but, of these, 238,000 had been auxiliaries recruited from the occupied lands.

After Bach-Zelewski was dismissed and heading for the exit past Goering's place in the dock, the Reichsmarshal, half rising in his seat, spat at him: *"Schweinhund Verräter!"* ("Filthy dog of a traitor!") Bach-Zelewski stopped dead in his tracks, flushed, then, after a momentary hesitation, continued. A buzz went through the room, and one of the guards started toward Goering; but Goering, with an angelic smile on his face, had already resumed his seat.

Andrus docked Goering's tobacco ration and exercise privileges for a few days; and, thereafter, witnesses were brought in and taken out through the door by the judges' bench, so as to obviate the possibility of a further confrontation.*

Taylor's presentation on the high command brought to an end the core of the American case, although the United States prosecution made major contributions to the French and Russian presentations on War Crimes and Crimes Against Humanity.

All in all, the American staff expressed the relief of a novice high-wire artist who has made it from one tower to another. Lieutenant Colonel John B. Street marveled: "It is amazing that the press has been so favorable when obviously the case went to trial without any real organization of evidence or any definite plan as to presentation." Roger Barrett, who had charge of the Defendants' Information Center, wrote: "In spite of all the bungling I really believe the evidence is in the record and the job is creditable. It certainly was done the hard way though. Our principal handicap was lack of leadership and direction. The deputy in charge [Storey] just wasn't a big enough man for the job."

The exodus of American lawyers, which had started before Christmas, accelerated. Storey departed in mid-January; and within a few weeks only 13 of the 150 attorneys were left. Jackson himself thought of returning to the Supreme Court during the French and Russian offerings and leaving Taylor in charge. The Supreme Court was divided 4–4 on a host of cases, and Jackson was needed to cast the deciding vote. Chief Justice Stone, however, did not want a man who was prosecuting one case simultaneously judging others. He advised Jackson he could either see the trial through or return to the Court. But he could not do both.

Jackson responded: "I think my choice must be to remain with this case to its finish. Regardless of whether it was wise to enter it in the beginning I am in it, and withdrawal would have some bad consequences."

---

*Bach-Zelewski's performance helped him to survive. Taylor was in the process of negotiating his extradition to Poland when the talks were broken off because of the Cold War. A denazification court sentenced him to ten years in prison in 1951, but suspended the sentence in consideration of the time he had already spent in custody. To purge his guilt feelings, he denounced himself publicly for mass murder in 1952, but was never prosecuted. In 1961 he was sentenced to three and a half years for his role in the Röhm massacre, and the next year he was tried again and condemned to life imprisonment for killing six German Communists in 1933.

He could not predict how much longer the trial would last, "but it now looks improbable final decision and sentence will be reached before July. The safest course is for you to write me off as a total loss for the rest of this term."

Obviously, Jackson could not continue as prosecutor of the other top Nazis destined for trial; and Taylor, agreeing to take charge of these cases, returned to the United States to recruit a new staff.

34   The Perversion of German Medicine

The French case was opened by François de Menthon on January 17. Forty-five years old, de Menthon was descended from a brother of Saint Bernard (who had come to the defense of Jews subjected to pogroms in Germany during the twelfth-century crusades). A professor of law and political economy, he had served in the French armed forces, been wounded and taken prisoner by the Germans, but had escaped in June of 1940. As a member of the underground, he had been co-director of the resistance newspaper *Combat*. In 1943 he had made his way to North Africa, where he had become minister of justice in the French provisional government. A staunch Gaullist, de Menthon was elected a deputy in 1946 and subsequently was runner-up in an election for the French presidency.

De Menthon viewed the trial in almost metaphysical terms. His perceptions, similar to those of Bernays, were that the civilized world was faced with a test of the human spirit. Although, like Sir Hartley Shawcross, he appeared only briefly in Nuremberg, and left the actual presentation of the French case to several assistant prosecutors, his address was one of the memorable statements of the trial.

"I propose today to prove to you," de Menthon commenced, "that all this organized and vast criminality springs from what I may be allowed to call a crime against the spirit. I mean a doctrine which, denying all spiritual, rational, or moral values by which the nations have tried, for thousands of years, to improve human conditions, aims to plunge humanity back into barbarism; no longer the natural and spontaneous barbarism of primitive nations, but into a diabolical barbarism, conscious of itself and utilizing for its end all material means put at the disposal of mankind by contemporary science. This sin against the spirit is the original sin of National Socialism from which all crimes spring.

"This monstrous doctrine is that of racism. . . . The individual has no value in himself and is important only as an element of the race. . . . Anyone whose opinions differ from the official doctrine is asocial or unhealthy. . . . National Socialism ends in the absorption of the personality of the citizen into that of the state, and in the denial of any intrinsic value of the human person.

"We are brought back, as can be seen, to the most primitive ideas of the savage tribe. All the values of civilization accumulated in the course of centuries are rejected, all traditional ideas of morality, justice, and law give way to the primacy of race, its instincts, its needs and interest. The individual, his liberty, his rights and aspirations, no longer have any real existence of their own.

"How can one explain how Germany, fertilized through the centuries by classic antiquity and Christianity, by the ideals of liberty, equality, and social justice, by the common heritage of western humanism to which she has brought such noble and precious contributions, could have come to this astonishing return to primitive barbarism? . . .

"Sacerdotal Judaism and Christianity in all its forms are condemned as religions of honor and brotherhood, calculated to kill the virtues of brutal force in man. A cry is raised against the democratic idealism of the modern era. . . . In the middle of the twentieth century Germany goes back, on her own free will, beyond Christianity and civilization to the primitive barbarity of ancient Germany. . . .

"The crime against race is punished without pity. The crime on behalf of race is exalted without limit. The regime truly creates a logic of crime which obeys its own laws, which has no connection whatsoever with what we consider ethical. With such a point of view, all horrors could have been justified and authorized. So many acts which appear incomprehensible to us, so greatly do they clash with our customary notions, were explained, were formulated in advance in the name of the racial community.

"The truly diabolical enterprise of Hitler and of his companions was to assemble in a body of dogmas formed around the concept of race all the instincts of barbarism, repressed by centuries of civilization, but always present in men's innermost nature.

"Without your judgment, history might incur the risk of repeating itself, crime would become epic, and the National Socialist enterprise a last Wagnerian tragedy.

"After your judgment, National Socialism will be inscribed permanently as the crime of crimes which could lead only to material and moral perdition, as the doctrine which they [the Germans] should forever avoid with horror and scorn in order to remain faithful, or rather become once more faithful to the great norms of common civilization."

For six weeks thereafter the court was exposed to one horror after another. The primary focus was on the images of savagery embodied by the concentration camps. Here, man had been dehumanized, reduced to a numbered object to be used in whatever manner his captors saw fit.

One offshoot of the euthanasia program conducted in the concentration camps had been the Final Solution. The other, equally sadistic in microcosm, had been the employment of human beings for medical experiments. After Major Monigan, during his interrogations, traced the course from one to the other, the Americans and French combined presented the case.*

On May 15, 1941, an air force physician, Dr. Sigmund Rascher, who was a friend of Himmler's, had written to the Reichsführer SS that he was attending a Luftwaffe medical course in Munich. "During this course, where researches on high altitude flights play a prominent part (determined by the somewhat higher ceiling of the English fighter planes), considerable regret was expressed at the fact that no test with human material had yet been possible for us, as such experiments are very dangerous and nobody volunteers for them. They are essential for researches on high altitude flight and cannot be carried out, as has been tried, with monkeys, who offer entirely different test conditions. Can you make available two or three professional criminals for these experiments?" If not criminals, then perhaps, Rascher suggested, feebleminded could be employed instead of being done away with uselessly in the euthanasia program.

Himmler was delighted. Hitler blamed high losses at the front on shortcomings in medicine, Dr. Brandt told Major Monigan. The Führer had remarked repeatedly: "The criminals are also here to serve their fatherland."

In order to understand fully what followed, Brandt related, "one has to see the whole of Himmler's personality." Like a schoolboy wishing to surprise his parents, he had always thought he could solve a problem better than anyone else, and derived immense satisfaction from launching secret projects that would enable him to tell Hitler, "I have done such and such." He experimented with running water over coal to obtain petroleum, with wheat cultivated without fertilizer, with cancer cures and with alchemy.

The Reichsführer SS opened Dachau to Rascher, and there the First Experimental Station of the Luftwaffe was established. A pressure chamber to simulate high altitude conditions was set up by the air force. Rascher experimented with the effect of various degrees of oxygen intake on subjects, and had air pumped out of the chamber to create a vacuum so that the men's lungs ruptured.

*The principal physicians involved in the medical atrocities were tried in one of the twelve subsequent Nuremberg cases.

"Some experiments gave men such pressure in their heads that they would go mad and pull out their hair in an effort to relieve the pressure," Anton Pacholegg, an inmate scientist who was assigned to assist Rascher, testified. "They would tear their heads and face with their fingers and nails in an attempt to maim themselves in their madness. These cases of extremes of vacuums generally ended in the death of the subject."

Himmler himself was fascinated by the experiments, and together with Karl Wolff and *Standartenführer* Wolfram Sievers, the head of the SS's Ancestral Heritage Institute—which had jurisdiction over medical experiments—frequently came to view them.

Rascher carried on for a year. On May 20, 1942, Field Marshal Erhard Milch, the operating head of the Luftwaffe, wrote Wolff: "Dear Wolffy! The altitude experiments carried out by the SS and air force at Dachau have been finished. Any continuation of these experiments seems essentially unreasonable. However, the carrying out of experiments of some other kind, in regard to perils at high seas, would be important."

To determine how German fliers downed in the ocean could be protected against exposure, Rascher submerged men into a vat of icy water, or, later, had them exposed all night to subzero temperatures, until their hands and feet froze white. Sometimes they were sprayed with water, until they turned virtually into blocks of ice. In an attempt to find the best means to revive the men, prostitutes were brought to Dachau from Ravensbrück concentration camp and made to cuddle the frozen men between their naked bodies. Rascher, however, reported: "Rapid rewarming was in all cases preferable to slow rewarming, because after removal from the cold water, the body temperature continued to sink rapidly. I think that for this reason we can attempt to dispense with the attempt to save intensely chilled subjects by means of animal heat . . . or women's bodies."

Rapid rewarming, Pacholegg explained, in water of varying temperatures meant "the victims came out looking like lobsters. Some lived but most of them died."

All of this impressed Himmler more than the Luftwaffe doctors, who accused Rascher of engaging in little more than sadistic quackery. Some even went so far as to include Himmler in this characterization. During an interrogation, Wolff proffered that it had been curiosity that had "led Himmler to take up similar hobbies and perform experiments on human beings." When the Luftwaffe, in November 1942, indicated no more interest in Rascher's experiments, Himmler addressed Milch:

"I personally assumed the responsibility for supplying asocial individuals and criminals who deserve only to die from concentration camps for these experiments. The difficulties are still the same now as before. In the 'Christian medical circles' the standpoint is being taken that it goes without saying that a young German aviator should be allowed to risk his life but that the life of a criminal is too sacred for this purpose, and one should not stain oneself with this guilt. I personally have inspected the experiments, and have—I can say this without exaggeration—participated in every phase of this scientific work in a helpful and inspiring manner.

"It will take at least another ten years until we can get such narrow-mindedness out of our people. But this should not affect the research work. I beg you to release Dr. Rascher, *Stabsarzt* in reserve, from the air force and to transfer him to me in the Waffen SS."

Milch made no objection. On August 31, 1942, he had written Himmler: "I have read with great interest the reports of Dr. Rascher and Dr. Romberg. I shall ask the two gentlemen to give a lecture combined with the showing of motion pictures for my men in the near future." But when Major Monigan questioned him about the experiments, Milch pretended he had never heard about either them or Dr. Rascher.

"I am always astounded by my fellow countrymen who did not know anything or pretended not to know anything," Ludwig Diels, who, as district president of Bonn, had received numerous reports about the euthanasia program and medical experiments, commented to Major Monigan.

Rascher next attempted to develop a chemical that could be taken internally to speed the clotting of blood. Inmates were shot, or subjected to amputations or other traumatic injuries simulating battlefield conditions. When it was known beforehand that a man could not survive, Rascher would make what he called a "leather inspection." Grabbing a man by the buttocks or thighs, he would say "Good," which meant that, after the victim had been killed, the skin was stripped from his body.

A Czech doctor, Franz Blaha, who had been head of the hospital at Iglau, Seyss-Inquart's birthplace, testified before the tribunal that he had been incarcerated at Dachau from 1941 to 1945. Presenting a wretched physical appearance, he said he had been assigned to perform autopsies, and had conducted twelve thousand all told—an average of nearly ten a day. On numerous occasions, Blaha recalled, he had been ordered by Rascher and another doctor to flay the skin off bodies:

"It was chemically treated and placed in the sun to dry. After that it was cut into various sizes for use as saddles, riding breeches, gloves, house slippers, and ladies' handbags. Tattooed skin was especially valued by SS men. Sometimes we did not have enough bodies with good skin and Rascher would say, 'All right, you will get the bodies.' The next day we would receive twenty or thirty bodies of young people. They would have been shot in the neck or struck on the head so that the skin would be uninjured. Also we frequently got requests for the skulls or skeletons of prisoners. In those cases we boiled the skull or the body. Then the soft parts were removed and the bones were bleached and dried and reassembled. In the case of skulls it was important to have a good set of teeth. So it was dangerous to have good skin or good teeth."

"I was in the office many times when human skin with blood still on it was brought into Rascher," Pacholegg noted. "After the bodies had been carted away, Rascher would inspect the skins carefully, holding them up to the light for flaws, and would pass on them before they were tanned. They were always stretched over small wooden frames when they came to Rascher. I saw the finished leather later made into a handbag that Mrs. Rascher was carrying."

One of Himmler's cherished goals was to find means of mass sterilization for all the *Untermensch* in the Greater German Reich, and he was delighted when a specialist on skin and venereal diseases suggested that extracts from two plants, Caladium and Dieffenbachia, native to North America but rare in Germany, could produce permanent sterility. "The thought alone that the three million Bolsheviks now in German captivity could be sterilized so that they would be available for work but precluded from propagation opens up the most far-reaching perspectives," the doctor pontificated.

Various operations and experiments to produce sterility were performed on Jewish youths in concentration camps. To deal with the *Mischlinge* (offspring of Jewish-Christian marriages), one imaginative physician proposed a harebrained scheme to hide an X-ray machine beneath a counter to which the *Mischlinge* would be required to report. While standing there, they would be given a squirt of X-rays that would sterilize them without their ever knowing what had happened.

At Goering's behest, Himmler agreed to make several hundred prisoners available to the director of the Hygienic Institute at the University of Strasbourg for the testing of various types of typhus vaccines. Supposedly, criminals were to be used, but since adults were too valuable as workers, Jewish children were sent from Auschwitz instead.

Most of these projects had, at least, a rational if perverse goal. But another physician at the University of Strasbourg, Dr. Hirt, well known for his work on cancer and microorganisms, simply wished to indulge his pseudo-anthropological hobby. "We have a nearly complete collection of skulls of all races and peoples at our disposal," he wrote Himmler. "Of the Jewish race, however, only very few specimens of skulls are available. The war in the East now presents us with the opportunity to overcome this deficiency. By procuring the skulls of the Jewish Bolshevik commissars, who represent the prototype of the repulsive, but characteristic subhuman, we have a chance now to obtain a palpable, scientific document. The best, practical method for obtaining and collecting the skull material could be handled by directing the Wehrmacht to turn over alive all captured Jewish Bolshevik commissars and to give them special close attention and care until a special delegate arrives. This special delegate, who will be in charge of securing the material, has the job of taking a series of previously established photographs, anthropological measurements, and in addition has to determine, so far as is possible, the background, date of birth, and other personal data of the prisoner. Following the subsequently induced death of the Jew, whose head should not be damaged, the delegate will separate the head from the body and will forward it to its proper point of destination in a hermetically sealed tin can."

Hirt's demands were so extensive—and he furthermore amended his request for not merely the heads, but the entire skeletons—that it was decided to ship the subjects live from Auschwitz to Natzweiler concentration camp near Strasbourg, and let Hirt conduct his own slaughter. Eichmann dispatched seventy-nine Jewish men, thirty Jewish women, two Poles, and four Asiatics to Hirt for skeletonization.

The cadavers, however, were still unstripped in early September 1944, when it seemed that the American army might overrun Strasbourg, and the SS officers involved became panicky. "Because of the vast amount of scientific research conducted therewith, the job of reducing the corpses to skeletons has not yet been completed," Sievers wrote. "The collection can be defleshed and thereby rendered unidentifiable. This, however, would mean that at least part of the whole work had been done for nothing, and that this singular collection would be lost to science, since it would be impossible to make plaster casts afterwards. The skeleton collection as such is inconspicuous. The flesh parts could be declared as having been left by the French at the time we took over the Anatomical Institute and would be turned over for cremating. Please advise me which of the three following proposals is to be carried out: 1. The collection as a whole is to be preserved. 2. The collection is to be dissolved in part. 3. The collection is to be completely dissolved."

Himmler decided that, in order to protect himself, science would, after all, have to be deprived of the unique collection. The bodies were ordered cremated. The job, however, was botched, and some of the remains were discovered by American troops.

Himmler assigned Dr. Ernst Grawitz, a boyhood friend whom he had made chief medical officer of the SS as well as president of the German Red Cross, overall responsibility for the experiments. By the spring of 1944, however, the projects—which included the testing of gases, cyanide-tipped bullets, and cyanide capsules for committing suicide—had grown so extensive that they were killing or incapacitating hundreds of camp inmates monthly. *Obergruppenführer* Oswald Pohl, head of the SS Economics and Administration Office, challenged Grawitz's decimation of his labor force. "Herewith, I explicitly forbid assignments of prisoners for experimental purposes without permission," Pohl ordered on May 12, 1944.

Grawitz blew himself and his family up with a couple of hand grenades at the end of the war, and Rascher was disposed of by order of Himmler. But the most prominent of the other 350 physicians survived to be assembled for Major Monigan's interrogation.

Dr. Brandt, though championing euthanasia, professed at first to have known nothing about the program's evolvement into vivisection. In response to Major Monigan's question, "What was the policy within Germany concerning medical experiments on human beings?" he replied:

"I have lately heard about it. First, quite independently of what actually has happened, the human being has always been used in some form for experimental purposes. It might sound primitive, but I want to mention every single operation as one such experiment. The jump from animal experiments to human experiments was for practical reasons actually needed."

Brandt expatiated pedantically and self-righteously on various classifications and subclassifications of vivisection. "It is my intention to justify the ethical considerations of the German doctor as a whole. There are sudden demands and new means of warfare and new symptoms that one has to look at in a separate existence and not connected with the ordinary, normal procedures in peacetime."

The reality was that Brandt had requested from Himmler prisoners on whom hepatitis experiments were to be conducted, and had stated: "One must reckon on cases of death. This illness has been very widespread in the past years, both amongst us in the Waffen SS and the police and the army, so that companies have been reduced by fifty percent for periods of up to six weeks."

Brandt acknowledged he had been present when Dr. Theodor Morrell, his rival and successor as Hitler's physician, had informed the Führer that he had invented a louse powder that would wipe out typhus. "I can remember a very peculiar dinner conversation," Brandt declared. "It was said that wherever there are horse blankets there are no lice. Himmler talked about it at supper. So the sweat of a horse must contain antigens."

Himmler had immediately demanded the implementation of a program to test and manufacture the powder. Though Morrell's nostrum was worthless, Hitler suspected that the medical profession was engaging in sabotage, and had ordered every soldier equipped with a packet. This order proved of greater benefit to Morrell, who made a fortune out of manufacturing the packets, than to the soldiers, who cynically observed that the lice seemed to thrive on the powder.

Strangely, however, Brandt could not recall the meetings he had had with Dr. Karl Gebhardt to initiate sulfa drug experiments at Ravensbrück concentration camp, or the prestigious conference that had followed, attended by all of the leading physicians of the Reich.

Gebhardt's father had been the Himmlers' family physician. And Gebhardt, an orthopedic surgeon, had benefited after the Nazi takeover by having a tuberculosis clinic at Hohenlychen, near Berlin, turned over to him for conversion into a hospital specializing in sports medicine for the 1936 Olympics. As a result of the publicity generated by the games, Gebhardt and Hohenlychen had become known throughout Europe, and he had treated many prominent foreign patients as well as German.

"Most of the leading personalities of this revolution, as is always the case in revolution, were not highly educated men," Gebhardt lectured Major Monigan. "Take Hess, for instance, who had no definite profession. Himmler had none. You can also take the Führer himself." Because of the prominence of Jewish physicians, the Nazi leaders had rationalized that traditional medicine was decadent; and, of course, if the Jews were to be eliminated from the profession, something would have to replace them. "These people had little regard for scientific medicine," Gebhardt continued, "and they were all attracted by 'natural medicine,' and they also had the feeling that progress and a reform were necessary in German medicine. They had a childish enthusiasm. All sorts of popular drugs, which were not approved by the medical profession allegedly because we did not understand them or were too conceited or were financially interested in the suppression of them, were used experimentally in concentration camps. The source of these experiments was Himmler's conception of medicine as pure mysticism. It was indicative of the general attitude of the Führer himself that at one time it was contemplated to make Streicher the head of the Public Health Department. Medical treatment is something that is needed by everybody, and they had homemade ideas on the kind of medicine that should be provided for the average man. For one thing, the services of the highly qualified physicians were accessible only to people who could pay a high price for them. What the National Socialists wanted to do was to introduce a popular medicine. It is a fact that there is an industry that makes a business and a profit out of producing all sorts of drugs and medicines which are of course more expensive than a simple man or woman can afford, and it must be admitted that a lot of things are sold by those industries which are not particularly good or necessary. I agree with Hess's point of view that reform is necessary. I disagree with their idea that such reforms could be introduced without the help of specialists."

Streicher had published articles against I.G. Farben and the Merck Chemical Company fully as splenetic as against the Jews. New chairs were endowed at universities for professors of herb cures. "The most absurd things occurred," Ludwig Diels recounted. He had once been prohibited from dismissing a medical officer who treated tuberculosis with pendulums. Another doctor, Werner Kirchert, informed Monigan: "Orders came through many times that this or that quack had to be employed; that this or that medicine had to be used; Himmler ordered that, in cases of frostbite, dog fat should be used."

The attack on the Soviet Union had overtaxed the depleted German medical profession to the point that, during the winter of 1941–42, the Wehrmacht medical department had collapsed, Gebhardt related. The practice had been to bring the wounded back to Germany for treatment; but when the transportation system broke down, tens of thousands died in field hospitals or during the journey. Gebhardt, who was of the old German school which believed that major operations should be performed on the spot, took a substantial number of surgeons and organized surgical hospitals near the front. "So, for instance, with a small wound in the arm, the whole arm could be split open so that it became like an opened orange and the open wound could be treated," he told Monigan.

But because of the primitive conditions that existed in the field hospitals and the large number of wounded—as many as two hundred frequently arrived within an hour—Gebhardt's solution proved impractical. The wounded continued to die of shock and gangrene. Other German doctors, having learned of the Allied success with sulfanilamide to inhibit infection in battlefield wounds, were urging Gebhardt to follow suit. But despite the fact that a German chemist and bacteriologist had developed sulfa drugs and that the German chemical industry had, at one time, led the world, the Nazi regime had created such havoc that the nation lacked facilities for mass manufacture of sulfa. "Therefore, we had to import sulfa from Switzerland," Gebhardt said, spending hard-to-get foreign exchange in the process. Furthermore, the doctors discovered that when sulfa was sprinkled onto an open wound, the effect was more often unfavorable than favorable.

Allied psychological warfare, in the meantime, conducted one of its most effective campaigns of the war. Hundreds of thousands of leaflets were dropped informing the German soldiers that every British and American serviceman, and even the supposedly Russian *Untermensch,* had with him a packet of sulfa powder that enabled him to survive if he were wounded, while the German soldier was condemned because his government was unable to provide him with the drug. The impact was enormous. "It was a crisis of our soldiers," Gebhardt declared. "Our soldiers didn't trust us anymore—they said the American and English soldiers have the drug which they use very successfully, and we don't have it, and therefore we have to die. There were only two things to do, either consider the war as lost, or from our point of view find out if these sulfa drugs are actually as good as they are supposed to be."

Gebhardt had been named supreme clinician of the SS. In July of 1942 he, Brandt, Grawitz, and other leading physicians in the Reich had met with Himmler. Himmler had asked Gebhardt to undertake experiments with sulfa on concentration camp inmates at Hohenlychen. The Reichsführer, Gebhardt recalled, had been in a euphoric mood: "Since fate had given him the task of doing the dirty work for the revolution, he told me many times that he was anxious to make the best of any chance to combine positive, constructive contributions with the sinister task of his. It gave him great comfort that the same concentration camps could be used to further science."

Gebhardt, who, as the representative of the Red Cross, traveled to foreign countries throughout the war, knew perfectly well what was going on, and did not want to compromise Hohenlychen by associating it with concentration camp science. He had had, however, no scruples about operating elsewhere: "I didn't see anything wrong in going ahead with these experiments and working on them just from the scientific point of view." He had offered, he told Major Monigan, to supervise them if they were done at nearby Ravensbrück, a concentration camp for women. Himmler ordered two young SS surgeons in his retinue, Fritz Fischer and Ludwig Stumpfegger, to perform the actual operations. Grawitz wanted the experiments conducted in secret, but Gebhardt, who had no intention of being deprived of credit for them, intended to publish the results.

"I might have refrained very easily from any participation," Gebhardt informed Monigan with egotistic ingenuousness. "I didn't want my two assistants to go ahead with these experiments by themselves, since I didn't think they were quite capable of achieving the same success which would have been achieved if I had worked on it myself; and since these human beings are going to be sacrificed anyway, I had considered it better to get some success out of it."

For six months Fischer simulated battlefield infections by slicing open the legs of women, stuffing them with wood shavings, dirt, glass, streptococcus, staphylococcus, and gangrene cultures, then sewing them up again. Later, Gebhardt, Fischer, and Stumpfegger embarked on a new line by attempting to transplant muscles and shoulder bones from one patient to another, with the predictable consequences. Those women who survived were horribly maimed and disfigured. Shortly before the end of the war Himmler ordered them shot, so that no witnesses would remain; but a few escaped.

In early May of 1943, Gebhardt, as the principal speaker before the Congress of Reich Physicians, proudly provided explicit details of the results of the Ravensbrück experiments. Virtually everyone of note in German medicine was there. A number of professors of medicine at various universities led a discussion afterward, and not one of them issued a word of criticism. The next day Gebhardt was feted by the German Orthopedic Society. Honors were showered upon him, and his reputation continued to grow.

And what had Gebhardt learned? "The point of issue for me was not the experiment," he pedantically told Monigan. "I, as a surgeon, must say that even today I can do without sulfanilamide." Its benefits, he thought, had been exaggerated. "I am rather an opponent of penicillin or sulfanilamide."

Fischer, posted to an SS combat division, received a measure of divine retribution when he lost his lower right arm in Normandy. Left to brood in his cell in Nuremberg, he slipped into fantasy and lunacy. "I have been working for nine years on the problem of cancer," he informed Monigan on November 5. "I have found a solution to the cancer problem, as to the problematic side of it as well as the therapeutic result. That means that the phenomenon of cancer is solved and the disease of cancer is curable from now on. This applies also to diseases that are named differently." No one else had been able to discover the solution, Fischer continued, "because everyone specializes, and individual specialists can't understand each other anymore."

A man of scarcely less imagination was Himmler's aide, Wolfram Sievers. On December 20 Sievers sent Monigan a statement that he had joined the SS in 1933 on orders of a secret resistance organization. While head of Himmler's Ancestral Heritage Institute he claimed to have helped numerous people, including Danish atomic scientist Niels Bohr, to escape, and had plotted the assassinations of both Hitler and Himmler, assassinations that, though Sievers had been one of Himmler's most frequent companions, had somehow never come off.

The septuagenarian, highly educated, English-speaking Dr. Claus Schilling epitomized the perversion of medicine by the Nazis. The former director of tropical medicine at the renowned Robert Koch Institute in Berlin, Schilling had spent many years in Africa. After retiring in 1936, he had gone to live in Italy. In 1941 he had met Dr. Leonardo Conti, the Reich public health chief, at an affair at the German embassy in Rome, and Conti had offered him the facilities at Dachau for malaria experiments.

Over the span of three years Schilling had induced malaria and experimented with various forms of treatment on more than one thousand inmates. Malaria, he explained to Monigan, was really not a fatal disease, and he had not lost any patients—a patent lie, since scores had died. Rascher, he admitted, had told him about his pressure chamber experiments, but since they had not been his affair, he had not inquired too deeply. Nor had he known anything about what went on in Dachau until after he had been imprisoned by the Americans: "When I came to Dachau, there was a certain rumor, but my will was not to occupy myself with what did not belong to my laboratory. I did my work in the camp, and didn't look right or left. When I read these descriptions, I said, how is it possible that I never noticed anything?"

Schilling had been condemned to death, along with twoscore other participants in Dachau atrocities, in a trial that had concluded in December.

Detailing his experiences at Dachau to the Nuremberg tribunal, Dr. Blaha described Schilling's malaria experiments, and phlegmonesulfa experiments by other doctors. "Forty healthy men were used at a time. All treatment was forbidden for three days, by which time serious inflammation and in many cases general blood poisoning had occurred. In some cases all the limbs were amputated. For these experiments, Polish, Czech, and Dutch priests were ordinarily used. Most of the six hundred to eight hundred persons who were used finally died. Most of the others became permanent invalids and were later killed."

Another doctor performed liver puncture experiments. A needle was jabbed into the liver of a person and a small piece of the liver was extracted. No anesthetic was used. "The experiment is very painful and often had serious results, as the stomach or large blood vessels were often punctured resulting in hemorrhage. All together about one hundred and seventy-five people were subjected to these experiments."

During one eighteen-month period, Dr. Blaha testified, "some five hundred operations on healthy prisoners were performed. These were for the instruction of the SS medical students and doctors, and included operations on the stomach, gall bladder, and throat. Many prisoners died on the operating table and many others from later complications."

Words poured out of Blaha in a torrent, and Lawrence had to halt him several times to permit the interpreters to catch up. "Very many visitors came to our camp," Blaha said, "so that it sometimes seemed to us that we were confined not in a camp but in an exhibition or in a zoo. At times there was a visit or an excursion almost every day from schools, from different military, medical, and other institutions, and also many members of the police, the SS, and the armed forces." Once, before he had been assigned to the autopsy room, Blaha related, he had been working in the fields. "We were pulling a heavy street roller, sixteen men; and a group of girls passed us who were on an excursion. Their leader said very loudly so that we could all hear it: 'Look, those people are so lazy that, rather than harness a big team of horses, they pull it themselves!'"

Two French physicians, Victor Dupont and Alfred Balachowsky, described their experiences at Buchenwald, paralleling those of Blaha at Dachau. Balachowsky closed the book on a controversy that had had its inception during the American introduction of the shrunken head and tattooed piece of skin from Buchenwald on December 13. At the time, both Kaltenbrunner's attorney, Kurt Kauffmann, and Bormann's attorney, Friedrich Bergold, had complained that the prosecution was not being entirely above board. Bergold protested "the prosecution's failure to mention a very important point, namely, that the German authorities indicted this inhuman SS leader [the Buchenwald commandant, Karl Koch] and his wife and condemned them to death. It is highly probable that the prosecution knew of this and that these horrible exhibits of perverted human nature, which were presented to us, were found in the files of the German court. If the prosecution had stated that this man was condemned to death, then, in the first place, the evidence against the defendant Kaltenbrunner would not have appeared so weighty, and second, public opinion would on the whole have been left with a different impression."

On January 14, Thomas Dodd had replied for the American prosecution: "I wish to say that we had no knowledge at all about this man Koch at the time that we offered the proof; didn't know anything about him except that he had been the commandant. But, subsequently to this objection we had an investigation made, and we have found that he was tried in 1944, indeed, by an SS court, but not for having tanned human skin nor having preserved a human head, but for having embezzled some money, for what—as the judge who tried him tells us—was a charge of general corruption, and for having murdered someone with whom he had some personal difficulties. Indeed, the judge, a Dr. Morgen, tells us that he saw the tattooed human skin and he saw a human head in Commandant Koch's office, and that he saw a lampshade there made out of human skin. But there were no charges at the time that he was tried for having done these things."

Koch, in fact, had been so corrupt and paranoid that it had been impossible for the SS administration to ignore his failings. He had extorted hundreds of thousands of marks from wealthy Jews who had been sent to Buchenwald after the *Kristallnacht,* he had operated a number of rackets in conjunction with the Nazi Party leader of Weimar, and he had had every prisoner who learned too much or might have become an embarrassment to him because of his activities killed. His guilty conscience had caused him to believe that one of the prisoners, a diminutive Jew with marked physical peculiarities, was spying on him not only within the camp but slipping out and following him all over Germany (and then voluntarily returning). To rid himself of this phantom, Koch had had the man murdered.

"Do you know anything about the fate of tattooed men?" Charles Dubost, a deputy French prosecutor, inquired of Dr. Balachowsky on January 29.

"Tattooed human skins were stored in Block 2, which was called at Buchenwald the Pathological Block," Balachowsky replied.

"Did they skin people?"

"They removed the skin and then tanned it."

"We were told that Koch, who was the head at that time, was sentenced for this practice."

"I was not a witness of the Koch affair, which happened before I came to the camp."

"So that even after he left there were still tanned and tattooed skins?"

"Yes, there were constantly tanned and tattooed skins, and when the camp was liberated by the Americans, they found in the camp, in Block 2, tattooed and tanned skins on 11 April 1945."

During the Russian case, commenced a few days later, the exposition of Nazi exploitation of the human being continued. A former British prisoner of war, John Henry Witton, who had been employed at the Danzig Anatomic Institute, provided details on the production of soap:

"The corpses arrived at an average of seven to eight per day. All of them had been beheaded and were naked. The corpses were unloaded as quickly as possible and taken down into the cellar. They were then put into large metal containers where they were then left for approximately four months. Owing to the preservative mixture in which they were stored, the tissue came away from the bones very easily. The tissue was then put into a boiler about the size of a small kitchen table."

Another British prisoner of war, William Neely, related in a deposition: "A machine for the manufacture of soap was completed sometime in March or April 1944. It consisted, as far as I remember, of an electrically heated tank in which bones of the corpses were mixed with some acid and melted down."

Sigmund Mazur, a German laboratory assistant at the Anatomic Institute, added to the account: "In February 1944 Professor Spanner gave me the recipe for the preparation of soap from human fat. According to this recipe five kilos of human fat are mixed with ten liters of water and five hundred or one thousand grams of caustic soda. All this is boiled two or three hours and then cooled. The soap floats to the surface while the water and other sediment remain at the bottom. After having cooled, the soap is poured into molds. I boiled the soap out of the bodies of women and men. The process of boiling alone took several days—from three to seven. During two manufacturing processes, in which I directly participated, more than twenty-five kilograms of soap were produced. The amount of human fat necessary for these two processes was seventy to eighty kilograms collected from some forty bodies. The finished soap then went to Professor Spanner, who kept it personally. I used this soap for my personal needs, for toilet and for laundry.

"In the same way as for human fat, Professor Spanner ordered us to collect human skin, which after having been cleaned of fat was treated by certain chemical products. The finished skin was packed in boxes and used for special purposes which I don't know."

One of the assistant Russian prosecutors, L. N. Smirnov, submitted a bar of the soap and a piece of skin as exhibits. The Russians dramatized their presentation by projecting slides of baskets full of guillotined heads found in Danzig, snapshots of mass executions taken by an *Obergruppenführer*, Karl Strock, picture after picture of gallows and the hanging of women, and an entire street festooned with bodies in Lvov. Goering grinned when the first slide was accidentally projected upside down, and pretended to read a book during the fifteen-minute presentation. But the judges were horrified. Two days later the Russians followed up with the Nazis' own newsreel of the destruction of Lidice.

35   "Night and Fog," and Counterterror

The more the progress of the war had turned against the Nazis, the more Hitler had lashed out in frustration against those who were hostages to his terror. Thus it had come to be that a major German defeat had frequently precipitated a new horror.

On December 7, 1941—two days after the Russians launched their counterattack in the battle for Moscow—Hitler had had Keitel promulgate the *Nacht und Nebel* (Night and Fog) Decree.

A court-martial had the proper deterrent effect, Hitler declared, only if the sentence was death and carried out within eight days of the crime. Preferably, Hitler would have done away with courts-martial altogether, for, he believed, "court-martial proceedings create martyrs. History shows that the names of such men are on everybody's lips, whereas there is silence with regard to the many thousands who have lost their lives in similar circumstances without court-martial proceedings. The only weapon to deal with terror is terror." Therefore, in every case of resistance in which the perpetrator was not condemned to death—even if he or she were acquitted!—"the disappearance of the accused without a trace" was to be effected. "No information whatsoever may be given about their whereabouts and their fate."

The occupation forces were directed to turn the prisoners over to the SD, which would transport them to a concentration camp in Germany. There, like the Jews, they would live and die as "nonpersons." They were to vanish as if swallowed by night and fog.

Tens of thousands of men and women were committed to Himmler's stygian realm on the basis of this decree. The Nazis even coined a new word to describe their fate: They were *"Vernebelt"*—transformed into mist!*

On January 28, a handsome, compelling, thirty-three-year-old French-woman, Marie Vaillant-Couturier, appeared to recount her experiences under the *Nacht und Nebel* decree. Arrested in February 1942 as a member of the resistance, she had been imprisoned for almost a year in Paris, and then, in January 1943, had been one of a group of 260 women transported to Auschwitz. Most in the group were intellectuals: doctors, teachers, and philosophers. Some had been acquitted by a German military tribunal, which, according to Hitler's directive, was irrelevant. Among them was Hélène Solomon, the daughter of an atomic physicist who had been a pupil of Curie. (Her husband, also a physicist, was tortured and shot by the Gestapo.)

"When we arrived at Auschwitz," Madame Vaillant related, "for twelve thousand internees there was only one tap of water, unfit for drinking, and it was not always flowing. As this tap was in the German washhouse we could reach it only by passing through the guards, who were German common-law women prisoners, and they beat us horribly as we went by. It was therefore almost impossible to wash ourselves or our clothes. For more than three months we remained without changing our clothes. When there was snow, we melted some to wash in. Later, in the spring, when we went to work we would drink from a puddle by the roadside and then wash our underclothes in it. We took turns washing our hands in this dirty water. Our companions were dying of thirst, because we got only a half a cup of some herbal tea twice a day.

"The work at Auschwitz consisted of clearing demolished houses,

---

*The Foreign Ministry periodically complained that "members of neutral countries also had been 'vernebelt' who, according to the basic decree, should not have been 'vernebelt.'"

road building, and especially the draining of marshland. This was by far the hardest work, for all day long we had our feet in the water. In the snow and mud of Poland leather shoes were completely destroyed at the end of a week or two. Therefore our feet were frozen and covered with sores. We had to sleep with our muddy shoes on, lest they be stolen, and when the time came to get up for roll call [at 3:30 AM] cries of anguish could be heard: 'My shoes have been stolen.' Then one had to wait until the whole block had been emptied to look under the bunks for odd shoes. Sometimes one found two shoes for the same foot, or one shoe and one sabot. One could go to roll call like that, but it was an additional torture for work, because sores formed on our feet which quickly became infected for lack of care."

On February 5, 1943, when there were rumors of rebellion, the entire population of the camp had been lined up on the frozen fields from three thirty in the morning until five in the evening while the SS searched the barracks. "When all the internees were back in the camp," Marie Vaillant narrated, "a party to which I belonged was organized to go and pick up the bodies of the dead which were scattered over the plain as on a battlefield. We carried to the yard of Block 25 the dead and the dying without distinction, and they remained there stacked up in a pile. One saw stacks of corpses piled up in the courtyard, and from time to time a hand or a head would stir among the bodies, trying to free itself. There were rats as big as cats running about and gnawing the corpses and even attacking the dying who had not enough strength left to chase them away.

"Another cause of mortality and epidemic was the fact that we were given food in large red mess tins, which were merely rinsed in cold water after each meal. As all the women were ill and had not the strength during the night to go to the trench which was used as a lavatory, the access to which was beyond description, they used these containers for a purpose for which they were not meant. The next day the mess tins were collected and taken to a refuse heap. During the day another team would come and collect them, wash them in cold water, and put them in use again."

After a time, Marie Vaillant had obtained assignment to the *Revier* (infirmary) where people "lay in appalling conditions, four in a bed of less than one meter in width, each suffering from a different disease, so that anyone who came for leg sores would catch typhus or dysentery from neighbors. The straw mattresses were dirty and were changed only when absolutely rotten. The bedding was so full of lice that one could see them swarming like ants. One of my companions, Marguerite Corringer, told me that when she had typhus, she could not sleep all night because of the lice. She spent the night shaking the blanket over a piece of paper and emptying the lice into a receptacle by the bed, and this went on for hours."

Experiments were conducted on sterilizing Jewish women with injec-

tions, operations, and X-rays. "The Jewish women, when they arrived in
the first months of pregnancy, were subjected to abortions. When their
pregnancy was near the end, after confinement, the babies were drowned
in a bucket of water. After a while another doctor arrived, and for two
months they did not kill the Jewish babies. But one day an order came from
Berlin saying that again they had to be done away with. Then the mothers
and their babies were called to the infirmary. They were put in a lorry and
taken away for the gas chamber."

During the arrival of the Hungarian Jews in June of 1944, Marie
Vaillant recalled, "an orchestra composed of internees, all young and
pretty girls dressed in little white blouses and navy blue skirts, played
during the selection, at the arrival of the trains, gay tunes such as 'The
Merry Widow,' the 'Barcarolle' from *The Tales of Hoffman,* and so forth.
From our block we could see after about three-quarters of an hour or an
hour after the arrival of a convoy, large flames coming from the crematoria,
and the sky was lighted up by the burning pits." When the Soviet army
captured Auschwitz in January of 1945, only six of thirty-five warehouses
had not been put to the torch by the retreating SS. In these, however, were
348,820 sets of men's clothing and 836,255 sets of women's clothing
stripped from the victims of the gas chambers.

"One night we were awakened by terrifying cries," Madame Vaillant
went on. "And we discovered, on the following day, from the men working in the *Sonderkommando*—the 'Gas Kommando'—that on the preceding
day, the gas supply having run out, they had thrown the children into the
furnaces alive."

At the end of four months, only fifty-two of the 260 women who had
arrived at Auschwitz on Madame Vaillant's transport were still alive. The
French resistance, however, succeeded in transmitting the names of the
transportees to England. Because of their prominence, they became the
vehicle for an intensive propaganda campaign by the BBC. Since stealth
and deviousness were the hallmark of the Nazi system, and Himmler did
not want well-known persons dying on his hands, orders arrived from
Berlin to preserve the remainder of the women. Conditions for the surviving fifty-two improved so dramatically that only three more died during
their remaining two years of captivity.

"It is difficult to convey an exact idea of the concentration camps to
anybody," Madame Vaillant concluded, "unless one has been in the camp
oneself, since one can only quote examples of horror; but it is quite impossible to convey any impression of that deadly monotony. If asked what was
the worst of all, it is impossible to answer, since everything was atrocious.
It is atrocious to die of hunger, to die of thirst, to be ill, to see all one's
companions dying around one and be unable to help them. It is atrocious

to think of one's children, of one's country which one will never see again, and there were times when we asked whether our life was not a living nightmare, so unreal did this life appear in all its horror.

"For months, for years we had one wish only: the wish that some of us would escape alive, in order to tell the world what the Nazi convict prisons were like everywhere, at Auschwitz as at Ravensbrück. There was the systematic and implacable urge to use human beings as slaves and to kill them when they could work no more."

Marie Vaillant's eloquence created a poignant air in the room. This was now simultaneously shattered and underscored by Hans Marx, the attorney for Streicher, who proceeded to make an incredible fool of himself as he conducted a cross-examination on behalf of the SS, whose counsel, Ludwig Babel, was absent.

What had been Madame Vaillant's profession, he asked?

"I was a journalist," she responded in German.

"Yes." Marx nodded, as if he had just elicited a devastating statement, then continued in his mincing, oleaginous way: "The fact of the matter is that you, in your statement, showed great skill in style and expression; and I should like to know whether you held any position such, for example, as teacher or lecturer?"

"No. I was a newspaper photographer." She destroyed Marx's thrust.

"How do you explain that you yourself came through these experiences so well and are now in such a good state of health?"

"First of all, I was liberated a year ago; and in a year one has time to recover. Secondly, I was ten months in quarantine for typhus and I had the great luck not to die of exanthematic typhus, although I had it and was ill for three and one-half months. Also, in the last months at Ravensbrück, as I knew German, I worked on the Revier roll call, which explains why I did not have to work quite so hard."

"How can you explain your very precise statistical knowledge, for instance, that seven hundred thousand Jews arrived from Hungary?"

"I told you that I have worked in the offices; and where Auschwitz was concerned, I was a friend of the secretary."

"It has been said that only three hundred and fifty thousand Jews came from Hungary," Marx remarked, as if this figure somehow mitigated the horror, "according to the testimony of the chief of the Gestapo, Eichmann." Marx thus managed to make three erroneous statements in one sentence, since Eichmann, of course, had never been chief of the Gestapo nor provided any figures, and Wisliceny had given 458,000 as the number.

"I am not going to argue with the Gestapo." Madame Vaillant was the essence of disdain. "I have good reasons to know that what the Gestapo states is not always true."

"How were you treated personally? Were you treated well?" Marx inquired, as if Marie Vaillant might have been the housekeeper of some noble family and he had never heard of the conditions in concentration camps.

"Like the others," Madame Vaillant replied curtly.

"Like the others? You said before that the German people must have known of the happenings in Auschwitz. What are your grounds for this statement?"

"I have already told you: To begin with there was the fact that, when we left, the Lorraine soldiers of the Wehrmacht who were taking us to Auschwitz said to us, 'If you knew where you were going, you would not be in such a hurry to get there.' Then there was the fact that the German women who came out of quarantine to go to work in German factories knew of these events, and they all said that they would speak about them outside.

"Further, the fact that in all the factories where the *Häftlinge* [the internees] worked they were in contact with the German civilians, as also were the *Aufseherinnen* [women supervisors], who were in touch with their friends and families and often told them of what they had seen."

"One more question." Marx could not seem to help ending with a final fatuity. "Up to 1942 you were able to observe the behavior of the German soldiers in Paris. Did not these German soldiers behave well throughout, and did they not pay for what they took?"

"I have not the least idea whether they paid or not for what they requisitioned. As for their good behavior, too many of my friends were shot or massacred for me not to differ with you."

"I have no further questions to put to this witness." Marx started to leave the lectern, took a few steps, then hesitated and turned back as if something else had occurred to him.

"If you have no further questions, there is nothing more to be said." Lawrence peered at him coldly, precipitating an outburst of derisive laughter that previously had been barely held in abeyance. "There is too much laughter in the court," Lawrence, who had firm conceptions of dignity, declared, though Biddle had difficulty keeping a straight face. "I have already spoken about that."

Four weeks later, a Russian witness, Severina Shmaglevskaya, duplicated Marie Vaillant's description of Auschwitz. Dwelling, once more, on sanitary conditions in the camp, she said: "In some cases the kitchen utensils and pots contained remains of food, and in others there was human excrement. Each of the workers received a pail of water, and had to wash a great number of these kitchen utensils during one half of the day. These kitchen utensils, which were sometimes very badly washed, were given to people who had just arrived at the concentration camp. From these pots and pans they had to eat, but often they caught dysentery and other diseases from the first day."

Since this account came a few minutes before the midday adjournment, and Lawrence always anticipated lunch with relish, he turned green. "Colonel Smirnov," the president of the court addressed the Russian assistant prosecutor, "I don't think the tribunal wants quite so much of the details with reference to these domestic matters."

In Denmark, where it was politically inexpedient to execute or *vernebel* thousands of people, Hitler had reverted to the gangsterism of the Röhm purge.

Denmark, because of its prudent submission to Nazi occupation in the spring of 1940, had been left nominally independent: its government, police, and minuscule armed forces had remained intact. Only a watchdog plenipotentiary, Werner Best, operating out of the Foreign Ministry, was installed to advise the government of Nazi wishes.

In the spring of 1943, however, Hitler received a slap in the face when the Danish Nazi Party garnered only 2.5 percent of the vote in the national elections; and in the following months the Führer imposed his authority on Denmark more and more. At the time of the Allied landing in Italy, Hitler demanded that the Danish government declare martial law. When it refused, he ordered the disarming and internment of the Danish armed forces, and introduced the SS and the Gestapo to the country. A few months later he was incensed when he learned that acts of sabotage and resistance continued to be dealt with according to Danish law.

Introduced at the trial were the minutes of a meeting on December 30, 1943, attended by Himmler, Kaltenbrunner, Keitel, Jodl, Best, and *Obergruppenführer* Gunther Pancke, who had taken over supervision of the Danish police. Hitler declared "there was only one way of dealing with saboteurs, namely to kill them, preferably at the moment when the crime was committed; otherwise, on arrest. Pancke replied that it was very difficult and dangerous to shoot people on arrest as they could not be sure when the arrest was made if the person arrested was really a saboteur. [But] Hitler demanded compensatory murders in a proportion of at least five to one."

To conduct this program of "counterterror," Kaltenbrunner summoned Alfred Helmut Naujocks, a thirty-year-old German-Lithuanian of such deviousness and double-dealing that Peter Lorre at his sleaziest would have had difficulty doing him justice. After joining the SS at the age of eighteen, he had been drafted into the SD by Heydrich in 1934, and a few months later had become the Nazi hit man and specialist in dirty tricks.*

In 1943 he was, in another of the Third Reich's Alice-in-Wonderland scenarios, chief of black market investigations in Belgium and northern France; his task, however, was not to stamp out the black market, but to conduct it himself for the benefit of Germany.

Naujocks went into action in Denmark enthusiastically. His first victim was Kaj Munk, a well-known pastor and poet, and hundreds of other Danes, picked for their prominence, followed. Whenever an installation or factory useful to the Germans was sabotaged by the resistance, Naujocks "countersabotaged" a nonmilitary target. Among the places his squad blew up were a glass factory, a movie company, a restaurant, and the famous Tivoli Amusement Park in Copenhagen.

Edgar Faure, a deputy French prosecutor who was subsequently to become prime minister of France, read a Danish police report to the Tribunal:

"A large number of persons, most of them well known, were murdered at intervals which grew steadily shorter. The doorbell would ring, for instance, and one or two men would ask to speak to them. The moment they appeared at the door they were shot by these unknown persons. Or, someone would pretend to be ill and go to a doctor. When the doctor entered the room, the unknown shot him."

Best had thought the operation madness, and tried to tone it down. In July of 1944, when the Danes staged a general strike, Ribbentrop had demanded to know from Best why, "contrary to the Führer's instructions you have continued to deal with sabotage activity by legal proceedings instead of simply by counterterror." When Best responded that the only effect of counterterror was to make the Danes lose respect for the Germans, Ribbentrop had no answer. "Do what you think is right and sensible. But the Führer's orders must be carried out," the foreign minister had declared contradictorily and incongruously.

---

*It would take a separate book to narrate Naujocks's story. Among his exploits were the simulated "Polish" attack on the small German radio station at Gleiwitz on August 31, 1939, and the kidnapping, in the "Venlo Incident" of November 12, 1939, of two British and a Dutch intelligence officer for the purpose of "proving" that the British and Dutch were conspiring together, so providing a pretext for the German attack on the Low Countries. By the fall of 1944 Naujocks had made so many and diverse enemies that he considered it expedient to defect to the Allies. To the British, he offered "to undertake the personal liquidation of Himmler." At the London Interrogation Center and at Nuremberg he helped put together the case against Kaltenbrunner, and his affidavit on the Gleiwitz raid was introduced at the trial. Shortly after the conclusion of the trial he escaped from custody and has not been heard from since.

Similar to "counterterror" in its underhanded barbarity was the Commando Order, issued by Hitler in the fall of 1942 as the Stalingrad disaster was unfolding.

In order to relieve pressure on the Soviets and placate Stalin, Prime Minister Churchill in mid-August ordered a sortie in force across the channel at Dieppe.

On August 19, five thousand Canadians, supported by tanks and artillery on the one hand and commando troops on the other, landed on one of the most heavily fortified areas of the coast. Even though given powerful air support, they suffered nearly 3,400 casualties.

Some of the German prisoners taken were handcuffed; and a few, who fell into the hands of the special forces, were trussed up in "death slings." "They were attached in such a way that they had a noose around their neck," Jodl explained to Colonel Hinkel. "They were lying on their bellies, and their legs were doubled up, and the other noose was around their legs. So that when the legs stretched out, the man would be strangled. In that way, three or four soldiers or members of the [construction] organization Todt choked. The Führer was furious."

To add fuel to Hitler's fury, the Germans discovered on one of the men a copy of the British *Handbook of Irregular Warfare*. This instructed the commandos "never to give the enemy a chance; the days when we could practice the rules of sportsmanship are over. For the time being every soldier must be a potential gangster.... The vulnerable parts of the enemy are the heart, spine, and privates. Kick him or knee him as hard as you can in the fork.... Remember you are out to kill."

In retaliation, Hitler ordered one thousand Canadian prisoners placed in chains. (The British thereupon shackled a comparable number of Germans, and it was a year before both sides retreated from the retrogression to medieval times.) The Führer was still fuming a month later when twelve commandos landed in Norway, killed a German sentry, threatened to chloroform a number of Norwegians, and blew up a power station vital to aluminum production.

Hitler told Jodl that, as a deterrent, all commandos would have to be shot. On October 7, the Führer had the Wehrmacht radio broadcast: "In the future all terrorist and sabotage units of the British and their associates who do not act like soldiers but like bandits will be mercilessly exterminated in battle." He directed Jodl to draw up the appropriate order that commandos "regardless whether as soldiers and irrespective of the kind of uniform are to be annihilated to the last man without mercy," since their actions "differ from the basic rules of warfare and [they] thus place themselves outside the rules of warfare." If they gave up, they were to be shot on the spot. "Whoever performs acts of sabotage as a soldier with the idea of surrendering without a fight after the act is successfully completed does not conduct himself as an honorable warrior." Hitler, as he had done in the Commissar Order and similar instances, made himself the unilateral arbiter of the Geneva Convention, and declared null and void whatever section was not convenient to him. When the Abwehr protested: "Sabotage is an essential part of conducting war at a time of total warfare; we ourselves have strongly developed this method of fighting," Jodl remarked cynically. "But the English are in much more need of it."

The first Allied soldiers to fall to the Commando Order were victimized ex post facto. The seven members of the team taken prisoner after the raid on the Norwegian power station were shot on October 30. A few days later, fourteen men who landed in Norway by glider were executed, though dressed in British uniforms. In the spring of 1943 ten fully uniformed Norwegian sailors from one of the torpedo boats using the fjords to conduct a kind of naval guerrilla warfare against German shipping were executed, and their bodies dumped at sea. A year later, fifteen members of the uniformed American "Ginny Mission," assigned to blow up a railroad tunnel in Italy, were shot after they surrendered. In the summer of 1944, the order was extended to members of Allied military missions operating with partisans in southeastern Europe, even though by then the worker shortage was so severe that the partisans themselves were shipped to German forced labor camps when captured.

When the Normandy invasion commenced, the question arose as to whether paratroopers were "commandos" who should be shot. Jodl, after checking with Hitler, ruled that those paratroopers who were regular members of combat units were not to be shot, but those landing in small units for sabotage and interdiction purposes behind the lines were. Thus, any paratrooper blown off course a few miles and unlucky enough to land outside of the immediate combat area was likely to be shot.

Since the Commando Order was unquestionably a violation of the Geneva Convention, Hitler decreed that it could be passed on only orally to units in the field. There was, consequently, wild confusion among the German troops about its application; and more often than not its implementation depended on caprice. During June of 1944 one SS panzer division executed no fewer than 107 Allied soldiers in thirty-one separate, documented incidents; and undoubtedly the actual number was greater.

Jodl claimed that the Commando Order was the only one of Hitler's directives to which he had had difficulty reconciling himself. This was curious because, ever since the start of Barbarossa, the Germans had been shooting prisoners of war almost routinely. When Hitler learned that "numerous German political refugees are supposed to be among the Free French units in Africa," he ordered that they were "to be disposed of without mercy in battle. Where this has not happened, they are to be shot retroactively on the command of the nearest German officer immediately and without further ado." During the summer of 1942, when Soviet prisoners of war, now being kept alive for use as laborers, staged frequent escapes, Keitel investigated the possibility of tattooing them on their buttocks so that, like stray cattle, they might more easily be identified and brought back. (This plan, because of its infeasibility, was never implemented.)

Early in 1944, when the German army was suffering a defeat along the Dnieper comparable to the disaster on the Volga the year before and the Soviets crossed the old Polish frontier, two-thirds of the distance from Stalingrad to Berlin, Hitler authored the *Kugel Erlass* (Bullet Decree). The *Kugel Erlass* stipulated that any officer or non-commissioned officer—except British or American—who escaped from a POW camp was to be shipped to Mauthausen concentration camp with the designation "*Stufe* III" (Third Degree). There they were either to be shot, or speedily starved and worked to death. To questions by the Red Cross or neutral powers, the Wehrmacht was directed to reply that the prisoners had "escaped and not been recaptured."

The immunity of the British and Americans, however, was temporary. On March 25, when the Russians were approaching the Romanian frontier and threatening Germany's oil supply, Hitler was in one of his most dyspeptic moods. The previous night, eighty Britons, Frenchmen, Greeks, Norwegians, Poles, Belgians, and Czechs—all officers of the Royal Air Force—had tunneled out of the Luftwaffe prison camp at Sagan in Silesia. The tunnel was discovered while the last four men were still in it. Fifteen other escapees were rounded up in the vicinity and returned to the camp. The remaining sixty-one scattered over Germany.

It was the hundredth tunnel dug at Sagan, and the first to be successfully completed. Since, however, there was a great shortage of barbed wire and the guards were largely overaged and undertrained, it was the third mass escape in Germany within a two-week period. Even though camp commanders were court-martialed when seven or more prisoners escaped at one time, this was another of those Hitlerian absurdities, for breakouts were so numerous that some officers had three or four actions pending against them simultaneously. Keitel, informed of the escape by Goering early on the morning of the twenty-fifth, was highly agitated. On the way up to the Obersalzberg for the day's conference with Hitler, Keitel told Jodl he did not intend to mention the escape to Hitler, for such occurrences always sent the Führer into a fury. In a day or two, perhaps, all of the escapees would have been recaptured, and the matter could be presented in a more favorable light.

Keitel was deluding himself. Since the SS and police were responsible for tracking down the prisoners, they had been notified immediately. A *Grossfahndung* (general hue and cry) had already been issued; and of course Himmler knew of it. Himmler had for a long time been lobbying to obtain control of the POW camps. Supported by Martin Bormann, he never missed an opportunity to needle the Wehrmacht about "coddling" the POWs. Every escape offered Himmler the opportunity to emphasize the incompetency of the Wehrmacht. Thus, while Keitel was in the midst of the situation conference with the Führer, Himmler appeared and sprang the news.

"This is unheard of!" Hitler exploded. "This is the tenth time that dozens of officers have escaped. These officers are an enormous danger! You don't realize," he told Keitel, "that in view of the six million foreigners who are prisoners and working in Germany, they are leaders who could organize an uprising. That is the result of this careless attitude of these commandants. These escaped air force officers are to be turned over to Himmler immediately."

Although Hitler's vision of a Spartacus-type rebellion led by escaped officers was another of his flights of imagination, each *Grossfahndung* did result in the mobilization of 40,000 to 100,000 men of the *Landeswacht* (home guard). Hundreds of thousands of man-hours in factories were consequently lost. Only three weeks before, Goering had come over to Himmler's side and supported the SS Reichsführer's desire to take over control of all stalags—except those holding British and American prisoners—so that the work output of the prisoners might be increased and man-hours lost through their escapes diminished.

Keitel protested that some of the flyers were already back in camp, and to remove them would cause enormous unrest among the POWs. Hitler grudgingly assented that the nineteen already recaptured might be left alone. The remainder, however, were a different matter. "Himmler," Hitler blazed, "they are to stay in your charge and you will never surrender them again!"

Keitel knew that any argument would merely harden the Führer's resolve. On the drive back down the mountain, the field marshal was in a state of hand-wringing despair. Once again Hitler was flouting the Geneva Convention. On previous occasions, it had always been Russians or citizens of occupied countries who had been affected, or there had at least been a rationalization that Hitler was engaging in a "reprisal." But there could be no such explanation for the placing of prisoners of war in concentration camps. The attempt of the POWs to escape was perfectly legal under international law. The British regarded it as a kind of sporting event, and had organized "escape committees" in every stalag. To Keitel it seemed impossible that the British government would not learn of the escape and wonder what had happened to the officers; and Jodl thought Hitler had abandoned every conception of human rights.

In actuality, as the two Wehrmacht commanders learned a day or two later, the Führer gave Himmler further instructions as soon as they left. In order to discourage future escapes, all the officers were to be shot upon recapture.

The executions commenced the next day, and were all carried out in the same way. As the men were purportedly being returned to camp, the vehicle carrying them stopped at an isolated spot, and they were let out to urinate. While they were relieving themselves, Gestapo agents shot them in the backs of their heads.

On Monday and Tuesday, a pair of tense conferences took place. One involved Keitel and General Westhoff, the acting commander of POW affairs. The second was between *Gruppenführers* Müller and Nebe, the heads of the Gestapo and Kripo (criminal police) on the one hand, and representatives of the Wehrmacht's Prisoner of War Department on the other. Müller announced that none of the prisoners would be returned to Sagan. Ten or fifteen, he reported, had already been killed while resisting or attempting to escape—a statement that fooled no one, and, according to the colonel representing the Luftwaffe, had a "shattering effect."

At the conference with Westhoff, Keitel declared that in the future all escaping officers—including British and American—would be taken over by the Gestapo, who would then determine whether they would remain in secret police custody or be returned to camp. "Gentlemen," he stated emphatically, "these escapes must stop. We must set an example." No written orders of any kind would be issued.

In response to the agitated Westhoff, who protested that he could not assume responsibility for such a course of affairs, Keitel snapped: "I don't give a damn! We discussed it in the Führer's presence and it cannot be altered." Finally, after a further series of questions, he admitted: "I can only tell you that the men who have escaped will be shot. Probably the majority of them are dead already."

Westhoff decided to demand, so as to protect himself, an order in writing. He himself prepared a draft, which he forwarded to Keitel. Where Westhoff noted that Keitel had said the escapees would be shot by the

Gestapo, Keitel corrected the sentence with his customary purple pencil: "I did not say shoot. I said turn over to the secret police."

On March 28, the order was issued as an adjunct to the *Kugel Erlass*. Those officers retained by the Gestapo—in principle, though not necessarily in practice, "plotters and escape leaders"—were to be transported to Mauthausen concentration camp. "The camp commandant of Mauthausen is to be informed that the prisoners are being handed over under Operation *Kugel.*" Status reports were to be made semiannually by the Gestapo.

By April 13, fifty of the escapees had been executed. Their names were posted at Sagan as a warning to the prisoners. Eight were never turned over to the Gestapo after being apprehended, and so survived. Only three made it out of Germany. A neutral Swiss representative responsible for checking on the welfare of Allied prisoners of war was told that the men had all been killed while trying to escape. The diplomat, however, had meantime learned that most of them had been gathered at one location, had been taken off under heavy guard, and killed shortly thereafter. He informed the British government. A great outcry was raised in the House of Commons. British Foreign Secretary Anthony Eden protested, via Switzerland, to Ribbentrop, who became very excited and demanded a detailed report from Keitel. Hitler ordered the drafting of a reply that was published in the newspapers but was such a transparent falsity that Westhoff and the other officers involved in POW affairs were thunderstruck. "We all clutched our heads—mad!" Westhoff recounted to Colonel Horace Williams, his interrogator at Nuremberg.

The Luftwaffe high command was up in arms over the order since it would be impossible to protect German airmen against retaliation by the Allies. Several generals appealed to Field Marshal Milch, who passed the request on to Goering. But Goering, in the face of British and American obliteration of German industry and cities, did not dare to risk the Führer's wrath.

Maurice Lampe, a French inmate at Mauthausen, told the tribunal what had happened to one group of forty-seven British, American, and Dutch officers who had been brought to the camp under the *Kugel Erlass* on September 6, 1944. Barefoot, they had been led the 186 steps down to the quarry, where stones weighing twenty-five kilograms (fifty-five pounds) were loaded onto slings on their backs. They were made to carry these at a trot up to the top, then forced to run back down. With every trip the load was increased. If they faltered, they were kicked and hit with a bludgeon:

"In the evening when I returned from the gang with which I was then working, the road which led to the camp was a bath of blood. I almost stepped on the lower jaw of a man. Twenty-one bodies were strewn along the road. Twenty-one had died on the first day. The twenty-six others died the following morning."

The murder of the Sagan airmen had given Hitler an opportunity to vent his spleen against the aspect of Allied warfare—the American and British strategic bombing—that had become the most sensitive issue with the Nazi hierarchy. Six months before, Jodl had, in effect, stated Hitler's opinion when he declared: "What weighs most heavily today are the enemy terror raids from the air on our homes, and so on our wives and children. In this respect the war—and this cannot be repeated often enough—has assumed, solely through the fault of England, forms such as are believed to be no longer possible since the days of racial and religious wars. The psychological, morale, and material effect of these terror raids is such that they must be relieved if they cannot be made to cease completely."

Jodl had prophesied that improvements in German air defenses would lead to an attrition rate of ten percent per raid on the bombing force, and that the Allies "might perhaps replace this loss in equipment but not in personnel"—a favorite topic among Hitler and the military, who were never able to train pilots and other specialists as fast as they were lost. Jodl's prediction, however, did not materialize. Now Hitler fumed: "Matters cannot go along like this any longer. The Luftwaffe has failed. What am I to do against the frightful bombing terror which is murdering German women and children? If those flyers realize that they will be liquidated as terrorists, they will think twice about flying here!"

At about the same time that the escape from Sagan took place, the United States daylight raids on the Continent had intensified. There was a notable increase in the use of long-range attack bombers, which engaged in low-level missions directed especially at railroads, trucks, and military vehicles. The consequence, as the Germans responded with light antiaircraft and machinegun fire, was that bullets and shrapnel, originating both from the planes and from the ground, made the vicinity of an attack hazardous for everyone. Civilians were being killed in France, Belgium, and other occupied countries as well as in Germany—as indeed they had been killed indirectly by Luftwaffe planes on strafing missions a few years earlier.

Western propaganda had in 1939 and 1940 depicted these incidents as deliberate massacres by the Nazis; and Goebbels naturally now engaged in like tactics. Thus Hitler, goaded by Goebbels and Martin Bormann, and furious that Wehrmacht officers were in whispered agreement with the British that the execution of the RAF POWs had been out-and-out murder, decreed a general campaign of killing downed airmen. He rationalized this order as a reprisal against "terror attacks." On May 21, Keitel directed a memorandum to the Wehrmacht Leadership Staff:

"The Führer has rendered the following decision with regard to measures to be taken against Anglo-American air crews. *In special instances* downed enemy airmen are to be shot without court-martial: (1) in the event of the shooting of our *own* downed air crews while parachuting to earth; (2) in the event of aerial attacks upon German planes which have made emergency landings; (3) in the event of attacks upon railway trains engaged in public transportation; (4) in the event of low-level aerial attacks upon individual civilians (farmers, workers, single vehicles, etc.)."

Jodl, who, like Keitel, was to a large degree demoralized, objected only halfheartedly that "to attack an airplane which has made an emergency landing cannot be classified as gangster methods, but is in complete agreement with the strictest standards of civilized warfare." He suggested that the order be preceded by a preamble justifying it on the basis the Allies were disregarding "the most primitive laws of civilization."

A few days later Goebbels initiated a propaganda campaign along the lines indicated by Jodl: "The enemy air terror pursues almost exclusively the aim of breaking the morale of the German civilian population. The enemy wages war against the defenseless, against women and children in particular, in order to compel the men of our country to yield. The Anglo-American terror fliers in the last few weeks, besides indiscriminately bombing the residential quarters of our cities, have taken to attacking the German civilian population openly, directly and without even any superficial respect for the international rules of warfare by strafing them and slaughtering them in cold blood. Enemy planes sweep low over villages, fields, and highways, and direct their machineguns upon harmless groups of people. This is naked murder. The Anglo-American pilots place themselves through such criminal modes of warfare outside of the pale of every internationally recognized rule of warfare. Last Sunday, for example, groups of playing children were attacked by strafing and suffered considerable casualties.

"No one will be astonished by the fact that the population has been seized with a terrible rage on account of these cynical crimes. It is only possible with the aid of arms to secure the lives of enemy pilots shot down during such attacks, for they would otherwise be killed by the sorely tried population. Who is right here? The murderers, or the victims who wish to defend themselves according to the principle: 'An eye for an eye, a tooth for a tooth'? It would be demanding too much of us if it were asked of us that we use German soldiers for the defense of murderers of children against parents seized with blind rage. It would be demanding too much of us to expect that we should silently accommodate ourselves as victims to this unlimited barbarity.

"We reach these conclusions in a completely objective manner. In these questions our people think much more radically than their government. It has always been our wish that the war should be conducted in a chivalrous manner. The enemy apparently does not want this. We can find means and ways to defend ourselves against these criminals. We owe this to our people which has in no way deserved to be declared fair game for the enemy killers."

If the piece was not shocking for its naked hypocrisy, it was only because its inverted logic had become standard in the Nazi regime. Instances of attempted lynchings had, in reality, rarely if ever occurred. Now, however, word was passed through the party apparatus that the damage resulting from bombing was so severe that an atmosphere had to be created in which civilians would lynch fliers before they were turned over to the Wehrmacht.

On May 30, Bormann notified party posts throughout the Reich that a number of Allied fliers had been lynched, and that "no police measures or criminal proceedings were involved"—it was the Nazi way of declaring open season on airmen, just as the prescient announcement of "spontaneous uprisings" had precipitated the *Kristallnacht* against the Jews. On June 3, a top secret order was issued to company commanders in the SS and the army that "value is no longer placed on imprisoned enemy aviators."

Keitel and Jodl both knew that the order made no sense, for if a plane engaged in a low-level attack were shot down, none of the crew would survive. In Jodl's opinion, the order "would only lead to a general murder of airmen." Since, however, it was impossible to argue with Hitler about the decree, per se, his acolytes scurried about trying to inject some order into the mayhem. It was perhaps symbolic of the lunacy of the Nazi era that on June 6, while the Allies were storming ashore in Normandy, Goering, Ribbentrop, Himmler, Kaltenbrunner, and Warlimont spent a good part of the day codifying the lynching of fliers. Ribbentrop, indeed, wished to make the order all-embracing, and urged that the crews of *all* planes shot down be executed. Goering, on the other hand, wanted nothing to do with the directive, and demonstrated his opposition by squelching Ribbentrop and limiting the order to the "terror fliers." The consensus, from which Goering passively though not actively dissented, was that "lynch law would have to be the rule."

Amid this Mad Hatter scheme of things, Keitel commented: "If you allow lynching at all, then you could hardly lay down rules for it." He was, nevertheless, concerned with what "rules" were to be followed in "the announcement of such cases as have led to lynch justice or to special treatment by the SD [so that] the intended deterrent effect to further acts of murder might be achieved." He noted, with considerable understatement, "It will have to be borne in mind that protests on the part of the enemy are to be expected from all quarters."

Since the mobs of enraged citizens visualized by Hitler and Goebbels failed to materialize, the sporadic lynchings that occurred were carried out by Nazi Party fanatics, local police, and even one of Goebbels's high-ranking SS aides, who forcibly removed a British flier from his guards, then shot him along the road.

Since there was no possibility of overtly opposing Hitler, the Luftwaffe commanders—like their army counterparts caught in similar dilemmas—simply failed to pass the order on through the chain of command. Eventually, in August, when Luftwaffe guards protected a captured flier against attack, Hitler learned the truth. Enraged, he expostulated that airmen in action against Russia had to reckon with the possibility of being beaten to death in case of an emergency landing, and airmen flying in the West should not claim special privileges. "The Luftwaffe are cowards, and afraid something might happen to them too," he shouted. "The whole thing is nothing more than a cowardly pact between the Luftwaffe and the British and American airmen!" Turning to Kaltenbrunner and a high-ranking air force general with him, he screamed: "I hereby order that all bomber crews who bailed out in the last few months, and those bailing out in the future, are to be turned over immediately by the Luftwaffe to the SD, and are to be liquidated by the SD. Anyone failing to carry out my orders or taking action against the population is liable to the death penalty and is to be shot!"

An hour or two later, Goering, who had not been present, called up one of his liaison officers with Hitler, and asked: "Tell me, has he gone quite mad now?"

Hitler's latest instructions—as happened occasionally when his orders passed beyond all bounds of reason—were never followed, and he did not press their implementation. Nevertheless, when Dresden was fire-bombed on February 9, 1945, in probably the most senseless raid of the war, his thoughts turned back once more to the handicaps of operating within the Geneva Convention. Some 25,000 civilians were killed in the bombing, and another 35,000 were missing. Goebbels, castigating Goering as a "parasite" bearing "the burden of guilt," suggested that several thousand Allied airmen be shot in retaliation. Since such a step would be a de facto renunciation of the Geneva Convention, Hitler directed Jodl to poll the heads of the army, navy, and air force. He himself was all in favor of the executions, not only as a measure of revenge, but because he expected the British and

Americans to shoot German prisoners in retaliation. The Allied action, Hitler thought, would have a stiffening effect on German troops, who currently were surrendering in droves in the West.

On February 20, Jodl gave Hitler the Wehrmacht operations staff report. The first question considered was resort to gas and bacteriological warfare, tests having been performed on concentration camp prisoners. *"The surprise introduction of gas and bacilli* for fighting the enemy can, in the present emergency, lead, owing to the surprise and shock effect, *to considerable initial successes,"* Jodl reported.

There were, however, *disadvantages:* "The enemy has air superiority. The German population which is at present crowded into a narrow area would, in a very short time, be subjected to counterblows. The German population in the enemy-occupied territory would also be affected by our own gas warfare. Finally, German gas warfare could not reach either Russia's wide spaces or, above all, the United States of America. The unrestricted use of all means of warfare has—according to experience—a much greater effect in a limited space than on an attacker, who can more easily escape the effects. *Conclusion:* the introduction of gas and bacilli as a war measure must work out to our disadvantage."

With regard to the effect on the soldiers, the experience of the war showed that the men in Italy and France often fought more stubbornly than those in Russia; for in the East the men were so fearful of being surrounded and captured that they fled at first indication of an enemy breakthrough. Hence, inducing apprehension about capture in the soldiers in the West would have a negative, not positive effect.

Although the Allies occasionally attacked ships, trains, and hospitals marked by a red cross, the report noted that the Germans had done the same, and had often misused the symbol as camouflage for their munitions, fuel, and military transports. (The "terror flier" decree nevertheless included airmen who attacked such transports.) In any case, the report ran cynically on, "The adherence to the obligations entered into in no way involves our having to enforce on ourselves any limitations prejudicial to the conduct of the war. Should the British, for instance, sink a hospital ship, this must be used as before for propaganda purposes but does not prevent us in any way from sinking a British hospital ship at once as a reprisal and then expressing our regret."

To sum up, there was no way Germany, which was already violating international law, could gain by formal renunciation of the convention. In fact, one of the studies by Jodl suggested "Germany will by no means free herself from the essential obligations of the laws of war by a denunciation of the convention."

In this fashion Hitler's threat to finally renounce all civilizing influences had been turned aside. Hitler's myrmidons always had a healthy respect when it came to taking actions against subjects of nations capable of retaliation. But only lonely German voices had protested the atrocities committed against minorities and the citizens of small countries trodden beneath the Nazi heel—the hapless people for whom neither humanity nor justice had existed in Hitler's *Weltanschauung.*

In his summation of the French case on War Crimes and Crimes Against Humanity, Dubost said: "The German people, whose military virtue we recognize, whose poets and musicians we love, whose application to work we admire, and who did not fail to give examples of probity in the most noble works of the spirit, this German people which came rather late to civilization, beginning only with the eighth century, had slowly raised itself to the ranks of nations possessing the oldest culture. Nevertheless, we behold the fact that millions of innocent men have been exterminated on the very soil of this people, by men of this people, in execution of a common plan conceived by their leaders, and this people made not a single effort to revolt.

"This is what has become of it because it has scorned the virtues of political freedom, of civil equality, of human fraternity. This is what has become of it, because it forgot that all men are born free and equal before the law.

"It allowed itself to be robbed of its conscience and its very soul. Evil masters came who awakened its primitive passions and made possible the atrocities which I have described to you. In truth, the crime of these men is that they caused the German people to retrogress more than twelve centuries.

"Their crime is that they conceived and achieved, as an instrument of government, a policy of terrorism toward the whole of the subjugated nations and toward their own people; their crime is that they pursued, as an end in itself, a policy of extermination of entire categories of innocent citizens. That alone would suffice to determine capital punishment."

37   *"A Most Terrible and Convincing Case"*

Goering, in response to Dubost, struck a heroic pose: "Everybody has to die sooner or later. And if I could have a chance to die as a martyr—why, so much the better. Do you think everybody has that chance? If I can have my bones put in a marble casket, that is, after all, a lot more than most people achieve. Of course, it may not even be my own bones. It is the same as Napoleon and Frederick the Great—the French have robbed their graves a dozen times—or like the pieces of wood from the True Cross. I've always said that if you put all the pieces of wood from the True Cross together you could build a forest!" He laughed. "No, it may not even be my own bones—but it is the idea behind it."

Ribbentrop thought that German actions had not been all that different from American and British: "Haven't you heard about how the Americans slaughtered the Indians? Were they an inferior race too? Do you know who started the concentration camps in the first place? The British. And do you know why? To force the Boers to give up their arms."*

Doenitz, who had initially characterized the indictment as "typical American humor," sadly shook his head. "I must say," he commented, "I was furious over the idea of being dragged to trial in the beginning because I did not know anything about these atrocities. But now, after hearing all this evidence—the double dealing, the dirty business in the East—I am satisfied that there was good reason to try to get to the bottom of the thing."

The profusion of evidence instilled in nearly everyone, including at least some of the defendants, an overwhelming feeling of abhorrence at the deviousness, mendacity, and inhumanity of the Nazi regime. Birkett called it "a most terrible and convincing case of complete horror and inhumanity in the concentration camps."

The reporters delighted in tearing apart the amateurish, fumbling efforts of the German counsel at cross-examination, over which Biddle kept shaking his head. "As usual the cross emphasizes prosecution's case," he wrote in his notes. "Counsel for SS asks stupid questions. . . . Counsel for Gestapo—cross-examination only underscores evidence. . . . Babel for the SS—as usual makes a fool of himself."

The most savage caricaturist would, indeed, have had difficulty drawing a portrait of greater imbecility, puerility, hypersensitivity, and irrelevant pendantry than that presented by Babel. Jacobus Vorrink, the president of the Dutch Socialist Party, describing the conditions of the German occupation, mentioned that "an author could not even publish a book without submitting it to some Nazi illiterate." Babel thereupon felt dutybound to defend the honor of German education and intelligence.

"Now, you used the word 'Nazi illiterate,'" he challenged. "Quite apart from, I would say, your not very friendly attitude towards us Germans, have you any justification for saying this? Have you met a single German who was illiterate?"

---

*The Boer War between Dutch settlers and British colonists in South Africa had evolved into guerrilla warfare between 1899 and 1902. The British had cleared the countryside and herded 120,000 women and children into concentration camps. Of these, approximately 20,000 died from disease and neglect.

Vorrink, given the opportunity, was pleased to define Nazi illiteracy for Babel: "By an 'illiterate Nazi' I meant a man who talks about things about which he has no knowledge, and the people who judge an author's work were people who had been set to read through the book to find out whether a Jew appeared in it and was presented as a good and humane character. According to the Nazi concept, such a book could not be published. I would add that I have used the word 'Nazi illiterate' from the days when there were found in the German cities, in the country of Goethe and Schiller, great piles of burned books, books that we had read and admired in Holland."

"I understand you to mean that you can bring no positive facts which might justify this derogatory word 'Nazi illiterate,'" Babel interpreted.

This kind of performance caused the Allied attorneys to roll their eyes; and Goering made no attempt to stifle his laughter at Babel.

When Marx was taken to task and threatened with ostracism by the *Berliner Zeitung* for his questioning of Marie Vaillant, Lawrence let it be known that the court would not permit the attorneys to be intimidated: "The tribunal desires to say in the plainest language that such conduct cannot be tolerated. The right of any accused person to be represented by counsel is one of the most important elements in the administration of justice. Counsel is an officer of the court, and he must be permitted freely to make his defense without fear from threats or intimidation. Counsel, in discharge of their duties under the charter, may count upon the fullest protection which is in the power of the tribunal to afford."

Such declarations, and Lawrence's repeated calling to account of the prosecution for attempted editorializing or introduction of one-sided or slanted evidence, greatly improved the morale of the defense attorneys and the accused, and bolstered their confidence in the fairness of the proceedings. A typical exchange occurred when Lieutenant Colonel William H. Baldwin, presenting the case against Frank, read portions of a forty-page report from Frank to Hitler, but did not mention that Frank was criticizing the atrocious conditions being described.

"Now, Lieutenant Colonel Baldwin," Lawrence intervened, "I asked you what was the whole content of the document from which you were reading this paragraph. According to counsel for Frank, the document, which is a very long document, shows that Frank was suggesting remedies for the difficulties which he here sets out. Is that so?"

"That is so, your honor," Baldwin agreed.

"Well, when you cite a small part of the document, you should make sure that what you cite is not misleading as compared to the rest of the document."

"I see, your honor. The purpose for which I introduced it was only to indicate a set of conditions which existed at a certain time. I naturally assumed that the defense, as Dr. Seidl has indicated, will carry on with the rest of the document as a matter of defense."

"Yes, of course, that is all very well, but the Defendant Frank's counsel will speak at some remote date; and it is not a complete answer to say that he will have an opportunity of explaining the document at some future date. It is for counsel for the prosecution to make sure that no extracts which they read can reasonably make a misleading impression on the mind of the tribunal."

"What is not satisfactory to the tribunal," Biddle chipped in, "is that you did not give us the real purport of the document."

When Commander Albrecht concluded his presentation of the case against Goering with a line from Byron, "He was the mildest mannered man who ever slit a throat or scuttled a boat," Lawrence ruled him out of order and directed the comment stricken from the record.

Though for an observer accustomed to courtroom procedure in democratic nations such actions by Lawrence were no more than what might be expected of any judge, for the Germans, having experienced twelve years of Hitler's Reich, they seemed like a revelation. Frank gushed: "It was wonderful how the judge pointed out that one quotation was taken out of context—just marvelous! So fair! So upright! It restores my faith in human nature."

Frank, together with Schirach, kept vacillating between renunciation of Hitler and support for Goering's view that Nazi Germany had been no more guilty of cynical opportunism, power politics, and brutality than any other nation. Goering kept exhorting his co-defendants to stick together and present a united front. Speer, conversely, having convinced Fritzsche to join him in his planned denunciation of Hitler, worked diligently on Frank and Schirach also to make their abnegations in court—the greater the number of defendants who abjured the Nazi system, the more would Speer be demonstrating to Jackson the effectiveness of his persuasion.

Gilbert, whose "observer" role had undergone a subtle change, was no longer entirely nonpartisan, since he prided himself in having become a kind of psychological father-confessor, helping the accused to perceive the enormity of the Nazi crimes. He advised Colonel Andrus that he believed it would be a good idea to reinstate some of the rules of solitary confinement that had existed before the start of the trial so as to diminish Goering's influence.

On February 15, Andrus prohibited further communication between the prisoners except in the courtroom, where he had no control. For lunch, Gilbert split the group into six different rooms, isolating Goering in one. Speer and Fritzsche were placed in another with Schirach and Funk, for the purpose of weaning the latter two away from Goering. The four military men were divided among four different groups to prevent them from consulting about their defense. Doenitz went with the Nationalists: Schacht, Papen, and Neurath. Keitel was joined to one hard-core group, including Frank, Seyss-Inquart, and Sauckel; and Jodl to another, consisting of Frick, Kaltenbrunner, and Rosenberg. The moralistic Raeder was subjected to the company of the obnoxious Streicher and the withdrawn Hess—who hated each other—and the rambling Ribbentrop. Raeder, presumably, was seated with the others to provide a symbol of sanity; and, as usual, he bore his tribulation with forbearance.

Schacht, on the other hand, was enraged that he should be subjected to the same restrictions as Goering and Frank. Shaking with anger, he screamed at the top of his lungs to Gilbert: "They threw me into jail like a *criminal!* With the most disgraceful, undignified, shameless treatment! Even in concentration camps I didn't have to sweep out my own cell and be forced to face this way or that way so that I couldn't sleep! I will have nothing more to do with any American institution. I will not even attend chapel anymore." When a photographer attempted to take his picture during lunch, he threw the coffee in his canteen cup at him, an act that caused him to have his privileges revoked for two days but earned him the plaudits of his co-defendants for the only time during the trial.

Though one-third of the defendants had excellent rapport with their attorneys, they were counterbalanced by an almost equally large group who did not see eye to eye with their counsel. Composing the former were Speer, Fritzsche, Schacht, Doenitz, Frank, Raeder, and Jodl; in the latter were Streicher, Hess, Ribbentrop, Frick, Kaltenbrunner, and Rosenberg.

Ribbentrop's lawyer, Fritz Sauter, who was also defending Funk and Schirach, had as much difficulty as Jackson or Amen getting the former foreign minister to speak factually or coherently. On January 8, the day after the evidence against Ribbentrop was presented, Sauter decided he would not be able to do justice to Ribbentrop's defense, and turned the case over to his young Munich associate, Martin Horn. Hess's attorney, Gunther von Rohrscheidt, was in a state of screaming frustration, since it was impossible for him to communicate with Hess at all. On January 23, Rohrscheidt, suffering what was perhaps a Freudian slip, broke his ankle and, vastly relieved, withdrew from the case. Hess's defense fell instead to Frank's attorney, Alfred Seidl, who was also an associate of Sauter, a fortuitous development that was to have a major impact on Hess's fate.

As they prepared their cases, the German attorneys continued to be bedeviled by disputations over documents. On January 9, Seidl and Sauter complained that they were still not receiving documents in German, as Lawrence had ordered. "It does not help us if agreements are made or regulations are issued, and in actual practice it is entirely different," Sauter appealed. "Last night, for example, we received a big volume of documents, all of which were in English. Now, in the evening in the prison we are supposed to spend hours discussing with our clients the results of the proceedings. In addition we are also required to talk over whole volumes of documents written in English, and that is practically impossible. Time and again these documents are not received until the evening before the day of the proceedings; and it is not possible, even for one who knows English well, to make the necessary preparations."

Lawrence had difficulty comprehending that, as a consequence of the general disorganization of the prosecution and the overwhelming work load of the tribunal's secretariat, his orders were not being complied with. The revelation that the German attorneys were not receiving the transcripts of the proceedings of December 18 until January 9 came as a shock. In the future, Lawrence directed, the transcripts were to be delivered without fail within forty-eight hours.

Matters improved somewhat after that, but the problem resurfaced during the French prosecution. Additionally, Dubost's declaration that the French prosecution was relying on only fifty of the two thousand German documents that they had examined stimulated the interest of the defense attorneys. Unaware that the French depended essentially on the Anglo-American documents, and that all two thousand were part of the hoard in the Document Room, the lawyers naturally suspected that material favorable to the defendants was being kept from them. During the last week in February, when the German lawyers were making application to the tribunal for the calling of their witnesses and assembly of their documents, Otto Nelte, Keitel's lawyer, addressed himself to the question: "There can be no doubt that these fifty documents were selected merely from the point of view of incriminating the defendant. On 11 February, if I remember correctly, I addressed myself to the French prosecution with a request to place at my disposal for examination the remaining one thousand nine hundred and fifty documents, which the French prosecution did not use. To date I have received no answer. The tribunal will appreciate the difficulty of my position. I know there are documents there which I am sure contain also exonerating facts. Yet I am not able to specify these documents. I beg the tribunal, therefore, for a ruling in this matter—that the prosecution should place at my disposal those documents for my perusal."

Dubost, hoisted upon his own hyperbole, could not reveal, as a matter of national pride, the truth of the matter. Stalling and evading, he succeeded in avoiding an unequivocal order from Lawrence to produce the documents; and the German attorneys, knowing there was something fishy, but hardly guessing what it was, were left with the feeling that they were being deprived of vital evidence.

Since it was up to the tribunal to have defense witnesses brought to Nuremberg, and to order searches for and translations of documents, the judges adopted a procedure for screening the counsels' requests for relevancy and redundancy, so that the secretariat would not be overwhelmed. Unfortunately, they also permitted the prosecution to comment upon the attorneys' applications. Fyfe, who represented the prosecutors in these meetings, assured everyone, "If there is any point of relevance in a witness for whom application is made, they [the prosecution] will not, of course, object." The lawyers were, nevertheless, distressed that, by being required to justify each witness, they had to reveal the outline of their cases beforehand.

Lawrence tried to reassure them: "The tribunal has already, in deciding provisionally upon the application for witnesses, acted in the most liberal way. The tribunal will allow any witness to be called whose evidence appears to be possibly relevant. That is all the tribunal can do because, as I have already stated, it is the tribunal who has to undertake the difficult task of securing these witnesses for the defendants."

It was true that, virtually without exception, the judges acted both liberally and impartially. Siemers, for example, representing Raeder, was delighted that, of the seventy documents he requested, all forty that he considered important were granted by the judges. Kranzbühler, defending Doenitz, received permission to examine the British Admiralty War Diary, and his assistant was flown to London for ten days.

But it was also true that the prosecution was able to obtain a blueprint of the defense each attorney intended to present. While the defense had not known until the day before of each prosecution witness's appearance—and Jackson had fought against providing the Germans with even that much notice—the prosecution, under the overall direction of Robert Kempner, began preparing material for cross-examination weeks ahead. Furthermore, many of the witnesses named by the defense counsel were incarcerated at Nuremberg or elsewhere, and had been questioned repeatedly by members of the prosecutorial staff, so that the prosecution knew more about them and their testimony than the defense.

Dix, and some of the other German lawyers, like Siemers and Sauter, had established an amicable working relationship with the prosecution. The more aggressive attorneys, however, thought Dix was too accommodating, and did not fight hard enough. They therefore shifted their support to Kranzbühler, who had the respect of the Allied attorneys, but was far more militant. Kranzbühler wished to submit evidence on the *Laconia* incident, in which an American plane had bombed several U-boats engaged in rescuing the survivors of a torpedoed British auxiliary cruiser, and to obtain an interrogatory from Admiral Chester W. Nimitz, the commander of the American Pacific fleet, for the purpose of demonstrating that German submarine practices had been no different from American. Franz Exner, defending Jodl, hoped to introduce the British commandos' *Handbook of Irregular Warfare.* Sauckel's counsel, Robert Servatius, wanted to bring up the fact that, since the end of the war, the Soviets had impressed tens of thousands of people for compulsory labor: "Part of the population of Königsberg is now in the Urals," he asserted.

Fyfe asked the judges to deny these, and all similar requests: "They fall under the general objection to *tu quoque* evidence which the prosecution has maintained throughout the trial."

Under Kranzbühler's leadership, however, the defense worked out an ingenious argument to get around the stricture on *tu quoque* (i.e., "If I am guilty, you are too"). The Germans did not desire to accuse the Allies of any illegal action—far from it! Kranzbühler declared: "I in no way wish to prove or even to maintain that the American Admiralty in its U-boat warfare against Japan broke international law. On the contrary, I am of the opinion that it acted strictly in accordance with international law. In the United States' sea war against Japan, the same question arises as in Germany's sea war against England, namely the scope and interpretation of the London Submarine Agreement of 1930. Through the interrogatory to Admiral Nimitz I want to establish that the American Admiralty in practice interpreted the London Agreement in exactly the same way as the German Admiralty, and thus prove that the German conduct of sea warfare was perfectly legal."

Exner argued, "If for instance, in the 'Close Combat Regulations,' English soldiers are ordered to perform actions for which our soldiers are censured, it would constitute a discrepancy of some importance. For in that case it would be obvious that the British government regarded such methods of warfare legitimate. If, however, such methods are legitimate for them, they must also be legitimate in our case, since it is impossible to have two standards in these matters." Servatius asserted that he wanted to show that the Hague Convention regarding land warfare was considered obsolete by the Soviets, and if it was obsolete for the Russians, it must be obsolete for the Germans too.

This was an argument that it was difficult for the prosecution to contend against. Rather than everyone having acted illegally, but only the Germans being brought to account, the defense attorneys were asserting that everyone had behaved *legally,* because evolution in warfare had made international law obsolete.

Lawrence was supportive of Fyfe, and even chipped in helpfully to supplement his arguments on occasion, but Biddle was clearly sympathetic to Kranzbühler. In the end, Kranzbühler was granted what he asked for, though Exner and Servatius fared less well.

The tribunal rejected a request by the attorneys for a three-week adjournment to prepare their cases. A major dispute broke out among the judges as to whether the defendants could testify in their own behalf. The Russians were adamant that the accused should not be given the opportunity to speak, save for a brief statement at the conclusion of the trial. This position shocked Parker to such an extent that, highly emotional, he threatened to resign if it were sustained. After a lengthy discussion, the western judges, outvoting the Russians, decided that the defendants could testify, but only under oath and subject to cross-examination. They were to be heard in the same order that they had been listed in the indictment and were seated in the dock.

On March 6, Stahmer was ordered to commence the defense of Goering the following day, although he had not yet spoken to all of his witnesses and his documents were not yet translated into the other languages. Though the judges had ruled that witnesses were to be brought to Nuremberg a week ahead of their appearance, Birger Dahlerus, Goering's 1939 contact with the British government, was not in sight and had not been heard from.

The defense's mood was, nevertheless, generally upbeat; and the Germans' morale was boosted immeasurably on the day the defense opened by a speech Winston Churchill had made, fortuitously, the day before in Fulton, Missouri.

IV

Defense

"From Stettin on the Baltic to Trieste on the Adriatic an iron curtain has descended across the continent. This is certainly not the liberated Europe we fought to build up. Nor is it one which contains the essentials of permanent peace," Churchill declared. Coming on top of a speech by Stalin three weeks earlier, in which he had said that World War II had by no means resolved the Communist-capitalistic conflict, Churchill's speech created a stir among the defendants. Goering boasted that he and Hitler had been right all along about the impossibility of a Soviet-Western alliance—the rift was simply coming a few months later than anticipated. Hess's prognostications were accorded new respect—perhaps the trial would break apart before its conclusion.

In the Palace of Justice there was an air of tension and suppressed excitement. A month before, the American CIC (Counter-Intelligence Corps) had uncovered an SS *Werwolf* organization, suspected of planning to disrupt the trial. Security, consequently, had been tightened. The corridors swarmed with MPs, and bodyguards were assigned to the judges and prosecutors.

During court hours a certain indulgence toward the defendants had gradually come to prevail. Fritzsche was the first to carry a blanket from his cell to sit upon, and when it was not taken from him, the others followed suit. To while away the long stretches of boredom in the dock, more and more of the defendants brought books, reading them under the cover of documents. If one of the accused managed to get hold of a newspaper, it was passed from hand to hand until all had devoured it—all, that is, except the bumbling Frick, who invariably was caught. Fritzsche tried to show him how to hold the paper as if it were a legal document, but it was hopeless—Frick was utterly artless. He became so absorbed in reading the newspaper that even when a guard took it away from him he kept on reading without knowing it was gone.

Caricatures of the principal accused, drawn by a newspaper artist, hung in the cafeteria: Goering's face was dominated by a diabolical grin; Schacht's long neck emerged out of a collar of plaster of Paris. Reporters laid bets on which of the prisoners would be hanged.

Though Goering at one point suggested they should all confine their court appearance to three words, "Lick my arse!" (the famous line of a sixteenth-century German warrior whom Goethe had made the hero of one of his plays), he prepared, for himself, an elaborate defense. Now that the Führer was dead, it was Goering's intent to demonstrate that he as much as Hitler had been responsible for the German resurgence and the Nazi triumphs between 1933 and 1941; but that he had had no culpability for the atrocities that followed.

Though the prosecution had offered most of its evidence against the defendants in summary form, simply referring to those portions of the overall case for which individuals were charged to have responsibility, the presentation had served to divide the defendants into roughly five groups.

The first consisted of Goering, Ribbentrop, Kaltenbrunner, Keitel, Jodl, Rosenberg, Frank, Sauckel, and Speer. Associated with varied and numerous atrocities, their names had come up repeatedly, and they seemed damned.

In the second were Hess and Streicher. Both had been close to Hitler and were fanatic Nazis. But they had had little executive power, and had faded out of the picture by the time Barbarossa had precipitated the avalanche of barbarities.

A third group consisted of Frick, Funk, Seyss-Inquart, Schirach, and Fritzsche. Administrators and ideologists, they were linked to some of the crimes. But they had been in the second rank of power, and their culpability seemed less than that of Goering, Ribbentrop, et al.

In a fourth, separate category were Raeder and Doenitz, who were charged with having conducted the naval campaign contrary to the laws of war.

Finally, there were the Nationalists, Schacht, Papen, and Neurath, accused of having lent themselves to Hitler's designs, and, especially, his preparations for the waging of aggressive war.

Since, in the minds of most of the defense as well as of the prosecution, there was little doubt that the essence of the Nazi regime's criminality had been proved, the task of the individual accused in attempting to show his innocence or mitigate his guilt was to disassociate himself from the group, to demonstrate that he had not participated in the alleged "common plan" and had not been involved in violations of international law or crimes against humanity. The impression that the defendants made on the stand would be, therefore, of critical importance.

This fact became evident as soon as the accused began presenting their witnesses, who, by and large, turned out to be a sorry lot. Since nearly all of them had been implicated in the regime's inhuman actions in one way or another, they entangled themselves under cross-examination in contradictions and generally turned out not to be credible.

Field Marshal Erhard Milch, who had been operating head of the Luftwaffe and was a key witness for Goering, offered a prime example. Milch's father had been a Jewish pharmacist, so Goering, at Milch's request, had arranged to have Milch simultaneously bastardized and Aryan-ized—an affidavit was produced that Milch's mother had committed adultery with a member of the minor nobility and that Erhard had been the offspring of the liaison. One of Goering's associates had once remarked, "When Milch pisses, ice comes out!" But as a witness Milch appeared as nothing but a dodging roadrunner, more apropos of Goering's depiction of him as "a fart out of my asshole!"

Implicated in the slave labor program as a member of the Central Planning Board, Milch denied that he had had any responsibility or that he had ever been cognizant that foreign workers were brought into Germany against their will. "I did not know that the workers who came from foreign countries had been deported; we were told that they had been recruited on a voluntary basis."

Milch claimed he had no recollection of the correspondence he had conducted with Himmler and Himmler's adjutant, Karl Wolff, about Rascher's experiments at Dachau. In response to Jackson's questions, he either could not remember or had never heard of atrocities, or had been on leave. "The only duty of a soldier is to obey," he stated, a line that emerged as one of the great platitudes of the trial.

Field Marshal Albert Kesselring, who had been a Luftwaffe general at the beginning of the war, testified about the circumstances surrounding the bombings of Warsaw, Rotterdam, and Coventry, and he was able to refute, quite convincingly, the allegations that these had been terror attacks.

Any advantage that might have accrued to Goering from the appearance of Birger Dahlerus, summoned to show how assiduously Goering had endeavored to avert war, was negated by Fyfe's cross-examination. Fyfe, after eliciting an acknowledgment from Dahlerus that he had realized, in September 1939, that Goering's aim had all along been to split Poland from Great Britain, continued: "He never told you that Hitler had said to him that Danzig was not the subject of the dispute at all? 'It is a question of expanding our living space in the East.' And I think he also did not tell you that Hitler had said on that day, 'Our task is to isolate Poland; the success of the isolation will be decisive.' He never spoke to you about isolating Poland?"

"He never indicated anything in that direction at all."

"Goering never told you that, at the time you were being sent to London, all that was wanted was to eliminate British intervention?"

"Not at all."

"Now, just let me put it to you"—Fyfe referred to Dahlerus's account in his book, *The Last Attempt*, of a meeting with Hitler—"how you described it, and you tell me if it is right. ' "If there should be a war," [Hitler] said, *"Dann werde ich U-Boote bauen, U-Boote, U-Boote!"** And he raised his voice each time.' "

"Yes."

" 'The voice became more indistinct and finally one could not follow him at all,' " Fyfe continued. " 'Then he pulled himself together, raised his voice as though addressing a large audience, and shrieked'—shrieked!— *'Ich werde Flugzeuge bauen, Flugzeuge bauen, Flugzeuge, Flugzeuge, und ich werde meine Feinde vernichten.'*† Just then he seemed more like a phantom from a storybook than a real person. I stared at him in amazement and turned to see how Goering reacted, but he did not turn a hair. His words became blurred and his behavior was that of a completely abnormal person. I realized that I was dealing with a person who could not be considered normal.' That was your considered view, was it not, Mr. Dahlerus?"

"It was the opinion I formed the first time I met him," Dahlerus agreed.

"That was the chancellor of Germany. Now I want you, for a moment, to deal with the foreign minister of Germany . . ." Fyfe brought out that Goering had told Dahlerus that Ribbentrop, who was unaware of Goering's negotiations with Dahlerus, had made a fanciful suggestion that Dahlerus' plane should be sabotaged because he thought Dahlerus was a British spy. Continuing his setting of the stage, Fyfe quoted Dahlerus's account of his meeting with Goering on September 1, 1939. " 'Finally he [Goering] called in the State Secretaries Körner and Gritzbach, gave them a long harangue, and presented each of them with a sword of honor, which he hoped they would carry gloriously through the war. It was as if all these people were in some crazy state of intoxication.' Are these your words?"

"Yes."

"So that, of the three principal people in Germany"—Fyfe unveiled the verbal snare he had prepared—"the chancellor was abnormal; the Reichsmarshal was in a crazy state of intoxication; and, according to the defendant Goering, the foreign minister was a would-be murderer who wanted to sabotage your plane?"

Dahlerus nodded assent.

To Carl Haensel, one of the defense attorneys, it seemed as if the specter of Hitler glided through the room, stopped behind Goering, and, like a vampire, sucked the words from his lips:

"Kalter Kaffee!"‡

---

*"Then I will build U-boats, U-boats, U-boats!"
†"I will build airplanes, airplanes, airplanes, and I will destroy my enemies."
‡"Cold coffee!" i.e., a served-over meal.

Following four days of testimony from his witnesses, Goering took the stand on Wednesday, March 13. Within a half hour it was evident that Jackson's position in his dispute with Donovan had been correct. To have called Goering as a prosecution witness would have been disastrous for the cause of the prosecution. Although Goering was nervous to begin with— his hands trembled and beads of sweat formed on his forehead—he quickly took command and established himself as a glib master at glorifying Hermann Goering and the Third Reich. For anyone not familiar with the history of the Nazi movement and its horrors, Goering's recitation made it appear as if National Socialism had been a macho, dynamic political force responsible for a national renaissance. Goering, his articulateness bolstered by an excellent memory, frequently expounded for ten or fifteen minutes in response to a single question by his attorney, Stahmer. He cleverly painted an analogy between the Führer Principle and the Presidency of the United States: "The Führer told me then that the simplest thing to do would be to take as example the United States of America, where the head of the state is at the same time also the head of the government. Thus, following the example of the United States, we combined the position of the head of the state with the head of the government, and he called himself Führer of the German people and Reich Chancellor of the German Reich."

To demonstrate the acceptance and legitimacy of the Nazi regime, Goering pointed out that foreign diplomats had frequently attended the Nuremberg rallies. The Soviet Union had congratulated Germany on its victory in Poland, and supported its right to reincorporate the territory detached by the Treaty of Versailles.

Like a preening peacock, Goering unfurled the feathers of his office. In contrast to his co-defendants, who almost to a man attempted to minimize their influence and the roles that they had played, Goering was anxious that no one in the world should be left in doubt about the immense powers he had wielded.

"With the dynamic personality of the Führer, unsolicited advice was not in order," Goering recited, "and one had to be on very good terms with him. That is to say, one had to have great influence, as I had—and I ask you to understand me correctly—as I had beyond doubt for many years, in order to come to him unsolicited, not only with advice, but also with suggestions or even persistent contradictions."

The entire charge that a conspiracy had existed was ridiculous, Goering asserted. "One can only talk of conspiracy here to the extent that this took place between the Führer and me until, say, 1941. There was no one who could even approach working as closely with the Führer, who was as essentially familiar with his thoughts, and who had the same influence as

I. Therefore at best only the Führer and I could have conspired. There is definitely no question of the others."

To hold Keitel, or any other military commander, responsible for waging an aggressive war was preposterous, Goering declared. "How does one imagine that a state can be led if, during a war, or before a war, which the political leaders had decided upon, whether wrongly or rightly, the individual general could vote whether he was going to fight or not, whether his army corps was going to stay at home or not, or could say, 'I must first ask my division.' Perhaps one of them would go along, and the others stay at home! That privilege in this case would have to be afforded the ordinary soldier too. Perhaps this would be the way to avoid wars in the future, if one were to ask every soldier whether he wanted to go home! Possibly, but not in a Führer state."

Modern warfare had made the Hague Convention obsolete, Goering asserted, and Churchill himself had said: "In the struggle for life and death there is in the end no legality." He himself, however, had always endeavored to keep warfare chivalrous. Complementing Kesselring, Goering denied that the German bombings of Warsaw, Rotterdam, and Coventry had been "terror attacks." Warsaw, Goering said, had been the principal base of the Polish air force, and was one of the country's key railroad centers. The commander at Warsaw had been called upon to surrender, but had refused. Goering continued: "Still we gave another warning. We dropped leaflets at first, not bombs, in which we urged the population not to fight. Secondly, when the commanding officer persisted in his stand, we urged the evacuation of the civilian population before the bombing. Then, after it was clearly stated in the last appeal that we would now be forced to make a heavy attack on the city if no surrender took place, we proceeded to attack first the forts, then the batteries erected within the city and the troops." The French military attaché in Poland had reported that the German air force had concentrated exclusively on military targets.

The bombing of Rotterdam Kesselring had attributed to "one of those unforeseeable coincidences of war which, I am sorry to say, occur in the armed services of all countries more frequently than one might think." When German parachute troops inside the city had been cut off and were under heavy fire, Goering had ordered three squadrons of planes dispatched to their support. In the meantime, negotiations for capitulation of the city had been initiated. Since, however, there was no direct radio communication between the planes and the troops in the city, the message had failed to reach the lead squadron in time; and, although the second and third waves were turned back, the first squadron had continued on to its target. When the oil and fat stored in a butter-manufacturing plant had ignited, a massive conflagration had resulted; and it was this fire that had been responsible for most of the damage and the casualties.

"The case of Coventry," which was known as "Little Essen," Kesselring had said, "was particularly fortunate as it presented an important military target and no one could speak of it as an attack directed against the civilian population." The British, naturally, had not seen things that way, and had made propaganda capital out of the bombing. Goering, however, pointed out, "There was located in and around Coventry an important part of the aircraft and aircraft accessories industry. I prepared that attack myself with both air fleets. That here the city itself was greatly affected resulted likewise from the fact that the industry there was widely spread over the city, with the exception of two new plants which were outside the city, and again in this case the damage was increased by the spreading of fire. If we look at German cities today, we know how destructive the influence of fire is."

Other actions that could not be dealt with in such straightforward fashion Goering tried to dismiss by ridicule, by placing the responsibility on others, by feigning ignorance, or by resorting, despite the tribunal's ruling, to the argument of *tu quoque*. German occupation of the Lowlands had occurred, Goering declared, because "information indicated that the chief of the French General Staff, Gamelin, as well as Admiral Darlan and the chief of the air force, Vuillemin, insisted on the occupation of Belgium under all circumstances for the security of France. How correct and absolutely clear it was became evident later when, after marching into France, we found the secret documents of the French General Staff, and also minutes of conferences which had taken place between the French and British governments in the so-called Supreme Military Council." Of course, the French plan had been predicated on the basis of the German threat; but that was not Goering's concern.

With respect to the *Kristallnacht*, he claimed that he had exercised a meliorating influence in the face of Goebbels' radical demands. Rationalizing his cooperation with Himmler, he declared: "That I requested inmates of concentration camps for the aviation industry is correct, and it is in my opinion quite natural because I was, at that time, not familiar with the details of the concentration camps." His intention to exploit the Soviet Union for the economic benefit of Germany, regardless of the consequences for the Russian population, he waved off with aplomb: "This is a rather unreliable document. We cannot tell clearly just who was present, where this was discussed, and who was responsible for the nonsense that is expressed in it. The feeding of several millions of people, that is, two or three, if I figure the entire troop deployment in Russia with all its staff, cannot possibly result in the starvation of many, many millions on the other side. It is impossible for one soldier on the one side to eat so much that on the other side there is not enough for three times that number. The fact is, moreover, that the population did not starve."

This was blatant speciosity mixed with outright prevarication, since it had been not only the German army but the German population that had been fed on the produce of the East, and millions of people—Jews, Poles, Russians, and Ukrainians—had starved in consequence.

Goering's direct examination by Stahmer lasted until midday of Monday, March 18. At 12:15 Jackson, carrying a thick folder of papers, moved to the lectern to commence the cross-examination. Fyfe, at a birthday party held for Jackson the month previous, had anticipated this moment by composing an ode on the style of "Horatius at the Bridge":

> The Reichsmarshal of Karinhall
> By all Valhalla swore—

Fyfe's epic started off, then projected Jackson into the arena like a gladiator:

> But the U.S. chief of counsel
> Set forth in brave array.
> He strapped the earphones on his head
> And girt him for the fray.

The pressure on Jackson was immense. He had anticipated the unanimous approval of his countrymen, but instead was being sniped at by various elements, particularly the military and business communities. *Fortune* magazine, deriding the presence of the Russians, suggested, "The very concept of international justice is being endangered by the Nuremberg novelty," and iterated that summary punishment would have been the preferable procedure. The *Army and Navy Journal* charged that Jackson was trying to establish principles "under which professional soldiers, sailors, and airmen shall be convicted as criminals on the mere ground of membership in high commands or general staffs. . . . Policy is the responsibility of political governments and in obedience to directives thereunder the military must obediently carry it out." The *Journal* proffered, in this respect, precisely the same argument as Goering and the defendants. Jackson had blasted back that the generals were not being indicted for membership in a profession, but for inhumane and monstrous outrages, and for conspiring to wage an unjust war: "The position of the author and those for whom he speaks so inaccurately seems to be that it is all right to punish somebody for illegal war making, shooting American prisoners of war, and murdering and enslaving civilians—so long as you don't get the men who actually did it." For the first time since the opening day of the proceedings the attention of the world was focused on Nuremberg. Now Jackson had the opportunity to vindicate himself and his concept of the trial.

This, then, was the moment of truth. Jackson, the professorial hunter, was expected to stalk and bring down Goering, who, with his surprisingly lithe movements and agile mind, resembled a catlike elephant. From the jam-packed gallery on the one side to the interpreting booth on the other, everyone felt himself involved in the drama. Birkett, wishing himself into the prosecutor's place, desired nothing so much as to see Goering savaged and the temple of National Socialism brought to its final ruin: "There are, in truth, two trials going on at the same time," he wrote, "the trial of the defendants in the dock and the greater trial of a whole nation and its way of thought. . . . If the leader of the surviving Nazis could be exposed and shattered, and the purposes and methods of the Nazi government revealed in their horrible crudity, then the whole free world would feel that this trial had served its supreme purpose; but if, for any reason, that design should fail, then the fears of those who thought the holding of any trial to be a mistake would be in some measure justified."

Those who knew Jackson well sensed trouble in the air. The trial had turned into a test of patience, but he was noted for his impulsiveness. Despite his great oratorical skills, he did not have the quick wit required for repartee. He lacked the knowledge and sense of European history that Birkett and Fyfe were steeped in. (Fyfe regularly tramped about the fields in the vicinity of Nuremberg retracing the battles of the Thirty Years' War.) Like most of the other members of the prosecution staff, Jackson's knowledge of the Nazi system and its personalities was limited. He could not identify Karl Saur, Speer's second in command. He referred to Dieter Wisliceny, one of his own key witnesses, as a *Gruppenführer* (major general) instead of as a *Hauptsturmführer* (captain), scarcely a minor discrepancy. While questioning Goering, he interrupted himself to ask, "Dalüge . . . who by the way was he?" although Dalüge, the chief of the uniformed police, had been incarcerated at Nuremberg and questioned by the Interrogation Division before being shipped off for trial to Czechoslovakia. He mixed up Ernst Thaelmann, the leader of the Communist Party and candidate for president in 1932, with Ernst Törgler, the Communist deputy accused in the Reichstag fire, giving Goering the opportunity to correct him. Time and again it was Goering who caught Jackson in error, rather than Jackson who trapped Goering in lies.

Birkett, in his diary, expressed his bitter disappointment: "Throughout this trial the dead Hitler has been present at every session, a dreadful, sinister, and in some respects an inexplicable figure; but Goering is the man who has really dominated the proceedings, and that remarkably enough, without ever uttering a word in public up to the moment he went into the witness box. That in itself is a very remarkable achievement and illuminates much that was obscure in the history of the past few years. He has followed the evidence with great intentness when the evidence required attention, and has slept like a child when it did not; and it has been obvious that a personality of outstanding though possibly evil qualities was seated there in the dock.

"But nobody appears to have been prepared for his immense ability and knowledge, and his thorough mastery and understanding of the detail of the captured documents.

"The cross-examination had not proceeded more than ten minutes before it was seen that he was the complete master of Mr. Justice Jackson. Suave, shrewd, adroit, capable, resourceful, he quickly saw the elements of the situation, and as his confidence grew, his mastery became more apparent.

"Mr. Justice Jackson, despite his great ability and charm, and his great powers of exposition, had never learned the very first elements of cross-examination as it is understood in the English courts. He was overwhelmed by his documents, and there was no chance of the lightning question following upon some careless or damaging answer, no quick parry and thrust, no leading the witness on to the prepared pitfall, and above all no clear overriding conception of the great issues which could have been put with simplicity and power."

The underlying error lay in Jackson's basic approach to the cross-examination. Under direct examination, Goering had not only admitted but boasted of his activities on behalf of the Nazi Party, his crushing of the opposition, and his role in the rearming of Germany, so there was no point in cross-examining him about these elements of his career. Jackson, however, rather than focusing on the aspects of Goering's activities which the Reichsmarshal clearly wanted to avoid and on which he was vulnerable, conducted the cross-examination like an examination-in-chief, leading Goering through his life as a Nazi from A to Z. His questions wandered hither and yon, bouncing sometimes like a marble in a pinball machine from the pointless to the irrelevant. Their impreciseness gave Goering the opportunity to expatiate at length, causing Jackson to express greater and greater irritation: "Can you answer my question? Time may not mean quite as much to you as it does to the rest of us. Can you not answer yes or no? Did you then know, at the same time that you knew the war was lost, that the German cities could not successfully be defended against air attacks by the enemy? Can you not tell us yes or no?"

Beyond the irrelevancy of such a question as to when Goering might have known that the German cities could not be defended—he was, after all, even in the broadest conception of the trial, accused of having conspired to launch a war, not of having failed to surrender—Jackson once more displayed his characteristic insensitivity with respect to the human element of the drama. Since Goering's life was at stake, he could scarcely be expected to be interested in shortening the trial's duration; and it seemed petty to cavil with him about the point. Lawrence, in fact, was moved to intervene on behalf of Goering:

"Mr. Justice Jackson, the tribunal thinks the witness ought to be allowed to make what explanation he thinks right . . ."

Far from destroying Goering, Jackson, cavalier and patronizing, generated sympathy for him.

Goering, furthermore, had the advantage, since he understood English, of being able to compose his replies while the questions were translated into German. Jackson, on the other hand, had to wait for Goering's responses to be rendered into English before he could comprehend. Goering's innate superiority in repartee was enhanced, and he seemed, consequently, more decisive and spontaneous than Jackson.

Late Tuesday afternoon, the second day of cross-examination, Jackson lost his composure entirely. Questioning Goering on mobilization preparations for the movement of troops into the Rhineland, he demanded to know why they had been "of a character which had to be kept secret from foreign powers?"

"I do not believe I can recall reading beforehand the publication of the mobilization preparations of the United States," Goering parried.

"Well, I respectfully submit to the tribunal that this witness is not being responsive, and has not been in his examination, and that it is . . ." As Jackson began to ramble, the judges looked astonished at him.

Since Goering continued to speak into his microphone simultaneously, the translating system—beset by periodic difficulties because people kept tripping over the cables on the floor and reconnecting them haphazardly so that Russian would be heard on the French channel and French on the Russian—flashed yellow and red lights like a short-circuited traffic signal.

"It is perfectly futile to spend our time if we cannot have responsive answers to our questions . . ." Jackson went on with his complaint, as Goering kept trying to interpose.

When, finally, order was restored, Jackson renewed his charge: "This witness, it seems to me, is adopting, and has adopted, in the witness box and in the dock, an arrogant and contemptuous attitude toward the tribunal which is giving him the trial which he never gave a living soul, nor dead ones either.

"I respectfully submit that the witness be instructed to make notes, if he wishes, of his explanations, but that he be required to answer my questions and reserve his explanations for his counsel to bring out."

Lawrence, thinking to give Jackson a chance to cool off, adjourned the trial a few minutes early. But Jackson, not to be deterred, returned to the attack immediately upon the trial's resumption the following morning.

"Now, representing the United States of America, I am confronted with these choices—to ignore that remark and allow it to stand for people who do not understand our system; or to develop at considerable expense of time, its falsity; or to answer it in rebuttal."

The judges were unable to fathom why Jackson should be so upset— Fyfe had told Biddle that Jackson was in a terrific state and seemed on the verge of flying completely off the handle. Lawrence was not pleased that Jackson was turning a petty aside into a major issue: "Surely it is making too much of a sentence the witness has said, whether the United States makes its orders for mobilization public or not. Surely that is not a matter of very great importance. Every country keeps certain things secret. Certainly it would be much wiser to ignore a statement of that sort."

Jackson, however, would not drop the issue. He wanted the tribunal to restrict Goering to answers of "yes" or "no." Birkett, anxious to maintain propriety in the trial and reduce prolixity, drafted a notice which he proposed that Lawrence read: "This trial is in danger of becoming unduly and unnecessarily prolonged because of the nonobservance of the essential rules of giving evidence, and the tribunal gives clear and firm notice that no irrelevancy in the answer of questions will be tolerated."

Biddle, on the other hand, characterizing Jackson's argument as "a silly speech," opposed putting a gag on Goering—such a ruling would place the tribunal in the worst possible light historically and politically, and make Goering a present of the very martyrdom he intended to achieve.

"I have never heard it suggested that the counsel for the prosecution has to answer every irrelevant observation made in cross-examination," Lawrence said. "The tribunal considers that the rule which it has laid down is the only possible rule and that the witness must be confined strictly to answering the question directly where the question admits of a direct answer, and that he must not make his explanation before he gives a direct answer; but, after having given a direct answer to any question, he may make a short explanation; and that he is not to be confined simply to making direct answers 'yes' or 'no.' "

The truth was that Goering, by nimbly dodging Jackson's sallies, and then obliquely harassing the prosecutor, had hit upon the ideal tactic to get Jackson's goat.*

---

*Shortly before Jackson's explosion the previous evening, Goering had pointed out that the *"freimachen"* of the Rhine, as written in a document referred to by Jackson, did not mean the "liberation" of the Rhine, as translated by the prosecution, but the "clearance" of the Rhine, an error that entirely blunted the thrust of Jackson's interrogation, and once more illustrated the sloppiness of some of the prosecution's preparations.

Noticeably angry at having his motion rejected by Lawrence, Jackson resumed his cross-examination. Before long, Goering received another opportunity to embarrass the prosecution. On December 22, he had been examined by members of an American team investigating cartels, and had been informed by them that the interrogation was in no way connected with the trial, that the information he provided would not be used in the trial, and that, therefore, the presence of his attorney was not necessary. In contravention of this pledge, Jackson, having had the session in the Palace of Justice's Interrogation Room bugged from the chamber above, now confronted Goering with his statements.

Cavalierly indignant, Goering declared: "Before the interrogation it was again confirmed to me that these statements should in no way be brought in in connection with this trial. However, that is all the same to me. You may produce them as far as I am concerned. But because of the method employed, I desire to have this made known here."

So it went. "And who was your Reich Commissar in Poland?" Jackson asked, giving Goering a chance for another comeuppance.

"There was no Reich Commissar in Poland. There was a governor-general in Poland, and that was Dr. Frank."

Repeatedly, Jackson was tripped up by his facts, submitted evidence of questionable reliability, drew unsupportable conclusions, or abruptly dropped a line of questioning. He attempted to link Schacht's arrest on July 23, 1944, with a letter Schacht had written Goering in November 1942, criticizing the conscription of teenagers. "The original promise of a short war has not been fulfilled," Schacht had declared. "The promised quick victory by the air force over England did not materialize. The public statement that Germany would remain free of enemy air raids has not been fulfilled. The repeated announcements that Russian resistance was definitely broken has proved to be untrue. The landings of the Allies in North and West Africa, declared to be impossible, have nevertheless been accomplished. The conscription of the fifteen-year-olds will be a heavy burden on the fighting morale of the German people, and increase the doubts of the termination of this war."

This letter, however, had resulted not in Schacht's arrest, but in his dismissal as minister without portfolio. By associating it with 1944 instead of 1942, Jackson displayed not only a dismaying lack of historical knowledge but unfamiliarity with the documents his own prosecutors had introduced. "Do you know when Schacht was sent to the concentration camp; do you know the date of that?" he demanded of Goering.

"Not exactly, but now that you remind me of it, I can say that this letter was certainly not written in 1944," Goering replied, "because in November 1944, I believe, Mr. Schacht was already in the concentration camp; consequently, it must date back to November 1943."

"And he was sent to the concentration camp shortly after dispatching that letter to you, wasn't he?"

"No, that is not correct."

It was, of course, self-defeating for a cross-examiner to keep tripping himself up. By permitting Goering to score repeatedly on secondary points, Jackson assisted him in diverting attention from the fact that he came off badly on the principal ones.

In preparation for Jackson's cross-examination, Sonnenfeldt, now elevated to the position of interrogator, had obtained an affidavit on the Reichstag fire from Colonel-General Franz Halder, the army's former chief of staff. At Hitler's birthday banquet in East Prussia on April 20, 1942, fifteen people, including Keitel, Jodl, and Speer, had been sitting at a large, rectangular table. An animated conversation had developed over the artistic value of the Reichstag building. One group had suggested that it had no artistic value, another that it was a historical monument. Then, Halder recalled, Goering had suddenly brought the conversation to a dead stop by bellowing: "The only one who really knows the Reichstag is I, for I set fire to it!"

A deadly hush had fallen over the gathering, Halder declared. Hitler had stirred his soup. Everyone had stared at Goering, who, his face turning purple, suddenly had seemed to realize that he had just admitted that the rumors which had swirled about this pivotal event for years were true; the conflagration that had panicked the nation and enabled the Nazis to initiate their program of repression and terror had been his handiwork—van der Lubbe had been nothing but a foil.

In response to Jackson's presentation of Halder's affidavit, Goering once more resorted to a sleight of words to distract attention from the corpus delicti: "I had no reason or motive for setting fire to the Reichstag. From the artistic point of view I did not at all regret that the assembly chamber was burned. I hoped to build a better one. But I did regret very much that I was forced to find a new meeting place for the Reichstag and that I had to give up my Kroll Opera House. The opera seemed to me much more important than the Reichstag."

The image of moderation in which he tried to cast himself was destroyed by the cross-examination on his chairmanship of the conference following the *Kristallnacht*. Reminded that he had told Heydrich, "I wish you had killed two hundred Jews instead of destroying such valuables," he could only respond lamely: "Yes. This was said in a moment of bad temper and excitement."

Faced with his directive of July 31, 1941, ordering Himmler and Heydrich to get on with the task of clearing the Jews out of the territory under the domination of the Third Reich, he was reduced to quibbling that the translation was incorrect because it stated that he demanded a "complete" or "final solution" rather than a "total solution of the Jewish question."

Goering's attempts to explain away, or to deny knowledge of or responsibility for such other actions as his looting of art from Jews and the occupied territories, and his participation in the July 16, 1941, conference organizing the economic rapine of the East, were similarly weak. He was unable to refute the charge that he had acquiesced to the Terror Flier Decree, but was reduced to caviling over the appropriateness of the language. By the time Fyfe took over the cross-examination from Jackson on the afternoon of March 20, Goering's contentiousness and resort to verbal distractions were wearing thin.

Fyfe undoubtedly exaggerated when he asserted that the whole fate of the trial now hung in the balance because Goering had bested Jackson, and the spirit of the other defendants had been buoyed. But there was no question that the tenor of the cross-examination changed when Fyfe took to the lectern.

Forty-five years old, the British prosecutor was stocky, baldheaded, and thick-lipped. Though he looked Jewish or Lebanese, his ancestry was Scottish Presbyterian. After matriculating at Oxford, he had become one of the most successful barristers in England, and subsequently had been elected to the House of Commons. A smooth, skillful interrogator, his questions had a cutting edge. He gave Goering no chance to counterpunch by finding weaknesses in the prosecution's attack. He successfully snared the Reichsmarshal for his role in the promulgation of the *Kugel Erlass* (Bullet Decree): "Then I am right, am I not, that the Soviet prisoners of war who escaped were to be, after their return to the camp, handed over to the Secret State Police. If they committed a crime, they were to be handed over to the Security Police, isn't that right?"

"Not exactly correct," Goering tried to weasel out.

Fyfe, however, had him. The Reichsmarshal, the fingers of his pawlike hand drumming nervously, watched with glinting eyes as Fyfe handed the document to a British secretary, who approached with feathered steps, laid the paper in front of Goering, then, elegant and sexy, retreated. "Read the next sentence," Fyfe directed him: " 'If a Soviet prisoner of war is returned to the camp, he has to be handed over to the nearest service station of the Secret State Police.' Your own sentence!"

Goering acknowledged that he had been aware of the forced labor program: "I said that I knew quite well that these workers were brought in and not always voluntarily. That I have never denied, and have even admitted it."

The British were obsessed with the shooting of the fifty Royal Air

Force officers who had escaped from Sagan; and Fyfe devoted the greater part of his cross-examination trying to establish Goering's complicity. Goering claimed that he had been on leave when the shootings occurred, and had found out about them too late to prevent them. Fyfe, never able to establish Goering's involvement conclusively, seized on the issue to indict Goering for his continuing support of Hitler. "Do you seek to justify and glorify Hitler after he had ordered the murder of these fifty young flying officers at Stalag Luft Number Three?"

"I am here neither to justify the Führer Adolf Hitler nor to glorify him. I am here only to emphasize that I remained faithful to him, for I believe in keeping one's oath not in good times only, but also in bad times when it is much more difficult."

"The Führer, at any rate, must have had full knowledge of what was happening with regard to concentration camps, the treatment of the Jews, and the treatment of the workers, must he not?"

"I already mentioned as my opinion that the Führer did not know about details in concentration camps, about atrocities as described here."

"I am not asking about details; I am asking about the murder of four or five million people. Are you suggesting that nobody in power in Germany, except Himmler and perhaps Kaltenbrunner, knew about that?"

"I am still of the opinion that the Führer did not know about these figures."

Goering was careful to qualify his statement: he was not so brazen as to claim that Hitler had not ordered or been aware of the Final Solution, merely that he had been uninformed about the millions that were involved —an assertion that, since Hitler was averse to personally besoiling himself with blood and guts, was quite likely true.

Pursuing Goering like a bloodhound, Fyfe put to him the minutes of a meeting Hitler and Ribbentrop had had with Hungary's Admiral Horthy on April 17, 1943. When Horthy had asked what he should do with the Hungarian Jews, Ribbentrop had declared that "the Jews should be exterminated or taken to concentration camps. There was no other possibility." Hitler, then, in the way of reassuring Horthy, had plunged into one of his monologues. "In spite of the fears which he had heard repeatedly in Germany," the minutes recorded the Führer as having said, "everything continued to go its normal way without the Jews. Where the Jews were left to themselves, as for instance in Poland, the most terrible misery and decay prevailed. They are just pure parasites. In Poland, this state of affairs had been fundamentally cleared up. If the Jews there did not want to work, they were shot. If they could not work, they had to perish. They had to be treated like tuberculosis bacilli, with which a healthy body may become infected. This was not cruel—if one remembered that even innocent creatures of nature, such as hares and deer, have to be killed so that no harm is caused by them. Why should the beasts who wanted to bring us bolshevism be more preserved? Nations which do not rid themselves of Jews perish. One of the most famous examples is the downfall of that people who were once so proud, the Persians, who now lead a pitiful existence as Armenians."

The passage, in addition to its screaming insanity, displayed a typical burst of Hitlerian ignorance in equating the Persians (Iranians) with the Armenians. "Do you still say that neither Hitler nor you knew of this policy to exterminate the Jews?" Fyfe demanded of Goering.

"For the correctness of the document—" Goering tried to launch into one of his diversions.

But Fyfe would not let him: "Will you please answer my question. Do you say neither Hitler nor you knew of the policy to exterminate the Jews?"

"As far as Hitler is concerned, I have said I do not think so. As far as I am concerned, I have said that I did not know, even approximately, to what extent these things were taking place."

"You did not know to what degree, but you knew there was a policy that aimed at the extermination of the Jews?"

"No, a policy of emigration, not liquidation of the Jews. I knew only that there had been isolated cases of such perpetrations."

On this rather unsatisfactory note, Fyfe ended his cross-examination. He was followed by Rudenko, who shed no further light on matters. Goering was permitted to get away with such assertions as, "The whole standard of living for the worker was raised. Up to that time the worker had been used and exploited." The Nazi government had brought great prosperity to Germany, he asserted. "The collapse was due only to the war's being lost."

This, of course, was an out-and-out inversion of the true state of affairs. The Nazis had succeeded in eliminating unemployment, but only at the cost of driving the nation to economic ruin. The real standard of living of the workers had declined. The prosperity of the Nazi *Bonzen* had been based largely on the despoliation of the Jews.

It was, in truth, the inability of the prosecution to demonstrate the interaction of the dynamic forces in the Third Reich that was the great failing of the trial. It had been the conjunction of Hitler's implacable, psychopathic hatred of the Jews and his commitment to war with Goering's corruption of the economy that had orchestrated the tragedy. Goering's directives of January 1939 and July 1941 on the Final Solution—or, as he termed it, the "total solution"—had not been haphazard, out-of-the-ordinary decrees. They were examples, rather, of the standard chain of command from Hitler the dictator to Goering the administrator to Himmler and Heydrich, the executors.

Goering's defense occupied two weeks. "Arrogant, crafty, intelligent," *Life* magazine commented, "Goering obviously enjoyed himself as he kept the courtroom spellbound for days. . . . Goering was anxious, whatever his fate, that history record him as an important world figure and as a German hero."

Jackson, on the other hand, Biddle noted, "looks beaten and dead tired." At its current pace, the trial promised to last as long as another year; and both the judges and the prosecution were determined to speed it up, though they differed on the manner in which that goal might be achieved. Jackson suggested that the defense not be permitted to read its documents into the record; that, instead, submission of the document books to the judges should suffice.

Dix retorted passionately: "I cannot consider it just and I cannot consider it fair if the prosecution had the right, for months, not only once but sometimes repeatedly and often, to bring their evidence to the knowledge of the public and of the world by reading it into the microphone; and in this regard it should be noted that, when these documents were presented, often only parts of documents were read which, in the opinion of the prosecution, were incriminating to the defendants, while those parts were omitted which, in our opinion, were exonerating for the defendants. The most important point of view is that of fairness and justice. The defense counsel must and would consider it a severe and intolerable limitation of the defense, if, contrary to the procedure exercised so far by the prosecution, it were deprived of the possibility of presenting, in its turn, at least the relevant parts of its own documentary evidence to the tribunal verbally and with comments." The president of the court at the Belsen trial, Dix remarked, had replied to press criticism about the length of the trial, " 'That no duration however long was to be regretted as long as it helped to reveal the truth in the end.' May I point out that the duration of the trial thus far was at any rate not brought about by the defense."

Once again, the judges ruled against Jackson, though Lawrence couched the decision in terms as diplomatic as possible. The defense would be granted the same right previously exercised by the prosecution to quote excerpts from documents. To speed the trial up, there would be restrictions on the frequently aimless and repetitious examination of witnesses by both the prosecution and the defense. A witness called by one defendant could be examined by a counsel for another defendant only if he had previously made application for and been granted the same witness by the tribunal. Cross-examination of the defense witnesses was to be limited to one prosecutor—a rule honored most often in its breach.

Furthermore, the trial of the Nazi organizations which Bernays had viewed as the heart and soul of the conspiracy, but which the judges tended to perceive as a nuisance and distraction from the twenty-one defendants in the dock, was shunted further to one side. Thousands of applications to testify were pouring in from members of the organizations interned in camps. The judges, therefore, authorized the organizations' defense counsels to visit the camps and gather evidence. A commission was formed, headed by Major Neave and other members of the tribunal's secretariat, to hear witnesses and screen evidence. The testimony was to be presented before the tribunal in summary form, along with a few key witnesses, at the conclusion of the case against the defendants. The loathsome Babel went off to make the rounds of internment camps, where he proceeded to hit up SS men for fees to augment his stipend from the tribunal. When this activity became known, a German court was charged with investigating the ethics of his behavior, and he was dismissed by the tribunal. His place as counsel for the SS was taken by Horst Pelckmann, a far more able attorney.

39   The Faithful Followers: Hess and Ribbentrop

Hess contributed to the shortening of the trial by presenting only a perfunctory defense. He could now scarcely remember from one day to the next. When his attorney, Seidl, refused to ask him the questions about extraterrestial influences and mesmeric forces that Hess wanted him to, Hess decided not to testify on his own behalf. As witnesses he called his mentally unbalanced brother and Professor Karl Haushofer. His brother did not appear, and Haushofer, who had suffered a stroke in November, could not bear the thought of testifying at Nuremberg. Shortly before midnight on March 9 he and his wife went out into their garden, paused by a statue of the Madonna, and drank a mixture of arsenic and liqueur. (Haushofer died from the potion. But his wife, who was of a more robust constitution, hanged herself from a bough projecting over a small creek.) When Hess was informed of the suicides, he stared blankly. He could not recall who the Haushofers were.

The case against Hess, presented by the British, was weak. Hess could not, of course, be connected with any of the principal Nazi atrocities committed after the attack on Russia, and he had not been present at any of the crucial meetings at which Hitler had spoken of his grandiose plans for aggression. He had clearly lived in the backwaters of power. The most serious charges against him were that he had been a slavish follower of the Führer and a dutiful supporter of the repressive measures taken against the Jews and Poles. Hess, Seidl told the court, "contests the jurisdiction of the tribunal where other than war crimes proper are the subject of the trial. However, he specifically assumes full responsibility for all laws or decrees which he has signed. For these reasons he does not desire to be defended against any charges which refer to the internal affairs of Germany as a sovereign state." This, in effect, was the sum of Hess's defense, though Seidl did submit three document books, one of which, dealing with the Treaty of Versailles, the tribunal refused to admit.

To Goering, Hess remarked, "I know now that the Nuremberg proceedings will never end—we will have to answer to a higher tribunal." Goering retorted sarcastically that, higher tribunals aside, Hess was first going to lie crushed like a pear beneath the foot of the Nuremberg court.

Ribbentrop's mental condition, like Hess's, continued to deteriorate; and his counsel, Martin Horn, joined the ranks of the attorneys questioning the sanity, or at least mental stability, of their clients. It was impossible for him to map out a coherent defense, Horn complained, because Ribbentrop was incapable of differentiating between fact and fiction—on the one hand, he denied categorically that he had attended conferences at which he was shown to have been present; on the other, he imagined himself into situations and activities that were out of the realm of fantasy. One day he would place the greatest stress on calling a witness to testify about what he had said at a certain meeting; and the next he would dispute that he had ever been at that meeting. He wrote a letter to the tribunal claiming that he was innocent—but simultaneously offering to let himself be tortured to death for any mistakes he might have made. Although the tribunal granted Ribbentrop ten witnesses, he decided, after many vacillations, to call only three; and these, it turned out, might have been better summoned by the prosecution. The defense witnesses boomeranged so consistently that only a fraction of those approved by the tribunal were ever put on the stand.

Horn's concern over the impression Ribbentrop would make was such that he told the tribunal that Ribbentrop was seriously ill and suffering from a speech impediment that would make testifying difficult for him. Horn suggested that, rather than ask Ribbentrop questions, he would put the answers to him instead, so that Ribbentrop could merely indicate his agreement or disagreement. The judges, refusing to approve this novel means of procedure, commissioned two doctors to examine the foreign minister. The doctors reported there was nothing organically wrong with him, but he was so terrified of being subjected to examination that he was half-paralyzed by fear.

Ribbentrop's first witness, his state secretary, Baron Steengracht von Moyland, provided a measure of hilarity, but otherwise became so overwhelmed with the necessity of disassociating himself from the charges against Ribbentrop that he abandoned his former chief.

"Now, witness, were you incarcerated at one time at a place known as Ashcan," Amen, referring to the code name for Mondorf, cross-examined Steengracht.

The baron, who had never heard of the code name, looked blankly at Amen: "In a refuse can?" he asked bewilderedly.

"Outside of Luxembourg."

"In a refuse can? I cannot remember it."

"Near Luxembourg."

"Locked in a refuse can? No, I can't remember it."

Ribbentrop, Steengracht asserted, had been "no typical exponent of National Socialism." Exploiting this appraisal, Amen inquired of Steengracht how he defined a "typical" National Socialist: "Do you consider Goering to be a typical Nazi?"

"By a typical Nazi one understands the 'average' Nazi. Goering is a unique person and one cannot compare his manner of living with other National Socialists."

"Well, are you acquainted with all of the gentlemen in the dock there in front of you?"

"Yes."

"Now, will you tell me which of those individuals you consider to be a typical Nazi, according to the standards which you applied yesterday to Ribbentrop?"

The reaction in the courtroom once more elicited from Lawrence a lecture on the necessity of maintaining propriety. "Colonel Amen, I do not want to interrupt your cross-examination, but I want to say there is too much laughter and noise in the court, and I cannot have it."

With some coaxing, Steengracht identified Rosenberg, Frank, Hess, Sauckel, Schirach, and Streicher as "typical Nazis."

Confronted with documents pertaining to anti-Jewish actions addressed to him or referred to him, Steengracht asserted, "I see this document today for the first time," or sloughed responsibility onto Rosenberg: "The Foreign Office could not exercise general control since all anti-Jewish questions were principally dealt with in Rosenberg's office."

Finally, throwing in the towel, Steengracht pleaded Ribbentrop guilty: "I should like to make a distinction between the real instincts of von

Ribbentrop and what he said when he was under Hitler's influence. I said already yesterday that he was completely hypnotized by Hitler and then became his tool."

"Yes." The assistant British prosecutor who was conducting this phase of the cross-examination nodded. "And from then on, he was prepared to do anything that Hitler wanted and was as violent a Nazi as anyone; isn't that right?"

"He followed blindly the orders given by Hitler."

Next came Ribbentrop's secretary of eleven years, Margaret Blank, who, it was said, had been in love with Ribbentrop. If so, her affection was deadly. Testifying as if she were speaking in Ribbentrop's behalf before a Nazi court, the words from her lips knotted themselves like a rope around Ribbentrop's neck. Responding to a question from Horn, she said: "As far as I can judge Herr von Ribbentrop always showed the greatest admiration and veneration for Adolf Hitler. To enjoy the Führer's confidence, to justify it by his conduct and work was his chief aim, to which he devoted all his efforts. To achieve this aim no sacrifice was too great. In carrying out the tasks set him by the Führer he showed utter disregard for his own person. When speaking of Hitler to his subordinates he did so with the greatest admiration. Appreciation of his services by the Führer, as for instance the award of the Golden Party Badge of Honor, the recognition of his accomplishments in a Reichstag speech, or a letter on the occasion of his fiftieth birthday, full of appreciation and praise, meant to him the highest recompense for his unlimited devotion."

"Is it true that Ribbentrop adhered to Hitler's views even if he himself was of a different opinion?" Horn continued.

"In cases of differences of opinion between himself and the Führer, Herr von Ribbentrop subordinated his own opinion to that of the Führer. Once a decision had been made by Adolf Hitler there was no more criticism afterward. Before his subordinates Herr von Ribbentrop presented the Führer's views as if they were his own."

A few minutes later, Horn, urged on by his friend Seidl, asked Fräulein Blank: "Do you know that, in addition to the Non-Aggression Pact and the trade agreement, a further agreement was concluded in Moscow?"

"Yes, there was an additional secret agreement."

By revealing to the world that Germany and the Soviet Union had agreed to divide Eastern Europe between them in 1939, Seidl aimed to blow Count One, the Conspiracy to Wage Aggressive War, right out of the trial: For if there had been a conspiracy, then one of the conspirators, the Soviet Union, was, in violation of all legal standards, participating in the prosecution and the judging of the case. If, on the other hand, the Moscow Pact had not constituted a conspiracy, then the Germans could be no more guilty than the Soviets. At the very least, Seidl aimed to hand the Russians a major propaganda defeat and widen the gap that was opening between the Soviet Union and the western nations. Seidl had first broached the matter of the secret agreement three days before by announcing he wished to introduce an affidavit from Friedrich Gaus, the chief of the Foreign Office's legal department, who had drawn up the pact between the Germans and the Russians. (Ribbentrop, thinking to mollify the Russians by not embarrassing them, had at first called Gaus as a witness, then changed his mind.) As soon as Horn broached the issue with Fräulein Blank, Rudenko was up like a shot:

"I consider the questions of the defense absolutely inadmissible and request that they be withdrawn."

"Is the alleged agreement between the Soviet government and Germany in writing?" Lawrence asked Horn.

"Yes. It was put down in writing, but I am not in possession of a copy of the agreement, and I should therefore like to ask the tribunal to allow me to obtain, at the appropriate time, an affidavit from Fräulein Blank who saw the original."

"Dr. Seidl, have you a copy of the agreement itself?" Lawrence inquired of Seidl.

"Mr. President, there are only two copies of this agreement. One copy was left in Moscow on 23 August 1939. The other copy was taken to Berlin by von Ribbentrop. According to an announcement in the press, all the archives of the Foreign Office were confiscated by the Soviet troops. May I, therefore, request that the Soviet government or the Soviet delegation be asked to submit to the tribunal the original of the agreement?"

"I asked you a question, Dr. Seidl. I did not ask you for an argument."

"I, myself, am not in possession of a copy of the agreement. The affidavit of Ambassador Gaus only states the contents of the secret agreement. He was able to give the contents of the secret agreement because he drafted it. The secret agreement, as drafted by Ambassador Gaus, was signed by Foreign Commissar Molotov and Herr von Ribbentrop. That is all I have to say."

Rudenko, in a state of great excitement, argued: "The presentation of such affidavits, which do not shed a true light on events, can be looked upon only as an act of provocation. This is clearly borne out by the fact that Ribbentrop himself repudiated this witness, even though his affidavits described Ribbentrop's activities, even though defense counsel for Hess has accepted testimonies from this witness and applied for their incorporation into the record, despite the fact that they contain no reference to Hess!"

Seidl was just as animated. Having previously requested that Molotov be summoned, he iterated: "I repeat my application that the Soviet Foreign Commissar Molotov be called and interrogated before this tribunal."

Lawrence held a hurried consultation with Biddle and the other judges, then adjourned the court to decide the question. As soon as the judges had retired, an anticipatory buzz erupted in the courtroom. Goering, speaking to no one in particular, remarked: "A woman is always more courageous than a man. On that you can rely."

"Is that intended as a needle for me?" Ribbentrop murmured half-heartedly.

To Rudenko's consternation, the judges ruled, upon returning, that Fräulein Blank could be questioned about the secret agreement. It now turned out, however, to Rudenko's vast relief, that all Fräulein Blank knew was that there had been "a special sealed envelope which was filed separately and bore an inscription something like 'German-Russian secret or additional agreement.'"

Fritzsche, projecting himself during the lunch hour back into his role as a radio commentator, recounted the incident with great enjoyment: "The defense counsel asked her if she knew about any secret treaty. The whole courtroom pricked up its ears. The Soviet prosecutor objects. The court recessed. They decided the question may be asked. The suspense is terrific. At last the world will know about the secret treaty with Russia. Yes, she knew it was in an envelope marked secret. That is all. You should have seen Biddle's face drop!" Fritzsche laughed: "What a letdown for the whole court! It was priceless!"

Ribbentrop himself made a terrible impression on the stand. Evasive and circumlocutious, he purported to be "frank" in a fashion that simply emphasized his doltish deviousness. As a subject for cross-examination, he was a prosecutor's dream. The British, who were assisted by Erich Kordt, a member of the Nationalist cabal who had been chief of Ribbentrop's personal staff until 1939, had primary cross-examination responsibility for the foreign minister. But the French, Americans, and Russians all took turns tearing him to pieces. As his words poured out, sometimes indistinctly, in long, convoluted sentences, even the Germans had difficulty making sense of what he was saying. Everyone grew weary of his long-winded, nonsensical exposition. Lawrence warned: "The tribunal has listened with great patience to a very great deal of detail. All I can say is that this exaggerated going into detail does not do the defendant's case any good."

Questioned about the numerous bloodthirsty statements he had made as foreign minister, he either could not remember them, or explained that he had not really meant them. He had not intended any harm to the Jews.

"I have never been anti-Semitic," Ribbentrop averred.

Faure, the deputy French prosecutor, challenged him with the minutes of the same conference between Hitler and Horthy previously put to Goering: " 'The foreign minister declared that the Jews were to be exterminated or sent to concentration camps. There was no other solution.' You did say that, did you not?"

"I definitely did not say it in those words," Ribbentrop replied, and continued with an utterly confusing declaration of what words he might have said it in.

"Well, defendant," Lawrence intervened, "the tribunal would like to know whether you did say to the Regent Horthy that the Jews ought to be taken to concentration camps?"

"I consider it possible that such may have been the case," Ribbentrop acknowledged, but then asserted that the record of the conference was inaccurate.

"Are you suggesting," Lawrence continued, "that Schmidt [the Foreign Ministry's chief interpreter, whom the court had heard a few days earlier as a Ribbentrop witness], who drew up this memorandum, invented the last few sentences, beginning with [Hitler's] words: 'If the Jews there did not want to work they would be shot. If they could not work they would have to perish. They had to be treated like tuberculosis bacilli . . .' Are you suggesting that Schmidt invented those sentences or imagined them?"

Ribbentrop, squirming beneath Lawrence's gaze, made a partial confession: "Mr. President, I should like to add that I myself was very grieved by these words of the Führer, and I did not quite understand them. These words were certainly not invented by Schmidt. The Führer did express himself in some such way at that time. That is true."

"You admitted that you knew of Hitler's policy to deport all Jews," Faure resumed, "and you admitted that insofar as you were competent as minister for foreign affairs, you assisted this policy, did you not? That is right, is it not?"

"As his faithful follower I adhered to the Führer's orders even in this field," Ribbentrop acknowledged.

Fyfe, referring to another of Ribbentrop's meetings with the Hungarians, suggested: "You want us to assume that you were telling lies to the Hungarians but you are telling the truth to this tribunal. That is what it comes to shortly, isn't it? That is what you want us to understand, isn't it?"

"I do not know whether one can talk of lies in this case, Mr. Prosecutor. This is a question of diplomacy. . . . Many things are said in diplomacy, every word of which is not weighed carefully."

"Tell me this: Every time today when you have been confronted with a document which attributed to you some harsh language or the opposite of what you have said here, you say that on that occasion you were telling a diplomatic lie. Is that what it comes to?"

When Ribbentrop failed to answer, Fyfe, snapping shut his folder of documents, concluded his cross-examination: "Thank you very much."

Ribbentrop returned to the dock in profound despair—it was as if he had just heard his death sentence pronounced. The attorneys, as well as the defendants, expressed unanimous dismay that such a man could have been foreign minister. Goering lectured him: "If you want to make great tirades, you have to be at least interesting!" Finally exploding in rage, he turned his back to Ribbentrop, and said nothing more.

The cross-examination showed up the defendants' characters in uncanny fashion, Fritzsche observed. Those in the dock watching their fellows unmasked and dissected never ceased to be amazed at the process. It was as if they were coming to know each other for the first time.

Ribbentrop was not the only one to employ sentences of monumental length, festooned with clauses like decorations from a Christmas tree; most of his fellow defendants and their attorneys had the same habit. Since, in German, the verb does not appear until the end of the sentence, the interpreters were reduced to desperation trying to untangle the clauses and phrases, and essential points frequently vanished in translation. Fritzsche drew up a paper, "Suggestions for Speakers," urging everyone to use shorter sentences and express himself more directly. But it was a hopeless task.

Birkett, though he could not speak German and hence was not aware of the cause for the mutilations in the translation, was in complete agreement with Fritzsche on the end result: "One of the tortures of this trial has been the language used by the interpreters into English," he chronicled. "Dr. Nelte has just said according to the interpreter, 'The evaluation of judgment is always subjective.' That is the sort of sentence which makes me despair of the record of this trial." Chafing, and irritated by his ulcer, Birkett gritted his teeth in frustration at what he perceived as Lawrence's lackluster performance—he could not help feeling that, by rights, he should be sitting in the president's chair.

"Although great efforts have been made to show the world that this is to be a fair trial," he mused, "I yet greatly fear that so far as the German people are concerned all these efforts will be in vain. It is difficult to see how the situation might be improved: but I think that if there had been a better tribunal much might have been done. The standard of the court does not compare favorably with the highest courts in England and there has been much weakness and vacillation, and, above all, a failure to appreciate that the trial is only in form a judicial process and its main importance is political. For that, of course, what was required was not only a knowledge of law but a knowledge of history, particularly German history, a knowledge of men and world affairs, and an instinct to apply these things at every stage of this most remarkable case."

40 "Destiny Took Its Tragic Course": Keitel

The evidence against Keitel, who followed Ribbentrop, was overwhelming. He had been present at nearly all of the conferences at which Hitler had articulated his barbarous concept of warfare, and many of the measures had been issued over his signature. From his days as a cadet, it had been his overriding desire to be "a good soldier." He prided himself on his appearance and the neatness of his cell. His self-discipline was exemplary. Mentally, however, he seemed to have progressed little since he was eighteen. "Nothing is more convincing to a soldier than success," he remarked; consequently, by 1941, he had been confident that Hitler "had the perceptions of a genius." On October 2, 1945, he had written a letter to Amen: "In carrying out these thankless and difficult tasks I had to fulfill my duty under the hardest exigencies of war, often acting against the inner voice of my conscience and against my own convictions. The fulfillment of urgent tasks assigned by Hitler demanded complete self-abnegation."

Keitel's superficiality and obtuseness seemed painted on his yellow-gray face as he sat rigidly erect in the witness box. In response to his attorney, Otto Nelte, he stepped out smartly: "It will not always be possible to separate clearly guilt and entanglement in the threads of destiny. But I do consider one thing impossible, that the men in the front lines and the leaders and the subleaders at the front should be charged with the guilt, while the highest leaders reject responsibility. That, in my opinion, is wrong, and I consider it unworthy. I am convinced that the large mass of our brave soldiers were really decent, and that wherever they overstepped the bounds of acceptable behavior, our soldiers acted in good faith, believing in military necessity and the orders which they received." For Keitel, this was a statement not only in behalf of all German fighting men, but, in particular, for his own three sons, one of whom had been killed in Russia during the summer of 1941, and another of whom had disappeared into a Soviet POW camp.

Immediately, however, Keitel began to qualify, in varying degrees, the responsibilities, which, he claimed, he accepted: "It is correct that there are a large number of orders, instructions, and directives with which my name is connected, and it must also be admitted that such orders often contain deviations from existing international law. On the other hand, there are a group of directives and orders based not on military inspiration but on an ideological foundation and point of view." He seemed to think that there were mitigating circumstances when murder was based on ideological grounds.

His explanation for his actions in the Terror Flier matter was vaguely confessional, and seemed like an echo from Ribbentrop's appearance: "I also wrote another note, and this refers to lynch law. It states: 'If you allow lynching at all, then you can hardly lay down rules for it.' To that I cannot say very much, since my conviction is that there is no possibility of saying under what circumstances such a method could be regulated or considered justified by mob justice, and I am still of the opinion that rules cannot be laid down, if such proceedings are tolerated.

"As these atrocities developed, one from the other, step by step, and without any foreknowledge of the consequences, destiny took its tragic course, with its fateful consequences," he acknowledged. Biddle regarded this as one of the most important declarations by a defendant during the course of the trial.

Nelte, in effect, was pleading Keitel guilty, but trying to stress extenuating circumstances.

"An honest man without a mind of his own," Papen appraised Keitel from the dock. "But anyway, an honest man."

"Sure," Schacht jibed, "an honest man, but not a man at all."

Keitel was so unsure of himself, so used to having his life and his thoughts directed by someone else, that, frequently, after giving an answer, he looked anxiously at Lawrence or Goering to see if they approved.

The initial cross-examination, conducted by Rudenko, was uneven, and Biddle criticized it as "a childish cross-examination, hardly ever directed to the facts."

Fyfe, following, slashed into Keitel with relish. Keitel admitted that he had signed the *Nacht und Nebel* decree; but, beyond that, he said little credible and nothing creditable about his role in a measure that had resulted, by September 1944, in 24,000 people being turned over to the SD by the Wehrmacht for *vernebeling* in concentration camps. "I learned here for the first time of the full and monstrous tragedy, namely, that this order, which was intended only for the Wehrmacht and for the sole purpose of determining whether an offender who faced a sentence in jail could be made to disappear by means of this *Nacht und Nebel* procedure, was obviously applied universally by the police, and so the horrible fact of the existence of whole camps full of people deported through the *Nacht und Nebel* procedure has been proved."

Turning to the Commando Order, Fyfe inquired witheringly of Keitel: "You were a field marshal, standing in the boots of Blücher, Gneisenau, and Moltke. How did you tolerate all these young men being murdered, one after the other, without making any protest?"

"I have stated here in detail my reasons for not making any further resistance or objections. I know that these incidents occurred and I know the consequences."

"But, field marshal, I want you to understand this. As far as I know, in the German military code, as in every military code, there is no obligation on the part of a soldier to obey an order which he knows is wrong, which he knows is contrary to the laws of war and law. It is the same in your army, and our army, and I think in every army, isn't that so?"

"I did not personally carry out the orders of 18 October 1942," Keitel responded, and launched into an evasive explanation that was really no answer at all.

Fyfe, determined to pull something more concrete out of him, continued: "I have given you only two cases; there are plenty more. The point I am putting to you is this: You were the representative, that you have told us a hundred times, of the military tradition. You had behind you an officer corps with all its—"

"No, Sir David," Keitel interrupted. "I must deny that. I was not responsible either for the navy or for the army or for the air force. I was not a commander; I was a chief of staff and I had no authority to intervene in the execution of orders in the various branches of the armed forces, each of which had its own commander in chief."

It was an incredible statement from a man who, whatever authority he had exercised in practice, had, at least in theory, been the highest-placed officer in the Wehrmacht.

"You were a field marshal, Kesselring was a field marshal, Milch was a field marshal—" Fyfe could only pity Keitel. "All, I gather, with military training behind them and all having their influence if not their command among the Armed Forces of Germany. How was it that there was not one man of your rank, of your military tradition, with the courage to stand up and oppose cold-blooded murder? That is what I want to know."

"I did not do it." Keitel wilted like a starched shirt in the tropics. "I made no further objection to these things. I can say no more and I cannot speak for others."

So it continued. In response to Fyfe's question whether he approved of the order, signed by him, calling for the execution of scores of hostages in retaliation for the life of each German, Keitel said: "It says only that hostages must be taken; but it says nothing about shooting them."

Goering, cursing in one and the same breath the wiliness of Fyfe and the stupidity of the defense attorneys, raged at Keitel for not putting up more of a fight: "You don't have to answer so damn directly! The question itself doesn't matter so much as the way you answer it. You can dodge around such dangerous questions and wait until they hand you one you have a good answer for and then sail into it!"

"But I can't make white out of black!" Keitel shot back. To Gilbert he said: "I could only tell them the way things were. The only thing that is absolutely impossible for me is to sit there like a louse and lie—that is absolutely impossible!"

Concluding his cross-examination on Monday, April 8, Fyfe was almost sympathetic: "Wouldn't it be fair to put it this way, that if you had known at the time all that you know now, you would have refused, even with all that you have told us, you would have refused to have anything to do with actions that produced concentration camps, mass murder, and misery to millions of people, or do you say that you still, knowing all that you know now, would have gone on with these actions?"

"No." Keitel agreed with Fyfe's premise. "I am convinced that if the German armed forces and their generals had known it, then they would have fought against these things."

Dodd, for the United States, said that he had just one question: "As an old professional soldier, you, of course, understood the traditions and indeed the principles of that profession that oblige a soldier not to carry out any order which he recognizes to be criminal in character."

"Yes, I understood that."

"You told us that some of these orders were violations of existing international law. An order issued in that form and on that basis is a criminal order, is an illegal order, is it not?"

"Yes, that is correct."

"Well, when you carried them out, you were carrying out criminal orders in violation of one of the basic principles of your professional soldier's code, no matter by whom they were issued."

"Yes," Keitel acknowledged.

Even in the courtroom, it was remarkable how Keitel was swayed by every prevailing breeze. Nelte did not wish the final impression of Keitel's appearance on the stand to be his admission that he had transmitted criminal orders; but he only compounded the negative image Keitel created by giving him another chance to "explain."

"I often had serious conflict of conscience," Keitel asserted. In the end, however, he had always permitted his scruples to be overcome by Hitler's argument that such measures were part of the military and political necessities of war. "Never did it enter my mind to revolt against the head of the state and the supreme commander of the armed forces, or refuse him obedience. As far as I am concerned, and as a soldier, loyalty is sacred to me. I may be accused of having made mistakes, and also of having shown weakness toward the Führer, Adolf Hitler, but never can it be said that I was cowardly, dishonorable, or faithless." He spoke with greater emotion and conviction than at any other time during his testimony.

Lakeitel to the last.

Tuesday, the ninth of April, was the trial's stormiest day. Court had just opened when Jackson strode to the lectern. His voice ringing with anger, he announced that the United States would, in the future, refuse to print and duplicate document books for the defendants. "Now, that is a drastic step, but I know of nothing less that I can do. We received from the General Secretary's office an order to print and have printed Document Book Number 1 for Rosenberg. That document book does not contain one item in its 107 pages that, by any stretch of the imagination, can be relevant to this proceeding. It is violent anti-Semitism and the United States simply cannot be put in the position of printing and disseminating to the press plain anti-Semitism. . . . Now, let us look at what we are actually asked here to disseminate: 'Actually, the Jews, like the Canaanites in general, like the Phoenicians and the Carthaginians, represent a bastard population.'" Jackson gave one example, then turned to another: " 'The Jews are arrogant in success, obsequious in failure, shrewd and crooked wherever possible, greedy, of remarkable intelligence, but nevertheless not creative.' Last night we received an additional order to print two hundred and sixty copies more of this sort of thing, and I have had to stop the presses." Jackson could perceive a thunder of criticism bursting over his head in the American press if he permitted his organization to be a party to the distribution of such material.

As commonly happened, Jackson's outburst set off a general brouhaha. The documents in question, previously disallowed as irrelevant by the tribunal, had actually been included in the document book by error. But before the matter was settled after an hour of heated argument, Fyfe was feeling aggrieved at Lawrence, Thoma repudiated his client, Rosenberg, and Dix came close to bringing the general resentment of the defense attorneys against the prosecution's mode of procedure out into the open.

Jackson refused to be swayed by Lawrence's initial suggestion that the imbroglio should be attributed to a misunderstanding and need not be pursued further. "Well, if your honor pleases, I do not think it is a mistake. What the issues here are—counsel says that he thinks he should try the new romanticism of Rosenberg. We are charging him for the murder of four or five million Jews. The question here is one of ideology. There is no purpose here in trying the question of anti-Semitism or the superiority of races, the fundamental difference in viewpoint. They believe—and, of course, if they can try this issue with this tribunal as a sounding board, it forwards their purpose—they believe in trying that issue. . . . We are in the very peculiar position, your honor, of being asked to be press agents for these defendants. The United States cannot be acting as press agents for the distribution of this anti-Semitic literature, which we have protested long ago was one of the vices of the Nazi regime, particularly after they have been argued on and have been denied by the court. This, it seems to me, is a flagrant case of contempt of court." Jackson rejected Lawrence's proposal that he and Thoma go over the documents together and attempt to work out their differences. "I would not even venture to sit down with Dr. Thoma, because we start from totally different viewpoints. He wants to justify anti-Semitism. I think it is not an issue here. It is the murder of Jews, of human beings, that is an issue here, not whether the Jewish race is or is not liked by the Germans."

Thoma was in agony. He had been a judge for nineteen years, and judge advocate general of the Luftwaffe from 1939 to 1941. Prior to the Nazi takeover, he had frequently been attacked by Streicher's *Der Stürmer* for his support of the Christian Socialist Party. Philosophically, as a militant Protestant, he could not have been more opposed to Rosenberg's anti-Judeo-Christian *Weltanschauung*, and had devoted great effort to urging Rosenberg to recant and throw himself on the mercy of the court. But when Rosenberg stuck to his beliefs, Thoma felt it to be his duty to defend him as vigorously as possible. Once again, the real roots of the controversary lay in the all-inclusive and ill-defined perimeters of the indictment.

"It says in the presentation of the case for the American prosecution," Thoma pointed out, "that Rosenberg remodeled the German educational system in order to expose the German people to the will of the conspirators and to prepare the German nation psychologically for a war of aggression." How could he defend Rosenberg against the charge of promulgating a perverse ideology if the defense was barred from referring to other ideologies?

"Secondly," Thoma continued, "one word more, I am forced to reply in person to the accusation raised by Mr. Justice Jackson—I must state something which I should normally not have said in this courtroom, namely, that I have told Herr Rosenberg repeatedly, 'Herr Rosenberg, I cannot defend your anti-Semitism; that, you have to do yourself.' For that reason I have limited my documents considerably, but have considered it my duty to place at Rosenberg's disposal every means necessary for him to defend himself on this point."

While Thoma directed himself to specific points, Dix launched into a lengthy and impassioned rebuttal to Jackson in general: "Very serious accusations against the defense have been raised. The expression was used that the prosecution was not the press agent of the defense. The accusation was raised that the defense were trying to make propaganda, and then these accusations reached their peak in the most serious charge which one can possibly make in reference to a participant in a trial, that of contempt of court.

"In the name of all defense counsel I oppose these heavy accusations with the best and strongest argument possible, that of an absolutely clean and pure conscience in this respect. I believe that we could avoid all these difficulties if we mutually agree that both parties, the prosecution and the defense, are working with good will and loyalty, and that the thought of deliberately disregarding the rulings of the tribunal is far from it. Errors and mistakes can always happen. May I just remind you that this leakage of news to the press was something that happened quite frequently at the beginning of the trial. I do not want to mention examples since the tribunal knows that it was not the defense. But I remind you that it was we, the defense, who quite energetically supported the ruling that only such matters should reach the press as had been introduced in the record here in the public sessions.

"I never considered that an insult, but rather merely the God-given dependence of human beings. For instance, it was impossible for me to get the charter, the basis of our trial, at the beginning of the trial. But eventually it was graciously placed at my disposal by the press.

"As to the particular accusation that National Socialist propaganda or that anti-Semitic propaganda is being made here, I think I can say, with a clear conscience, that none of the defense counsel has ever dreamed of trying to use this courtroom to make ideological propaganda for the dead —I emphasize the word *dead*—world of the Third Reich. That would not only be wrong; it would be worse than a wrong; I might say, using Talleyrand's words, that it would be unbearable stupidity to do a thing like that."

Dix expressed the hope that Jackson would "make a statement in order to clear the atmosphere in regard to this accusation which is extremely painful not only for the defense but also for the entire court."

"I certainly do not want to be unfair to our adversaries; I know they have a very difficult job," Jackson declared grudgingly. "I shall withdraw all characterizations and let what I have to say stand on the facts."

He was, however, still seething during the noon recess, and stormed in to see Biddle and Parker in what, Biddle recorded, was "a very wild and uncontrolled mood. Apparently the criticism of his cross-examination of Goering has gotten way under his skin. He threatens to resign—this is not new. He talks about refusing any printing of documents which he does not approve—irrespective, apparently, of what we order! He says Lawrence always rules against the Americans. (This is absurd.) Bob still contends the defendants are engaged in active propaganda, that the tribunal is falling into disrepute, and that Thoma violated an order."

Parker and Biddle tried to cool him off, told him they would help to prevent unnecessary printing, and agreed that Lawrence was too easygoing.

The fact of the matter was that Jackson was in such a general state of discontent that anything was liable to set him off. On April 5, the British attorney general and prosecutor-in-chief, Sir Hartley Shawcross, had come to Nuremberg to discuss the preparation of future, additional trials. The French strongly favored the holding of another trial, and the British felt duty-bound to support them. The Russians were noncommittal. Everyone agreed, in general, that if another trial was to be held, it should focus on the industrialists. Jackson's views, however, of the four-power procedure and the International Military Tribunal had become thoroughly jaundiced. Privately, he held the opinion that the United States should, in the future, go its own way and dispose of the 350 prisoners it held classified as major war criminals in perhaps sixteen separate, American-staged trials. Officially, he conveyed his viewpoint in a long message to the War Department on April 8:

"My position was stated to be, first, that no commitment by the United States to participate in another international trial exists and none should be made until the result of this trial is known. Second, one trial will accomplish one of the primary purposes, which was to authenticate and document the history of the Nazi conspiracy, aggression, and atrocities. Third, if this tribunal should hold the case against Schacht insufficient, the precedent would embarrass the trial and probably preclude the conviction of other industrialists. Fourth, that the United States has not undertaken to act as host at Nuremberg to more than one trial which has involved very considerable cost, and that I am not now prepared to recommend a repetition."

Jackson went on to detail his grievances against the tribunal. It was permitting the defendants to call too many witnesses, to introduce too many documents, and to make long speeches. "These speeches are not damaging to our legal case, but they do have a bad effect in restoring these Nazis in the favor of the German people and in complicating the future problem of Germany. The judges, including our own, seem unaware of the consequences of this course and usually meet our objections to it with unfavorable or at least indecisive rulings. This course can go so far as to discredit this trial until the public will not tolerate another and I am not prepared to say that I would recommend another before this bench.

"From the point of view of proving our case for history I am completely satisfied and would think another trial would add little relatively to that.

"Rumors about the judges' attitude float about Nuremberg just as they do about any county seat. Without relying too much on them it is possible of course that some defendants, possibly Schacht, will be acquitted. In that event we should certainly not proceed with weaker cases before an International Military Tribunal."

Jackson was, furthermore, disgruntled with Telford Taylor and with Biddle. In mid-March, Jackson had wired Washington to inquire what had happened to Taylor, who had not yet returned to Nuremberg from his recruiting trip. The delay in appointing him to head the follow-up trials was becoming embarrassing, Jackson declared.

Taylor, it turned out, was balking at going back to Europe without his wife. Army regulations now permitted the spouses of officers to accompany their husbands. But Jackson remained adamant that he didn't want the wives of any of his personnel in Nuremberg—scuttlebutt had it that he refused to have his own wife intrude into his comfortable domestic arrangements.

The army, overriding Jackson's objections, authorized Taylor to return to Nuremberg *with* his wife, and both were expected momentarily as Jackson unburdened himself to Biddle on April 9. Biddle's wife had just arrived, together with the wife of Herbert Wechsler, Biddle's principal assistant. To accommodate them, Biddle had appropriated the Villa Conradti,* used as a VIP guest house but seldom occupied, for himself and Wechsler. Jackson accused Biddle of causing dissension and lowering the morale of his organization by bringing his wife to Nuremberg. "Bob certainly has it in for me," Biddle wrote in his notes. "He's very bitter. He seems to me unfair and unhappy. I am sorry for him."

41   A Breath of Ashes: Kaltenbrunner

On the heels of Jackson's eruption, the court was treated to an extraordinary appearance on the stand by Kaltenbrunner, as well as the presentation of the trial's most dramatic witness.

After Heydrich had been assassinated in late May of 1943, Himmler had left the post of chief of the RSHA vacant for more than six months.

---

*The Villa Conradti was the property of a wealthy industrialist, and was furnished with a mixture of the exquisite and gauche. Its most notorious feature was a huge painting on the guest room ceiling directly over the four-poster bed. A rippling, naked, Nordic male was depicted passionately kissing a young woman clad like Lady Godiva in nothing but her tresses. Parker, shocked to his southern core, characterized it as "a picture of a nude woman that any man of culture would have been ashamed to have in his house." Novelist Rebecca West, who stayed with the Biddles while reporting on the trial for *The New Yorker*, referred to it as "Sauckel's dream."

As head of the Security Police, Heydrich had grown far too independent and powerful for Himmler's liking. Himmler, therefore, had hesitated to give someone else the opportunity to emulate Heydrich. Finally, he had jumped Kaltenbrunner, who was *Höhere SS und Polizeiführer* in Vienna, over a host of officers with more seniority, because Kaltenbrunner, though a capable administrator with a good record in intelligence gathering, was a weak, high-living alcoholic who presented no threat.

Following the July 20 assassination attempt on Hitler, however, Kaltenbrunner had taken personal charge of the investigation. Reporting daily to Hitler, Kaltenbrunner, like Heydrich before him, had become more and more independent of Himmler. The latter devoted his time mostly to the Waffen SS and finally assumed command of an army, first in the west and then along the Vistula. Drifting away from Hitler, Himmler had gradually become interested in trying to save himself by reaching an accommodation with the West. Kaltenbrunner, on the other hand, had applied himself to carrying out Hitler's orders. So that, during the last months of the Nazi regime, a cleavage had developed in the SS.

Both Kaltenbrunner and his attorney, Kurt Kauffmann, were tall men with burning eyes, both were in their early forties, and both had the appearance of fanatics. Kauffmann, a one-time Nazi and five-year veteran of the Wehrmacht, had acquired a profound distaste for his client. Innately, Kauffmann was as anxious as the prosecution to expose the rottenness of the Nazi leadership, and professionally he was, like many of the attorneys, frustrated and disillusioned by his client's unwillingness to face or speak the truth. While Goering lied with cunning and Ribbentrop in bewilderment, Kaltenbrunner prevaricated brazenly. Penned, with his huge frame, in the witness chair like a lassoed wild horse, he snarled at the questions, pawed at them, and with incredible evasiveness circled around them without ever providing any answers. Kauffmann seemed, rather than to be examining him, to play the role of prosecutor in cross-examination.

Repeatedly, either Kauffmann, Lawrence, or both, tried to haul Kaltenbrunner back from the tangents he galloped off on.

"I am now reading a particularly incriminating passage—" Kauffmann referred to the Commissar Order. "It can be assumed obviously that you, too, must have been informed about this extremely grave situation, which was inhuman and prohibited by international law, does it not?"

"I was not informed of it," Kaltenbrunner replied.

Following the noon recess, the contest resumed: "I am asking you an especially important and incriminating point, it seems to me." Kauffmann took up the matter of executions. "Was the regular channel from Himmler through Kaltenbrunner to Müller?"

Kaltenbrunner went off again, twisting and turning, backtracking and crisscrossing his path, so that the judges, whose comprehension of the structure of Himmler's organization was still shaky, could not follow him at all. "The prosecution endeavors to shift the entire guilt," he spoke animatedly, gesturing with his hands, "for the destruction of human life from the WVHA [The SS Economic and Administration Department] to the RSHA [Reich Main Security Office] and, if the high tribunal wants to find the truth—"

"Just a minute!" Lawrence, who had lost Kaltenbrunner some way back, interposed. "This is again a long, argumentative speech. The only question which arises, it seems to me, is: Did a conference take place between Kaltenbrunner, Pohl, and the chief of the concentration camps? That is the only question of fact."

Confused by Kaltenbrunner's meanderings, Lawrence had misquoted the question, but Kauffmann seconded him: "I am of the same opinion. Please answer 'yes' or 'no' to the question which was just put to you. Did such conferences between Pohl, Müller, and yourself take place?"

"I never had conferences with Pohl and Müller. I had to have semiannual conferences with Pohl because Pohl was, as chief of the WVHA, the finance minister for the entire SS and police, and the funds for my entire intelligence service had to come from Pohl insofar as the Reich Finance Minister did not provide for all the personnel."

When, during one of twenty-two interrogations, Colonel Brookhart had asked Kaltenbrunner, "How often did you visit Mauthausen?" Kaltenbrunner had responded:

"Never! I think I was there twice and that was only because I had to arrange something about a stone contract that had to do with Vienna, and then I did not consider this camp as healthy because typhus was prevailing there. I did not enter the camp itself."

"How do you know its conditions then?" Brookhart had been curious. "According to the adjutant of the camp, you visited several times while you were the chief of the RSHA."

"No." Kaltenbrunner had shaken his head. "I have not been in the camp, but—" He thought the matter over. "I have been perhaps eleven kilometers away in a farmhouse where I was invited to a wedding."

Eventually, he had recalled that he had once gone to Mauthausen to talk with the camp commander, Ziereis, but that had been strictly because they had a mutual interest in hunting and target practice.

"Ziereis shot at big clay pigeons," Kaltenbrunner had remarked.

A number of witnesses, including a former guard, Alois Höllriegel, avowed that Kaltenbrunner had visited the concentration camp several times, and that executions by various means had been demonstrated for his edification. Photographs had been taken of Kaltenbrunner at the camp. A former Austrian cabinet member named Karwinsky, who had known Kaltenbrunner during the 1930s, declared: "I saw Kaltenbrunner again in the Mauthausen camp, when I was severely ill and lying on rotten straw with several hundred seriously ill persons, many of them dying. The prisoners, suffering from hunger oedemata and from the most serious intestinal sicknesses, were lying in unheated barracks in the dead of winter. The soiled straw was not renewed for weeks, so that a stinking liquid was formed, in which worms and maggots crawled around. There were no medical attendants or medicine. Conditions were such that ten to twenty persons died every night. Kaltenbrunner walked through the barracks with a brilliant suite of high SS functionaries, saw everything, must have seen everything."

Kaltenbrunner denied it all, denied he had ever been in Mauthausen itself, denied that he had ever witnessed an execution, and launched into what was supposed to be a refutation of Karwinsky's testimony with an incredible exposition of a time that he had been a prisoner in an Austrian concentration camp under Schuschnigg's regime and had staged a hunger strike. The inanity of Kaltenbrunner's verbosity was breathtaking.

Kaltenbrunner achieved the acme of the ridiculous after Amen, in cross-examination, quoted to him an affidavit by a high Gestapo official (and close co-worker of Kaltenbrunner's), Josef Spacil*: " 'On occasion of meetings of the office chiefs, *Gruppenführer* Müller frequently consulted Kaltenbrunner as to whether this or that case should be specially treated or if special treatment was to be considered. Both Müller and Kaltenbrunner proposed in my presence special treatment or submission to the Reichsführer SS for approval of special treatment for certain cases which I cannot specify in detail. I estimate that in approximately fifty percent of the cases special treatment was approved.' Are the contents of that affidavit true or false, defendant?"

"You will see immediately that the tragic expression 'special treatment' is given here an absolutely humorous turn," Kaltenbrunner answered, as everyone in the courtroom stared at him in disbelief. Far from indicating execution, Kaltenbrunner explained, "special treatment" meant that the person should be lodged at a fashionable Alpine resort. "Especially qualified and distinguished personalities were accommodated there—I would mention Monsieur Poncet and Monsieur Herriot [two French statesmen] and many more. They had three times the normal rations for diplomats, which is nine times the rations of the ordinary Germans during the war. They were daily given a bottle of champagne. That is what is meant here by 'special treatment.' "

*Spacil had had responsibility for the section forging and passing foreign bank notes.

From the very beginning of his interrogation Kaltenbrunner had denied that he had signed any of the thousands of documents that bore his signature, and hour after hour was spent in virtually futile pursuit of the subject.

"I must say that not once in my whole life did I ever see or sign a single protective custody order," he declared vigorously, though *Standartenführer* Willy Litzenberg, head of one of the Gestapo sections, declared: "Kaltenbrunner was the only man who could decree protective custody. I can't understand how Kaltenbrunner can say he knew nothing about it."

"You will admit that, naturally, this statement of yours is not very credible," Kauffmann proposed to Kaltenbrunner. "It is a monstrosity that the office chief should not know that such orders were signed with his name. How do you explain this fact, a fact which appears from the documents which bear your signature?"

Kaltenbrunner put the entire blame on the Gestapo chief, Müller, who, he proclaimed, had for more than two years illegally affixed his signature upon thousands and thousands of documents without his finding out about it. "He had never informed me of this and he never had authority from me to do this. To the contrary, this was out of the question and, on the other hand, superfluous, because he was immediately under Himmler and he had authority from Himmler, so that he might just as well have written 'Himmler.' I admit that this remains a fact about which the tribunal will not believe me, but nevertheless it was so."

Questioned on a communication between the Gestapo and the Wehrmacht, he flip-flopped from one position to another like a fish pulled out of the water. After first appearing to acknowledge his signature, he changed his mind: "I did not say that this is my signature. I only said it resembles my signature; and I also said it is possible that it is only a facsimile. I cannot recall a letter of such contents signed by me."

After he had rambled on for some time, Lawrence, who was acquiring a particular distaste for Kaltenbrunner, admonished: "Answer questions and do not make speeches." Taking a hand in the cross-examination, Lawrence asked: "Are you saying that the signature on the document is not yours, or that you may have signed it without looking at the decree? Which are you saying?"

"Your lordship, this document and this decree were never submitted to me. To sign such a document would have been completely against my inner attitude toward the entire problem."

"I am not asking you what your inner attitude is. I am asking you whether the name on it is written by your hand."

"No."

Goering, Fritzsche, and some of the other defendants grinned at the great signature battle. The matter was not really very mysterious. Of course, Kaltenbrunner had not personally signed the tens of thousands of protective custody orders; these had been routinely stamped with his facsimile. The official who had been authorized to issue the decrees with Kaltenbrunner's signature was interned in a camp near Nuremberg. He had already been questioned by American officers and could speedily have put an end to Kaltenbrunner's denials—but, as in the case of Eichmann, there was a breakdown in communications, and he was never called.

Kaltenbrunner asserted he had known nothing about the Final Solution until months after taking office.

"It is natural to assume," Kauffmann suggested, "if I place myself in the position of the prosecution, that you must have had knowledge of the 'final solution.' Did not Himmler at some time put to you clearly what this 'final solution' was?"

"No, not in this form. I said yesterday that on the basis of all information which accumulated during the summer and autumn of 1943, including reports from enemy broadcasts and foreign news, I came to the conviction that the statement regarding the destruction of Jews was true. I immediately went to see Hitler, and the next day Himmler, and complained to both of them saying that I could not for one single minute support any such action."

Ohlendorf had previously declared that, as was evident to anyone with an iota of common sense, all Kaltenbrunner's protestations were prevarications: "As chief of the Security Police and SD, Kaltenbrunner had knowledge of the program for extermination of the Jews. He knew that the Reichsführer SS had been charged with the responsibility of exterminating the Jews and that this program was also carried out by the *Einsatzkommando* of the Security Police and SD, as well as in concentration camps to which the Security Police sent Jews for extermination. I will have to sharply contradict statements of Kaltenbrunner to the effect that he might try to shake off any of the responsibility."

Kauffmann had asked to have Ohlendorf, Wisliceny, Schellenberg, and Höllriegel recalled for cross-examination; but he dropped the request after becoming convinced that they were speaking the truth and Kaltenbrunner was lying.

When Kaltenbrunner denied that he had had any responsibility for or connection with the destruction of the Warsaw ghetto, Amen confronted him with an affidavit from Karl Kaleske, the adjutant to the *Höhere SS und Polizeiführer* in Warsaw: "With every SS group there were from four to six Security Policemen, because they knew the ghetto very well. These Security Policemen were under Doctor Hahn, commander of the Security Police of Warsaw. Hahn received his orders not from the *SS und Polizei-*

führer of Warsaw, but directly from Kaltenbrunner in Berlin. Doctor Hahn frequently came to our office and told the *SS und Polizeiführer* that he had received such and such an order from Kaltenbrunner."

"These statements are, without exception, wrong!" Kaltenbrunner gesticulated.

"Just like all the other statements of all the other persons that have been read to you today? Is that correct?"

"This statement is not correct. It is not true and can be refuted." Kaltenbrunner launched into another of his expositions. "It is not correct and this witness does not know—"

"Well, you said that six times!"

"—does not know the conditions."

"Well, how about General Stroop? Did he know anything about it?"

"He would have to confirm my statement at least that he was subordinated to the *Höhere SS und Polizeiführer* in the government-general and that he was not subordinated to me. I should be very glad if he could confirm that immediately. From your words I must assume that he is in custody here."

"Well, he is not in custody here, but fortunately we have an affidavit from him." Amen read: " '*Obersturmbannführer* Dr. Hahn was commander of the Security Police of Warsaw at that time. Hahn gave the Security Police their orders concerning their tasks in this action. These orders were not given to Hahn by me, but came from Kaltenbrunner in Berlin. For example, in June or July of that same year, I was together with Hahn in Kaltenbrunner's office and Kaltenbrunner told me that while Hahn and I must work together, all basic orders to the Security Police must come from him in Berlin. All executions were ordered by the Reich Main Security Office, Kaltenbrunner.' Do you say that statement of Stroop is true or false?"

"It is untrue and I request that Stroop be brought here!" Kaltenbrunner did not budge an inch.

It was he, Kaltenbrunner claimed, who had been responsible for bringing the mass executions of Jews to an end in the fall of 1944; and he then plunged into a contradictory, almost incomprehensible account of the negotiations the American Jewish Joint Distribution Committee and the Swiss Union of Orthodox Rabbis had succeeded in opening with Himmler during the summer of 1944. The conduit was a seventy-five-year-old, right-wing Swiss banker, Jean Marie Musy, who was personally acquainted with Himmler but had a son serving in the American Air Force. On October 30, Musy, using as bait a five million Swiss franc account established by the United States in Switzerland, had persuaded Himmler to issue an order halting the extermination of the Jews. (Tens of thousands, nevertheless, died, together with other concentration camp inmates, in the ensuing months from starvation and disease.) Though Kaltenbrunner had opposed the accord, he now claimed it was he who had been responsible for terminating the Final Solution.

On and on his words tumbled. His blood-red eyes protruded from his elongated face, and the pitch of his voice kept rising. "I ask you, sir, not to take me unawares and maneuver me into a position where I might go to pieces! I shall not break down!" he bellowed. "I shall not break down! I swear to you and I have sworn to help you establish the truth!"

A stark silence encompassed the court as the interpreters incongruously, like a faint echo, continued to provide the translations over the earphones.

The matter of the Jews and of Kaltenbrunner's signature were combined, finally, in a letter he had written to a friend, *Brigadeführer* Blaschke, the mayor of Vienna, informing him about twelve thousand Hungarian Jews who were being dispatched to work camps near the city. The letter was signed with the intimate *"Dein,"* used only between family members or close friends. It seemed that this signature, at least, Kaltenbrunner would have to acknowledge.

"Now do you recall that communication?" Amen asked.

"No."

"Do you deny having written that letter?"

"Yes."

"Is that not your signature?"

"No, that is not my signature. It is a signature either in ink or it is a facsimile, but it is not mine."

"Now, would it not be an absolutely ridiculous and unthinkable thing that a stamp or a facsimile would be made up which contained not only a signature but the expression *'Dein'* above the signature?"

"That would be nonsensical, I wholly agree with that; but I did not say that it must be a facsimile signature. I just said it is not my signature." As the other defendants laughed in disbelief, Kaltenbrunner explained that someone in his office, knowing he was on familiar terms with Blaschke, must not only have written the letter without his knowledge, but forged his signature, *"Dein* Kaltenbrunner."

"Is it not a fact that you are simply lying about your signature on this letter in the same way that you are lying to this tribunal about almost everything else you have given testimony about?" Amen impaled him. "Is that not a fact?"

"Mr. Prosecutor, for a whole year I have had to submit to this insult of being called a liar!" The words rushed out, until it seemed that Kaltenbrunner might momentarily suffer another hemorrhage. "For a whole year I have been interrogated hundreds of times both here and in London, and I have been insulted in this way and even much worse. My mother, who died in 1943, was called a whore, and many other similar things were hurled at me. This term is not new to me, but I should like to state that in a matter of this kind I certainly would not tell an untruth—"

Paying no attention to the blinking yellow light, he continued for several minutes, gesturing and protesting, until Lawrence, almost gently, advised him: "You must try to restrain yourself. And when you see the light, speak slower. You know about the light, do you not?"

"It would take a novelist to have any idea of the truth about Kaltenbrunner," Amen remarked at the close of the session.

"That concludes the cross-examination, except for one point," Amen announced. "There is a witness named Höss, who is called on behalf of the defendant, and through whom I would like to introduce two exhibits. If he is not to be called, however, then I would like to introduce those exhibits through the defendant. So I am wondering whether we could obtain a definite statement as to whether or not the witness Höss is actually to be called by the defense."

"Dr. Kauffmann, are you proposing to call Höss?" Lawrence inquired.

"Yes," Kauffman replied.

Rudolf Franz Ferdinand Höss, commandant of Auschwitz, had been captured by the British in May of 1945, but, together with thousands of other prisoners, released. He had been working on a farm near Flensburg when rearrested on March 11, 1946. Brought to Nuremberg on April 1, he was questioned by a number of interrogators, including Brookhart and Sonnenfeldt.

Like Ohlendorf and Eichmann, Höss, born forty-six years before in Baden, near the French border, was an unremarkable man. His father had been a bigoted, sexually suppressed, fanatic Catholic, who, after fathering Rudolf and his younger sister, had taken an oath of celibacy and dedicated Rudolf to God, intending that he should become a priest. Assuming the mantle of a saint, the father had proclaimed Rudolf's sister an angel, and made Rudolf's boyhood a torture of penitence, prayer, lies, and guilt feelings. Höss, consequently, had developed a passionate hatred for both his father and his sister. At the age of seventeen he had escaped by enlisting in the cavalry, and had seen service in Iraq and Palestine. Following the armistice, he had joined one of the *Freikorps* and fought against the Poles in Upper Silesia. Climaxing the first part of his life, he had in 1923, under the direction of Martin Bormann, participated in the murder of a suspected informant named Kadow.

Sentenced to ten years, he had been released after five. Himmler had enlisted him as a noncommissioned officer in the Dachau guards when the concentration camp had been established. Moving steadily up the ladder, he had, after four years as commander of Auschwitz, ended his career as the coordinator between the RSHA and WVHA on concentration camp affairs.

Höss, who had briefly attended high school and could understand English, had a simplistic intelligence marred by occasional lapses of memory.*

"Didn't you exterminate about three million Jews in Auschwitz?" Sender Jaari, a sarcastic, hard-drinking Finn, who had advanced from interpreter to interrogator, inquired of Höss prior to his court appearance.

"No. I never said three million."

"What did you say?"

"Two million."

"You said two and a half million were gassed."

"Yes."

"And half a million just died because of disease and epidemics."

"Yes."

"Is that three million all together, or isn't it?"

"Yes. But not three million were exterminated."

"So in Auschwitz everything was orderly and nice. Some people worked under the most comfortable circumstances and others were gassed under the most comfortable circumstances?"

"Yes," Höss agreed.

"Every German in Upper Silesia, just to keep it down to a limited area, knew about the extermination of Jews in Auschwitz, right?"

"Yes. They all assumed that, but not one of them knew exactly what happened."

"Didn't they know it or did they?"

"I can only emphasize that these things were based on assumption. The people saw the trains arriving. They saw the fires burning. They could smell the stench, and from all these things they concluded what was going on."

Höss had lived with his wife and five children just outside the camp compound at Auschwitz. Two months after the first of the permanent gassing installations and crematoria had been constructed in the fall of 1942, the Gauleiter of Upper Silesia had asked Frau Höss at a dinner one night what she thought of her husband's work. Although she had been subjected to hints before, this was the first time that anyone had brought

*He made a number of statements whose erroneous nature was established by the testimony at the Auschwitz trial in the early 1960s.

up the subject directly, and she pretended ignorance. The gauleiter, then, teasingly, painted a fairly graphic picture of the exterminations for her. When she and Höss returned home, she asked her husband if what the gauleiter had said was true. Höss admitted that it was. After that, they no longer slept together, and a few months later Höss took a beautiful camp inmate, Eleanor Hodys, as his mistress. When the girl became pregnant, he had the baby aborted. By that time he had violated the SS code to such a degree that, without Himmler's protection, he could have been tried and condemned to death.

A few days after arriving in Nuremberg, Höss had been confronted with *Scharführer* Otto "Crazy Dog" Moll, the noncom who had been in charge of the gassing and burning of the bodies. Moll was upset that he was handcuffed to a guard and Höss was not: "It hurts me to see that he, the commandant, is running around free when I have to go around shackled to a guard. I asked many times why these things had to be done," Moll pleaded, "why they could not be stopped. I even asked Höss and he answered that he himself did not like them, but he himself had strict orders and nothing could be done about it. He, like the rest of us, suffered by this work and none of us were really sane any more."

"Is that right, Höss?" Brookhart asked him.

"Yes, others also said that, and already testified to that in the Reich."

"When do you think you lost your sanity, Höss?"

"I think you mean that just when our nerves started to crack," Höss amended. "I can testify that I was not healthy in 1942. There were strict orders and they had to be followed. Many of the others felt as I did, and subordinate leaders came to me in the same manner as Moll did and discussed it and they had the same feeling."

Two-thirds of the victims had generally been women and children, but in the transports from the Ukraine and Hungary the percentage of children had been particularly high and the work of extermination especially wearing on the SS and their Jewish *Sonderkommando*. Moll, soaked with alcohol, had not seemed to have any compunctions about his task at Auschwitz, but now raged: "Only the highest places in the Reich, the Reich government, Hitler, Himmler, von Ribbentrop, or the other bastards, could ever have ordered such things. I do not know just what these men are saying in their defense now, or if they claim today they know nothing of it, if they say that I don't have the faintest idea why they should be masters or representatives of the German people. Kaltenbrunner, Pohl, Schmauser, Himmler, or whatever their names may be, who sat in the high places, used us small people as tools to carry out their operations."

"Kaltenbrunner said that he knew nothing about this."

"I don't believe that."

"Kaltenbrunner is saying that today, what do you think of that?"

"You have to understand me, I was always a small man, he was a high officer. Now they are trying to leave us in the lurch, we have been condemned to death, now they may be exonerated. It is not only us that hate the name of Kaltenbrunner, but the name of Kaltenbrunner was terror for all of us, terror for all of Germany and terror for all of Europe. Kaltenbrunner was the right hand of Himmler. We had his people in every town, every village, and every hamlet. We used to call them Kaltenbrunner's commissars, they were everywhere; they were stationed there to listen. Kaltenbrunner would send his spies and suppress the people. I believe that now this man is saying he does not know any of this, but he must know all!"

Since the prosecution had concluded their case, they could not call Moll; but Kauffmann—as well as the attorneys for several other defendants —intended to have Höss corroborate that the secrecy attached to the Final Solution had been so great that Kaltenbrunner could not have known about it. It was like opening the floodgates of a dam to wash away the bloodstains of a murder; and of all the blunders committed by the defense it was probably the worst.

"Witness, your statements will have a far-reaching significance," Kauffmann initiated his questioning of Höss. "You are perhaps the only one who can throw some light upon certain hidden aspects, and who can tell which people gave the orders for the destruction of European Jewry, and can further state how this order was carried out and to what degree the execution was kept a secret."

Himmler, Höss averred, "told me that I was not even allowed to say anything about it to my immediate superior, *Gruppenführer* Glücks. This conference concerned the two of us only, and I was to observe the strictest secrecy."

"What was the position held by Glücks, whom you have just mentioned?" Kauffmann asked.

"*Gruppenführer* Glücks was, so to speak, the inspector of concentration camps at that time, and he was immediately subordinate to the Reichsführer."

Himmler, Höss said, had visited Auschwitz, and Eichmann had come repeatedly, but Kaltenbrunner had never been there.

"Did you ever talk to Kaltenbrunner with reference to your staff?"

"No, never."

"Is it right for me to assume that administration and feeding of concentration camps were exclusively under the control of the Main Economic and Administrative Office?"

"Yes."

"A department which is completely separated from the RSHA?"

"Quite correct."

Höss, anxious to justify the "correctness" of the concentration camp system, asserted: "These so-called ill treatments and this torturing in concentration camps, stories of which were spread everywhere among the people, and later by the prisoners that were liberated by the occupying armies, were not, as assumed, inflicted methodically, but were excesses committed by individual leaders, subleaders, and men who laid violent hands on internees."

In actuality, the atrocities had been inflicted methodically, and individuals had committed excesses because they were condoned, a fact that was later demonstrated graphically at the trial of Auschwitz personnel.*

Kauffmann's attempt to show that it was not Kaltenbrunner but Müller who, as head of the Gestapo, had been responsible for exterminations and executions was destroyed by Amen in cross-examination:

"Is it not a fact that all of these execution orders which you testify

*Some examples:

A dozen boys aged eight to fourteen had been brought to Auschwitz for stealing coal. When Himmler heard that they had been assigned to various men's barracks, he had agonized about the potential for immorality. The boys had been taken to the *Revier* (infirmary) and spritzed—injected with phenol. Thus, the morality of the camp had been preserved.

More than sixteen thousand Gypsies had been locked up in Auschwitz although, unlike the Jews, they had not been considered "enemies of the Reich," but merely out of place in the Nazi scheme of things. (Some men, either part or full Gypsies, serving in the Wehrmacht had returned home during the war to discover that their families had disappeared; others, even though wounded and decorated, had themselves been shipped off to concentration camps.) By August of 1944 the Gypsies had been reduced to four thousand in number. Because of the filth and starvation, they had been ravaged by diseases unknown to medicine since the Dark Ages. When Himmler had come to Auschwitz and seen children with grotesquely twisted bodies, with faces without noses and teeth protruding through skinless cheeks, he had taken pity. Everyone in the Gypsy compound was to be gassed, he had ordered, as a "humanitarian solution."

Interrogations had been conducted by means of the Boger Swing, devised by the SS man in charge of security, Wilhelm Boger. The victim had his hands and feet trussed together like a pig, and he or she had then been lifted on a pole that was placed across two bars. As the person dangled suspended with his head hanging down, he had been beaten on his buttocks and his sides until his bones were crushed, or until he "confessed." Frequently the victims had not known what to confess to, and Boger had not cared. The person could admit to anything he wanted—it was the "confession" that was important.

One excruciatingly painful method of execution had been death by starvation. Victims had been placed in standing cells constructed like cupboards in which it was impossible to sit or lie down, and had there been abandoned to waste away. Sometimes Boger had heightened the agony by forcing the prisoners to first eat a "Boger salad," a plate of highly salted and spiced herring, which added the tortures of thirst to those of starvation.

Medical experiments and the tanning of skin had taken place at Auschwitz as in other concentration camps. Max Kasner, a hospital orderly, recalled being detailed to a corpse removal squad one day: "On the left lay about seventy exceptionally beautiful dead women. The breasts of the dead women had been cut off, as had been the flesh from many parts of their bodies—the sides, for example. The yard sloped steeply and the drains were clogged with blood. We waded in blood over our ankles. You must keep in mind that we hospital aides were dressed in white. We looked like butchers."

were signed by Müller were also signed by order of, or as representative of, the chief of the RSHA, Kaltenbrunner?"

"Yes," Höss responded in his high-pitched, almost adolescent voice.

"In other words, Müller was merely signing as the representative of the chief of the RSHA, Kaltenbrunner? Is that not correct?"

"I must assume so."

With Höss nodding assent, his affidavit was introduced paragraph by paragraph: "I commanded Auschwitz until 1 December 1943, and estimate at least 2,500,000 victims were executed and exterminated there by gassing and burning, and at least another half million succumbed to starvation and disease, making a total dead of about 3,000,000. This figure represents about seventy or eighty percent of all persons sent to Auschwitz as prisoners.

"While Kaltenbrunner was chief of RSHA, orders for protective custody commitments, punishment, and individual executions were signed by Kaltenbrunner or by Müller, chief of the Gestapo, as Kaltenbrunner's deputy.

"Pohl, as chief of WVHA, and Kaltenbrunner, as chief of RSHA, often conferred personally and frequently communicated orally and in writing concerning concentration camps.

"The 'final solution of the Jewish question' meant the complete extermination of all Jews in Europe.

"Children of tender years were invariably exterminated since by reason of their youth they were unable to work. We were required to carry out these exterminations in secrecy but, of course, the foul and nauseating stench from the continued burning of bodies permeated the entire area, and all of the people living in the surrounding communities knew that exterminations were going on at Auschwitz."

Words dripped from Höss's mouth like tears of blood; he closed the circle of witnesses on the Final Solution. Goering's sarcastic scoffing of a few weeks earlier that it was technically impossible to kill so many people echoed hollowly and cynically. An English reporter told Carl Haensel, the assistant attorney for the SS, that it was incredible that the defense should have called such a witness: "You would have to sit a virgin with blue eyes on the witness stand after this to believe they could not be guilty."

The defense attorneys shuddered and were nauseated. "The contrast between Höss and his actions and the innocent posture of the defendants was all the more embarrassing," Haensel remarked. "It rained blood, one breathed ashes, the smell of burned corpses poisoned the atmosphere."

42 "A Thousand Years of Guilt": Rosenberg and Frank

After the tempest of Kaltenbrunner and Höss, the defense of Rosenberg was almost placid, despite the fact that Thoma called his client "an arrogant heathen."

"He ought to be glad I have *not* presented so many documents to show what a vicious anti-Semite he is," Thoma confided to Gilbert. "I have found the most damaging documents against him myself, and he ought to be glad that I have *not* presented them! I told him, 'For God's sake, Rosenberg, you want me to make them think that you disapprove of the extermination, and didn't know anything about it, and yet you want me to present the documents to show that the extermination was justified!' He makes me sick!"

"The old boy wants to talk about the philosophy of the French Revolution," Biddle commented wryly, after the tribunal rejected Rosenberg's request to trace the history of anti-Semitism. Fyfe, objecting to a number of witnesses Rosenberg wanted to call, remarked: "The only evidence is that Rosenberg wouldn't hurt a fly, and that the witnesses have seen him not hurting flies."

Rosenberg was a master of euphemism, a bureaucratic pedant, whose seemingly endless sentences snaked about, intertwined, and stuck to each other like overboiled spaghetti; even Thoma had difficulty deciphering his answers. By his rationalization, sophistry, and halfhearted attempts at justification of Nazi barbarism, he created, in his own fashion, as negative an impression as Kaltenbrunner.

"In regard to the extermination of one hundred and seventy thousand civilians, I cannot take any position as to what transpired in the police camps on grounds of police security," he asserted. "I would like to point out, however, that according to official statements of the indigenous administration, in the first place more than forty thousand Estonians in Estonia and more than forty thousand Latvians in Latvia were deported to the interior of Soviet Russia after the Red Army occupied these countries." He had never heard of more than two concentration camps, Oranienburg and Dachau, Rosenberg claimed, and Himmler had cheerfully invited him to inspect the latter: " 'Why don't you come to Dachau and take a look at things for yourself? We have a swimming pool there, we have sanitary installations—irreproachable; no objections can be raised.' " He had not, however, accepted, Rosenberg said. "I desisted for reasons of good taste; I simply did not want to look at people who had been deprived of their liberty."

Actions against the Jews had been justified by international law, according to Rosenberg: "It is a recognized principle of international law that, in war, reprisals may be taken by resorting to the same procedures and the same concepts as primarily used by the enemy. Since time immemorial the Jews have, in their Jewish laws codified in the Talmud, applied the principle that all non-Jews are to be considered as so much cattle, as outlaws; and the property of non-Jews should be dealt with as a thing which has been abandoned, that is to say, as derelict property."

It was, perhaps, fitting if specious that Rosenberg should cite the religious conflicts of medieval times in his attempt to justify the Nazi policies. On December 18, 1941, he had addressed himself to Hitler: "I beg the Führer to permit the seizure of all Jewish home furnishings of Jews in Paris who have fled or will leave shortly and those of Jews living in all parts of the occupied West to relieve the shortage of furnishings in the administration in the East."

The possessions of the Jews sent to concentration camps had been, in fact, employed for the benefit of German families who had been bombed out: "I received a mission from the Führer and while I was well aware that it was something quite exceptional and against the law," Rosenberg had related during one of his interrogations, "yet the situation in Germany was so terrible—"

"In other words you didn't concern yourself with its legal aspects; is that it?" Colonel Hinkel had asked.

"I admit that in this case."

He had thought it better to retaliate specifically against the Jews than against the French in general for acts of resistance. "I suggest to the Führer," he had written, "that, instead of executing one hundred Frenchmen, we shoot in their place one hundred Jewish bankers, lawyers, etc. It is the Jews in London and New York who incite the French Communists to commit acts of violence, and it seems only fair that the members of this race should pay for this. It is not the little Jews but the leading Jews in France who should be held responsible."

In court, Rosenberg attributed his recommendation to an error of judgment. Dodd, cross-examining him, tried to pin him down:

"You said you thought that was what? A little bad judgment, or not quite just, or something of the kind? Is that right?"

"I stated that it was humanly unjust."

"It was murder, isn't that what it was, a plan for murder? Yes or no?"

"No. But I consider the shooting of hostages, which was publicly made known by the Armed Forces, as an obviously generally accepted fact under the exceptional conditions of war."

Rosenberg repeatedly complained about the translation back and forth between German and Russian. Regarding the *Ausrottung* of the Jews, he quibbled over the semantics: "We are speaking here of extermination of Jewry; there is also still a difference between 'Jewry' and 'the Jews.'"

"I asked you if it was not a fact that at that time and later on Jews were being exterminated in the Occupied Eastern Territories which were under your ministry?" Dodd persisted. "Will you answer that yes or no?"

"Yes."

"I think you will agree that in the Ukraine your man Koch was doing all kinds of terrible things, and now I don't understand that you dispute that Lohse and Kube were helping to eliminate or liquidate the Jews, and that Bräutigam, an important member of your staff, and that Leibbrandt, another important member of your staff, were informed of the program. So that five people at least under your administration were engaged in this kind of conduct, and not small people at that."

When Rosenberg started to reply tangentially, Lawrence intervened: "Will you answer the question first? Do you agree that these five people were engaged in exterminating Jews?"

"Yes. They knew about a certain number of liquidations of Jews. That I admit, and they have told me so, or if they did not, I have heard it from other sources."

Rosenberg had planned the pillage and exploitation of Russia, he had projected that millions upon millions of people would die as a result, he had been informed early of the brutal slaughter of all kinds of men under the Commissar Order, and even when he had objected to the insensate barbarism because it was bad politics he had not had the spine to take action.

"I did not see in Adolf Hitler a tyrant," Rosenberg told the court, "but like many millions of National Socialists I trusted him personally on the strength of the experience of a fourteen-year-long struggle. I served Adolf Hitler loyally, and what the party may have done during those years, that was supported by me too."

In a conversation with Fritzsche he was even more emphatic: "No matter how often I go over everything in my mind, I still cannot believe that there was a single flaw in that man's character."

On the surface, there was a stark difference between Frank and the defendants who had preceded him. He was the first of the accused to reject and denounce Hitler. He had Goering's cunning and intelligence, and Hitler's ability to assess an audience and play to it. While Keitel and Rosenberg had sat rigidly erect in the witness box and Kaltenbrunner had crouched tensely, Frank seemed relaxed, his keen black eyes scanning the entire room. Lawrence had made it clear during Rosenberg's appearance, chiding prosecution and defense alike, that the tribunal was tired of prolixity, repetition, and irrelevancies; so Frank answered questions fairly succinctly.

Beyond and beneath his sense of theater, however, Frank was only marginally different from the others. Forced into speaking the truth by the twelve thousand pages of his journal, he nevertheless resorted to mendacity whenever he thought he would not be caught.

To Seidl's question, "Did you ever participate in the annihilation of Jews?" Frank responded: "I say yes; and the reason why I say yes is because, having lived through the five months of this trial, and particularly after having heard the testimony of the witness Höss, my conscience does not allow me to throw the responsibility solely on these minor people. I myself have never installed an extermination camp for Jews, or promoted the existence of such camps; but if Adolf Hitler personally has laid that dreadful responsibility on his people, then it is mine too, for we have fought against Jewry for years; and we have indulged in the most horrible utterances—my own diary bears witness against me. Therefore, it is no more than my duty to answer your question in this connection with 'yes.' A thousand years will pass and still this guilt of Germany will not have been erased!"

Frank made it seem as if he were voluntarily taking the burden upon his shoulders out of a sense of duty and noblesse oblige, while, in actuality, he had been involved in all phases of Jewish existence and its extermination, and his remarks on the Final Solution might have filled a volume by themselves.

Biddle, who called his statement "a cheap dramatic confession," and the other judges were not fooled.

All Frank could do now was to assert that his utterances had exceeded his atrocities: "Some of the words are terrible. I myself must admit that I was shocked at many of the words which I had used. It was a wild and stormy period filled with terrible passions, and when a whole country is on fire and a life and death struggle is going on, such words may easily be used."

The one point Frank could cite in his favor was that he had fought a running battle against Himmler, and in 1942 had spoken out against the SS state. (The prosecution failed to point out that in so doing Frank had merely been trying to protect himself against charges of corruption by

Himmler.*) "Without law—or contrary to law—no German Reich is conceivable," Frank stated. "It is intolerable that a state should be able to deprive a member of the community of honor, liberty, life, and property, declare him an outlaw, and condemn him without first giving him the opportunity to reply to the accusations made against him. . . . If justice is not supported, the state loses its moral foundation. It sinks into the abyss of darkness and horror. . . . The Police State must never exist. Never!"

Lawrence, addressing himself to the critical point, asked: "Dr. Seidl, are there any passages in these documents which express the opinion that the same principles ought to be applied to others than fellow Germans?"

The answer, of course, was in the negative.

Frank's testimony precipitated a storm of dissension among his fellow defendants. "According to your diary, you damned well knew what was happening!" Fritzsche accosted him when he returned from the stand. "It would have been more honorable to say so, and not to try to hide among the millions of our nation whom you are trying to burden with a thousand years of guilt."

43   The Venomous Vulgarian: Streicher

Of all the defendants, the one who most typified the stormtrooper was Julius Streicher, the former Gauleiter of Nuremberg. One of nine children he had, like his father, become a schoolteacher at the age of eighteen. Six years later, in 1909, he had been assigned to an elementary school in a working-class district of Nuremberg. During World War I he had risen from lance corporal to lieutenant—an extraordinary advance in the Imperial Army, where officers were a breed apart—and received several decorations, including the Iron Cross First Class.

After the war he had started a right-wing working-class movement in Nuremberg. As a speaker able to rouse the masses, he had been second only to Hitler. His group, actually, had been more numerous than the National Socialists when, in 1921, Streicher had taken them into the Nazi Party in a body.

As a leader in his own right, Streicher had maintained a certain independence and had been one of the few men on familiar *"du"* terms

*Himmler had had one of Frank's principal subordinates, Dr. Karl Lasch, governor of Radom, arrested for corruption. After several weeks of intensive questioning, Lasch had broken down and, in order to save himself, made a confession, implicating Frank. Himmler had thereupon had Lasch transported to Auschwitz, where he had been given a pistol with one shot and instructed to commit suicide.

with Hitler. Even while continuing to work as a schoolteacher, he had
begun publishing a small-time scandal sheet, *Der Stürmer*. A parody of *True
Confessions*, its formula had consisted of tales in which golden-haired German girls are menaced by swarthy and lecherous (but rich) Jews. One of
the excerpts from Streicher's writings introduced by the prosecution declared:

"The male sperm in cohabitation is partially or completely absorbed
by the female and thus enters her bloodstream. One single cohabitation of
a Jew with an Aryan woman is sufficient to poison her blood forever.
Never again will she be able to bear purely Aryan children, even when
married to an Aryan. They will all be bastards.

"Now we know why the Jew uses every artifice of seduction in order
to ravish German girls at as early an age as possible; why the Jewish doctor
rapes his female patients while they are under anesthetic . . ."

Though Hitler had delighted in Streicher's vulgarity, no one had
taken *Der Stürmer* seriously except the pubescent youth and harried house-
wives for whom it represented daring reading.

Since Streicher was abhorred by the Nationalists, Hitler had kept him
away from Berlin, and Streicher had never attained national power. In
Nuremberg, on the other hand, he had operated like a cross between a
feudal lord and an old-fashioned machine boss. In addition to the numerous offices he maintained about the city, he had held court in taverns and
beer halls. People had been hired and fired at his word. His reach had
extended into every government department, including the police and the
courts. At the Palace of Justice, where he had frequently been an accused
in libel cases, he had interrupted trials with speeches, and influenced the
outcome. Once he had even stormed into the office of the police president
of Nuremberg and threatened to thrash him, whereupon the official had
vowed to shoot him dead on the spot.

No one in Nuremberg had dared oppose him openly, including his
bitter enemy, the *Höhere SS und Polizeiführer*. Circulation of *Der Stürmer*,
which had never been more than a few thousand before 1935, had soared
to 600,000 after Streicher hired a promotion director. A renegade Jew,
Jonas Wolk, had been employed to research Hebrew writings and purported Jewish atrocities of the Middle Ages. These had been sensationalized in every issue. From sales of *Der Stürmer* and "voluntary payments"
extorted from businesses, Streicher's income had ballooned to over a million marks a year.

A sexually obsessed sadist who always carried a whip and frequently
used it, Streicher had occasionally conducted inquiries into the practices
of adolescent boys. When one youngster had not known what he meant by
"masturbation," Streicher had provided him with a graphic description,

followed by a whipping. The Gauleiter was so proud of his own sexual prowess, including his nocturnal emissions, that he had been known to save the semen for display. He had had several mistresses, and a network of informants among Nuremberg's prostitutes and lowlife.

Between Streicher the vulgarian and Goering the venal sybarite there had been an antipathy exacerbated by Goering's ownership of Veldenstein and his periodic visits to Nuremberg. At the time of Goering's marriage to Emma, *Der Stürmer* had published a photograph of her shopping at a Jewish store—it had been a dig not only at Emma's numerous Jewish friends, but Goering's own relationship to Epenstein. Three years later, when Emma was awaiting the birth of her child, Streicher had suggested the possibility that the pregnancy was a product of artificial insemination. Such an allegation had gone beyond the permissible in the Nazis' inner feuds; and the hierarchy had waited for Streicher to take a misstep. This had come on the heels of the *Kristallnacht*.

Throughout the Gau the Jews' property had been confiscated at ten percent or less of its value. One or another of the Nazi leaders had either obtained title or wound up with the profits from the transactions. Streicher himself had extorted industrial shares worth 112,000 marks from a Jewish banker who had been arrested.

This was precisely the kind of malfeasance that Goering, arrogating the right to the spoils for himself, had prohibited. Various Nuremberg agencies, including the SS and Gestapo, had forwarded reports to Goering. Goering and Hess had persuaded Hitler, with great difficulty, that the charges must be investigated. Hess had suspended Streicher from his position as Gauleiter. Goering had convened a commission which, in view of Streicher's predilection for adolescents, had placed the investigation in the hands of Josef Meisinger, head of the Gestapo's Office for the Suppression of Homosexuality. Among the specifications against the man who for fifteen years had accused the Jews of sacrificing Christian children had been a complaint of child murder. (Streicher had managed to pin this on one of his lieutenants, who had committed suicide.) After a four-month investigation and a trial before the Supreme Party Court, Streicher had been found guilty of most of the charges.* He had been ostracized and removed from all his party offices, but permitted to continue as publisher of *Der Stürmer*.

After he was incarcerated at the Palace of Justice, Streicher became the talk of the jail. He loved to attract an audience by performing exercises

---

*Included was one that he had ordered his subordinates to turn in their wedding rings so he could have them fashioned into a gift for Hitler's fiftieth birthday, but instead had used the gold to have a brooch made for his girl friend.

in the nude in his cell. He washed his face and brushed his teeth in the toilet bowl, a practice that might have given those Germans who considered the Russians barbarians for engaging in the same custom pause for reflection.

Hitler's onetime adjutant, Fritz Wiedemann, observed: "Streicher is either insane or a very great criminal. I rather think the former is the case."

Streicher's lawyer, sixty-three-year-old Hans Marx, suspected likewise. Prior to the start of the trial he had requested "that the tribunal consider whether a psychiatric examination of the defendant Streicher would not be proper. I deem it necessary as a precaution in my own interest, since my client does not desire examination of this sort, and is of the opinion that he is mentally completely normal. I myself cannot determine that; it must be decided by a psychiatrist."

Colonel Pokrovsky, the assistant Soviet prosecutor, had supported Marx. Streicher had told Pokrovsky, as he did everyone else, that he was really a Zionist at heart. This led Pokrovsky to observe: "This testimony immediately produced certain doubts as to the mental stability of the defendant." Pokrovsky thought that Streicher was probably shamming: "It is not the first time that persons now standing trial have attempted to delude us about their mental condition." An examination should be conducted immediately, Pokrovsky had urged, "to establish definitely whether he is or is not in full possession of his mental capacities."

During the examination by American, French, and Russian psychiatrists, Streicher at one point had been asked to undress. When the attractive Russian interpreter had stepped to the door and turned her back, Streicher had jeered: "What's the matter? Are you afraid of seeing something nice?"

The commission had concluded that Streicher, though an obsessed and compulsive neurotic, was not psychotic; and Lawrence ruled that he was fit to stand trial.

The charges against Streicher were presented by Lieutenant Colonel J. M. Griffith-Jones of the British prosecution: "It may be that this defendant is less directly involved in the physical commission of crimes against Jews. The submission of the prosecution is that his crime is no less the worse for that reason. No government in the world, before the Nazis came to power, could have embarked upon and put into effect a policy of mass extermination without having a people who would back them and support them. It was to the task of educating people, of producing murderers, educating and poisoning them with hate, that Streicher set himself. In the early days he was preaching persecution. As persecution took place he preached extermination and annihilation; and, as we have seen in the ghettos of the East, as millions of Jews were being exterminated and annihilated, he cried out for more and more.

"That is the crime that he has committed. It is the submission of the prosecution that he made these things possible—made these crimes possible—which could never have happened had it not been for him and for those like him. Without him, the Kaltenbrunners, the Himmlers, the General Stroops would have had nobody to carry out their orders. The effect of this man's crimes, of the poison that he has injected into the minds of millions and millions of young boys and girls and young men and women lives on. He leaves behind him a legacy of almost a whole people poisoned with hate, sadism, and murder, and perverted by him."

"I did not intend to advocate or to inflame but to enlighten," Streicher responded. "We educated no murderers. The content of the articles which I wrote could not have educated murderers. What happened during the war—well, I certainly did not educate the Führer. The Führer issued the order on his own initiative."

The conflict between Streicher and Marx was, if anything, more acerbic than that between Kaltenbrunner and Kauffmann, or Rosenberg and Thoma. "My defense counsel has not conducted and was not in a position to conduct my defense in the way I wanted," Streicher, who had suffered a mild heart attack in the courtroom on January 24, complained immediately after taking his oath. Marx, Streicher claimed, was being intimidated by commentary in the press and on the radio: "The announcer said, 'There are camouflaged Nazis and anti-Semites among the defendants' counsel.' That these terroristic attacks were made with the intention of intimidating the defendants' counsel is clear. I wish to say that I have not been afforded the possibility of making an unhampered and just defense before this International Military Tribunal."

Marx at once became extremely excited and concerned with justifying himself: "As attorney and as defense counsel of a defendant I have to reserve for myself the right how I shall conduct the defense. If Herr Streicher is of the opinion that I am incapable, or not in a position to conduct his defense, then he should ask for another defense counsel. I am not terrorized by any journalist."

Lawrence, expressing the full confidence of the court in Marx, tried to calm him, but the contention and bickering between Marx and Streicher continued. Turning to an issue of Der Stürmer that had accused the Jews of ritual murder, Marx inquired: "Why did you now in 1935 stir up again this doubtlessly very grave issue?"

"I should like to ask my counsel to express no judgment as to what I have written," Streicher objected. "To question me, but not to express judgment. The prosecution are going to do that."

This, naturally, set Marx off again, and a few minutes passed before the proceedings settled down, and Streicher answered: "That ritual murder issue [of *Der Stürmer*] refers to court files which are located in Rome. There are pictures in it which show that in twenty-three cases the Church itself has dealt with this question. The Church has canonized twenty-three non-Jews killed by ritual murder. But in this connection I should like to say that we never wanted to assert that all Jewry was ready now to commit ritual murders. But it is a fact that within Jewry there exists a sect which engages in these murders, and has done so up until the present."

This was more than Jackson could stand. Chief Justice Stone had collapsed and died the previous week, everyone was aware that Jackson was one of the principal candidates to succeed him, and that a bitter struggle was taking shape between Jackson's proponents and opponents. (It was suggested that if Jackson were elevated to the chief justiceship, Parker would get Jackson's place as an associate justice, but Parker noted, "I am not building any hopes on getting the appointment.") Jackson felt more than ever that every aspect of the trial was under microscopic scrutiny and might tip the balance for him or against him. Wishing to squelch Streicher, he injected himself quite irrelevantly into the dispute between Streicher and his counsel: "Now this is not an orderly way to make charges against the Jewish people. It seems to me that, having appointed counsel to conduct his case, he has shown repeatedly that he is not willing to conduct his case in an orderly manner and he ought to be returned to his cell and any further statements that he wishes to make to this court transmitted to his counsel in writing. This [Streicher's allegation regarding ritual murder] is entirely unfair and in contempt of court."

Streicher, actually, despite his argumentativeness, was sticking more to the point than most of the defendants who had preceded him, and Lawrence did not deem Jackson's suggestion that he should be hustled back to his cell worthy of comment. "Dr. Marx, I think you had better continue," he directed the attorney.

The point at issue was whether Streicher had promoted the extermination of the Jews. Had he learned of their fate in the East, and then continued to urge their *Vernichtung?*

" 'Never since the beginning of the world and the creation of man has there been a nation which dared to fight against the nation of bloodsuckers and extortionists who, for a thousand years, have spread all over the world. It was left to our Movement to expose the eternal Jew as a mass murderer,' " Griffith-Jones quoted Streicher's writings to him. "Is it right that for fourteen years you have been repeating, 'German people, learn to recognize your true enemy' and in doing so, is it true that you had been preaching religious hatred?"

"No, it is not preaching hatred; it is just a statement of fact."

" 'There must be a punitive expedition against the Jews in Russia,' " Griffith-Jones quoted from a May 1939 article in *Der Stürmer*, " 'a punitive expedition which will provide the same fate for them that every murderer and criminal must expect, death sentence and execution. The Jews in Russia must be killed. They must be utterly exterminated. Then the world will see that the end of the Jews is also the end of bolshevism.' Do I understand you to say now, to have said in the evidence, that you never knew that Jews were being exterminated in thousands and millions in the Eastern Territories? Did you never know that?"

"No."

Streicher testified that he had been a reader of the *Israelitisches Wochenblatt (Israel Weekly)* published in Switzerland, and Griffith-Jones challenged him: "Are you really saying that those copies of the *Israelitisches Wochenblatt*, which you and your editors were reading, contained nothing except for a hint of disappearance, with no mention of figures or murder? Is that what you are telling this tribunal?"

"Yes, I stick to that, certainly."

Strictly speaking, Streicher was telling the truth. For although the Jewish paper had begun to report the methodical extermination of Jews in 1941 and 1942, it had not been until the distribution of the Weczler-Vrba report and the capture of Maidanek by the Russians in the summer of 1944 that the full truth and the details of the Final Solution had become known.

Link by link, nevertheless, Griffith-Jones tightened the chain around Streicher. In the spring of 1943 an article in *Der Stürmer* had declared: "When Adolf Hitler stepped before the German people twenty years ago to submit to them the National Socialist demands which point the way into the future, he also made the promise which was to have the gravest repercussions: that of freeing the world from its Jewish tormentors. How wonderful it is to know that this great man and leader is following up this promise with practical action. It will be the greatest deed in the history of mankind."

In May of 1943, Streicher's paper had carried a firsthand report from the Jewish ghettos: "*Der Stürmer* sent its photographic reporter to various ghettos in the East. Nothing can surprise him easily. But what our contributor saw in these ghettos was a unique experience for him. He wrote, 'What my eyes and my Leica camera saw here convinced me that the Jews are not human beings but children of the devil and the spawn of crimes. . . . It is hard to see how it was possible that the scum of humanity was for centuries looked upon as God's chosen people by the non-Jews. . . . This satanic race really has no right to exist.' "

"Now," Griffith-Jones demanded, "you have heard of what was happening in the ghettos in the East during 1942 and 1943? Are you telling this tribunal that your photographer went with his camera to those ghettos and found out nothing about the mass murder of Jews?"

"Yes, otherwise he would have reported to us about it."

Griffith-Jones turned to August 1943, and again quoted *Der Stürmer:*

"The Swiss Jewish newspaper [*Israelitisches Wochenblatt*] goes on to say, 'The Jews of Europe, with the exception of those in England and of insignificant Jewish communities in the few neutral countries, have disappeared, so to speak. The Jewish reservoir of the East that was able to counterbalance the force of assimilation in the West no longer exists.'

" 'This is not a Jewish lie; it is really true that the Jews have, so to speak, disappeared from Europe, and that the Jewish reservoir of the East from which the Jewish pestilence spread for centuries among the European nations has ceased to exist.' "

"The word 'disappear,' after all," Streicher retorted, "does not mean extermination en masse."

"Very well." Griffith-Jones went on to the edition of March 2, 1944: " 'Eternal night must come over the born criminal race of Jews so that eternal day may bless awakening non-Jewish mankind.' "

"That is an anti-Semitic play of words," Streicher said jauntily.

"It may be an anti-Semitic play of words, but the only meaning it can have is murder. Is that not true?"

"No."

"You know, do you not, even if you do not believe the full figures, that millions of Jews have been murdered since the beginning of the war? Do you know that? You have heard the evidence, have you not?"

"Yes," Streicher agreed. "I have to say, the only evidence for me is the testament of the Führer. There he states that the mass executions took place upon his orders. That I believe. Now I believe it."

As defense witnesses, Streicher called Ernst Hiemer, an editor of *Der Stürmer,* and Friedrich Strobel, a Nuremberg jurist. Streicher had declared, "I first heard of the mass murders and mass killings at Mondorf," but Hiemer contradicted him. "Streicher at first refused to credit these reports in the Swiss press and called them premeditated lies. He declared that these reports were being printed merely for the purpose of undermining the prestige of the German people abroad. It is true Streicher soon changed his opinion. He began to doubt that his opinion was right and finally he believed that the occurrences in concentration camps, as pictured in the Swiss press, did after all correspond to the fact. Streicher said that Himmler was the only man who could have authorized such crimes."

"And when was that, approximately?" Marx inquired.

"I cannot give you the exact date, but I believe it was in the middle of 1944."

Nevertheless, after that, in the September 14, 1944 issue, *Der Stürmer* had editorialized, "Bolshevism cannot be vanquished. It must be destroyed. The same is true of Judaism. It cannot be vanquished, disarmed, or rendered powerless. It must be exterminated."

Strobel, seeming more like a prosecution than a defense witness, testified that at a meeting in Nuremberg on December 3, 1938, Streicher had declared that it was "impossible to fight a power like world Jewry" with outrages like those of the *Kristallnacht.* "I wondered at the time whether Streicher really had a lucid interval and realized how harmful that anti-Jewish action was," Strobel commented, "or whether merely his vanity was wounded, or whether he felt that a too quick radical extermination of the Jews would put an end also to his own importance."

44 *An Irregular Witness: Frick and Schacht*

Aside from Hess, the only defendant not to take the stand was Wilhelm Frick. Believing that the prosecution had introduced little evidence linking him directly to War Crimes or Crimes Against Humanity, Frick, taking into consideration the experiences of the other defendants on the stand and his own during interrogation, decided that the safest course was not to subject himself to cross-examination.

The prosecution accused him of being the Nazis' "administrative brain," but Frick believed that in drawing up and signing Hitler's laws he had done nothing wrong, since the legislation had been legally approved by the cabinet. Evasive, excitable, forgetful, and maudlin, he had protested at an interrogation that he had played no part in Goering's anti-Jewish laws following the *Kristallnacht:* "I was passive in the whole affair, and I just signed the law. It would not have made any difference if I signed the law or not." Prior to his indictment, he had pleaded: "At my age of almost sixty-nine years, I simply couldn't be considered a dangerous person, and wonder whether it would not be possible to consider my release."

Robert Kempner, for the prosecution, had linked Frick with the euthanasia program because the Interior Ministry had had jurisdiction over nursing homes and asylums. "In fact," Kempner said, "the defendant Frick not only had jurisdiction over these establishments, but he was one of the originators of a secret law organizing the murdering."

In this, the prosecution was, of course, wrong, since Hitler had initiated the program with nothing more than a few words to Bouhler and Brandt; Frick had been entirely bypassed. A German tribunal, the Berlin Court of Assizes, had already ruled that no legislation had ever been enacted, and had consequently sentenced two participants in the killings to death.* But since Frick made no attempt to refute the charge, the impression of Frick's involvement stuck in the minds of the judges and ultimately had considerable influence on their verdict.

The point on which several interrogators had hammered at Frick was that, as minister of the interior, he had had jurisdiction over Himmler. Repeatedly Frick had denied that this was so.

"You were responsible for all the conduct and conditions in every concentration camp throughout the Reich as minister of the interior, were you not?" Thomas Dodd had challenged.

"Unfortunately not. It completely escaped my control," Frick had replied.

"Whether it escaped your control or not, wasn't Himmler under you?"

"Formally yes, but he made himself completely independent because he was always in the entourage of the Führer."

"I know. You always answer by saying it was done by Himmler. You knew about his camps and his treatment of people who were confined in those camps."

"No, that is not so. Whenever I got complaints about conditions in concentration camps and I tried to make investigations, I was told this is not a government matter. It is a party matter. Concentration camps did not even appear in a state budget. They were part of the SS budget."

In an effort to prove that he had had no control over Himmler, Frick called as his only witness Hans Bernd Gisevius, whose appearance was one of the most irregular of any trial ever held.

A fervent Nationalist, Gisevius, after passing his law examination in 1933, had joined the Gestapo. Caught in the intrigues and infighting between the Gestapo, the SS, and the SA in 1934, he had incurred the wrath of Gestapo Chief Rudolf Diels, who at one time had even issued a warrant for his arrest. Escaping into the national Ministry of Interior, Gisevius had become Frick's expert on the Gestapo. When Frick had attempted to curb the abuses relating to protective custody orders, Gisevius's machinations had earned him the enmity of Heydrich. From 1935 to 1936 he had worked in the Berlin criminal police under the venal police president of the city, Graf von Helldorf. During this time he had met Schacht, and ingratiated himself with the financier by debugging his home of the listening devices planted by the SD.

Gisevius had thus been drawn into the ring of the conservative opposition. At the start of the war he had been absorbed into the Abwehr, where

---

*Several others had been convicted and condemned to death in the Hadamar trial, where the prosecutor was Leon Jaworski, subsequently to gain fame in the Watergate scandal.

Colonel Hans Oster, Admiral Wilhelm Canaris's deputy, had operated at the nerve center of the conspiracy. Two years later Gisevius had been posted, ostensibly as vice-consul but actually as a military intelligence officer, to Zurich, Switzerland. In 1943 he had made contact with Allen Dulles and tried to sell him on the idea of a western accommodation with the conspirators in order to keep the Soviets out of Germany.

A few days prior to the attempted assassination of Hitler on July 20, 1944, Gisevius, scheduled to become head of the new government's Reichs-kommissariat for Purgation and Restoration of Public Order—more commonly known as the police—had returned to Germany. After the failure of the plot, he had gone underground and eventually made his way back to Switzerland with forged papers supplied to him by Dulles.

Together with his fellow conspirator, Count Fabian von Schlabren-dorff—who had miraculously survived after being tortured by the Gestapo and sentenced to be executed—Gisevius, under the direction of Major Monigan, had helped prepare the indictment and gather the evidence against Goering, Keitel, Kaltenbrunner, Ribbentrop, and several other defendants. At a time in August and September when the prosecutors had been striving to educate themselves and organize the mass of documents into a coherent case, Gisevius and Schlabrendorff had provided invaluable guidance and assistance.

No one but Jackson and a few key members of his staff were, of course, aware of the role Gisevius had played in the preparation of the case; and Jackson only compounded the deception when later, upon initiating his "cross-examination" of Gisevius, he offered:

"The tribunal should perhaps know your relations with the prosecution. Is it not a fact that within two months of the surrender of Germany I met you at Wiesbaden, and you related to me your experiences in the conspiracy?"

"Yes," Gisevius replied.

"And you were later brought here and after coming here you were interrogated by the prosecution, as well as by the counsel for Frick and for Schacht?"

"Yes."

That was as far as Jackson's moiety of revelation went in a trial in which one of the key issues was the casuistry of the Nazi regime.

Although the truth lay beyond their ken, several of the defendants, most notably Goering, anticipated Gisevius's testimony with great unease. In his recently published book, *Kampf bis zum Letzen* (entitled *To the Bitter End* in the United States), Gisevius, who blamed the Reichsmarshal for the thwarting of his career, characterized Goering as a "blood-drenched scoundrel." Quartered in the Guest House, Gisevius was irate to find his old antagonist, Diels, a celebrity there. How could Schacht be imprisoned and Diels, playing Casanova and hobnobbing with newsmen at the Faber Castle, have the run of Nuremberg, Gisevius demanded to know!

From the moment he took the stand, Gisevius seemed more a prosecution witness against Goering than a defense witness for Frick. His replies to Frick's unexceptional and easygoing lawyer, Otto Pannenbecker, were lengthier and more tangential than the responses of Goering or Streicher, but Lawrence was inclined to let him narrate as he wished. Describing the events of 1933 and 1934, Gisevius declared: "It was the Prussian minister of the interior, Goering, who considered this secret state police as his special preserve. During those months nothing happened in this office which was not known or ordered by Goering personally. The defendant Goering gave the Political Police so-called open warrants for murder, with which all that had to be done was to fill in the names of those who were to be murdered."

Gisevius wandered from one thing to another and touched briefly on the Reichstag fire and the Röhm purge. After having been on the stand somewhat less than an hour, he introduced the subject of the war minister, Blomberg. "I intentionally mention Blomberg's name, and ask to be permitted to pause here to tell the tribunal about an incident which occurred this morning. I was in the room of the defendants' counsel and was speaking to Dr. Dix. Dr. Dix was interrupted by Dr. Stahmer, counsel for Goering. I heard what Dr. Stahmer told Dr. Dix—"

"May I ask whether a personal conversation which I had with Dr. Dix has anything to do with the taking of evidence?" Stahmer materialized at the lectern.

"I am not speaking—" Gisevius tried to go on.

Lawrence intervened: "Witness, don't go on with your evidence while the objection is being made. Yes, Dr. Stahmer."

"I do not know whether it is in order when giving evidence to reveal a conversation which I had with Dr. Dix in the defense counsels' room."

"May I say something to that?" Gisevius interposed.

"Will you kindly keep silent." Lawrence peered at him over his glasses.

"May I finish my statement?"

"Will you keep silent, sir!"

"This morning in the room of the defense counsel," Stahmer resumed, "I had a personal conversation with Dr. Dix concerning the Blomberg case. That conversation was not intended to be heard by the witness."

"This incident has been reported to me," Jackson injected himself, "and I think it is important that this tribunal know the influence—the threats that were made at this witness in this courthouse while waiting to testify here, threats not only against him but against the defendant Schacht. I ask that this tribunal allow Dr. Gisevius, who is the one representative of democratic forces in Germany, to take this stand to tell his story."

The tale as it unfolded—though blown considerably out of proportion—generated a sensation. Everyone in the courtroom was agog as Stahmer continued: "Goering told me that it was of no interest to him if the witness Gisevius did incriminate him, but that he did not want Blomberg, who died recently*—and I assumed it was only the question of Blomberg's marriage—he, Goering, did not want these facts concerning the marriage of Blomberg to be discussed here in public. He merely wanted the deceased Blomberg to be spared. If Schacht did not prevent that—I was speaking only of Schacht—then he, Goering, in his turn, would have no consideration for Schacht—would no longer have any consideration for Schacht. That is what I told Dr. Dix for reasons of personal etiquette."

Dix's version sounded more menacing: "My colleague, Stahmer, approached me and said he would like to speak to me. I replied that at the moment I was having an important and urgent conversation with Gisevius and asked whether it could wait. Stahmer said 'No,' and that he must speak to me at once. I then took my colleague Stahmer aside. He said to me, 'Listen, Goering has an idea that Gisevius will attack him as much as he can. If he attacks the dead Blomberg, however, then Goering will disclose everything against Schacht—and he knows lots of things about Schacht which may not be pleasant for Schacht.' I could only interpret that information to mean that I should notify Gisevius of this development promised by Goering. Why should he [Stahmer] inform me at that time, unless he meant that the mischief hinted at and threatened by Goering might possibly be avoided—in other words, that the witness Gisevius, on whom everything depended, should think twice before making his statement? I did not have the slightest doubt that what Stahmer meant by his words to me was that I should convey them to Gisevius."

Goering had blundered terribly. Beyond the fact that he could not, since his day as a witness was past, have done anything to harm Schacht, he had, by attempting to silence Gisevius, revealed himself as the man of machination and intimidation that he was charged with being, and so made Gisevius's account all the more credible.

Gisevius returned to his testimony: "The whole thing gave me the feeling that I was under pressure. I know quite well why Goering does not want me to speak about that affair. To my thinking, it is the most corrupt thing Goering ever did, and Goering is just using the cloak of chivalry by pretending that he wants to protect a dead man, whereas he really wants

---

*Blomberg had succumbed in the witness wing at Nuremberg six weeks previously.

to prevent me from testifying in full on an important point—that is, the Fritsch crisis."

Turning, momentarily, from the Blomberg-Fritsch crisis, Gisevius asserted that he and Frick had attempted to combat and control Himmler and the Gestapo through the Ministry of the Interior, but had been foiled by Goering. "It was Goering who forbade Himmler to answer, and who protected Himmler when he refused to give any information in reply to our inquiries."

Having given Gisevius the opportunity to excoriate Goering, Pannenbecker concluded his questioning without materially benefiting the defense of Frick.

Dix then took over the microphone on behalf of Schacht. Until 1936, Gisevius said, Schacht had held the opinion "that Goering was the conservative strongman whose services one ought to use, and could use, to oppose the terror of the Gestapo and the State by establishing orderly conditions. I contradicted Schacht vehemently regarding his views about the defendant Goering. I warned him. I told him that in my opinion Goering was the worst of all, precisely because he was hiding under the middle-class conservative cloak. I implored him not to effect his economic policy with Goering, since this could only come to a bad end.

"Schacht—for whom much may be said, but not that he is a good psychologist—denied this emphatically. Only then in the course of 1936 he began to realize more and more that Goering was not supporting him against the party, but that Goering supported the radical elements against him, only then did Schacht's attitude begin to change gradually, and he came to regard not only Himmler but also Goering as a great danger."

On the afternoon of the second day of Gisevius's appearance, Jackson initiated his "cross-examination."

"Now, was the defendant Frick fully informed as to the facts which you know about the illegal conduct of the Gestapo?" Jackson asked.

"Yes. I had to submit to him all the material that arrived which was important."

"Now, was Frick informed of your conclusions about the Röhm purge?"

"Yes, because on the Sunday, while the murders were continuing, I spoke to Frick about the murders of Strasser, Klausner, Schleicher, and the many other murders; and Frick was particularly disgusted at the murder of Strasser,* because he considered that an act of personal revenge by Goering and Himmler."

*Gregor Strasser, leader of the Nazi left-wing faction, had ranked second in the party to Hitler until December 1932, when he had resigned following a dispute with Hitler and Goering over the advisability of the Nazis' joining a proposed Schleicher cabinet.

"But when Frick signed the decree, along with Hitler, declaring these murders legitimate and ordering no prosecutions on account of those murders, Frick knew exactly what had happened from you; is that the fact?"

"He knew it from me, and he had seen it for himself."

"And then came Kaltenbrunner." Jackson bridged the years. "Did you notice any improvement after the appointment of Kaltenbrunner?"

"Kaltenbrunner came and things became worse from day to day. More and more we learned that perhaps the impulsive actions of a murderer like Heydrich were not so bad as the cold, legal logic of a lawyer who took over the administration of such a dangerous instrument as the Gestapo. These gentlemen lunched together, and Nebe* often came to me from such luncheons so completely exhausted that he had a nervous breakdown."

"Now, I want to ask you some questions about the defendant Keitel. Of course, we have heard that Hitler was the actual head of the state, but I want to ask whether Keitel occupied a position of real leadership and power in the Reich."

"Keitel occupied one of the most influential positions in the Third Reich. I would like to say at this point that I was a very close friend of four of the closest collaborators of Keitel. It may be that Keitel did not influence Hitler to a great extent. But I must testify here to the fact that Keitel influenced the OKW and the army all the more."

To each of Jackson's questions, whether Keitel had received reports on "a systematic program of murder of the insane," "the persecution and the murder of the Jews," "the atrocities that were committed in Poland against the Poles," or "the forced enslavement of millions of foreign workers," Gisevius snapped "*Jawohl*" ("Yes, indeed"), as if he were mentally clicking his heels.

Biddle mistrusted Gisevius, calling him "too facile a witness—fluent, detailed, much too pat." Nevertheless, Biddle thought that, on the whole, Gisevius was telling the truth, and assessed him as "the most damaging witness against Goering."

Among the defendants, Speer and Schacht gloated at Goering's discomfiture, while Keitel was dismayed at the testimony about Blomberg: "It is an unheard-of disgrace to dig this scandal out into the open like this! I have been an honorable soldier for forty-four years, and now they are trying to make a monkey of me and my whole tradition."

Schacht rubbed his hands together: "Now all the rotten business is coming to light. It was so stupid of the prosecution to indict me! My

*Nebe, chief of the Kripo and onetime *Einsatzgruppe* commander, had been a friend of Gisevius's.

witness is their best witness," he exclaimed, little realizing the true implication of his words.

Schacht posed a dilemma for Jackson. A month before, Don Heath,
the director of political affairs for the American Military Government, had
met with Jackson and Captain Sam Harris, the assistant American prosecutor responsible for the case against Schacht. Heath, who had been
Schacht's contact at the American embassy in Berlin prior to Pearl Har-
bor, pleaded the financier's case. Schacht, Heath said, had started to turn
from Hitler in 1936, and by January of 1939 had been an out-and-out
opponent.

Furthermore, in contrast to evidence that kept turning up against the
other defendants, additional material on Schacht tended to exculpate him.
An investigator examining the files of Hans Lammers, the state secretary
in the Reich Chancellery, informed Harris: "The documents contained in
the Lammers files are not suited as evidence for the prosecution. On the
contrary, part of this file would constitute excellent evidence for the defense." Schacht's reluctance to reveal his role as an informant—a revelation that would virtually have assured his acquittal—was not the prosecution's problem. But, even so, Jackson had doubts that Schacht could be
convicted.

Nevertheless, since the United States, pursuing the economics case,
had primary responsibility for cross-examining Schacht, Funk, and Speer,
Jackson considered it a matter of personal honor to take on Schacht himself.

Unfortunately for Jackson, he had had little involvement in the investigation of the case against Schacht, so most of his knowledge was second-
hand. Harris prepared a fifty-page analysis, plus a hundred pages of excerpts from interrogations, to brief Jackson. Harris recommended that
Jackson limit his cross-examination to a few points on which Schacht
seemed vulnerable. The theme of the examination should be, Harris
quipped, "Figures don't lie, but liars often figure."

During direct examination by Dix, Schacht demonstrated that his
reputation for articulateness, adroit phraseology, and cutting sarcasm was
well deserved. He left no doubt of his sentiments toward Hitler and the
Nazis: "Only one thing did most of the leaders of the party have in common with the old Teutons, and that was drinking," he said. "Excessive
drinking was a main part of the Nazi ideology."

Hitler, Schacht continued, "did not have sufficient school education,
but he read an enormous amount later, and acquired a wide knowledge.
He juggled with that knowledge in a masterly manner in all debates,
discussions, and speeches.

"No doubt he was a man of genius in certain respects. He had sudden ideas of which nobody else had thought and which at times were useful in solving great difficulties, sometimes with astounding simplicity, sometimes, however, with equally astounding brutality.

"He was a mass psychologist of really diabolical genius. While I myself and several others were never captivated in personal conversations, still he had a very peculiar influence on other people, and particularly he was able—in spite of his screeching and occasionally breaking voice—to stir up the utmost overwhelming enthusiasm of large masses in a filled auditorium.

"He promised equal rights for all citizens, but his adherents, regardless of their capabilities, enjoyed privileges before all other citizens. He promised to put the Jews under the same protection which foreigners enjoyed, yet he deprived them of every legal protection. He had promised to fight against political lies, but together with his minister Goebbels he cultivated nothing but political lies and political fraud. He promised the German people to maintain the principles of positive Christianity, yet he tolerated and sponsored measures by which institutions of the church were abused, reviled, and damaged. Also, in the foreign political field he always spoke against a war on two fronts—and then later undertook it himself. He despised and disregarded all laws of the Weimar Republic, to which he had taken the oath when he became chancellor. He mobilized the Gestapo against personal liberty. He pardoned criminals and enlisted them in his service. He did everything to break his promises. He lied to and deceived the world, Germany, and me."

Spotlighting the fallacy in the argument of many of his fellow defendants that they were bound by the oath of allegiance that they had taken to Hitler, Schacht pointed out that Hitler himself had taken the oath to the Weimar constitution and that this constitution had never been repealed, but that Hitler had violated it repeatedly. Ministers, Schacht said, could not evade their responsibilities by referring to the Führer Principle: "The responsibility of the ministers continued to exist, my own also, and was kept down only by the terror and the violent threats of Hitler. I would never keep an oath of allegiance to a perjurer, and Hitler turned out to be a perjurer a hundredfold."

On several occasions Jackson objected to the direction and scope of Dix's questions. Birkett noted: "He has done this in a most petulant and aggressive manner, and is obviously suffering from frayed nerves. This is the result of his failure against Goering, and he seems to fear a similar failure against Schacht."

Almost to a man, Schacht's fellow defendants were pulling for Jackson as he began his cross-examination. Jackson intended to reveal Schacht as a man of expediency and duplicity, who had joined Hitler in a search for power and had left him not because of disagreement over principles, but because Schacht had been frustrated by Goering. After establishing that Schacht had supported Hitler for the chancellorship, Jackson charged: "Now, let me get you correctly. When you saw Hitler was going to win, you joined him?"

"No. I did not join Hitler when I saw that he would win, but when I discovered that he had won."

"Oh, well, I'll accept the amendment," Jackson agreed, then turned to the question of Schacht's integrity: "Now, I understood you to say in your testimony that you really didn't have anything to do socially with Hitler or with the other Nazis and that you refused their invitation to lunch at the Reich Chancellery; and one of the chief reasons was that those present showed such abject humility to Hitler. Did you say that?"

"Yes."

"Now, I want to read to you from your speech on the occasion of the Führer's birthday: 'We are meeting together here to remember with respect and love the man to whom the German people entrusted the control of its destiny more than four years ago. With the limitless passion of a glowing heart and the infallible instincts of a born statesman, Adolf Hitler, in a struggle which he led for fourteen years with calm logic, has won for himself the soul of the German people.' "

"I do not believe that anyone, on the occasion of the birthday celebration of the head of a state, could say anything different," Schacht replied. Earlier, on October 16, he had explained his deception during an interrogation by Murray Gurfein: "I didn't want to commit suicide, sir." When Gurfein had retorted, "You must have understood that the risk of voluntary association with power is that you cannot escape the obligation to it," Schacht had said: "If you have to deal with normal and honest men, I think you are right. If you have to deal with a gangster, then it is very difficult to stick to honesty yourself without risking your life."

Was it not true, Jackson asked Schacht, that he had informed Goering: "I have full sympathy for your activities. I do believe, however, that in a totalitarian state it is wholly impossible to conduct two divergent economic policies."

"Yes. The differences which led to my resignation resulted from the fact that Goering wanted to assume command over economic policies while I was to have the responsibility for them. And I was of the opinion that he who assumed responsibility should also have command."

"Now, is it not a fact that your controversy with Goering was a controversy of personal character for control," Jackson continued, "and not a controversy as to the question of armament? You both wanted to rearm as rapidly as possible."

"I do not want to continue that play with words as to whether it was personal or anything else, Mr. Justice. I had differences with Goering on the subject; and if you ask whether it was on armament, speed, or extent, I reply that I was at greatest odds with Goering in regard to these points. I have never denied that I wanted to rearm in order to gain equality of position for Germany. I never wanted to rearm any further. Goering wanted to go further; and this is one difference which cannot be overlooked."

In that case, Jackson said, he would be forced to reveal the opinion Schacht had expressed about Goering during an interrogation: " 'Whereas I have called Hitler an amoral type of person, I can regard Goering only as immoral and criminal. Endowed by nature with a certain geniality which he managed to exploit for his own popularity, he was the most egocentric being imaginable. The assumption of political power was for him only a means to personal enrichment and personal good living. The success of others filled him with envy. His greed knew no bounds. His predilection for jewels, gold, and finery, etcetera, was unimaginable. Only as long as someone was useful to him did he profess friendship. Goering's knowledge in all fields in which a government member should be competent was nil, especially in the economic field, though he created an immense official apparatus and misused his powers as lord of all economy most outrageously. In his personal appearance he was so theatrical that one could only compare him with Nero. A lady who had tea with his second wife reported that he appeared at this tea in a sort of Roman toga and sandals studded with jewels, his fingers bedecked with innumerable jeweled rings and generally covered with ornaments, his face painted and his lips rouged.' "

Titters swept the courtroom as Jackson placed the paper aside. Goering, beneath the scrutiny of the judges, squirmed uneasily in the dock. "This is no place to bring up a thing like that, even if it is true," he mumbled. "I don't know why he brought that up."

Though Jackson exposed Schacht's hypocrisy, he failed to heed Harris's admonition to restrict the cross-examination to a few points. He was hopelessly outmatched when he invaded Schacht's territory of finance and economics. As Schacht and Jackson fired volleys back and forth in English, Lawrence warned them to slow down so that the interpreting system could keep up. But Schacht found sardonic pleasure in the translators' difficulties, and later recalled: "I did not need them, and I did not mind much whether they found their task easy or difficult."

Attempting to distinguish between the German nation and the Hitler government, Schacht pointed out that he had been a servant of the state, not of the government: "I hope that I shall still receive my pension. It has nothing to do with the regime. How else should I pay my expenses?"

"Well, they may not be very heavy, Doctor," Jackson suggested.

"Just a minute!" Lawrence killed the ensuing merriment. "It is quite unnecessary for anyone present in the court to show his amusement by laughter."

Though Jackson had objected angrily during Schacht's examination by Dix to any mention of the western powers' complicity in Hitler's expansionist policy, he himself gave Schacht the very opportunity to make the point he had been wanting to. Jackson charged that Schacht had furthered German absorption of the Sudetenland by amalgamating the territory's banks with the Reichsbank: "That is what you did after this wrong and reprehensible act had been committed by Hitler, did you not?"

"It is no 'wrong and reprehensible' act committed by Hitler, but Hitler received the Sudeten German territory by way of treaty. There can be no talk of injustice. I cannot believe that the Allies have put their signature to a piece of injustice."

"The taking over of Czechoslovakia representing your idea of justice?"

"I have already told you that Germany did not 'take over Czechoslovakia,' but that it was indeed presented to Germany by the Allies on a silver platter."

"Are you now saying that that was an act of justice, or are you condemning it? Are you today for it, or against it?"

"I cannot answer your question for the reason that, if someone gives me a present, such as this, I accept it gratefully."

"Even though it does not belong to them to give?"

"Well, that I must naturally leave up to the donor."

"Were you in this court when Goering testified to his threat to bomb Prague—the beautiful city of Prague?"

"Thanks to your invitation, I was here."

"Yes. I suppose you approve that use of the force which you had created in the Wehrmacht?"

"No, no, that was an atrocious thing."

"Well, we have found something we agree on, Doctor. You knew of the invasion of Poland?"

"Yes."

"You regarded it as an unqualified act of aggression on Hitler's part, did you not?"

"Absolutely."

"The same was true of the invasion of Luxembourg, was it not?"

"Absolutely," Schacht replied, then continued with the same response as Jackson went down his list of nations invaded by Hitler, concluding with Russia.

"And you have left out Norway and Belgium," Schacht reminded him.

"Yes; well, I got to the end of my paper. The entire course was a course of aggression?"

"Absolutely to be condemned."

"And the success of that aggression at every step was due to the Wehrmacht, which you had to do so much with creating?"

"Unfortunately," Schacht assented.

Jackson scored by drawing the admission from Schacht that when he had administered the oath to the employees of the Austrian National Bank following the Anschluss and had led them in a triple *"Sieg Heil!"* he himself had no longer had faith in the Führer. But Jackson, as customary, did not know when to stop and damaged his own argument by summarizing: "And so, Dr. Schacht, we are to weigh your testimony in the light of the fact that you preferred, over a long period of time, a course of sabotage of your government's policy by treason against the head of the state, rather than open resignation from his cabinet?"

It was, after all, only a week before that Jackson had praised Gisevius, Schacht's confederate, as "the one representative of democratic forces in Germany."

The judges clearly gave the nod to Schacht. "Schacht is much too clever for him," Biddle thought.

"I have been right much impressed by him," Parker wrote. "He is a man of real ability and evidently tried to prevent some of the Nazi outrages."

Birkett noted that the prosecution had failed to destroy Schacht's defense that his contribution toward rearmament had not been illegal, per se, and that he had divorced himself from the regime when its criminal tendencies had become manifest. "In this particular contest between Schacht and Jackson, Schacht most certainly held his own," Birkett decided. "Nothing occurred during the cross-examination other than a strengthening of Schacht's defense."

45   *Blood on the Gold: Funk*

Walther Funk followed Schacht onto the witness stand as he had succeeded him in the Hitler administration; and there could have been no starker example of the manner in which men of talent had been precipitated out of the regime in favor of sycophantic sybarites. Slumping down into his chair as if attempting to hide in it, the flabby, hypochondriac Funk mumbled and slurred his words so badly that the interpreters and stenographers had difficulty understanding him. Parker called him "a pitiful little man in bad health"—precisely the impression Funk wanted to create.

Born in the East Prussian capital of Königsberg in 1890, Funk was a talented pianist with an expert knowledge of classical music. After studying law, philosophy, and political economy at various German universities, he had in 1920 gone to work for Hugenberg's *Berliner Boersenzeitung,* a respected, conservative financial journal, and two years later had become its editor. One of the wide circle of businessmen and industrialists who believed Hitler could be used to combat the Communists, he had found the Nazis' comprehension of economics minimal, and undertaken to educate them in the benefits of private enterprise.

When Hitler had become chancellor, Funk had been appointed press chief. Subsequently, Goebbels, who had no interest in administration, had left the running of the Propaganda Ministry to Funk.

Upon Schacht's refusal to ruin the economy by continuing excessive expenditures for armaments, Hitler had casually come up to Funk during a performance of *La Bohème* and told him: "I shall have to make you minister of economy after all." A year later, Funk had taken over Schacht's position as Reichsbank president as well. "Who would ever have thought I'd land up here!" Funk marveled.

Like Goering, Funk had been addicted to jewelry and high living, and carried a watch made out of a glittering dollar gold piece. He loved cigars, drinking, and all-night parties. A talking compendium of risqué jokes, Funk had attempted to pass himself off as one of the world's great lechers. These sexual pretensions had caused considerable merriment in the higher Nazi echelons, where he had been well known as a homosexual. When, at the time of the Fritsch crisis, the Berlin police president, Helldorf, had informed Goebbels that he also had a dossier on Funk, Goebbels had shrugged. "The only thing that could be done," the propaganda minister had said, "was to arrange an automobile accident, and that would be no way to treat an *alte Kämpfer* like Funk."

Following Goering's conference in the wake of the *Kristallnacht,* Funk had busied himself implementing Goering's edict to remove the Jews from the economy. At Goering's birthday parties, he had always been the master of ceremonies, gilding the Reichsmarshal with the most fulsome praise. On his fiftieth birthday Hitler and Goering had presented him with 800,000 marks and a 110-acre estate, including a twenty-two room mountainside mansion, near Bad Tölz in Bavaria.

When, in mid-October, Funk had been brought to Nuremberg from the hospital where he had been treated for his bladder infection, he had complained interminably to his interrogator, Murray Gurfein: "I am stuck in a very cold cell, and if this continues for two or three days, we shall have the old trouble all over again. I must request you to deal with me softly, as I am very ill."

"All the decrees excluding the Jews from industry were yours, were they not?" Gurfein had asked.

"Yes. We had to do this because otherwise Jewish property would have been free for everybody to loot, and we had to do something to protect it." "Protection," in the Nazi lexicon, had meant expropriation for the benefit of the bigwigs.

"You know the looting and all that was done at the instigation of the party, don't you?"

"Yes, most certainly." Funk had broken into sobs. "That was when I should have left in 1938. Of that I am guilty." Funk had all but beaten his breast. "I am guilty. I admit that I am a guilty party here."

On the stand, Funk, recalling his interrogation by Gurfein, recounted: "When I was reproached with these measures of terror and violence against the Jews I suffered a spiritual breakdown, because at that moment it came to my mind with all clearness that the catastrophe took its course from here on down to the horrible and dreadful things of which we have heard here and of which I knew, in part at least, from the time of my captivity. I felt a deep sense of shame and a personal guilt at that moment, and I feel it also today."

The core of the case against Funk, which Dodd led up to gradually, then suddenly sprang during a discussion about gold and foreign exchange, was that Funk had made an agreement with Himmler to "launder" through the Reichsbank the valuables taken off concentration camp victims.

"When did you start to do business with the SS, Herr Funk?" Dodd unleashed his surprise.

"I have never done that."

"Yes sir, business with the SS. Are you sure about that? I want you to take this very seriously. It is about the end of your examination, and it is very important to you. I ask you again, when did you start to do business with the SS?"

Ironically, it was Funk and his lawyer, Fritz Sauter, who had led the prosecution to the man, Emil Puhl, former vice-president of the Reichsbank, who became the most damaging witness against Funk. When Sauter had sent out an interrogatory to be answered by Puhl, the prosecution had taken the opportunity to question Puhl themselves.

"We have been trying for a long time to put this part of this case together," Dodd explained to the court, "and we have finally succeeded."

Directing himself once more to Funk, Dodd continued: "Well, now let us see. You were not ordinarily in the habit, in the Reichsbank, of accepting jewels, monocles, spectacles, watches, cigarette cases, pearls, diamonds, gold dentures, were you?"

"If that happened, then the Reichsbank committed an illegal act. The Reichsbank was not authorized to do that."

"And is it your statement that if it was done you did not know anything about it?"

"No," Funk said, meaning "yes."

Funk was returned to the dock while the lights were turned out and a brief motion picture was shown of the contents of the Reichsbank vaults in Frankfurt. American soldiers appeared. The doors of a vault swung open. Huge, tightly packed bags with *Deutsche Reichsbank* lettered on their sides dropped to the floor. The seals on the bags were broken, and rings, bracelets, jewelry, watches, bank notes, gold coins, and gold teeth poured out as if from a cornucopia.

The lights were switched on again. Funk, shattered, tottered back to the witness chair.

"I ask you again now, did you ever hear of anybody depositing his gold dentures in a bank for safekeeping?" Dodd resumed. There was no response from Funk. "You saw that film, and you saw the gold bridgework, and the other dental work. Certainly nobody ever deposited that with a bank. And not only did people not deposit gold teeth, but they never deposited eyeglass rims, did they, such as you saw in the picture?"

"That is right. These things are, of course, no regular deposits. That goes without saying." Funk could only repeat that he had not been informed and knew nothing about these transactions.

"Well, now, let us see what your assistant, Mr. Puhl, says about that, the man who you told us yesterday was a credible gentleman, and whom you asked the tribunal to call as a witness on your behalf."

In the summer of 1942, Puhl recounted, "Funk told me that he had arranged with Reichsführer Himmler to have the Reichsbank receive in safe custody gold and jewels for the SS. Funk directed that I should work out the arrangements with Pohl, who, as head of the economics sections of the SS, administered the economic side of the concentration camps.

"I asked Funk what the source was of the gold, jewels, bank notes, and other articles to be delivered by the SS. Funk replied that it was confiscated property from the Eastern Occupied Territories, and that I should ask no further questions. I protested against the Reichsbank handling this material. Funk stated that we were to go ahead with the arrangements for handling the material, and that we were to keep the matter absolutely secret.

"On the same day Pohl telephoned me and asked me if I had been advised of the matter. I said I would not discuss it by telephone. He then came to see me. The material deposited by the SS included jewelry, watches, eyeglass frames, dental gold, and other gold articles in great abundance, taken by the SS from Jews, concentration camp victims, and other persons. This was brought to our knowledge by SS personnel who attempted to convert this material into cash and who were helped in this by the Reichsbank personnel with Funk's approval and knowledge."

"I declare that this affidavit by Herr Puhl is not true." Funk's voice shook. "I never exchanged a word with Herr Puhl regarding precious stones and jewelry. It is incredible to me that a man who most certainly also carried out certain functions in his agreement with the SS—that is, with Herr Pohl—now tries to put the blame on me. On no account will I take this responsibility and I request that Herr Puhl be called here."

"What would you say if I tell you that Herr Puhl said that there were all together some seventy-seven shipments of materials such as you saw here this morning? Do you say that is untrue, or do you agree with it?"

"That might be quite true, but I was never informed about these things. I did not know at all that any jewelry, watches, cigarette cases, and so forth were delivered to the Reichsbank. That is news to me."

"Did you know that anything came from concentration camps to the Reichsbank?"

"Yes, the gold, of course."

"Gold teeth?"

"I have said that—no."

Dodd turned next to an inventory of one shipment of valuables from the Reichsbank to the municipal pawnshops. Listed were thousands of rings, watches, earrings, broaches, wrist watches, candlesticks, goblets, eating utensils, and pearls. "Do you want this tribunal to believe that employees and people in your bank were sending lists out to municipal pawnbrokers without its ever coming to your attention?"

"I know nothing at all about these events."

"All right. You know you did on one occasion at least, and possibly two, break down and weep when you were being interrogated, and you said 'I am a guilty man.' " Dodd bored in relentlessly. "Is it not a fact that this matter that we have been talking about has been on your conscience all the time and that was really what is on your mind, and it has been a shadow on you ever since you have been in custody? And is it not about time that you told the whole story?"

"I cannot tell more to the tribunal than I have already said, that is the truth. Let Herr Puhl be responsible before God for what he put in the affidavit. It is absolutely clear that Herr Puhl is now trying to put the blame on me and to exculpate himself. If he has done these things for years with the SS, it is his guilt and his responsibility."

"You are trying to put the blame on Puhl, are you not?"

"No. He is blaming me and I repudiate that."

"The trouble is, there was blood on this gold, was there not, and you knew this since 1942?" Dodd made a final attempt to break Funk down.

"I did not understand." Funk failed to grasp Dodd's metaphor, and tears welled in his eyes.

That night the members of the court were exposed to a poignant performance at the Nuremberg Opera House. In place of the usual fare of operettas, opera, and classical music performed by German musicians, the Opera House presented on the eve of V-E Day the survivors of a Jewish concentration camp orchestra. Organized in Kaunas, the capital of Lithuania, soon after the ghetto had been established in 1941, they had survived by performing at executions and other grisly functions at the bidding of the Nazis. When the ghetto had been liquidated in June of 1944, the thirty-five players had been transported to and marched from concentration camp to concentration camp. In June of 1945 the twelve survivors had reassembled to offer, in addition to such standards as Meyerbeer, Rossini, and Leoncavallo, songs from the ghetto and marches from the concentration camps.

Ghetto, I will never forget you—
Dark and crooked ghetto streets, death looms from every corner.
No home, no parents, hungry, forgotten by God and men.

Barbarians have come and destroyed from the face of the earth everything that has been created
Then they led us 1, 2, 3, 1, 2, 3—my steps seem to cry
Where is your wife, your child, your family? Where to? Why? What for?
But the liberation will come and then to the tune of 1, 2, 3, we will march through the gates of the ghetto.

Night. The old Bible is in front of me and I keep reading.
"My people, you will be like the sand of the sea and the stars in the sky."
The Almighty is never mistaken. We are like the sand because everyone seems to be able to tread on us. God Oh God, where are the stars? Where are they?

When Puhl arrived in court, he tacked first this way then that, attempting to avoid the shoals of his own involvement. Sauter suggested: "You first heard that these articles belonged to concentration camp victims at your interrogation?"

"Yes," Puhl agreed.

"And when did you learn what was contained in this deposit; when did you know that, to pick out one example, gold teeth were contained in it?"

"Not at all."

"So of this, too, you heard only after your arrest?"

"Of the details, yes."

"You say in the affidavit that Funk told you that matters should be kept absolutely secret; that is the wording. Will you say now whether this is true or whether it is a misunderstanding?"

"That it should be kept secret? No."

"Yes."

"Of course, this matter was to be kept secret, but then everything that happens in a bank must be kept secret."

"Witness, this statement cannot of course satisfy us." Sauter underscored Puhl's evasiveness.

Dodd confronted Puhl with an affidavit, executed in the meantime by Albert Thoms, one of Puhl's subordinates. Thoms detailed the instructions given him by Puhl, and the discussions they had held of the manner in which the property should be disposed. An account had been set up under a fictitious name, "Max Heiliger." "After one or two deliveries, most of the people in the *Hauptkasse* and almost everybody in my office knew all about the SS deliveries." Some of the items were stamped 'Lublin,' or 'Auschwitz,' Thoms avowed. "We all knew that these places were the sites of concentration camps. It was the tenth delivery, in November 1942, that dental gold appeared. The quantity of the dental gold became unusually great."

Puhl, looking at the floor, now changed his account. "It is obvious," he said, "that the desire for secrecy came from the SS."

"Herr Puhl, look up at me a minute, will you?" Dodd tried to get Puhl to meet his eyes. "Didn't you tell Lieutenant Meltzer, Lieutenant Margolies, and Dr. Kempner, when they were all together with you, that all of this business with the SS was common gossip in the Reichsbank? These gentlemen who are sitting right here."

"There was a general whisper in the bank about this transaction; but details were, of course, not known."

"Are you worried about your part in this?"

"No. I myself, once the matter had been set in motion, had nothing further to do with it."

"You know, when the defendant Funk was on the stand, he said that you were the one who first told him about the SS business. You were quite upset when we told you that Funk had said that you were the man who originated this."

"Yes."

"You got terribly upset about it. Don't you remember that?"

"Yes." Puhl nodded.

Thoms, following Puhl to the stand, avowed that he had informed Puhl of the nature of the SS shipments: "I am firmly convinced that when he walked through the strongrooms, Herr Puhl must have seen these objects, as they were lying quite openly on the table and everyone who visited the strongroom could see them."

It was evident that Funk, Puhl, and Thoms were all lying about the extent of their knowledge—though at the beginning they undoubtedly had not been fully aware of the manner in which the SS had acquired their booty. It was not until several weeks later that another, unexpected witness provided more definitive testimony against Funk.

46   A Question of Equivocation: Doenitz and Raeder

The two admirals, Raeder and Doenitz, were the responsibility of the British. Raeder, born in 1876, was a man of the Victorian era, and represented the Nationalists with their puritan morals and imperialist values. Doenitz, fifteen years younger, typified the disillusionment of the World War I generation, which had adopted Nazism as the revolutionary movement that would sweep away the wreckage of the decadent past and promote the resurgence of the nation.

After receiving a classical education in Latin and Greek, Raeder, the son of a school principal, had, at the age of eighteen, enrolled as a naval cadet. Learning English and Russian, and serving as navigation officer on the Kaiser's yacht, he had been tabbed as an outstanding officer, destined for a high command. During World War I he had been captain of a cruiser.

The Treaty of Versailles had reduced Germany to a cockleshell navy and left Raeder, his hopes dashed, an embittered man given to garrulous bromides. Appointed commander of the sea arm in 1927, he had welcomed Hitler because of the Führer's rearmament program. Though Raeder's daughter and her husband, who was one-fourth Jewish, abhorred the Nazi regime and had emigrated, the navy commander on March 12, 1939, had hailed Hitler:

"The Führer has shown his people that in the National Socialist racial community lie the greatest and invincible sources of strength. The German people and its Führer have done more for the peace of Europe and for the entire world than some neighbors are capable of realizing. This is the reason for the clear and unsparing summons to fight bolshevism and international Jewry, whose race-destroying activities we have sufficiently experienced. This task demands that the young soldier should also be taught National Socialist ideology and the problems of life. The armed forces and the party thus become more and more united in attitude and spirit. This is the work and entire merit of one man, whose genial leadership has led a whole nation in a few years from the deepest night into the brightest future. It was the Führer who has led his faithful followers from victory to victory."

For Goering, on the other hand, Raeder had no use whatever. While serving with the Luftwaffe commander on the court of honor that had exonerated Fritsch, Raeder had become convinced that Goering had engineered the affair, and was a threat to the Wehrmacht officer corps. The antagonism between the two men had reached a climax in February 1940, when the overenthusiastic Luftwaffe had sunk two of Germany's limited number of destroyers. Goering had tried to blame the mishap on the navy's carelessness and inadequate identification signals. Raeder, livid, had retorted that Goering was "sabotaging naval warfare," and suggested that the proper action would be "to arraign the supreme commander of the air force before a court-martial."

As an imperialist, Raeder supported Hitler's expansionist policy, and, in fact, when it came to the interests of the navy, was prepared to go him one better. On October 3, 1939, a few days after the Soviet Union had obtained naval bases in Estonia, Raeder had raised the question with Hitler of demanding similar bases in Norway. Hitler, however, had not been interested in extending the war to the north. It was only after Russia had attacked Finland, and the western powers had started laying plans to send troops across northern Norway in support of the Finns, an action that would simultaneously have cut off Germany's ore supplies, that Hitler had changed his mind.

The British and French military commanders had, as usual, moved with glacial indecision; and when, early in March of 1940, the Russians had cracked the Finnish defenses and the Finns had sued for peace, both the Allies and the Germans had been left suspended in mid-plan. "Conclusion of peace between Finland and Russia deprives England, but us too, of any political basis to occupy Norway," Jodl had written in the War Diary.

The British, nevertheless, had decided to go ahead and mine Norwegian territorial waters, then meet the expected violent German reaction by sending a limited number of troops to Norwegian ports. Hitler, conversely, had proceeded with full-scale preparations for invasion.

The German and the British ships had actually crossed each other during the initiation of operations the first week of April. Amid the islands and the fjords of the rugged coast, the two fleets had fought some of the fiercest and bloodiest naval battles in history. Though the Wehrmacht had won the land war, the British, once again, had triumphed at sea. By the end of the campaign, Raeder had lost more than a third of his fleet. Three cruisers and ten destroyers had been sunk, and two battlecruisers and one pocket battleship had been knocked out of action for months. The ultimate result had been that, though Hitler had gone through the motions of ordering Operation Sea Lion, neither he nor Raeder had believed that an invasion of the British Isles was a practical possibility.

When, between Christmas and New Year's of 1942–43, a flotilla of German vessels had failed to carry through an attack on an Allied Arctic convoy, Hitler, enraged, had threatened to scrap the German surface fleet. This had been too much for Raeder—even though Hitler had obviously not meant what he said—and he had induced the Führer to permit him to retire.

Doenitz, who replaced Raeder, had been more attuned to the demands of modern naval warfare than Raeder, but his mind was shallow even when measured by Nazi standards. After first serving on a cruiser in World War I, he had joined the submarine service in 1916, and two years later received his first command. Approximately a month before the end of the war, Doenitz's U-boat had attacked a British convoy in the Mediterranean and been hit in the ensuing action. The submarine, after plummeting stern first toward the bottom, had, at a moment when all those aboard believed themselves doomed, shot up as precipitately as it had plunged, and crashed to the surface. Doenitz, taken prisoner by the British, had been so affected by the experience that he had been confined for nine months in a lunatic asylum, and been repatriated to Germany as insane.

Remaining in the navy after recovering, Doenitz had, in 1935, been picked to head the submarine arm. Because of Raeder's concentration on surface ships, Germany had had in 1939 but forty-eight submarines, only about half of which were fit for service in the Atlantic. The situation had been so bad that, in November, Raeder had asked Hitler to explore the possibility of buying submarines from Russia. Hitler had rejected the suggestion, noting: "The Russians should not see any weakness with us."

Not until 1942 had the stepped-up submarine program initiated in 1939 begun to take effect. Because of the changed conditions of combat between the two wars—notably the equipping with wireless and arming of all British merchant ships—there were, unlike World War I, few surface attacks by submarines. Most ships were torpedoed without warning, and, following the sinking, the U-boats simply slipped away. Though the United States had violated international law by launching an undeclared war against German submarines in the Atlantic in 1941, Hitler had wanted at all cost to avoid an incident that might precipitate American entry into the war, and refused Raeder and Doenitz permission to retaliate. All in all, until 1942 submarine warfare had been conducted as decently as possible under the circumstances, and there had not been a single verified incident of a submarine attacking the survivors of a torpedoed ship.

Then, in the fall of 1942, an action had occurred off the coast of Africa that reflected new realities and simultaneously altered perceptions.

On September 12 a U-boat had torpedoed a British auxiliary warship, the *Laconia*, which, in addition to 750 crewmen and military personnel, had had 1,800 Italian prisoners of war, 100 Polish guards, and 80 civilian men, women, and children aboard. The sea was calm, and nearly everyone, except the Italian prisoners locked in the hold, had gotten off the ship. (Of the Italians, only some 450 managed to escape.) There had been, consequently, about 1,400 people on boats, rafts, and flotsam in the water.

When the submarine commander, Werner Hartenstein, had radioed Germany to report the situation, Doenitz, violating his own standing instructions, had dispatched two additional U-boats to assist in the rescue, and the Vichy government had directed vessels from Dakar. With Doenitz's permission, Hartenstein had sent out an SOS in English, and guaranteed the safety of any ship responding. Three days later, however, only the other submarines had shown up. More than 400 survivors had been taken aboard the three vessels, which had also hitched strings of lifeboats to their sterns, and begun slowly towing them the several hundred miles to Africa. Hartenstein had bedecked his U-boat with a huge Red Cross flag.

On the sixteenth, this unusual procession had been spotted by a four-engined B-24 Liberator bomber stationed on Ascension Island in the mid-South Atlantic. The squadron commander, believing that the subs were rescuing the Italian prisoners of war and would endanger two British merchantmen on their way to pick up the Allied survivors, had ordered the plane to attack.

Despite the frantic efforts of a British officer in one of the lifeboats to signal the B-24, the Liberator had made five low-level strafing and bombing runs. Hartenstein's sub had been hit and damaged, several lifeboats had been smashed or overturned, and, as blood spread over the water, sharks had swarmed to the scene. The U-boats had cut loose the lifeboats, placed some of the excess passengers aboard the subs back on rafts, and broken off the rescue.

Doenitz, who had risked Hitler's wrath to authorize the rescue, had now reaped the tirade, and been forced into acknowledging the correctness of Hitler's view that in war the overriding consideration was the destruction of the enemy. On September 17 Doenitz had radioed his submarine commanders:

"No attempt must be made to rescue members of ships sunk, and this includes picking up persons in the water and putting them in lifeboats, righting capsized lifeboats, and handing over food and water. Rescue runs counter to the most elementary demands of warfare for the destruction of enemy ships and crews.

"Be harsh. Bear in mind that the enemy takes no regard of women and children in his bombing attacks on German cities."

Three and a half months later, Hitler, emphasizing once more that the way to win the war was by terrorization, had told Japanese Ambassador Oshima that henceforth ships would be sunk "with the intention of killing as many of the crew as possible. Once it gets around that most of the seamen are lost in the sinkings, the Americans will soon have difficulties enlisting people." It would not matter, therefore, how many ships the United States built, because there would be no crews to man them. In the summer of 1943, Ribbentrop, complaining that, despite Hitler's assurances, eighty-seven percent of the crews of ships sunk were being rescued, had asked Doenitz if the casualty rate could not be increased.

The fact was that Doenitz had been struggling merely to keep the submarine fleet operational in the face of Allied countermeasures. In January of 1943 Germany had had 212 submarines. But, Doenitz informed the Nuremberg tribunal, in the spring of 1943 "the airplane, the surprise by airplane, and the equipment of the planes with radar—which in my opinion is, next to the atomic bomb, the decisive war-winning invention of the Anglo-Americans—brought about the collapse of U-boat warfare." The effectiveness of the air war had been accentuated by the Ultra code breakers, who intercepted the subs' reports of their positions. Between February and May, Doenitz had lost eight-five submarines, forty percent of his fleet. Losses in May had been so high—thirty-eight boats—that on the twenty-fourth Doenitz had withdrawn the U-boats from the North Atlantic.

With the help of Speer, Doenitz's engineers had designed a new snorkel submarine, able to cruise indefinitely beneath the water. But by May of 1945 only one of these vessels had been sent to sea, and none ever fired a torpedo at an Allied ship.

Although a total of 2,472 Allied ships had been sunk during the war, Doenitz had lost 650 subs in the process, and presided over little more than a suicide service. The life expectancy of a submarine and its crew had been two missions. Of the 40,000 men who served on the U-boats, 25,000 had been killed and 5,100 taken prisoner.

Shortly prior to the selection of the defendants in August 1945, the British Admiralty had recommended against indicting Doenitz: "The Admiralty opinion is that if criminality is to be attached to any German naval leader, it should be Raeder. Unless additional information implicating

Doenitz in political as distinct from military acts of criminality has been uncovered, it is believed that there is insufficient evidence to convict him or to warrant his being tried. If, as it has been somewhat facetiously said, we should have some defendants whom we can acquit, then we should be worried lest we afford other defendants the opportunity to profit through such defense evidence as Doenitz can undoubtedly introduce in his behalf."

That assessment, however, had been made prior to a full investigation of the 1944 *Peleus* incident. After sinking the Greek steamer *Peleus* in the Mediterranean, Lieutenant Heinz Eck, a U-boat commander, had cruised through the wreckage for five hours, directing his men in the machinegunning of the survivors. Three badly wounded seamen had, nevertheless, eventually been plucked from the water by the British; and Eck and his crew had, following a later action, been captured in Africa upon beaching their damaged craft.

At his trial in October 1945, Eck had explained that he had taken the action solely to prevent Allied planes from spotting the wreckage and, consequently, searching out his submarine. Prior to his execution on November 30, he had provided a deposition for Kranzbühler. In this he stated that he had issued the order entirely on his own volition, not as the result of any instructions by Doenitz, even though, before leaving port, he had been briefed by the flotilla commander, Captain Karl Moehle, and informed like his fellow submarine captains:

"Rescue runs counter to the most elementary demands of warfare for the destruction of enemy ships and crews."

When British interrogators had charged Moehle with being the author of the order and thus sharing the guilt with Eck, Moehle had denied the accusation, and replied that he had merely passed on the instructions he had received by wire from Doenitz. "It was perhaps even the intention," Moehle suggested during interrogation, "that this order could be interpreted in two ways and the reason may be that, in the first place, it contravened international laws of warfare, and second, that it was an order which must give rise to serious conflicts of conscience in commanding officers." Nevertheless, Moehle declared, it had been clear to anyone familiar with the manner in which Doenitz issued orders "that the High Command regarded as desirable that not only ships but also their crews should be regarded as objects of attack, that is, that they should be destroyed. At that time, German propaganda was continually stressing the shortage of crews for enemy merchant ships and the consequent difficulties. I too understood the order in that way."

In a courtroom suddenly filled with naval brass, Moehle, one of the most decorated officers in the German navy, stated unequivocally: "The order meant in my opinion that it was desirable in the case of sinking of merchantmen that there should be no survivors."

Kranzbühler, however, sailing in familiar waters, conducted probably the cleverest cross-examination of the trial. "How many ships did you sink?" he asked Moehle.

"Twenty ships."

"After sinking ships, did you destroy the rescue equipment or fire at the survivors?"

"No."

"Did you have an order to do that?"

"No."

Having established that Moehle himself had never fired on anyone in the water—though his combat service had ended in the spring of 1941—Kranzbühler, speaking in short, clipped sentences, proceeded to place the burden for the new orders and the changes in the conduct of submarine warfare on the Allies: "Do you know that the order of September 1942 was given in consequence of an incident in which German U-boats, contrary to orders, had undertaken rescue measures? And the U-boats were then attacked by Allied aircraft?"

"Yes, sir," Moehle replied.

The second witness against Doenitz was Lieutenant Peter Heisig, who had stepped forward in a futile attempt to save a friend, August Hoffmann, who, as executive officer on Eck's submarine, had been sentenced to death along with Eck and another man. Heisig, who was in a British POW camp, had volunteered that Eck had, in fact, acted according to Doenitz's instructions. Doenitz had addressed his graduating officer class in the autumn of 1942, Heisig related, and told it that the Allies were launching over a million tons of shipping a month, more than was possible for the U-boats to destroy even under the best of circumstances. "The bottleneck of the Allies lay only in the problem of personnel for these newly built ships. He therefore demanded that we should from now on carry on total warfare against ships and crew. That meant, so far as possible, no seaman from a sunk ship was to get home anymore. In this way it would be impossible for the opponent to make use of his newly built ships, since no more crews would be available. After the sinking of a ship, every possibility of rescue must be denied to the crew, through the destruction of every means of saving life. I later discussed these remarks of Admiral Doenitz's with the others, and all present unanimously and unambiguously took them to mean that after the sinking of a ship, all possibility of escape, whether in boats, in rafts, or by any other means was to be denied to the crew, and the destruction of the crew was to be attempted by every means. This mode of warfare was for me as for most of my comrades completely new. Owing to Admiral Doenitz's authoritative position, it was nevertheless fully and completely accepted by many of them."*

As with Moehle, Kranzbühler conducted a crisp cross-examination of Heisig to make his point, and did not go one step beyond.

"Do you maintain that the speech of Grand Admiral Doenitz mentioned in any way that fire should be opened on shipwrecked sailors?"

"No; we gathered that from his words; and from his reference to the bombing war, we gathered that total war had now to be waged against ships and crews. That is what we understood, and I talked about this to my comrades. We were convinced that Admiral Doenitz meant that. He did not express it clearly."

"Do you think that the prohibition of rescue measures is identical with the shooting of shipwrecked sailors?"

"We came to this—"

"Please, answer my question. Do you think these two things are identical?"

"No."

"Thank you."

Under interrogation by Colonel Hinkel before the start of the trial, Doenitz had first lied about the post-*Laconia* order and exclaimed: "Such an order was never given!" Then, faced with the entry in the Naval War Diary, he had justified it: "It is very contradictory that in the war one side is going to save the other side, and during this the other side is coming to bomb us. That is the real reason for this entry." During a subsequent session, he had become highly excited: "I saved, saved, and saved! I didn't see any help from you! Now when you come and take exception to it, you do it against a man who was constantly saving the best he could. It was quite clear to me that the time had passed where I was able to be on the surface and to do things like that. You had your powerful air force against me!"

In the courtroom, Doenitz admitted under cross-examination by Fyfe that Heisig could, in essence, be right about his speech: "It may well be that the subject of America's new construction program and the manning of the new ships by trained crews was discussed. I have always taken the

*In the witness wing at Nuremberg, Heisig, prior to his appearance, was the object of intimidation by a clique of fellow prisoners that included Gunther Hessler—Doenitz's son-in-law—Field Marshal Albert Kesselring, Alfred Naujocks, General Heinz Guderian, and others. Taunted as "Doenitz's gravedigger," he was told that he was much too young to realize what the war had been about, and should refuse to testify.

"My fellow inmates are gradually beginning to get on my nerves," Heisig wrote his mother. "They were all at one time in either high or top positions in the Nazi government. But now they are all innocent little lambs who never harmed a flea. Cowards!"

view that losses of crews would make replacements difficult, and this is stated in my war diary together with similar ideas, and perhaps I said something of the kind to my midshipmen."

Building on Kranzbühler's cross-examination of Heisig, however, Doenitz asserted that Heisig had misinterpreted his words: "During cross-examination he has submitted here that I have not said anything about fighting against shipwrecked personnel; secondly, everything else he said is so vague that I do not attach much value to its credibility."

If that were the case, Fyfe hammered at Doenitz, then Moehle was an amazing example of misconception: "He commanded the U-boat flotilla from 1942 until the end of the war. That is nearly three years; and as he told us, he has a number of decorations for gallant service. Are you telling the tribunal that Commander Moehle went on briefing submarine commanders on a completely mistaken basis for three years without any of your staff or yourself discovering this? You saw every U-boat commander when he came back."

"I could not know that he had these doubts. He had every opportunity of clearing up these doubts, and I did not know, and nobody on my staff had any idea that he had these thoughts."

The question of submarine warfare aside, Doenitz had been a fanatic Nazi overawed by the Führer. Hitler, Doenitz offered, had had "extraordinary intelligence and energy and a practically universal knowledge, [he was a man] from whom power seemed to emanate, and who was possessed of a remarkable power of suggestion."

In contrast to most of the opportunists around the Führer, Doenitz had never wavered in defeat. "Adolf Hitler is the only statesman of stature in Europe," he had orated in 1944. He had referred to the July 20 conspirators as "a small mad clique of generals . . . rascals and henchmen of our enemies whom they served with unprincipled, dastardly, and false cleverness." On February 20, 1945, he had told German youth over the radio: "You have been so very fortunate as to be placed by destiny in the greatest era of our people. Now I come to the most important point. Your moral bearing. You must be attached body and soul and with all the forces of your heart and character to the Führer. You must regard yourselves as *his* children, whom nothing on earth could ever make waver in their unconditional loyalty. This is the greatest and finest thing in a man's life—unconditional and loyal devotion to the great man who is his leader."

Responding to Hitler's proposal to renounce the Geneva Convention, Doenitz had suggested: "It would be better to carry out measures considered necessary without warning, and at all costs to save face with the world."

"That means, put in blunt and brutal language," Fyfe interpreted, "don't denounce the convention, but break it whenever it suits you, doesn't it?"

A mere two weeks before the final collapse, Doenitz had spoken in praise of murder: "In a prison camp in Australia, a petty officer acting as camp senior officer had all Communists among the inmates systematically done away with in such a way that the guards did not notice. This petty officer is sure of my full recognition for his decision and execution. After his return, I shall promote him with all means, as he has shown he is fitted to be a leader."

To Fyfe's charge that this was the advocacy of political killing, Doenitz could only reply halfheartedly that he had not really meant "Communists" but "spies."

On May 10, 1945, two days after the Nazi surrender, Doenitz had written in his diary: "The foundation for the further existence of the German people is the national spirit which National Socialism created. It must be maintained."

In the end, the personality and skill of Kranzbühler had more to do with the outcome of the case against Doenitz than the evidence against the admiral. It was because Kranzbühler had caught favor in the eye of Biddle that the American judge, pleading personal privilege, had overcome the reluctance of Lawrence and Birkett to permit an interrogatory to be submitted to Admiral Chester W. Nimitz, commander of the American Pacific Fleet during the war.

To the question, "Was it customary for submarines to attack merchantmen without warning?" Nimitz replied: "Yes, with the exception of hospital ships and other vessels under safe conduct voyages for humanitarian purposes."

"Were, by order or on general principles, the U.S. submarines prohibited from carrying out rescue measures toward passengers and crews of ships sunk without warning in those cases where by doing so the safety of their own boat was endangered?"

"On general principles, the U.S. submarines did not rescue enemy survivors if undue additional hazard to the submarine resulted, or the submarine would be prevented from accomplishing its further mission," Nimitz responded. "Therefore, it was unsafe to pick up many survivors."

Kranzbühler thus won his point. Circumventing the barrier to *tu quoque*, he had obtained affirmation that American submarine practices had paralleled the German, that none of the combatants had attempted to rescue survivors if their own vessels had been endangered, and that therefore, in practice, if not strictly in theory, German naval warfare had been "legal." In a case as massive and complex as this, in which few defendants won even minor points, it was striking to have one succeed in a major. It was natural, therefore, that Nimitz's reply carried great weight with the judges.

Raeder was not so fortunate, even though he was able to demonstrate that in emphasizing the importance of Norwegian bases he had merely pointed out the obvious—the only reason the Germans had arrived before the Allies was because of their greater ruthlessness and resolution.

During his interrogation in Moscow, Raeder had unburdened himself of some of his feelings about his fellow leaders in the Wehrmacht; and these opinions were now read in court. "Speer flattered Doenitz's vanity, and vice versa," Raeder declared. "Doenitz's strong political party inclination brought him difficulties as head of the navy. His last speech to the Hitler Youth, which was ridiculed in all circles, gave him in the navy the nickname of 'Hitlerbube Doenitz.' "*

Keitel, Raeder said, was "a man of unimaginable weakness, who owes his long stay in his position to this characteristic. The Führer could treat him as badly as he wished—he stood for it."

"Goering," Raeder asserted, "had a disastrous effect on the fate of the German Reich. His main peculiarities were unimaginable vanity and immeasurable ambition, running after popularity and showing off, untruthfulness, impracticality, and selfishness. He was outstanding in his greed, wastefulness, and soft unsoldierly manner."

"A pissed-off jealous old man!" Doenitz, who had to sit brushing shoulders with Raeder for another three months, exploded.

Keitel could not understand how Raeder could have dissembled respect and friendship for him through all the years they had worked together, and was devastated by Raeder's statement. "My defense has entered a new phase under wholly altered circumstances," he enigmatically told his counsel, Otto Nelte, unrealistically failing to accept the fact that his defense had, for all practical purposes, been concluded. More than anything, these revelations, coming one by one, shattered the remnants of trust among the defendants—even those who maintained a semblance of unity wondered what each truly thought about the others.

In the end, it was a relatively minor point, but one on which the British were highly sensitive, that militated heavily against Raeder.

On the opening day of the war, a German submarine had sunk the British passenger liner *Athenia* under the mistaken impression that it was an auxiliary cruiser. About a hundred Americans had been on board, and, because of the resemblance to the *Lusitania* incident of World War I, a great hue and cry had resulted. The Germans, from the beginning, had

---

*"Hitlerboy Doenitz."

denied responsibility. When, however, the U-boat had returned to port on September 27, 1939, its shamefaced commander had admitted that he had torpedoed the ship in error. The situation had contained the potential for such diplomatic dynamite that Hitler had ordered Raeder and Doenitz to suppress all facts. In a schoolboyish forgery, the log of the submarine had been altered to expunge the record of the torpedoing. Compounding the deception, Goebbels, on October 23, had asserted in a brazen and clumsy piece of propaganda: "Churchill sank the *Athenia*." Alleging that Churchill had placed a bomb aboard the ship, Goebbels had characterized him as a "criminal" and a "murderer."

Raeder, professing himself a man of probity and integrity, told the court that Goebbels's propaganda ploy had come as a complete surprise to him. He would, he said, have intervened had he known about it beforehand.

When Fritzsche later took the stand, Lawrence exhibited an intense interest in the subject. In response to Lawrence, Fritzsche declared that he had kept making inquiries to the navy about the *Athenia:* "The answer was always the same. No German submarine was near the place of the catastrophe."

"And are you saying that that liaison officer of the navy told you that after the twenty-third of October, 1939?"

"Yes."

"Did he continue to tell you that?"

"Yes."

"That is all," Lawrence concluded. It was evident that Raeder had never attempted to halt Goebbels's outrageous deception. Thus, so far as Lawrence was concerned, Raeder's posture as a man of character was destroyed.

One of the witnesses called by Raeder was Ernst von Weizsäcker, formerly state secretary in the Foreign Office. Alfred Seidl, the attorney for Hess and Frank, grasped the opportunity to renew his campaign to embarrass the Russians and, if possible, generate dissension between the Soviets and their western Allies. A slight, diminutive, bespectacled member of the Nazi Party, Seidl was the bete noire of the tribunal. Buzzing about like a persistent gnat, he pursued his goal of demonstrating that either the Conspiracy to Launch Aggressive War had been nonexistent, or else had included the Russians. "Obviously Seidl is trying to cause trouble in the tribunal," Biddle noted.

Seidl's aggressiveness made some of the other German attorneys uncomfortable, and his high-pitched laugh, resembling Frank's, left them uneasy. But he had gained adherents among members of the American prosecution who shared his distaste for the Russians—there was a staunchly anti-Communist group gathered about Father Walsh and Thomas Dodd—and one of them slipped him a copy of the second secret protocol negotiated between the Germans and the Russians following the conclusion of the campaign against Poland. In essence, this added little to the covert addendum to the Moscow Pact which Seidl had already succeeded in introducing; but it gave him one more opportunity to needle the Russians.

"Do you know, I have him now, I have him truly," he exulted conspiratorially to Carl Haensel, the assistant attorney for the SS. "There exist two secret protocols. We have the text now. What will they do?"

Rudenko protested: "We are examining the matter of the crimes of the major German war criminals. We are not investigating the foreign policies of other states. Second, the document is—in substance—a forged document and cannot have any probative value."

Rudenko had nothing to back up his claim that the document was forged; and Seidl pointed out that it was the prosecution that had introduced the Moscow Pact as part of its charge of aggressive war. Lawrence maneuvered out of the situation by procrastinating action on the admissibility of the document, but permitting Seidl to question Weizsäcker about his knowledge of the treaties, a decision that, in practice, gave Seidl what he wanted.

Though Weizsäcker did little more than corroborate what had previously been stated about the division of the eastern spoils, his testimony—added to the revelation of the Soviets' offer of Murmansk as a submarine base to the Germans—demonstrated the extent of Stalin's cooperation with Hitler. The discomfiture of the Russians in Nuremberg was great, and the pending testimony on the Katyn Forest massacre promised to increase it further. A few days after Weizsäcker's appearance, N. D. Zorya, one of the assistant Soviet prosecutors, shot himself. (His death was officially described as an accident.)

As each of the defendants concluded his appearance, he lost much of his interest in the proceedings, and the entire front row of the dock and a portion of the second was now encompassed in apathy. Hess had never been present in the courtroom in any form but physical. Ribbentrop, glassy-eyed from his diet of sleeping pills, appeared spectral, as if playing the role of his own ghost. Rosenberg, who seemed to the judges to be constantly writing, was in reality entertaining himself by drawing sketches. Frank, abandoning the trial for euphoric flights into literature and music, floated off into the world of his visions. Funk looked as if, like Humpty Dumpty, he had fallen off a wall and would never be put back together again. Schacht regarded both his fellow prisoners in the dock and the proceedings with disdain. The snap had even gone out of Goering, who, brooding, spent long periods slumped down in his corner as if in a bathtub. The lassitude spread through the courtroom and threatened to become generalized—the seldom-used interpreter sitting behind the American and French judges took to slumbering much of the day, and was left undisturbed until his persistent snoring became an embarrassment to the tribunal.

Sometimes it seemed as if the mood in the courtroom was influenced as much by the weather as by the proceedings—spring arrived in early April, the windows in the Palace of Justice were thrown open, and the fragrance of hawthorne invaded the corridors. The budding of the flowers and leafing out of the trees intensified everyone's awareness of the trial's duration. In the fields, women spread liquid manure, carried in great vats on ox carts, over the spongy soil; and the very atmosphere took on a pungent aroma. Golden broom and milky lupine rippled in waves over the countryside. Saffron crocuses carpeted the banks of the Pegnitz River, teeming with fish. It was the stream of Goering's youth, and from the windows of the lunchroom he could follow its course as it wended its way from Veldenstein, thirty miles distant.

47   The American: Schirach

For six months Goering and Speer had grappled over the soul of Schirach, the Reichsmarshal attempting to stiffen his backbone, the armaments minister urging him to recant. The youngest of the defendants, Schirach was three-quarters American. His paternal grandfather, emigrating from Germany, had served as a major in the Union Army during the Civil War, lost a leg, and been selected as one of the honorary pallbearers at Lincoln's funeral. Marrying into the wealthy Norris family, which owned a locomotive works in Philadelphia, he had ultimately taken his bride back to Germany. Baldur's father, Carlo, an officer in the Imperial Army, had visited the United States during the 1890s, and also married an American, the daughter of a New York lawyer. (She was killed during an Allied air raid.)

Baldur had been born in Berlin in 1907—the year before his father resigned his commission to become director of the court theater at Weimar —and had grown up in that peculiarly romantic, anachronistic society cherished by the German nobility. Insulated as much as possible from a century of industrialization, it was as if they had been cast away on an

island since the Napoleonic Wars. When the illusions of glory that led
Germany into World War I had been dissipated and the postwar world had
thundered in on them, they had seemed helpless to cope with it. With the
end of the monarchy, Carlo had found himself unemployed; and though
he had been rehired when the theater later reopened, Baldur's older
brother Karl had been so traumatized that, in 1919, he had committed
suicide. Baldur, influenced by dramas of love and glory, was to spend his
entire life hovering between reality and make-believe.

According to his own account, he had begun to sort things out and
develop his *Weltanschauung* upon reading, at the age of seventeen, *The
International Jew*, Henry Ford's offshoot of the *Protocols of the Wise Men of
Zion*. In 1925 Hitler, on a motor trip from Munich to Berlin, had appeared
in Weimar, and his passion for the theater had brought him into the
Schirach home. The eighteen-year-old Baldur had joined the party, and
two years later, at the suggestion of Hitler, entered Munich University to
organize a National Socialist Student Bund. In October 1931, Hitler had
appointed him leader of the Hitler Youth (a name originated by Streicher)
with the rank of *Gruppenführer* in the SA. Puffed up with his importance,
the twenty-four-year-old major general had raced from one point to the
other in the country to make speeches.

Prior to the Nazi takeover, membership in the Hitler Youth had
numbered only 110,000 of the more than 4.5 million boys and girls enrolled
in the various German youth organizations. By 1939, however, the Hitler
Youth had encompassed 9 million of the 10 million Aryan children. Day
in and day out they had been drilled in such ditties as:

> We are the rollicking Hitler Youth;
> We have no need of Christian truth;
> No evil old priest these ties can sever;
> We're Hitler's children now and ever.

As early as November 6, 1933, Hitler had boasted: "When an opponent declares, 'I will not come over to your side,' I calmly say: 'Your child
belongs to me already.' In a short time they will know nothing else."

Regarding Schirach as his protégé, Hitler had given his blessing to the
Youth leader's marriage to Henriette Hoffmann, the daughter of photographer Heinrich Hoffmann. Thinking of himself as a writer, Schirach had
composed poesy in praise of Hitler, and published volumes on the Hitler
Youth and on Nazi education.

After the armistice with France in 1940, Schirach, who had served as
a lieutenant in a machine-gun company, had been appointed Gauleiter of
Vienna. There he became notorious for spouting such puerile nonsense as
"Vienna cannot be conquered with bayonets, only with music," and

"Every boy who dies at the front is dying for Mozart." In the fashion of the German nobility and the Nationalist upper classes, he had abhorred "rowdy" anti-Semitism; and when as patron of the arts, he had presented composer Richard Strauss with a diamond-tipped baton, he had not hesitated to gallantly kiss the hand of Strauss's Jewish daughter-in-law.

On the other hand Schirach had, like Frank, held the view that the Jewish masses must disappear; *how* they were to vanish was not his problem. In November 1940 Schirach had informed the Führer that there were still sixty thousand Jews, most of them unfit for forced labor, in Vienna. A few days later, on December 3, Hitler had advised Schirach, "The sixty thousand Jews still residing in the Reichsgau Vienna will be deported most rapidly to the general-government because of the housing shortage prevalent in Vienna." Subsequently, at the time the liquidation of the Warsaw ghetto was being conducted, Schirach had boasted: "If anyone reproaches me with having driven from this city, which was once the European metropolis of Jewry, tens of thousands upon tens of thousands into the ghettos of the East, I feel myself compelled to reply: I see in this an action contributing to European culture."

As the war progressed, Schirach's romantic notions and mildly modernistic view on art had gradually led to a decline in his standing. Hitler's most serious disenchantment with the Schirachs, however, had stemmed from an action not of Baldur's, but of Henriette's.

In mid-1943, Henriette, who was permitted to travel freely about Europe, had gone to Portugal and then to Amsterdam. In Lisbon she had picked up a copy of *Life* magazine that included a vivid description of atrocities. The message of the article in *Life* had been reinforced in Amsterdam, where she had been accidentally exposed to a procession of Jewish women and children being marched off by the SS, and later taken to a schoolroom where the benches had been covered with displays of wedding rings, jewelry, and precious stones stripped from the victims.

"Do you want any diamonds?" an SS officer had asked her. "They go at a ridiculous price."

A short time later when Henriette and Baldur had been guests of Hitler on the Obersalzberg, Henriette had attempted to show him the copy of *Life*. Hitler, thrusting the magazine aside as if it were an adder, had shouted: "You people must learn to hate, all of you! You are much too sentimental!"

As the end neared, Schirach, envisioning himself, flag in hand, baring his breast against the Russians, had vowed that he would die defending Vienna to the last. "This was pretty awkward for us," Rudolf Mildner, the head of the Gestapo in Vienna revealed to an interrogator in Nuremberg, "because it meant that we would have had to remain in Vienna too."

To the relief of the Gestapo, Schirach, reconsidering, had discarded his uniform and slunk away to Innsbruck. There, adopting the pseudonym Richard Falk, he had prepared to launch a new career as a writer, and had embarked on a mystery entitled *The Secrets of Myrna Loy.* * His face, however, was well known; and, fearful that he might be recognized and receive summary justice from the French occupation troops or the Austrian anti-Nazis, he had decided that he would fare better with the Americans. On June 4, 1945, he had crossed over into the American zone, identified himself at a local post, and offered his services for the reeducation of German youth in the ways of democracy.

In court, Schirach, concluding finally that it was better to try to survive with Speer than to go down with Goering, cast himself as a misguided youth who had evolved into a harmless functionary. Although, as Gauleiter and *Reichstatthalter* (governor) of Vienna he had been the most powerful Nazi in Austria, he claimed: "My principal activities in Vienna were social work and cultural work." He tried to explain away the fact that he had been on the distribution list for *Einsatzgruppen* reports and had received Goebbels's directive to the gauleiters on the extermination of the Jews by pleading that the *Einsatzgruppen* reports had gone to a subordinate, and all responsibility for the Austrian portion of the Final Solution had lain with Eichmann's deputy in Vienna, Alois Brünner, who had already been condemned to death.

It was an immense piece of luck for Schirach, as for Speer, that the prosecution failed to present evidence on his attendance at the 1943 Posen meeting, where Himmler had made it a point to explain to the Reich's leaders the meaning of the Final Solution. His dramatic "confession" was, consequently, unlike Frank's *mea culpa,* accepted with some credence by the judges: "Before God, before the German nation, before my German people, I alone bear the guilt of having trained our young people for a man whom I for many long years had considered unimpeachable, for a man who murdered by the millions," Schirach told the court.

"[Auschwitz was] the greatest, the most devilish mass murder known to history. But that murder was not committed by Höss; Höss was merely the executioner. The murder was ordered by Adolf Hitler, as is obvious from his last will and testament. He and Himmler jointly committed that crime which, for all time, will be a stain in the annals of our history. It is a crime which fills every German with shame.

"The youth of Germany is guiltless. Our youth was anti-Semitically inclined, but it did not call for the extermination of Jewry.

"If anti-Semitism and racial laws could lead to an Auschwitz, then

*Myrna Loy was a prominent American film star of the era.

Auschwitz must mark the end of racial politics and the death of anti-Semitism. Hitler is dead. I never betrayed him; I never tried to overthrow him; I remained true to my oath as an officer, a youth leader, and an official. I was no blind collaborator of his; neither was I an opportunist. Hitler's racial policy was a crime which led to disaster for five million Jews and for all the Germans. The younger generation bears no guilt. But he who, after Auschwitz, still clings to racial politics has rendered himself guilty."

48   The Political General: Jodl

In many ways, General Alfred Jodl—together with Goering, Schacht, and Speer one of the four outstanding personalities in the dock—was the antithesis of Schirach. Giving no ground, he defended to the last the actions of the Wehrmacht. With his haggard face and drawn mouth, he looked like a man who had never smiled in his life, but had survived on a diet of bitter persimmons.

Unquestionably brilliant, his intelligence manifested itself in his relations with other people in an irritating superciliousness. Militant, cynical, and outspoken, he had a proclivity for self-righteous rationalization. During the presentation of his defense, his wife, Luise, was admitted into the courtroom as secretary to his two attorneys, Franz Exner and Hermann Jahrreiss. Succeeding in smuggling a tiny bunch of flowers into the court, she left them on the witness stand with a note: "Be patient and do not lose your temper."

After December 1941, when Hitler had started devoting most of his time to the war against the Soviet Union, Jodl had become the de facto director, if not commander, of German operations in the West. His responsibilities had included supervision of Wehrmacht propaganda, and, from 1944 on, questions of international law.

It was Jodl's contention that his task in preparing the plans for all of Hitler's aggressions had been purely technical; but he effectively destroyed his own defense by exhibiting an impressive knowledge of the diplomatic and political ramifications of the actions, which he attempted to justify.

"Jodl gives the impression that he was much more than a mere soldier," Birkett recorded. "He shows considerable political knowledge, much ingenuity, and remarkable shrewdness."

The Anschluss, Jodl declared, had consisted of "a triumphal march, such as the world probably has seldom seen—even though no one likes to acknowledge it today. It was characterized by my suggestion to the chief of the operations department of the army that he should have bands marching at the head of the columns and that all drivers should be sure to wear goggles, otherwise they might be blinded by the flowers thrown at them." Considering the course of subsequent events, such an ironic exposition was inappropriate in the extreme, but Jodl lacked awareness of his abrasiveness.

Each Nazi aggression had entangled Jodl further in the strands of his own complicity. His most irritating and irrational contention was that Barbarossa had been "undeniably a purely preventive war"—an assertion based on nothing but Hitler's paranoid fear that Stalin, who had shown himself his match for ruthlessness and opportunism, might some day attack or threaten to attack the Reich when it was fully engaged with Britain.

Jodl was cross-examined by Fyfe's principal assistant, the rugged "Khaki" Roberts, whose sarcasm was a match for Jodl's cynicism. Roberts cited Hitler's Partisan Order that resistance should not be punished "by legal prosecution of the guilty, but by the occupation forces spreading such terror as is alone appropriate to eradicate every inclination to resist," and then suggested: "That is a terrible order, is it not?"

"No, it is not at all terrible," Jodl disagreed, "for it is established by international law that the inhabitants of an occupied territory must follow the orders and instructions of the occupying power, and any uprising, any resistance against the army occupying the country is forbidden. The principle of such warfare is an eye for an eye and a tooth for a tooth, and this is not even a German principle."

"I will not argue about it, witness. I gather you approve of the order."

"I approve it as a justified measure conforming to international law and directed against a widespread resistance movement which employed unscrupulous methods." It was as if Jodl had shut out from his mind all the evidence of the atrocious conduct of antipartisan warfare, during which tens of thousands of the innocent had been murdered from one end of Europe to the other.

Despite his support of terror tactics, Jodl was not above claiming credit for himself for the order of May 6, 1944, directing that in the future "all partisans captured in enemy uniform or civilian clothing or surrendering during combat are to be treated in principle as prisoners of war." Jodl explained that he had taken "this unusual step because I became convinced, after the shooting of the English Air Force officers at Sagan, that the Führer no longer concerned himself with the idea of human rights." In reality, the directive had been part of the change in policy forced upon the Nazi regime by the necessity of utilizing all available manpower for war production.

"Had you thought that he was humane up to March of 1944?" Roberts questioned.

"Before this time, I personally knew of no action of his which could not be justified legally, at least under international law." The fact that Jodl seemed to speak with sincerity only increased the puzzlement of the judges as to where Jodl might have been keeping himself the past few years.

"This was—would you agree with me—that this was sheer murder of these fifty airmen?" Roberts demanded of Jodl.

"I completely agree with you; I consider it sheer murder."

"How could you honorable generals go on serving a murderer with unabated loyalty?"

"I did not serve with unabated loyalty after this event, but I did everything in my power to avoid further injustice."

Jodl counted among his achievements the fact that Hitler had been dissuaded from his idea of renouncing the Geneva Convention. Advising against the renunciation, Jodl had written: "Just as it was a mistake in 1914 that we ourselves solemnly declared war on all the states which had for a long time wanted to wage war on us, and through this took the whole guilt of the war on our shoulders, so it would be a mistake now to repudiate openly the obligations of international law and thereby to stand again as the guilty party before the outside world. Adherence to the accepted obligations does not demand in any way that we should have to impose on ourselves any limitations which will interfere with the conduct of the war."

"That is not very honorable, is it?" Roberts suggested.

"I can only say that this was the sole method which achieved success with the Führer, and by its use success was, in fact, achieved. If I had come to him with moral or purely legal arguments, he would have said, 'Leave me alone with this foolish talk.' "

"But, you see, you were deploring there the fact that you told the world the truth in 1914. In 1914 you said that you regarded treaties only as a scrap of paper. You are saying now, 'What a pity we told the world the truth in 1914.' "

Again, as in the case of so many of the other defendants, the court was confronted with the puzzle: Was Jodl telling the truth now when he said he had lied to Hitler; or had he meant what he said to Hitler, and was lying now; or, quite likely, had he been so corrupted by a system in which mendacity was part of life and hypocrisy a pervasive force that he could not himself separate honest declarations from dissimulations?

In contrast to the witnesses who had preceded him, Jodl—in addition to going into trances—spoke so deliberately that Lawrence suggested: "Defendant, it is not necessary to speak so slowly, if you can speak a little faster"; and Goering remarked: "I wish he would talk faster and get on with it. He makes me nervous."

Jodl admitted to Gilbert that he was torn between admiration and hatred for Hitler. Unable to make up his mind which feeling he wanted to convey, Jodl left the judges likewise confused. When Hitler had first come to power, Jodl told the court, "I very often said that I looked on him as a charlatan [but] in the course of the years I became convinced that he was not a charlatan but a man of gigantic personality who, however, in the end assumed infernal power."

It was quite plausible to accept Jodl's contention that his perception of Hitler had undergone such transformation. Even now, however, his predominant view of the Führer seemed to be one of admiration. Following the July 20 assassination attempt, he had stated: "The Führer did not come to power by force, but borne up by the love of the German people."

"Do you remember saying that?" Roberts asked.

"Yes, and that is true. He came to power, borne up by the love of the German people. He was almost overwhelmed by this love of the people and of the soldiers."

"Borne up by the love of the German people?" Roberts bored in. "You have forgotten the SS, the Gestapo, and the concentration camps for political opponents, have you not?"

"I have told you how unfortunately little I knew of all these things, almost nothing," Jodl replied weakly. "Of course, with the knowledge of these things, all this takes on a different aspect."

Why, Roberts inquired, had Jodl declared that " 'the twentieth of July was the blackest day which German history has seen as yet, and will probably remain so for all times'? Why was it such a black day for Germany? Because somebody tried to assassinate a man whom you now admit was a murderer?"

He had objected, Jodl replied, because he himself had almost been "blown up in a cowardly, insidious manner by one of my own comrades —should I perhaps approve of it? If the man with a pistol in his hand had shot the Führer and had then given himself up, it would have been entirely different."

"Do you think it is any more dastardly than shooting those fifteen American soldiers who landed in the north of Italy to destroy a military target, shooting them like dogs?"

"That also was murder, undoubtedly. But it is not the task of a soldier to be the judge of his commander in chief. May history or the Almighty do that."

Once more, as so often in this trial, the reluctance of the former German leaders to make a commitment was manifested. Clearly, Jodl had not known because he had not wanted to know, because knowledge would have demanded the taking of a stand, while ignorance did not. "As for the ethical code of my action"—he retreated like a turtle into his shell—"I must say that it was obedience. That I was far from extending this code of obedience to the blind code of obedience imposed on the slave has, I consider, been proved beyond all manner of doubt. Nevertheless, you cannot get around the fact that there can be no other course for a soldier but obedience."

49   The Fox and the Goat: Speer and Sauckel

Thomas Dodd had presented the evidence against Sauckel and Speer as an entity under the charge of slave labor. Considering Speer the more important of the two men, the American prosecution had asserted: "Unlike Sauckel, Speer's criminal activity went substantially beyond the realm of slave labor. His was one of the masterminds in the plan for the systematic robbery and spoliation of the lands overrun by the German war machine."

Sauckel himself stated: "The others only got whatever was left, because Speer told me once in the presence of the Führer that I am here to work for Speer and that, mainly, I am his man."

Sauckel's attorney, Robert Servatius, had applied for some thirty witnesses and affidavits, but received almost no response, for everyone summoned was afraid of being prosecuted later. "I may even have to consider withdrawing my motion altogether because I have to admit that the amount of material reaching me is very small," Servatius chagrinedly told the court.

Those witnesses for Sauckel that were brought to Nuremberg through the medium of the tribunal's secretariat more often than not turned out to be the subjects of erroneous identification. "Yesterday the witness Hildebrandt arrived, but it was again the wrong Hildebrandt," Servatius complained. "This is the third witness who has appeared here in this comedy of errors. It was the wrong one for Mende, the wrong for Stothfang, and the wrong one for Hildebrandt."

The bald-headed Sauckel provided, with his Hitler mustache, an unpleasant reminder of the Nazi era. He had difficulty uttering his thoughts coherently, and, as unlikely as it might seem, was even less comprehensible than Ribbentrop or Rosenberg. Time and again Servatius, who had studied in London and Moscow and spoke English, French, and Russian, warned him: "The interpreters cannot translate your long sentences properly. You must make short sentences and divide your phrases, otherwise no one can understand you and your defense will suffer a great deal.

. . . Herr Sauckel, you must formulate your sentences differently, the interpreters cannot translate them. You must not insert one sentence into another."

Servatius's exhortations were, to a large extent, futile. Sauckel's intertwined verbiage was compounded by his transparent evasiveness; seldom did he provide a direct answer.

In his proletarian heart, Sauckel had wished that all workers, foreign as well as German, should be treated humanely; and Speer had spoken in his favor at Dustbin: "I must emphasize that Sauckel always did his best to secure decent treatment and food for the foreign workers in Germany. He worked on this with all his energy." But in his Nazi soul Sauckel had subordinated his humanitarian instincts to the ruthless exploitation of men, women, and children. In demanding that workers "must be fed, housed, and treated in such a way that with the least possible effort the greatest possible results will be achieved," Sauckel claimed, on the witness stand, he had merely been following the principles of Henry Ford's efficiency engineering.

His contention that "I had no police facilities at my disposal" was specious, since by Hitler's directive Sauckel had had only to give orders and all German agencies had been required to comply with them. Sauckel had fixed the quotas, they had been broken down as the demands were passed from one subordinate agency to the next, and had manifested themselves at the lowest level in call-up notices like the following: "Should you disobey this compulsory service decree, the members of your family (parents, wife, brothers, sisters, and children) will be placed in a punitive camp and will be liberated only after you have presented yourself. I reserve for myself the right to confiscate your personal and real property as well as the personal and real property of the members of your family. Moreover you will be punished with confinement and prison, or with penal servitude, or with internment in a concentration camp."

"The threat of such penalties in this form was completely unknown to me," Sauckel asserted. "If I had learned of it, I would have stopped it immediately."

Biddle, dissatisfied with the questioning of both the prosecution and the defense, launched into the deftest cross-examination of the trial.

At a meeting of the Central Planning Board on March 1, 1944, Sauckel had stated: "The most abominable point against which I have to fight is the claim that there is no organization in these districts properly to recruit Frenchmen, Belgians, and Italians and to dispatch them to work. So I have even proceeded to employ and train a whole staff of French and Italian agents of both sexes who for good pay, just as was done in olden times for shanghaiing, go hunting for men and dupe them, using liquor as well as persuasion in order to dispatch them to Germany."

"Who appointed these agents that worked as private recruiting agents?" Biddle wanted to know. "Who appointed them?"

"In those countries, the commissioner for labor allocation appointed them—" Sauckel started to take off into another of his long-winded explanations; but Biddle cut him short:

"I see. And they would be paid on, I think you said, a commission basis; is that right? Every workman they brought in, they would get a fee for, is that right?" Biddle indicated that Sauckel's recruiters had been bounty hunters.

"Yes. I do not know the details myself anymore, but for the most part that is correct."

"Now, I take it when you used the word 'shanghai,' that simply means private recruiting with force."

"No—"

"Now, wait a minute. Can you shanghai a man without using force? You do not mean you shanghaied them by persuasion? Did you?"

"Yes, for I wanted to recruit these French associations in just this voluntary, friendly way, over a glass of beer or wine in a cafe. I don't mean shanghai in the bad sense as I recall it being used from my sailor day. Never, your honor, in France or anywhere else, did I order men to be shanghaied, but rather—"

"Oh, I know you did not order it!" Biddle's scalpel was so sharp that Sauckel did not even realize he was being dissected. "You mean that 'shanghai' just meant that you had a friendly glass of wine with a workman and then he joined up? Was that what you meant?"

"I understood it in that way."

"Was it contrary to German law?"

"It was against my convictions and contrary to German laws."

"Now, let us see where the police came in," Biddle continued. "If any man resisted being brought in as a workman, or did not register, or did not live up to his contract, he became a criminal. That was when the police came in. The police were there simply to see that the law was not broken. That is right, isn't it? That was their function?"

"No, that was not my task; that was the task of the service authorities," Sauckel, once more displaying a guilty conscience, proffered a denial to a question he had not been asked.

"Well, why do you always say, 'It was not my task.' I did not ask you if it was your task. I am just talking about the police; I am not talking about you. Now, when those labor decrees were violated, then it was that the police began to function. Isn't that right?"

"That would have been the normal way, the correct way."

"Good. . . . Now there were also what you call the labor training camps. . . . To whom were they subordinate?"

"They were subordinate exclusively to the police, that is, as far as I know, to *Gruppenführer* Müller."

"And I presume that they were staffed and officered by the SS, as were the other concentration camps?"

"I have to assume that also, but I cannot say definitely because I have never seen any such camps."

"So when a man was sent to a labor training camp, he was not sent simply to labor; he was being punished, wasn't he, for having broken the law? So, although part of your duty was to look after the foreign laborers who were brought over here, that stopped after they were turned over to the police, and you had no more jurisdiction; is that right?"

"That is right," Sauckel agreed, but emphasized that once the workers had been employed they had passed out of his domain, a point that Biddle failed to grasp. (Ley's suicide had aborted the presentation of evidence on the *Deutsche Arbeiter Front*; and the judges, therefore, were deprived of information on one of the three sides of the labor-industrial triangle composed of Sauckel, Speer, and Ley.)

"I think we are very clear, or comparatively so, as to the numbers that were brought in," Biddle continued, the total having been established at approximately five million. "I want to know how many were voluntary and how many were involuntary."

At a meeting of the Central Planning Board in the spring of 1944, Sauckel had declared: "Of the five million foreign workers who came to Germany, less than two hundred thousand came voluntarily."

This figure, like a number of other expressions attributed to him, Sauckel now contended, was unquestionably due to a clerical error. "That is an utterly impossible proportion."

"Quite!" Biddle agreed. Biddle next turned to the fact that, in contradiction to Sauckel's claim that he had had no enforcement police of his own, he had, in actuality, formed a contingent of about a thousand men trained by the SS in France. "Why did you organize this police corps? Why did you do it? I thought you kept away from police measures."

"In order to have protection for these people and for these places which frequently were raided, demolished, or harassed by the resistance movement."

"I see what you mean. This was an organization to protect the recruiting that was going on; is that right?"

"Yes."

"Well, then, either it was the police, or it was the military, or it was some other force which was going to carry out your forcible recruiting; is that right?" Biddle concluded rhetorically.

Speer, it seemed, would find it impossible to disassociate himself from Sauckel's guilt. On June 28, 1945, at one of his first interrogations at Dustbin,* Speer had related frankly that the ties between the armament industry and Sauckel had been very strong. The Central Planning Board, controlled by Speer, had established production goals, and estimated the number of workers that would be required. Allocations for the armament industry had represented by far the largest demand. On October 18, shortly after being brought to Nuremberg, Speer had told Murray Gurfein: "I do not wish to give the impression that I want to deny the fact that I demanded manpower and foreign labor from Sauckel very energetically."

"Is it clear to you, Mr. Speer," Gurfein had asked, "that in 1942 when the decisions were being made concerning the use of forced foreign labor, that you participated in the discussions yourself?"

"Yes."

"So that I take it the execution of the program of bringing foreign workers into Germany by compulsion under Sauckel was based on earlier decisions that had been made with your agreement?"

"Yes," Speer had acknowledged.

During the course of his accretion of power, Speer had brought the number of workers under his control from 2.5 million to 14 million, and striven to place Sauckel more and more under his domination. The contest between Speer and Sauckel had been all the more unequal because Speer had camped out at Hitler's headquarters and had had continual access to Hitler, while Sauckel had seldom seen the Führer. Every dispute between Speer and Sauckel had, therefore, been resolved in favor of Speer.

Since Speer, in addition to his involvement in the forced labor program, had been partnered with Himmler in the massive use of concentration camp inmates for war production, and had violated the Geneva Convention by illegal employment of prisoners of war, the outlook for his defense seemed bleak. Speer's lawyer, Hans Flächsner, was pessimistic; and Biddle noted that Speer—whose heart was beating wildly even though he had downed a couple of tranquilizers—looked "utterly crushed" as he took the stand.

Speer, however, proved himself the cleverest of the accused. Georg Thomas, the head of the Wehrmacht's economics and armaments office, characterized him as a masterful liar, as adept at prevaricating by omission as commission. By pretending frankness he aimed, first of all, to disarm the opposition. He then tried to mask the truth with flurries of statistics,

---

*As previously pointed out, the Nuremberg prosecution was deprived of access to the material from Dustbin.

profound generalities that at first glance seemed relevant but in actuality evaded the question, and by a subtle shifting of responsibility.

"I had no influence on the methods by which workers were recruited," Speer contended. "Besides, this was no concern of mine. . . . Of course, I expected Sauckel to meet above all the demands of war production, but it cannot be maintained that he primarily took care of my demands, for beginning with the spring of 1943 I received only part of the workers I needed. It is also clear that the German labor reserves had not been fully utilized. In January 1943 these German reserves were still ample. I was interested in having German workers—including, of course, women—and this nonutilization of German reserves also proves that I cannot be held solely responsible for covering the essential needs, that is, for demanding foreign labor."

In reality, the "German labor reserve" had consisted almost entirely of untrained teenagers, women, and old people, none of whom had been of much use to Speer. Speer needed skilled workers and heavy laborers, and to get them he had engaged in such tricks as endeavoring to obtain from French industry lists of technicians held prisoner of war under the guise that they were to be repatriated. "The French firms know exactly which prisoners of war are smelters," he had directed one of his subordinates in November 1942. "Unofficially, you should create the impression that they would be released. They give us the names, and then we get them out. Have a try!"

The impression Speer hoped, nevertheless, to generate, and in large measure succeeded in creating on the tribunal, was one of having attempted to exercise a moderating influence on Sauckel's radical roundups, which had purportedly exceeded the requirements of war industry. But few of Speer's assertions, wrapped skillfully in casuistry, could have withstood close examination. When Speer declared, "It cannot be maintained that he primarily took care of my demands," the statement was based on the fact that *only* forty percent of the impressed laborers had been assigned to tasks *directly* concerned with war production. Hundreds of thousands of others, however, had gone to supporting industries; and even women put to work as agricultural laborers had formed part of Speer's manpower requisitions, since men needed for coal mining and other heavy labor could not be transferred from farms until the women replaced them. Directly and indirectly, Speer had utilized eighty to ninety percent of the foreign workers brought in by Sauckel. When, for example, in early 1944, the official in charge of coal production, the most critical of the German basic industries, had requested 25,000 more men, and asked that the fulfillment of this need not be made dependent on the recruiting of foreign laborers, Speer had replied: "Nothing doing!"

Like other members of the regime with a modicum of common sense, Speer had come to disapprove of Sauckel's mindless roundups because they interfered with production and augmented the ranks of the resistance. (At Dustbin, he had told an interrogator: "We were often of the opinion that Sauckel richly deserved a high decoration from your side.") Consequently, in mid-1943, he had decreed that Sauckel could no longer transport men from French, Belgian, and Italian factories essential to the German war effort. Taking men from a French factory and putting them to work in a German was a practice that had never made any sense. Beyond the fact that it had merely transferred manpower from one place to another, and so had not augmented total production, it had had the deleterious effect of causing tens of thousands of workers to disappear into the countryside, and thus wreaked havoc with efficiency.

Speer, however, had not had the least moral or humanitarian objections to Sauckel's recruiting practices. Early in 1943, after the Germans had occupied southern France and Speer had stripped the machinery from factories for shipment to Germany, he had notified Sauckel: "It is no longer necessary to give special consideration to Frenchmen in the further recruiting of specialists and helpers in France. The recruiting can proceed with emphasis and sharpened measures." Beyond the five percent of the labor force he had declared off limits, Speer had not cared whom Sauckel dragooned to Germany, and, in fact, had continued to demand as many men from him as always. But since Sauckel with his narrow mind had opposed the institution of so-called *Sperrbetrieben* (blocked factories) from which he could not remove workers, because his own task had been made more difficult, Speer in the courtroom exploited his establishment of the *Sperrbetrieben* to cast himself as a man of reason. Before the development of the blocked factories, Speer told the court, "between eighty thousand and one hundred thousand workers came, for instance, from France to Germany every month. After the establishment of the blocked factories, this figure decreased to the insignificant number of three thousand or four thousand a month."

This was a gross exaggeration, since the largest number of French laborers—aside from prisoners of war—working in Germany had been 764,000, and at least a third of these had previously been POWs. Sauckel had had great difficulty in getting as many as a quarter million men out of France in any one year. Furthermore, prior to the Allied landing, transports of French laborers to Germany had continued to average about six thousand, not three thousand or four thousand, a month.

Sauckel, however, could not be saddled with the onus for Speer's agreement with Himmler on concentration camp labor. Speer's relationship with Himmler had dated from the latter 1930s, when Himmler, not unlike the ancient Egyptian slave masters, had set his victims to quarrying building materials for the monstrous monuments that Speer was supposed to raise for the Führer. It was necessary, Himmler had told the SS, "to exploit them [the camp inmates] for the great folk community by having them break stones and bake bricks so that the Führer can erect his grand buildings." Then, in February 1942, when Speer had taken over as armaments minister, Himmler's output of stones and bricks had been applied to the construction of the new factories that Germany desperately needed.

Six months later, in September 1942, when the roundup of Jews for "extermination through work" had reached its initial peak, Himmler had suggested that the burgeoning camp population be employed for arms manufacture on the premises. Speer, perceiving that Himmler, in addition to making a botch of things, would establish an arms industry beyond his control, had objected: "I pointed out to the Führer that, apart from an insignificant amount of work, no possibility exists of organizing armaments production in the concentration camps, because (1) the machine tools required are missing; (2) there are no suitable premises. Both of these assets would be available in the armament industry, if use could be made of them by a second shift."

Speer had suggested that the logical procedure would be to transfer workers from factories in suburbs and small towns to plants in the cities, and have them replaced by concentration camp laborers. Speer had succeeded, furthermore, in frustrating Himmler's attempt to expand his power: "I pointed out to the Führer," he had written, "the difficulties which I expect to encounter if Reichsführer SS Himmler should be able, as he requested, to exercise authoritative influence over these factories. The Führer, too, does not consider such an influence necessary."

To placate Himmler, Hitler had agreed to Speer's compromise "that Reichsführer SS Himmler derive advantage from making his prisoners available; he should get equipment for his divisions."

Responding in court to the questioning of Flächsner, Speer denied "the main accusation by the prosecution that I deliberately increased the number of concentration camps, or caused them to be increased." This was a typical Speer equivocation, separating cause from effect and contradicting a statement he himself had made to Gurfein: "We were anxious to use workers in concentration camps in factories and to establish small concentration camps near the factories in order to use the manpower that was available there."

It was thus that the concentration camp system had spread like a disease, feeding hundreds of satellite camps throughout the Third Reich. At the same time, new factories had been erected at the site of major concentration camps, notably Dachau, Mauthausen, Buchenwald, Dora, and Auschwitz. Speer himself had been vitally interested in the hydrogenation and Buna plants constructed by I. G. Farben at Auschwitz for the conversion of coal to gasoline and the manufacture of artificial rubber. An entirely new compound, Monowitz, had been added to Auschwitz and Birkenau to house the laborers.

Functioning as a giant labor procurement organization for Speer's industries, the SS had siphoned people into one concentration camp after another. *Obergruppenführer* Oswald Pohl, chief of economics and administration for the SS, had called attention to "a marked change in the structure of the concentration camps. The custody of prisoners for the sole reasons of security, education, or as a preventive measure is no longer the main consideration. The importance now lies in the economic side."

Speer himself had urged at a meeting of the Central Planning Board that incarceration in concentration camps should be held as a club over the heads of workers, German and foreign alike: "There is nothing to be said against the SS and police taking drastic steps and putting those known as slackers into concentration camps. There is no alternative. Let it happen several times and the news will soon go around."

At an interrogation on April 5, Höss had told Brookhart, Sonnenfeldt, and Jaari, "We had a lot to do with Speer," and related that Speer and Pohl had conferred regularly on the use of concentration camp labor. On the heels of Höss's capture, an intensive manhunt had been launched for Pohl, and he had been arrested at the end of May. Questioned by Brookhart on June 8, a few days before Speer took the stand, Pohl had related that Himmler had told him at the time of Kaltenbrunner's appointment: "The procurement of manpower is getting more and more difficult. I have therefore agreed with Speer that he would procure labor from the concentration camps to a still increased extent." Speer's demands, Pohl complained, had become insatiable. Speer had met frequently with Himmler, and the Reichsführer SS had made the armaments minister exaggerated promises.

In the area under the jurisdiction of the Dachau concentration camp, Speer had wanted to dig two huge subterranean warehouses, for which he requested one hundred thousand laborers. Himmler had agreed to furnish these, though Dachau had contained only thirty thousand prisoners.

"They could not have delivered so many inmates. Where should they take the hundred thousand from?" Pohl rhetorically shook his head.

The answer was that Himmler had robbed Speer to provide Speer. The practice of dragging people off to concentration camps for the minutest infraction had reached gigantic proportions. It had not been until May 1944, Speer informed the court, that he had realized that Himmler was engaged in an action that, like Sauckel's transfer of workers from essential French industry to German, had added nothing to the sum total of production. The information, Speer declared, "greatly upset me because, after all, this is nothing more than kidnapping. I had an estimate submitted to me about the number of people thus being removed from the economic system. The round figure was thirty thousand to forty thousand a month."

At a meeting with Hitler on June 5, 1944, Speer, pointing out the disruptions in production that resulted, had demanded that the workers be returned to their places of employment. Hitler, seemingly, had agreed with Speer; but, as was customary with problems of this kind, he had referred Speer to their author, Himmler. Himmler had denied that the SS and police had taken anywhere near so many foreign workers into custody. He had promised that he would investigate abuses; and that, as was usual with complaints made to Himmler about Himmler, had been the end of the matter.

In August of 1943, the partnership between Himmler and Speer had entered a new dimension with the initiation of construction on an underground factory at Nordhausen in the heart of the Harz Mountains of Thuringia for the purpose of producing V-bombs. Himmler's construction chief, Hans Kammler, had been placed in charge of the project, and made jointly and directly responsible to Himmler and Speer.

V-weapons had fallen under Speer's jurisdiction since they had been developed by the army. Up to that time, however, Goering had successfully resisted Speer's attempts to take over Luftwaffe production also. But on February 14, 1944, following devastating Allied raids on aircraft plants, Goering had wired Himmler: "I ask you to put at my disposal as great a number of concentration camp convicts as possible for air armament. The situation of the air war makes subterranean transfer necessary."

Goering's request had given Speer his opening. Nine days later he and Milch, who had shifted his primary allegiance from Goering to Speer, had agreed to form a new "Fighter Aircraft Staff," combining the resources of the Luftwaffe, the armaments ministry, and the SS for the manufacture of the new jet planes.

Goering, perceiving that this development would result in the final transfer of power over the economy and production from himself to Speer, had refused to acquiesce. On March 5, Speer, Milch, and Goering's adjutant, Bodenschatz, had met with Hitler to discuss this impasse, as well as Goering's proposal to boost output by placing all prisoners of war except British and American under the control of the SS. On March 18, Speer had gone to Klessheim Castle near Salzburg, an hour's drive from Berchtesgaden, for five days. Another guest at Klessheim had been Hungarian Admiral Horthy. Ribbentrop and Himmler had arrived, Keitel and Jodl had, of course, already been with Hitler, and the Führer and his acolytes had conducted a grand strategy meeting to discuss what was to be done in Hungary.

A month later, on April 17, Speer had sent a memorandum to Himmler: "I have in conjunction with Field Marshal Milch informed the Führer on the work of the Fighter Staff [whose chairman was Speer] in pointing to the extraordinarily pleasing and successful cooperation of the newly created organization. The total subterranean security of the most sensitive work will be concluded by the end of the year."

A second huge underground installation was to be built in Bohemia-Moravia. Since manpower was in short supply everywhere, the memorandum had continued: "If the labor cannot be supplied there either, the Führer wants to get in touch in person with the Reichsführer SS and will cause him to provide the approximately one hundred thousand men required through the securing of corresponding Jewish contingents from Hungary. The Führer demands that a meeting take place with him shortly in order to discuss the details in the presence of the men concerned."

Although Speer had already extracted thousands of Jews from Hungary for use in mines and other enterprises, he had contended during his questioning by Gurfein, "I did not write this," and, as repeatedly happened during the trial of the Nazi leaders, had attempted to pin responsibility on one of his subordinates. "Saur [Speer's deputy and technical director] was the author of this document. It is out of the question that I participated because I was sick at the time." He had, he averred, not known anything about the Hungarian Jews until he recovered. On the witness stand he declared: "From January until May 1944 I was seriously ill," thus giving the judges to understand that he had been out of touch with things.

This was Speer at his most skilled mendacity; for, although he had been hospitalized and on vacation during the first four months of 1944, he had been anything but out of action. On January 18, seeking treatment for an arthritic knee and general exhaustion, he had moved into Gebhardt's Hohenlychen clinic. Bringing his secretaries with him, he had had a telephone line installed to his ministry, and conducted business without interruption. "The conferences, telephone calls, and dictation continued from my bed often did not stop before midnight," he recalled in his memoirs. Though felled by pulmonary difficulties for a few days in February, he had recovered shortly, and a month later been well enough to travel. After participating in the conference on Hungary, he had gone to recuperate in Merano, Italy, for a month.

It was from there that he had directed the dispatch to Himmler of the memorandum on the Fighter Aircraft Staff. When Goering had objected to Speer's control over the underground jet plane factory, Speer had threatened to resign. Hitler, panic-stricken, had dispatched Milch and

Saur to Merano to assure the armaments chief of Hitler's esteem and complete support. Thus fortified, Speer had flown to Berchtesgaden on April 25, and met Hitler in an extraordinary session, in which he had been able to dictate his own terms. His triumph over Goering had been complete. Not only the construction of the new facilities, but all Luftwaffe production had shortly fallen into his domain; and three days later, on April 28, Eichmann had dispatched the first fifteen hundred Jewish laborers from Hungary to Auschwitz.

So much for Speer's inactivity during his illness.

In December 1943, a month before he had admitted himself to Hohenlychen, Speer had visited Nordhausen. "When you inspected establishments, did you ever see concentration camp inmates?" Flächsner inquired of him.

"Of course, when on inspection tours of industries, I occasionally saw inmates of concentration camps, who, however, looked well fed."

When Biddle suggested that perhaps he did not have a good comprehension of conditions in concentration camps, Speer stated: "It was known in Germany that a stay in a concentration camp was an unpleasant matter. I also knew that, but I did not know any details."

"Well, is not 'unpleasant' putting it a little mildly?"

"I must say that during the time in which I was a minister, strange though it sounds, I became less disturbed about the state of concentration camp inmates than I had been before, because I heard only good and calming reports about the concentration camps from official sources."

"Herr Speer, what do you know about the working conditions in subterranean factories?" Flächsner inquired.

"The most modern equipment for the most modern weapons had been housed in subterranean factories. Since we did not have many of these subterranean works at our disposal, we had to house in the main this latest equipment there. This equipment required perfect conditions of work—air which was dry and free from dust—good lighting facilities, fresh air installations, so that the conditions which applied to such a subterranean factory would be about the same as those on a night shift in a regular industry. I should like to add that, contrary to the impression which has been created here in court, these subterranean factories, almost without exception, were staffed with German workers, because we had a special interest in having these modern installations manned by the best workers which were at our disposal."

This was a typical Speerism—part out-and-out lie, part evasion by tangential generalization.

In his memoirs, Speer painted an entirely different picture: "The conditions for these prisoners were in fact barbarous, and a sense of profound involvement and personal guilt seizes me whenever I think of them. As I learned from the overseers after the inspection was over, the sanitary conditions were inadequate, disease rampant; the prisoners were quartered right there in the damp caves, and as a result the mortality among them was extraordinarily high. That same day I allocated the necessary materials and set all the machinery in motion to build a barracks camp immediately on an adjacent hill. In addition, I pressed the SS camp command to take all necessary measures to improve sanitary conditions and upgrade the food. They pledged that they would do so."

Deftly gliding into another subject, Speer left the impression that, as soon as he had gained knowledge of the conditions, he had taken measures to alleviate them. This, in fact, was simply mendacity in another variation. The truth had been as grim as anything at Auschwitz.

Upon returning from Nordhausen to Berlin, Speer had complained to his friend Dr. Karl Brandt and to Hitler that production was deteriorating and priceless, irreplaceable technicians and experts were being lost because of the atrocious working conditions; an effort should be made, Speer had declared, to improve the health of the workers. Brandt had dispatched Dr. Poschmann, chief medical officer in Speer's organization, to Nordhausen to investigate.

To Allied investigators, Poschmann described his visit as the most terrifying experience of his life. Contrary to Speer's assertion that the workers had been mainly German, the work force had consisted, except for guards and supervisors, entirely of fifty-two thousand concentration camp inmates representing eighteen nationalities, including thousands of Hungarian Jews. They existed like human moles. Once they were marched into the dripping limestone caverns, they did not emerge—except for one brief roll call weekly—for three months. Worked a minimum of seventy-two hours a week, they were fed a diet, providing little protein and no vitamins, of eleven hundred calories daily. One pallet had been provided for every three men, and they slept in eight-hour shifts. Lung and heart diseases were epidemic because of the dampness and intense air pressure. Muscles and bones deteriorated. Forced to stoop continuously, men eventually had been unable to straighten up at all, and walked about with the posture of apes. Deaths averaged 180 a day. When a deputation of prisoners petitioned for improved conditions, Kammler had responded by turning machine guns on them, killing eighty. Mass executions had occurred frequently, and continued unabated until the end of the war. When Poschmann expressed concern that a single case of typhoid might spread like wildfire and wipe out the entire labor force, Kammler had retorted that nothing of the sort could happen: At the first sign of typhoid the entire section, and everybody in it, would be walled up, and that would end the threat.

Poschmann had returned to Brandt in a state of despair. Brandt thereupon had talked to Himmler. Himmler had rejected any interference: "I want to point out to you that this matter has nothing to do with you. If something has to be put right, it will be done by Kammler himself."

When it had become evident to Brandt that Himmler had no intention of taking corrective measures, Brandt had informed Hitler. Hitler had told him to go and see Himmler. When Brandt replied that he had already spoken to the Reichsführer SS, Hitler had waved him off: "Leave it. Himmler will put it right."

With that, the prisoners at Nordhausen had been condemned to their fate. Conditions had continued unimproved until the end of the war.

Clearly, Speer had reason to be pessimistic, and to view Jackson's cross-examination with trepidation. But all the heart and fire had gone out of the American prosecutor. On June 6, President Truman had ended the suspense and Jackson's hopes by designating Secretary of the Treasury Fred Vinson as his nominee for Chief Justice of the United States. Parker commented: "I think it is a fine appointment but I feel sorry for Bob Jackson. It means, most probably, that his life's ambition has passed him by when he thought, and everybody else thought, that he had it in his grasp. Black is responsible for defeating him; and the only comfort to him is that Black did not get the chief's place. That would have created an intolerable situation for Jackson."

Unquestionably, Black and Douglas had been lobbying hard behind the Washington scene against Jackson's appointment. Doris Fleeson had carried a column on the "Blood Feud," Drew Pearson had predicted in his column that Black and Douglas would resign if Jackson were appointed, and in a story in the March 16 edition of the Washington *Star* Black had vented his "fiery scorn" at what he called Jackson's "open and gratuitous insults [and] slur upon his personal and judicial honor."*

As soon as Vinson's nomination was announced, Jackson struck back at Black by issuing a lengthy statement from Nuremberg. He had refused to bow before Black's bullying or his threats, Jackson declared: "His position came to this: I must join in covering up the facts or have war. I refuse to buy my peace at that price. If war is declared on me, I propose to wage

---

*Aside from the deep philosophical divisions and clashes of temperament between Jackson on the one hand and Black and Douglas on the other, the feud stemmed from a case in which Black's former law partner, Cranston Harris, had represented the United Mine Workers against the Jewel Ridge Coal Company. When Black had voted with the 5–4 majority in favor of the UMW, the coal company, charging conflict of interest on Black's part, had petitioned for a rehearing. In rejecting the petition, Jackson had written that the Supreme Court did not have jurisdiction over excluding one of its members, thus indicating that, ethically, he thought Black should have disqualified himself.

it with the weapons of the open warrior, not those of the stealthy assassin." Black had twice voted and provided the majority in cases in which he might have had a personal interest: "I want that practice stopped."

Parker thought that the dispute, which was the talk of Nuremberg and Washington, was "a most interesting row! My sympathies are all with Jackson, but if he had asked me I would have advised him not to make this attack. Everybody will think he was motivated by pique at not being appointed chief justice and was trying to get even. He certainly shows Black up in an ugly light, but I don't think he has helped himself any."

For Speer, however, it was one more stroke of luck; because, with that explosion, all the animosity seemed to go out of Jackson. In place of the bellicose questioner of Goering and Schacht, the man who confronted Speer appeared to regard him almost with compassion as a fellow sufferer in the game of life. Cross-examining Speer, Jackson at times sounded more like Speer's advocate than his prosecutor.

Speer, having made his approach to Jackson more than six months earlier, conversely offered in his testimony two crucial statements that delighted Jackson's ears. In one, he denounced the oath of loyalty to Hitler which many of the defendants had stressed: "There is one loyalty which everyone must keep; and that is loyalty toward one's own people. That duty comes before everything. If I am in a leading position and if I see that the interests of a nation are acted against in such a way, then I too must act. That Hitler had broken faith with the nation must have been clear to every intelligent member of his entourage, certainly at the latest in January or February 1945. Hitler had once been given his mission by the people; he had no right to gamble away the destiny of his people with his own." In the other statement, Speer depreciated the Führer Principle: "Even in an authoritarian system the leaders must accept a common responsibility, and it is impossible for them to dodge that common responsibility after the catastrophe, for if the war had been won the leaders would also presumably have laid claim to common responsibility."

Never questioning Speer's veracity or confronting him with contradictory evidence, Jackson couched his questions in such a way as to give Speer the benefit of every doubt. On the subject of Speer's cooperative ventures with Himmler, he all but congratulated Speer on the good bargain he had struck. (Originally Speer provided Himmler with only five percent of arms output in return for the concentration camp labor, but the proportion multiplied manifold as Himmler expanded the Waffen SS.) When it came to Speer's complicity in the removal of Jews, Jackson made it seem as if Speer himself had been a victim: "As I understand it, you were struggling to get manpower enough to produce the armaments to win a war for Germany."

"Yes," Speer agreed.

"And this anti-Semitic campaign was so strong that it took trained technicians away from you and disabled you from performing your functions. Now, isn't that the fact?"

Momentarily Speer, suspecting a trap, was bewildered: "I did not understand the meaning of your question."

"Your problem of creating armaments to win the war for Germany was made very much more difficult by this anti-Jewish campaign which was being waged by other of your co-defendants."

"That is a certainty." As the realization came to Speer that Jackson was a friendly inquisitor, his face lit up, and an immense burden lifted from his shoulders: "And it is equally clear that if the Jews who were evacuated had been allowed to work for me, it would have been a considerable advantage to me."

Jackson asked no questions about Nordhausen, and only one about the Hungarian Jews: "As I understand it, you knew about the deportation of one hundred thousand Jews from Hungary for subterranean aircraft factories, and you told us in your interrogation of 18 October, 1945 that you made no objection to this. That is true, is it not?"

"That is true, yes," Speer agreed, ecstatic to get off so easily.

Jackson was anxious to introduce into the record affidavits, obtained since the conclusion of the prosecution's case, on the condition of foreign laborers at the Krupp Works, and used Speer as a medium to accomplish this goal. In contrast, however, to the wide-ranging charges against the other defendants, Jackson was careful to qualify: "I am not attempting to say that you were personally responsible for these conditions." A few minutes later he iterated: "I am not suggesting—I repeat I am not suggesting—that this was your responsibility. I am suggesting that it is the responsibility of the regime." Within a half hour, in response to an objection by Flächsner to one of the documents, he said for the third time: "I am not prosecuting him with personal responsibility for these conditions."

Finally, incongruously, Speer voiced the opinion that his responsibility had been greater than Jackson suggested: "First I should like to say, as you have so often mentioned my nonresponsibility, that if in general these conditions had been true, on the basis of my statement yesterday I should consider myself responsible. I refuse to evade responsibility. But the conditions are not what they are said to have been here. There are only individual cases which are quoted."

Obviously, Speer could, without great difficulty, have been exposed; but the interaction between Speer and Jackson created a marked impression on spectators and judges alike. Even Fyfe was to some degree taken in; though one of the assistant British prosecutors, Lieutenant Colonel

Griffith-Jones, who had cross-examined Streicher, had no such illusions.

"He was by far the most attractive personality among the defendants," Fyfe wrote, "yet he was prepared to sanction any amount and any treatment of slave labor to maintain his production of war material. My wife was one of many people who were profoundly impressed by Speer's evidence and manner, and remarked to Griffith-Jones that he would be the sort of man Germany would need in the future. Griffith-Jones replied by producing a length of blood-stained telephone wire, about ten feet long, which had been picked up at Krupp's, and which had been used to flog workers. Nevertheless, Speer's consciousness of, and deep shame for, his own and Germany's crimes were in marked contrast with the attitudes of the rest of the defendants, and made him a civilized and sympathetic character."

50 Step by Step: Seyss-Inquart, Papen, Neurath, and Fritzsche

The defenses of the remaining four men in the dock, Seyss-Inquart, Papen, Neurath, and Fritzsche, were unremarkable, and, in the overall context of the trial, unimportant.

Limping to the witness stand, his eyes swimming like egg yolks behind his thick glasses, Seyss-Inquart presented the image of a colorless bureaucrat, neither evil nor immoral: a politically vapid, lukewarm Nazi who had not joined the party until two months after the Anschluss which he had brokered. Chosen as *Reichstatthalter* of Austria by Hitler, he had been caught between the Austrian Nazi Party veterans, who considered him an upstart, and the German carpetbaggers imported by Josef Bürckel, the Rhineland leader whom Hitler installed as Gauleiter. (Since Bürckel had previously supervised the reintegration of the Saarland into the Reich, Hitler regarded him as an expert on annexation.) A year after the Anschluss, Seyss-Inquart had been so beleaguered by attacks from both sides that, fearful of losing his position, he had appealed to Goering and Himmler (who had made him an honorary *Gruppenführer* in the SS).

"I know that I am not of an active fighting nature," he had admitted, then hedged, "unless final decisions are at stake." Although he did not expect everyone to understand why he had not committed himself completely to the Nazi cause, he asserted that the correctness of his approach had been demonstrated by the fact that "if some people are already tired out from the struggle and some have been killed in the fight, I am still around somewhere ready to go into action. I followed [the path] calmly and would without hesitation follow it again because I am satisfied that at one point I could serve the Führer as a tool in his work."

Flattering Himmler, Seyss-Inquart had noted: "Even if I am not energetic in all circumstances, I still act sensibly. In any event, I am also harmless."

Goering and Himmler had been charmed by Seyss-Inquart's sycophancy, and Hitler had always had room for a willing tool. After first appointing Seyss-Inquart Frank's deputy in Poland, the Führer, on May 12, 1940, had made him Reich Commissioner for the Netherlands. Ruling over a people Hitler regarded as full-fledged Aryans, Seyss-Inquart had tried to follow as moderate a policy as he was permitted by the Führer. Nevertheless, he had cooperated with Himmler when the SS, in February 1941, had shipped six hundred Jewish youths to Mauthausen in retaliation for Jewish resistance to a Nazi pogrom. When the Dutch had staged a sympathy strike, Seyss-Inquart had broken it by imposing a massive fine and threatening the strikers with the death penalty. "The Jews are the enemy of National Socialism with whom no armistice or peace can be made," he had declared. "We will smite the Jews where we meet them and whoever goes along with them must take the consequences."

On the other hand, Seyss-Inquart had persuaded most Dutch officials to remain at their posts (including the half-Jewish secretary-general of agriculture, fisheries, commerce, and industry) and governed through them. Hitler, Goebbels had recorded, "is full of praise for Seyss-Inquart. He governs the Netherlands very cleverly. . . . [He is] a master in the art of alternating gingerbread with whippings, and of putting severe measures through with a light touch."

When Dutch resistance had intensified as the war progressed, Seyss-Inquart's reputation had suffered in consequence. In conjunction with the Allied airborne landings at Arnhem and Nijmegen in September 1944, the underground had orchestrated sabotage, assassinations, and a general transportation strike. When the airborne attack had failed, Seyss-Inquart had retaliated by ordering a roundup of all ablebodied men up to age forty for labor in Germany. To break the strike, he had confiscated much of Dutch shipping and embargoed the transportation of food. Twenty-five thousand people, a large part of them children, had died of malnutrition during the winter of 1944–45 as a result.

At the beginning of April 1945, Seyss-Inquart had joined with Speer in frustrating Hitler's scorched-earch policy, and delayed blowing up the great North Sea dams, destruction of which would have placed a large part of northern Holland under water. Hitler had still thought highly enough of him to name him foreign minister in his "will," and Seyss-Inquart had reciprocated by proclaiming: "After the heroic death of our Führer, we shall never cease to fight."

Although Seyss-Inquart had been indicted for his role in the Anschluss as much as for his administration of Holland, it was his actions in the Netherlands on which he was going to be primarily judged.

Heydrich had insisted that, for security purposes, the Jews had to be treated like other enemy aliens, Seyss-Inquart stated: "For that reason, in March of 1941 I ordered that the Jews in the Netherlands be registered. And then things went on step by step." The ultimate step had been the shipment of 110,000, of whom no more than five or six thousand had survived, to concentration camps. "It is rather difficult for me to speak about it now because it sounds like mockery," Seyss-Inquart related to the court. "I was told that the Jews were to be sent to Auschwitz. I had people sent from the Netherlands to Auschwitz. They came back with the report that that was a camp for eighty thousand people with sufficient space. The people were comparatively well off there. For example, they had an orchestra of one hundred men."

At least a quarter million Dutchmen had been impressed for labor in Germany, and during the last nine months of the war four thousand Dutch men and women had been shot. Seyss-Inquart, however, claimed that these executions had been the doing of the security police, and he had had no authority to intervene. In contrast, he asserted, during the first four years of occupation when he had had control over death sentences, "There were less than eight hundred cases—that is to say, less than were caused by a bombing attack on the town of Nijmegen."

During his interrogation by Dodd the previous September, Seyss-Inquart had claimed: "I have done many things in Holland which have been good."

"And you have done many things in Holland which have been bad."

"They were perhaps only harsh."

"It is easy to tell you are a lawyer," Dodd had concluded. The impression Seyss-Inquart made on the judges was much the same.

Papen and Neurath represented the aristocracy's accommodation with Hitler. Together with Fritzsche, they professed themselves not to be anti-Semitic, though Papen told the court that he had deplored "the overwhelming influence of the Jewish element in the spheres which form the nation's public opinion, such as press, literature, theater, film, and especially law. There seemed no doubt in my mind that this foreign monopoly was unhealthy and that it should be remedied in some way. But as I said, that had nothing whatever to do with the racial question." Neurath contended: "I have never been anti-Semitic. My Christian and humanitarian convictions prevented that. A repression of the undue Jewish influence in all spheres of public and cultural life, as it had developed after the First World War in Germany, however, I regarded as desirable." Fritzsche declared: "I was not anti-Semitic. But I was anti-Semitic in this sense: I wanted a restriction of the predominant influence of Jewry in German politics, economy, and culture, such as was manifested after the First World War. I wanted a restriction based on the ratio of Jews to Germans."

The eminence of Jews in German life had been unquestionable— Goebbels had estimated that before 1933 they accounted for forty percent of literary output—but none of the defendants attempted an explanation of how, in the less than one and a half centuries since Napoleon had ended their ghettoization, they could have achieved such importance. Unless they had had a compact with the devil—which is what Streicher implied —their rise could have stemmed only from their dedication to education, hard work, and pursuit of excellence; but such an acknowledgment would, of course, have been the antithesis of the Nazi rationale and "racial" *Weltanschauung*. During an interrogation Frick confessed: "The party attitude against the Jews originally arose out of the fact that they were powerful politically and the party wanted to get into power, and they had to dispose of the Jews in politics to do so." So the Nationalist reactionaries and the Nazis had joined in proclaiming achievement by a minority as immoral, and finally legislating it as illegal.

Long quotations by Papen's lawyer, Egon Kubuschok, from Papen's 1934 Marburg speech, which had helped precipitate the Röhm purge, drew ripples of admiration in the court. " 'They opposed equality before the law,' " Kubuschok read, " 'which they criticized as liberal degeneration, whereas in reality it is the prerequisite for any fair judgment. These people suppressed that pillar of the state which always—and not only in liberal times—was called justice. The mistaking of brutality for vitality would reveal a worship of force which would be dangerous to a people. . . . If we want a close connection with and a close association among the people, we must not underestimate the good sense of the people; we must return their confidence and not try to hold them everlastingly in bondage. . . . The people know what great sacrifices are expected from them. They will bear them and follow the Führer in unflinching loyalty . . . if every word of criticism is not taken for ill will, and if despairing patriots are not branded as enemies of the state.' "

Fyfe, however, cross-examining Papen, exposed him as a hypocrite, compromising his principles to preserve his position. "Herr Jung had helped you considerably with the composition of the Marburg speech, had he not?" Fyfe asked Papen. "He was shot after the thirtieth of June, was he not?"

"Yes."

"He was a man for whom you not only had great affection, but for whose political views you had great respect and agreement, is that not so?"

"Perfectly right, yes."

"You have told us about Herr von Bose. He was shot. . . . Von Bose and Jung had been working with you in close cooperation and if anyone knew whether they were innocent men or not it was you. Why did you, with that knowledge, agree with Hitler to carry on as vice-chancellor and then to enter the foreign service?"

"I have stated that I had resigned," Papen evaded Fyfe's question.

"You see what I am putting to you? I am putting to you quite clearly that all you cared about was your own personal position. You were prepared to serve these murderers so long as your own dignity was put right."

Turning to Papen's letter of abject rapprochement to Hitler after having offered his resignation, Fyfe demanded: "Why did you write stuff like that to the head of a gang of murderers who had murdered your collaborators? Why did you write to him: 'The crushing of the revolt, your courageous and firm personal intervention have met with nothing but recognition throughout the entire world.' Why did you write it?"

"Because at that time it was my opinion that there actually had been a revolution and that Hitler had crushed it," Papen squirmed.

"Well, now, you knew very well that Hitler was worried from the point of view of foreign opinion as to publicity being given to the effect of a break between you and him. Herr von Papen, if you, as an ex-chancellor of the Reich and, as you said yourself, one of the leading Catholic laymen of Germany, an ex-officer of the Imperial Army, had said at that time 'I am not going to be associated with murder, cold-blooded murder as an instrument of policy,' you might at some risk to yourself have brought down the whole of this rotten regime, might you not?"

"That is possible, but had I said it publicly, then quite probably I would have disappeared somewhere just as my associates did."

Fyfe continued detailing Papen's accommodation with Hitler even after his aide Tschirschky had fled in 1935 to escape from the Gestapo, and Ketteler, Papen's secretary and the fiancé of his daughter, had been murdered in 1938. "Why didn't you after this series of murders which had gone on over a period of four years, why didn't you break with these people and stand up like General Yorck or any other people that you may think of from history, stand up for your own views and oppose these murderers? Why didn't you do it?"

He had done it for love of country, Papen asserted: "I did my duty—

my duty to Germany, if you wish to know. I can understand very well, Sir David, that after all these things we know today, after the millions of murders which have taken place, you consider the German people a nation of criminals, and that you cannot understand that this nation has its patriots as well. I did these things in order to serve my country, and I should like to add, Sir David, that up to the time of the Munich Agreement, and even up to the time of the Polish campaign, even the major powers tried, although they knew everything that was going on in Germany, to work with this Germany. Why do you wish to reproach a patriotic German with acting likewise?"

Fyfe refused to accept this argument, though in many ways it was a valid one. "The major powers have not had their servants murdered, one after the other, and were not close to Hitler like you!" he accused Papen. "You had seen your own friends, your own servants, murdered around you. You had the detailed knowledge of it, and the only reason that could have led you on and made you take one job after another from the Nazis was that you sympathized with their work. That is what I am putting against you, Herr von Papen."

Neurath, Fyfe made clear, had served Hitler just as slavishly as a respectable, conservative front man. Beyond that, he had associated himself far more closely than Papen with Hitler's policies, and shared responsibility for the repression of the Czech population.

Neurath claimed, like so many others, that he had been serving not Hitler but Germany, and had retained his position in Czechoslovakia as long as possible in order to provide a moderating influence: "I had to stay as long as I could in order to prevent this country, which was entrusted to Germany, from coming under the definite domination of the SS. Everything that happened to the country after my departure in 1941 I had actually prevented through my presence; I believed that by remaining I not only rendered a service to my own country but to the Czech people as well. I believe that by my persevering in office I prevented much of the misery which befell the Czech people after I left."

When he became excited, Neurath stuttered badly; and though his age did not show in his face, he exhibited a number of signs of incipient senility. His mind wandered, and Lawrence had to remind him that it was not sufficient merely to shake his head when responding to questions.

Despite his protestations of benevolence toward the Czechs, Neurath had recommended, along with his state secretary, Karl Frank, that the population should, as far as possible, be assimilated and *Germanized*. "Such a Germanization provides for," Frank had written, "(1) the changing of the nationality of racially suitable Czechs; (2) the expulsion of racially unassimilable Czechs and of the intelligentsia who are enemies of the Reich, or 'special treatment' for these and all destructive elements; (3) the recolonizing of the territory thus freed with fresh German blood."

Neurath attempted to blame these recommendations and all other repressive acts on Frank, who had been executed in Prague on May 22. But Fyfe had no difficulty in impeaching Neurath, who had sent his own, parallel memorandum along with Frank's.

"I will read the words again," Fyfe announced. "I have read them three times: 'I enclose another memorandum on the same question which my State Secretary K. H. Frank has drawn up independently of me and which in its train of thought leads to the same result, and with which I fully agree.'"

"I have just now told you that I no longer agree with these statements today," Neurath retorted, as if all culpability could be erased by an admission that one has erred and changed his mind.

No one except the Russians was interested in Fritzsche, and the incongruity of his inclusion in the trial with the leaders of the Third Reich was emphasized even more sharply when he took the stand. Fritzsche had never met most of his co-defendants before being brought to Nuremberg, and only with Funk had he had more than a passing acquaintance. In Moscow, at the prompting of the Soviets, he had exaggerated his importance; in Nuremberg, conversely, he depreciated the role he had played as the country's leading radio commentator.

The truth lay somewhere between. Like Funk, Fritzsche had been employed during the 1920s by Hugenberg. In the summer of 1932 the Papen government had contracted with him to initiate a program, "Political Newspaper Review," on the radio, and in May of 1933 Goebbels had placed him in charge of the wireless service of the Reich Broadcasting Company. Moving up steadily in the ranks, he had had, from 1939 until November 1942, direct responsibility for the German press.

During the Stalingrad offensive he had gone to the Ukraine to conduct propaganda, and received reports on the extermination of Jews. Though he claimed that he had investigated and been able to discover nothing except that hostages had been executed, he most surely lied, for the shootings had been so widespread and the stories of them so notorious that only a mentally incompetent blind and deaf man would have had difficulty uncovering the evidence.

Subsequently, as Plenipotentiary for the Political Organization of the Greater German Radio, Fritzsche had had authority over all political domestic and foreign broadcasts, and continued to harp on the theme, "The guilty ones are exclusively the Jews and the plutocrats."

No one on the Allied side believed him when he asserted his ignorance of the Final Solution. But, as Jackson had stated a number of times, the defendants were not being tried for what they had thought or what they had said, but for what they had done. Fritzsche was far too slick for the clumsy, dialectic-laced cross-examination of the Russian prosecution. Having observed the trial for eight months, he knew just what to say to impress the judges:

"It was always and it still is my conviction that no oath relieves a man of his general duties to humanity. No one is made an irresponsible tool by an oath. My oath would never have made me carry out an order if I had recognized it to be criminal.

"If the German people had learned of these mass murders, they would certainly have no longer supported Hitler. They would probably have sacrificed five million for a victory, but never would the German people have wished to bring about victory by the murder of five million people.

"I should like to say further that this murder decree of Hitler's seems to me the end of every race theory, every race philosophy, every kind of race propaganda, for after this catastrophe any further advocacy of race theory would be equivalent to approval in theory of further murder. An ideology in the name of which five million people were murdered is a theory which cannot continue to exist."

51   The Katyn Forest Massacre

The evidence on the Katyn Forest massacre followed the defense of Fritzsche. Under direct orders from the Kremlin, Rudenko had insisted on charging the Germans—and Goering in particular—with responsibility for the Katyn killings. All Jackson's power of persuasion had not been able to dissuade Rudenko; and Katyn consequently had become an albatross hung around their own necks by the Russians, and a continuing source of contention for the judges.

On February 14, the Soviet prosecution had alleged: "One of the most important criminal acts for which the major war criminals are responsible was the mass execution of Polish prisoners of war shot in the Katyn Forest near Smolensk by the German fascist invaders." The Germans, the Russians contended, had overrun three camps containing the Polish officers, engaged in railway construction, west of Smolensk, and had executed the prisoners in the autumn of 1941. In the spring of 1943, according to the Soviets, the Germans had opened the graves, transported the bodies of other POWs to Katyn for the purpose of augmenting the number of victims, and employed five hundred Russian prisoners of war—who themselves had later been shot—to exhume the graves. The unit responsible for the executions had been disguised under the name of "Staff 537, Engineer Construction Batallion." The entire elaborate operation had been carried out for the purpose of conducting anti-Communist propaganda.

Jackson, learning that the War Department had a file on Katyn, had sent his son Bill to Washington to bring the material back to Nuremberg. The most convincing document in the collection was a report by Lieutenant Colonel John Van Vliet, Jr., who had been a German prisoner of war. The first week of May 1943, Van Vliet had been among a number of American and British officers flown to Smolensk by the Germans for the purpose of inspecting the site of the massacre and, hopefully, providing propaganda statements for the Germans. None of the officers had ever said a word in behalf of the Germans, but Van Vliet had become convinced by what he had seen that the Germans were telling the truth. The dead men had been dressed in winter clothing, and none of the newspapers or letters found on the bodies had been dated later than April or May 1940.

In a heated closed session on March 12, the tribunal had granted Stahmer's application for witnesses on behalf of Goering to refute the Russian charges. Nikitchenko was incensed and had called the action "flagrantly in violation of the charter." A month later, Rudenko had petitioned for a reversal of the action on the basis that the judges had exceeded their authority, misconstrued the charter, and were grossly in error. Biddle had suggested, tongue in cheek, that Rudenko's language was so intemperate that it constituted an attack on the integrity of the court, and that Rudenko should be held in contempt. By a three to one vote the judges had called Rudenko's assertion that the report of the Soviet's Extraordinary State Commission constituted "irrefutable evidence of the facts found [a contention] unsupported by the charter and intrinsically unreasonable in itself."

All through the month of June the Soviets attempted unsuccessfully to preclude any airing of the controversy in court and to obtain a reversal of the tribunal's decision to permit each side to present three witnesses.

The testimony offered by both sides on July 1 and 2 was anything but conclusive; the German witnesses, however, proved far more credible. Colonel Friedrich Ahrens had been the commander of Signal Regiment 537, which had established its headquarters in the so-called Dnieper Castle at the southern edge of the forest. The "castle," a large two-story building of about fifteen rooms, including a movie theater, a rifle range, and a sauna, had previously been an NKVD installation. All through 1942, Ahrens said, he had heard rumors about executions committed in the area by the Soviets, but had taken no further interest until one day early in 1943 he had observed a wolf digging up bones from a mound. After he reported the incident to army headquarters, an exhumation team had been sent, and had discovered several ditches in which bodies had been piled in layers five to seven deep, as well as one or two smaller graves containing the remains of civilian men and women.

From the statements of the witnesses it seemed evident that no shootings had taken place after mid-September 1941; but since the Wehrmacht had captured the area in July, there was a gap in knowledge of about two months. Most incriminating for the Germans was the fact that the victims had been shot with German-manufactured ammunition; and though this facet of the massacre was explicable by the shipment of munitions from Germany to Russia, Goebbels himself, perturbed by the news, had written: "Unfortunately German munitions were found in the graves of Katyn. The question of how they got there needs clarification. If it were to come to the knowledge of the enemy, the whole Katyn affair would have to be dropped."

The three Russian witnesses detracted from, rather than added to, the Soviet case. Victor Prosorovski, the chairman of the Soviet commission that had investigated the site, merely iterated the commission's findings. Doctor Marko Markov, a Bulgarian who had served on the International Medical Commission established by the Germans to conduct autopsies on the corpses, had signed the International Commission's report indicating that the guilt for the murders lay with the Soviets; but now, since Bulgaria had come into the Soviet orbit, he took the same facts and tried to explain them in favor of the Russians. Boris Bazilevsky, a Smolensk professor who had collaborated with the Germans and served as deputy mayor during the occupation, but had purportedly been accepted back without rancor or penalty by the Soviets, had not been in the Katyn Forest and did not know its geography, but testified that a member of the German command had remarked to him "that Russians would at least be allowed to die in the camps while there were proposals to exterminate the Poles."

Aside from the fact that the Russians were clearly apprehensive about any examination of the affair, and that two of their witnesses were of doubtful reliability, the preponderance of circumstantial evidence weighed heavily against them: (1) although the Soviets purported to have found letters and documents on the bodies dated as late as the summer of 1941, all communications between the dead men and their families had ceased as of April 1940; (2) following the German attack, the Russians had impressed all Poles whom they could round up into the Red Army, and it is inconceivable that fifteen thousand Polish officers, had they still been alive, would not have been enlisted in the Soviet forces; (3) it is even more unbelievable that the group would have been left behind to be captured by the Germans; (4) the Nazis, dripping blood all over the East, were certainly of no mind to publicize their own atrocities—in fact, it had been upon the heels of the Katyn discovery that Himmler had embarked upon his manic attempt to dig up and burn hundreds of thousands of bodies to cover the tracks of the *Einsatzgruppen;* (5) if the Russians had not been responsible, then what had happened to the other ten thousand Polish officers who had disappeared, but whose bodies had not been at Katyn?

In the final analysis, Katyn demonstrated that, ideologies aside, the practices of tyrannies tend to be much the same.

52 *The Poisoned Chalice: The Case of the Organizations*

One month of the summer was devoted to the defense of the organizations and another to the closing arguments by the defense and prosecution. Although the world at large took little note of the trial of the organizations, this aspect of the case was followed with anxiety by the German people; for some four million men stood to be branded as criminals if the organizations to which they had belonged were found guilty of having been part of the conspiracy.

"These organizations penetrated the whole German life," Jackson charged. "The country was subdivided into little Nazi principalities of about fifty households each. A thousand little Führers dictated; a thousand imitation Goerings strutted; a thousand Schirachs incited the youth; a thousand Sauckels worked slaves; a thousand Streichers and Rosenbergs stirred up hate; a thousand Kaltenbrunners and Franks butchered and killed; a thousand Schachts and Speers and Funks administered and supported and financed this movement.

"They served primarily to exploit mob psychology and to manipulate the mob. These organizations indoctrinated and practiced violence and terrorism. They provided the systematized, aggressive, and disciplined execution throughout Germany and the occupied countries of the plan for crimes which we have proven. It seems beyond controversy that to punish a few top leaders but to leave this web of organized bodies in the midst of postwar society would be to foster the nucleus of a new Nazidom. These organizations are the carriers from this generation to the next of the infection of aggressive and ruthless war. The next war and the next pogroms will be hatched in the nest of these organizations as surely as we leave their membership with its prestige and influence undiminished by condemnation and punishment."

Hans Laternser, the counsel for the general staff and high command, responded for the defense. "In Germany, as in almost all other states, the punishment of groups and organizations is not known at all, only the punishment of individuals is known." The same prosecution which had condemned the Nazi thesis of collective guilt was nevertheless urging collective condemnation. "I believe it is permissible to say that neither England nor America would ever be willing to pass such a law for their own population." A member of an organization would be able to exculpate himself only if he could prove that he had been forced to join under duress, or that extenuating circumstances mitigated his complicity. "Thus the unique situation arises that the tribunal would pass verdicts on all those members without knowing whether or not numerous innocent members would be affected thereby."

Jackson was prepared to exclude from condemnation members who did not have "knowledge of the criminal aims and activities" of the organization, as well as those who had merely performed clerical and housekeeping functions.

Assistant Secretary of War Howard C. Petersen, however, warned Jackson that any attempt to separate the guilty from the innocent within the organizations by providing hearings for individuals was unfeasible. "The problem is one of reconciling our aims and our resources. On the one hand we want to punish thousands of criminals and to do so promptly and with justice. On the other hand, we are growing weaker every day in the manpower required. Our resources today by way of a going organization or competent personnel for it are practically nil."

Eight attorneys and twenty-three assistants represented the organizations. They collected affidavits containing more than 313,000 signatures. Included were 96,000 declarations of ignorance from SS men avowing that they had no knowledge of atrocities. Over six hundred persons were brought to Nuremberg as potential witnesses. Of these, the commission headed by Major Neave heard one hundred and one—one for the Reich cabinet, twenty-two for the political leadership, twenty-nine for the SS, six for the SD, thirteen for the Gestapo, seventeen for the SA, and thirteen for the high command. From this number, the defense attorneys selected twenty-two to appear before the tribunal.

With two or three exceptions, the presentation of evidence in defense of the organizations seemed like a replay of what had gone before. The witnesses once more purported to know nothing, were overwhelmingly unbelievable, and fell apart under cross-examination. The prosecution used the opportunity to cross some *t*'s and dot some *i*'s, and to buttress the cases against Kaltenbrunner and Funk.

When Freiherr von Eberstein, a member of the nobility who had been the *Höhere SS und Polizeiführer* in Munich, took the stand in behalf of the organizations, Elwyn Jones exploited the opportunity to read into the record an affidavit by Oswald Pohl on his transactions with Funk:

" 'Through my activity as Chief of the WVHA I remember clearly two large business deals between my office and the Reich Ministry of Economics and the Reichsbank of Herr Walther Funk. One deal concerned textiles from persons killed in concentration camps. In this connection Himmler endeavored to procure through the Reich Minister of Economics, Walther Funk, a higher allotment of uniform cloth for the SS. I informed Funk of my instructions that I was to ask him for more textiles for SS uniforms, since we had been able to deliver such large quantities of old textiles due to the actions against Jews. It was openly discussed that we perhaps deserved privileged treatment on account of the deliveries of old clothes of dead Jews. It was a friendly conversation between Funk and myself and he said to me that he would settle the matter favorably with the officials concerned.

" 'The second business deal between Walther Funk and the SS concerned the delivery of articles of value from dead Jews to the Reichsbank. I discussed with the Reichsbank director, Emil Puhl, the manner of delivery. In this conversation no doubt remained that the objects to be delivered were the jewelry and valuables of concentration camp inmates, especially of Jews, who had been killed in extermination camps. It was an enormous quantity of valuables, since there was a steady flow of deliveries for months and years. A part of these valuables from people killed in death camps I saw myself when Reichsbank President Funk and Vice-President Puhl invited us to an inspection of the Reichsbank vault and afterward to lunch. Puhl himself led us on this occasion and showed us gold ingots and other valuable possessions of the Reichsbank. I remember exactly that various chests containing objects from concentration camps were opened. After we had inspected the various valuables, we went upstairs into a room in order to have lunch with Reichsbank President Funk. I sat beside Funk and we talked, among other things about the valuables which I had seen in his vault. On this occasion it was clearly stated that a part of the valuables which we had seen came from concentration camps."

Funk's attorney, Sauter, had no intention of summoning Pohl for cross-examination, but obtained permission to recall Funk to the stand. Funk reiterated that he had known only in the vaguest way about the business between the SS and the Reichsbank.

"Do you know of any reason why he should fabricate testimony like this against you?" Dodd asked Funk. "Why should he lie about you in this terrible way? Can you give a suggestion, any motive, any cause?"

"In my opinion the motive is purely psychological, because people who are in the terrible situation that Pohl is in, who are indicted for the murder of millions, usually attempt to incriminate others. We know that."

"Are you sure you were in the Reichsbank in those days?" Dodd looked quizzically at Funk when Funk replied to one question after another, "I knew nothing about those things, nothing at all."

In an attempt to prove that the exterminations had been illegal, so far as the SS organization was concerned, Horst Pelckmann, the attorney for the SS, called Gunther Reinecke, the chief judge of the Supreme SS and Police Court, and his principal investigator, *Obersturmbannführer* (Lieutenant Colonel) Georg Konrad Morgen, of the Criminal Police.

Reinecke testified that in 1941 he had launched an investigation into the gigantic corruption that had spread throughout the concentration camp system following the arrest of wealthy Jews on the heels of the *Kristallnacht.*

It was during the course of these investigations, Reinecke asserted, that his men had uncovered the machinery for mass extermination. Pohl had pretended to cooperate, but had been in reality "head of that criminal clique. He was not only caught in the death machinery of the concentration camps, but he became at the same time the most corrupt person in the whole Reich. When toward the end of 1944 the legal authorities succeeded, on the strength of individual facts, in cornering the criminals Pohl and Grawitz, and also Müller from the Gestapo, who was covering up many of the crimes, it was for the first time that these men referred to orders from above. The investigations which the legal authorities then commenced along a new line collapsed together with the German war machine."

The situation described by Reinecke was, of course, ludicrous—another excerpt from the Nazi theater of the absurd. Since the death of Heydrich, Pohl had been, as director of the SS economics empire and controller of the purse strings, the most powerful man in the organization next to Himmler. Müller had been responsible for internal security; and Ernst Grawitz, the SS's chief medical officer, had been Himmler's confidant. Nothing short of a revolution could have brought the removal of these men, who had only been carrying out Himmler's directives. Reinecke, in essence, was stating: "We have found the criminals, and they are we." In mid-1944, Himmler had ordered that, with the conclusion of the case against the Buchenwald commander, Koch, the investigation should be brought to a close.

Biddle, not satisfied with Reinecke's answers during either the direct or cross-examinations, embarked upon one of his own periodic inquiries: "Well, now, you have not told us what conditions you found in the camps. You said they were very bad. What were they; what was going on in the camps?"

"We discovered through our investigations that in the camps there was to some extent a regular system of killing which was in use."

"And as a result of discovering that there was a regular system of killing you thought there must be an order to that effect, although you never found it, is that right?"

"Yes, your lordship. The fact that an order from above was in existence became known to us at the end of 1944."

Morgen, who, as an official of the Kripo, had been in charge of the inquiry, was more specific. "Through these investigations I gained insight into the extremely dark and dismal side of the concentration camps. The concentration camps were establishments which, to put it mildly, were bound to give rise to crimes. The prisoner was sent to the concentration camp through the Reich Security Main Office [RSHA]. A political agency decided about his freedom, and its decision was final. Thereby the prisoner was deprived of all legal rights. Once in the concentration camp, it was almost impossible to regain freedom, although at regular intervals the cases were reviewed. The procedure was so complicated that, aside from exceptional instances, the great majority could have no hope. The camp, the Reich Security Main Office, and the agency which had assigned the individual to the camp had to agree to his release. Only if these three agencies reached an agreement could a release be effected. Thereby, not only the reason for the arrest was taken into consideration, but through a monstrous order of SS *Obergruppenführer* Pohl, the production side was also important. If a prisoner was needed in the camp because he was a good man, even though all conditions for release existed, he could not be released."

Morgen had spent most of his time, eight months, at Buchenwald, and two months at Dachau, but had had his attention directed toward Wirth's concentration camp empire of Maidanek, Treblinka, Belzec, and Sobibor by one of the more remarkable reports in the history of the Third Reich. Toward the end of 1943, Morgen related, he had received a communication from the commander of the Security Police in Lublin: "He reported that in a Jewish labor camp in his district a Jewish wedding had taken place. There had been eleven hundred invited guests at this wedding. What followed was described as quite extraordinary owing to the gluttonous consumption of food and alcoholic drinks. Among these Jews were members of the camp guard, that is to say some SS men, who joined in this revelry. I thought that this report would give me a clue to another big case of criminal corruption. With this in mind, I went to Lublin. I found out the camp and the commander, who was *Kriminalkommissar* Wirth. I asked Wirth whether this report was true or what it meant. To my great astonishment, Wirth admitted it. I asked him why he permitted members of his command to do such things, and Wirth then revealed to me that on the Führer's order he had to carry out the destruction of Jews.

"I asked Wirth what this had to do with the Jewish wedding. Wirth said that he had four extermination camps and that about five thousand Jews were working at the extermination of Jews and the seizure of Jewish property. In order to win Jews for this business of extermination and plundering of their brethren of race and creed, Wirth gave them every freedom and, so to speak, gave them a financial interest in the spoliation of the dead victims. As a result of this attitude, this sumptuous Jewish wedding had come about." Morgen continued, detailing the deception employed in directing Jews into the gas chambers.

"Did you ask Wirth how he arrived at this devilish system?" Pelckmann wanted to know.

"When Wirth took over the extermination of the Jews, he was already a specialist in mass destruction of human beings. He had previously carried out the task of getting rid of the incurably insane. By order of the Führer himself, whose order was transmitted through the Chancellery of the Führer, he had, at the beginning of the war, set up a detachment for this purpose. This system Wirth now employed with a few alterations and improvements for the extermination of Jews. He was also given the assignment by the Führer's Chancellery to exterminate the Jews."

"The statements which Wirth made for you must have surpassed human imagination. Did you immediately believe Wirth?"

"At first Wirth's description seemed completely fantastic to me, but in Lublin I saw one of his camps. From the piles of things—there was an enormous number of watches piled up—I had to realize that something frightful was going on here. I saw and watched his couriers arrive. They actually came from Berlin, Tiergartenstrasse, the Führer's chancellery, and went back there. I investigated Wirth's mail and I found in it confirmation of all this."

"You mentioned the Jewish prisoners who aided in the killing. What became of these people?"

"Wirth told me that at the end of the actions he would have these prisoners shot and in doing so would despoil them of the profit which he had allowed them to make. He did not do this all at once, but by means of the deceptive methods already described he lured and segregated the prisoners and then killed them individually."

Despite the macabre fascination of Morgen's testimony and the further corroboration it provided of the destruction of the Jews, it was to a considerable extent a distortion. Morgen's purpose was to attempt to demonstrate that the Final Solution had been conducted outside the sphere of the General SS and the Waffen SS, and his testimony was slanted toward this end. He had, in reality, only a superficial knowledge of Wirth's and Höss's operations—he had initiated his investigation of Auschwitz only at a late date, while tracking a massive gold-smuggling operation from the concentration camp to Bohemia and Moravia. Wirth's Jewish *Sonderkommando* had numbered a few hundred, not five thousand, and Wirth certainly had not killed hundreds, much less thousands, of men individually by means of subterfuge. Morgen was not even familiar with Höss's rank, referring to him as a *Standartenführer* (colonel) instead of a *Hauptsturmführer* (captain). He had never been in Birkenau, but confused it with Monowitz, the I.G. Farben–operated camp on the other side of Auschwitz. "The extermination camp Monowitz lay far away from the concentration camp," Morgen said. "It was situated on an extensive industrial site and was not recognizable as such and everywhere on the horizon there were smoking chimneys. The camp itself was guarded on the outside by special troops of men from the Baltic—Estonians, Lithuanians, Latvians—and also Ukrainians. The entire technical arrangement was almost exclusively in the hands of the prisoners."

Had things been as Morgen would have had them, no more than one or two SS officers and noncoms would have been involved in the entire operation.

"Were there no officers of the SS there at all?" Lawrence inquired.

"One officer, the commander of this company, I believe, a *Hauptsturmführer* Hartenstein, or something like that," Morgen responded, failing to realize that Hartenstein had, in fact, been the commanding officer of Birkenau.

The guards and operating personnel, Morgen asserted entirely falsely, had included no Germans. The men from the Baltic countries and the Ukraine had been *disguised* in SS uniforms, he claimed. "They could not be members of the General SS. As far as I could learn, they were volunteers and draftees who had been recruited in the Baltic countries where they had carried out security tasks, and who were then somehow especially selected and sent to Auschwitz and Monowitz. These were special troops, who had only this particular task and no other. They were completely outside of the Waffen SS."

"Did you ask questions as to why they were put into SS uniforms?" Lawrence queried.

"No, I did not ask that question. I assumed that this was done for camouflage reasons so that this extermination camp would not be distinguished outwardly from the other labor camps and the concentration camp itself. As a soldier it was incomprehensible to me that this damage to the reputation of the SS was tolerated, as it had nothing to do with this extermination."

"Now, witness, under normal circumstances what would you have had to do after you had learned of all these terrible things?" Pelckmann resumed the questioning.

"Under normal circumstances I would have had to have *Kriminalkommissar* Wirth and Commander Höss arrested and charged with murder."

"Did you do that?"

"No."

"Why not?"

"The circumstances prevailing in Germany during the war were no longer normal in the sense of state legal guarantees. No court-martial in the world could bring the supreme commander, let alone the head of the state, to court. It was not possible for me as *Obersturmbannführer* to arrest Hitler, who, as I saw it, was the instigator of these orders."

Of course, by 1944, residents of foreign nations had—in contrast to Morgen's assertions—made up a majority of the complement of the SS, and been completely integrated into the organization. Lawrence did not understand Morgen's testimony at all, and even Pelckmann—though leaning heavily upon it to show that Höss and Wirth had received their orders directly from Himmler outside of the regular SS channels—regarded it with a grain of salt.

"The result of the prosecution's evidence," Pelckmann admitted, "forces the defense to the conclusion that crimes in considerable extent were committed by members of the SS, but not that the whole SS organization is criminal."

"It cannot be denied that the name of the SS is connected with these murders and misdeeds," he continued later. "In the face of all the world this confession must be made in this trial. And just as every German must be ashamed that such horrible and inhuman things occurred in his country, even more should every SS man search himself and examine to what extent he is politically or morally guilty for these happenings. He should again look back upon his whole life and study when, where, and how he might have deviated from the road of true humanity—perhaps only in heart and mind.

"I indict every one of these murderers and criminals who belong to that organization or one of its units—and there are more than a few of them.

"I acquit the thousands and hundreds of thousands of those who served in good faith, and who therefore share only morally and metaphysically, not criminally, the guilt which the German people must bitterly bear.

"One must be acquainted with the German mentality," Pelckmann suggested to the tribunal, to be able to understand how "the psychopathological seducer of a people, Adolf Hitler," had been able to deceive and exploit the nation. Anti-Semitism, Pelckmann suggested, "is based on the inferiority complex of the average man, on his mistrust of the Jews' superiority in certain intellectual fields." Hitler had been motivated by a fiery hatred, "that hatred which sprang from the feeling of inferiority of him who recognized the superiority of the penetrating intellect over dark impulses." The SS, however, had been beguiled, "for anti-Semitism was preached to the SS merely as the other side of race eugenics on which emphasis was laid."

That was one side of Pelckmann's argument. The other was that the SS had been, at most, an unwitting tool, and the real guilt lay with other of the indicted organizations: "A reign of terror may well have been exercised through arrest and the putting of individuals in concentration camps, but that was not a function of any branch of the SS organization, but rather of the Ministry of the Interior, of the police, and the RSHA (Gestapo)."

Despite Pelckmann's intelligence and penchant for honesty, he seemed unable to grasp that it had been the SS, in all its various forms, which had operated the concentration camps, and that organizations like the Gestapo and the police had been staffed in whole or in part *by* the SS.

The futility of Pelckmann's endeavor was demonstrated as the attorney for each organization attempted, in his turn, to pass the poisoned chalice to another. Hans Laternser, representing the High Command, denounced the SS leaders, and charged that they were "trying for the last time in their hatred to draw the military leaders into their own disaster. . . . The abysmal hatred of the mass murderers from the circle around Himmler is persecuting them even to this very courtroom."

Rudolf Merkel pleaded that the Gestapo "became the scapegoat for all misdeeds in Germany and the occupied territories, and today it is made to bear responsibility for all evil." Merkel ascribed responsibility for the *Nacht und Nebel* operation to the Wehrmacht, and for the Commissar Order to the Wehrmacht and the SD, though, in fact, the Gestapo had been the principal agency concerned in both cases. Underscoring the confusion and lack of comprehension still prevalent among the participants in the trial, Merkel asked: "How could Gestapo officials know what was going on behind the barbed wire of the concentration camps, how could they know of the executions, asphyxiations, and ill treatment of the detainees since no official had access to a concentration camp, and the Gestapo had nothing to do with the administration of the concentration camps?"

In reality, the Gestapo had exercised political control over the camps and had held the power of life and death over the inmates. The fact that, as the trial grew to a close, Merkel still did not understand this was revealing and dismaying. Capping his inane misconstruction, Merkel, running wild with Morgen's testimony, fantasized a fictitious "Kommando Reinhard," supposedly "independent of any police office" and controlled by Wirth. "By a hitherto unknown system of deception it allowed these camps to be run by the Jews themselves," he asserted.

When Hans Gawlik, defending the SD, echoed the denials of the other organization attorneys, Lawrence, who himself had never quite succeeded in unraveling the intricacies of Himmler's SS structure, interrupted: "Dr. Gawlik, the tribunal understands that the SS, the Gestapo, and the SD all disclaim responsibility for the *Einsatzgruppen.* Could you tell the tribunal who is responsible for the *Einsatzgruppen?*"

"The *Einsatzgruppen,* in my opinion," Gawlik replied, "were organizations of a special kind which were directly under Himmler."

"Can you tell the tribunal who were the individual men who composed the *Einsatzgruppen?*" Lawrence was not to be turned aside. "Did they consist of SS or SA or SD or the Wehrmacht?"

"I do not remember them exactly, your Lordship, but I do know that they included Waffen SS, Criminal Police, Gestapo, SD . . ." Gawlik ticked off one organization after another.

"Counsel for the Gestapo has argued that the Gestapo was erroneously blamed for the crimes committed in the occupied territories," Dodd summarized for the prosecution, "but he said, interestingly enough, that the SS committed these crimes. And then counsel for the SS argued before the tribunal that the SS was erroneously blamed and the SD committed the crimes. And then counsel for the SD says to the tribunal that the SD was erroneously blamed and the Gestapo was really to blame after all. Counsel for the SS blames the Gestapo for the running of the concentration camps and counsel for the Gestapo says no, it was the SS who ran the concentration camps. Now the fact is that all of these executive agencies participated in the commission of these vast crimes against humanity.

"It is a strange feature of this trial that counsel for the respective organizations have not sought to deny these crimes but only to shift responsibility for their commission. The military defendants blame the political leaders for initiating wars of aggression; the Gestapo blames the soldiers for the murder of escaped prisoners of war; the SA blames the Gestapo for concentration camp murders; the Gestapo blames the leadership corps for anti-Jewish pogroms; the SS blames the cabinet for the concentration camp system; and the cabinet blames the SS for the exterminations in the East. The fact is that all these organizations united in carrying out the criminal program of Nazi Germany. They are to blame. When the membership of these organizations swore an oath of obedience to Hitler, they united themselves for all times with him, his work, and his guilt."

Complementing Dodd, Taylor concluded: "This was not war; it was crime. This was not soldiering; this was savagery. These things need to be said. We cannot here make history over again, but we can see that it is written true."

During the languid summer days, when senses in the courtroom were dulled by the hypnotizing hum of the ventilating system and the warm air stirring gently, the judges periodically had difficulty not merely staying alert, but awake. When Konrad Morgen was on the stand, Lawrence dozed docilely as the SS major described the ideal conditions provided for the inmates at Buchenwald: "They had regular mail service. They had a large camp library, even books in foreign languages. They had variety shows, motion pictures, sporting contests, and they even had a brothel. Nearly all the other concentration camps were similar to Buchenwald."

At the word "brothel" Lawrence stirred, like a slumbering dog conditioned to respond to certain stimuli. "What was it they even had?" He looked up.

"A brothel," Morgen repeated; but since Lawrence seemed still somewhat bewildered, Biddle, nudging him, whispered: "Brothel, Geoffrey, brothel."

"What?" Lawrence, hard of hearing, leaned closer.

"Bordello, brothel, whorehouse!" Biddle expatiated, as a titter swept through the courtroom, since Biddle had accidentally tripped the switch on his microphone.

Such small diversions were now as much of the life of the court as the great issues to be decided by the judges. When Field Marshal Gerd von Rundstedt was on the stand, Biddle observed that the American soldier standing guard behind him was the field marshal's nephew, though Rundstedt was unaware of this. When, during the middle of another session, Biddle had to hurry off to the bathroom, Goering, with a leer, swiveled about to remark upon Biddle's departure to Raeder, and was tapped on the shoulder by one of the guards. As Birkett watched, Goering carefully and deliberately flicked the spot on his shoulder, as if to rid himself of the contamination.

Goering's interest in the legs of the women continued unabated; though, in contrast to so many of the other Nazi leaders, Goering had never been known as a lascivious man. One young, attractive interpreter from Minneapolis, noted for her towering hairdos and the dramatic manner in which she performed her translations, became famed as "The Passionate Haystack." But when Biddle, at a party, asked her to dance, she proved uncommunicative and stiff. Far more intriguing was a striking, dark Czech girl, Leba Barbanova, with whom Biddle conversed in French. *"Mademoiselle,"* he complimented her on the dance floor, *"vous dansez comme une ange."*

With a smile she replied: "But, *monsieur,* would that be fun? I am reliably informed that angels do not have bodies."

A diminutive Russian major, emboldened by vodka, launched a determined assault on Parker's secretary, a prim, straitlaced spinster. "Really, I love you!" he protested. "This house is your home. Have more vodka."

The further the summer advanced, and the closer the trial moved to its conclusion, the more numerous the parties grew. There were sedate parties at which Elwyn Jones sang Welsh hymns and Telford Taylor, a violin virtuoso, played Mozart and Bach; and Fyfe, who was spending his spare time writing a book for his young daughter, withdrew to a corner to scribble a few lines. There were lively parties with fireworks and high jinks on the Fourth of July and Bastille Day. There were Russian all-night parties at which Volchkov quoted Russian proverbs: "It is midnight—time for the children to go to bed—then the grownups stay for breakfast."

"I am exceedingly weary today in consequence of a very late night at our party last night and a trifle too much indulgence in White Ladies," Birkett recorded on the day in mid-August when Funk retook the stand to refute Pohl's affidavit. "Fellow sufferers in this last respect are General Nikitchenko and Colonel Volchkov of the Russian delegation. I have the greatest difficulty in keeping awake and the documents which are being discussed by Dr. Servatius are of such surprising dullness that the temptation to sleep is quite overpowering."

53   *"A Mad and Melancholy Record"*

The final arguments of the defense attorneys were notable for their prolixity, reams of irrelevancies, and plethora of banalities. Though the lawyers protested that the fourteen court days allotted by the tribunal were not enough, if measured by content four would have been too many.

Stahmer and Kauffmann, the counsel for Goering and Kaltenbrunner, both soared into the metaphysical. When Kauffmann went on and on about "surging waves of a furious torrent" and "demoniacal depths [in] which lurk those who hate the true God," Lawrence, after listening at length, finally suggested:

"Is it not time that you came to the case of the defendant that you represent? The tribunal proposes, as far as it can, to decide the cases which it has to decide in accordance with law and not with the sort of very general, very vague and misty philosophical doctrine with which you appear to be dealing."

A number of the attorneys pleaded for leniency by depreciating their clients. Thoma thought Rosenberg had exaggerated his importance because "he does not want to be pictured as though nobody paid any attention to his books, his speeches, and his publications."

Marx suggested that Streicher "was a fanatic" who suffered from "a sort of mental cramp." Sauter called Funk "a topic which unfortunately is especially dry and prosaic."

Siemers sanctimoniously proffered: "Raeder cannot be a criminal, since all his life he has lived honorably and as a Christian. A man who believes in God does not commit crimes, and a soldier who believes in God is not a war criminal."

Servatius, continuing his inept conduct of Sauckel's case, maintained that his client was misunderstood. When Sauckel had advocated that "one should handcuff the workers in a polite way," Servatius argued, "the point in question was merely a comparison between the clumsy manner of the police and the obliging manner of the French; handcuffing was not thereby especially advocated as a method of mobilization: clean, correct, and Prussian on the one hand, while at the same time obliging and polite on the other; that is how the work was to have been done."

Since Speer's case followed Sauckel's throughout the trial, Flächsner, characterizing Speer as moderate and rational in contrast to the brutal Sauckel, stuck to his stratagem of seeking to exonerate Speer at Sauckel's expense. The prosecution could not have done a better job of undercutting Sauckel.

Kranzbühler for Doenitz and Dix for Schacht maintained their reputations for skill and persuasiveness. Kranzbühler emphasized the facts in favor of Doenitz, skirted around those that were detrimental, and manipulated analogy in subtle fashion. The fact that eighty-seven percent of the sailors from sunken ships had survived, Kranzbühler argued, "is simply not compatible with an order for destruction." If there had been isolated incidents in which men were attacked in the water, these had occurred on both sides. Referring to "cases in which Allied forces had allegedly shot at German shipwrecked crews," Kranzbühler contended "that every one of these instances is better than that of the prosecution, and some appear rather convincing."

Dix painted a graphic picture of incongruity: "There in the dock sit Kaltenbrunner and Schacht. Whatever the powers of the defendant Kaltenbrunner may have been, he was in any case Chief of the Reich Security

Main Office. Until those May days of 1945, Schacht was a prisoner of the Reich Security Main Office in various concentration camps. It is surely a rare and grotesque picture to see jailer and prisoner sharing a bench in the dock.

"The charge against him was high treason against the Hitler regime. Since the summer of 1944 I was assigned to defend Schacht before Adolf Hitler's People's Court; in the summer of 1945 I was asked to conduct his defense before the International Military Tribunal. This, too, is in itself a self-contradictory state of affairs. . . .

"No criminal charge whatsoever can be brought against Schacht personally. To the extent that he erred politically, he is in all candor prepared for the verdict of history. Yet even the greatest dynamics of international law cannot penalize political error."

Keitel's attorney, Otto Nelte, acknowledged Germany's responsibility, but pleaded for understanding: "The misery, the misfortune that has fallen on the entire human race is so great that words do not suffice to express it. The German people, especially after having learned the catastrophes that have befallen the nations in the West and East and the Jews, is shaken by horror and pity for the victims. But while other nations are able to look upon all this misery and all this misfortune as a chapter of the past, there still rests upon this nation the gloom of despair. By affirming the guilt of the entire nation the verdict of this tribunal would perpetuate this despair. The German people does not expect to be acquitted. It does not expect the cloak of Christian charity and oblivion to be spread over all that has happened. The German nation is ready to the last to take the consequences upon itself. It hopes, however, that the soul and heart of the rest of mankind will not be so hardened that the existing tension, in fact the existing hatred, between this nation and the rest of mankind will remain."

When, following the defense, the prosecution opened its final argument, Jackson again came to the fore. Impassioned and exhaustive, driven sometimes to exaggeration and lack of objectivity in his fervent partisanship, he displayed himself once more the master of rhetoric: "In eight months we have introduced evidence which embraces as vast and varied a panorama of events as have ever been compressed within the framework of a litigation. It is impossible in summation to do more than outline with bold strokes the vitals of this trial's mad and melancholy record, which will live as the historical text of the twentieth century's shame and depravity.

"It is common to think of our own time as standing at the apex of civilization. The reality is that in the long perspective of history the present century will not hold an admirable position, unless its second half is to redeem its first. These twoscore years in the twentieth century will be reported in the book of years as one of the most bloody in all annals. Two World Wars have left a legacy of dead which number more than all the armies engaged in any way that make ancient or medieval history. No half century ever witnessed slaughter on such a scale, such cruelties and inhumanities. The terror of Torquemada pales before the Nazi inquisition. If we cannot eliminate the causes and prevent the repetition of these barbaric events, it is not an irresponsible prophecy to say that this twentieth century may yet succeed in bringing the doom of civilization.

"Of one thing we may be sure, the future will never have to ask, with misgiving, what the Nazis could have said in their favor. The fact is that the testimony of the defendants has removed any doubt of guilt which, because of the extraordinary nature and magnitude of these crimes, may have existed before they spoke. They have helped write their own judgment of condemnation.

"We are not trying them for the possession of obnoxious ideas. It is their right, if they choose, to renounce the Hebraic heritage in the civilization of which Germany was once a part. Nor is it our affair that they repudiated the Hellenic influence as well. The intellectual bankruptcy and moral perversion of the Nazi regime might have been no concern of international law had it not been utilized to goosestep the *Herrenvolk* across international frontiers. It is not their thoughts, it is their overt actions which we charge to be crimes.

"The time has come for final judgment, and if the case I present seems hard and uncompromising, it is because the evidence makes it so.

"A glance over the dock will show that, despite quarrels among themselves, each defendant played a part which fitted in with every other, and that all advanced the common plan.

"The large and varied role of Goering was half militarist and half gangster. He stuck his pudgy finger in every pie. In order to entrench that power he contrived to have the Reichstag burned, established the Gestapo, and created the concentration camps. He was equally adept at massacring opponents and at framing scandals to get rid of stubborn generals. He built up the Luftwaffe and hurled it at his defenseless neighbors. He was among the foremost in harrying Jews out of the land. By mobilizing the total economic resources of Germany he made possible the waging of the war which he had taken a large part in planning. He was, next to Hitler, the man who tied the activities of all the defendants together in a common effort.

"The zealot Hess, before succumbing to wanderlust, was the engineer tending the party machinery. Keitel, the weak and willing tool, delivered the armed forces, the instrument of aggression, over to the party and directed them in executing its felonious designs.

"Kaltenbrunner, the grand inquisitor, took up the bloody mantle of

Heydrich to stifle opposition and terrorize compliance. It was Rosenberg, the intellectual high priest of the 'master race,' who provided the doctrine of hatred which gave the impetus for the annihilation of Jewry, and who put his infidel theories into practice against the Eastern Occupied Territories. The fanatical Frank proceeded to export his lawlessness to Poland, which he governed with the lash of Caesar, and whose population he reduced to sorrowing remnants. Frick, as the ruthless organizer, helped the party to seize power, supervised the police agencies to ensure that it stayed in power, and chained the economy of Bohemia and Moravia to the German war machine.

"Streicher, the venomous vulgarian, manufactured and distributed obscene racial libels which incited the populace to accept and assist the progressively more savage operations of 'race purification.' As minister of economics Funk accelerated the pace of rearmament, and as Reichsbank president he banked for the SS the gold teeth fillings of concentration camp victims—probably the most ghoulish collateral in banking history. It was Schacht, the facade of starched respectability, who in the early days provided the window dressing, and whose wizardry later made it possible for Hitler to finance the colossal rearmament program, and to do it secretly.

"Doenitz, Hitler's legatee of defeat, promoted the success of the Nazi aggressions by instructing his pack of submarine killers to conduct warfare at sea with the illegal ferocity of the jungle. Raeder, the political admiral, stealthfully built up the German navy in defiance of the Versailles Treaty, and then put it to use in a series of aggressions which he had taken a leading part in planning. Von Schirach, poisoner of a generation, initiated the German youth in Nazi doctrine, trained them in legions for services in the SS and Wehrmacht, and delivered them up to the party as fanatic, unquestioning executors of its will.

"Sauckel, the greatest and cruelest slaver since the Pharaohs of Egypt, produced desperately needed manpower by driving foreign people into the land of bondage on a scale unknown even in the ancient days of tyranny in the Kingdom of the Nile. Jodl, betrayer of the traditions of his profession, led the Wehrmacht in violating its own codes of military honor in order to carry out the barbarous aims of Nazi politics. Von Papen, pious agent of an infidel regime, held the stirrups while Hitler vaulted into the saddle.

"Seyss-Inquart, spearhead of the Austrian fifth column, took over the government of his own country only to make a present of it to Hitler, and then, moving north, brought terror and oppression to the Netherlands. Von Neurath, the old school diplomat, who cast the pearls of his experience before Nazis, guided Nazi diplomacy in the early years, soothed the fears of prospective victims, and, as Reich Protector of Bohemia and Moravia, strengthened the German position for the coming attack on Poland. Speer joined in planning and executing the program to dragoon prisoners of war and foreign workers into German war industries, which waxed in output while the laborers waned in starvation. Fritzsche, radio propaganda chief, by manipulation of the truth goaded German public opinion into frenzied support of the regime and anesthetized the independent judgment of the population, so that they did without question their masters' bidding. And Bormann, who has not accepted our invitation to this reunion, sat at the throttle of the vast and powerful engine of the party, guiding it in the ruthless execution of Nazi politics, from the scourging of the Christian Church to the lynching of captive Allied airmen.*

"These men destroyed free government in Germany and now plead to be excused from responsibility because they became slaves. They are in the position of the fictional boy who murdered his father and mother and then pleaded for leniency because he was an orphan.

"What these men have overlooked is that Adolf Hitler's acts are their acts. It was these men among millions of others, and it was these men leading millions of others, who built up Adolf Hitler and vested in his psychopathic personality not only innumerable lesser decisions but the supreme issue of war or peace. They intoxicated him with power and adulation. They fed his hate and aroused his fears. They put a loaded gun in his eager hands. It was left to Hitler to pull the trigger, and when he did they all at that time approved. His guilt stands admitted, by some defendants reluctantly, and some vindictively. But his guilt is the guilt of the whole dock, and of every man in it. . . .

"No one lives who, at least until the very last moments of the war, outranked Goering in position, power, and influence. No soldier stood above Keitel and Jodl, and no sailor above Raeder and Doenitz. Who can be responsible for the diplomacy of duplicity if not the foreign ministers, von Neurath and Ribbentrop, and the diplomatic handyman, von Papen? Who should be answerable for the oppressive administration of occupied countries if gauleiters, protectors, governors, and commissars such as Frank, Seyss-Inquart, Frick, von Schirach, von Neurath, and Rosenberg are not? Where shall we look for those who mobilized the economy for total war if we overlook Schacht and Speer and Funk? Who was the master of the great slaving enterprise if it was not Sauckel? Where shall we find the hand that ran the concentration camps if it was not the hand of Kaltenbrunner? And who whipped up the hate and fears of the public, and

*Erich Kempka, Hitler's chauffeur, testified on July 3 that he had seen Bormann apparently killed in an explosion while attempting to flee from Berlin.

manipulated the party organizations to incite these crimes, if not Hess, von Schirach, Fritzsche, Bormann, and the unspeakable Julius Streicher?

"The defendants have been unanimous, when pressed, in shifting the blame on other men, sometimes on one and sometimes on another. . . . The chief villain on whom blame is placed—some of the defendants vie with each other in producing appropriate epithets—is Hitler. He is the man at whom nearly every defendant has pointed an accusing finger.

"I shall not dissent from this consensus. It may well be said that Hitler's final crime was against the land he had ruled. He was a mad messiah who started the war without cause and prolonged it without reason.

"I admit that Hitler was the chief villain. But for the defendants to put all blame on him is neither manly nor true. Other legs must run his errands; other hands must execute his plans. On whom did Hitler rely on such things more than upon these men in the dock?

"The fact is that the Nazi habit of economizing in the use of truth pulls the foundations out from under their own defenses. Lying has always been a highly approved Nazi technique. Hitler, in *Mein Kampf,* advocated mendacity as a policy. Nor is the lie direct the only means of falsehood. They all speak with a Nazi doubletalk with which to deceive the unwary. In the Nazi dictionary of sardonic euphemisms 'final solution' of the Jewish problem was a phrase which meant extermination; 'special treatment' of prisoners of war meant killing; 'protective custody' meant concentration camps. Rosenberg was stated by his counsel to have always had in mind a 'chivalrous solution' to the Jewish problem. When it was necessary to remove Schuschnigg after the Anschluss, Ribbentrop would have had us believe that the Austrian chancellor was resting at a 'villa.' It was left to cross-examination to reveal that the 'villa' was Buchenwald concentration camp. The record is full of other examples of dissimulations and evasions.

"This was the philosophy of the National Socialists. It is against such a background that these defendants now ask this tribunal to say that they are not guilty of planning, executing, or conspiring to commit this long list of crimes and wrongs. They stand before the record of this trial as bloodstained Gloucester stood by the body of his slain king. He begged of the widow, as they beg of you: 'Say I slew them not.' And the queen replied, 'Then say they were not slain. But dead they are . . .' If you were to say of these men that they are not guilty, it would be as true to say that there has been no war, there are no slain, there has been no crime."

For the defendants, the effect of Jackson's speech was like a dousing with ice water, Fritzsche recorded. Sitting on edge, some took notes, listened intently for mention of their own names, flushed when Jackson's epithets applied to them, and reacted angrily to what they considered unfair characterizations. Some of the accused kept count of the number of times each was mentioned—Goering's name, cited forty-two times, naturally led the list; and Schacht's came in a distant second. Only Speer expressed satisfaction with Jackson's speech—an approval that, Goering suggested, probably derived from the fact that he, Schirach, and Schacht had made a deal with the prosecution.

54   Epitaph on Ideals

On Saturday, the thirty-first of August, the day on which the tribunal was to adjourn to start deliberations on the verdict, the defendants were each allotted fifteen minutes to rebut the prosecution's argument and offer their own final statements. Once more the court was filled to capacity. Birkett, noting that "for some of them it is the last public statement they will ever make," was very much aware of "the solemnity of the occasion. When one considers that these men have fallen from high place and power, that they now contemplate the ruins of everything for which they once cared and share the sufferings and humiliations of the German people, and know that their person, fortune, and fate are being weighed in the balance, one cannot refrain from some admiration for their outward fortitude."

Remarkably, the majority of the accused said little, and several contented themselves with a paragraph or two. Seyss-Inquart, with a surprisingly admirable outburst of principle for a man who had spent his life as a fence-sitting opportunist, virtually sealed his own doom: "To me [Hitler] remained the man who made Greater Germany a fact in German history. I served this man. And now I cannot today cry 'Crucify him!' since yesterday I cried 'Hosannah!'"

Speer, speaking prophetically on the basis of his own experience, warned: "Today the danger of being terrorized by technocracy threatens every country in the world. Hitler not only took advantage of technical developments to dominate his own people—he almost succeeded, by means of his technical lead, in subjugating the whole of Europe. In five or ten years the technique of warfare will make it possible to fire rockets from continent to continent with uncanny precision. A new large-scale war will end with the destruction of human culture and civilization. Nothing can prevent unfettered engineering and science from completing the work of destroying human beings, which it has begun in so dreadful a way in this war. Therefore this trial must contribute toward preventing such degenerate wars in the future, and toward establishing rules whereby human beings can live together."

Frank gave himself and his country up to God: "At the beginning of our way we did not suspect that our turning away from God could have such disastrous, deadly consequences. I beg of our people not to continue in this direction, be it even a single step; because Hitler's road was the way without God, the way of turning from Christ, and, in the last analysis, the way of political foolishness, the way of disaster, and the way of death. His path became more and more that of a frightful adventurer without conscience or honesty, as I know today at the end of this trial."

But then, having once more recanted, Frank retracted part of his recantation and turned accuser:

"There is still one statement of mine which I must rectify. On the witness stand I said that a thousand years would not suffice to erase the guilt brought upon our people because of Hitler's conduct in this war. Every possible guilt incurred by our nation has already been completely wiped out today, not only by the conduct of our wartime enemies toward our nation and its soldiers, which has been carefully kept out of this trial, but also by the tremendous mass crimes of the most frightful sort which —as I have now learned—have been and still are being committed against the Germans by the Russians, Poles, and Czechs, especially in East Prussia, Silesia, Pomerania, and the Sudetenland. Who shall ever judge these crimes against the German people?"

Schacht, rising, heaped brimstone on Jackson with such indignation that at least one of the judges, Birkett, was impressed: "The prosecution has branded me in the world press for a whole year as a robber, murderer, and betrayer. It is this accusation alone which I have to thank for the fact that in the evening of my life I am without means of subsistence and without a home. But the prosecution are mistaken if they believe that they can count me amongst the pitiful and broken characters. To be sure, I erred politically. I never claimed to be a politician, but my economic and financial policy of creating work by assisting credit proved brilliantly successful. My political mistake was not realizing the extent of Hitler's criminal nature at an early enough time. But I did not stain my hands with one single illegal or immoral act. The terrorism of the Gestapo did not frighten me. For terrorism must always fail before the appeal to conscience. At the conclusion of this trial I stand shaken to the very depths of my soul by the unspeakable suffering which I tried to prevent with all my personal effort and with all obtainable means, but which in the end I failed to prevent—not through my fault."

The most eloquent words were, curiously, spoken by Sauckel—revealing a previously unfathomed complexity of character—and the two army officers, Jodl and Keitel. "I have been shaken to the very depths of my soul by the atrocities revealed in the trial," Sauckel said. "In all humility and reverence, I bow before the victims and the fallen of all nations, and before the misfortune and suffering of my own people, with whom alone I must measure my fate.

"My error was perhaps the excess of my feelings and my confidence in, as well as my great veneration of Hitler. I knew him only as the champion of the German people's right to existence and saw him as the man who was kind to workers, women, and children, and who promoted the vital interests of Germany. The Hitler of this trial I could not recognize. Perhaps my loneliness and submersion in the world of my imagination and my work was a further defect. I only became a National Socialist because I condemned class struggle, expropriation, and civil war, and because I firmly believed in Hitler's absolute desire for peace and understanding with the rest of the world. I had no part in any conspiracy against peace or against humanity, nor did I tolerate murders or mistreatment. Perhaps in the eyes of Himmler and Goebbels I was a hopeless utopian— they were my foes. I myself am prepared to meet any fate which providence has in store for me, just like my son, who was killed in the war."

Keitel, ramrod erect as always, confessed: "I believed, but I erred, and I was not in a position to prevent what ought to have been prevented. That is my guilt.

"It is tragic to have to realize that the best I had to give as a soldier, obedience and loyalty, was exploited for purposes which could not be recognized at the time, and that I did not see that there is a limit set even for a soldier's performance of his duty. That is my fate.

"From the clear recognition of the causes, the pernicious methods, and the terrible consequences of this war, may there arise the hope for a new future in the community of nations for the German people."

Jodl addressed himself more specifically to the problems of the military: "It is my unshakable belief that later historians will arrive at a just and objective verdict concerning the higher military leaders and their assistants, for they, and the entire German Wehrmacht with them, were confronted with an insoluble task, namely, to conduct a war which they had not wanted under a commander in chief whose confidence they did not possess and whom they themselves trusted only within limits; with methods which frequently were in contradiction to their principles of leadership and their traditional, proved opinions; with troops and police forces which did not come under their full command; and with an intelligence service which in part was working for the enemy. They did not serve the powers of hell and they did not serve a criminal, but rather their people and their fatherland.

"In a war such as this, in which hundreds of thousands of women and children were annihilated by layers of bombs or killed by low-flying aircraft, and in which partisans used every—yes, every—single means of violence which seemed expedient, harsh measures, even though they may appear questionable from the standpoint of international law, are not a crime in morality or in conscience. For I believe and avow that a man's duty toward his people and fatherland stands above every other. To carry out this duty was for me an honor, and the highest law. May this duty be supplanted in some happier future by an even higher one, by the duty towards humanity."

In Birkett's opinion, "Keitel bore himself like a brave soldier and spoke bravely too." Biddle, referring to Jodl, mused: "I am always struck by the apparently sincere and passionate idealism of so many of the defendants—but what ideals!"

Goering's final words were so prosaic, so lacking in fire and memorableness, that, afterwards, it was easier to comprehend Hitler's dominance over him: "I wish to state expressly that I condemn these terrible mass murders to the utmost, and cannot understand them in the least. But I should like to state clearly once more before the high tribunal that I have never decreed the murder of a single individual at any time, and neither did I decree any other atrocities or tolerate them, while I had the power and knowledge to prevent them. I did not want a war, nor did I bring it about. The only motive which guided me was my ardent love for my people, its happiness, its freedom, and its life."

Hess was a special case. His mind had deteriorated steadily during the course of the trial. On August 2 Seidl, convinced that he was now quite mad, had petitioned the court for a full psychiatric examination of him.

The judges turned the matter over to Gustav Gilbert, who recommended against another examination on the curious grounds that psychiatrists were unlikely to be able to reach a consensus: "Lay discussion of psychiatric concepts does not help throw any light on this case, because psychiatrists themselves are not in agreement on the definition of terms like 'psychopathic constitution', 'hysterical reaction,' etc. and these terms have entirely different meanings in English and in German usage." Gilbert was of the opinion that Hess was not insane in the legal sense of being incapable of distinguishing right from wrong, and that he had not been "insane at the time of the activities for which he had been indicted." Although Hess could not remember from one day to the next, or even from the morning until the afternoon, his state of mind was symptomatic of hysterical amnesia, not of insanity, and a further psychiatric report was likely merely to reiterate the conclusions of the one submitted to the tribunal in November.

This, however, was an oversimplification, as it became evident from the moment Lawrence intoned: "I call on the defendant Rudolf Hess."

"First of all, I should like to make a request to the High Tribunal that

I may remain seated because of my state of health," Hess responded, though there was nothing organically wrong with him.

"Certainly." Lawrence nodded.

Hess now indicated that, since the others had concluded their defenses, he was ready to commence his. To start with, he pointed out that all of his prognostications had materialized; that he had predicted "that some of the defendants would act rather strangely: They would make shameless utterances about the Führer; they would incriminate their own people; they would partially incriminate each other, and falsely at that. Perhaps they would even incriminate themselves, and also wrongly."

The explanation for these, and other inexplicable occurrences, Hess solemnly decared, harked back to the Moscow purge trials of the late 1930s: "These were characterized by the fact that the defendants accused themselves in an astonishing way. At the end, when death sentences were passed upon them, they clapped in frenzied approval to the astonishment of the world. But some foreign press correspondents reported that one had the impression that these defendants, through some means hitherto unknown, had been put into an abnormal state of mind, as a result of which they acted the way they did."

Evidently, Hess indicated, this mysterious, mesmeric force had been abroad in the world ever since, and had infiltrated the minds of Germany's leaders, as well as unknown multitudes of other men, thus providing the answer to "the hitherto inexplicable actions of the personnel in the German concentration camps, including the scientists and physicians who made these frightful and atrocious experiments on the prisoners, actions which normal human beings, especially physicians and scientists, could not possibly carry out.

"But this is also of equally great significance in connection with the actions of the persons who undoubtedly gave the orders and directions for the atrocities in the concentration camps and who gave the orders for shooting prisoners of war and lynchings and other such things, up to the Führer himself.

"I recall that the witness Field Marshal Milch testified here that he had the impression that the Führer was not normal mentally during the last year, and a number of my comrades here have told me that during the last years the Führer's eyes and facial expression had something cruel in them, and even had a tendency toward madness."

Goering kept tugging at Hess's sleeve and whispering, "Stop! Stop!" but Hess continued happily oblivious until, after some twenty minutes, Lawrence indulgently interposed and notified Hess that the tribunal could not permit him to continue *ad infinitum:* "The tribunal, therefore, hopes that the defendant Hess will conclude his speech."

Jerked back to reality, Hess protested that he had been unable to conduct his defense because "it was impossible for me to persuade my counsel to declare himself willing to put the proper questions to me; it was likewise impossible for me to get another counsel to agree to put these questions to me." Finally he concluded: "I was permitted to work for many years of my life under the greatest son whom my people have brought forth in its thousand-year history. I am happy to know that I have done my duty to my people, my duty as a German, as a National Socialist, as a loyal follower of my Führer. I do not regret anything. If I were to begin all over again, I would act just as I have acted, even if I knew that in the end I should meet a fiery death at the stake. No matter what human beings may do, I shall some day stand before the judgment seat of the Eternal. I shall answer to Him, and I know He will judge me innocent."

Thus, after 216 days of testimony, Lawrence announced: "The tribunal will now adjourn until 23 September, in order to consider its judgment. On that date the judgment will be announced."

V

Judgment

55   *Deliberation*

On September 2, Colonel Andrus suggested to the tribunal that the regulations for the prisoners be relaxed while the verdict was being determined, and that they be permitted daily visits with their families. After the judges assented, each defendant was allowed to speak to his wife and children for one hour a day through the grille in the partitioned conference room.

The corridors of the Palace of Justice rang with the voices of children. Schacht's four- and five-year-old daughters by his second wife played with seven-year-old Edda Goering and Ribbentrop's youngest child. Almost a year and a half had passed since the children had seen their fathers, and some could scarcely remember them. At one meeting, Schacht's four-year-old suddenly stood up and whispered conspiratorially through the grille: "I like you very much."

Goering, with old-fashioned gallantry, stood up and bowed whenever one of the women he knew passed by on the other side of the partition. Keitel and Papen refused to see their wives under circumstances which they considered degrading. Raeder was visited by his son and daughter, but the most strenuous effort by the American military authorities to discover from the Russians the whereabouts of his wife and have her brought to Nuremberg were unsuccessful—the Soviets, whose behavior made the Sphinx seem scrutable, returned all inquiries with the notation "Address Unknown."*

In the prison, one cell was set aside as a common room. There, three or four of the defendants were permitted to gather together for an hour at a time. Chess and cards were made available, but left unused—the prisoners felt a tremendous need to talk to each other and purge themselves of their feelings about the trial. Some of them, like Keitel and Ribbentrop, made perfunctory efforts to write justifications; but only Frank, who had been working on his memoirs for the past several months, tried to complete them before the announcement of the verdict.

One beautiful, sunny day when the strains of the organ could be heard in the exercise yard, Keitel circled round and round a small plot of lawn, then, when the attention of the guards was momentarily diverted, stooped

*In actuality, Frau Raeder, who had voluntarily accompanied her husband to Moscow, had been returned to the vicinity of Berlin and was being held under house arrest by the NKVD. In August and September of 1946 she was seriously ill, but nine more months passed before the Americans were able to discover where she was, and she was not released until 1950.

furtively and straightened up with a four-leaf clover. "Do you think it will bring me luck?" he plaintively asked Fritzsche. An instant later a guard appeared and took it away from him—the prisoners were forbidden to pick anything up.

Neurath kept studying the reports from the manager of his estate and worrying why the cattle were not doing better. Streicher, suffering from terrible nightmares, kept repeating: "I am going to celebrate Christmas in Valhalla!" Goering, who had refused to speak to Schirach after Schirach had joined Speer and Fritzsche and "confessed," held out his hand and said: "Let's bury it, Schirach. I know you are a patriot. Let's not spoil these last days before we're hanged."

In their consultation room in the Palace of Justice, the judges were closeted under conditions of the strictest security. Only two interpreters accompanied them. The contents of the wastebaskets were burned after each session. The clerical staff working on the various drafts of the judgment were isolated in a villa in the suburbs. In actuality, since it would have been impossible to render a judgment and opinion in a case as massive and complex as this in a period of only three to four weeks, the work had been initiated after Fritzsche's appearance in June, and Biddle's assistants, Jim Rowe and Adrian Fisher, together with Parker's aide, Robert Stewart, had been preparing analyses of the guilt of the individual defendants since May.*

The most vexing problem involved the concept of the conspiracy and the guilt of the organizations. At the initial meeting on June 27, de Vabres, who had not played an aggressive role during the trial but was a recognized authority on international law, moved that Count One, the Conspiracy to Commit Aggressive War, be stricken. De Vabres argued that the crime of conspiracy did not exist in international law and that the evidence had shown that there had been no common plan. No practical purpose would be served by a finding of "conspiracy," since all of the defendants had been involved individually in waging aggressive war, in crimes against humanity, or in war crimes.

"I was very much influenced by his argument and said so," Biddle wrote one of his advisers, Herbert Wechsler (who had returned to his post at Columbia University). Excising the charge of conspiracy would elimi-

---

*Rowe, a thirty-seven-year-old skiing enthusiast from Montana, had clerked for Supreme Court Justice Oliver Wendell Holmes, then been an administrative assistant to President Roosevelt and an assistant attorney general under Biddle; Fisher, thirty two years old, was a graduate of Harvard Law School, had clerked for Supreme Court Justices Louis Brandeis and Felix Frankfurter, and had been an official in the State and War departments. Both had served in the armed forces. Stewart was still on active service as a major in the army.

nate many difficulties, Biddle believed, "and get rid of all the trash and looseness gathered in the indictment. Will you think about this?"

The debate continued throughout the summer. Biddle was more and more inclined to concur with the French; but Parker resolutely advocated the other side of the issue. Parker hated immorality and injustice. For him, the trial had been one long exposure of viciousness and cruelty, of human degradation such as he had never in his most fantastic thoughts believed existed; and he had become firmly convinced that what the tribunal was confronted with was a conspiracy of evil. The conspiracy had been proved "beyond all peradventure," he maintained, issuing the phrase in his southern accent with the archaic majesty of an Elizabethan canon.

Birkett agreed passionately with Parker from a historical perspective. Count One was the basis of the indictment, he contended. If Count One were rejected, the heart would be torn out of the body of the trial: "If you say this dreadful war isn't planned, you bring about a national disaster. You acquit the party. Do you want to acquit the Nazi regime?" Such an action would do grievous injury to the world and infinite harm to the tribunal. Lawrence, Nikitchenko, and Volchkov sided with Parker and Birkett. Weeks of discussion merely hardened the positions of the British and Parker on the one hand, and the French on the other. Both sides seemed to be going to extremes, Biddle observed at a judges' conference on August 19, and pleaded for understanding. Wechsler's opinion, beefed up with inputs from Rowe, Fisher, and Stewart, was that the evidence had indicated many plans, including one to prepare and wage war, but not a single great conspiracy. Hitler's strategy had undergone continual evolution. Its key feature had been its impermanence. The attack on Norway had been "decided upon unexpectedly, to everybody's surprise, save that of Raeder and Rosenberg, who instigated it. The attack against the USSR was dreaded and disapproved of by the Führer's principal collaborators: Goering, Ribbentrop, Keitel, Raeder. How, then, can one speak of a conspiracy? Only one voice was heard, namely Hitler's. The defense has rightly maintained that the existence of a conspiracy or common plan is incompatible with the Führer principle."

Using Wechsler's opinion as a basis, Biddle suggested a compromise. It was his belief, Biddle declared, that there had been no conspiracy to commit War Crimes or Crimes Against Humanity, and he asked that this issue be voted on first.

Biddle's colleagues concurred with him, and decided to limit the application of conspiracy to the charge of waging aggressive war.

Next came the problem of deciding when the conspiracy had been initiated. This was a question to which the prosecution had never really applied itself; and Biddle noted that Fyfe's assertion that the common plan had had its inception with the formation of the Nazi Party was "very vague and unsatisfactory."

Finally, the judges concluded that the Hossbach Meeting on November 5, 1937, had marked the first time that Hitler had specifically spelled out his aggressive intentions, and that the conspiracy, therefore, stemmed from that date.

To resolve the impasse between the French and the British, Biddle worked out an equivocal compromise: "It is not necessary to decide whether a single master conspiracy between the defendants has been established by the evidence. But the evidence establishes with certainty the existence of many separate plans rather than a single conspiracy embracing them all." Based on this finding, the tribunal convicted eight of the defendants on Count One—a judgment that many jurists found difficult to accept.

By excluding Crimes Against Humanity from the conspiracy, the judges unwittingly cut the ground from the case against the organizations; for no matter how pernicious the SD and Gestapo had been, they had *not* been part of a conspiracy to wage aggressive war.

Though Biddle was as convinced as anyone that wholesale atrocities had been committed by members of the SS, the SD, and the Gestapo, he argued that group criminality did not exist; and that, in a case that pitted human rights and the liberty of the individual against the collectivism and the impersonal tyranny of the state, no greater incongruity or injustice could be perpetrated than to condemn hundreds of thousands of people without trial. His eloquence almost swayed Parker, who contended that the organizations could be connected only with War Crimes and Crimes Against Humanity. Thus, the tribunal was left with the head of one animal and the tail of another—a conspiracy to wage aggressive war, and a group of organizations with complicity for charges on which the tribunal had ruled that there had been no conspiracy.

Birkett opposed Biddle on the organizations as he had on conspiracy. To avoid declaring the organizations criminal would be a great political mistake, he argued; and the French were inclined to back him. The evil connected with the names of the Gestapo and the SS were so great, Falco proffered, that the French public would never accept their seeming exoneration, and he and de Vabres would be ostracized. Biddle found himself alone against the other seven judges on the issue. Negotiating skillfully and exercising great power of persuasion, he succeeded, nevertheless, in pulling the teeth out of the judgment on the organizations.

The Russians wanted to convict all seven indicted groups; but the western judges had little difficulty agreeing on acquitting three of them. The membership of the Reich Cabinet and the high command (and general staff) had been so small that any individuals who had committed crimes could be identified and tried, and it was therefore purposeless to declare the organizations guilty. The SA had been emasculated by Hitler. On the other hand, the judges unanimously held the Gestapo, the SD, and the leadership corps of the Nazi Party culpable. The SS was troublesome, because although it had started out as an elitist, voluntary association, it had later embraced hundreds of thousands of draftees. The judges decided to include in their findings only those members who had joined prior to the start of the war.

The consensus worked out by Biddle stated: "A criminal organization is analogous to a criminal conspiracy in that the essence of both is cooperation for criminal purposes. The group must be formed or used in connection with the commission of crimes denounced by the charter." The declaration then continued with baffling contradiction to all but neutralize itself. Membership in one of the convicted organizations was criminal, per se, the judges ruled, and could be punished with any sentence, including death. The tribunal, however, excluded from condemnation "persons who had no knowledge of the criminal purposes or acts of the organization, and those who were drafted by the state for membership, unless they were personally implicated in the commission of acts declared criminal." Membership alone was not enough for the finding of guilt, they said, in an amazing and clear-cut demonstration of judicial schizophrenia.

The net effect was a statement in principle that was inoperative in practice, since none of the Allied governments had any interest in setting up the huge and expensive organizations that would have been required to administer the judgment. By his maneuvering, Biddle had killed Bernays's central concept of the trial, supported by Secretary of War Stimson and by Jackson, that the Nazi era represented a conspiracy carried out through the medium of the organizations, and that only by a conspiracy indictment could the atrocities the Nazis had committed against their own people be brought before an international tribunal. No more convincing refutation could have been provided of the criticism that the trial was a cut-and-dried affair, or that the judges were handmaidens of the victorious nations, or that they would not mete out justice impartially.

The findings on individual guilt were, in general, much less troublesome. The judges had no difficulty agreeing on the conviction of sixteen of the defendants at their very first meeting.

Biddle and Parker relied heavily on the analyses prepared by Rowe, Fisher, and Stewart. Biddle concurred with Rowe's conclusion absolving Goering of the charge of "terror bombing" Warsaw, Rotterdam, and Coventry. The testimony had been completely convincing as to Warsaw. The city, after numerous warnings, had been raided when it refused to surrender. "This is accepted military doctrine throughout the world."

With regard to the attack on Rotterdam, the analysis noted: "This sort of mistake was so common throughout the war because of the difficulty of air-ground visual and radio communications that his [Goering's] explanation must be accepted as true in the absence of *conclusive* proof by the prosecution that the attack was completely political.

"Coventry was an aircraft center with the industry widely dispersed and therefore an acceptable, indeed necessary military target."

The testimony as to whether Goering could have prevented the shooting of all or some of the escaped fliers from Sagan had been conflicting, and, the analysis suggested, "the evidence is not sufficiently clear to convict Goering on this."

In the conflict between Gisevius and Goering, Rowe, though suspecting Gisevius's motives, believed that "Goering was the kind of man Gisevius said he was." Parker considered Goering nothing but a schemer and a liar, and assessed his responsibility for the Final Solution as second only to Hitler's: "Goering vigorously denied that he knew anything about these murders and attributes the responsibility to Hitler, Himmler, and Goebbels. It is difficult to believe that a man so intimately in touch with every phase of the life of Germany could have been ignorant of such a widespread operation as the wholesale extermination of the Jews."

"Goering was often, indeed almost always, the moving force, second only to his leader," Rowe summarized. "He was the prime conspirator. He was the leading war aggressor. He was the director of the slave labor program and the creator of the oppressive program against the Jews and other races."

This statement can be faulted for the conclusion that Goering was the leading war aggressor (which he certainly was not), and, to a certain extent, on his involvement with the slave labor program, but otherwise was amply substantiated. The judges unanimously found Goering guilty and condemned him to death.

The Allied Control Council had decreed that the executions should be performed by one of the traditional German methods, hanging or guillotining, unless the tribunal specified otherwise. Nikitchenko spoke up against guillotining, and no one argued with him. De Vabres, characterizing Goering as a high-class brigand who had a certain nobility, preferred shooting him. Biddle retorted that shooting should be applied only as an indication of mitigation. The judges voted seven to one that Goering should be hanged.

Hess, despite his disordered mind, generated no sympathy. For this state of affairs, Seidl, who had repeatedly baited the Russians and antagonized the other judges, was more to blame than Hess. By his maneuvers and efforts to expose the Soviets, while presenting only a perfunctory defense, Seidl had conveyed an image of Hess magnified in importance; and Hess himself had provided the finishing touches in his final speech— none of the judges were of a mind to deal lightly with a man who had reaffirmed his faith in the Führer and said he had no regrets. Nikitchenko and Volchkov thought he should be executed; Lawrence, Biddle, Parker, and Falco voted for life imprisonment; de Vabres suggested a sentence of twenty years; and Birkett, not wishing to involve himself in condemning a lunatic, abstained. The consensus was that Hess should be imprisoned for life.

There was unanimous agreement that Ribbentrop, Kaltenbrunner, and Streicher were guilty and should be hanged, and only a smattering of dissent on Keitel, Jodl, Rosenberg, Frank, Frick, and Seyss-Inquart.

"Rosenberg was one of the second string trying to squeeze his way into the huddle with the big boys," Stewart, with a penchant for football terminology, wrote. The importance of his work had probably been exaggerated, but he had "really made the grade in the action against the USSR. He was definitely one of the boys who made the plans." Streicher well deserved the title of "Jew Baiter Number One. A cheerleader never carries the ball nor calls a play, yet by his continual goading of the crowd to frenzied excitement he is a personality in his team's success."

Seyss-Inquart was disposed of with the observation that it was "no defense that he was less brutal than Himmler."

No one disagreed that Keitel should be executed, but the two French judges thought that he had, at least, comported himself honorably, and deserved to be shot rather than hanged. De Vabres and Falco also dissented from the death verdict on Jodl, for whom, de Vabres believed, a sentence of twenty to thirty years would be appropriate.

Biddle, as a compromise, suggested: "Hang Keitel, shoot Jodl." When, however, the Russians and the British—the principal victims of war crimes—remained adamant, the American and French judges gave way, and agreed to sentence both men to death by hanging.

Funk very nearly shared the same fate. At the initial discussion of his sentence, only de Vabres and Parker believed that he should be spared execution. Parker persuaded Biddle to hold Funk's case in abeyance for a day; and Biddle, after reviewing the evidence, concluded that, though Funk was as morally guilty as anyone, he had not participated directly in atrocities. Over the opposition of the Russian judges, who continued to propose death, the westerners voted to sentence Funk to life imprisonment.

In every case de Vabres, the most compassionate of the judges, pro-

posed a milder sentence than the others. On the other hand, he joined with
the two Russian judges in not wishing, as a matter of principle, to acquit
anyone. He was of the rather odd opinion that the tribunal would be
making a statement of morality, not merely of law, and that, regardless of
individual culpability, the crimes had been of such enormity that anyone
who had played the most remote role in their commission must be convicted.

In practice, the judges balloted as individuals. But when a diversity
of opinion appeared on several of the defendants, Nikitchenko proposed
that, if a formal vote by nation were required, a 2–2 tie should not be
interpreted as acquittal, but, in effect, as a "hung jury." The possibility of
the defendant's retrial would then be left open. By a vote of 3–1, the
western powers arrayed against the Russians, the judges rejected this
conception. If the vote on any defendant was 2–2, the charges against him
would be dismissed.

With respect to Raeder and Doenitz, the evidence seemed to indicate
that Doenitz was the more political and culpable of the two. But what
stuck in the minds of the judges was that Raeder had been the original
proponent of the invasion of Norway.

Doenitz, on the other hand, found an advocate in Biddle, who was
very much influenced by Rowe's findings in favor of the admiral: "The
prosecution charge that Doenitz and Raeder deliberately waged unrestricted submarine warfare contrary to international law has not been
maintained," Rowe wrote. "Most international law experts share the German view that an armed merchant ship is not entitled to protection. The
defense met every specification raised by the prosecution—and also made
attempts to discuss the international law involved, an attempt not duplicated by the prosecution. The preponderance of evidence clearly favors
the defense. The prosecution has failed to make its case beyond a reasonable doubt."

Numerous tragedies had occurred on both sides because identification
of ships was extremely difficult, Rowe reminded the judges. "The incredibly large number of cases on the Allied side of mistaken identification were
throughout the war the curse of the American and British navies, causing
the loss of thousands of Allied lives by their own guns." Furthermore, the
United States had, if anything, pursued submarine warfare more mercilessly than the Germans: "Unrestricted submarine warfare was carried on
throughout the war in the Pacific and Indian oceans by Great Britain and
the United States in a particularly ruthless way. The United States began
even though the Japanese restricted submarines to attacks on warships
exclusively. Nor should the actions of the United States Navy in the
summer of 1941 against German submarines, which did not fight back, be

forgotten. It remains offensive to the Anglo-American concept of justice to punish men for doing exactly what one has done himself."

On this reasoning, Biddle argued vigorously for Doenitz's acquittal: The essence of the charge against Doenitz was the practice of submarine warfare—the rest of the specifications were trifling. Nimitz had given precisely the same orders as Doenitz. "Germany waged a much cleaner war than we did."

Once more, however, Biddle was in the lone minority. Lawrence viewed Doenitz as "a typical National Socialist—harsh and inhumane." Parker thought that Doenitz had, in his espousal of Nazism, "stepped outside his profession," and refused to believe that the United States Navy was capable of the ruthlessness manifested by Doenitz. De Vabres took the middle ground: Doenitz was guilty, but there had been extenuating circumstances, and he should receive a light sentence.

A term of ten years was agreed on for Doenitz; but Raeder received life.

In assessing the respective culpabilities of Sauckel and Speer, Fisher and Rowe had not been swayed by Speer's protestations. Sauckel, Fisher wrote, "never had the responsibility for any major policy decisions but was always used to execute policies which had been decided on by more powerful men such as Goering and Speer." There was, however, "little to be said on the question of mitigation," because Sauckel had practiced "complete ruthlessness and unfeeling efficiency in application of a program which took five million into slave labor and countless numbers to their death."

If Sauckel deserved no mercy, Speer's guilt was overwhelming: "Speer aggrandized control over labor to himself, and took the position he had authority over Sauckel to provide laborers, and got his way over Sauckel's objections. Sauckel continually told Speer the laborers were being obtained by force. Speer continually kept the pressure on Sauckel and overstepped the bounds of his authority. The violence used in recruiting was largely in response to his high demands for labor. It does not appear that his views as to treatment differed from those of Sauckel.

"A strong argument will be made for Speer on the question of mitigation. However, Speer was the leading figure in the slave labor program, and is a man of sufficient intelligence fully to realize the moral implications of what he was doing."

None of the judges had anything good to say of Sauckel, and he was condemned to death. Speer's personality had, however, impressed several of the tribunal's members, and their emotions tended to play as great a role in their judgment as the evidence that had been presented. Though Biddle and the Russians argued that Speer was as culpable as Sauckel and should share his fate, Birkett, who identified with Speer, suggested a sentence of ten years. Parker noted that Speer had renounced Hitler and seemed genuinely repentant. Lawrence proposed fifteen years, to which de Vabres, Falco, and Parker acquiesced. Biddle and Nikitchenko contended that, taking the extent of Speer's complicity into account, this was a mere slap on the wrist, and at first refused to budge. After lengthy debate, a sentence of twenty years was agreed upon.

The evidence analysis against Schirach was damning: "The warped outlook of an entire generation in Germany is von Schirach's responsibility. The evidence compels rejection of von Schirach's contention that the evacuation of the Jews from Vienna was carried out by the RSHA without involvement on his part. The mass of evidence shows that von Schirach was personally concerned with the deportations. He is guilty of Crimes Against Humanity, Slave Labor, and the Final Solution." At first he seemed destined to be condemned to death or to life imprisonment. Biddle, Birkett, and de Vabres, however, were inclined to be lenient; and with some reluctance on the part of Lawrence, and the usual opposition of the Russians, a sentence of twenty years was approved.

Neurath, after a spirited debate, received fifteen years.

The cases of Schacht and Papen crystallized the diverse perspectives of the judges.

In his memorandum on Schacht, Fisher observed: "The tribunal has decided that the evidence does not establish one great conspiracy for *Lebensraum* and world domination, but several to make war on individual countries." Schacht had already resigned as economics minister by the time of the Hossbach Meeting in November 1937, determined by the judges to mark the inception of the conspiracy. "It follows that Schacht must be acquitted because there is no evidence he participated in the conspiracy to make war. The only evidence is that he helped finance the rearmament program—but there is no evidence that this was with the intention to wage war."

Lawrence thought Schacht should be set free. Parker, who agreed with Lawrence, squared off against de Vabres. Parker was as committed to his conviction that it would be immoral to condemn an innocent man, as de Vabres was adamant that it would be shocking to sentence Keitel to death while acquitting Schacht, since both, at one time, had traveled in the same boat. Biddle tended to agree with de Vabres. Birkett was diametrically opposed to de Vabres's thesis of guilt in principle. If Schacht were not guilty, then he must be acquitted. If he were guilty, he deserved severe punishment. There had been a great body of testimony in Schacht's favor, Birkett declared.

Nikitchenko, who wanted to execute Schacht, privately asked Biddle how much he ought to come down. Biddle replied that he would suggest a stiff term as a compromise and see what happened. De Vabres announced that he would agree to an absolute maximum of ten years—considering Schacht's age, any longer sentence would be the equivalent of life imprisonment. Volchkov voiced his agreement, and Biddle indicated he would not object. Hard bargaining with Lawrence, Parker, and Birkett produced a compromise sentence of eight years.

On von Papen, the British and American judges split with the French and Russian. Biddle and Parker argued that Papen had not been a conspirator, that he had not promoted the Anschluss, and had been as surprised by it as everybody else.

Papen's guilt, Falco suggested, was equivalent to Schacht's, and he should received approximately the same sentence. De Vabres however, contended that Papen's complicity had been greater than Schacht's. Papen was immoral and corrupt, and the practical effect of his actions had been to make him an accomplice in the events leading toward war. "What are we here for if not to put morals into international law?" de Vabres demanded of his fellow judges.

Birkett said he had searched the evidence without being able to find anything on which to convict Papen: "We come down to the dislike of the kind of man Papen is." But Papen could not be convicted on his personality.

Lawrence was disturbed: "I dislike Papen more than I dislike Schacht." He felt, nevertheless, compelled to vote for acquittal. The result was a 2–2 tie—the Americans and British arrayed against the French and the Russians. The verdict would be announced as acquittal.

Lawrence then observed that in his opinion it would be unfortunate to acquit only Papen; and, since Schacht had been convicted, Fritzsche ought to be let off.

Nikitchenko could not understand the logic of this. Why was it necessary to acquit Fritzsche just because of Papen?

Parker, more rational than Lawrence, argued that Fritzsche was being offered as a sacrifice in place of Goebbels, and that a man should not be convicted for what he said and wrote unless it was an incitement to crime. By a 3–1 vote of the western judges against the Russians, Fritzsche was adjudged not guilty.

When the judges reconvened on Friday the thirteenth, Lawrence confided to Biddle that de Vabres had changed his mind on Schacht—he still believed all of the defendants should be convicted; but, since Papen had been acquitted, Schacht would have to be too, since he was less guilty than Papen.

Lawrence himself rationalized that "the unity of judgment" demanded the discharge of all three defendants with small responsibilities.

Biddle, who, despite, his amicable relations with Lawrence, did not think too highly of his legal ability, noted it was "shoddy to base Schacht's fate on that of others."

Nikitchenko, terribly upset at de Vabres's change of heart, which produced another acquittal on a 2–2 tie—the French and British versus the Americans and Russians—criticized a vote not based on the evidence as unjust. Suggesting that it was the last straw, he announced he would dissent. Biddle hoped he would not air the tribunal's linen in public; but Nikitchenko, setting his jaw, declared that he *must* dissent on several cases, including Schacht's, and would protest the interpretation that a 2–2 tie amounted to an acquittal.

Then, with tensions manifest and September 23 little more than a week off, the judges decided to give themselves an additional week to iron out their differences. Judgment day was postponed until September 30.

56   Verdict

The delay, seeming to indicate that the judges were having difficulty reaching a decision, raised the spirits of the defendants and their families. Saturday the twenty-eighth was the final day the defendants were permitted to be with their wives and children; and Sunday an atmosphere of gloom pervaded the cell block. On Monday the prisoners returned to their familiar places in the courtroom.

The judges arrived in black, bulletproof cars escorted by machinegun-mounting, siren-blaring jeeps. A number of members of the prosecution team, including Colonel Storey, who had long since returned to the United States, came back to Nuremberg for the pronouncing of the judgment. Andrus placed his entire complement of guards on alert. Requests for passes were in such demand that even Biddle could not get an extra pair of tickets.

The tension was extraordinary. People who had become used to the constant buzz and desultory activity during the sessions of the past few months found the deathly stillness unnerving.

To the frustration of many in the audience and the aggravated anxiety of the men in the dock, the entire first day was devoted to the judges' findings on the law of the case, their verdict on the organizations, and their review of the evidence and justification in support of their decisions. The members of the tribunal expected their judgment to become a landmark in the history of international law and relations, and were highly conscious of the drama of the moment—they were not merely pronouncing a verdict on the past but offering a guidepost for the future. Each, including the alternate judges, read a section in turn.

Although Biddle had found it impossible to define precisely what constituted a war of aggression—a definition that experts on international law still cannot agree on—the judgment declared: "To initiate a war of aggression is not only an international crime; it is the supreme international crime differing only from other war crimes in that it contains within itself the accumulated evil of the whole." The tribunal rejected the defense's contention that no crime can be committed if no law has been established prohibiting an act: "To assert that it is unjust to punish those who in defiance of treaties and assurances have attacked neighboring states without warning is obviously untrue, for in such circumstances the attacker must know that he is doing wrong, and so far from it being unjust to punish him, it would be unjust if his wrongs were allowed to go unpunished."

Therefore, all those who had participated in the planning and prosecution of aggressive war were guilty: "Hitler could not make aggressive war by himself. He had to have the cooperation of statesmen, military leaders, diplomats, and businessmen. When they, with knowledge of his aims, gave him their cooperation, they made themselves party to the plan he had initiated. They are not to be deemed innocent because Hitler made use of them, if they knew what they were doing."

Although the judges had held some vigorous arguments among themselves over the attacks on Norway and Greece, they pronounced that every German assault on a neutral, from Poland in 1939 to Russia in 1941, had constituted an instance of aggressive war.

Parker, reading the section on War Crimes and Crimes Against Humanity, enunciated the words with barely concealed indignation: "The evidence relating to War Crimes has been overwhelming. War Crimes were committed on a vast scale, never before seen in the history of war. They were perpetrated in all the countries occupied by Germany, and on the High Seas, and were attended by every conceivable circumstance of cruelty and horror. There can be no doubt that the majority of them arose from the Nazi conception of 'total war.' Everything is made subordinate to the overmastering dictates of war. Rules, regulations, assurances, and treaties all alike are of no moment; freed from the restraining influence of international law, the aggressive war is conducted by the Nazi leaders in the most barbaric way. War Crimes were committed when and wherever the Führer and his close associates thought them to be advantageous. They were for the most part the result of cold and criminal calculation."

Though the SA, the Reich Cabinet, and the general staff and high command were acquitted as groups, Lawrence excoriated the generals as individuals: "They have been responsible in large measure for the miseries and sufferings that have fallen on millions of men, women, and children. They have been a disgrace to the honorable profession of arms. Without their military guidance the aggressive ambitions of Hitler and his fellow Nazis would have been academic and sterile. Many of these men have made a mockery of the soldiers' oath of obedience to military orders. When it suits their defense, they say they had to obey; when confronted with Hitler's brutal crimes, which are shown to have been within their general knowledge, they say they disobeyed. The truth is they actively participated in all these crimes, or sat silent and acquiescent, witnessing the commission of crimes on a scale larger and more shocking than the world has ever had the misfortune to know."

None of the defendants slept much that night, and they all looked haggard the next morning. As if by design, fall had descended abruptly on the city. Nuremberg was enshrouded in a light mist through which the broken towers and jagged sculptures of rubble appeared and disappeared in shifting, surrealistic images. On this day the judges, faced with the task of pronouncing sentence, were as taut as the defendants. Biddle felt sick, and Birkett had difficulty looking at the men in the dock.

Goering, his eyes—like those of Frank, Doenitz, and Schirach—hidden behind dark glasses, sat slumped dejectedly, his head bowed, the earphones held to his right ear. Hess, as indifferent as always, irritatedly brushed Goering off when Goering attempted to attract his attention, and refused to put on the headphones at all. Keitel remained rigid and expressionless, as he had since the first day of the trial. Funk, as usual, twisted and fidgeted. Streicher, his arms crossed, leaned back pugnaciously; he had acquired the habit of chewing gum from the American secretaries, and his jaws worked perpetually like those of a masticating cow.

The entire proceedings were broadcast on the German radio; and the wives of the defendants, still not permitted into the courtroom, sat transfixed by their receivers.

Lawrence began at 9:30 AM with the fifteen-hundred-word judgment on Goering. For reasons of Allied sensitivity, no mention was made of the fact that the Luftwaffe had, essentially, been exonerated in the bombings of Warsaw, Rotterdam, and Coventry. Otherwise, Goering was convicted on all four counts: "By the decree of 31 July, 1941, he directed Himmler and Heydrich to 'bring about a complete solution of the Jewish question in the German sphere of influence in Europe.' There is nothing to be said in mitigation. For Goering was often, indeed almost always, the moving force, second only to his leader. On some specific cases there may be conflict of testimony, but, in terms of the broad outline, his own admissions are more than sufficiently wide to be conclusive of his guilt. His guilt is unique in its enormity. The record discloses no excuses for this man."

The verdict made it clear that Goering could expect no mercy in the sentencing, which was to follow after the midday break. In adjudging Hess guilty, the judges conceded "that Hess acts in an abnormal manner, suffers from loss of memory, and has mentally deteriorated during this trial. But there is nothing to show that he does not realize the nature of the charges against him, or is incapable of defending himself. There is no suggestion that Hess was not completely sane when the acts charged against him were committed."

Ribbentrop, Keitel, Rosenberg, Jodl, and Neurath joined Goering in being convicted on all four counts. Ribbentrop, the judgment declared, "played an important part in Hitler's 'final solution' of the Jewish question. Von Ribbentrop participated in all of the Nazi aggressions from the occupation of Austria to the invasion of the Soviet Union. There is abundant evidence, moreover, that von Ribbentrop was in complete sympathy with all the main tenets of the National Socialist creed."

"There is nothing in mitigation," Lawrence declared in the verdict on Keitel. "Superior orders, even to a soldier, cannot be considered in mitigation where crimes as shocking and extensive have been committed, consciously, ruthlessly, and without military excuse or justification."

Rosenberg, Nikitchenko read, had occasionally "objected to the excesses and atrocities committed by his subordinates, but these excesses continued and he stayed in office until the end." Biddle, passing judgment on Frank, observed: "It is undoubtedly true that most of the criminal program charged against Frank was put into effect through the police [and] it therefore may well be true that some of the crimes committed in the General Government were committed without the knowledge of Frank, and even occasionally despite his opposition. But it is also true that Frank was a willing and knowing participant in the use of terrorism in Poland; in the economic exploitation of Poland in a way which led to the death by starvation of a large number of people; in the deportation into Germany as slave laborers of over a million Poles; and in a program involving the murder of at least three million Jews."

When de Vabres mentioned Frick's name, Frick jerked erect as if he had been jabbed: Frick's principal guilt, de Vabres stated, lay in the fact that he had known of the atrocities committed in the concentration camps and had done nothing to stop them. The euthanasia program had been conducted "under Frick's jurisdiction. He had knowledge that insane, sick, and aged people, 'useless eaters,' were being systematically put to death. Complaints of these murders reached him, but he did nothing to stop them."

"With knowledge of the extermination of the Jews in the Occupied Eastern Territory," Lawrence declared in pronouncing judgment on Streicher, "this defendant continued to write and publish his propaganda of death. Streicher's incitement to murder and extermination at the time when the Jews in the East were being killed under the most horrible conditions clearly constitutes persecution on political and racial grounds in connection with war crimes, and constitutes a Crime Against Humanity."

Funk, Nikitchenko read, had either known or deliberately closed his eyes to what was going on in the Reichsbank.

As Biddle followed with the judgment on Schacht, Schacht sat back listening, a slight, Mona Lisa–like smile on his face as if he had never doubted the outcome—little did he realize by what quirk of fortune he had been saved. "The Tribunal finds that Schacht is not guilty on this indictment," Biddle concluded as a murmur swept through the courtroom, "and directs that he shall be discharged by the marshal when the tribunal presently adjourns."

The judgment on Doenitz reflected the tribunal's doubts and disagreements. "The Tribunal is of the opinion that the evidence does not establish with the certainty required that Doenitz deliberately ordered the killing of shipwrecked survivors," de Vabres observed. "The orders were undoubtedly ambiguous, and deserve the strongest censure."

Announcing the verdict on Jodl, de Vabres said, "Participation in such crimes as these has never been required of any soldier and he cannot now shield himself behind a mythical requirement of soldierly obedience at all costs as his excuse for commission of these crimes. There is nothing in mitigation."

Papen, Lawrence noted, "engaged in both intrigue and bullying. But the Charter does not make criminal such offenses against political morality, however bad these may be."

Sandwiched between the convictions of Seyss-Inquart and Neurath, Biddle announced the verdict on Speer: "As the dominant member of the Central Planning Board, Speer took the position that the Board had authority to instruct Sauckel to provide laborers for industry under its control and suceeded in sustaining this position over the objection of Sauckel. Sauckel obtained the labor and allocated it to the various industries in accordance with instructions supplied by Speer. Speer knew when he made his demands on Sauckel that they would be supplied by foreign laborers serving under compulsion." Biddle cited in mitigation that Speer had not been "directly concerned with the cruelty in the administration of the slave labor program, that Speer's establishment of blocked industries did keep many laborers in their homes, and that in the closing stages of the war he was one of the few men who had the courage to tell Hitler that the war was lost and to take steps to prevent the senseless destruction of production facilities."

Fritzsche, the judges announced, had engaged in acerbic propaganda statements, "but the Tribunal is not prepared to hold that they were intended to incite the German people to commit atrocities on conquered peoples, and he cannot be held to have been a participant in the crimes charged."

When the court recessed at midday, the press was permitted access to the three acquitted men. Schacht became the center of a maelstrom of reporters and photographers. Even in this moment of triumph, the businessman within him was irrepressible: He swapped his comments and autographs for cigarettes and chocolates—the effective currency of the period. Dodd, who had been Papen's interrogator, congratulated him and presented him with a box of Havana cigars. Fritzsche was so overwhelmed that his head was literally reeling—politically oriented through and through, he had doubted that, as a matter of policy, the tribunal would acquit anyone; and, of course, his testimony had been full of evasions and prevarications.

For the last time the defendants ate together. The eighteen convicted men stole envious glances at the places of Schacht, Papen, and Fritzsche, where Colonel Andrus had placed three oranges.

During the judgment, the tribunal had singled out Goering, Keitel, and Jodl as men for whom no extenuating circumstances existed; conversely, it had remarked that it perceived mitigating factors in the actions of Doenitz and Speer. Flächsner told Speer he regarded this as a favorable omen—probably Speer would receive only a light sentence of four or five years; and Speer, whose outsized imagination was already starting to regenerate itself, envisioned the United States calling upon him to participate in the development of Alaska, where he would build new cities.

At 2:30 PM, Goering, handcuffed to a guard, was taken on the elevator to the second floor, and brought alone into the court.

The atmosphere was eery as Goering stood there like a villainous star making his final bow before an audience that, save for an occasional cough or the rustle of a paper, appraised him in silent censure. As Goering placed the headphones to his right ear, Lawrence began to read the sentence. Suddenly Goering motioned anguishedly—the cord was not connected, and he could hear nothing.

After the cord had been plugged in, Lawrence began over again, and intoned: "Defendant Hermann Goering, on the count of the indictment on which you have been convicted, the International Military Tribunal sentences you to death by hanging."

Goering saluted and disappeared from the courtroom stage. Seventeen times more the door slid open to admit the convicted. Each of the men, after being sentenced, was taken directly back to jail without seeing his fellow defendants, so that those waiting below did not know what had occurred.

Hess once more refused to place the earphones on his head, but stood, rocking back and forth on his heels and looking at the ceiling. He heard not a word, and was marched off, as he had been marched in, with his reverie unbroken. Seven times in a row after Hess, Lawrence pronounced the death sentence. Ribbentrop appeared, carrying a bundle of documents under his free arm, as if he were on his way to a conference. Kaltenbrunner smiled slightly. Frank, seeming disoriented, at first faced the far wall, and was spun around by the guard toward the judges. Funk, upon hearing his life sentence pronounced, broke into sobs and bowed toward the judges.

Nikitchenko announced his dissent on the acquittals of Schacht, Papen, and Fritzsche, and on Hess's life sentence—the Russians wanted Hess executed. At 3:40 PM the Nuremberg tribunal adjourned for the last time. The reporters stampeded out of the courtroom to file their stories. Within three or four days the judges, the VIPs, and most of the prosecution staff were gone, departing gladly with an almost unseemly haste.

57   Execution

"Death!" Goering whispered as he returned to his cell, his face drained of blood and his hands shaking—despite all of his bravado and speculation that there would be busts of himself in every German home, he had never expected to be sentenced to die. Sauckel trembled and perspired as if he were in the grip of a fever, then broke down and cried bitterly. Keitel and Jodl were stunned that they were to be hanged and not shot—that was a disgrace they thought they might have been spared.

The seven sentenced to imprisonment were immediately separated from the eleven condemned to death and moved to cells on the second floor. Speer, glad enough to have survived, overtook Hess, laboring up the narrow, serpentine staircase with a table.

"What did you get, Herr Hess?" Speer asked.

Hess looked at Speer as if he were asking the most irrelevant and frivolous question: "I have no idea," he answered absentmindedly. "Probably the death penalty."

Papen, as a gesture of empathy, sent his orange to Neurath; Fritzsche his to Schirach. Schacht, with no one to relate to among the defendants, carefully peeled and munched on his. Andrus prepared to release the three acquitted men as soon as their attorneys arranged for transportation. But, as the afternoon progressed, an angry crowd of Germans, protesting the acquittals, gathered in front of the Palace of Justice.

Among the most outraged was Wilhelm Högner, the Bavarian prime minister. Arriving in Nuremberg at the conclusion of the trial, he found himself a resident of the Guest House alongside Heinrich Hoffmann, who was telling concentration camp victims who had lost their entire families that "Hitler adored children"; everything that had happened had been due to the perversions of Himmler, Bormann, and Kaltenbrunner, Hoffmann maintained. Högner had no intention of being as indulgent as the Americans, and ordered the arrest of Hoffmann. Schacht, Papen, and Fritzsche were also to be taken into custody and held for trial by a denazification court, as soon as the Americans relinquished custody of them.

Dix, therefore, recommended to Schacht that he spend the night in the confines of the jail; Papen and Fritzsche likewise chose to stay. Andrus gave them cells, whose doors were not locked, on the third floor; and there they remained.

Not until three days later did Schacht and Fritzsche decide to emerge into the hostile environment. The Americans provided delivery vans, one for each man, and they were spirited off during the midnight hours. Schacht went to the house where his wife was living, Fritzsche to the home of his attorney, Heinz Fritz. American military police guarded the doors which, within the hour, were besieged by Bavarian gendarmes with warrants for the arrest of the men. After an incongruous confrontation between the American and the German police, an accommodation was reached, leaving the two men momentarily at liberty, but under surveillance.

Papen had more difficulty finding a refuge, and occupied a cell in the Nuremberg jail for several more weeks. Finally, the police president of Nuremberg, who had known Papen in his army days, offered to take him in until the authorities decided how to proceed.

As soon as Luise Jodl heard the sentences pronounced over the radio, she embarked on a desperate attempt to save her husband. In an eloquent plea to Field Marshal Montgomery, she wrote that never before in history had a chief of the general staff been treated like a criminal; how could Jodl, who had been regarded as an honorable soldier when he signed the surrender at Reims, now be condemned to death?

To be certain that Montgomery received her letter, she hurried to the Grand Hotel in order to present it personally to the departing British delegation. The old porter, whom she knew, admitted her. A brilliant victory and farewell celebration was in progress. Frocked waiters bore silver trays arrayed with champagne glasses. From the ballroom, conversation and laughter bubbled out into the corridor. A young British captain appeared. "What can I do for you, ma'am?" he inquired.

Frau Jodl explained her petition. He took the letter, disappeared, then returned shortly to say that Maxwell Fyfe himself had promised to deliver it. She sent cables to Churchill, Eisenhower, Stalin, French Marshal Juin, and other high-ranking officers. Churchill and Eisenhower both responded. Churchill said that he had passed her message on to Prime Minister Attlee; Eisenhower replied that he was too unfamiliar with the case to make a judgment—a dismaying but not surprising declaration—but had forwarded her petition to the Allied Control Council.

The attorneys hardest hit by the verdicts and sentences were Exner and Jahrreiss (Jodl), Servatius (Sauckel), and Gustav Steinbauer (Seyss-Inquart). Exner as a family friend of the Jodls felt a personal responsibility and a personal loss; but, beyond that, Exner, as a professor of criminal law, and Jahrreiss, as a professor of international law, had difficulty reconciling the judgment with their training and experience. Working around the clock to compose their official appeal, which had to be submitted by October 5, they wrote: "The judgment is completely incomprehensible to Jodl and to us. Jodl *must* feel himself to be the victim of a new concept of justice. It may be safely said that no lawyer would have dared to say in 1939 that the rulers of a state could be punished as individual criminals for preparing an aggressive war. The simplest proof that 'aggression' is a crime only for the vanquished is furnished by the case of Russia. The judgment makes him a martyr."

It was a well-reasoned plea; but it had all been said before and rejected. Perhaps it was unfortunate that the tribunal had not paid greater heed to de Vabres's exhortations and emphasized morality more in their judgment. For clearly what the judges had said, implicitly as well as explicitly, was that he who lends himself to an infernal regime himself becomes corrupted. Obedience to Satan does violence to God.

The maudlin, romantic Steinbauer, whose performance through the trial had been less than amateurish, claimed that Seyss-Inquart deserved mercy because he had forced ninety thousand Austrian Jews to emigrate prior to the war: "All of these people were saved from a terrible fate." Dwelling in fables, the lawyer penned: "When I was a schoolboy the children were told that, once upon a time, when our old Kaiser had rejected a plea for mercy a tear fell from his eye and wiped out the signature."

Finally awakening to the fact that Speer had unburdened a considerable part of his culpability onto Sauckel, Servatius asked how it was possible to reconcile Speer's and Sauckel's sentences: "Sauckel had nothing to do with concentration camp labor—this was a secret enterprise of Himmler who collaborated directly with Speer. One cannot fail to contrast the personalities of Speer and Sauckel. Sauckel was a tireless worker, and carried out his task with a strict sense of duty without looking to the right or the left. As a workingman he remained a stranger among the leaders. Speer was a close friend of Hitler."

Horn and Thoma could think of nothing better than to ask consideration for their clients on the basis that they were spineless fools.

"A man of such weakness of character whose ruin was brought about by the diabolical figure of Hitler has some call on clemency," Horn wrote of Ribbentrop.

"Rosenberg is certainly one of the most colorless personalities among the defendants," Thoma echoed. "By will and intelligence he is of the subaltern type. His poverty of ideas is the reason why he had so little true success in his numerous offices. It is further significant that he is not willing to admit that he was insignificant. He resented my attempt to bring this out. In reality, weak will and lack of insight are the basic traits of his character."

Seidl used his lengthy appeals for Frank and Hess to cudgel the Soviet Union one last time, though he surely realized that he could accomplish nothing but to stoke a conflagration. Hess, Seidl pointed out, was the only defendant to be convicted solely on the basis of Counts One and Two, the Conspiracy to Commit Aggressive War and the Crimes Against Peace. But Hess had not participated in a single conference with Hitler that formed the foundation for these charges. To the contrary, it had been Stalin and Molotov who had conspired with Hitler against Poland and the Baltic countries.

By the time Seidl was finished, the Russians would have gladly hanged him and his clients together.

Others, like Goering and Streicher, declined to appeal. (Their attorneys filed pleas on their behalf anyway.) Keitel and Jodl asked to be shot instead of hanged. Raeder, pleading old age, requested that his life sentence be "commuted" to execution by firing squad.

Though neither the condemned men nor their attorneys knew it, it was all an exercise in futility. Jackson opposed any commutation of the sentences: "Clemency is a matter of grace, not of right," he declared. "None of the defendants have rendered any service whatever to the prosecution." The rules of the Allied Control Council stipulated that a unanimous vote was required for any mitigation of the sentences; and the Soviets, of course, were not about to grant mercy.

The eleven condemned to death were no longer permitted to exercise in the yard. Whenever one emerged from his cell, he was handcuffed to a guard. For a few minutes a day, one at a time, they were marched up and down in the center of the cell block in lock step with a military policeman. When they saw their attorneys in the Palace of Justice, a GI sat with each of them like a Siamese twin joined at the wrist.

Kaltenbrunner, damning Kauffmann, confided to the assistant SS attorney, Carl Haensel: "If they knew what I still know, if the court knew what I could still say, if they would let me speak, they would not hang me!" Of all the defendants, he remained perhaps the most enigmatic figure: a rawboned man exuding an aura of suppressed violence and madness, his intelligence entangled in the web of his emotional breakdown.

"Why didn't you say so when you had the chance?" Haensel asked.

For a long time Kaltenbrunner sat transfixed in thought, as if he did not intend to respond; then suddenly he burst out: "The trial is a play, and one wants to win." Once more he submerged himself in brooding, then started up, terror in his face, as if he had seen a vision of hell: "Canaris did the same in my place. He also denied everything until the end. We both, together, only we both, know the past as it truly was."

One day the Countess Gisela von Westaup-Wolf, Kaltenbrunner's mistress and mother of his one-and-a-half-year-old twins, appeared. Begging to be allowed to speak to him, she shed copious tears. They were of no avail; for the time when she might have been allowed to speak to him was past.

The Allied Control Council ordered the executions carried out on the fifteenth day after sentencing. The condemned, however, were not informed of the date. Kaltenbrunner, Ribbentrop, Sauckel, and Streicher were in such a state of anguish that it was questionable whether they would retain their sanity till the fatal day. Ribbentrop, suffering from excruciating headaches, kept asking, "When?" Sauckel, agonizing over what would happen to his wife and the seven children still living with her, wept periodically. Though the men were given sleeping pills, Streicher was visited by demons in the middle of the night—on two or three occasions his screaming and raging awakened the whole cell block.

"It is all right to hang a man, but why torture him?" he remarked, as if his nightmares were being conjured by Andrus.

Frank, on the other hand, was almost serene. Reading *The Song of Bernadette*, he identified himself with the martyrs of the Church. Seyss-Inquart viewed his execution with the fatalistic objectivity of a person who is, at one and the same time, both an actor in and the director of a tragedy. He asked that those of the condemned who wished be allowed to meet with each other and to take cold showers daily—he said that, as Reich Commissar of the Netherlands, he had permitted these practices, and the men destined for execution had been grateful to him. (Andrus authorized the showers, but prohibited the meetings.) "You may be convinced, colonel," Seyss-Inquart wrote, "that I myself as well as all my fellow sufferers expect calmly the end of an inevitable and, in a certain sense, necessary event, and will certainly do nothing which could render your task more difficult."

The British and French were so apprehensive about demonstrations or a possible attempt to rescue the prisoners that they insisted that no prior announcement of the executions be made. On October 11 the attorneys were informed that the appeals had been denied. (The only one seriously considered was Jodl's request to be shot instead of hanged, and this was turned down by the British and the Russians, as it had been during the deliberations of the judges.)

The lawyers passed the news on to the families; and Gilbert, followed by Andrus, went around to the cells to inform the condemned.

Lying in their bunks, reading aimlessly and occasionally writing fretfully, the men seemed in a state of suspended animation. Some were stamp collectors, and continued carefully to detach the stamps from the letters they received. In addition to Gilbert, Father O'Connor and the Reverend Charles Gerecke, the Lutheran pastor from Missouri, frequently dropped by. The music from the organ in the prison chapel pervaded the cells in accompaniment to the wan autumn sunlight.

Jodl, taking a hot shower, thought wrily that for once he did not have to spare the soap. In these last hours of his life the soul of the poet conquered the cynical warrior—it was his misfortune that he had suppressed his instincts until it was too late. To Luise he wrote that he felt like a monk in his cell: it was not a prison but a refuge. He kept it so clean and orderly, he remarked, that even his mother would have been proud of him.

On Saturday, October 12, the prisoners were granted their final visits with their families; and the rumor swept the cell block that the executions would be carried out on Monday. But Monday, of course, came and went. It was only after the lights were directed onto the floors of the cells that night that the truck with its load of lumber was driven to the far side of the gymnasium behind the prison wing. All night the carpenters worked where the MPs had played basketball the evening before. Three gallows, painted black, were erected, eight feet high and eight feet square. A heavy iron ring was suspended from each crossbeam to hold the ropes. On the east side of the walkway leading from the prison to the Palace of Justice an opening was cut to permit a turn toward the gym. Despite Andrus's efforts to keep his prisoners in ignorance, the faint sounds of carpentry penetrated into the cells like distant drums of death throughout the night.

When, on Tuesday, the former Nazi leaders were told that their final meetings with their attorneys were at hand, they divined their executions were imminent. The routine of the prison was, nevertheless, maintained throughout the day and evening.

As darkness settled, the witnesses and officials gathered. The delegation from the Allied Control Council consisted of four generals, one from each of the occupying powers. Bavarian Prime Minister Högner and the prosecutor general of Nuremberg represented Germany. Eight reporters were chosen to provide pool coverage for the press; but no photographers were permitted into the gym. As if a supernatural director were orchestrating the drama, a chill, wind-whipped rain ensheathed the prison.

Ominously, the prison clock tolled the hours. The lights in the cells were turned down as always at 9:30 PM. But there was no way to completely mask the comings and goings, the clanging of doors and the tread of footsteps. In the prison office at the end of the corridor Andrus checked once more over the details with the Quadripartite Commission. Tossing restlessly, the condemned lay on their bunks. Shortly before 10:30 PM, Goering, clad in silk, pale blue pajama tops and black bottoms, went to the toilet alcove, where only his legs were visible to the guard. Cracking open the meerschaum pipe which he had never let out of his sight during his imprisonment, he extracted a cyanide capsule.* (The periodic searches of the prisoners and their effects had been far from exhaustive. Speer, for example, had had a cyanide capsule secreted in a tube of toothpaste in case he was sentenced to death.)

Placing the capsule in his mouth, Goering returned to his bunk. At quarter to eleven he crushed the glass between his teeth. Within seconds his body went into convulsions and his breath rattled in his throat.

"Chaplain, Goering's having a fit!" the excited guard called out to Pastor Gerecke. Gerecke rushed into the cell. A few seconds later he was followed by Andrus. Goering's lips were drawn back in a grimace over his tightly clenched teeth. One eye was open and one closed. His toes curled downward out of his pajama trousers. From his mouth came the essence of almonds. On the floor lay the broken pipe. Within moments he was dead.

Andrus immediately ordered the remaining ten condemned men handcuffed to guards. All pretenses were dropped, though the machinery of execution could not legally begin to function until midnight—the start of the fifteenth day. The Reverend Gerecke and Father O'Connor went from cell to cell. (They were rejected by Rosenberg, Streicher, and Jodl.) At midnight the mess tins were brought in with the traditional, ghoulish

---

*That Goering had the capsule in his pipe was Schirach's contention, and seems more logical than Andrus's far more elaborate version, which would have required Goering to shift the capsule from place to place during his imprisonment, and occasionally even swallow it and retrieve it from his stool.

last supper. The Nazi leaders were ordered to get dressed in their court clothes, neatly pressed as always. Streicher, refusing, battled and yelled as the guards struggled to get him into his pants, shirt, and coat. On the second tier Hess, awakened by the ruckus, called out: "Bravo, Streicher!"

A few minutes before 1 AM, Andrus, at the head of an official party of a dozen men, went from cell to cell and read the sentences again to each man: "Death by hanging!"

"*Tod durch den Strang!*" the interpreter repeated.

Keitel knelt down in his cell to pray with Gerecke, but could not go on; his voice choked, and sobs racked his body. Tears burst in a torrent from the eyes of the man who had remained stonefaced throughout the trial.

The sequence of execution followed the same order as the presentation of the cases. So, with Goering dead, Ribbentrop was the first to go. At five minutes past one Andrus called: "Joachim von Ribbentrop!" The ashen-faced Ribbentrop, held by a soldier on either side and trailed by Gerecke, followed Andrus out of the prison wing and down the steps to the familiar walkway. A few paces took them to the new doorway that opened toward the gym.

The brilliant, stark lighting of the gymnasium slapped at Ribbentrop's eyes, and he flinched. The three black gallows, standing in a row, seemed with their black drop cloths like living, skirted idols ready to swallow and digest the condemned in their wombs. Behind several tables sat the witnesses, reporters, and representatives of the Allied Control Commission. The chill damp air was permeated with the odor of cigarettes, coffee, and whiskey. It was a grim, pitiless scene. But for those who had sat through the horrors and tortures of the trial, who had learned of men dangled from butcher hooks, of women mutilated and children jammed into gas chambers, of mankind subjected to degradation, destruction, and terror, the scene conjured a vision of stark, almost biblical justice.

The execution party, led by a lieutenant colonel, took charge of Ribbentrop. "Ask the man his name," the colonel demanded superfluously. Then Ribbentrop, his hands now tied behind his back with black shoelaces, was led the thirteen steps up the farthest of the gallows, where the United States Army's official hangman, assisted by two volunteers, one German and one American, waited.

When asked whether he had anything to say, Ribbentrop responded in a surprisingly firm voice: "God protect Germany. My last wish is that Germany's unity shall be preserved and that an understanding be reached between East and West."

Sergeant John Woods, a paunchy and ruddy-faced Texan, who had already hanged 347 men in his fifteen-year career, stepped forward and placed the noose over Ribbentrop's head. An assistant fastened a GI belt around Ribbentrop's ankles. A black hood was dropped over Ribbentrop's head. The colonel gave a cutting motion with his hand. Woods pulled the lever. At 1:14 Ribbentrop plunged from view as if sucked down into the netherworld.

A minute later Keitel was marched in through the doorway. Having regained his composure, he militarily snapped out, when asked his name: "Wilhelm Keitel!" The noose and hood had already been placed over his head when he shouted out: *"Alles für Deutschland! Deutschland über Alles!"** At 1:20 he plummeted through the trap door, leaving behind an eery echo of his voice.

Kaltenbrunner, next in the macabre relay, was brought in while Ribbentrop and Keitel were still hanging, not yet dead, on the adjacent gallows. (Though the condemned's necks were broken and they were instantly rendered unconscious, Ribbentrop did not die until eighteen minutes and Keitel twenty-four minutes after they had been hanged.) Periodically, an American and a Russian doctor disappeared behind the drop cloths to check on whether the men had succumbed.

Ribbentrop was cut down at 1:35. At 1:49, Rosenberg, who had always envied the foreign minister his position, became with unintentional but biting irony his successor on the scaffold.

Streicher, blazing defiance, refused to give his name, then spat at Woods: "The Bolsheviks will hang *you* one day!" Just before he fell to his death, Streicher once more demonstrated his fascination with and knowledge of Judaism. "Purim Festival, 1946!" he called out, referring to the celebration commemorating the deliverance of Persian Jews from the king's prime minister, Haman, who had advocated their extermination, but had instead himself been hanged, together with his ten sons.

All but one of the cells were left in a state of disarray: personal objects scattered about, and the mess tins with the remnants of the final meal standing ungathered for more than a day. Jodl, however, departed with everything spic and span, as if he expected an inspection while he was gone and would return shortly.

Seyss-Inquart, subjected to a wait of two hours, carefully marked a cross on October 16 of the calendar he had kept on the wall of the cell. Limping heavily toward the scaffold, he observed: "I hope that this execution will be the last act of the tragedy of the Second World War. I hope that out of this disaster, wisdom will inspire the people, which will result in understanding between the nations, and that peace on earth will be finally established. I believe in Germany."

At three minutes before three he was declared dead. The bodies of the

---

*"Everything for Germany! Germany above all!"

ten hanged men, together with Goering's, were laid out in an adjacent room, where they were photographed, clothed and unclothed, from various angles by a volunteer from the Signal Corps. (The surgeon general of the United States had requested that their brains be excised and shipped to Washington for study, but his application was denied.) At four o'clock the corpses were loaded onto two trucks, which, under heavy escort, swung out through the gates into the mist and rain. At dawn the convoy arrived at Dachau. The crematorium was fired up once again. At the end of the day the ashes of the dead were dropped into a brook on the outskirts of Munich. Symbolically, the cradle of the Nazi movement became the grave of its leaders.

58   Requiem for the Reich

Throughout the trial the specter of Hitler had inhabited the courtroom. Hitler was the sun about which his minions had revolved, and once he was gone they wobbled and spun aimlessly, lost in the void. Papen complained:

"One of the most grotesque aspects of the trial was that no accusation was leveled at Hitler, either in the indictment or the verdict. Hitler should have been the chief defendant in the trial, even though he was dead."

The question was, of course, whether the International Military Tribunal was supposed to be a court of justice or a historical inquest. On the Allied side, such men as Birkett and General Donovan, who considered it the latter, were the exception. Whether Hitler had or had not been indicted was, in fact, irrelevant; but the failure to produce an explanation for the phenomenon of Hitler was a major deficiency. The Germans, desperately seeking some logic for the depths to which they had descended, would have welcomed an analytical inquiry. Neurath's attorney, Otto von Lüdinghausen, asked the judges to investigate "how it could happen that an intellectual, high-ranking people—a people who gave so much to the world in terms of cultural and spiritual gifts as the German people—that it could hail a man such as Hitler, follow him into the bloodiest of all wars, giving him the best it had? Not until you, your Honors, have taken this into consideration and examined this question will you be able to establish a just verdict . . . a judgment which will stand the test of history."

Since the structure of government in the Third Reich had depended on personal power to an extent unique in the history of industrial nations, much of the answer lay in the psychology of Hitler.

His ancestors had been Austrian peasants. According to Hans Frank's account, *Im Angesicht des Galgens (In the Sight of the Gallows)*, written at

Nuremberg, Hitler's paternal grandmother, Maria Schicklgruber, had worked as a domestic for a Jewish family named Frankenreither in Vienna or Graz. In 1837, at the age of forty-two, Maria Schicklgruber had become pregnant. The family had provided a pension for her, leading Frank to intimate that the father of the child had likely been the Frankenreithers' young son. Since the Frankenreithers' financial assistance to Fräulein Schicklgruber would, however, have been customary in any case if she had worked for them for some twenty or twenty-five years, the pension cannot be said to be conclusive indication of the child's paternity.

Five years later Maria Schicklgruber, who soon thereafter died, had married Johann Hiedler; and several decades afterward the illegimate child, Alois, who was to become the father of the Führer, had been legitimized under the name Hitler.

Alois Hitler, breaking the pattern of his peasant forebears, had succeeded in obtaining an education, and had afterwards joined the Austrian civil service, where he had steadily advanced in rank, and eventually become a customs inspector.

Adolf had been born in 1889 when Alois was fifty-two and his third wife, Clara, who was either his niece or (more likely) his stepniece, was twenty-nine. Before his death in 1903, Alois, a whip-wielding drunkard, brutalized Adolf, a mischievous and highly imaginative child, who grew up hating his father.

Adolf Hitler was an unremarkable student, but nevertheless continued through *Realschule* (nonclassical high school). His education, therefore, was more extensive than the average child's of that era. It came as a shock to him that when he went to Vienna at the age of seventeen his talent and schooling were adjudged inadequate for admission as a student of painting or architecture. Since Jews dominated commerce and the professions to a remarkable degree in the city, the conjunction of their success with the rejection suffered by Hitler planted the seed of that hatred that was to mature later.

In the spring of 1913 Hitler had departed precipitately from Vienna for Munich, a move that has never been satisfactorily explained but was probably grounded in the fact that he had contracted syphilis. Reports to this end were prevalent in the Strassers' circle in Munich; and Himmler's masseur-confidant Felix Kersten stated that Himmler was in possession of a twenty-six-page medical file in which it was revealed that Hitler had been infected about the time of World War I. The disease had then become latent until 1937, when it had reappeared.*

---

*If Hitler had come down with syphilis in 1913, a short time before he was ordered to report for a preinduction medical examination by the Austrian army, a logical explanation for his flight to Munich would be provided, since the discovery of his plight would have proved unbearably humiliating for him. Early in 1914 the Austrian authorities tracked him

Hitler's encounter with Rosenberg in 1919 and exposure to the *Protocols of the Wise Men of Zion*, as well as to Wilhelm Marr's theory of anti-Semitism, had led him to synthesize out of these and his personal experiences his own distorted *Weltanschauung*. Through the device of the Jewish "plot" fabricated in the *Protocols* he had been able to reconcile his contempt for the eastern Jews, steeped in their archaic habits and mired in poverty, with the envy he felt for the middle-class Austro-German Jews. The hatred engendered by his father could be rationalized by the blemish of Jewish "blood." Even the spread of venereal disease was ascribed by him to the machinations of the Jews.* Sharing Streicher's lurid sexual obsessions, he combined Jews, syphilis, and national degeneracy in a wild, irrational passage of *Mein Kampf*:

> Running parallel to the political, ethical, and moral contamination of the people there had been for many years a no less terrible poisoning of the health of the national body. . . . Especially in the big cities, syphilis was beginning to spread more and more, while tuberculosis steadily reaped its harvest of death . . .
>
> Particularly with regard to syphilis, the attitude of the leadership of the nation and the state can only be designated as total capitulation. . . . This Jewification of our spiritual life and mammonization of our mating instincts will sooner or later destroy our entire offspring. . . . The question of combating syphilis should have been made to appear as *the* task of the nation. Not just *one more* task. To this end, its injurious effect should have been thoroughly hammered into people as the most terrible misfortune, and this by the use of all available means, until the entire nation arrived at the conviction that everything—future or ruin—depended on the solution of this question.
>
> The struggle against syphilis and the prostitution which prepares the way for it is one of the most gigantic tasks of humanity, gigantic because we are facing not the solution of a single question but the elimination of a large number of evils which bring about this plague as a resultant manifestation. For in this case the sickening of the body is only a consequence of the sickening of the moral, social, and racial instincts.

Even as a youth Hitler had exhibited symptoms of paranoia and a tendency toward exaggerated, abnormal fantasies. The evidence is strong that these proclivities were exacerbated in him during the 1930s by an attack of general paresis, a syphilis-engendered mental disease sometimes manifesting itself twenty to twenty-five years after infection.

---

to the Bavarian capital and threatened him with arrest if he did not report. By then, the overt symptoms might well have disappeared, though the examining physician found him to be in such a debilitated condition as to be unfit for service.

*Ironically, syphilis had been visited upon the Spanish conquistadors by the American Indians and imported to Europe *after* the Jews had been expelled from Spain. Not only could the Jews have scarcely been more innocent bystanders, but Salvarsan, the first effective treatment for syphilis, was devised by a Nobel Prize–winning German-Jewish bacteriologist, Paul Ehrlich, in 1910.

At the beginning of 1937, Hitler had added Dr. Theodor Morrell, a noted Berlin specialist on skin and venereal diseases, to his medical staff. Some of the members of the Führer's entourage considered Morrell a quack because of his habit of administering shots to Hitler. (Goering jibed at him as "Herr Reich Injection Master.") But fever therapy, or injections of arsenic and bismuth, were at the time the only known treatment for general paresis. Though such therapy can momentarily arrest and bring a remission in the disease, each attack damages the person's brain further.

Megalomania, paranoia, and a blunting of the moral senses are classically associated with the affliction. According to the *Textbook of Abnormal Psychology*, the paretic is extremely domineering, irritable, full of grandiose delusions, and likely to feel that he is an object of persecution: "A loss of judgment is one of the first abnormalities to appear in general paresis and one which continues throughout the course of the illness. The paretics will not notice contradictions or unclearnesses in their own thinking or in the conversations of others. . . . They complacently bring forth some absurd plan, disposing of obvious objections in an irrational fashion. . . . Mentally they seem to be in a sort of dream world in which their own ideas, wishes, fears, and everyday occurrences are mixed up with no distinction between fact and fancy. . . . [The paretic] will be changeable, easily angered, sulky, emotionally excited at small events, will lose control of his temper or will have fits of crying and wailing with self-pity. . . . He will be careless in the face of danger, lack foresight with respect to approaching difficulty, and be quickly reassured after severe misfortune. . . . Abrupt alteration of emotions is common.

"As the disease progresses the *motor symptoms* become more and more pronounced. The disturbance of speech becomes quite obvious. . . . Movements are slow, clumsy, and awkward. . . . His gait is unsteady and shuffling. . . . His features become flabby and expressionless while his voice is monotonous or tremulous . . ." Parkinson's disease is sometimes a concomitant.

The textbook description is strikingly applicable to Hitler's symptoms and behavior from the 1930s on to the last year of his life, when his speech became blurred, his hands trembled, and he shuffled instead of walked.

That something was radically wrong was lost neither on his intimates who retained some objectivity nor on people who only occasionally came into his presence. "We often say that genius and insanity are closely related," Speer observed in a monograph written at Dustbin. "This could have been applied to Hitler at a pretty early stage." Even before the war Hitler had had periods of mental disturbance. Sometimes in the midst of an important report or discussion, people became aware that he was staring rigidly at some fixed point in space; and no one knew how much, if anything, he had heard. By 1944, Speer said, Hitler "often reminded me of a senile man."

Fritz Wiedemann, Hitler's lieutenant during World War I and adjutant from 1933 to 1938, declared during an interrogation: "You can understand Hitler's policies only if you accept the fact that he wasn't quite sound in his head. A completely split personality. On the one hand he was very charming, especially towards women, and on the other hand he was crazy, stark crazy!"

Wilhelm Scheidt, the Wehrmacht historian, told Colonel Hinkel: "You have to take the nature of Hitler himself, who often liked to talk to himself, and during these talks to himself sometimes developed plans that could actually be realized, and other plans which were so fantastic that nobody ever believed that it would be possible to carry them through. You have to consider that Hitler was really an actor, and an actor with many variations, and he really tried to deceive people about his intentions."

General Lahousen related to Colonel Amen, "Hitler had the habit of interrupting people and then taking over the conversation from them, leaving others speechless. He would not talk to anybody in the room, but rather talk to himself, in the form of a soliloquy. And this is the way in which he went on."

Keitel confided to Thomas Dodd: "He was full of ideas. He had a thousand ideas. It was very difficult to report to him. When you reported, he started talking very soon. After the second or third sentence, he interrupted me and started to talk to himself. Then lots of ideas came up. After such a report, one was very confused to figure out what he really wanted. It was all very irrational. I did not know what he wanted."

It had been an unsettling and flabbergasting experience to have the dictator of the Reich suddenly divide into Hitler and the Führer, and hear the two personalities carry on a conversation with each other to the exclusion of everyone else. "The generals do not recognize you fully," Hitler had said to the Führer, Keitel recounted; and the Führer, agreeing, had complained that the army's leaders still looked upon him as the corporal of World War I instead of a military genius comparable to Hannibal or Napoleon.

General Geyr von Schweppenburg, the former German military attaché in London and later panzer commander in Normandy, declared: "He was a maniac. From the medical point of view, at least from the end of 1941."

It was the combination of irrationality and ruthlessness that had been in large part responsible for Hitler's successes until 1941. His wild, emotional outbursts, so novel and uncharacteristic of the German, had fascinated his audiences and enveloped them in his passion. Hampered by neither ethics nor morality, he had manipulated people against themselves, and exploited their vices and weaknesses to gain his own ends. Whatever they wanted to hear he had told them, regardless of what his intentions were; he had never held himself to what he said from one day to the next. His brutal, nihilistic, kill-or-be-killed view of mankind had left room for neither compromise nor peace. "One might accuse me of wanting to fight again and again," he had told his generals on November 23, 1939. "In struggle I see the fate of all beings."

His adversaries, unable to come to grips with the fact that they were dealing with a mentally unbalanced man, had been swept aside by the shock and unexpectedness of his actions. His critics had been disarmed by his triumphs. His adherents had been reinforced in their conviction that he was a man of genius not to be judged by ordinary standards.

Since any man who retained his critical faculties or a sense of ethics departed or was weeded out, the circle surrounding Hitler had come to reflect the aberrant characteristics of the Führer himself. Of the chief wielders of power in the Reich, Goering, Himmler, Heydrich, and Ley were all abnormal to a greater or lesser degree, as were such others of Hitler's companions as Hess and Streicher. Bormann was a sadist and convicted murderer who brutalized everyone, including his family. The rest of the entourage consisted of vapid conduits like Keitel or bewildered mimics like Ribbentrop. Only Speer had retained a measure of balance, but in the exultation of power he had been corrupted like everyone else.

Ribbentrop's state secretary, Baron Steengracht von Moyland, remarked to Colonel Brundage:

"Everything looks amazing, but it is like an insane asylum where the inmates have taken over the administration, and have made the sensible people inmates."

What had taken place in this culture of lunacy was not that the ordinary human sensibilities had disappeared, or that the denizens had been unable to distinguish between right and wrong, or moral and immoral actions, but that Hitler had convinced them that commonly accepted ethics and morality were Judeo-Christian inventions to be superseded by new doctrines based on utilitarianism and necessity. The way had been opened for a pedantic theoretician like Karl Brandt to initiate the killing of more than a quarter million people in the euthanasia program. It had been but one step further to take another group of "useless eaters," Jewish women and children, and subject them to the same process of extermination.

Seyss-Inquart's lament that things had proceeded "step by step" was a refrain repeated by both the defendants and other Nazis at Nuremberg —how could they have foreseen that the Nuremberg Laws would be followed by other measures, each more repressive than the one before, until the process had ended in the charnelhouse of Auschwitz? There was not a single dissenting voice that, had they known what lay ahead when they took the first step, they would have drawn back.

But this is like the member of a robber band trying to beg off because he himself has not killed or anticipated that the end result would be murder—he is a criminal nonetheless. The Nationalists could not excuse themselves on the argument that they had only wanted to deprive Jews of their political rights and their property, not of their lives; that they had been beguiled and betrayed by Hitler—it was they who, flaunting their purported Christian morality, had shared his totalitarian philosophy and ambitions, and subverted democracy. Knowing very well that they were entering into a pact with the devil, they could not, after he had created a hell on earth, disentangle themselves from complicity because they had deluded themselves that they could control and exploit him. The path to perdition commences the moment it is postulated that a person or group of persons is inferior or deserving of discrimination; that one man is placed above criticism and beyond control. At Dustbin, Speer said: "The possibility of the absolute rule of one man, surrounded by weaklings, must be prevented for all time to come. On this question there should not even be the opportunity of a free choice."

Other defenses advanced by the accused were, in general, just as specious and flimsy.

The argument that one's oath commits oneself to faithfulness and obedience irrespective of circumstances or the orders given is, prima facie, indefensible. One cannot excuse murder on the basis of having pledged oneself to Cain, or the slaughter of children because one enlisted in the service of Gilles de Rais when he was the lieutenant of Joan of Arc and is therefore committed to him even after he develops into Bluebeard.

The defense of superior orders can be valid only when a person has no volition to refuse, or no capability of forming an independent judgment. In none of the Articles of War of the belligerent powers was a soldier —and certainly not a high-ranking officer—constrained to obey an illegal or criminal order. No less a Nazi than Goebbels—complaining about the Allied "terror fliers"—cited this fact:

"It is not provided in any military law that a soldier in the case of a despicable crime is exempt from punishment because he passes the responsibility to his superior, especially if the orders of the latter are in evident contradiction to all human morality and every international usage of warfare."

Hitler himself never pushed one of his aides beyond his principles—

if it became clear that an act went against a man's conscience, Hitler either dropped the matter or, more frequently, found someone with fewer scruples. No concentration camp guard was punished for a refusal to engage in murder, savagery, or sadism. Those who participated did so of their own volition. The only ones under physical compulsion were the inmates, for whom most of the ghastliest tasks in the machinery of horror were reserved.

Conversely, if obedience to superior orders is no justification, the superior who gives these orders cannot be above the law. The so-called immunity of the head of state was nothing more than a relic from the days of "the divine right of kings." If the leader of a nation is liable for corrupt and unlawful acts committed against his own countrymen, it would be incongruous to excuse him on the basis that he has only employed the power at his command against the people of other nations.

Finally, there was the defendants' plea of ignorance. Not even Goering and Kaltenbrunner admitted to having known what went on in concentration camps, and Speer pretended that in his relations with Himmler he had never realized the depravity involved.

These were, of course, out-and-out lies. The excuses of other men, like Ribbentrop and Funk, were reminiscent of a man who knows that he is living with a murderer, but is careful not to descend into the cellar, where the bodies are being buried. When more than 45,000 members of the Waffen SS had served in concentration camps, when *Einsatzgruppen* reports had been extensively distributed among the leadership, when thousands of men had witnessed the exterminations in the East, when Himmler had made an unequivocal declaration to the party leaders, when Goebbels had been forced to issue broadsides in response to rumors, and when reports from foreign sources had been readily available to any top Nazi who wished to educate himself, whatever ignorance had existed had been voluntary. Though Hitler, as part of his plan to appear indispensable and preclude the formation of any coalition against him, had compartmentalized the government, and not everyone had necessarily known about every barbarity,* the general pattern had remained a mystery to no one in a position of authority.

As to what the German people had known, it was probably more than they liked to admit and less than the Allies believed. "Those with real knowledge did not dare to speak, and everyone else preferred not to hear,"

---

*For example, Ohlendorf, who was perhaps the best-informed man in the Reich and an expert on extermination, had never heard, specifically, of Maidanek. Wisliceny, though intimately familiar with Maidanek and Auschwitz, was ignorant of Treblinka, because it had lain outside his domain.

Papen wrote. See no evil, hear no evil, and speak only of trivialities had been the pattern for survival in the Third Reich.

Of greater relevancy to the question of culpability is, What could the people have done had they known?

The answer, from a practical standpoint, is nothing. Successful rebellion requires mass alienation from the reigning government, discontent born of hunger and desperation, the existence of a revolutionary leadership, and a concurrent breakdown of existing authority. None of these elements had been present in the Third Reich, due in large part to Hitler's cold-blooded starvation and spoliation of other peoples to keep the Germans fed and supplied, as well as the Germans' fear that defeat would place them in even greater peril than dictatorship. The Nationalist resistance, in addition to being essentially incompetent, had had no popular base, and had all too often been reduced to rationalizing its continuing symbiosis with the Nazis.

Albrecht Haushofer had personified the dilemma and impotence of the decent German when he had written after a meeting with Odilo Globocnik or Ernst Zörner, the overlords of the Lublin area:

"I sit at a table with a man whose duty it will be, in the Jewish ghetto of Lublin, to let a greater part of the German Jews deported there freeze to death and starve according to program. By one frivolous sentence— whether he had properly considered that for the sixty- and seventy-year-old people the costs of transport would no longer be worthwhile—I can perhaps achieve that at least the old ones will be spared. But in such a case I quite plainly could not endure an emotional observation of the whole process from a personal angle."

Except for the unreconstructed Nazis, the Germans have come to look upon the Nuremberg tribunal as a requisite historical event, the beginning of a process of exorcism from Nazi deviltry. Herbert Kraus, the associate counsel for Schacht, said it "unmasked an abyss of moral abominations." Otto Kranzbühler called it "the painful starting point for building the relations that exist today between Germany and her western Allies."

Although they criticized some of the trial procedures, and disagreed with the concept and validity of the prosecution on aggressive war, most of the defense attorneys regarded the tribunal as having acted equitably, and praised the verdict. Theodor Klefisch, associate defense counsel for the SA, wrote that the tribunal had "no equal in the history of nations." It had met the requirements of impartiality and justice with consideration and dignity. "It opens the eyes of young people and of adults to a despotism which pressed for war by enslaving justice and freedom through terror, corruption, faithlessness, lies, and disregard for the most sacred human rights; and by this criminal madness delivered the German people into inexpressible misery."

Kranzbühler said: "The members of the government who themselves created the law may not cite for their justification the state law for which they themselves are responsible. . . . Hitler's decrees were a protection neither for himself nor his subordinates. . . . The newly created notion . . . of a crime against humanity . . . was necessary and could not be avoided after the experience of the immediate past and present."

In 1952, the First Criminal Senate of the German Federal Court held the acts of the Nazi Reich to have been invalid because they violated all legal and moral tenets irrespective of nationality. "There would have been no difficulty in finding twenty-four defendants in the IMT guilty according to German law," Carl Haensel, associate counsel for the SS, declared.

But what of the others?

From the evidence presented, it was clear that beyond the twenty-one men tried, decision makers and perpetrators of major criminal acts ranged into the hundreds, their deputies into the thousands, and the rank and file directly involved into the tens of thousands. Of the concentration camp guards, no more than a couple of hundred were put on trial. Over 2,700 additional war crimes cases, most of them involving multiple defendants, were docketed, and 1,900 were under active investigation. But as, during the summer of 1946, the principal trial drew to a close, there was widespread disagreement among the Allies on how to proceed.

Telford Taylor prepared a plan to bring two hundred to four hundred more Nazi leaders before a half-dozen tribunals distributed throughout the four zones of occupation. But the United States Army objected because of the expense involved. The Russians, strapped for foreign exchange, did not want to participate in any further trials unless they were held in Berlin. General Clay, supporting the Soviets, thought a transfer to Berlin would remove a great burden from the U.S. zone. Jackson, however, now caught up in the Cold War, had earlier remarked, "This would be nearly impossible from my viewpoint," and was adamantly opposed. The British and French, trying to determine whether to retain part of their prosecutorial staffs in Nuremberg, pressed for a decision.

When the impasse between Jackson, Taylor, and Clay was not resolved, the other Allied powers were eliminated perforce. Taylor and his deputy, Captain Drexel Sprecher, together with their new staff of thirty-five attorneys, were left with the cases and defendants on their hands.

On October 17, the day after the executions, President Truman officially appointed Taylor as Jackson's successor. Taylor had five additional courtrooms prepared in the Palace of Justice. On October 26, indictments were filed against Karl Brandt, Karl Gebhardt, Wolfram Sievers, Viktor Brack, and nineteen other defendants involved in the euthanasia extermination and concentration camp medical experiments. During the course of the next two and one half years, under conditions that gradually became more and more adverse, Taylor prosecuted a total of 185 accused in twelve separate cases.

Three judges were brought to Nuremberg from the United States for each trial, and their judgments tended to reflect the tide of events. The menace presented by the Soviet Union blurred the inhumanities of the Nazi era. The McCarthyite chorus attributed the trials to a Communist plot. Senator William Langer of North Dakota declared: "It is the Communists' avowed purpose to destroy the western world, which is based on property rights. It was intended to try the accused as aggressors, convict them of having started the war, and then confiscate their property."

Representative John J. Rankin of Mississippi, venting an American bigotry that would have brought smirks to the faces of Hitler and Goering, articulated a neo-Nazi line in the Congress of the United States: "I desire to say that what is taking place in Nuremberg, Germany, is a disgrace to the United States. . . . A racial minority, two and a half years after the war closed, are in Nuremberg not only hanging German soldiers but trying German businessmen in the name of the U.S."

In actuality, no German soldiers were hanged, and the German industrialists who had robbed the populations of the occupied lands, exploited the slave laborers, and built the factories to work concentration camp inmates to death were universally receiving light sentences—in most cases the men were released shortly after trial in consideration of the time they had been held in captivity. The prosecution in the I.G. Farben case developed overwhelming evidence of the defendants' complicity in the crimes of Auschwitz, yet twelve were found not guilty, five received sentences of one to four years, and six of five to eight years. One of the judges, Louisiana State University Law School Dean Paul Hebert, issued a withering blast at his two midwestern colleagues, accusing them of bias in favor of the accused.

Charles F. Wennerstrum, an Iowa judge who presided over the trial of army leaders involved in mass executions and the rounding up of slave laborers, returned to America early in 1948 to denounce the trials and the American prosecution. Taylor, who by then was frustrated, fed up, and to some extent heartsick at the lack of interest in the execution of justice prevalent in the United States, replied to Wennerstrum: "Your behavior arises out of a warped, psychopathic mental attitude."

By 1949 the Cold War had undermined any further inclination for prosecution, and the next year the start of the Korean War completed the process of diverting the world's attention. The Russians, for their part, were more interested in trials for their political impact than for the pursuit of justice, and failed to respond to American efforts aimed at bringing to account the personnel of Buchenwald and Nordhausen, which lay in the Soviet zone.

Some of the leading perpetrators, such as *Obergruppenführer* Karl Wolff, once ticketed as Heydrich's successor, and Hinrich Lohse, whose culpability as Rosenberg's commissioner of the *Ostland* had been no less than that of such executed defendants as Seyss-Inquart, Jodl, and Streicher, walked off scot-free.

The United States set up a clemency board which reduced one sentence after another. Of the men convicted in the followup cases at Nuremberg, only twelve—Oswald Pohl, seven of the accused in the medical case, and Otto Ohlendorf and three other *Einsatzgruppe* leaders—were executed.

Men who had received life sentences were almost invariably paroled after ten years, if not sooner. Indeed, by 1951 only a few of those convicted were still in jail.

About half of the top leadership of the SS, including Eichmann's deputies and the commanders of *Einsatzgruppen,* survived or disappeared. The principle of prima facie guilt for members of convicted organizations broke down in practice. Though Bernays was undoubtedly right that normal judicial procedures could not have coped with the multitude of crimes, the solution devised was equally impractical, and in actuality gave the guilty a chance to escape by blending into the mass. Fewer than one million of the nearly 3.5 million persons charged before denazification courts were brought to trial, and of these only 9,600—including Schacht, Papen, and Fritzsche—spent any time in confinement. By 1949 all but 300 had been freed.

There was no mechanism at all for determining from among the millions of displaced persons in Germany those who had been impressed as slave laborers and those who had been volunteers in the SS or collaborators of the Nazis in some other capacity. Though the latter were supposedly barred from entry into the United States, background investigations were only rarely performed. It was more important for an immigrant to affirm that he was not a Communist—which he could do easily enough if he had been a member of the Waffen SS guarding concentration camps, or of the indigenous militia hunting down partisans, or of the *Einsatzgruppe* auxiliaries exterminating Jews. How many war criminals were able to slip into the United States is anyone's guess; but the occasional case that has achieved notoriety undoubtedly represents only the tip of the iceberg.

Until 1958, the United States refused to turn over to German legal authorities records of investigations for possible prosecution of individuals. The German government did not, in any case, press the issue. Only after the publicity of the Eichmann trial in 1961 was the pursuit vigorously renewed. By then, even when the perpetrators could be found, it was difficult to reconcile the generally hardworking husbands and fathers who appeared as defendants with the brutal and bloody killers of a quarter century before. Public opinion tended as often as not to sympathize more with the defendants than with their far-away, long-dead victims. Although the German prosecutors were dedicated, sentences were frequently incongruously light and more in the nature of moral judgments than of punishment.

Of the seven Nuremberg defendants incarcerated at the Spandau Prison in Berlin, the ailing Neurath was, in 1954, the first to be released. Raeder, though sentenced to life imprisonment, followed the next year, thus preceding Doenitz, who completed his ten-year term in 1956. Funk, his health deteriorating, was paroled in 1957. (Neurath died in 1956, and Funk and Raeder in 1960.) Schirach and Speer both served their full twenty-year sentences.

In no one was the evil induced by the Nazi era and the schizophrenia it had generated more personified than in Speer. The first twenty-six years of his life he had been a patrician; the next fourteen he had spent in the service of Mephistopheles; twenty-one years of atonement had followed. In his last fifteen years he sought to explain the earlier sixty-one, carving out a highly successful career as an author on the basis of his experiences with Hitler, and to a large extent rehabilitating himself in the eyes of the world. As time passed, it was more and more difficult to perceive in the grandfatherly, genteel, and pleasant Speer one of the principal perpetrators of the Nazi horrors. He himself had difficulty coming to terms with his own guilt. "I do not believe there can be any atonement in this lifetime for sins of such huge dimensions," he said, and expressed himself haunted by the picture of a Jewish family on the threshold of the gas chamber: "I could not rid my mind of that photograph. I would see it in my cell at night. I see it still. It has made a desert of my life." Yet he could not get himself to take the final step and admit that this photograph was not merely symbolic of the regime among whose leaders he had been, but was the imprint of his own involvement with Himmler's labor program, of which the killing of the "useless eaters" had been an integral part.

After Doenitz and Speer died within a few months of each other in 1981, the last Nuremberg survivor was, ironically but perhaps fittingly, the lunatic, hypochrondiac Hess. With all his purported ailments and paranoid fears of being poisoned, he seemed to thrive in Spandau, where his behavior had often driven his fellow prisoners into a fury. Though his guilt was less than that of some who escaped punishment altogether and many others long since released, he has since 1966 been the solitary inmate of Spandau, the central figure in what is surely one of the most extraordinary chapters in the history of penology.

The truth is that Hess turned his face from the world long ago, and seemingly has no desire to return to it. With Seidl's concurrence, he has steadfastly maintained that his imprisonment is illegal and refused to petition the trial powers for release.

"What, basically, did Nuremberg accomplish?" Francis Biddle asked in a report to President Truman upon his return to the United States. "The conclusions of Nuremberg may be ephemeral or they may be significant. That depends on whether we now take the next step. I suggest that the time has now come to set about drafting a code of international criminal law."

At first it seemed as if the United Nations might act on Biddle's proposal. On December 11, 1946, the General Assembly affirmed without dissent the judgment of the tribunal, and decided to embody the principles in "a general codification of offenses against the peace and security of mankind, or of an international criminal code."

Once more, predictably, it was far easier to agree in principle than to implement the principles with a machinery of enforcement. In December 1948 the United Nations passed a Genocide Convention, calling upon every state to take action against groups committed to the destruction of people on religious, ethnic, national, or racial grounds. But the United States, where segregation still held sway, refused to ratify the convention, and the Soviet Union did so only with reservations. Again, it seemed, as it had after World War I, that the United States would not commit itself to practice what it preached.

But if Nuremberg could be resisted, it could not be ignored. The American government found it more and more impolitic to conduct two policies: one for international consumption, and the other for domestic accommodation. Anticipating the United Nations' passage of the Genocide Convention and a Declaration of Human Rights, President Truman in 1948 desegregated the armed services. In 1954, the Supreme Court unanimously held school segregation unconstitutional. It was one of the last cases in which Justice Jackson participated, and he made it clear that the Nuremberg experience and the "awful consequences of racial prejudice revealed by . . . the Nazi regime" influenced his decision.

Despite the lack of an international criminal code and the obsolescence of several clauses of the Hague and Geneva conventions, most nations, including the United States, have agreed through treaty to outlaw the barbaric practices that came to light at Nuremberg. Reprisals may not be taken against hostages and prisoners of war. Forced labor is outlawed. Guerrillas, providing they operate in identifiable combat units and according to accepted customs of war, are to be granted equal status with regular soldiers. The armed forces regulations of all of World War II's major combatants now state that orders that would embrace the commission of a crime are illegal and need not be obeyed. Morality and humanity, as universally accepted, are supreme, and not to be superseded.

On the other hand, it is also true that the more things change, the more they remain the same.

What greater irony than the fact that the Jews, whom Hitler equated with bolshevism, have been the principal sufferers of repression in the Soviet Union! The truth is that they have been victimized there as in Germany and other totalitarian states because as a concentrated element of the educated middle class they have always been movers in the striving for liberty, and represent a thorn to the ambitions of dictators and would-be dictators.

Although territorial aggrandizement as practiced before World War II has fallen into disrepute, power politics in the name of self-interest has continued as before, and none of the Nuremberg prosecuting nations has been without sin. The United States has, on and off, practiced ideological imperialism. The French, in attempting to perpetuate colonialism, engaged in some of the same kinds of terror for which the Nuremberg defendants were condemned. The British, French, and Israelis attacked Egypt in 1956. The Soviets have crushed nationalist movements in East Germany, Hungary, Czechoslovakia, Poland, and Afghanistan. Brushfire wars have proliferated.

Guerrilla wars, whether in Southeast Asia, Africa, Central America, or Lebanon, continue to be fought with untrammeled savagery; and generally it is the noncombatants, caught between the opposing forces, who suffer the most. The genocide in Cambodia exceeded, proportionately, Hitler's exterminations in eastern Europe. In Argentina, Chile, Iran, and a host of other nations, political opposition has been crushed with Gestapo tactics. The Christian Falangist action in the Beirut refugee camps had all the elements of a German ghetto clearance; and the Nuremberg tribunal would doubtlessly have considered the Begin government culpable for its involvement.

Thus, while many of the principles of Nuremberg have been incorporated into international law, practices have changed little. The impact of Nuremberg has faded. Nuremberg has become an abstract concept rather than a dire precept. Jimmy Carter, the American President most dedicated to the principles of Nuremberg, received more criticism than praise for his policy.

The world, however, can ignore the lessons of Nuremberg only at its peril. The balance of nuclear terror has been accepted as part of life on the presumption that safeguards and the sanity of the world's leaders will preclude the unleashing of a holocaust. But what would happen if Hitler were regenerated in the guise of another dictator—if there were to be another all-powerful leader who grows more and more lunatic in office, and cannot be removed? Had Hitler possessed atomic weapons and believed it to his advantage to use them, he would have had no scruples about doing so. What if a paranoid tyrant, surrounded by toadies and nonentities, labors under the delusion he is about to be subjected to attack and orders a "retaliatory" strike? Nor, with the spread of nuclear technology, need such a mental case be master of one of the great nations.

Though the horror to surpass all horrors and essence of the "crime of crimes" denounced by the French prosecutor, de Menthon, was the Final Solution of the Jewish Question, it must be remembered that millions of others—the mentally retarded, the Gypsies, the slave laborers, the prisoners of war, first from the Soviet Union and then from all nations—were also victims of Nazi barbarities. The begetters of the ultra–right-wing movement that denies the holocaust and attempts to sanitize the Nazi regime and sugarcoat the culpability of its leaders are the successors to the proponents of the *Protocols of the Wise Men of Zion*. In place of the fiction that the Jews are conspiring to dominate the world, they propound the Big Lie that the holocaust is a myth, devised by the Jews for ulterior purposes. The new anti-Semites use the same techniques as the old, and their goal is also the same: to denigrate and discredit not only the Jewish faith but all men of liberal and democratic persuasion, so as to pave the way for a recrudescence of persecution and tyranny. They mock concentration camp survivors like Marie Vaillant, who said at Nuremberg: "For months, for years we had only one wish: the wish that some of us would escape alive, in order to tell the world what the Nazi convict prisons were like everywhere, at Auschwitz as at Ravensbrück."

In lockstep with these pernicious propagandists march the neo-Nazis and the Ku Klux Klan, demonstrating for "Aryan" supremacy, urging the deportation of Jews and blacks, employing Hitlerian euphemisms, and manipulating democratic processes and guarantees in the same manner as Hitler a half century ago. Never let it be forgotten that Hitler exploited the freedom granted him by the Weimar constitution to destroy the republic. The rise of a new Hitler in an industrial nation may be remote, but it is not impossible. Given the proper combination of circumstances, no country, including the United States, is immune.

Horst Pelckmann, the counsel for the SS, said in his final argument:

"This trial should be the last warning to those who do not heed the demands voiced by the world and all its peace-loving citizens for freedom of speech and religion, for freedom from want and freedom from fear"; and Karl S. Bader, a German legal expert, wrote: "Nobody who considers the years 1933 to 1945 will in future time be able to pass by this material, tremendous in its extent and value for the perception of the errors of man."

De Menthon's words are as applicable today as they were when he challenged the judges in 1946 to make their judgment "one of the foundations . . . to which nations aspire on the morrow of this frightful torment. The need for justice of the martyred peoples will be satisfied, and their sufferings will not have been useless to the progress of mankind."

Notes

The following abbreviations are employed in the Notes:

IMT   International Military Tribunal, *Trial of the Major War Criminals;* the published transcript of the trial.

NCA   Nazi Conspiracy and Aggression, the 10-volume compendium of the prosecution's documents.

RG 238   Record Group 238, the collection of documents in the National Archives specifically pertaining to the Nuremberg trial.

Int.   The Interrogation Records in RG 238.*

Interviews   References to author's interviews.

      The Interrogation Division of the International Military Tribunal questioned nearly 200 persons, including 22 defendants. A list of the principal interrogators and the people they questioned is provided as an aid to using the Notes.

INTERROGATOR	DEFENDANTS AND CASES FOR WHICH RESPONSIBLE
Col. John Harlan Amen	Goering and Hess
Lt. Col. Smith W. Brookhart	Kaltenbrunner, and SS and Gestapo personnel
Col. Howard Brundage	Streicher, Ribbentrop, and foreign ministry officials
Thomas Dodd	Keitel, Papen, Seyss-Inquart, and the Anschluss of Austria
Col. Murray I. Gurfein	Schacht, Speer, Funk, and the economics case
Lt. Col. Thomas Hinkel	Doenitz, Jodl, Frank, Rosenberg, Schirach, particularly War Crimes in the East and Crimes Against the Jews
Major John J. Monigan	Ley, Sauckel, Neurath, the labor case, and medical experiments
Henry Sackett	Frick and the Nazi administration

*Except in rare instances, the interrogations are identified according to the person questioned, the interrogator, and the date. When the date or another piece of data is missing, this is due to the fact that the National Archives requires Xeroxing to be performed by a member of the staff, a process that can take as long as eight weeks. When this material ultimately reached me at my home, it did not contain all the identifying data; and since some defendants were interrogated as many as thirty times, I was not always able to pin down specific dates. Such material is indicated by "X" (Xeroxed). A few other documents in RG 238 were subject to the same problem.

Col. Curtis L. Williams   War Crimes
                                 (Fritzsche and Raeder, captured by the Soviets,
                                 were questioned only cursorily at Nurem-
                                 berg.)

Interrogations: General

Wilhelm Abegg—former state secretary of Prussia

Max Amann—friend of Hitler and chief of Nazi party publishing empire

Ernst von Bohle—Nazi party Foreign Political Bureau official and aide to Rudolf
    Hess

Gottfried Boley—Ministerialrat in the Reich chancellery

Hildegarde Brüninghoff—secretary to Robert Ley

Walter Buch—chief justice of the Supreme Party Court; father-in-law of Martin
    Bormann

Josef Buehler—Hans Frank's state secretary in Poland

Hans Conrad—Ribbentrop's doctor

Richard Walter Darre—minister of agriculture

Hildegarde Fath—secretary to Rudolf Hess

Hans Ficker—privy counselor at Reich Chancellery

Veli Gajun Chan—president of National Liberation Movement of Turkestan

Joachim von zur Gathen—interpreter in Oberkommando der Luftwaffe, ques-
    tioned about the "terror flier" decree

Bertus Gerdes—Nazi party staff leader in Munich

Martin Gerken—engineer imprisoned at Mauthausen

Hans Gisevius—participant in the July 20 plot; he helped prepare the prosecution
    case

Ulrich Goerdeler—son of Karl Goerdeler, former price commissioner and mayor
    of Leipzig executed for complicity in the July 20 plot

Louise Guyon Zesbron—SS secretary and friend of top SS leaders

Karl Haberstock—Berlin art dealer who acquired art for Goering

General Kalman Hardy—commander of Hungarian river forces

Karl Haushofer—famous geopolitician who influenced Hess and Hitler

Hans Hemmen—Foreign Office official and president of the German Economic
    Armistice Delegation in France

Walter Hofer—art expert employed by Goering

Heinrich Hoffmann—Hitler's photographer and confidant; father-in-law of Bal-
    dur von Schirach

Admiral Nicholas Horthy—Hungarian regent

Wilhelm Keppler—state secretary for special purposes in foreign office

Helen Kraffczyk—secretary to Hans Frank

Eugen Kumming—Wehrmacht interpreter questioned on Commissar Order

Hans Heinrich Lammers—state secretary in Reich Chancellery and member of
    Hitler's inner circle; later sentenced to life imprisonment

Louis P. Lochner—Associated Press correspondent in Berlin

Bruno Lohse—art historian who worked for Goering

Roswell D. McClelland—representative of the War Refugee Board in Switzerland

Elmar Michel—ministerial director in Reich ministry of economics, questioned about Sauckel

Baron Adolf Steengracht von Moyland—state secretary in foreign office

Jean Marie Musy—right-wing Swiss banker instrumental in negotiating a halt to the Final Solution

Wilhelm August Patin—a former priest who was Himmler's cousin, and who was employed by the Reichsführer SS to investigate the clergy

Emil Puhl—vice-president of the Reichsbank

Friedrich Rainer—Austrian lawyer, high Nazi party official, and close friend of Seyss-Inquart; later executed for his actions as Gauleiter of Trieste

Ernst Ranis—head of Nazi economic looting operation in occupied territories

Theresa Reinwald—secretary for Supreme Party Court

Hans Rotacker—Kreisleiter questioned about terror flier actions

Julius Schaub-Keitel—personal adjutant to Hitler

Arthur Scheidler—high-ranking official questioned about the Sagan killings

Moritz von Schirrmeister—Goebbels's personal press expert

Paul Otto Schmidt—foreign ministry chief interpreter

Johann Schneider—killer of an Allied flier

Christiana Schroeder—secretary to Hitler

Laura Schroedl—former personal secretary to Hess

Franz Xavier Schwarz—Nazi party treasurer

Franz Seldte—minister of labor

Karl Stroelin—mayor of Stuttgart

Wilhelm Stuckart—state secretary in ministry of interior

Fritz Thyssen—industrialist who bankrolled the Nazis and Goering before breaking with the party in 1939

Siegfried Uiberreither—gauleiter of Styria

Gabor Vajna—Hungarian minister of interior

Fritz Wiedemann—Hitler's lieutenant in World War I and adjutant from 1935 to 1939

Interrogations: Wehrmacht

Field Marshal Werner von Blomberg—former minister of war

Karl Bodenschatz—Goering's adjutant

Friedrich von Boetticher—former German military attaché in Washington

Berndt von Brauchitsch—aide to Goering

Field Marshal Walther von Brauchitsch—former German army commander on the eastern front

Herbert Buechs—Luftwaffe general staff officer

Admiral Leopold Buerkner—OKW liaison with foreign office

General Alexander von Falkenhausen—military governor of Belgium

General Nikolaus von Falkenhorst—German commander in Norway

Colonel General Heinz Guderian—panzer commander and inspector general
Lt. Gen. Heinz von Gyldenfeld—Army staff officer
Colonel General Franz Halder—former army chief of staff
Lieutenant Peter Heisig—submarine commander who testified against Admiral
    Doenitz
Field Marshal Albert Kesselring—German commander in Italy
Major General Erwin Lahousen—Abwehr officer who became the first prosecu-
    tion witness
Field Marshal Erich von Manstein—leading army commander dismissed by Hitler
    in 1944
William Mantel—judge advocate general of the German army
Erhard Milch—Goering's state secretary and operating head of the Luftwaffe
Helmut Pirner—officer who testified on Hitler's reaction to comparison of Ger-
    man and Soviet tank production
General Hermann Reinecke—ardent Nazi who was chief of the National Socialist
    Leadership staff (political indoctrination) of the Wehrmacht
Major General Hans Roettiger—chief of staff of the German forces in Italy
Otto Salman—submarine commander
William H. Scheidt—Wehrmacht historian
Field Marshal Hugo Sperrle—leading Luftwaffe commander
General Leo Geyr von Schweppenburg—former German military attaché in Lon-
    don and panzer commander in Normandy
Major General Walter Warlimont—Jodl's deputy
General Adolf Westhoff—chief of German Department of Prisoner of War Affairs
Siegfried Westphal—high-ranking German officer in Italy
Ernst Zolling—Rommel staff officer

Interrogations: SS and Gestapo

Obergruppenführer Erich von dem Bach-Zelewski—chief of the anti-partisan
    forces
Kurt Becher—adjutant to Hermann Fegelein, Himmler's liaison with Hitler
Gruppenführer Gottlob Berger—chief of the SS Hauptamt and the Waffen SS
Rudolf Bilfinger—Gestapo official
Kurt Daluge—chief of the uniformed police and later Protector of Bohemia and
    Moravia; subsequently executed by the Czechs
Rudolf Diels—first chief of the Gestapo
Gruppenführer Joseph Sepp Dietrich—head of Hitler's bodyguard, and later SS
    group commander
Brigadeführer Werner Doerffler-Schuband—Waffen SS general
August Eigruber—Gauleiter of Upper Austria
Brigadeführer Werner Grothmann—Himmler's adjutant
Margaret Himmler—estranged wife of Heinrich Himmler
Alois Höllriegel—Mauthausen Concentration Camp guard
Wilhelm Hoettl—SD intelligence officer and protégé of Kaltenbrunner

Rudolf Höss—commandant of Auschwitz

Hildegarde Kunze—secretary in Eichmann's department

Willy Litzenberg—Gestapo sub-department chief

Gruppenführer Benno Martin—Höhere SS and Polizeiführer in Nuremberg

Standartenführer Rudolph Mildner—wide-ranging Gestapo officer subsequently executed in Poland for his complicity in Auschwitz and other atrocities

Scharführer Otto Moll—head of the gassing squad at Auschwitz

Alfred H. Naujocks—chief of the Nazis' dirty-tricks department

Brigadeführer Otto Ohlendorf—chief of SD internal intelligence

Obergruppenführer Oswald Pohl—head of the SS economics and administration department; executed after being convicted in a follow-up case at Nuremberg

Brigadeführer Ernst Rode—adjutant to Bach-Zelewski

Hauptsturmführer Werner Roepert—Himmler's radio operator

Brigadeführer Walter Schellenberg—chief of the SD foreign intelligence department

Sturmbannführer Otto Skorzeny—SS special-forces leader who rescued Mussolini

Hauptsturmführer Dieter Wisliceny—Eichmann deputy

Obergruppenführer Karl Wolff—Himmler adjutant and later SS commander in Italy

Interrogations: Euthanasia and Medical Experiments

Dr. Karl Brandt—Reich Commissioner for Sanitation and Health, and Hitler's personal doctor

Dr. Karl Brunner—physician at the Hohenlychen clinic

Dr. Leonardo Conti—Commissioner of Public Health

Ludwig Diels—Bonn district president who provided information on medical practices and experiments

Dr. Fritz Fischer—doctor involved in vivisection at Ravensbrück Concentration Camp

Dr. Karl Gebhardt—internationally known surgeon and close friend of Himmler; he became supervisor of experiments on prisoners at Ravensbrück Concentration Camp

Dr. Eugen Haagen—participant in typhus-vaccine experiments on inmates at Natzweiler Concentration Camp

Dr. Werner Kirchert—SS doctor involved in the euthanasia program

Dr. Hermann Pfannmüller—institution psychiatrist associated with the euthanasia program

Dr. Claus Schilling—specialist in tropical medicine executed for his malaria experiments at Dachau

Standartenführer Wolfram Sievers—chief of SS department that supervised medical experiments on prisoners

Dr. Karl Taubock—physician involved in sterilization experiments

Dr. Percival Traite—doctor at SS Medical Academy

Chapter 1. Escape from Auschwitz

Page   Identification—Source

3   and Novaky—Wisliceny by Brookhart, Nov. 14, 1945.

3   arms factories—Ibid.

3   for Auschwitz—RG 238, Box 45, "Testimony of First Escapee."

3   prisoners of war—Höss by Jaari and Sam Harris, Apr. 1, 1946.

3   (in the birches)—Wisliceny by Brookhart, Nov. 14, 1945.

5   were killed—RG 238, Box 45, "Testimony of First Escapee."

5   for miles—Egbert Papers, "Transport."

5   going on—Höss by Jaari, Sam Harris, and Brookhart, Apr. 1 and 30, 1946.

6   madcap inflation—RG 238, Box 45, "Testimony of Second Escapee."

6   were transported—Wisliceny by Brookhart, Nov. 15, 1945.

7   people simultaneously—Höss by Jaari, Sam Harris, and Brookhart, Apr. 1 and 2, 1946.

7   already dead—Naumann, pp. 212, 213.

7   of convenience—Ibid., p. 75.

8   to Budapest—Ibid., p. 290.

8   the President—RG 238, Box 44, Wheeler to Jackson, Aug. 28, 1945; and Box 45, May 10, 1945.

8   other leaders—RG 238, Box 40, State Department cables of Apr. 14, May 25, and June 17, 1944.

9   are stopped—RG 250.1, Box 7.

9   recovered inmates (fn)—Naumann, p. 210.

9   ordered them out—NCA, 2604 PS, Deposition of Rudolf Kastner, Sept. 13, 1945.

Chapter 2. The Sword of Justice

9   Christian faith—Bernays Papers, Box 2, Tab A.

10   mass executions—RG 250.0, Box 7, Eden Statement of Dec. 17, 1942.

10   to justice—Bernays Papers, Box 2, Tab D, Statement of Nov. 1, 1943.

10   meeting in London—Bernays Papers, Box 2, Tab D, Henry L. Stimson, Francis Biddle, & Edward R. Stettinius Memorandum for the President, Jan. 22, 1945.

10   the punishment—Bernays Papers, Box 2, Tab E.

10   calculated policy—RG 238, Box 226, "Combat Crimes."

10   like circumcision—Rauschning, p. 223.

11   conscience and morality—Ibid., p. 225.

11   been proved—Churchill, p. 693.

11   summarily shot—RG 238, Box 7, Statement of Dec. 7, 1943.

11   crimes sprang—Bernays Papers, Box 1, Bernays to wife, June 10, 1945.

12   their members—Ibid.

13   destructive scale—RG 238, Box 7, Bernays Memo of Jan. 4, 1945.

13   under duress—Bernays Papers, Box 4, Memo for the President: "Trial and Punishment of War Criminals," Nov. 27, 1944.

14   of a trial—RG 238, Box 21, Rosenman to Herbert Wechsler, Apr. 23, 1945; and RG 260, Box 2, Report of Rosenman–Simon Conference, Apr. 5, 1945.

14   preferable course—RG 238, Box 21, Rosenman to Herbert Wechsler, Apr. 23, 1945.

14   organized to convict—RG 238, OCC 000.7, Excerpt from Address delivered by Robert H. Jackson to American Society of International Law, Apr. 13, 1945.

15   for expedition—RG 238, Box 11, Jackson Memo to President Truman, Apr. 29, 1945.

15   personal assistance—RG 238, Box 12, Minutes of Staff Conference of May 16, 1945.

15   the prosecution—RG 238, Box 12, Telephone conversation between Brig. Gen. John Weir and Lt. Col. Joseph Hodgson, May 17, 1945.

16   Jackson's counterpart—RG 238, OCC 000.7, Jackson Report to President Truman, June 7, 1945.

16   the material—Bernays Papers, Box 4, Telford Taylor Memo, "An Approach to the Preparation of the Prosecution of Axis Criminality."

16   the defendants—State Department Files, East–West Prosecution, Box 3695, Memo of June 14, 1945.

17   occupied Poland—Bernays Papers, Box 4, Minutes of Meeting of June 21, 1945.

17   their cases—Bernays Papers, Box 4, Alderman to Jackson, June 25, 1945.

18   open comment—Bernays Papers, Box 1, Bernays to wife, June 22, 1945.

18   Crimea [Yalta] Declarations—Jackson, *Report*, Meeting of June 29, 1945.

19   unnecessary delays—Ibid.

19   master planners—Ibid.

19   200,000 trials—Jackson, *Report*, Meeting of July 2, 1945.

19   tried in London—Jackson, *Report*, Meeting of July 3, 1945.

19   appall you—Jackson, *Report*, Meeting of July 7, 1945.

20   American bombing—Fyfe, p. 90.

20   during the war—RG 238, Box 9, Report of J. D. Beam, British Foreign Office, July 26, 1945; and Interrogation of Dr. Karl Brandt at Ashcan.

21   its realization—Bernays Papers, Box 1, Bernays to wife, July 22, 1945.

21   about that—Bernays Papers, Box 1, Bernays to wife, July 29, 1945.

23   war of aggression—Jackson, *Report*, Meeting of July 19, 1945.

23   *not* be agreeable—Jackson, *Report*, Meeting of July 25, 1945.

23   this thing across—Jackson, *Report*, Meeting of July 24, 1945.

23   in our support—Jackson, *Report*, Meeting of July 23, 1945.

23   were bandits—Jackson, *Report*, Meeting of July 25, 1945.

23   at the polls—Ibid.

23   disposition of it—Ibid.

24   Military Tribunal—Jackson, *Report*, Meeting of Aug. 2, 1945.

24   filing cards—Bernays Papers, Box 1, Bernays to Col. R. Ammi Cutter, July
        9, 1945.

25   killings, lootings, etc.—Bernays Papers, Box 2, Lt. Walther Rothschild to
        Bernays, July 25, 1945.

25   minor miracle—Bernays Papers, Box 1, Bernays to Col. R. Ammi Cutter,
        July 9, 1945.

25   efficient approach—Bernays Papers, Box 3, Bernays Notes on Meeting of
        Aug 9, 1945.

25   general infection—Bernays Papers, Box 1, Bernays to wife, July 27,
        1945.

25   only a dreamer—Bernays Papers, Box 1, Bernays to wife, Aug. 3, 1945.

26   reasons of health—Bernays Papers, Box 1, Bernays to Jackson, Aug. 15,
        1945.

26   wrote him—Bernays Papers, Box 1, Lt. Col. John Street to Bernays, Aug.
        29, 1945.

Chapter 3. The Accused

26   Stood at 122—Bernays Papers, Box 3, Bernays to Jackson, Aug. 15, 1945.

26   objection to them—Bernays Papers, Box 4, Tab 5, Alderman Memo for
        Jackson, June 23, 1945.

26   been added—Bernays Papers, Box 4, Draft Indictment of Defendants, Aug.
        8, 1945.

27   to be selected—RG 238, Box 9, Kaplan to staff, June 26, 1945.

27   seventy-three names—RG 238, Box 9, OCC Memo to War Department,
        Aug. 16, 1945.

27   occupation zone—Dennett, p. 87.

27   twenty-two defendants—RG 238, Box 9, List of Aug. 25, 1945.

28   for Alfried's—State Department Files, East–West Prosecution, Box 3696,
        List of Aug. 28, 1945.

Chapter 4. The Prisoners of Ashcan

31   party for him—Egbert Papers; Mosley, pp. 314, 322.

31   is forgotten—Baldur von Schirach, p. 319.

32   Patch snapped—Egbert Papers.

32   Heinrich Himmler—Heydecker & Leeb, p. 33.

32   by the war—RG 238, Box 21, Statement of Paul Sixus.

32   blurted out—Heydecker & Leeb, p. 34.

33   his uniform—Andrus, pp. 30–33.

34   Russian prisoners—Ibid., p. 54.

34   consequently a washout—Ibid., pp. 58–61.

34   to Nuremberg—Ibid., p. 59.

34   a chute, sir?—Ibid., p. 63.

35   devil a little—*Time*, Oct. 1, 1945.

Chapter 5. The Documentation Division

37   pages each—RG 238, Box 42, Marburg Documentation Center.

37   Galician Jews—RG 238, Box 42, Gurfein to Jackson and Donovan.

37   be enlarged—RG 238, Box 44, Third Army Documentation Center, July 14, 1945.

37   who or where—Brookhart Interview.

38   evidentiary value—RG 238, Box 205, OCC General Memorandum No. 2, Sept. 22, 1945.

38   in writing—Bernays Papers, Box 1, Maj. Frank Wallis to Bernays, Oct. 10, 1945.

Chapter 6. Goering and Hess: The Flight from Reality

38   and the ego—Bernays Papers, Box 1, Bernays to Wheeler, June 6, 1946.

39   Henry Kissinger (fn)—Sonnenfeldt Interview.

39   Goering continued—Int. of Goering by Amen, Aug. 27, 1945.

39   these details—Int. of Goering by Amen, Sept. 7, 1945.

40   out of it—Ibid.

40   you needed it—Int. of Goering by Amen, Aug. 28, 1945.

40   youth in Austria—Int. of Goering by Amen, Oct. 3, 1945.

41   ist ein Jude—Mosley, p. 7.

42   Excellent propaganda!—Fest, The Face of the Third Reich, p. 74.

43   accepted custom—Mosley, p. 113.

44   the savior—Fest, The Face of the Third Reich, p. 190.

44   fine arts—Int. of Keitel by Dodd, Oct. 10, 1945.

44   own family—Hess Int. File: Erich Lipman to Lt. Blumenstein, Third Army Documentation Center, Oct. 29, 1945.

46   one great deed—Manvell and Fraenkel, Hess, p. 79.

47   into infinity—Rees, p. 28.

47   for the worse—Ibid., p. 59 et seq.

47   iron tablets—Int. of Hess by Amen, Oct. 30, 1945.

49   to his son—Int. of Hess by Amen, Oct. 9, 1945.

49   his intellect—Walsh Papers, Box 13, Diary Entry of Oct. 9, 1945.

50   give to him—Int. of Hess by Amen, Oct. 10, 1945.

50   to give me—Int. of Hess by Amen, Oct. 15, 1945.

Chapter 7. Ribbentrop: The Wandering Aryan

52   him as Fatzke—RG 238, Box 16, Memoirs of Princess Hohenlohe-Waldenburg.

52   Ribbentrop too!—Shirer, p. 410.

52   watching him—RG 238, Box 16, Memoirs of Princess Hohenlohe-Waldenburg.

52   Wandering Aryan—Fest, The Face of the Third Reich, p. 181.

52 than Bismarck—Speer, *Inside the Third Reich*, p. 338.

53 meaningless claptrap—Ribbentrop, p. X.

53 in the meantime—Speer, *Inside the Third Reich*, p. 246.

53 shall I do?—RG 238, Box 7, Murphy to State Department, Aug. 19, 1945; Kelly, pp. 103, 111; Andrus, pp. 40, 99.

54 this very day—Int. of Ribbentrop by Brundage, Aug. 29, 1945.

54 were going on—Int. of Ribbentrop by Brundage, Aug. 30 and Oct. 8, 1945.

54 coming to you—Int. of Ribbentrop by Brundage, Sept. 10, 1945.

55 to explain—Int. of Ribbentrop by Brundage, Aug. 29, 1945.

55 for Brundage—Int. of Conrad by Brundage, Sept. 14, 1945.

55 to say more—Walsh Papers, Box 13, Diary Entry of Sept. 20, 1945.

55 American forces—Int. of Ribbentrop by Jackson, Oct. 5, 1945.

55 losing war—State Department Files, East–West Prosecution, Box 3697, Jackson to President Truman, Oct. 12, 1945.

58 dismissed him—Int. of Ribbentrop by Jackson, Oct. 5, 1945.

58 dismiss anyhow—Int. of Ribbentrop by Amen, Oct. 7, 1945.

Chapter 8. Jackson: The Labors of Hercules

59 American hands—RG 238, Box 205, Jackson to Storey, Sept. 17, 1945.

59 supplemental evidence—Bernays Papers, Box 1, Wallis to Bernays, Oct. 10, 1945.

60 total of 108—State Department Files, East–West Prosecution, Wendelin to Holmes, Aug. 14, 1945; RG 238, Box 231, IBM to Jackson, Aug. 8, 1945, and Charles Horsky to Jackson, Aug. 19, 1945.

60 Shea replied—RG 238, Box 10, Teletype of Aug. 15, 1945.

60 Girls' Town—Bernays Papers, Box 1, Katherine Fite to Bernays, Oct. 22, 1945.

60 168 people—Fyfe, 102.

60 insurance collectors—Bernays Papers, Box 1, Lt. Col. Andy Wheeler to Bernays, Oct. 12, 1945.

60 concentration camp—Ibid.

61 out of him—Sonnenfeldt Interview.

61 carried the field—Dennett, p. 93.

Chapter 9. The Judges

62 both races—Langston Hughes, *Fight for Freedom* (New York: Berkeley Medallion Books, 1962), p. 74.

63 at Nuremberg—Parker Papers, Parker to Biddle, Sept. 14, 1945.

63 in a sense—Parker Papers, Parker to Jacob Billikopf, Sept. 17, 1945.

63 less enthusiasm—Parker Papers, Parker to wife, Oct. 3, 1945.

63 lynching party—*Justices of the Supreme Court*, vol. III, p. 2345.

63 rolling sea—Parker Papers, Parker to wife, Oct. 3, 1945.

64 in myself—Hyde, p. 494.

64   Foreign Office—Hyde, p. 495.

65   poppy red—Biddle, *In Brief Authority*, p. 380.

66   a 3–1 majority—Jackson, *Report*, Charter of Tribunal, Article 4 c.

66   with satisfaction—Biddle Papers, Notes on Conference, Oct. 13, 1945.

66   United States—State Department Files, East–West Prosecution, Box 3697,
      Jackson to President Truman, Oct. 12, 1945.

66   run the show—Biddle Papers, Notes on Conference, Oct. 13, 1945.

66   eleven thousand—Biddle Papers, Organizational Meeting Notes, Oct. 14,
      1945.

68   others agreed—Biddle Papers, Notes on Conference, Oct. 15, 1945.

68   except conquest—State Department Files, East–West Prosecution, Box
      3697, Jackson to President Truman, Oct. 12, 1945.

69   legal standards—State Department Files, East–West Prosecution, Box
      3697, Hentig to President Truman, Sept. 30, 1945.

69   the tribunal—Biddle Papers, Notes on Organizational Meetings, Oct. 21,
      1945.

Chapter 10. Ley: The Disaster of Anti-Semitism

70   United States—Shirer, p. 364; U. S. Department of Labor, *Handbook of
      Labor Statistics, 1968*, p. 166.

70   155 marks ($62)—Grunberger, 198.

71   ten billion marks—Int. of Ley by Monigan, Oct. 6, 1945.

71   money back—Shirer, 368.

71   sensible thing—Grunberger, 334.

71   and the Jew—RG 238, Box 31, *Der Angriff*, Jan. 31, 1940.

71   actually dead—RG 238, Box 88, Ley References.

72   attack the enemy—Speer, *Spandau*, p. 473.

72   burst out—Heydecker & Leeb, p. 28.

72   the plant—RG 238, Box 181, Ley Papers, Aug. 18, 1945.

72   right to it—RG 238, Box 181, Ley Papers, "Dialogue with Inge," Aug. 14,
      1945.

73   close proximity—RG 238, Box 181, Ley Papers, "My Political Testament."

73   where perpetrated—IMT, vol. 1, pp. 173–174.

74   over the radio—RG 238, Box 181, Ley Papers, "Defense," Oct. 24, 1945.

74   his mouth—Kelley, p. 170; Gilbert, p. 6.

74   unmarked grave—RG 238, Box 181, Report on Suicide of Dr. Robert Ley
      by Col. B. C. Andrus.

Chapter 11. The Krupp Fiasco

77   would kill him—Biddle Papers, Notes on Conference, Oct. 21, 1945.

77   the question—IMT, vol. 2, p. 14.

77   falls sick—IMT, vol. 2, p. 10.

77   without delay—IMT, vol. 2, p. 8.

77   was unconscionable—Biddle Papers, Notes on Conference, Nov. 16, 1945.

77   of Alfried—Biddle Papers, Notes on Conference, Nov. 14 and 16, 1945.

Chapter 12. *Attorneys for the Defense*

77   voted down—Biddle Papers, Notes on Conference, Oct. 10, 1945.

78   this evening—Int. of Goering by Amen, Oct. 19, 1945.

78   about the Jews—Int. of Frank by Hinkel, Sept. 6, 1945.

79   from God—Walsh Papers, Folder 72, Frankfurt-am-Main Address, Oct. 31, 1935.

79   barbed wire—Int. of Frank by Hinkel, Sept. 13, 1945.

79   replied blandly—Ibid.

79   foreign press—Int. of Frank by Hinkel, Sept. 10, 1945.

79   that happened—Int. of Frank by Hinkel, Sept. 13, 1945.

80   them quietly—Int. of Frank by Hinkel (X).

80   writing and printing—Int. of Frank by Hinkel, Oct. 8, 1945.

80   never did—Int. of Frank by Hinkel, Sept. 1, 1945.

80   of the Jews—Int. of Frank by Hinkel (X).

81   quest for power—Gilbert, p. 20.

81   real jam—Biddle Papers, Notes on Conference, Oct. 21, 1945.

83   the same job—Int. of Doenitz by Hinkel, Oct. 24, 1945.

83   friends of Hitler—Biddle Papers, Notes on Conference, Oct. 29, 1945.

83   tribunal pays—Biddle Papers, Minutes of Oct. 19 Meeting.

83   with counsel—Biddle Papers, Minutes of Oct. 30 Meeting.

84   the deliberations—Biddle Papers, Minutes of Nov. 1 Meeting.

84   under the Nazis—State Department Files, East–West Prosecution, Box 3701, Robert Murphy to Secretary of State, Aug. 8, 1947.

85   the Middle Ages—Parker Papers, Parker to wife, Oct. 22 and 27, 1945; Jeannie Beam to Mrs. Parker, Nov. 6, 1945.

85   their countrymen—Biddle Papers, Notes on Conference, Nov. 14, 1945; Biddle, *In Brief Authority*, p. 374.

86   during the trial—Biddle Papers, Notes on Conference, Nov. 13, 1945.

86   political trial—Egbert Papers, Personal Details of Defense Counsel, Mar. 22, 1946.

86   particularly repulsive (fn)—Kraus, "The Nuremberg Trial after Seventeen Years," p. 234.

87   comprehended the other—IMT, vol. 2, pp. 18–19.

Chapter 13. *Discord on the Prosecution*

88   Information Center—RG 238, Box 205, OCC General Memorandum, Nov. 3, 1945.

88   from the Russians (fn)—Walsh Papers, Diary Entry of Feb. 12, 1946.

88   from the room—Storey, pp. 102, 104.

88   for the case—RG 238, Jackson to War Department, Nov. 1, 1945 (X).

89   tearfully grateful—Fyfe, 104.

89   and organizations—Bernays Papers, Box 4, Storey and Wheeler Memo for Jackson, "Proposed Plan of Trial Organization," Oct. 15, 1945.

89   trial counsel—RG 238, Box 211, Oct. 26, 1945.

90   someone else—Walsh Papers, Diary Entry of Sept. 20, 1945.

90   lack of precedent—Walsh Papers, Diary Entry of Nov. 4, 1945.

91   the corridors—RG 238, Box 201, Storey Memo of Nov. 12, 1945.

91   the Margolieses—Interviews with Tom Harris and Daniel Margolies.

92   back to Moscow—Biddle, *In Brief Authority*, pp. 376–377.

92   Are Trying!—Ibid., p. 428; Storey, p. 107.

Chapter 14. The Eve of Trial

94   to hang me!—Egbert Papers.

94   two nails—Andrus, p. 125.

95   fits of bawling—Int. of Kaltenbrunner by Brookhart, Nov. 10, 1945.

Chapter 15. The Conspiracy

101   Happy Hooligan—Andrus, p. 93.

102   near-genius range—Gilbert, p. 31.

105   you hang us!—Ibid., p. 36.

105   paid to Reason—IMT, vol. 2, p. 99.

105   cruelty of power—Ibid.

106   ancient East—IMT, vol. 2, pp. 99–100.

106   innumerable events—IMT, vol. 2, p. 100.

106   to do justice—IMT, vol. 2, p. 101.

106   of the law—IMT, vol. 2, p. 102.

106   illegal or criminal—IMT, vol. 2, p. 150.

107   terrible war—IMT, vol. 2, p. 105.

107   aggressive war—IMT, vol. 2, p. 178.

107   the conspiracy—IMT, vol. 5, p. 42.

107   National Socialist movement—IMT, vol. 5, p. 50.

107   Hitler himself—IMT, vol. 5, p. 42.

109   unclean weapons—Heiden, p. 15.

109   final aims—Hitler, p. 308.

109   the World War—Toland, p. 188.

110   the right place—Fest, *Hitler*, p. 133.

110   on March 4—IMT, vol. 2, p. 179.

110   of the race—IMT, vol. 1, p. 174.

111   bold measures—IMT, vol. 2, p. 109.

111   preparation for war—IMT, vol. 5, p. 119.

112   *Doktor Schacht*—Schacht, p. XII.

112   iron discipline—Fest, *Hitler*, p. 310.

113   entered upon it—IMT, vol. 6, p. 77.

113 need a hat—Fest, *Hitler*, p. 337.

114 seriously injured—Fest, *Hitler*, p. 338.

114 government buildings—Int. of Wilhelm Abegg, former state secretary of Prussia, by Hinkel, Dec. 9, 1945.

115 becoming chancellor—NCA, EC 456, Schacht to Hitler, Nov. 12, 1932.

115 coalition cabinet—NCA, 3901 PS, Petition to Hindenburg, November 1932.

116 party dictatorship—Fest, *Hitler*, p. 350.

116 he declared—Fest, *Hitler*, p. 366.

117 informed the court—IMT, vol. 2, p. 187.

117 offered in evidence—IMT, vol. 2, p. 188.

117 worthy of recital—IMT, vol. 2, p. 187.

117 Party of Germany—NCA, 351 PS, Minutes of January 30, 1933 session of cabinet.

118 a real one—IMT, vol. 2, p. 110.

119 been arrested—Reed, p. 118.

119 very night—Diels, p. 95.

119 Goering echoed—Tobias, p. 90.

119 and the State—NCA, 1390 PS, Feb. 28, 1933.

119 violent overthrow—NCA, 2050 PS, Weimar Constitution.

120 and the State—NCA, 2001 PS, Mar. 24, 1933.

121 be re-educated—IMT, vol. 2, p. 189.

121 in crises—Fest, *Hitler*, p. 547.

121 nothing more—NCA, 1856 PS, Goering Speech at Frankfurt-am-Main, Mar. 3, 1933.

121 to do so—NCA, 2324, *Aufbau einer Nation*, pp. 86–87.

Chapter 16. *"A Ring of Evil Men"*: The Röhm Purge

121 told the court—IMT, vol. 5, p. 352.

121 for Goebbels—NCA, 2029 PS, 2030 PS, and 2034 PS, Reichs Ministry for Enlightenment and Propaganda, Mar. 1933.

122 in prison—NCA, 1652 PS, Mar. 21, 1933.

122 beyond censure—NCA, 1393 PS.

122 supervisory personnel—*Neues Tagebuch*, Apr. 6, 1934.

122 all positions—NCA, 1397 PS, Apr. 7, 1933.

122 were dissolved—IMT, vol. 2, p. 194.

122 the Führer—NCA, 2231 PS, July 14, 1933.

122 from the state—NCA, 1395 PS, Dec. 1, 1933.

123 into quasi-colonies—IMT, vol. 2, p. 194; NCA, 2005 PS, Second Law Integrating the Länder with the Reich, Apr. 7, 1933.

123 general population—NCA, 2022 PS, Apr. 25, 1933.

123 seventy-five percent!—Grunberger, p. 322.

123 or painter—NCA, 2415 PS, Nov. 1, 1933.

123 to the court—IMT, vol. 2, p. 112.

124   providing work—Shirer, p. 286.

124   seven hundred persons—NCA, 2472 PS and 2544 PS, Affidavits of Rudolf
       Diels.

124   Berlin alone—Höhne, p. 85.

124   his control—Diels, p. 253.

126   the German people—Shirer, 290.

127   biological decline—Fest, *The Face of the Third Reich*, p. 261.

127   by propaganda—IMT, vol. 16, pp. 292–295.

128   informed the court—IMT, vol. 2, p. 192.

128   is done for—Fest, *Hitler*, p. 412.

128   all a misunderstanding—NCA, 3300 PS, Papen Monograph, "Austria,"
       May 3, 1945.

129   emergency defense—NCA, 2057 PS, July 3, 1934.

129   is his lot—Fest, *Hitler*, p. 468.

129   entire world—NCA, D 716, Papen to Hitler, July 12, 1934.

130   three months—NCA, 1723, Minister of Interior Protective Custody Re-
       port, Jan. 25, 1938.

130   protective custody—NCA, 775 PS, Memorandum of the Minister of the
       Interior.

130   in the Reich—Ibid.

Chapter 17. The Hossbach Meeting: A Split in the Alliance

133   prosecution related—IMT, vol. 2, p. 219.

134   *must be awaited*—NCA, EC 433, Schacht's Königsberg speech, Aug. 18,
       1935.

135   makes us fat!—Mosley, p. 204.

135   I never would—Int. of Schacht by Gurfein, Oct. 16, 1945.

135   I hated him—Int. of Schacht by Hinkel, Oct. 11, 1945.

135   of the year—NCA, EC 286, Schacht to Göring, Apr. 2, 1937.

135   paper money—Schacht, p. 342.

135   captured documents—IMT, vol. 2, p. 262.

136   could react—NCA, 386 PS, Hossbach Notes on Conference with Hitler,
       Nov. 5, 1937.

Chapter 18. Goering's Coup: The Blomberg–Fritsch Crisis

137   of the Hunt—NCA, 2836 PS, Affidavit of Offices and Positions.

137   and of God—Fest, *The Face of the Third Reich*, p. 75.

138   embroidered nightshirts—RG 238, Box 16, Memoirs of Princess Hohen-
       lohe-Waldeburg.

138   silk stockings—Ibid.; Fest, *The Face of the Third Reich*, p. 78.

139   Blomberg's resignation—Shirer, p. 429.

140   was von Fritsch—Höhne, p. 239.

140   Schmidt averred—Bewley, p. 210.

140   He did it!—Höhne, p. 244.

140   military staff—NCA, 1377 PS, Decree Concerning the Leadership of the Armed Forces, Feb. 4, 1938.

140   faithful executives—IMT, vol. 7, p. 106.

141   for the post—NCA, 3704 PS, Blomberg Statement of Nov. 7, 1945.

141   but to tremble—Fest, *Hitler,* p. 544.

141   we can do—von Hassell, p. 23.

Chapter 19. Goering as Machiavelli: The Anschluss

141   that is splendid!—NCA, 3300 PS, op. cit.

142   war machine—IMT, vol. 5, p. 352.

142   is our enemy—Schuschnigg Interrogation File, Schuschnigg Statement, p. 123.

143   German troops—Int. of Edmund von Glaise-Horstenau by Williams, Nov. 6, 1945.

143   telephone conversations—IMT, vol. 2, p. 414.

144   take over—NCA, 2949 PS, Transcript of Conversations, Mar. 13, 1938.

144   assumed power—NCA, 4005 PS, Speech by Friedrich Rainer, Mar. 11, 1942.

145   decisive factor—NCA, 2949 PS, op. cit.

145   telephone conversations—IMT, vol. 2, p. 414.

145   history this way—Gurfein Interview.

146   a little tedious—IMT, vol. 2, p. 226.

146   here in court—IMT, vol. 2, p. 190.

146   to read English—IMT, vol. 2, p. 191.

146   relied upon—IMT, vol. 2, p. 251.

147   photostatic copies—IMT, vol. 2, p. 252.

147   are imposed—IMT, vol. 2, p. 215.

147   every document—IMT, vol. 2, p. 251.

147   mechanical problem—Ibid.

147   transcript in German—IMT, vol. 2, pp. 255–256.

147   Storey replied—IMT, vol. 2, p. 292.

147   to the press—Biddle Papers, Notes on Evidence, Nov. 26, 1945.

148   will be done—IMT, vol. 2, pp. 292–293.

148   the presentation—Egbert Papers, Nov. 27, 1945.

148   on the stand—IMT, vol. 2, p. 322.

148   motion picture—IMT, vol. 2, p. 431.

149   spoiled everything—Gilbert, pp. 46–49.

Chapter 20. Conflict: Donovan versus Jackson

150   foreign witnesses—State Department Files, East–West Prosecution, Box 3698, Jackson to President Truman, Dec. 1, 1945, with Enclosures (hereafter referred to as "Jackson-Donovan"); Donovan to Jackson, Nov. 27, 1945.

150   is unfair—Ibid.

151   Nuremberg and leave—Jackson-Donovan: Donovan to Jackson, Nov. 7, 1945.

151   Colonel Storey—Jackson-Donovan: Jackson to Donovan, Nov. 8, 1945.

152   experienced them—Jackson-Donovan: Schacht to Donovan, Nov. 14, 1945.

152   his position—Jackson-Donovan: Donovan to Jackson, Nov. 14, 1945.

152   *admit* that (fn)—Interviews with Brookhart and Sonnenfeldt.

153   in his place—Kalnoky, p. 94.

154   better days—Jackson-Donovan: Int. of Lahousen by Amen.

154   or his counsel—Jackson-Donovan: OCC Memo of Nov. 24, 1945, Subject: Witnesses.

154   not be lost—Jackson-Donovan: Donovan to Jackson, Nov. 24, 1945.

155   have responsibility—Jackson-Donovan: Jackson to Donovan, undated.

155   mine does not—Jackson-Donovan: Donovan to Jackson, Nov. 27, 1945.

156   other counts—IMT, vol. 2, pp. 436–437.

156   accept that—IMT, vol. 2, p. 436.

156   reasons is bunk—Biddle Papers, Notes on Evidence, Nov. 30, 1945.

157   Lahousen protested—IMT, vol. 3, pp. 22–25.

158   with death—IMT, vol. 3, p. 23.

158   would be limited—RG 238, Box 180, Report of Hess Psychiatric Examination, Nov. 20, 1945.

158   homeopathic remedies—IMT, vol. 2, pp. 484–485, 493, 495.

159   good faith—IMT, vol. 2, p. 496.

159   as a defense—Biddle Papers, Notes on Evidence, Nov. 30, 1945.

160   supplemental rations—Fritzsche, pp. 51–52.

Chapter 21. The Rape of Czechoslovakia

160   European developments—NCA, 388 PS, Case Green Directive, Apr. 21, 1938.

161   near future—IMT, vol. 3, p. 42.

161   than October 1—NCA, 2360 PS, May 30, 1938.

161   younger generation—Int. of Wiedemann by Brundage, Oct. 9, 1945.

161   the United States—NCA, EC 419, Schwerin-Krosigk to Hitler, Sept. 1, 1938.

162   Jewish fiends—Toland, p. 646; Shirer, p. 519.

162   at an end—NCA, 2358 PS, Sportspalast Speech of Sept. 26, 1938.

162   would follow—Shirer, 539.

162   Of course not—IMT, vol. 16, p. 646.

162   not fighting—Schmidt, p. 105–107.

163   his fingers—Gilbert, p. 91.

Chapter 22. Kristallnacht: *The Plot Against the Jews*

163   warlike undertaking—IMT, vol. 3, p. 89.

163   were insignificant—IMT, vol. 2, p. 236.

164   order again—NCA, 1301 PS, Goering Conference of Oct. 14, 1938.

165   not animals—Levin, pp. 78–79.

165   discouraged either—NCA, 3063 PS, Nazi Supreme Party Court: Report
        About the Events . . . of 9 Nov. 1938.

166   of this night—NCA, 374 PS, TWX series of orders signed by Heydrich and
        Müller concerning treatment of Jews, Nov. 9–11, 1938.

166   not be mistreated—NCA, 765 PS, Teletype from Heydrich to SD and
        police re: "Measures about Jews Tonight," Nov. 10, 1938.

168   concentration camps—NCA, 3063 PS, op. cit.; L 202, report of David H.
        Buffum, United States consul, to State Department, "Anti-semitic On-
        slaught as Seen from Leipzig," Jan. 4, 1939.

168   hair disturbed—Manvell and Fraenkel, *Goebbels,* p. 144.

168   stinking lies—Ibid., p. 149.

168   pretty reading—IMT, vol. 4, p. 554.

173   Take him!—NCA, 1816 PS, Stenographic Report of Meeting on "The
        Jewish Question" under Chairmanship of Field Marshal Goering, Nov.
        12, 1938.

173   from them—NCA, 1415 PS, Police Report of the Appearance of Jews in
        Public, Nov. 25, 1938.

173   movie houses—NCA, 2612 PS, *Völkischer Beobachter,* Dec. 5 and 6, 1938.

173   higher education—NCA, 2683 PS, *Völkischer Beobachter,* Nov. 15 and 16,
        1938.

174   with the government—NCA, 1409 PS, Compulsory Deposit of Securities
        by Jews, Dec. 3, 1938.

174   their emigration—NCA, 2876 PS, Tenth Decree Relating to the Reich
        Citizenship Law, July 4, 1939.

174   villa in Berlin—NCA, 1759 PS, Affidavit of U. S. diplomat Raymond Geist.

174   Gauleiter admitted—Int. of August Eigruber by Williams, Nov. 3, 1945.

174   civilized world—NCA, L 202, op. cit.

174   dreadful experiences—NCA, 2604 PS, Report of Samuel Honahen to State
        Department, Nov. 12, 1938.

175   to have them—NCA, L 205, George Rublee to Acting Secretary of State,
        Dec. 8, 1938.

175   fire and sword—*Das Schwarze Korps,* Nov. 24, 1938.

Chapter 23. Schacht: *An Economy in Ruins*

175   this protection—NCA, EC 450, Report of Dodd-Schacht-Fuller Confer-
        ence.

175   with shame—Schacht, p. 358.

175   known that—IMT, vol. 12, p. 562.

176   the proceeds—Int. of Schacht by Gurfein, Oct. 17, 1945.

176   and persecution—RG 238, Box 8, Horsky Interview of George Rublee, Oct. 19, 1945; Box 19, Gilbert Cable to Secretary of State, Nov. 30, 1938; NCA, 3358 PS, The Jewish Question as a Factor in German Foreign Policy in 1938, Jan. 25, 1939.

177   *are exhausted*—NCA, EC 369, President of the Reichsbank to the Führer, Jan. 7, 1939.

177   must be restored—Ibid; Schacht, p. 369.

177   take his leave—Schacht, p. 359.

178   race in Europe—NCA, 2663 PS, Reichstag Speech of Jan. 30, 1939.

178   very shortly—Shirer, p. 592.

178   feared greatly—NCA, 2801 PS, Minutes of Meeting between Goering and Slovak Minister Durkansky, undated.

178   and Moravia—NCA, 2798 PS, German Foreign Office Minutes of Meeting between Hitler and Hacha, Mar. 15, 1939.

178   this problem—NCA, 2119 PS, Führer Decree of Mar. 16, 1939.

179   ever were made—*British Black Book*, vol. 5, p. 712.

179   this effect—Shirer, p. 611.

179   on September 1—Gisevius, p. 363.

Chapter 24. *"War Is Still a Law of Nature"*: The Moscow Pact

180   escape accusation—IMT, vol. 3, p. 92.

180   with justice—IMT, vol. 3, p. 104.

180   a new crime—IMT, vol. 3, p. 106.

180   Hitler's name—IMT, vol. 3, p. 143.

181   towards each other—IMT, vol. 3, pp. 144–145.

181   with the other—IMT, vol. 10, p. 354.

182   international press—IMT, vol. 3, p. 220.

182   to the court—IMT, vol. 2, p. 277.

182   ethical justification—NCA, L 211, Direction of War as a Problem of Organization, Apr. 19, 1938.

183   against England—NCA, L 79, Minutes of Conference, May 23, 1939.

184   Wednesday, August 23—Shirer, p. 703.

185   protocol concluded—Shirer, p. 720.

185   we must act—NCA, 798 PS, Führer Speech to the Commanders-in-Chief, Aug. 22, 1939.

185   was doubtful—IMT, vol. 9, p. 679.

186   obligation to Poland—Shirer, 726.

186   British intervention—IMT, vol. 3, p. 248.

186   great nation—IMT, vol. 3, p. 253.

Chapter 25. Keitel and Jodl: "A Child's Game in a Sandbox"

187   that way—NCA, 1780 PS, Jodl Diary Entry of Aug. 10, 1938.

187   air force—IMT, vol. 15, p. 294.

188   command had been—Int. of Guderian, Warlimont, and Bach-Zelewski by Capt. Walter Rapp, Nov. 25, 1945.

188   Adolf Hitler—NCA, 1954, PS, Int. of Keitel by Col. Boheslav Ecer, Aug. 3, 1945.

188   such utterances—Int. of Jodl by Hinkel, Aug. 29, 1945.

188   unscrupulous as himself—IMT, vol. 5, p. 36.

188   territorial-seizing operation—NCA, 388 PS, Draft for New Directive, Case Green, May 20, 1938.

189   artillery standards—Int. of Keitel by Dodd, Aug. 30, 1945.

189   'extermination of folkdom'—IMT, vol. 2, pp. 478–479 and vol. 3, pp. 20–21.

190   England and France—Shirer, p. 846.

190   fall asleep—Int. of Jodl by Hinkel, Aug. 30, 1945.

190   Channel coast—NCA, 1796 PS, Notes to the War Diary, Sept. 1939.

191   against England—NCA, C 62, Directive No. 6 on the Conduct of the War, Oct. 9, 1939.

191   we have won—Ibid.

191   own accord—NCA, EC 606, Conference of Gen. Georg Thomas with Goering, Jan. 30, 1940.

191   god of war—NCA, 1796 PS, Jodl War Diary Entry of Feb. 13, 1940.

191   Thomas Dodd—Int. of Keitel by Dodd, Aug. 30, 1945.

192   simply ridiculous—Int. of Jodl by Hinkel, Aug. 29, 1945.

192   he declared—Shirer, p. 991.

192   similar rejection—Shirer, p. 989.

192   British fleet—NCA, 442 PS, General Order No. 16, Preparation of Landing Operations against England, July 16, 1940.

194   in comparison—Int. of Jodl by Hinkel, Aug. 30, 1945.

194   new variation—Ibid.

194   in Romania—NCA, C 170, Diary of Naval Operations Staff, Entry 79, first week of Sept., 1940.

194   that fall—IMT, vol. 15, p. 391; and Int. of Jodl by Hinkel, Aug. 30, 1945.

194   forced upon us—NCA, C 53, Keitel Directive of Sept. 20, 1940.

195   armament orders—NCA, 3579 PS, Schnurre Memorandum of Sept. 28, 1940.

195   across the Soviet Union—NCA, 2353 PS, Basic Facts for a History of the German War and Armaments Economy.

195   against the Soviet Union—Int. of Jodl by Maj. Gen. Alexandrov, Nov. 8, 1945.

196   synthetic factories—NCA, 1456 PS, Memorandum, Chief of Armaments Economic Agency, June 20, 1941.

196   be attacked—IMT, vol. 15, p. 392; Int. of Field Marshal Walther von Brau-
            chitsch by Hinkel, Nov. 19, 1945.
196   Alderman elaborated—IMT, vol. 2, p. 294.
196   Volga-Archangelsk—NCA, 446 PS, Directive No. 21, Dec. 18, 1940.
197   branded a defeatist!—Cecil, p. 197.
197   allied power—Int. of Jodl by Hinkel, Sept. 10, 1945.

Chapter 26. *"The Train of the Dead"*

197   more often—Donovan Papers, Donovan to wife Mary, Oct. 19, 1945.
197   Academy Award—Donovan Papers, Donovan to Mary, Nov. 18, 1945.
197   for Jackson (fn)—Donovan Papers, Donovan to Mary, Sunday (probably
            Oct. 27, 1945).
198   population here—IMT, vol. 3, p. 406.
198   their children—Ibid.
198   biological potentialities—IMT, vol. 3, p. 407.
198   to catch dogs—IMT, vol. 3, p. 424.
198   to Germany—IMT, vol. 3, p. 432.
199   in our history—IMT, vol. 3, pp. 500–501.
199   Christmas tree—IMT, vol. 3, p. 513.
199   the population—IMT, vol. 3, p. 562.
199   household articles—IMT, vol. 3, p. 515.
199   is hanging—IMT, vol. 3, p. 453.
199   *Furchtbar! Furchtbar!*—Gilbert, p. 68.
199   the whole thing!—Gilbert, p. 78.
199   just in him—Gilbert, p. 80.
199   were murdered—Gilbert, p. 71.
200   of the defendants—IMT, vol. 3, p. 209.
200   to historians—Egbert Papers, Jackson Memo of Dec. 6, 1945.
200   to introduce—Bernays Papers, Box 1, Lt. Col. John Street to Bernays, Jan.
            29, 1947.
201   main points—Bernays Papers, Box 1, Wheeler to Bernays, Dec. 2, 1945.
201   seemed astonished—IMT, vol. 3, p. 341.
201   Reich cabinet—IMT, vol. 4, p. 110.
201   ministers thought?—IMT, vol. 4, p. 114.
202   at the moment—IMT, vol. 4, p. 92.
202   be cumulative—IMT, vol. 4, p. 109.
202   third sentence—IMT, vol. 4, p. 86.
202   be executed—Fritzsche, p. 32.
203   like murderers—Gilbert, pp. 88–89.
203   in a limousine!—Ibid., p. 83.
203   Goering, Ribbentrop—Ibid., p. 82.
203   almighty God!—Ibid., p. 44.
204   about all this—Ibid., p. 86.
204   Get the bastards!—Kalnoky, p. 120.

Chapter 27. The Ravages of Euthanasia

205   able to work—IMT, vol. 5, p. 362.

205   and posterity—Hitler, p. 255.

205   surgical operation—NCA, 3067 PS, July 14, 1933.

205   ever permitted—NCA, L 305, Petition of Stefan Berens from Gestapo
       Office, Cologne.

205   not be employed—NCA, 2442 PS, Dr. O. Steche, "Guide to Racial Science
       and Heredity," 1937.

206   war casualties—Int. of Pfannmüller by Monigan, Sept. 8, 1945.

206   guaranteed existence—*Justiz und Nationalsozialistisches Verbrechen*, vol. 5, p.
       175.

206   mercy death—NCA, 630 PS, Letterhead of Adolf Hitler, Sept. 1, 1939.

207   died from gas—Pfannmüller by Monigan, Sept. 8, 1945.

207   on the list—IMT, vol. 7, p. 97.

208   more the better—Ibid.

208   down with it—NCA, M 152, Bishop Wurm to Reich Minister of Interior
       Frick, July 19, 1940.

209   of last year—NCA, 1696 PS, Augsburg Social Welfare Association to Di-
       rector, Kaufbeuren Hospital, May 6, 1941.

209   primitive races?—NCA, M 152, Bishop Wurm to Frick, Sept. 5, 1940.

209   great indignation—NCA, 842 PS, Kreisleiter Walz to Area Staff Leader; D
       906, Situation Report, Kreisleitung of Ansbach, Dec. 30, 1940.

209   excellent health—NCA, D 906, op. cit.

209   punishable by death—NCA, 615 PS, Bishop Hilfrich to Reich Minister of
       Justice.

210   front crippled—NCA, 3701 PS, Correspondence between Tiessler and
       Bormann, Aug. 12 and 13, 1941.

210   'natural death'—NCA, 3816 PS, Affidavit of Gerhard Schmidt, director of
       Haar-Egglfing, Mar. 28, 1946.

210   as this one—Int. of Brandt by Monigan (X).

211   support them—Ibid.

Chapter 28. Frank: The Ant and the Aphid

211   Reich territories—Höhne, p. 304.

212   *without any reason*—NCA, D 419, Army District Command XXI to C-of-C
       of the Reserve Army, Nov. 23, 1939.

212   support themselves—NCA, 2233G PS, Frank Diary.

212   thousands succumbed—NCA, 2613 PS, *The Black Book of Poland.*

212   hysterical women—NCA, 1918 PS, Himmler Address to SS Leibstandarte
       Adolf Hitler at Metz.

212   the man himself—IMT, vol. 5, p. 77.

212   German Reich—NCA, 2233H PS, Protocol of the Conference of Depart-
       ment Heads, Oct. 10, 1939.

213   eternal nomad—Davidson, p. 432.

213   were arrested—NCA, 4043 PS, Statement of Father Mizgalski Gerard, July
       1, 1946.

213   taken place—Int. of Frank by Hinkel, Sept. 10, 1945.

213   biological propagation—NCA, 661 PS, Secret Resettlement Thesis for the
       Academy of German Law, Jan. 1940.

213   labor-short Reich—NCA, 1375 PS, Goering to Four-Year Plan Representa-
       tives in Cracow, Jan. 25, 1940.

213   soon as possible—NCA, EC 305, Meeting under the Chairmanship of Field
       Marshal Goering on Questions Concerning the East, Feb. 12, 1940.

214   draconian action—NCA, 2233L PS, Frank Journal, Jan. 19, 1940.

214   refuse to enlist—NCA, 2233N PS, Frank Journal, April–June, 1940.

214   thousands of Poles—IMT, vol. 12, p. 39.

214   were shot—Höhne, p. 305.

214   ashamed of it—IMT, vol. 12, p. 39.

215   be attained—NCA, 2233C PS, Frank Journal, Oct. 7, 1940.

Chapter 29. Barbarossa: The Commissar and Partisan Orders

215   as a state—Hitler, pp. 654–655.

216   sufficient proof—NCA, 1519 PS, Treatment of Political Commissars, Mar.
       31, 1941.

216   Defendant Rosenberg—IMT, vol. 3, p. 351.

216   be a Russian (fn)—Rauschning, p. 132.

216   our soul (fn)—NCA, 2891 PS, Excerpts from Alfred Rosenberg's *Myth of
       the Twentieth Century* (Munich: Hoheneichen Verlag, 1941), p. 215.

216   of the sexes (fn)—NCA, 2891 PS, op. cit., p. 533.

216   Roman philosophy (fn)—NCA, 2891 PS, op. cit. p. 514.

217   Central Asia—NCA, 1015 PS, Rosenberg Memo of Apr. 2, 1941, on the
       USSR.

217   enough already—NCA, EC 3, Economic Notes for Reporting Period of
       August 15–September 16; Sept. 18, 1941.

217   any feelings—NCA, 1058 PS, Rosenberg Talk to Staff, June 20, 1941.

218   also of Europe—NCA, EC 126, Economic Policy Directive for Economic
       Organization East, May 23, 1941.

218   crashing down—Clark, p. 43.

218   to exploit it—NCA, L 221, Memorandum for the Record, July 16, 1941.

218   frontiers accordingly—Ibid.

219   population to resist—NCA, C 52, Supplement to Order No. 33, July 23,
       1941.

219   threaten mutiny—NCA, 886 PS, Decree for the Conduct of Courts Martial
       in the District "Barbarossa," May 13, 1941.

219   German army—Int. of Jodl by Hinkel, Aug. 29, 1945.

219   fanatic communists—NCA, 502 PS, Directive for the Chief of the Security
       Police, July 17, 1941.

219   entrusted to them—Ibid.

220   Russian captivity—NCA, EC 338, Directive for the Treatment of Soviet
         Prisoners of War, Sept. 15, 1941.

220   back the measures—Ibid.

220   have him executed—Int. of Lahousen by Amen, Sept. 5, 1945.

220   size of his shoes—IMT, vol. 2, p. 458.

221   become epidemic—Int. of Veli Gajun Chan by Hinkel, Sept. 14, 1945.

221   execute Turks—Int. of Veli Gajun Chan by Hinkel, Sept. 21, 1945.

221   in the camps—Int. of Veli Gajun Chan by Hinkel, Sept. 14, 1945.

222   pick them up—Naumann, pp. 59, 112, 134.

222   were left—NCA, 081 PS, "Prisoners of War," Feb. 28, 1942.

222   became epidemic—Lahousen Affidavit, Lahousen Interrogation Records,
         Nov. 20, 1945.

222   to the opera—Ciano, 443.

224   a German sentry—Ciano, p. 465.

224   for survival—Clark, p. 207.

224   to be met—NCA, 294 PS, Memorandum of Otto Bräutigam, Oct. 25, 1942.

224   who opposes us—NCA, L 221, op. cit.

225   considered as proper—NCA, 389 PS, Directive on Communist Insurgents
         in the Occupied Areas.

225   own advantage—Ibid.

225   weeks thereafter—IMT, vol. 15, p. 329; Int. of Keitel by Maj. Gen. Alexan-
         drov, Nov. 9, 1945.

226   of the war—Reitlinger, *The House Built on Sand*, p. 111.

226   housing shortage—NCA, 053 PS, Report No. 10 of Capt. Girus Koch, Oct.
         5, 1941.

226   Asiatic-Jewish danger—NCA, D 411, Commander of Troops in the East-
         ern Territories, Oct. 10, 1941.

Chapter 30. Einsatzgruppen

226   throughout the East—NCA, D 411, op. cit., Oct. 28, 1941.

227   German administration—NCA, 3257 PS, Report of Armaments in the
         Ukraine, Dec. 2, 1941.

227   have to cease—NCA, 878 PS, Jews in the Newly Occupied Eastern Ter-
         ritories, Sept. 12, 1941.

227   essential production—NCA, 212 PS, Directive for the Handling of the
         Jewish Question.

228   of the problem—NCA, 3663 PS and 3666 PS, Correspondence between
         Rosenberg and Lohse, Oct. 31–Dec. 18, 1941; D 841, Deposition of Wal-
         ter Kurt Dietmann.

228   physician-short Reich—NCA, L 180, Report of Einsatzgruppe A, The
         Situation in Lithuania, Oct. 15, 1941.

228   German hospitals—NCA, 1381 PS, Second Report of the Reich Minister
         for the Occupied Eastern Territories, Dec. 1942.

229   as volunteers—NCA, 3047 PS, Report of Master Sergeant Soennecken, Oct. 24, 1941.

230   like a revolution—NCA, 1104 PS, Carl to Kube, Oct. 31, 1941.

230   Reichsmarshal—Ibid.

230   superior offices—NCA, 3428 PS, Kube to Lohse, July 31, 1942.

231   around the child—IMT, vol. 4, pp. 254–256.

232   before them—NCA, 2992 PS, Affidavit of Hermann Friedrich Gräbe, Nov. 10, 1945.

233   assured Brookhart—Int. of Ohlendorf by Brookhart, Nov. 9, 1945.

233   or a lunatic—Jaari Memo to Brookhart, Mar. 8, 1946, in Ohlendorf Interrogation File.

233   the Holy Grail—Höhne, p. 236.

235   at the front—IMT, vol. 4, pp. 316–322.

235   murderous orders?—Gilbert, p. 61.

236   of the dying—IMT, vol. 7, pp. 494–496.

236   lying in filth—IMT, vol. 4, p. 334.

236   longer noticed—NCA, 501 PS, Becker to Obersturmbannführer Rauch, May 16, 1942.

236   have been saying—IMT, vol. 4, pp. 327–328.

238   corresponding sentence—IMT, vol. 4, p. 354.

Chapter 31. Speer and Sauckel: Slave Labor

238   left behind—NCA, 2353 PS, op. cit.

239   his memoirs—Speer, *Inside the Third Reich,* p. 63.

240   every other nation—Ibid., p. 109.

240   unrequited love—Ibid., p. 188.

240   my plans—Speer, Ibid., p. 247.

241   his own way—NCA, 1452 PS, Conference of the Chiefs with the Chief of the Department, Mar. 24, 1942.

241   labor camps—NCA, 1520 PS, Memorandum of Conference between Hitler, Rosenberg, Bormann, and Lammers, May 8, 1942.

242   great demand—NCA, EC 194, Keitel Directive on Use of POWs in War Industry, Oct. 3, 1941.

242   fill the gaps—NCA, 016 PS, Sauckel's Labor Mobilization Program, Apr. 20, 1942.

243   people's state—Int. of Sauckel by Monigan, Sept. 11, 1945.

243   official appointment—Int. of Sauckel by Monigan, Sept. 12, 1945.

243   all soldiers now—Int. of Sauckel by Monigan (X).

243   for its execution—IMT, vol. 3, p. 404.

244   German "race"—NCA, EC 68, Directive on Treatment of Foreign Farm Workers of Polish Nationality, Mar. 6, 1941.

244   be minimal—NCA, EC 194, Keitel Directive on Use of POWs in War Industry, Oct. 31, 1941.

244   as workers—NCA, 1201 PS, Report of B. D. Gotha.

244   like flies—NCA, 294 PS, op. cit.

244   Soviet Union—NCA, EC 318, Conference of Presidents under the Chairmanship of Sauckel, Apr. 15, 1942.

244   decisive importance—NCA, 3787 PS, Meeting of the Reich Defense Council (undated).

244   national life—NCA, 016 PS, op. cit.

244   fifteen and thirty-five—NCA, 025 PS, The Importation of Domestic Workers from the East into the Reich, Sept. 4, 1942.

245   presents to friends—Int. of Sauckel by Monigan, Sept. 28, 1942.

245   Hitler decreed—NCA, 025 PS, op. cit.

245   Germany for work—NCA, 016 PS, op. cit.

245   each month—Int. of Sauckel by Monigan, Sept. 17, 1945.

245   as assistants—NCA, 1296 PS, Employment of Foreign Laborers in Germany, June 27, 1942.

245   slave trade—NCA, 294 PS, op. cit.

245   to monasteries—NCA, 018 PS, Rosenberg to Sauckel, Dec. 21, 1942.

246   catch dogs—Ibid.

246   industrial workers—NCA, 084 PS, Present Status on the Question of Eastern Laborers, Sept. 30, 1942.

246   surviving like this—NCA, 054 PS, Report to Reich Minister for the Occupied Eastern Territories Concerning Treatment of Ukrainian Specialists, Oct. 7, 1942.

246   as much food—Int. of Sauckel by Monigan, Sept. 28, 1945.

246   than myself—Int. of Sauckel by Monigan, Sept. 21, 1945.

246   food balance—NCA, 1193 PS, Letter of Nov. 14, 1941, transmitting Report of Conference on Employment of Soviets, Nov. 7, 1941.

247   never murmur—NCA, D 305, Statement of Heinrich Buschauer, Oct. 5, 1945.

247   to the Russians—NCA, 1193 PS, op. cit.

247   baking ovens—NCA, D 288, Statement of Dr. Wilhelm Jaeger, Oct. 15, 1945.

248   for eating—NCA, D 313, Statement of Dr. Apolinary Gotowicky, Oct. 13, 1945.

248   for three thousand workers—NCA, D 288, op. cit.

248   was eighteen months—NCA, D 313, op. cit.

248   in the Reich—NCA, 1296 PS, op. cit.

248   two million foreigners—NCA, 017 PS, Sauckel to Gauleiter Meyer, Oct. 3, 1942.

248   with Hitler—Int. of Sauckel by Monigan, Sept. 17, 1945.

248   that direction—Int. of Goering by Amen, Oct. 1, 1945.

249   great epidemics—NCA, 025 PS, Conference with Plenipotentiaries for Labor Mobilization, Sept. 4, 1942.

249   Dutchmen or Italians—Cecil, 207.

249   more and more—NCA, 294 PS, op. cit.

249   of the dull—Lochner, p. 325.

250   correct principles!—Int. of Sauckel by Monigan, Sept. 17, 1945.

250   treated as correctly—NCA, 407 PS, Sauckel to Hitler, Mar. 10, 1943.

250   Bolshevik worlds—NCA, 1290 PS, Sauckel to Hitler, April 14, 1943.

250   treasonable crimes—NCA, 205 PS, Bormann's Memorandum concerning
       the General Principles for the Treatment of Foreign Laborers, May 5,
       1943.

250   definite promise—NCA, 1292 PS, Führer Conference on the Allocation of
       Labor, Jan. 4, 1944.

250   and liquor—Int. of Obergruppenführer Karl Wolff by Brundage, Sept. 18,
       1945.

250   labor service—NCA, 3819 PS, Sauckel to Hitler, Mar. 17, 1944.

250   German industry—NCA, 2520 PS, Approximate Number of Foreigners
       Sent to Work for the German War Effort.

251   for industrialists—Egbert Papers, Ohlendorf Notes on Corruption, Aug.
       11, 1945.

251   bunch of crooks—FIAT, Entry 160, Box 12, Report by O. Hoeffding, Aug.
       1, 1945.

251   manage that too—Speer, *Inside the Third Reich*, p. 389.

251   after Goering—CIOS Interrogation of Speer, May 28, 1945.

251   in the billions—Speer, *Inside the Third Reich*, p. 440.

252   be with us—*The Observer*, April 9, 1944.

252   not poisoned—NCA, 007 PS, Himmler to Prützmann, Höhere SS und
       Polizeiführer in the Ukraine, Sept. 7, 1943.

252   will meet him—Speer, *Inside the Third Reich*, p. 514.

252   people to survive—Ibid., p. 554.

252   been killed—Ibid., p. 557.

252   scorched-earth policy—Ibid., p. 582.

253   his memoirs—Ibid., p. 622.

253   war criminal—FIAT, Entry 160, Box 12, Report by O. Hoeffding, Aug. 1,
       1945.

253   Nuremberg prosecution—FIAT, Entry 160, Box 12, Speer Interrogation
       by Dr. Fred Kaufmann, Sept. 5, 1945.

253   visualize very well—Miale, p. 262.

254   here who will—Speer, *Inside the Third Reich*, p. 642.

254   testify to that—RG 238, Box 183, Speer to Jackson, Nov. 17, 1945.

254   such a possibility—Ibid.

255   were innocent—IMT, vol. 4, p. 343.

255   state of mind—Speer, *Inside the Third Reich*, p. 543.

255   government in Germany—Int. of Ohlendorf by Brookhart, Oct. 27, 1945.

255   in his book (fn)—Speer, *Inside the Third Reich*, p. 547.

256   through the floor!—Gilbert, pp. 102–103.

256   these measures—Speer, *Inside the Third Reich*, p. 405.

256   *of the earth*—Toland, pp. 1051–1052.

Chapter 32. "The Final Solution of the Jewish Question"

257   very well—IMT, vol. 4, p. 355.

257   occupied by Germany—IMT, vol. 4, p. 356.

257   every responsibility (fn)—Int. of Wisliceny by Brookhart, Nov. 17, 1945.

258   known to me—IMT, vol. 4, p. 358.

258   carried out—IMT, vol. 4, p. 359.

258   confirmed bureaucrat—IMT, vol. 4, p. 361.

258   country altogether—IMT, vol. 7, p. 40.

259   their destruction—IMT, vol. 4, p. 357.

259   final solution—*The Black Book of Poland*, p. 57.

259   influence in Europe—NCA, 710 PS, Goering to Heydrich, July 31, 1941.

260   no precedent—*Justiz und Nationalsozialistisches Verbrechen*, vol. 1, p. 473.

260   liquidate them yourselves—NCA, 2233 D PS, Frank Journal, Sept. 9, 1941.

261   absolutely possible—Ibid.

261   their annihilation—Ibid.

261   two months before—Protocol of the Conference on the Final Solution of the Jewish Question, Jan. 20, 1942: Ludwigsburg Prosecutor's Office.

261   the old idiots!—Int. of Wisliceny by Jaari, Apr. 2, 1946.

261   military colonies—NCA, 910 PS, Report of Dr. Self, Mar. 27, 1942; Kersten, p. 134.

262   from Asia!—Kersten, p. 133.

262   Viktor Brack—Kempner, *Eichmann und Komplizen*, p. 102.

262   untalented disciple—IMT, vol. 20, p. 502.

262   he did not (fn)—Int. of Brandt by Monigan (X).

262   Jewish bacillus—Lochner, p. 148.

263   official exchange—Jewish Encyclopedia, "Warsaw," vol. 16, pp. 350–351.

263   chickens and geese—Höhne, p. 320.

263   notices the war—NCA, 3815 PS, Lasch Interrogation by the SS.

263   values here?—NCA, 3257 PS, Inspector of Armaments, Ukraine to General Thomas, Dec. 2, 1941.

263   by 75 percent—NCA, 1381 PS, Political and Economic Problems of the Military and Civilian Administration of the Occupied Eastern Territories, Dec. 1942.

265   be speeded up—NCA, 2233E PS, Cabinet Session of Aug. 24, 1942.

265   war machine—Int. of Frick by Sackett, Oct. 3, 1945.

265   concentration camp—IMT, vol. 6, p. 191.

265   at Auschwitz—Naumann, p. 114.

265   foreign countries—Hausser, p. 237.

266   production of V-rockets—Int. of Obergruppenführer Oswald Pohl by Brookhart, June 8, 1946; Int. of Ohlendorf by Brookhart, Nov. 9, 1945.

266   exploited for profit—Int. of Pohl by Brookhart, June 8, 1946.

266   petty offenses—Int. of Höss by Jaari, Apr. 2, 1946.

267   from evacuation—Höhne, p. 379.

267   business affairs—Ibid.

267   Aryan workers—Ibid., p. 380.

267   on November 15—Eisenbach, p. 19.

268   ruthless severity—NCA, 3244 PS, Decrees, Regulations, and Announcements, Oct. 9, 1942.

268   Polish Jews—Lochner, p. 251.

268   are assigned—NCA, 1472 PS, Cable for Gestapo Chief Müller, Dec. 16,
1942.

269   never be written—IMT, vol. 3, p. 500.

269   single action—Levin, p. 147.

269   on January 22—NCA, 1061 PS, Jürgen Stroop, "The Warsaw Ghetto is No
More."

270   Police Stroop—IMT, vol. 3, p. 553.

271   in his report—IMT, vol. 11, p. 382.

271   for preservation—Jewish Encyclopedia, "Warsaw," vol. 16, p. 354.

272   security police—NCA, L 18—Disposition of Jewish Labor, Oct. 23, 1942.

272   work the machines—Int. of Kaltenbrunner by Brookhart, Oct. 12, 1945.

272   Ukrainian state?—NCA, 1384 PS, Minutes of Führer Conference of June
8, 1943.

273   we had seen—IMT, vol. 7, pp. 446–447, 592–595.

273   Final Solution—Brookhart Interview.

273   extraordinary satisfaction—IMT, vol. 4, p. 371.

273   other countries (fn)—Int. of Wisliceny by Brookhart, Nov. 15, 1945.

273   like a Jew—Int. of Wisliceny by Josef Maier, Mar. 5, 1946, and by Jaari,
Mar. 21, 1946.

Chapter 33. Partisan Warfare

274   been a sham—RG 238, Box 193, Taylor-Kaplan Memorandum to Jackson,
Oct. 22, 1945.

274   and valuable—RG 238, Box 193, Taylor Memorandum to Jackson, "Preparation of Case against German High Command," Dec. 7, 1945.

275   in the East—Höhne, p. 363.

275   one thousand a month—NCA, 3711 PS, Statement of Wilhelm Scheidt,
Nov. 25, 1945.

275   to the Germans—NCA, 265 PS, Report on Situation in the General District Zhitomir, June 30, 1943.

276   or by courtmartial—Int. of Keitel by Maj. Gen. Alexandrov, Nov. 9,
1945.

276   village burned—NCA, 886 PS, Führer Decree of May 13, 1941; D 729,
Conversation between Goering and Mussolini, Oct. 23, 1942.

276   Ukrainians perished—NCA 1526-V PS—Letter from Ukrainian Main
Committee to Frank, Feb. 1943.

276   thirteen years—Ibid.

276   war victims—NCA, 2233 AA PS, Frank Journal, Jan. 25, 1943.

277   commissioner by force—NCA, 3012 PS, To All Group Leaders of the Security Service–SD, Mar. 19, 1943.

277   such measures—NCA, D 729, op. cit.

277   security police—Statement of Bach-Zelewski (X), Bach Interrogation File.

277   carried off—NCA 3943 PS, Report from the Eastern Occupied Territories, No. 46, Mar. 24, 1943.

278   believe such things—IMT, vol. 38, pp. 373, 371.

278   reopened to traffic—IMT, vol. 7, p. 474.

278   about to rise—NCA, L 37, Collective Responsibility, July 19, 1944.

278   spits of meat—Int. of General Heinz Guderian by George Sawicki, Jan. 29, 1946.

278   their surrender—Statement of Bach-Zeleswki (X), Bach Interrogation File.

279   stop looting—Ibid; Int. of Brigadeführer Ernst Rode by George Sawicki, Jan. 28, 1946.

279   incur no penalty—IMT, vol. 5, p. 405.

280   in the church—Brown, pp. 697–702.

280   military reasons—IMT, vol. 6, pp. 413–414.

280   professed ignorance—Int. of Bach-Zelewski, Guderian, and Walter Warlimont by Capt. Walther Rapp, Nov. 25, 1945.

280   thought on that!—Guderian by Sawicki, Jan. 29, 1946.

280   anything about it—Int. of Bach-Zelewski et al., op. cit.

280   anxious to testify—Int. of Bach-Zelewski by Rapp, Dec. 5, 1945.

281   anti-partisan warfare—Bach-Zelewski Statement (X) in Bach Interrogation File.

281   expected of him—IMT, vol. 4, p. 414.

281   stinking neck!—Gilbert, p. 114.

281   dirty pig that!—Ibid.

281   been channelled—IMT, vol. 4, p. 488.

281   partisan warfare?—IMT, vol. 4, p. 493.

282   cleverest of men—Höhne, p. 545.

282   our philosophy—IMT, vol. 4, p. 494.

282   has to come—Ibid.

282   three divisions—IMT, vol. 4, p. 495.

282   occupied lands—Höhne, p. 369; Hilberg, p. 244.

283   to presentation—Bernays Papers, Street to Bernays, Feb. 11, 1946.

283   for the job—Bernays Papers, Roger Barrett to Bernays, Feb. 11, 1946.

284   of this term—RG 238, Box 38, Jackson to Stone, Mar. 14, 1946.

Chapter 34. The Perversion of German Medicine

284   that of racism—IMT, vol. 5, p. 373.

285   human person—IMT, vol. 5, p. 374.

285   primitive barbarism?—IMT, vol. 5, p. 375.

285   modern era—IMT, vol. 5, p. 376.

285   ancient Germany—IMT, vol. 5, p. 378.

285   racial community—IMT, vol. 5, p. 422.

285   innermost nature—IMT, vol. 5, p. 423.

285   common civilization—IMT, vol. 5, p. 426.

286   euthanasia program—NCA, 1602 PS, Rascher to Himmler, May 15, 1941.

286   and alchemy—Int. of Brandt by Monigan (X).

287   of the subject—NCA, 2428 PS, Deposition of Anton Pacholegg, May 13, 1945.

287   be important—NCA, 343 PS, Milch to Wolff, May 20, 1942.

287   women's bodies—NCA, 1618 PS, Rascher Report, Sept. 10, 1942.

287   of them died—NCA, 2428 PS, op. cit.

287   human beings—Int. of Wolff by Brundage, Sept. 7, 1945.

288   the Waffen SS—NCA, 1617 PS, Himmler to Milch, Nov. 1942.

288   near future—NCA, 343 PS, Milch to Himmler, Aug. 31, 1942.

288   or Dr. Rascher—Int. of Milch by Monigan, Oct. 23 and 24, 1945.

288   Major Monigan—Int. of Ludwig Diels by Monigan, Oct. 30, 1945.

288   from his body—NCA, 2428 PS, op. cit.

289   good teeth—IMT, vol. 5, p. 171.

289   was carrying—NCA, 2428 PS, op. cit.

289   doctor pontificated—NCA, 035 PS, Dr. Pokorny to Himmler, Oct. 1941.

289   Auschwitz instead—Int. of Haagen by Monigan, Nov. 14, 1945; NCA, 008 PS, Sievers to Pohl, May 19, 1944.

290   sealed tin can—NCA, 085 PS. Unknown to Sturmbannführer Brandt, Securing Skulls of Jewish Bolshevik Commissars, Feb. 9, 1942.

290   for skeletonization—NCA, 086 PS, Sievers to Brandt, Nov. 2, 1942; 087 PS, Sievers to Eichmann, June 21, 1943.

290   completely dissolved—NCA, 088 PS, Sievers to Brandt, Sept. 5, 1944.

290   ordered cremated—NCA, 091 PS, Hauptsturmführer Berg to Brandt, Oct. 12 and 21, 1944.

291   on May 12, 1944—NCA, 1751 PS, Assignment of Prisoners for Experimental Purposes, May 12, 1944.

293   help of specialists—Int. of Gebhardt by Monigan, Oct. 18, 1945.

293   with pendulums—Int. of Ludwig Diels by Monigan, Oct. 30, 1945.

293   should be used—Int. of Werner Kirchert by Monigan, Oct. 6, 1945.

293   told Monigan—Int. of Gebhardt by Monigan, Oct. 18, 1945.

293   shock and gangrene—Int. of Fisher by Monigan, Sept. 20, 1945.

293   from Switzerland—Int. of Gebhardt by Monigan, Oct. 18, 1945.

294   have to die—Int. of Gebhardt by Monigan, Sept. 25, 1945.

294   supposed to be—Int. of Gebhardt by Monigan, Sept. 22, 1945.

294   further science—Ibid.

294   out of it—Int. of Gebhardt by Monigan, Sept. 22.

294   them up again—Int. of Fisher by Monigan, Sept. 20, 1945.

295   and disfigured—Ibid.

295   or sulfanilamide—Int. of Gebhardt by Monigan, Oct. 18, 1945.

295   any more—Int. of Fischer by Monigan, Nov. 5, 1945.

295   never come off—RG 238, Sievers Interrogation File, Sievers to Monigan,
        Dec. 20, 1945.
296   noticed anything—Int. of Schilling by Monigan, Sept. 5, 1945.
296   later killed—IMT, vol. 5, p. 171.
296   later complications—IMT, vol. 5, p. 170.
296   armed forces—IMT, vol. 5, p. 175.
297   pull it themselves—IMT, vol. 5, p. 191.
297   different impression—IMT, vol. 3, p. 594.
297   these things—IMT, vol. 5, pp. 200–201.
298   man murdered—Höhne, pp. 384–386.
298   on 11 April 1945—IMT, vol. 6, pp. 311–312.
298   kitchen table—IMT, vol. 7, p. 599.
298   melted down—IMT, vol. 7, p. 600.
299   don't know—IMT, vol. 7, pp. 598–599.
299   bodies in Lvov—IMT, vol. 7, pp. 548–550.

Chapter 35. "Night and Fog," and Counterterror

299   (Night and Fog) Decree—NCA, L 90, Prosecution of Offenses within the
        Occupied Territories, Dec. 12, 1941.
300   terror is terror—NCA, 666 PS, Directive for Prosecution of Offenses
        Against the Reich or Occupation Authorities, Dec. 7, 1941; 668 PS,
        Letter from Chief of the Sipo and SD, plus OKW Letter re: Prosecution
        of Offenses against the Reich and Occupation Forces, June 24, 1942.
300   their fate—NCA, 833 PS, Prosecution of Crimes against the Reich, Feb. 7,
        1942.
300   been 'vernebelt'! (fn)—NCA, D 767, Criminal Acts by Non-German Civil-
        ians in the Occupied Territories, Sept. 13, 1941.
300   by the Gestapo—IMT, vol. 6, pp. 204–205.
301   in the water—IMT, vol. 6, p. 207.
301   lack of care—IMT, vol. 6, p. 209.
301   chase them away—IMT, vol. 6, p. 208.
301   use again—IMT, vol. 6, pp. 208–209.
301   on for hours—IMT, vol. 6, p. 210.
302   gas chamber—IMT, vol. 6, p. 212.
302   burning pits—IMT, vol. 6, p. 215.
302   the gas chambers—IMT, vol. 7, p. 588.
302   furnaces alive—IMT, vol. 6, p. 216.
302   of captivity—IMT, vol. 6, p. 219.
303   work no more—IMT, vol. 6, p. 228.
304   about that—IMT, vol. 6, pp. 229–230.
305   domestic matters—IMT, vol. 8, p. 321.
305   national elections—IMT, vol. 6, p. 506.
305   five to one—IMT, vol. 7, pp. 46–47.
306   liquidation of Himmler (fn)—Int. of Naujocks by Brookhart, Oct. 10,
        1945.

306   in Copenhagen—Ibid; Int. of Standartenführer Rudolph Mildner by Henry Kudsk, Mar. 4, 1946.

306   shot him—IMT, vol. 7, p. 45.

306   and incongruously—Höhne, p. 498.

Chapter 36. War Crimes

307   was furious—Int. of Jodl by Hinkel, Oct. 1, 1945.

307   out to kill—Davidson, p. 383.

307   aluminum production—IMT, vol. 15, p. 488.

307   exterminated in battle—NCA, 1263 PS, Appendix 2, Führer Headquarters, Oct., 1942.

308   honorable warrior—NCA, 1265 PS, Treatment of POWs, Oct. 15, 1942.

308   need of it—NCA, 1263 PS, op. cit.

308   on October 30—IMT, vol. 15, p. 488.

308   British uniforms—IMT, 508 PS, Landing of British Freight Gliders in Norway, Nov. 21, 1942.

308   dumped at sea—NCA, D 919, Extract from War Crimes Trial, Oslo (undated); 526 PS, Top Secret: Saboteurs in Norway, May 10, 1943; IMT, vol. 15, pp. 488–489.

308   they surrendered—NCA, 2510 PS, Deposition of Major Frederick W. Roche.

308   when captured—NCA, 537 PS, Treatment of Members of Foreign Military Missions, July 30, 1944; 1279 PS (same title), July 27, 1944.

308   to be shot—NCA, 531 PS, Treatment of Commandos, June 23, 1944; 532 PS (same title), June 24, 1944.

308   was greater—NCA, 2997 PS, Court of Inquiry re: Shooting of POWs by 12th SS Panzer Division.

309   further ado—NCA, 4067 PS, Teletype to FRR Panzer Army, Africa, June 9 (no year).

309   never implemented—IMT, vol. 10, pp. 563–564.

309   been recaptured—NCA, L 158, Measures to be Taken Against Escaped Officers and Non-Commissioned Officer POWs, Mar. 28, 1944.

309   two-week period—IMT, vol. 11, pp. 192–193; Int. of Keitel by Williams, Nov. 10, 1945.

309   them simultaneously—Int. of Major General Adolf Westhoff by Williams, Nov. 2, 1945.

310   favorable light—IMT, vol. 15, p. 439.

310   Himmler immediately—IMT, vol. 15, p. 439.

310   (home guard)—NCA, D 731, Statement of Obersturmbannführer Ernst Walde, Dec. 13, 1945.

310   escapes diminished—IMT, vol. 9, p. 103.

310   them again!—Int. of Keitel by Hinkel, Nov. 10, 1945.

311   every Stalag—Int. of Westhoff by Williams, Nov. 2, 1945.

311   human rights—IMT, vol. 15, p. 476.

311   their heads—IMT, vol. 11, p. 9.

311   "shattering effect"—NCA, D 731, op. cit.

311   dead already—Int. of Westhoff by Williams, Nov. 2, 1945.

312   secret police—Ibid; IMT, vol. 11, pp. 166–167.

312   by the Gestapo—NCA, L 158, op. cit; IMT, Vol. 9, pp. 591–592.

312   interrogator at Nuremberg—Int. of Westhoff by Williams, Nov. 2, 1945.

312   on to Goering—NCA, D 730, Statement of Lt. Gen. Walther Grosch, Dec. 7, 1945.

313   following morning—IMT, vol. 6, p. 186.

313   cease completely—NCA, L 172, The Strategic Position in the Fifth Year of the War, Nov. 7, 1943.

313   flying here!—IMT, vol. 15, p. 588.

313   few years earlier—NCA, D 780, Concerning the Treatment of Enemy Terror Airmen, June 20, 1944.

314   single vehicles, etc.—NCA, 731 PS, Memorandum of May 21, 1944.

314   laws of civilization—Ibid.

315   enemy killers—NCA, 1676 PS, A Word on the Enemy Air Terror, May 29, 1944.

315   enemy aviators—NCA, 057 PS, Justice Exercised by the People against Anglo-American Murderers, May 30, 1944.

315   murder of airmen—IMT, vol. 15, pp. 339–340; NCA, 745 PS, Enemy Aviators Who Have Been Shot Down, June 12, 1944.

315   be the rule—NCA, 735 PS, Treatment of Enemy Aviators, June 6, 1944.

315   rules for it—IMT, vol. 10, p. 552.

315   all quarters—NCA, 730 PS, Treatment of Enemy Aviators, June 15, 1944.

316   along the road—Int. of Westhoff by Brookhart, Jan. 10, 1946.

316   special privileges—IMT, vol. 9, p. 357.

316   to be shot!—IMT, vol. 15, p. 586.

316   quite mad now?—IMT, vol. 15, p. 589.

317   in retaliation—Toland, p. 1165.

317   of the convention—NCA, D 606, Denunciation of Agreements Based on International Law, Feb. 20, 1945.

318   capital punishment—IMT, vol. 6, p. 426.

Chapter 37. "A Most Terrible and Convincing Case"

319   idea behind it—Gilbert, p. 172.

319   their arms—Ibid., p. 152.

319   of the thing—Ibid., Gilbert, pp. 174, 176.

319   concentration camps—Hyde, p. 505.

319   prosecution's case—Biddle, Notes on Evidence, Jan. 11, 1946.

319   stupid questions—Biddle, Notes on Evidence, Jan. 28, 1946.

319   underscores evidence—Biddle, Notes on Evidence, Jan. 29, 1946.

319   fool of himself—Biddle, Notes on Evidence, Feb. 2, 1946.

320   Babel interpreted—IMT, vol. 6, p. 498.

320   Tribunal to afford—IMT, vol. 8, p. 532.

321   of the document—IMT, vol. 5, p. 81.

321   from the record—Storey, p. 140.

321   human nature—Gilbert, p. 117.

322   chapel any more—Ibid., p. 154.

323   necessary preparation—IMT, vol. 5, p. 22.

323   within forty-eight hours—IMT, vol. 5, p. 44.

323   for my perusal—IMT, vol. 8, p. 231.

324   of course, object—IMT, vol. 8, p. 166.

324   the defendants—IMT, vol. 8, p. 163.

324   by the judges—Lippe, 251.

325   throughout the trial—IMT, vol. 8, p. 594.

325   perfectly legal—IMT, vol. 8, pp. 548–551.

325   these matters—IMT, vol. 8, pp. 594–595.

326   to cross-examination—Biddle Papers, Notes on Evidence, Feb. 21 and 23, 1946.

Chapter 38. The Catlike Elephant: Goering

329   its conclusion—Fritzsche, pp. 32–33.

329   "Lick my arse!"—Gilbert, p. 113.

331   ice comes out!—Mosley, p. 293.

331   my asshole!—Ibid., p. 306.

331   voluntary basis—IMT, vol. 9, p. 87.

331   of the trial—IMT, vol. 9, p. 119.

331   direction at all—IMT, vol. 9, p. 479.

331   Not at all—IMT, vol. 9, p. 480.

332   minister of Germany—IMT, vol. 9, p. 481.

332   your words?—IMT, vol. 9, p. 482.

332   nodded assent—IMT, vol. 9, p. 483.

332   *Kalter Kaffee!*—Haensel, *Das Gericht vertagt sich*, p. 31.

333   German Reich—IMT, vol. 9, p. 254.

333   Treaty of Versailles—IMT, vol. 9, pp. 264, 312.

333   persistent contradictions—IMT, vol. 9, p. 370.

334   of the others—IMT, vol. 9, p. 401.

334   Führer state—IMT, vol. 9, p. 311.

334   no legality—IMT, vol. 9, p. 364.

334   and the troops—IMT, vol. 9, p. 338.

334   military targets—IMT, vol. 9, p. 337.

334   might think—IMT, vol. 9, p. 177.

335   civilian population—IMT, vol. 9, p. 178.

335   of fire is—IMT, vol. 9, p. 341.

335   Military Council—IMT, vol. 9, p. 319.

335   concentration camps—IMT, vol. 9, p. 354.

336   did not starve—IMT, vol. 9, pp. 350–351.

336   for the fray—Fyfe, p. 108.

336   preferable procedure—*Fortune,* "The Nuremberg Novelty," Dec. 1945.

336   carry it out—*Army and Navy Journal,* Dec. 1, 1945.

336   actually did it—Bosch, p. 169.

337   measure justified—Hyde, pp. 503, 509.

337   way was he—IMT, vol. 9, p. 538.

337   correct him—IMT, vol. 9, p. 433.

338   simplicity and power—Hyde, pp. 510–511.

338   yes or no?—IMT, vol. 9, p. 431.

339   thinks right—IMT, vol. 9, p. 421.

339   to bring out—IMT, vol. 9, pp. 507–508.

340   in rebuttal—IMT, vol. 9, p. 509.

340   of that sort—IMT, vol. 9, p. 511.

340   will be tolerated—Hyde, p. 512.

340   'yes' or 'no'—IMT, vol. 9, pp. 511–512.

340   prosecution's preparations (fn)—IMT, vol. 9, p. 512.

341   known here—IMT, vol. 9, p. 551.

341   Doctor Frank—IMT, vol. 9, p. 565.

341   of this war—NCA, 3700 PS, Schacht to Goering, Nov. 3 (1942).

342   not correct—IMT, vol. 9, pp. 556–557.

342   fire to it—NCA, 3740 PS, Halder Affidavit, Mar. 6, 1946; RG 238, Box 195,
        Sonnenfeldt Memorandum to Amen, Mar. 7, 1946.

342   the Reichstag—IMT, vol. 9, p. 434.

342   temper and excitement—IMT, vol. 9, p. 538.

343   the Jewish question—IMT, vol. 9, p. 519.

343   been buoyed—Fyfe, pp. 112, 114.

343   own sentence!—IMT, vol. 9, p. 581.

343   admitted it—IMT, vol. 9, p. 613.

344   these figures—IMT, vol. 9, p. 614.

345   as Armenians—IMT vol. 9, pp. 617–618.

345   such perpetrations—IMT, vol. 9, p. 619.

345   and exploited—IMT, vol. 9, p. 265.

345   being lost—IMT, vol. 9, p. 653.

346   German hero—*Life,* Apr. 1, 1946.

346   dead tired—Biddle Papers, Notes in Evidence, Mar. 21, 1946.

346   the defense—IMT, vol. 9, pp. 662–664.

Chapter 39. The Faithful Followers: Hess and Ribbentrop

347   a small creek—Walsh Papers, Box 8, Heinz Haushofer to Father Walsh,
        Mar. 14, 1946.

348   refused to admit—IMT, vol. 9, pp. 692–693.

348   Nuremberg court—Haensel, *Das Gericht vertagt sich,* p. 85.

349   paralyzed by fear—RG 238, Box 182, Ribbentrop Folder, Mar. 26, 1946;
        IMT, vol. 10, p. 93.

349   can't remember it—IMT, vol. 10, p. 147.

349   National Socialism—IMT, vol. 10, p. 110.

349   cannot have it—IMT, vol. 10, p. 136.

349   "typical Nazis"—IMT, vol. 10, pp. 137–138.

349   Rosenberg's office—IMT, vol. 10, p. 129.

350   given by Hitler—IMT, vol. 10, p. 135.

350   were his own—IMT, vol. 10, pp. 186–187.

350   secret agreement—IMT, vol. 10, p. 190.

351   be withdrawn—Ibid.

352   this tribunal—IMT, vol. 10, pp. 191–192.

352   murmured half-heartedly—Haensel, *Das Gericht vertagt sich,* p. 139.

352   additional agreement—IMT, vol. 10, p. 193.

352   was priceless!—Gilbert, p. 224.

352   any good—IMT, vol. 10, p. 278.

353   did you not?—IMT, vol. 10, p. 409.

353   those words—Ibid.

353   concentration camps?—IMT, vol. 10, p. 411.

353   imagined them?—Ibid.

353   Ribbentrop acknowledged—IMT, vol. 10, p. 412.

353   weighed carefully—IMT, vol. 10, p. 361.

354   very much—IMT, vol. 10, p. 394.

354   nothing more—Haensel, *Das Gericht vertagt sich,* p. 140.

354   first time—Fritzsche, p. 165.

354   hopeless task—Ibid., p. 82.

354   this trial—Hyde, p. 513.

355   remarkable case—Hyde, p. 515.

Chapter 40. *"Destiny Took Its Tragic Course": Keitel*

355   he remarked—Keitel, p. 243.

355   of a genius—Int. of Keitel by Hinkel (X).

355   self-abnegation—IMT, vol. 10, p. 626.

355   they received—IMT, vol. 10, p. 470.

356   ideological grounds—IMT, vol. 10, p. 471.

356   are tolerated—IMT, vol. 10, p. 552.

356   fateful consequences—IMT, vol. 10, p. 537.

356   man at all—Gilbert, p. 237.

356   they approved—Lippe, p. 209.

356   to the facts—Biddle Papers, Notes on Evidence, Apr. 5, 1946.

356   been proved—IMT, vol. 10, p. 545.

357   speak for others—IMT, vol. 10, pp. 643–644.

357   shooting them—IMT, vol. 10, p. 646.

358   Keitel shot back—Gilbert, pp. 248–249.

358   absolutely impossible!—Gilbert, p. 244.

358   these things—IMT, vol. 11, p. 24.

358   Keitel acknowledged—IMT, vol. 11, p. 25.

359   or faithless—IMT, vol. 11, p. 27.

359   plain anti-Semitism—IMT, vol. 11, p. 73.

359   stop the presses—IMT, vol. 11, p. 74.

360   that issue—IMT, vol. 11, p. 76

360   contempt of court—IMT, vol. 11, p. 77.

360   by the Germans—IMT, vol. 11, p. 79.

360   this point—IMT, vol. 11, p. 85.

361   like that—IMT, vol. 11, pp. 83–84.

361   entire court—IMT, vol. 11, p. 84.

361   on the facts—IMT, vol. 11, p. 85.

362   violated an order—Biddle Papers, Notes on Evidence, Apr. 9, 1946.

363   Military Tribunal—RG 238, Jackson to War Department, Apr. 8, 1946 (X).

363   on April 9—RG 260, OMGUS, 000.5 War Crimes, Box 2, Jackson to
        AGWAR, Mar. 15, 1946; Charles Fahey to Gen. Clay, Mar. 16, 1946; RG
        84, Box 750, AGWAR to OMGUS, Mar. 23, 1946.

363   sorry for him—Biddle Papers, Notes on Evidence, Apr. 9, 1946.

363   in his house (fn)—Parker Papers, Parker to wife, Nov. 18, 1946.

363   "Sauckel's dream" (fn)—Biddle, *In Brief Authority*, p. 427.

Chapter 41. A Breath of Ashes: Kaltenbrunner

364   incriminating passage—IMT, vol. 11, p. 251.

364   Kaltenbrunner replied—IMT, vol. 11, p. 252.

364   to Müller?—IMT, vol. 11, p. 262.

365   the personnel—IMT, vol. 11, p. 263.

365   to a wedding—Int. of Kaltenbrunner by Brookhart, Oct. 3, 1945.

365   had remarked—Int. of Kaltenbrunner by Brookhart, Oct. 8, 1945.

365   his edification—IMT, vol. 4, pp. 386–390.

366   seen everything—IMT, vol. 11, pp. 322–323.

366   'special treatment'—IMT, vol. 11, pp. 338–339.

367   it was so—IMT, vol. 11, p. 243.

367   signed by me—IMT, vol. 11, p. 366.

367   make speeches—IMT, vol. 11, p. 367.

367   by your hand—IMT, vol. 11, p. 364.

368   never called—Hoettl, p. 314.

368   such action—IMT, vol. 11, p. 305.

368   the responsibility—Int. of Ohlendorf by Brookhart, Nov. 3 and 9, 1945.

369   be refuted—IMT, vol. 11, p. 352.

369   about it—IMT, vol. 11, p. 353.

369   budge an inch—IMT, vol. 11, pp. 354–355.

369   of the Jews—Int. of Jean Marie Musy by Maj. Robert Haythorne, Oct. 26
        and 29, 1945.

370   establish the truth—IMT, vol. 11, pp. 335–336.

371   do you not?—IMT, vol. 11, pp. 348–349.

371   the session—Fritzsche, p. 186.
371   Kauffmann replied—IMT, vol. 11, p. 378.
372   Höss agreed—Int. of Höss by Jaari, Apr. 3, 1946.
372   was going on—Int. of Höss by Jaari, Apr. 8, 1946.
374   must know all!—Int. of Höss and Moll by Brookhart, Apr. 16, 1946.
374   kept a secret—IMT, vol. 11, p. 397.
374   the Reichsführer—IMT, vol. 11, p. 398.
375   Quite correct—IMT, vol. 11, p. 402.
375   on internees—IMT, vol. 11, p. 404.
375   been preserved (fn)—Naumann, p. 157.
375   "humanitarian solution" (fn)—Höss, pp. 137–138.
375   of starvation (fn)—Naumann, pp. 144–145.
375   like butchers (fn)—Ibid., p. 271.
376   assume so—IMT, vol. 11, p. 414.
376   at Auschwitz—IMT, vol. 11, pp. 416–417.
376   the atmosphere—Haensel, *Das Gericht vertagt sich*, p. 183.

Chapter 42. "A Thousand Years of Guilt": Rosenberg and Frank

377   makes me sick!—Gilbert, pp. 347–348.
377   hurting flies—Biddle Papers, Notes on Evidence, Mar. 4, 1946.
377   these countries—IMT, vol. 11, pp. 497–498.
378   their liberty—IMT, vol. 11, pp. 512–513.
378   derelict property—IMT, vol. 7, p. 62.
378   in this case—Int. of Rosenberg by Hinkel, Sept. 25, 1945.
379   conditions of war—IMT, vol. 11, pp. 562–563.
379   yes or no?—IMT, vol. 11, p. 555.
379   other sources—IMT, vol. 11, pp. 561–562.
379   by me too—IMT, vol. 11, p. 516.
379   man's character—Fritzsche, p. 147.
380   been erased!—IMT, vol. 12, p. 13.
380   dramatic confession—Biddle, *In Brief Authority*, p. 446.
380   easily be used—IMT, vol. 12, p. 28.
381   commit suicide (fn)—Int. of Mildner by Brookhart, Oct. 23, 1945.
381   never exist. Never!—IMT, vol. 12, p. 153.
381   fellow Germans?—IMT, vol. 12, p. 155.
381   years of guilt—Fritzsche, p. 205.

Chapter 43. The Venomous Vulgarian: Streicher

382   under anaesthetic—IMT, vol. 5, p. 95.
382   at his word—Int. of Gruppenführer Benno Martin by Brundage, Oct. 19, 1945.
382   on the spot—Int. of Obergruppenführer Karl Wolff by Brundage, Sept. 5, 1945.

382   marks a year—IMT, vol. 12, p. 342; Int. of Martin by Brundage, Oct. 22,
            1945.
383   by a whipping—NCA, 1757 PS, Report of Goering's Commission.
383   lowlife—Int. of Martin by Brundage, Oct. 19 and 20, 1945.
383   been arrested—NCA, 1757 PS, op. cit.
383   Der Stürmer—Höhne, p. 238.
383   girl friend (fn)—Int. of Martin by Brookhart, Nov. 10, 1945.
384   in his cell—Andrus, p. 107.
384   for reflection—RG 238, Box 184, Amen note to Bill Jackson, Apr. 30, 1946.
384   is the case—Int. of Fritz Wiedemann by Lt. John D. Martin, Nov. 10, 1945.
384   by a psychiatrist—IMT, vol. 2, p. 22.
384   mental capacities—IMT, vol. 2, p. 24.
384   something nice?—Gilbert, p. 9.
384   stand trial—IMT, vol. 2, p. 156.
385   perverted by him—IMT, vol. 5, p. 118.
385   Streicher responded—IMT, vol. 12, p. 318.
385   own initiative—IMT, vol. 12, p. 322.
385   Military Tribunal—IMT, vol. 12, p. 306.
385   any journalist—IMT, vol. 12, p. 307.
385   to do that—IMT, vol. 12, p. 336.
386   until the present—IMT, vol. 12, p. 337.
386   the appointment—Parker Papers, Parker to wife, May 5, 1946.
386   contempt of court—IMT, vol. 12, p. 337.
386   better continue—Ibid.
386   religious hatred?—IMT, vol. 12, p. 347.
387   statement of fact—IMT, vol. 12, p. 348.
387   know that?—IMT, vol. 12, pp. 358–359.
387   that, certainly—IMT, vol. 12, p. 360.
387   history of mankind—IMT, vol. 12, p. 367.
388   extermination en masse—IMT, vol. 12, pp. 370–371.
388   I believe it—IMT, vol. 12, pp. 376–377.
388   at Mondorf—IMT, vol. 12, p. 322.
388   middle of 1944—IMT, vol. 12, p. 408.
389   be exterminated—IMT, vol. 12, p. 406.
389   own importance—IMT, vol. 12, pp. 400–401.

Chapter 44. An Irregular Witness: Frick and Schacht

389   administrative brain—IMT, vol. 5, p. 352.
389   law or not—Int. of Frick by Sackett, Oct. 8, 1945.
389   my release—Int. of Frick by Sackett, Sept. 25, 1945.
389   the murdering—IMT, vol. 5, p. 362.
390   killings to death—Haensel, "The Nuremberg Trial Revisited," p. 250.
390   the SS budget—Int. of Frick by Dodd, Sept. 6, 1945.
391   and for Schacht—IMT, vol. 12, p. 357.

391   "blood drenched scoundrel"—Gisevius, p. 367.

392   Goering personally—IMT, vol. 12, p. 169.

392   to be murdered—IMT, vol. 12, p. 170.

393   tell his story—IMT, vol. 12, pp. 176–177.

393   personal etiquette—IMT, vol. 12, pp. 177–178.

393   to Gisevius—IMT, vol. 12, pp. 178–179.

394   Fritsch crisis—IMT, vol. 12, p. 180.

394   our inquiries—IMT, vol. 12, p. 181.

394   a great danger—IMT, vol. 12, p. 191.

395   for himself—IMT, vol. 12, pp. 254–255.

395   all the more—IMT, vol. 12, p. 265.

395   clicking his heels—IMT, vol. 12, pp. 269–271.

395   against Goering—Biddle, *In Brief Authority,* pp. 438–439.

395   whole tradition—Gilbert, p. 297.

396   of his words—Ibid., p. 293.

396   out-and-out opponent—RG 238, Box 183, Memo of Conversation between Jackson, Don Heath, and Capt. Sam Harris, Mar. 29, 1946.

396   for the defense—RG 238, Box 183, Hans Nathan to Capt. Sam Harris, Jan. 2, 1946.

396   often figure—RG 238, Box 183—Sam Harris Memo for Jackson on Schacht cross-examination, Apr. 27, 1946.

396   Nazi ideology—IMT, vol. 12, p. 445.

397   filled auditorium—IMT, vol. 12, p. 451.

397   Germany, and me—IMT, vol. 12, p. 454.

397   threats of Hitler—IMT, vol. 12, p. 458.

397   a hundredfold—IMT, vol. 12, p. 519.

397   against Schacht—Hyde, p. 516.

398   the amendment—IMT, vol. 12, pp. 568–569.

398   the German people—IMT, vol. 12, p. 578.

398   anything different—Ibid.

398   your life—Int. of Schacht by Gurfein, Oct. 16, 1945.

398   have command—IMT, vol. 13, pp. 3–4.

399   be overlooked—IMT, vol. 13, p. 7.

399   lips rouged—IMT, vol. 13, p. 8.

399   brought that up—Gilbert, pp. 314–315.

399   easy or difficult—Schacht, p. 429.

400   by laughter—IMT, vol. 13, p. 28.

400   of injustice—IMT, vol. 13, p. 22.

400   to the donor—IMT, vol. 13, p. 25.

401   Schacht assented—IMT, vol. 13, pp. 22–23.

401   from his cabinet—IMT, vol. 13, p. 34.

401   Biddle thought—Biddle Papers, Notes on Evidence, May 3, 1946.

401   Nazi outrages—Parker Papers, Parker to wife, May 3, 1946.

401   Schacht's defense—Hyde, p. 517.

Chapter 45. Blood on the Gold: Funk

402   bad health—Parker Papers, Parker to wife, May 4, 1946.

402   after all—Int. of Funk by Sackett, Nov. 5, 1945.

402   Funk marveled—Lochner, p. 82.

402   like Funk—Gisevius, p. 221.

403   to protect it—Int. of Funk by Gurfein and Brookhart, Oct. 19, 1945.

403   guilty party here—Int. of Funk by Gurfein, Nov. 8, 1945.

403   also today—IMT, vol. 13, p. 120.

403   with the SS?—IMT, vol. 13, p. 162.

403   finally succeeded—IMT, vol. 13, p. 163.

404   meaning "yes"—IMT, vol. 13, p. 167.

405   and knowledge—IMT, vol. 13, pp. 170–171.

405   called here—IMT, vol. 13, p. 172.

405   these things—IMT, vol. 13, p. 173.

405   said that—no—IMT, vol. 13, p. 176.

405   these events—IMT, vol. 13, pp. 174–175.

406   not understand—IMT, vol. 13, pp. 178–179.

406   Where are they?—RG 238, Box 192, Nuremberg Opera House Program,
        May 7, 1946.

407   details, yes—IMT, vol. 13, p. 570.

407   satisfy us—IMT, vol. 13, pp. 571–572.

407   unusually great—IMT, vol. 13, p. 581.

407   not known—IMT, vol. 13, p. 584.

408   Puhl nodded—IMT, vol. 13, p. 585.

408   could see them—IMT, vol. 13, p. 603.

Chapter 46. A Question of Equivocation: Doenitz and Raeder

410   to retire—Int. of Raeder by Monigan, Nov. 8, 1945.

410   as insane—Egbert Papers, Biographical Reports.

410   in the Atlantic—NCA, C 170—Naval War Diary, Nov. 10, 1939.

410   weakness with us—Int. of Doenitz by Hinkel, Nov. 3, 1945.

411   to retaliate—Int. of Doenitz by Hinkel, Sept. 18, 1945; Shirer, p. 1153.

411   off the rescue—IMT, vol. 13, pp. 282–291; RG 238, Doenitz Interrogation
        File, Memorandum from Lt. Comdr. John P. Bracken to Jackson, Aug.
        24, 1945.

412   German cities—IMT, vol. 13, p. 278.

412   enlisting people—IMT, vol. 13, p. 373.

412   not be increased—IMT, vol. 13, p. 293.

412   U-boat warfare—IMT, vol. 13, p. 279.

412   Allied ship—Lt. Comdr. A. N. Glennon, "The Weapon That Came Too
        Late," United States Naval Institute Proceedings, Mar. 1961, pp. 85–93.

412   taken prisoner—IMT, vol. 13, pp. 267, 295.

413   in his behalf—RG 238, Doenitz Interrogation File, Memorandum from Bracken to Jackson, Aug. 24, 1945, and enclosed Admiralty Report.

413   ships and crews—IMT, vol. 5, p. 220; and NCA, D 630, Extract from Bd U War Diary, Sept. 17, 1942.

413   commanding officers—NCA, 382 PS, Moehle Statement of July 19, 1945.

413   in that way—Ibid.

414   no survivors—IMT, vol. 5, p. 234.

414   Moehle replied—IMT, vol. 5, p. 237.

415   many of them—NCA, D 566, Affidavit of Peter Heisig, Nov. 27, 1945.

415   Cowards! (fn)—RG 238, Heisig Interrogation File, Heisig to Capt. Walther Rapp and Lt. Michael Read, Dec. 5, 1945; Letter to his mother, Dec. 16, 1945.

415   Thank you—IMT, vol. 5, pp. 227–228.

415   never given!—Int. of Doenitz by Hinkel, Sept. 28, 1945.

415   this entry—Int. of Doenitz by Hinkel, Oct. 9, 1945.

415   against me!—Int. of Doenitz by Hinkel, Oct. 22, 1945.

416   my midshipmen—IMT, vol. 13, p. 384.

416   its credibility—Ibid.

416   these thoughts—IMT, vol. 13, p. 385.

416   power of suggestion—IMT, vol. 13, p. 301.

416   stature in Europe—NCA, D 650, Second Baltic Order of the Day, Apr. 19, 1945.

416   false cleverness—Egbert Papers, Doenitz Biographical Report.

416   his leader—RG 238, Box 18, Doenitz Speech to German Youth over Radio, Feb. 20, 1945.

417   doesn't it?—IMT, vol. 13, p. 347.

417   be a leader—NCA, D 650, op. cit.

417   but "spies"—IMT, vol. 13, p. 394.

417   be maintained—RG 238, Doenitz Interrogation File, Memorandum from Bracken to Jackson, Aug. 24, 1945.

417   many survivors—IMT, vol. 17, pp. 378–380.

418   'Hitlerbube Doenitz'—Int. of Raeder by Monigan, Nov. 10, 1945.

418   unsoldierly manner—IMT, vol. 14, p. 225; RG 238, Raeder Interrogation File, Raeder's Moscow statement.

418   months, exploded—Gilbert, p. 346.

418   Otto Nelte—Keitel, p. 235.

419   and a "murderer"—IMT, vol. 5, pp. 264–265.

419   it beforehand—IMT, vol. 14, p. 80.

419   was destroyed—IMT, vol. 17, p. 235.

419   Biddle noted—Biddle Papers, Notes on Evidence, June 3, 1946.

420   will they do?—Haensel, Das Gericht vertagt sich, p. 121.

420   probative value—IMT, vol. 14, p. 284.

Chapter 47. The American: Schirach

422   make speeches—NCA, 1458 PS, Schirach, *The Hitler Youth*, ch. 2.

422   now and ever—IMT, vol. 14, p. 476.

422   nothing else—NCA, 2441 PS, Ziemer, *Education for Death*, p. 48.

423   for Mozart—Fishman, p. 75.

423   prevalent in Vienna—NCA, 1948 PS, Dr. Fischer to the Reichstatthalter in Vienna, Nov. 7, 1940; 1950 PS, Lammers to Schirach, Dec. 3, 1940.

423   European culture—NCA, 3048 PS, Schirach Speech of Sept. 14, 1942.

423   ridiculous price—Grunberger, p. 104.

423   too sentimental!—Fishman, p. 69.

423   Vienna too—Int. of Mildner by Brookhart, Nov. 3, 1945.

424   of democracy—Baldur von Schirach, p. 317.

424   cultural work—IMT, vol. 14, p. 414.

424   condemned to death—IMT, vol. 14, pp. 487–491.

425   himself guilty—IMT, vol. 14, pp. 432–433.

Chapter 48. The Political General: Jodl

425   your temper—Biddle Papers, Notes on Evidence, June 8, 1945.

425   remarkable shrewdness—Hyde, p. 518.

426   thrown at them—IMT, vol. 15, p. 356.

426   preventive war—IMT, vol. 15, p. 394.

426   unscrupulous methods—IMT, vol. 15, p. 479.

426   prisoners of war—IMT, vol. 15, p. 337.

426   human rights—IMT, vol. 15, p. 336.

427   further injustice—IMT, vol. 15, p. 496.

427   of the war—IMT, vol. 15, pp. 506–507.

427   truth in 1914—IMT, vol. 15, p. 507.

427   little faster—IMT, vol. 15, p. 320.

427   me nervous—Gilbert, p. 360.

428   infernal power—IMT, vol. 15, p. 552.

428   different aspect—IMT, vol. 15, pp. 509–510.

428   was a murderer?—IMT, vol. 15, pp. 508–509.

428   Almighty do that—IMT, vol. 15, p. 509.

429   but obedience—vol. 15, p. 383.

Chapter 49. The Fox and the Goat: Speer and Sauckel

429   war machine—IMT, vol. 4, p. 531.

429   am his man—IMT, vol. 3, p. 486.

429   told the court—IMT, vol. 11, p. 607.

429   for Hildebrandt—IMT, vol. 15, p. 2.

430   into another—IMT, vol. 14, pp. 622–623.

430   all his energy—FIAT, Entry 160, Box 12, Speer Interrogation of Aug. 20, 1945.

430   efficiency engineering—IMT, vol. 14, p. 626.

430   at my disposal—IMT, vol. 15, p. 9.

430   it immediately—IMT, vol. 15, p. 166.

430   to Germany—IMT, vol. 3, pp. 432–433.

431   Who appointed them?—IMT, vol. 15, p. 192.

431   allocation appointed them—IMT, vol. 15, p. 193.

431   in that way—Ibid.

431   German laws—IMT, vol. 15, p. 194.

431   correct way—IMT, vol. 15, p. 196.

431   they subordinate—IMT, vol. 15, pp. 197–198.

432   such camps—IMT, vol. 15, p. 198.

432   That is right—IMT, vol. 15, p. 199.

432   were involuntary—IMT, vol. 15, p. 200.

432   impossible proportion—IMT, vol. 15, p. 202.

432   is that right?—IMT, vol. 15, pp. 202–203.

432   concluded rhetorically—IMT, vol. 15, p. 207.

433   largest demand—FIAT, Entry 160, Box 12, Interrogation of June 28, 1945.

433   had acknowledged—Int. of Speer by Gurfein, Oct. 18, 1945; IMT, vol. 3, pp. 486–487.

433   took the stand—Biddle Papers, Notes on Evidence, June 21, 1945.

433   as commission—RG 238, Box 8, CIOS Interrogation of General Georg Thomas, July 11 and 18, 1945.

434   concern of mine—IMT, vol. 16, p. 457.

434   foreign labor—IMT, vol. 16, p. 456.

434   Have a try!—IMT, vol. 9, p. 111.

434   in by Sauckel—Ibid.

434   Nothing doing!—IMT, vol. 3, p. 490.

435   from your side—FIAT, Entry 160, Box 12, Interrogation of Aug. 20, 1945.

435   sharpened measures—NCA 556-13 PS, Sauckel Note for the Files, Jan. 4, 1943.

435   thousand a month—IMT, vol. 16, p. 460.

435   four thousand, a month—NCA, 2520 PS, Approximate Number of Foreigners Put to Work for the German War Effort.

436   grand buildings—IMT, vol. 4, p. 202; Manvell and Fraenkel, *Himmler*, p. 99.

436   his divisions—IMT, vol. 3, p. 463.

436   to be increased—IMT, vol. 16, p. 463.

436   available there—NCA, 3720 PS, Testimony of Albert Speer, Oct. 18, 1945.

437   economic side—IMT, vol. 3, p. 461; NCA, R 129, Pohl to Himmler, Apr. 30, 1942.

437   soon go around—IMT, vol. 3, p. 440.

437   camp labor—Int. of Höss by Brookhart et al., Apr. 5, 1946.

437   increased extent—Int. of Pohl by Brookhart, June 8, 1946.

437   shook his head—Ibid.

438   of the matter—IMT, vol. 16, p. 474.

438   Himmler and Speer—Int. of Pohl by Brookhart (X).

438   transfer necessary—NCA, 1584-I PS, Goering to Himmler, Feb. 14, 1944.

438   of the SS—IMT, vol. 9, p. 103.

439   done in Hungary—Int. of Arthur Scheidler by Jaari, Apr. 10, 1946.

439   men concerned—NCA, 1584-III PS, Speer to Himmler, Apr. 17, 1944.

439   with things—NCA, 3720 PS, op. cit.; IMT, vol. 16, p. 478.

439   his memoirs—Speer, *Inside the Third Reich,* p. 421.

440   his own terms—Ibid., pp. 421–441.

440   looked well fed—IMT, vol. 16, p. 442.

440   official sources—IMT, vol. 16, p. 588.

440   at our disposal—IMT, vol. 16, pp. 443–444.

441   would do so—Speer, *Inside the Third Reich,* pp. 474–475.

442   of the war—NCA, 2222 PS, Headquarters, 12th Army Group, Report of Investigation of Alleged War Crimes, May 25, 1945; Int. of Brandt by Monigan, Sept. 29, 1945; FIAT, Report No. 77 on Speer et. al., Mar. 18, 1946.

442   for Jackson—Parker Papers, Parker to wife, June 9, 1946.

443   practice stopped—Parker Papers, Jackson Press Release, June 10, 1946.

443   himself any—Parker Papers, Parker to wife, June 12 and 14, 1946.

443   with his own—IMT, vol. 16, p. 504.

443   common responsibility—IMT, vol. 16, p. 586.

444   advantage to me—IMT, vol. 16, p. 520.

444   off so easily—Ibid.

444   these conditions—IMT, vol. 16, p. 537.

444   of the regime—IMT, vol. 16, p. 538.

444   these conditions—IMT, vol. 16, p. 545.

444   which are quoted—Ibid.

445   sympathetic character—Fyfe, p. 129.

Chapter 50. Step by Step: Seyss-Inquart, Papen, Neurath, and Fritzsche

446   in his work—NCA, 2219 PS, Seyss-Inquart to Goering, July 14, 1939.

446   also harmless—NCA, 3271 PS, Seyss-Inquart to Himmler, Aug. 19, 1939.

446   Nazi pogrom—IMT, vol. 15, p. 667.

446   the consequences—NCA, 3430 PS, Speech of Mar. 12, 1941.

446   very cleverly—Lochner, p. 475.

446   light touch—Ibid., p. 426.

446   as a result—IMT, vol. 16, p. 192.

447   cease to fight—Egbert Papers, Seyss-Inquart Biographical Report.

447   step by step—IMT, vol. 15, p. 667.

447   of one hundred men—IMT, vol. 15, p. 668.

447   town of Nijmegen—IMT, vol. 15, p. 649.

447   had concluded—Int. of Seyss-Inquart by Dodd, Sept. 18, 1945.

448 racial question—IMT, vol. 16, p. 274.
448 as desirable—IMT, vol. 16, p. 596.
448 Jews to Germans—IMT, vol. 17, p. 166.
448 to do so—Int. of Frick by Sackett, Sept. 2, 1945.
448 of the state—IMT, vol. 16, pp. 292–295.
449 He was shot—IMT, vol. 16, p. 358.
449 Fyfe's question—IMT, vol. 16, p. 362.
449 was put right—IMT, vol. 16, p. 363.
449 Papen squirmed—IMT, vol. 16, p. 364.
449 associates did—IMT, vol. 16, p. 365.
450 Herr von Papen—IMT, vol. 16, p. 416.
450 after I left—IMT, vol. 17, p. 16.
451 German blood—IMT, vol. 17, pp. 64–65.
451 statements today—IMT, vol. 17, p. 66.
451 and the plutocrats—NCA, 3064 PS, Broadcast of Jan. 8, 1944.
452 to be criminal—IMT, vol. 17, p. 138.
452 five million people—IMT, vol. 17, p. 181.
452 continue to exist—Ibid.

Chapter 51. The Katyn Forest Massacre

452 fascist invaders—IMT, vol. 7, p. 425.
453 of the charter—Biddle Papers, Notes on Evidence, Mar. 13, 1946.
453 unreasonable in itself—Biddle Papers, Notes on Conference, Apr. 6, 1946.
454 to be dropped—Lochner, p. 354.
454 exterminate the Poles—IMT, vol. 17, p. 325.

Chapter 52. The Poisoned Chalice: The Case of the Organizations

455 ruthless war—IMT, vol. 8, pp. 354–355.
455 and punishment—IMT, vol. 8, p. 356.
456 individuals is known—IMT, vol. 8, p. 434.
456 own population—IMT, vol. 8, p. 435.
456 affected thereby—IMT, vol. 8, p. 434.
456 housekeeping functions—IMT, vol. 8, p. 446; RG 238, Box 198, Assistant Secretary of War Howard C. Petersen to Jackson, Feb. 18, 1946.
456 practically nil—RG 238, Box 198, Petersen to Jackson, Feb. 18, 1946.
456 the tribunal—Biddle Papers, Notes on Conference, Final Report by Neave, Aug. 15, 1946.
457 concentration camps—IMT, vol. 20, pp. 314–317.
458 nothing at all—IMT, vol. 21, pp. 241–243.
458 war machine—IMT, vol. 20, pp. 439–440.
459 end of 1944—IMT, vol. 20, p. 479.
459 not be released—IMT, vol. 20, p. 497.
460 come about—IMT, vol. 20, pp. 492–493.

460   the Jews—IMT, vol. 20, pp. 494–495.

460   of all this—IMT, vol. 20, p. 495.

460   them individually—IMT, vol. 20, p. 502.

461   of the prisoners—IMT, vol. 20, p. 504.

461   Morgen responded—IMT, vol. 20, p. 505.

461   ask that question—IMT, vol. 20, p. 504.

461   this extermination—IMT, vol. 20, p. 505.

462   these orders—IMT, vol. 20, p. 506.

462   is criminal—IMT, vol. 21, p. 588.

462   heart and mind—IMT, vol. 21, p. 604.

462   bitterly bear—IMT, vol. 21, p. 618.

463   Adolf Hitler—IMT, vol. 21, p. 573.

463   intellectual fields—IMT, vol. 21, p. 569.

463   emphasis was laid—IMT, vol. 21, p. 570.

463   RSHA (Gestapo)—IMT, vol. 21, p. 598.

463   own disaster—IMT, vol. 22, p. 82.

463   very courtroom—IMT, vol. 22, p. 90.

463   for all evil—IMT, vol. 21, p. 500.

463   concentration camps—IMT, vol. 21, p. 519.

464   he asserted—IMT, vol. 21, p. 533.

464   after another—IMT, vol. 22, p. 21.

465   and his guilt—IMT, vol. 22, pp. 262–263.

465   written true—IMT, vol. 22, p. 297.

465   Biddle expatiated—IMT, vol. 20, p. 494; Biddle, *In Brief Authority*, p. 464.

465   of the contamination—Hyde, p. 518.

466   and stiff—Biddle, *In Brief Authority*, p. 398.

466   have bodies—Ibid., p. 421.

466   more vodka—Ibid., p. 423.

466   for breakfast—Ibid.

466   quite overpowering—Hyde, p. 521.

Chapter 53. "A Mad and Melancholy Record"

466   the true God—IMT, vol. 18, p. 40.

467   to be dealing—IMT, vol. 18, p. 43.

467   his publications—IMT, vol. 18, p. 69.

467   mental cramp—IMT, vol. 18, p. 219.

467   dry and prosaic—IMT, vol. 18, p. 220.

467   war criminal—IMT, vol. 18, p. 430.

467   have been done—IMT, vol. 18, p. 495.

467   rather convincing—IMT, vol. 18, p. 356.

468   state of affairs—IMT, vol. 18, p. 270.

468   political error—IMT, vol. 18, p. 272.

468   will remain—IMT, vol. 17, pp. 606–607

469   doom of civilization—IMT, vol. 19, p. 397.

469   to be crimes—IMT, vol. 19, p. 399.

469   makes it so—IMT, vol. 19, p. 400.

469   willing tool—IMT, vol. 19, p. 415.

471   Allied airmen—IMT, vol. 19, pp. 416–417.

471   every man in it—IMT, vol. 19, p. 424.

472   Julius Streicher—IMT, vol. 19, p. 426.

472   without reason—IMT, vol. 19, p. 429.

472   in the dock—IMT, vol. 19, p. 430.

472   concentration camps—IMT, vol. 19, p. 431.

472   and evasions—IMT, vol. 19, pp. 431–432.

472   been no crime—IMT, vol. 19, p. 432.

473   with the prosecution—Gilbert, p. 422.

Chapter 54. Epitaph on Ideals

473   outward fortitude—Hyde, pp. 521–522.

473   cried Hosannah!—IMT, vol. 22, p. 405.

473   live together—IMT, vol. 22, pp. 406–407.

474   German people?—IMT, vol. 22, pp. 384–385.

474   brilliantly successful—IMT, vol. 22, p. 389.

474   through my fault—IMT, vol. 22, p. 390.

475   measure my fate—IMT, vol. 22, p. 396.

475   or mistreatment—IMT, vol. 22, p. 397.

475   were my foes—IMT, vol. 22, p. 398.

475   in the war—IMT, vol. 22, p. 399.

475   German people—IMT, vol. 22, p. 378.

476   towards humanity—IMT, vol. 22, p. 400.

476   bravely too—Hyde, p. 522.

476   what ideals!—Biddle Papers, Notes on Evidence, Aug. 31, 1946.

476   to prevent them—IMT, vol. 22, p. 366.

476   and its life—IMT, vol. 22, p. 368.

476   been indicted—IMT, vol. 1, pp. 166–167: Report of Prison Psychologist on
       Mental Competence of Defendant Hess, Aug. 17, 1946.

477   toward madness—IMT, vol. 22, pp. 368–370.

477   "Stop! Stop!"—Fritzsche, p. 317.

477   his speech—IMT, vol. 22, p. 372.

478   questions to me—Ibid.

478   me innocent—IMT, vol. 22, p. 373.

478   will be announced—IMT, vol. 22, p. 410.

Chapter 55. Deliberation

481   very much—Schacht, p. 442.

481   until 1950 (fn)—RG 260, OMGUS, 000.5 War Crimes, Box 3.

482   anything up—Fritzsche, p. 315.

482   in Valhalla!—Ibid., p. 314.

482   we're hanged—Baldur von Schirach, p. 333.

483   about this?—Biddle Papers, Box 1, Biddle to Herbert Wechsler, July 10, 1946.

483   all peradventure—Biddle, p. 468.

483   Nazi regime?—Biddle Papers, Notes on Judgment, Aug. 15, 1946.

483   Führer principle—Parker Papers, Herbert Wechsler Comment on Lawrence's Memorandum, "The Form of the Judgment and Opinion," April 12, 1946.

483   aggressive war—Biddle Papers, Notes on Judgment, Aug. 19, 1946.

484   and unsatisfactory—IMT, vol. 8, pp. 217–218; Biddle Papers, Notes on Evidence, Feb. 25, 1946.

484   embracing them all—IMT, vol. 1, p. 225.

485   justice impartially—Biddle Papers, Notes on Judgment, Sept. 3 and 13, 1946; Biddle, *In Brief Authority*, pp. 469–473; IMT, vol. 1, pp. 256–257.

486   Goering on this—Biddle Papers, Defendants, Summary of Evidence, Rowe Memorandum on Goering.

486   of the Jews—Parker Papers, Box 60, Parker Draft on Goering.

486   other races—Biddle Papers, Defendants, Summary of Evidence, Rowe Memorandum on Goering.

486   him to death—Biddle Papers, Notes on Judgment, Meetings on Individuals, Sept. 2, 10, and 11, 1946.

486   should be hanged—Ibid.

487   imprisoned for life—Ibid.

487   and Seyss-Inquart—Ibid.

487   made the plans—Biddle Papers, Defendants, Summary of Evidence, Stewart Memorandum on Rosenberg.

487   team's success—Biddle Papers, Defendants, Summary of Evidence, Stewart Memorandum on Streicher.

487   than Himmler—Parker Papers, Box 60, Unsigned Memorandum on Seyss-Inquart.

487   be appropriate—Biddle Papers, Notes on Judgment, Meetings on Individuals, Sept. 10 and 11, 1946.

487   death by hanging—Ibid.

487   life imprisonment—Ibid.

488   be dismissed—Biddle Papers, Notes on Judgment, Meeting on Individuals, Sept. 9, 1946.

489   done himself—Biddle Papers, Defendants, Summary of Evidence, Rowe Memorandum on Doenitz.

489   than we did—Biddle Papers, Notes on Judgment, Meeting on Individuals, Sept. 9, 1946.

489   received life—Ibid.

489   to their death—Biddle Papers, Defendants, Summary of Evidence, Fisher Memorandum on Sauckel.

489   he was doing—Biddle Papers, Defendants, Summary of Evidence, Fisher Memorandum on Speer.

490   was agreed upon—Biddle Papers, Notes on Judgment, Meeting on Individuals, Sept. 11, 1946.

490   was approved—Biddle Papers, Defendants, Summary of Evidence, Unsigned Memorandum on Schirach; Notes on Judgment, Meeting on Individuals, Sept. 9, 1946.

490   fifteen years—Biddle Papers, Notes on Judgment, Meeting on Individuals, Sept. 11, 1946.

490   to wage war—Parker Papers, Box 60; Biddle Papers, Defendants, Summary of Evidence, Fisher Memorandum on Schacht.

490   Birkett declared—Biddle Papers, Notes on Judgment, Meeting on Individuals, Sept. 6, 1946.

491   eight years—Biddle Papers, Notes on Judgment, Meeting on Individuals, Sept. 11, 1946.

491   as acquittal—Biddle Papers, Notes on Judgment, Meetings on Individuals, Sept. 6 and 11, 1946.

491   adjudged not guilty—Biddle Papers, Notes on Judgment, Meetings on Individuals, Sept. 9 and 11, 1946.

492   to an acquittal—Biddle Papers, Notes on Judgment, Meeting on Individuals, Sept. 13, 1946.

Chapter 56. Verdict

493   of the whole—IMT, vol. 1, p. 186.

493   go unpunished—IMT, vol. 1, p. 219.

493   they were doing—IMT, vol. 1, p. 226.

493   criminal calculation—IMT, vol. 1, pp. 226–227.

494   misfortune to know—IMT, vol. 1, pp. 278–279.

495   for this man—IMT, vol. 1, p. 282.

495   were committed—IMT, vol. 1, p. 284.

495   National Socialist creed—IMT, vol. 1, pp. 287–288.

495   or justification—IMT, vol. 1, p. 291.

495   until the end—IMT, vol. 1, p. 296.

495   three million Jews—IMT, vol. 1, p. 298.

495   to stop them—IMT, vol. 1, p. 301.

496   Crime Against Humanity—IMT, vol. 1, p. 304.

496   in the Reichsbank—IMT, vol. 1, p. 306.

496   presently adjourns—IMT, vol. 1, p. 310.

496   strongest censure—IMT, vol. 1, p. 313.

496   in mitigation—IMT, vol. 1, p. 325.

496   these may be—IMT, vol. 1, p. 327.

497   production facilities—IMT, vol. 1, pp. 331–333.

497   crimes charged—IMT, vol. 1, p. 338.

497   death by hanging—IMT, vol. 1, p. 365.

Chapter 57. Execution

498   been spared—Gilbert, pp. 431–433.

498   death penalty—Speer, *Spandau,* pp. 1, 2.

500   he inquired—Jodl, p. 318.

500   Allied Control Council—Ibid., p. 319.

500   him a martyr—Biddle Papers, Appeals from Judgment, Franz Exner and
       Hermann Jahrreiss for Jodl.

500   the signature—Biddle Papers, Appeals from Judgment, Gustav Steinbauer
       for Seyss-Inquart.

501   friend of Hitler—Biddle Papers, Appeals from Judgment, Robert Servatius
       for Sauckel.

501   of his character—Biddle Papers, Appeals from Judgment, Alfred Thoma
       for Rosenberg.

501   Baltic countries—Biddle Papers, Appeals from Judgment, Alfred Seidl for
       Frank and Hess.

501   to the prosecution—RG 2600, OMGUS, 000.5 War Crimes, Box 3, Jackson
       to Petersen, Sept. 17, 1946.

502   truly was—Haensel, *Das Gericht vertagt sich,* p. 167.

502   why torture him?—Andrus, p. 104.

503   more difficult—Ibid., p. 179.

503   proud of him—Jodl, pp. 320–333.

504   cyanide capsule—Baldur von Schirach, p. 336.

504   he was dead—Andrus, p. 190.

505   "Bravo, Streicher!"—Speer, *Spandau,* p. 10.

505   interpreter repeated—Andrus, p. 193.

505   von Ribbentrop!—Ibid., p. 194.

505   demanded superfluously—Ibid.

505   East and West—Ibid., p. 195.

506   "Purim Festival, 1946!"—Ibid., p. 197.

506   believe in Germany—Ibid.

506   declared dead—RG 84, U. S. Political Adviser for Germany, Box 750, Oct.
       16, 1945, lists the times of execution and deaths of all the condemned.

Chapter 58. Requiem for the Reich

507   he was dead—Papen, p. 555.

507   test of history—IMT, vol. 19, p. 221.

508   had reappeared—Kersten, pp. 165–166.

509   entire offspring—Hitler, pp. 246–247.

509   this question—Ibid., p. 250.

509   racial instincts—Ibid., p. 256.

510   conversations of others—Carney Landis & Marjorie Bolles, *Textbook of
       Abnormal Psychology* (New York: Macmillan, 1950), p. 218.

510   fact and fancy—Ibid.

510   quite obvious—Ibid., p. 220.

510   or tremulous—Ibid., p. 221.

511   a senile man—FIAT, Entry 160, Box 12, Speer Monograph for O. Hoeff-
       ding, Aug. 1, 1945.

511   stark crazy!—Int. of Wiedemann by Lt. John B. Martin, Nov. 10, 1945.

511   his intentions—Int. of Scheidt by Hinkel, Nov. 7, 1945.

511   he went on—Int. of Lahousen by Amen, Sept. 19, 1945.

511   what he wanted—Int. of Keitel by Dodd, Oct. 10, 1945.

511   end of 1941—Int. of Geyr von Schweppenburg in POW camp, Aug. 7,
       1945.

512   of all beings—NCA, 789 PS, Conference with the Führer, Nov. 23, 1939.

512   people inmates—Int. of von Moyland by Brundage (X).

513   a free choice—FIAT, Speer Monograph, op. cit.

513   usage of warfare—NCA, 1676 PS, A Word on the Enemy Air Terror, May
       28–29, 1944.

515   personal angle—Douglas-Hamilton, p. 106.

515   moral abominations—Kraus, p. 234.

515   western Allies—Kranzbühler, "Nuremberg, Eighteen Years Afterwards,"
       p. 347.

516   inexpressible misery—Theodor Klefisch in *Juristische Rundschau*, Aug. 1947,
       pp. 45–49.

516   nor his subordinates—Otto Kranzbühler in Benton & Grimm, p. 120.

516   past and present—Ibid., p. 119.

516   of nationality—Kraus, pp. 236–237.

516   the SS, declared—Haensel, "The Nuremberg Trial Revisited," p. 251.

516   active investigation—RG 238, Box 38, Jackson to War Department, May 4,
       1946.

516   from my viewpoint—RG 238, Box 38, Jackson to War Department, Feb.
       11, 1946.

516   for a decision—RG 260 OMGUS, 000.5 War Crimes, Box 3, OCC Budget
       Estimates, Aug. 8, 1946; Memorandum of Maj. Gen. H. R. Bull, GSC
       Chief of Staff, Aug. 24, 1946.

517   their property—Bosch, p. 84.

517   name of the U.S.—Ibid., p. 83.

517   the accused—Appleman, p. 180.

517   mental attitude—Interview with General Taylor; Appleman, p. 190.

518   the Soviet zone—RG 260 OMGUS, 000.5 War Crimes, Box 2, Memoran-
       dum of Ben A. Smith Jr., Chief, War Crimes Branch, Oct. 31, 1946.

518   scot free—Hilberg, pp. 710, 715.

518   still in jail—Ibid., pp. 696–698.

518   or disappeared—Höhne, p. 581.

518   had been freed—Hilberg, p. 701.

519   of my life—*Los Angeles Times*, Sept. 2, 1981.

520   for release—Speer, *Spandau*, p. 470.

520   criminal law—Biddle Papers, Trial Documents, Biddle Report to President Truman, Nov. 9, 1946.

520   criminal code—*History of United Nations War Crimes Commission*, (London: H. M. Stationery Office, 1948), p. 260.

520   the Nazi regime—Richard Kluger, *Simple Justice*, (New York: Alfred A. Knopf, 1976), p. 690.

522   as at Ravensbrück—IMT, vol. 6, p. 286.

523   freedom from fear—IMT, vol. 21, p. 617.

523   errors of man—Karl S. Bader, Professor of Jurisprudence at the University of Mainz, in Benton & Grimm, p. 154.

523   progress of mankind—IMT, vol. 5, p. 426.

Bibliography

Andrus, Burton, C. *I Was the Nuremberg Jailer* (New York: Coward, McCann & Geoghegan, 1969).

Appleman, John Alan. *Military Tribunals and International Crimes* (Indianapolis and New York: Bobbs-Merrill Co., 1954).

Arendt, Hannah. *Eichmann in Jerusalem* (New York: Viking Press, 1963).

Armstrong, John A. *Soviet Partisans in World War II* (Madison: University of Wisconsin Press, 1964).

Aronson, Shlomo. *Reinhard Heydrich und die Frühgeschichte von Gestapo und SD* (Stuttgart: Deutsche Verlagsanstalt, 1971).

Bach-Zelewski, Erich von dem. *Leben eines SS Generals* (New York: Aufbau [Reconstruction], 1946).

Benton, Wilbour, and Grimm, George, eds. *German Views of the War Trials* (Dallas: Southern Methodist University Press, 1955).

Berthold, Will. *Brigade Dirlewanger* (Aktueller Buchverlag, 1961).

Best, S. Payne. *The Venlo Incident* (London: Hutchinson, 1950).

Bewley, Charles. *Hermann Goering and the Third Reich* (New York: Devin-Adair Co., 1962).

Biddle, Francis. *A Casual Past* (Garden City, N.Y.: Doubleday, 1961).

———. *In Brief Authority* (Garden City, N.Y.: Doubleday, 1962).

Böberach, Heinz. *Meldungen aus dem Reich* (Neuwied and Berlin: Hermann Luchterhand Verlag, 1965).

Bosch, William J. *Judgment on Nuremberg* (Chapel Hill: University of North Carolina Press, 1970).

Bräutigam, Otto. *So hat es sich zugetragen* (Würzburg: Holzner Verlag, 1968).

Bross, Werner. *Gespräche mit Hermann Goering während der Nürnberger Prozesse* (Flensburg and Hamburg: Wolff Verlag, 1960).

Broszat, Martin. *German National Socialism* (Santa Barbara: Clio Press, 1966).

Brown, Anthony C. *Bodyguard of Lies* (New York: Harper & Row, 1975).

Buchheim, Hans. *SS und Polizei im Nationalsozialistischen Staat* (Selbstverlag der Studiengesellschaft für Zeitprobleme, 1964).

Buchheim, Hans, et al. *Anatomy of the SS State* (New York: Walker & Co., 1968).

Calvocoressi, Peter. *Nuremberg* (New York: Macmillan, 1948).

Cecil, Robert. *The Myth of the Master Race: Alfred Rosenberg and Nazi Ideology* (New York: Dodd, Mead & Co., 1972).

Ciano, Count Galeazzo. *Ciano's Diary* (London and Toronto: Heinemann, 1947).

Clark, Alan. *Barbarossa* (New York: William Morrow & Co., 1965).

Cohn, Norman. *Warrant for Genocide* (New York: Harper & Row, 1967).

Crankshaw, Edward. *Gestapo* (New York: Viking Press, 1956).

Cyprian, T. *Nazi Rule in Poland* (Warsaw: Polonia, 1961).

Dahlerus, Birger. *The Last Attempt* (London: Hutchinson, 1948).

Dallin, Alexander. *German Rule in Russia* (New York: Macmillan, 1957).

Davidson, Eugene. *The Trial of the Germans* (New York: Macmillan, 1967).

Dawidowicz, Lucy. *The War Against the Jews* (New York: Holt, Rinehart & Winston, 1975).

Degrelle, Leon. *Die Verlorene Legion* (Stuttgart: Veritas Verlag, 1955).

Delarue, Jacques. *The History of the Gestapo* (London: Macdonald, 1964).

Dennett, Raymond, ed., *Negotiating with the Russians* (Boston: World Peace Foundation, 1951).

De Vabres, Donnedieu. *Le Procès de Nuremberg* (Paris: Editions Montchrestien, 1947).

Dicks, Henry V. *Licensed Mass Murder* (London: Sussex University Press, 1972).

Diels, Rudolf. *Lucifer ante Portas* (Stuttgart: Deutsche Verlagsanstalt, 1950).

Dixon, Aubrey C., and Heilbronn, Otto. *Communist Guerrilla Warfare* (New York: Frederick A. Praeger, 1955).

Dodd, Thomas J. "The Nuremberg Trials," *Journal of Criminal Law and Criminology*, vol. 37 (January 1947).

Doenitz, Karl. *The Doenitz Memoirs* (Cleveland and New York: World Publishing Co., 1959).

Douglas-Hamilton, James. *Motive for a Mission* (London: Macmillan-St. Martin's Press, 1971).

Dulles, Allen. *Germany's Underground* (New York: Macmillan, 1947).

Ehrhardt, Helmut. *Euthanasie und Vernichtung Lebensunwerten Lebens* (Stuttgart: 1965).

Eisenbach, Arthur. *Operation Reinhard* (Poznan: Instytut Zachodni).

Erhard, Hans. "The Nuremberg Trial against the Major War Criminals and International Law," *American Journal of International Law*, vol. 43 (April 1949).

Fest, Joachim C. *The Face of the Third Reich* (New York: Pantheon Books, 1970).

———. *Hitler* (New York: Harcourt Brace Jovanovich, 1974).

Fishman, Jack. *The Seven Men of Spandau* (London: W.H. Allen, 1954).

Fitzgibbons, Louis. *Katyn* (London: Tom Stacey, 1971).

Ford, Corey. *Donovan of OSS* (Boston: Little, Brown, 1970).

Frank, Hans. *Das Dienstagebuch des Deutschen Generalgouverneurs in Polen, 1939–1945* (Stuttgart: Deutsche Verlagsanstalt, 1975).

———. *Im Angesicht des Galgens* (Munich: Beck Verlag, 1953).

Frischauer, Willi. *Hermann Goering* (New York: Ballantine Books, 1951).

Fritzsche, Hans. *The Sword in the Scales* (London: Allan Wingate, 1953).

Fyfe, Maxwell (Earl of Kilmuir). *Political Adventure: The Memoirs of the Earl of Kilmuir* (London: Weidenfeld & Nicolson, 1964).

Galland, Adolf. *The First and the Last* (New York: Ballantine Books, 1957).

Gallo, Max. *The Night of Long Knives* (New York: Harper & Row, 1972).

Gerhart, Eugene C. *Robert H. Jackson, America's Advocate* (Indianapolis and New York: Bobbs-Merrill, 1958).

Gilbert, G. M. *Nuremberg Diary* (New York: Farrar, Straus & Co., 1947).

Gisevius, Hans Bernd. *To the Bitter End* (Boston: Houghton Mifflin Co., 1947).

Goodspeed, D. J. *Ludendorff* (Boston: Houghton Mifflin Co., 1966).

Göring, Emmy. *My Life with Göring* (London: David Bruce and Watson, 1972).

Grunberger, Richard. *The Twelve Year Reich*. (New York: Holt, Rinehart & Winston, 1971).

Haensel, Carl. *Das Gericht vertagt sich* (Hamburg: Claasen Verlag, 1950).

———. "The Nuremberg Trial Revisited," *De Paul Law Review*, vol. 13 (1963).

Halder, General Franz. *Hitler as Warlord* (London: Putnam. 1950).

Harris, Whitney. *Tyranny on Trial* (Dallas: Southern Methodist University Press, 1954).

Hassell, Ulrich von. *The Von Hassell Diaries, 1938–1944* (Garden City, N.Y.: Doubleday, 1947).

Hausser, Paul. *Waffen SS im Einsatz* (Göttingen: Plesse Verlag, 1953).

Heiden, Konrad. *Der Führer* (Boston: Houghton Mifflin Co., 1944).

Hess, Ilse. *Prisoner of Peace* (London: Britons, 1954).

Heydecker, Joe, and Leeb, Johannes. *The Nuremberg Trials* (London: Heinemann, 1962).

Hilberg, Raul. *The Destruction of the European Jews* (Chicago: Quadrangle Books, 1961).

Hitler, Adolf. *Mein Kampf* (Boston: Houghton Mifflin Co., 1943).

Höhne, Heinz. *The Order of the Death's Head* (New York: Coward, McCann & Geoghegan, 1970).

Höss, Rudolf. *Commandant of Auschwitz* (London: Weidenfeld and Nicolson, 1953).

Hoettl, Wilhelm. *The Secret Front* (London: Weidenfeld and Nicolson, 1953).

Hoffmann, Heinrich. *Hitler Was My Friend* (London: Burke, 1955).

Horthy, Admiral Nicholas. *Memoirs* (London: Hutchinson, 1956).

Hossbach, Friedrich. *Zwischen Wehrmacht und Hitler, 1934–1938* (Wolfenbütteler Verlagsanstalt, 1949).

Hyde, H. Montgomery. *Norman Birkett* (London: Hamish Hamilton, 1964).

International Military Tribunal. *Trial of the Major War Criminals* (Nuremberg, 1947). (42 volumes.)

Jackson, Robert H. *The Nuernberg Case* (New York: Alfred A. Knopf, 1947).

———. *Report of the United States Representative to the International Conference on Military Tribunals* (Washington, D.C.: Department of State, 1949).

Jewish Black Book Committee. *The Black Book* (New York: Duell, Sloan & Pearce, 1946).

Jodl, Luise. *Jenseits des Endes* (Vienna, Munich, Zurich: Verlag Fritz Molden, 1976).

Justiz und Nationalsozialistisches Verbrechen (Amsterdam: University Press, vols. 1–10).

Kalnoky, Ingeborg. *The Guest House* (Indianapolis and New York: Bobbs-Merrill Co., 1974).

Keitel, Wilhelm. *The Memoirs of Field Marshal Keitel* (New York: Stein & Day, 1966).

Kelley, Douglas M. *Twenty-two Cells in Nuremberg* (New York: Greenberg Publisher, 1947).

Kempner, R. W. *Eichmann und Komplizen* (Stuttgart: Europa Verlag, 1961).

———. *SS im Kreuzverhör* (Munich: Rütten & Loening Verlag, 1964).

Kersten, Felix. *The Kersten Memoirs* (London: Hutchinson, 1956).

Kesselring, Albert. *A Soldier's Record* (New York: William Morrow & Co., 1954).

Kintner, Earl, ed. *Hadamar Trial of Alfons Klein et al.* (London: William Hodge, 1948).

Kogon, Eugen. *The Theory and Practice of Hell* (London: Secker & Warburg, 1951).

Komorowsky, Eugen. *Night Never Ending* (Chicago: Joseph L. Gilmore, 1974).

Kordt, Erich. *Wahn und Wirklichkeit* (Stuttgart: Union Deutsche Verlags Gesellschaft, 1947).

Kramarz, Joachim. *Stauffenberg* (New York: Macmillan, 1967).

Kranzbühler, Otto. "Nuremberg, Eighteen Years Afterwards," *De Paul Law Review,* vol. 14 (1964).

Kraus, Herbert. "The Nuremberg Trial of the Major War Criminals, Recollections after Seventeen Years," *De Paul Law Review,* vol. 13 (1963).

Krüger, Dr. Kurt. *I Was Hitler's Doctor* (New York: Biltmore Publishing Co., 1941).

Kruuse, Jens. *Oradour sur Glane* (Fayard, 1969).

Kubizek, August. *Young Hitler* (London: Alan Wingate, 1954).

Kurland, Philip B. "Robert H. Jackson" in *The Justices of the Supreme Court,* vol. iv; Leon Friedman and Fred L. Israel, eds.

Lang, Jochen von. *The Secretary: Martin Bormann* (New York: Random House, 1979).

Langbein, Hermann. *Der Auschwitz Prozess* (Frankfurt: Europäische Verlaganstalt, 1965).

Laternser, Hans. *Verteidigung Deutscher Soldaten* (Bonn: Girardet Verlag, 1950).

Lawrence, Lord Justice. "The Nuremberg Trial," *International Affairs,* vol. 23 (April 1947).

Le Chêne, Evelyn. *Mauthausen* (London: Methuen & Co., 1971).

Lerner, Daniel. *The Nazi Elite* (Stanford: Stanford University Press, 1951).

Leventhal, Harold, et al. "The Nuremberg Verdict," *Harvard Law Review,* July 1947.

Levin, Nora. *The Holocaust* (New York: Thomas Y. Crowell Co., 1965).

Lippe, Viktor von der. *Nürnberger Tagebuch Notizen* (Frankfurt-am-Main, 1951).

Lochner, Louis P., ed. *The Goebbels Diaries* (New York: Doubleday, 1948).

Manchester, William. *The Arms of Krupp* (New York: Bantam Books, 1970).

Manvell, Roger, and Fraenkel, Heinrich *Dr. Goebbels* (New York: Simon & Schuster, 1960).

———. *Hess* (London: McGibbon & Kee, 1971).

———. *Himmler* (New York: G. P. Putnam's Sons, 1965).

———. *The Men Who Tried to Kill Hitler* (New York: Coward, McCann & Geoghegan, 1964).

Mendelsohn, John. *Trial by Document* (Washington, D.C.: unpublished Ph.D. thesis in National Archives Library, 1974).

Miale, Florence. *The Nuremberg Mind* (New York: New York Times Book Co., Quadrangle Books, 1975).

Morgenthau, Henry G. *Germany Is Our Problem* (New York: Harper & Brothers, 1945).

Mosley, Leonard. *The Reich Marshal* (Garden City, N.Y.: Doubleday, 1974).

Musmanno, Michael A. *The Eichmann Kommandos* (Philadelphia: MacRae Smith Co., 1961).

Naumann, Bernd. *Auschwitz* (New York: Frederick A. Praeger, 1966).

Nazi Conspiracy and Aggression (Washington, D.C.: U. S. Government Printing Office, 1947). (10 volumes.)

Neave, Airey. *Nuremberg* (London: Hodder & Stoughton, 1978).

Nelte, Otto. *Das Nürnberger Urteil und die Schuld der Generale* (Hannover: Verlag des Anderen Deutschlands, 1947).

Organisationsbuch der NSDAP (Munich: Zentralverlag der NSDAP, 1938).

Pannenbecker, Otto. "The Nuremberg War Crimes Trial," *De Paul Law Review,* vol. 14 (1964).

Papen, Franz von. *Memoirs* (New York: E. P. Dutton & Co., 1953).

Parker, John J. "The Nuremberg Trial," *Journal of the American Judicature Society*, vol. 30 (December 1946).

Pearlman, Moshe. *The Capture and Trial of Adolf Eichmann* (New York: Simon & Schuster, 1963).

Picker, Henry. *Hitler's Table Talk* (London: Weidenfeld & Nicolson, 1953).

Raeder, Erich. *My Life* (Annapolis: U. S. Naval Institute, 1960).

Rauschning, Hermann. *The Voice of Destruction* (New York: G. P. Putnam's Sons, 1940).

Reed, Douglas. *The Burning of the Reichstag* (London: Victor Gollancz, 1934).

Rees, John R., editor. *The Mind of Rudolf Hess* (New York: W. W. Norton, 1948).

Reitlinger, Gerald. *The Final Solution* (New York: Beechurst Press, 1953).

———. *The House Built on Sand* (New York: Viking Press, 1960).

———. *The SS, Alibi of a Nation* (London: Heinemann, 1956).

Ribbentrop, Joachim von. *The Ribbentrop Memoirs* (London: Weidenfeld & Nicolson, 1953).

Ritter, Gerhard. *The German Resistance* (New York: Frederick A. Praeger, 1958).

Schacht, Hjalmar. *Account Settled* (London: Weidenfeld & Nicolson, 1948).

———. *Confessions of the Old Wizard* (Boston: Houghton Mifflin Co., 1956).

Schellenberg, Walter. *The Schellenberg Memoirs* (London: Andre Deutsch, 1956).

Schirach, Baldur von. *Ich glaubte an Hitler* (Hamburg: Mosaik Verlag, 1967).

Schirach, Henriette. *Der Preis der Herrlichkeit* (Wiesbaden: Limes Verlag, 1956).

Schlabrendorff, Fabian von. *The Secret War Against Hitler* (New York: G. P. Putnam's Sons, 1965).

Schmidt, Paul. *Hitler's Interpreter* (London: Heinemann, 1951).

Shirer, William L. *The Rise and Fall of the Third Reich* (New York: Fawcett Publications, 1960).

Smith, Bradley. *Reaching Judgment at Nuremberg* (New York: Basic Books, 1976).

Speer, Albert. *Inside the Third Reich* (New York: Avon Books, 1971).

———. *Spandau* (New York: Pocket Books, 1977).

Steinbauer, Gustav. *Ich war Verteidiger in Nürnberg* (Klagenfurt: E. Kaiser Verlag, 1950).

Steinbock, Johann. *Das Ende von Dachau* (Österreicher Kulturverlag, 1948).

Steiner, Jean. *Treblinka* (New York: Simon & Schuster, 1967).

Stimson, Henry L. "The Nuremberg Trial, Landmark in Law," *Foreign Affairs*, vol. 25 (January 1947).

Stimson, Henry L., and Bundy, McGeorge. *On Active Service in Peace and War* (New York: Harper & Brothers, 1947).

Storey, Robert. *The Final Judgment* (San Antonio: Naylor Co., 1958).

Taylor, Telford. *Final Report to the Secretary of the Army* (Washington, D.C.: U. S. Government Printing Office, 1949).

———. *Munich* (New York: Doubleday, 1979).

———. *Nürnberg and Vietnam* (Chicago: Quadrangle Books, 1970).

———. *Sword and Swastika* (New York: Simon & Schuster, 1952).

———. *War Crimes and International Law* (Carnegie Endowment for International Peace, no. 450, April 1949).

Tobias, Fritz. *The Reichstag Fire* (New York: G. P. Putnam's Sons, 1964).

Toland, John. *Adolf Hitler* (New York: Ballantine Books, 1977).

Trials of War Criminals before the Nuremberg Military Tribunals (Washington, D.C.: U. S. Government Printing Office, 1951–1952). (15 volumes.)

U. S. House of Representatives. *Report of the Select Committee on the Katyn Forest Massacre* (82nd Congress, 1951–1952).

Warlimont, Walter. *Inside Hitler's Headquarters* (New York: Frederick A. Praeger, 1964).

Wiedemann, Fritz. *Der Mann der Feldherr werden wollte* (Velbert, 1964).

Wighton, Charles. *Heydrich* (London: Oldham, 1962).

Winterbotham, F. A. *The Ultra Secret* (London: Weidenfeld & Nicolson, 1974).

Wittlin, Tadeusz. *Time Stopped at 6:30* (Indianapolis and New York: Bobbs-Merrill Co., 1965).

Zawodny, Janusz. *Death in the Forest* (Notre Dame University Press, 1962).

Ziemer, Gregor. *Education for Death* (London, New York, Toronto: Oxford University Press, 1941).

Index